CO-AYR-810

# Introduction to Psychology
## Gateways to Mind and Behavior

**TWELFTH EDITION**

**Dennis Coon**

**John O. Mitterer**
Brock University

Prepared by

**Jori H. Reijonen**
Western Michigan University

**WADSWORTH**
CENGAGE Learning

Australia • Brazil • Japan • Korea • Mexico • Singapore • Spain • United Kingdom • United States

ISBN-13: 978-0-495-80429-1
ISBN-10: 0-495-80429-0

**Wadsworth**
10 Davis Drive
Belmont, CA 94002-3098
USA

Cengage Learning is a leading provider of customized learning solutions with office locations around the globe, including Singapore, the United Kingdom, Australia, Mexico, Brazil, and Japan. Locate your local office at: **www.cengage.com/international**

Cengage Learning products are represented in Canada by Nelson Education, Ltd.

To learn more about Wadsworth, visit
**www.cengage.com/wadsworth**

Purchase any of our products at your local college store or at our preferred online store
**www.ichapters.com**

Printed in the United States of America
1 2 3 4 5 6 7 8 12 11 10 09

# Table of Contents

# Introduction to Psychology and Research Methods

# Chapter Overview

Psychology is the scientific study of behavior and mental processes. Psychologists engage in critical thinking as they gather and analyze empirical evidence to answer questions about behavior. Psychology spans a wide variety of specialty areas of research, including animal behavior, animals as models of human behavior, and human behavior. As a science, psychology's goals are to describe, understand, predict, and control behavior.

Critical thinking—the ability to reflect on, actively evaluate, compare, analyze, critique, and synthesize information—is central to the scientific method, to psychology, and to effective behavior in general. To judge the validity of a claim, it is important to gather evidence for and against the claim and to evaluate the quality of the evidence.

Psychology differs from commonsense and false explanations of behavior. Numerous pseudopsychologies are frequently confused with valid psychology. Belief in a pseudopsychology is based in part on uncritical acceptance, the fallacy of positive instances, and the Barnum effect.

The scientific method is important to psychologists because scientific research provides the highest quality information about behavior. In the scientific method, systematic observation is used to test hypotheses about behavior and mental events. Important elements of a scientific investigation include observing, defining a problem, proposing a hypothesis, gathering evidence, testing the hypothesis, publishing results, and forming a theory. Concepts must be defined operationally before they can be studied empirically. The results of scientific studies are made public so that others can evaluate them, learn from them, and use them to produce further knowledge.

Psychology became a science when researchers began to directly study and observe psychological events. The first psychological laboratory was established in Germany by Wilhelm Wundt, who studied conscious experience. The first school of thought in psychology was structuralism. Structuralism was followed by functionalism, behaviorism, and Gestalt psychology, psychodynamic approaches and humanism.

There are three complementary perspectives in modern psychology. The biological perspective includes biopsychology and evolutionary psychology. The psychological perspective includes behaviorism, cognitive psychology, the psychodynamic approach, and humanism. The final perspective is called the sociocultural perspective. Today there is an eclectic blending of many viewpoints within psychology. Most of what we think, feel, and do is influenced by the social and cultural worlds in which we live.

Although psychologists, psychiatrists, psychoanalysts, and counselors all work in the field of mental health, their training and methods differ considerably. Clinical and counseling psychologists, who perform psychotherapy, represent only two of dozens of specialties in psychology. Other representative areas of specialization include industrial, educational, consumer, school, developmental, engineering, medical, environmental, forensic, community, psychometric, and experimental psychology. Psychological research may be basic or applied.

Experiments involve two or more groups of subjects that differ only with regard to the independent variable. Effects on the dependent variable are then measured. Extraneous variables are held constant. Because experiments are set up so the independent variable is the only possible cause of a change in the dependent variable, clear cause-and-effect connections can be identified. To be taken seriously, the results of an experiment must be statistically significant. Researchers in psychology follow ethical guidelines in order to protect the rights, dignity, and welfare of participants.

Research participant bias is a problem in some studies. The placebo effect is also a factor, especially in experiments involving drugs. A related problem is researcher bias. Researcher expectations can create a self-fulfilling prophecy. If a double-blind procedure is used, neither subjects nor researchers collecting data know who was in the experimental or control group, allowing the researcher to draw valid conclusions.

Psychologists sometimes use nonexperimental research methods, which usually cannot demonstrate cause-and-effect relationships. Naturalistic observation is a starting place in many investigations. Two problems with naturalistic observation include the effects of the observer on the observed and observer bias. In the correlational method, relationships between two traits, responses, or events are measured and a correlation coefficient is computed to gauge the strength and direction of the relationship. Correlations allow prediction but do not demonstrate cause-and-effect. Case studies provide insights into human behavior that can't be gained by other methods. In the survey method, people in a representative sample are asked a series of carefully worded questions. Obtaining a representative sample of people is crucial when the survey method is used to study large populations.

Information in the mass media about psychology and psychological research varies greatly in quality and accuracy. It is wise to think critically and to be skeptical about such information in order to separate facts from fallacies. Problems in media reports are often related to biased or unreliable sources of information, uncontrolled observation, misleading correlations, false inferences, oversimplification, use of single examples, and unrepeatable results.

# Learning Objectives

*Theme: Psychology is a science and a profession. Scientific observation is the most powerful way to answer questions about behavior.*

| |
|---|
| **GQ: What is psychology and what are its goals?** |
| LO 1.1 Define *psychology*, explain reasons for studying it, and how psychology can be both a science and a profession. |
| LO 1.2 Explain the problem with using common sense as a source of information. |
| LO 1.3 Describe what behavior is and differentiate *overt* from *covert* behavior. |
| LO 1.4 Explain what *empirical evidence* is and give an example of it. Explain how this search for empirical evidence set psychology apart from other fields of study and why some topics in psychology are difficult to study. |
| LO 1.5 Explain why and how animals are used in research and define the term *animal model* in your discussion. List a way in which psychological research may benefit animals. |
| LO 1.6 List and explain the four goals of psychology and its ultimate goal, including why the word *control* has a special meaning for psychologists which is distinct from the everyday meaning of the word. |
| **GQ: What is critical thinking?** |
| LO 1.7 Define the term *critical thinking* and describe its four basic principles. |
| **GQ: How does psychology differ from false explanations of behavior?** |
| LO 1.8 Indicate the foundations and fallacies of each of the following *pseudopsychologies*: a. *palmistry*; b. *phrenology*; c. *graphology*; and d. *astrology*. Explain why these *pseudopsychologies* continue to thrive even though they have no scientific basis. |
| **GQ: How is the scientific method applied in psychological research?** |
| LO 1.9 List and define the six steps of the *scientific method*. Include the concepts of *hypothesis, operational definition*, and *theory formulation*. Explain the importance of publication and describe the parts of a research report. |
| **GQ: How did the field of psychology emerge?** |
| LO 1.10 Use the following schools of psychology to answer the five questions below: *structuralism, functionalism, behaviorism, Gestalt psychology, psychodynamic* school, and *humanism*. a. its founder; b. reasons it was founded; c. its goal; d. its impact on modern psychology; e. its possible value in psychotherapy. |
| LO 1.11 Describe the role of women in psychology's early days and contrast it to today. |
| **GQ: What are the contemporary perspectives in psychology?** |
| LO 1.12 Briefly describe the three major perspectives in modern psychology and explain what it means to be *eclectic*. |
| LO 1.13 Explain how understanding human diversity may help us better understand ourselves and the behavior of others. Define the terms *cultural relativity* and *norms*. |
| **GQ: What are the major specialties in psychology?** |
| LO 1.14 Write a brief summary of each of the following areas of specialization in psychology: a. *developmental*; b. *learning*; c. *personality*; d. *sensation* and *perception*; e. *comparative*; f. *biopsychology*; g. *cognitive*; h. *gender*; i. *social*; j. *cultural;* and k. *evolutionary*. |
| LO 1.15 Characterize the differences in training, emphasis and/or expertise among *psychologists, psychiatrists, psychoanalysts, counselors*, and *psychiatric social workers*. Describe the roles of *clinical* and *counseling* psychologists, the largest areas of specialization among psychologists, and their major sources of employment. Define the term *"scientist-practitioner" model* and list the three points in the professional code for psychologists established by the APA. |
| LO 1.16 Differentiate *basic* from *applied research*. |
| **GQ: How is an experiment performed?** |
| LO 1.17 List and describe the three *variables* in the *experimental method*. Explain the nature and purpose of the *control group* and the *experimental group* and why subjects are randomly assigned to the groups. |
| LO 1.18 Explain what *statistically significant* results are, why the *replication* of results is important, and the value of *meta-analysis*. |

| |
|---|
| **GQ: What is a double-blind experiment?** |
| LO 1.19 Describe the *single-blind* and *double-blind* experimental approaches and how they control for the *placebo effect*, *research participant bias*, and the *researcher bias*, respectively. Include the concept of *self-fulfilling prophecy*. |
| **GQ: What nonexperimental research methods do psychologists use?** |
| LO 1.20 Describe the technique of *naturalistic observation* including its advantages and disadvantages. Include the terms *observer effect* and *observer bias*. Explain what the *anthropomorphic fallacy* is and how it can lead to problems in psychological research. Define the term *observation record*. |
| LO 1.21 Describe what a *correlational study* is and its advantages and disadvantages. Explain what a *correlation coefficient* is, what it means, how it is expressed numerically and as a graph, and how it does NOT show causation. |
| LO 1.22 Briefly describe the *clinical method* of research including when it is used and its advantages and disadvantages. |
| LO 1.23 Briefly describe the *survey method* of investigation including its advantages and disadvantages, a definition of *population* and *sample*, and a discussion of *courtesy bias*, *gender bias*, and *Internet surveys*. |
| **GQ: How good is the psychological information found in the popular media?** |
| LO 1.24 List the suggestions that will help you become a more critical reader of psychological information in the popular press. |

# RECITE AND REVIEW

## Psychology—The ABCs of Behavior: Pages 12-17

What is psychology and what are its goals?

1.  Psychology is both a science and a(n) _____ .

2.  Psychology is defined as the scientific study of behavior and _____ processes.

3.  Psychologists study overt and covert _____ .

4.  Psychologists seek empirical _____ based on scientific observation.

5.  Scientific observation is _____ so that it answers questions about the world.

6.  Answering psychological questions requires a valid research _____ .

7.  Developmental psychologists study the course of human _____ .

8.  Learning theorists study how and why _____ occurs.

9.  Personality _____ study personality _____ and dynamics.

10. Sensation and perception psychologists study the _____ organs and perception.

11. Comparative psychologists study different species, especially _____ .

12. Biopsychologists study the connection between biological processes and _____ .

13. Cognitive psychologists are mainly interested in _____ .

14. Gender psychologists study differences between _____ and _____ .

15. Social psychologists study _____ behavior.

16. Cultural psychologists study the ways that _____ affects _____ .

4

17. Evolutionary psychologists are interested in patterns of behavior that were shaped by
_____ .

18. Other species are used as _____ models in psychological research to discover principles that apply to human behavior.

19. Psychology's goals are to describe, _____ , predict, and _____ behavior.

# Critical Thinking—Take It with a Grain of Salt: Pages 16-17
What is critical thinking?

1. Critical thinking is the ability to _____ , compare, _____ , critique, and synthesize information.

2. Critical thinking involves a willingness to _____ claims and _____ .

3. Scientific observations usually provide the highest quality _____ about various claims.

# Pseudopsychologies—Palms, Planets and Personality: Pages 17-19
How does psychology differ from false explanations of behavior?

1. _____ beliefs are sound practical beliefs that are based on our _____ experiences without scientific observation.

2. Palmistry, phrenology, graphology, and astrology are _____ systems or pseudopsychologies.

3. Belief in pseudopsychologies is encouraged by uncritical acceptance, the fallacy of positive instances, and the _____ effect, named after a famous showman who had "something for everyone."

# Scientific Research—How to Think Like a Psychologist: Pages 19-20
How is the scientific method applied in psychological research?

1. Scientific investigation in psychology is based on reliable evidence, accurate description and _____ , precise definition, controlled observation, and repeatable results.

2. Six elements of a scientific method involve observing, defining a(n) _____ , proposing a hypothesis, gathering evidence/testing the hypothesis, publishing _____ , and forming a theory.

3. To be scientifically _____ , a hypothesis must be testable.

4. Psychological concepts are given operational _____ so that they can be observed.

5. A(n) _____ is a system of ideas that interrelates facts and concepts.

6. Published research reports usually include the following sections: a(n) _____ , an introduction, a methods section, a(n) _____ section, and a final discussion.

## A Brief History of Psychology—Psychology's Family Album: Pages 23-26

How did the field of psychology emerge?

1. Historically, psychology is an outgrowth of philosophy, the study of _____ , reality, and human nature.

2. The first psychological _____ was established in Germany by Wilhelm _____ .

3. Wundt tried to apply scientific methods to the study of conscious _____ by using introspection or "looking inward."

4. Functionalism was concerned with how the mind helps us _____ to our environments.

5. Behaviorism was launched by John B. _____ .

6. Behaviorists objectively study the relationship between _____ and _____ .

7. The modern behaviorist B. F. Skinner believed that most behavior is controlled by _____ reinforcement.

8. Cognitive behaviorism combines _____ and conditioning to explain behavior.

9. Gestalt psychology emphasizes the study of _____ units, not pieces.

10. According to the Gestalt view, in psychology the whole is often _____ than the sum of its parts.

11. The psychoanalytic approach emphasized the _____ origins of behavior.

12. Psychoanalytic psychology, developed by Austrian physician Sigmund _____ , is an early _____ approach.

13. Humanistic psychology emphasizes _____ , subjective experience, human potentials, and personal _____ .

14. Psychologically, humanists believe that self-_____ and self-evaluation are important elements of personal adjustment.

15. Humanists also emphasize a capacity for self-actualization—the full development of personal _____ .

## Psychology Today—Three Complementary Perspectives on Behavior: Pages 26-28

What are the contemporary perspectives in psychology?

1. Much of contemporary psychology is an eclectic _____ of the best features of various viewpoints.

2. Five main streams of thought in modern psychology are behaviorism, _____ , the psychodynamic approach, biopsychology, and _____ psychology.

3. Cognitive _____ attempts to uncover the relationship between mental events and neural activities in the brain.

4. Positive psychology focuses on topics that relate to _____ human functioning.

5. To fully understand behavior, psychologists must be aware of human _____ as well as human universals.

6. Our behavior is greatly affected by cultural _____ and by social norms ( _____ that define acceptable behavior).

# Psychologists—Guaranteed Not to Shrink: Pages 29-31
What are the major specialties in psychology?

1. Psychologists who treat emotional problems specialize in _____ or counseling psychology.

2. Psychiatrists typically use both _____ and psychotherapy to treat emotional problems.

3. Freudian psychoanalysis is a specific type of _____ .

4. Both counselors and psychiatric social workers have _____ degrees.

5. Some of the major _____ in psychology are clinical, counseling, industrial-organizational, educational, consumer, school, developmental, engineering, medical, environmental, forensic, psychometric, and experimental psychology.

6. Scientific research in psychology may be either _____ or applied.

# The Psychology Experiment—Where Cause Meets Effect: Pages 32-35
How is an experiment performed?

1. _____-and-effect relationships in psychology are best identified by doing a controlled _____ .

2. In an experiment, conditions that might affect behavior are intentionally varied _____ . Then, changes in behavior are observed and recorded.

3. In an experiment, a variable is any condition that can _____ , and that might affect the outcome of the experiment (the behavior of subjects).

4. Experimental conditions that are intentionally varied are called _____ variables.

5. _____ variables measure the results of the experiment.

6. Extraneous variables are conditions that a researcher wishes to _____ from affecting the outcome of the experiment.

7. Extraneous variables are controlled by making sure that they are the same for all _____ in an experiment.

8. Subjects exposed to the independent variable are in the _____ group. Those not exposed to the independent variable form the _____ group.

9. Extraneous variables that involve personal _____ , such as age or intelligence, can be controlled by randomly assigning subjects to the experimental and control groups.

7

10. If all extraneous variables are _____ for the experimental group and the control group, any differences in behavior must be caused by differences in the _____ variable.

11. The results of an experiment are statistically _____ when they would occur very rarely by _____ alone.

12. Meta-analysis is a statistical technique to _____ the results of many studies.

# Double Blind—On Placebos and Self-Fulfilling Prophecies: Pages 35-36
What is a double-blind experiment?

1. Experiments involving drugs must control for the _____ effect that is always present when drugs are involved in a study.

2. In a(n) _____-blind study, subjects don't know if they are getting a drug or a placebo. In a(n) _____-blind study, neither experimenters nor subjects know who is receiving a real drug.

3. Researchers must minimize the experimenter effect (the tendency for people to do what is _____ of them).

4. In many situations, the experimenter effect leads to self-fulfilling _____ .

# Nonexperimental Research Methods—Different Strokes Pages 37-42
What nonexperimental research methods do psychologists use?

1. Naturalistic observation refers to actively observing behavior in _____ settings.

2. Two problems with naturalistic studies are the effects of the observer on the observed (the observer _____ ) and _____ bias.

3. Problems with naturalistic studies can be minimized by keeping careful observational _____.

4. In the correlational method, the _____ between two traits, responses, or events is measured.

5. Correlation coefficients range from +1.00 to –1.00. A correlation of _____ indicates that 6. there is no relationship between two measures.

6. Correlations of +1.00 and –1.00 reveal that _____ relationships exist between two measures.

7. The closer a correlation coefficient is to plus or _____ 1, the stronger the measured relationship is.

8. A positive correlation shows that _____ in one measure correspond to increases in a second measure.

9. In a negative correlation, increases in one measure correspond to _____ in a second measure.

10. Correlations allow us to make _____ , but correlation does not demonstrate causation.

11. Graphing a linear relationship between two measures forms a straight line. When curvilinear relationships are graphed, a(n) _____ line results.

12. Clinical psychologists frequently gain information from _____ studies.

13. Case studies of the four Genain sisters who developed schizophrenia by the age of 25 are valuable since they allow scholars to investigate the relationship between mental disorder and _____ .

14. Case studies may be thought of as _____ clinical tests.

15. In the survey method, information about large populations is gained by asking people in a representative _____ a series of carefully worded questions.

16. _____ in research can occur when the race, ethnicity, age, sexual orientation, and gender of researchers and participants are not representative.

17. _____ bias refers to the tendency for women to be under-represented as researchers and as participants in research.

18. The value of surveys is lowered when the sample is biased and when replies to questions are _____ because of _____ (a tendency to give socially desirable answers).

# Psychology in the Media—Separating Fact from Fiction: Pages 43-44
How good is psychological information found in the popular media?

1. _____ and critical thinking are called for when evaluating claims in the popular media.

2. You should be on guard for _____ or biased sources of information in the media.

3. Many claims in the media are based on unscientific observations that lack _____ groups.

4. In the popular media, a failure to distinguish between correlation and _____ is common.

5. Inferences and opinions may be reported as if they were _____ observations.

6. Single cases, unusual _____ , and testimonials are frequently reported as if they were valid generalizations.

# CONNECTIONS

## Psychology—The ABCs of Behavior: Pages 12-17

What is psychology and what are its goals?

1. _____ biopsychology
2. _____ psychology
3. _____ personality theorist
4. _____ social psychologist
5. _____ commonsense beliefs
6. _____ scientific observation
7. _____ understanding
8. _____ EEG
9. _____ empirical evidence
10. _____ comparative psychology
11. _____ description
12. _____ control

a. investigates attitudes and persuasion
b. brain waves
c. systematic observation
d. animal behavior
e. detailed record
f. human and animal behavior
g. "why" questions
h. brain and behavior
i. direct observation
j. traits, dynamics, individual differences
k. influencing behavior
l. proof based on everyday experiences

## Critical Thinking—Take It with a Grain of Salt: Pages 16-17

What is critical thinking?

1. _____ faith
2. _____ reflect
3. _____ empirical testing
4. _____ authority
5. _____ critical thinking

a. expertist
b. evaluating claims and evidence
c. supporting evidence
d. heart of critical thinking
e. religious beliefs

## Pseudopsychologies—Palms, Planets and Personality: Pages 17-19

How does psychology differ from false explanations of behavior?

1. _____ uncritical acceptance
2. _____ fallacy of positive instances
3. _____ Barnum effect
4. _____ phrenology
5. _____ graphology
6. _____ astrology
7. _____ pseudopsychology

a. looks at positions of the planets
b. handwriting analysis
c. analysis of the shape of skulls
d. unfounded systems
e. stated in general terms
f. remembering things that confirm expectations
g. believe positive descriptions of oneself

## Scientific Research—How to Think Like a Psychologist: Pages 19-20

How is the scientific method applied in psychological research?

1. _____ theory
2. _____ common sense
3. _____ operational definition
4. _____ scientific method
5. _____ hypothesis
6. _____ replicate

a. repeat
b. map of knowledge
c. unscientific information
d. controlled observation
e. specific procedure
f. tentative statement

## A Brief History of Psychology—Psychology's Family Album: Pages 23-26

How did the field of psychology emerge?

1. _____ Wundt
2. _____ Titchener
3. _____ James
4. _____ Darwin
5. _____ Maslow
6. _____ Pavlov
7. _____ Skinner
8. _____ Wertheimer
9. _____ Ladd-Franklin
10. _____ Freud

a. father of psychology
b. natural selection
c. behaviorism
d. functionalism
e. conditioned responses
f. Gestalt
g. color vision
h. introspection
i. psychoanalysis
j. self-actualization

## Psychology Today—Three Complementary Perspectives on Behavior: Pages 26-28

What are the contemporary perspectives in psychology?

1. _____ sociocultural perspective
2. _____ psychological perspective
3. _____ eclectic
4. _____ biological perspective
5. _____ positive psychology
6. _____ social norms

a. draws from a variety of perspectives
b. part of neuroscience
c. includes psychodynamic perspective
d. focus on optimal behavior
e. stresses impact of context
f. rules defining acceptable behavior expectations

## The Psychology Experiment—Where Cause Meets Effect and Double Blind—On Placebos and Self-Fulfilling Prophecies: Pages 32-36

How is an experiment performed? What is a double-blind experiment?

| | | | |
|---|---|---|---|
| 1. | _____ single blind experiment | a. | effect on behavior |
| 2. | _____ identify causes of behavior | b. | experimental method |
| 3. | _____ independent variable | c. | varied by experimenter |
| 4. | _____ dependent variable | d. | excluded by experimenter |
| 5. | _____ extraneous variables | e. | reference for comparison |
| 6. | _____ control group | f. | done by using chance |
| 7. | _____ random assignment to groups | g. | control for placebo effects |
| 8. | _____ placebos | h. | control for placebo effects |
| 9. | _____ double-blind experiment | i. | control for research bias |

## Nonexperimental Research Methods—Different Strokes: Pages 37-42

What nonexperimental research methods do psychologists use?

| | | | |
|---|---|---|---|
| 1. | _____ survey methods | a. | strength and direction of relationship |
| 2. | _____ correlation | b. | participation is voluntary |
| 3. | _____ case studies | c. | clinical method |
| 4. | _____ gender bias | d. | representative of population |
| 5. | _____ valid sample | e. | inaccurate answers |
| 6. | _____ courtesy bias | f. | public poling techniques expectations |
| 7. | _____ ethical research | g. | under representation of women |
| 8. | _____ Jane Goodall | h. | detailed summary |
| 9. | _____ observational record | i. | naturalistic observation |

## Psychology in the Media—Separating Fact from Fiction: Pages 43-44

How good is psychological information found in the popular media?

| | | | |
|---|---|---|---|
| 1. | _____ sleep learning device | a. | health department seeks Klingon interpreter |
| 2. | _____ psychic advisers | b. | use Barnum effect |
| 3. | _____ urban legend | c. | shown by research to be of little value |
| 4. | _____ inference | d. | necessary for true experiment |
| 5. | _____ lunar effect | e. | supposed effect of moon on behavior |
| 6. | _____ control group | f. | intepretation |

# CHECK YOUR MEMORY

## Psychology—The ABCs of Behavior: Pages 12-17
What is psychology and what are its goals?

1. Psychology can best be described as a profession, not a science. TRUE or FALSE

2. Psychology is defined as the scientific study of human behavior. TRUE or FALSE

3. Although it is a covert activity, dreaming is a behavior. TRUE or FALSE

4. The term *empirical evidence* refers to the opinion of an acknowledged authority. TRUE or FALSE

5. The term *data* refers to a systematic procedure for answering scientific questions. TRUE or FALSE

6. Cognitive psychologists are interested in researching memory, reasoning, and problem solving. TRUE or FALSE

7. Animal models are used to discover principles that can be applied to animals only. TRUE or FALSE

8. Naming and classifying are the heart of psychology's second goal, understanding behavior. TRUE or FALSE

9. Control refers to a psychologist's ability to alter conditions that affect a participant's behavior. TRUE or FALSE

## Critical Thinking—Take It With a Grain of Salt: Pages 16-17
What is critical thinking?

1. Statements like "The more motivated you are, the better you will do at solving a complex problem" are commonsense beliefs that have been shown to be true. TRUE or FALSE

2. Critical thinking utilizes commonsense beliefs as the foundation for evaluating and judging the quality of evidence obtained. TRUE or FALSE

3. Critical thinking is the ability to make good use of intuition and mental imagery. TRUE or FALSE

4. Critical thinkers actively evaluate claims, ideas, and propositions. TRUE or FALSE

5. A key element of critical thinking is evaluating the quality of evidence related to a claim. TRUE or FALSE

6. Critical thinkers recognize that the opinions of experts and authorities should be respected without question. TRUE or FALSE

## Pseudopsychologies—Palms, Planets and Personality: Pages 17-19

How does psychology differ from false explanations of behavior?

1.   Pseudoscientists test their concepts by gathering data.  TRUE or FALSE

2.   Phrenologists believe that lines on the hands reveal personality traits.  TRUE or FALSE

3.   Graphology is only valid if a large enough sample of handwriting is analyzed.  TRUE or FALSE

4.   Astrological charts consisting of positive traits tend to be perceived as "accurate" or true, even if they are not.  TRUE or FALSE

5.   The Barnum effect refers to our tendency to remember things that confirm our expectations.  TRUE or FALSE

## Scientific Research—How to Think Like a Psychologist: Pages 19-20

How is the scientific method applied in psychological research?

1.   The scientific method involves testing a proposition by systematic observation.  TRUE or FALSE

2.   An operational definition states the exact hypothesis used to represent a concept.  TRUE or FALSE

3.   Operational definitions link concepts with concrete observations.  TRUE or FALSE

4.   A hypothesis provides a map of knowledge.  TRUE or FALSE

5.   Mehl's study did not find that women talk more than men.  TRUE or FALSE

6.   Freudian personality theory is easily testable and falsifiable.  TRUE or FALSE

## A Brief History of Psychology—Psychology's Family Album Pages 23-26

How did the field of psychology emerge?

1.   In 1879, Wundt established a lab to study the philosophy of behavior.  TRUE or FALSE

2.   Wundt used introspection to study conscious experiences.  TRUE or FALSE

3.   Edward Titchener is best known for promoting functionalism in America.  TRUE or FALSE

4.   The functionalists were influenced by the ideas of Charles Darwin.  TRUE or FALSE

5.   Behaviorists define psychology as the study of conscious experience.  TRUE or FALSE

6.   Watson used Pavlov's concept of conditioned responses to explain most behavior.  TRUE or FALSE

7.   Believing that human's behaviors are controlled by rewards, B. F. Skinner invented the "Skinner box" to study primarily animals' responses.  TRUE or FALSE

8. Cognitive behaviorism combines thinking and Gestalt principles to explain human behavior. TRUE or FALSE

9. Margaret Washburn was the first woman in America to be awarded a Ph.D. in psychology. TRUE or FALSE

10. Mary Calkins was the first woman president of the American Psychological Association in 1905, and did early research on memory. TRUE or FALSE

11. Women account for approximately 75 percent of college students who major in psychology today. TRUE or FALSE

12. "The whole is greater than the sum of its parts" is a slogan of structuralism. TRUE or FALSE

13. Freud's psychodynamic theory of personality focused on the unconscious thoughts, impulses, and desires with the exception of sex and aggression since they describe negative views of human behavior. TRUE or FALSE

14. According to Freud, repressed thoughts are held out of awareness in the unconscious. TRUE or FALSE

15. Carl Jung and Erik Erikson were two neo-Freudians who firmly believed in Freud's psychodynamic theory. TRUE or FALSE

16. Humanists generally reject the determinism of the behavioristic and psychodynamic approaches. TRUE or FALSE

# Psychology Today—Three Complementary Perspectives on Behavior: Pages 26-28
What are the contemporary perspectives in psychology?

1. The five major perspectives in psychology today are behaviorism, humanism, functionalism, biopsychology, and cognitive psychology. TRUE or FALSE

2. Cognitive neuroscience studies the relationship between mental events and the environment. TRUE or FALSE

3. Humanism offers a positive, philosophical view of human nature. TRUE or FALSE

4. Positive psychology focuses on the negative aspects of the self in order to achieve one's happiness and well-being. TRUE or FALSE

5. The cognitive view explains behavior in terms of information processing. TRUE or FALSE

6. To understand behavior, psychologists must be aware of the cultural relativity of standards for evaluating behavior. TRUE or FALSE

## Psychologists—Guaranteed Not to Shrink: Pages 29-31
What are the major specialties in psychology?

1. Most psychologists work in private practice. TRUE or FALSE

2. The differences between clinical and counseling psychology are beginning to fade. TRUE or FALSE

3. To enter the profession of psychology today you would need to earn a doctorate degree.
   TRUE or FALSE

4. The Psy.D. degree emphasizes scientific research skills. TRUE or FALSE

5. More than half of all psychologists specialize in clinical or counseling psychology. TRUE or FALSE

6. Clinical psychologists must be licensed to practice legally. TRUE or FALSE

7. Studying ways to improve the memories of eyewitnesses to crimes would be an example of applied research. TRUE or FALSE

## The Psychology Experiment—Where Cause Meets Effect Pages 32-35
How is an experiment performed?

1. Extraneous variables are those that are varied by the experimenter. TRUE or FALSE

2. Independent variables are suspected causes for differences in behavior. TRUE or FALSE

3. In an experiment to test whether hunger affects memory, hunger is the dependent variable.
   TRUE or FALSE

4. In an experiment, subjects are randomly assigned to the experimental and control groups.
   TRUE or FALSE

## Double Blind—On Placebos and Self-Fulfilling Prophecies: Pages 35-36
What is a double-blind experiment?

1. A person who takes a drug may be influenced by his or her expectations about the drug's effects.
   TRUE or FALSE

2. Neither the single-blind nor the double-blind experiment can control for the placebo effect since it is always present when drugs are involved in a study. TRUE or FALSE

3. In a single-blind experiment, the experimenter remains blind as to whether she or he is administering a drug. TRUE or FALSE

4. Subjects in psychology experiments can be very sensitive to hints about what is expected of them.
   TRUE or FALSE

# Nonexperimental Research Methods—Different Strokes: Pages 37-42

What nonexperimental research methods do psychologists use?

1. Jane Goodall's study of chimpanzees made use of the clinical method. TRUE or FALSE

2. Concealing the observer helps reduce the observer effect. TRUE or FALSE

3. Anthropomorphic error refers to attributing animals' behaviors, thoughts, emotions, and motives to humans. TRUE or FALSE

4. A correlation coefficient of +.100 indicates a perfect positive relationship. TRUE or FALSE

5. Strong relationships always produce positive correlation coefficients; weak relationships always produce negative correlations. TRUE or FALSE

6. Perfect correlations demonstrate that a causal relationship exists. TRUE or FALSE

7. The best way to identify cause-and-effect relationships is to perform a case study. TRUE or FALSE

8. Phineas Gage is remembered as the first psychologist to do a case study. TRUE or FALSE

9. Case studies may be inconclusive because they lack formal control groups. TRUE or FALSE

10. The case study of the four Genain sisters who developed schizophrenia by the age of 25 is an example of environmental (nature) influence. TRUE or FALSE

11. Gender bias in research occurs when researchers assume that there are no differences between men and women; therefore results based on men cannot be applied to women. TRUE or FALSE

12. Representative samples are often obtained by randomly selecting people to study. TRUE or FALSE

13. Representative sampling is an advantage of web-based research. TRUE or FALSE

14. A tendency to give socially desirable answers to questions can lower the accuracy of surveys. TRUE or FALSE

# Psychology in the Media—Separating Fact from Fiction: Pages 43-44

How good is psychological information found in the popular media?

1. The existence of extrasensory perception was confirmed by recent experiments. TRUE or FALSE

2. Psychological courses and services offered for profit may be misrepresented, just as some other products are. TRUE or FALSE

3. At least some psychic ability is necessary to perform as a stage mentalist. TRUE or FALSE

4. Successful firewalking requires neurolinguistic programming. TRUE or FALSE

5. Violent crime rises and falls with lunar cycles. TRUE or FALSE

6. If you see a person laughing, you must infer that he or she is happy. TRUE or FALSE

7. Individual cases and specific examples tell us nothing about what is true in general.
   TRUE or FALSE

8. Information found on the Internet such as "Learn to speak Klingon" is usually accurate, therefore verification is not necessary. TRUE or FALSE

# FINAL SURVEY AND REVIEW

## Psychology—The ABCs of Behavior
What is psychology and what are its goals?

1. Psychology is both a(n) _____ and a(n) _____ .

2. Psychology is defined as the scientific study of _____ and _____ processes.

3. Psychologists study _____ and covert _____ .

4. Psychologists seek empirical evidence based on scientific _____ .

5. Scientific observation is _____ so that it answers questions about the world.

6. Answering psychological questions requires a valid research _____ .

7. _____ psychologists study the course of human development.

8. _____ theorists study how and why learning occurs.

9. Personality _____ study personality _____ and dynamics.

10. Sensation and _____ psychologists study the _____ organs and perception.

11. _____ psychologists study different species, especially animals.

12. _____ study the connection between biological processes and _____ .

13. _____ psychologists are mainly interested in thinking.

14. _____ psychologists study differences between males and females.

15. Social psychologists study _____ behavior.

16. _____ psychologists study the ways that culture affects _____ .

17. Evolutionary psychologists are interested in patterns of _____ that were shaped by _____ .

18. Other species are used as _____ models in psychological research to discover principles that apply to _____ behavior.

19. Psychology's goals are to _____ , understand, _____ , and control behavior.

18

## Critical Thinking—Take It With a Grain of Salt: Pages 16-17
What is critical thinking?

1. Critical thinking is the ability to evaluate, _____ , analyze, _____ , and synthesize information.

2. Critical thinking involves a willingness to _____ claims and _____ .

3. _____ observations usually provide the highest quality _____ about various claims.

## Pseudopsychologies—Palms, Planets and Personality
How does psychology differ from false explanations of behavior?

1. _____ beliefs are sound practical beliefs that are based on our _____ experiences without scientific observation.

2. Palmistry, phrenology, graphology, and astrology are false systems, or _____ .

3. Belief in pseudo-psychologies is encouraged by uncritical acceptance, the fallacy of _____ instances, and the _____ effect, named after a famous showman who had "something for everyone."

## Scientific Research—How to Think Like a Psychologist
How is the scientific method applied in psychological research?

1. Scientific investigation in psychology is based on reliable evidence, accurate description and _____ , precise definition, controlled observation, and _____ results.

2. Six elements of a scientific method involve observing, defining a(n) _____ , proposing a hypothesis, gathering evidence/testing the _____ , publishing results, and forming a theory.

3. To be scientifically _____ , a hypothesis must be testable.

4. Psychological concepts are given _____ definitions so that they can be observed.

5. A(n) _____ is a system of ideas that interrelates facts and concepts.

6. Published research reports usually include the following sections: an abstract, a(n) _____ , a(n) _____ section, a results section, and a final discussion.

## A Brief History of Psychology—Psychology's Family Album
How did the field of psychology emerge?

1. Historically, psychology is an outgrowth of _____ , the study of philosophy, reality, and human nature.

2. The first psychological _____ was established in Germany by Wilhelm _____ .

3. Wundt tried to apply scientific methods to the study of conscious _____ by using _____ or "looking inward."

4. Functionalism was concerned with how the mind helps us _____ to our environments.

5. Behaviorism was launched by John B. _____ .

19

6. Behaviorists objectively study the relationship between _____ and _____ .

7. The modern behaviorist B. F. Skinner believed that most behavior is controlled by _____ .

8. Cognitive behaviorism combines _____ and _____ to explain behavior.

9. Gestalt psychology emphasizes the study of _____ units, not pieces.

10. According to the Gestalt view, in psychology the _____ is often greater than the sum of its parts.

11. The psychoanalytic approach emphasized the _____ origins of behavior.

12. Psychoanalytic psychology, developed by Austrian physician Sigmund _____ , is an early _____ approach.

13. Humanistic psychology emphasizes _____ , subjective experience, human _____ , and personal growth .

14. Psychologically, humanists believe that self-image and _____ are important elements of personal adjustment.

15. Humanists also emphasize a capacity for _____ —the full development of personal potential.

# Psychology Today—Three Complementary Perspectives on Behavior
What are the contemporary perspectives in psychology?

1. Much of contemporary psychology is an _____ blend of the best features of various viewpoints.

2. Five main streams of thought in modern psychology are _____ , humanism , the psychodynamic approach, _____ , and cognitive psychology.

3. Cognitive _____ attempts to uncover the relationship between mental events and _____ activities in the brain.

4. _____ psychology focuses on topics that relate to optimal human functioning.

5. To fully understand behavior, psychologists must be aware of human _____ as well as human universals.

6. Our behavior is greatly affected by cultural _____ and by social _____ ( rules that define acceptable behavior).

# Psychologists—Guaranteed Not to Shrink
What are the major specialties in psychology?

1. Psychologists who treat _____ problems specialize in _____ or counseling psychology.

2. Psychiatrists typically use both _____ and psychotherapy to treat emotional problems.

3. Freudian _____ is a specific type of psyhotherapy .

4. Both counselors and psychiatric social workers have _____ degrees.

20

5.  Some of the major _____ in psychology are clinical, counseling, industrial-organizational, educational, consumer, school, developmental, engineering, medical, environmental, forensic, psychometric, and experimental psychology.

6.  Scientific research in psychology may be either _____ or _____.

# The Psychology Experiment—Where Cause Meets Effect

How is an experiment performed?

1.  _____ -and-effect relationships in psychology are best identified by doing a controlled _____ .

2.  In an _____, conditions that might affect behavior are intentionally varied _____ . Then, changes in behavior are observed and recorded.

3.  In an experiment, a(n) _____ is any condition that can change , and that might affect the outcome of the experiment (the behavior of subjects).

4.  Experimental conditions that are intentionally varied are called _____ variables.

5.  _____ variables measure the results of the experiment.

6.  _____ variables are conditions that a researcher wishes to prevent from affecting the outcome of the experiment.

7.  Extraneous variables are controlled by making sure that they are the same for all _____ in an experiment.

8.  Subjects exposed to the _____ variable are in the experimental group. Those not exposed to the independent variable form the _____ group.

9.  Extraneous variables that involve personal _____ , such as age or intelligence, can be controlled by _____ assigning subjects to the experimental and control groups.

10. If all extraneous variables are _____ for the experimental group and the control group, any differences in behavior must be caused by differences in the _____ variable.

11. The results of an experiment are _____ significant when they would occur very rarely by _____ alone.

12. _____ is a statistical technique to combine the results of many studies.

# Double Blind—On Placebos and Self-Fulfilling Prophecies

What is a double-blind experiment?

1.  Experiments involving drugs must control for the _____ effect that is always present when drugs are involved in a study.

2.  In a(n) _____ study, subjects don't know if they are getting a drug or a placebo. In a(n) _____ study, neither experimenters nor subjects know who is receiving a real drug.

3.  Researchers must minimize the _____ effect (the tendency for people to do what is expected of them).

4.  In many situations, the experimenter effect leads to self-fulfilling _____ .

# Nonexperimental Research Methods—Different Strokes: Pages 37-42
What nonexperimental research methods do psychologists use?

1. _____ observation refers to actively observing behavior in natural settings.

2. Two problems with naturalistic studies are the effects of the observer on the observed (the _____ effect ) and _____ bias.

3. Problems with naturalistic studies can be minimized by keeping careful observational _____.

4. In the correlational method, the _____ between two traits, responses, or events is measured.

5. Correlation coefficients range from +1.00 to _____ . A correlation of _____ indicates that there is no relationship between two measures.

6. Correlations of _____ and –1.00 reveal that _____ relationships exist between two measures.

7. The closer a correlation coefficient is to _____ or minus 1, the stronger the measured relationship is.

8. A(n) _____ correlation shows that increases in one measure correspond to increases in a second measure.

9. In a negative correlation, increases in one measure correspond to _____ in a second measure.

10. Correlations allow us to make _____ , but correlation does not demonstrate _____ .

11. Graphing a linear relationship between two measures forms a straight _____. When curvilinear relationships are graphed, a _____ line results.

12. Clinical psychologists frequently gain information from _____ studies.

13. Case studies of the four Genain sisters who developed schizophrenia by the age of 25 are valuable since they allow scholars to investigate the relationship between mental disorder and _____ .

14. Case studies may be thought of as _____ clinical tests.

15. In the _____ method, information about large populations is gained by asking people in a
16. representative _____ a series of carefully worded questions.

17. _____ in research can occur when the race, ethnicity, age, sexual orientation, and gender of researchers and participants are not representative.

18. _____ bias refers to the tendency for women to be under-represented as researchers and as participants in research.

19. The value of surveys is lowered when the sample is biased and when replies to questions are _____ because of _____ (a tendency to give socially desirable answers).

# Psychology in the Media—Separating Fact from Fiction: Pages 43-44
How good is psychological information found in the popular media?

1. _____ and _____ thinking are called for when evaluating claims in the popular media.

22

2. You should be on guard for unreliable or _____ sources of information in the media.

3. Many claims in the media are based on unscientific observations that lack _____ groups.

4. In the popular media, a failure to distinguish between _____ and _____ is common.

5. Inferences and opinions may be reported as if they were _____ observations.

6. Single cases, unusual _____ , and testimonials are frequently reported as if they were valid _____.

# MASTERY TEST

1. Observable actions are to _____ behavior as internal activities are to _____ behavior.
   a. covert; covert
   b. covert; overt
   c. overt; overt
   d. overt; covert

2. Who among the following would most likely study the behavior of gorillas?
   a. developmental psychologist
   b. comparative psychologist
   c. environmental psychologist
   d. forensic psychologist

3. An engineering psychologist helps redesign an airplane to make it safer to fly. The psychologist's work reflects which of psychology's goals?
   a. understanding
   b. control
   c. prediction
   d. description

4. Who among the following placed the greatest emphasis on introspection?
   a. Watson
   b. Wertheimer
   c. Washburn
   d. Wundt

5. Which pair of persons had the most similar ideas?
   a. Titchener—Skinner
   b. James—Darwin
   c. Watson—Rogers
   d. Wertheimer—Maslow

6. The behavioral definition of psychology clearly places great emphasis on
   a. overt behavior.
   b. conscious experience.
   c. psychodynamic responses.
   d. introspective analysis.

7. As a profession, psychology is fully open to men and women, a fact that began with the success of
   a. O'Sullivan-Calkins.
   b. Tyler-James.
   c. Ladd-Franklin.
   d. Neal-Collins.

8. The idea that threatening thoughts are sometimes repressed would be of most interest to a
   a. structuralist.
   b. psychoanalyst.
   c. humanist.
   d. Gestaltist.

9. "A neutral, reductionistic, mechanistic view of human nature." This best describes which viewpoint?
   a. psychodynamic
   b. cognitive
   c. psychoanalytic
   d. biopsychological

10. Which of the following professional titles usually requires a doctorate degree?
    a. psychologist
    b. psychiatric social worker
    c. counselor
    d. all of the preceding

11. Who among the following is most likely to treat the physical causes of psychological problems?
    a. scientist-practitioner
    b. psychoanalyst
    c. forensic psychologist
    d. psychiatrist

12. More than half of all psychologists specialize in what branches of psychology?
    a. counseling and comparative
    b. applied and counseling
    c. psychodynamic and clinical
    d. counseling and clinical

13. When critically evaluating claims about behavior, it is important to also evaluate
    a. the source of anecdotal evidence.
    b. the credentials of an authority.
    c. the quality of the evidence.
    d. the strength of one's intuition.

14. Which of the following pairs is most different?
    a. pseudo-psychology—critical thinking
    b. graphology—pseudo-psychology
    c. palmistry—phrenology
    d. psychology—empirical evidence

15. The German anatomy teacher Franz Gall popularized
    a. palmistry.
    b. phrenology.
    c. graphology.
    d. astrology.

16. Marla tends to believe flattering descriptions of herself more than unflattering descriptions of herself, a tendency called
    a. the Barnum effect.
    b. the astrologer's dilemma.
    c. the fallacy of positive instances.
    d. uncritical acceptance.

17. Descriptions of personality that contain both sides of several personal dimensions tend to create
    a. an illusion of accuracy.
    b. disbelief and rejection.
    c. the astrologer's dilemma.
    d. a system similar to phrenology.

18. If an entire population is surveyed, it becomes unnecessary to obtain a
    a. control group.
    b. random comparison.
    c. random sample.
    d. control variable.

19. Control groups are most often used in
    a. naturalistic observation.
    b. the clinical method.
    c. pseudoscience.
    d. experiments.

20. Concealing the observer can be used to minimize the
    a. observer bias effect.
    b. double-blind effect.
    c. observer effect.
    d. effects of extraneous correlations.

21. A psychologist studying lowland gorillas should be careful to avoid the
    a.   anthropomorphic error.
    b.   participant bias.
    c.   Barnum effect.
    d.   fallacy of positive instances.

22. Testing the hypothesis that frustration encourages aggression would require
    a.   a field study.
    b.   operational definitions.
    c.   adult subjects.
    d.   perfect correlations.

23. In experiments involving drugs, experimenters remain unaware of who received placebos in a _____ experiment.
    a.   zero-blind
    b.   single-blind
    c.   double-blind
    d.   control-blind

24. A saline injection is 70 percent as effective as morphine in relieving pain, which is an example of the
    a.   placebo effect..
    b.   self-fulfilling prophecy.
    c.   operational definition.
    d.   dependent variable.

25. In psychology, the _____ variable is a suspected cause of differences in _____.
    a.   independent; the control group
    b.   dependent; the experimenter effect
    c.   independent; behavior
    d.   dependent; correlations

26. A person who is observed crying may not be sad. This suggests that it is important to distinguish between
    a.   individual cases and generalizations.
    b.   correlation and causation.
    c.   control groups and experimental groups.
    d.   observation and inference.

27. In an experiment on the effects of hunger on the reading scores of elementary school children, reading scores are the
    a.   control variable.
    b.   independent variable.
    c.   dependent variable.
    d.   reference variable.

26

28. Which of the following correlation coefficients indicates a perfect relationship?
    a. 1.00
    b. 100.0
    c. −1
    d. both a and c

29. Jane Goodall's studies of chimpanzees in Tanzania are good examples of
    a. survey research.
    b. experimental studies.
    c. correlational studies.
    d. naturalistic observation.

30. To equalize the intelligence of members of the experimental group and the control group in an experiment, you could use
    a. extraneous control.
    b. random assignment.
    c. independent control.
    d. random selection.

31. Which method would most likely be used to study the effects of tumors in the frontal lobes of the brain?
    a. sampling method
    b. correlational method
    c. clinical method
    d. experimental method

32. Cause is to effect as the _____ variable is to the _____ variable.
    a. extraneous; dependent
    b. dependent; independent
    c. independent; extraneous
    d. independent; dependent

33. The specific procedures used to gather data are described in which section of a research report?
    a. introduction
    b. abstract
    c. method
    d. discussion

34. Which of the following correlations demonstrates a cause-effect relationship?
    a. -.98
    b. 1.00
    c. .50
    d. none of the above

35. A graph of a perfect negative relationship would form a
    a. straight line.
    b. circle.
    c. horizontal line.
    d. U-shaped line.

36. A researcher statistically combines the results of all of the published results concerning the effects of sugar on hyperactive behavior in children. In order to draw a conclusion about the effects of sugar on hyperactivity, the researcher has used
    a. the double-blind technique.
    b. experimental replication.
    c. natural clinical trials.
    d. meta-analysis.

37. Appreciating an orchestra playing Mozart's fifth symphony more than a musician playing a solo on a clarinet is best explained by _____ psychology.
    a. Gestalt
    b. cognitive
    c. behavioral
    d. biopsychology

38. An in-depth study on the life history of the four Genain sisters is an example of the
    a. survey method.
    b. correlational method.
    c. scientific method.
    d. clinical method.

39. The case of the four identical Genain sisters who all developed schizophrenia suggests that their disorder was influenced by
    a. only environmental conditions.
    b. only hereditary factors.
    c. both environmental and hereditary factors.
    d. neither environmental or hereditary factors.

40. Carlie believes that blind people have unusually sensitive organs of touch. She based her beliefs on personal experiences and everyday observation. Carlie's sound practical belief is an example of
    a. common sense.
    b. scientific observation.
    c. uncritical acceptance.
    d. representative sample.

41. Protecting a client's welfare is part of a psychologist's professional code of
    a. specialization.
    b. ethics.
    c. research.
    d. knowledge.

42. To control for placebo effects, a _____ study is used.
    a. correlational
    b. single-blind
    c. clinical case
    d. Web-based

43. Which term refers to the tendency for women to be under-represented as psychological researchers and as participants in research?
    a. experimenter bias
    b. observer bias
    c. gender bias
    d. male bias

# SOLUTIONS

## RECITE AND REVIEW

### Psychology—The ABCs of Behavior Pages 12-17
What is psychology and what are its goals?

1. profession
2. mental
3. behavior
4. evidence
5. planned or structured
6. method
7. development
8. learning
9. theorists; traits
10. sense (or sensory)
11. animals
12. behavior
13. thinking
14. males; females
15. social
16. culture; behavior
17. evolution
18. animal
19. understand; control

### Critical Thinking—Take It with a Grain of Salt: Pages 16-17
What is critical thinking?

1. evaluate; analyze
2. evaluate; evidence
3. evidence

### Psuedopsychologies—Palms, Planets and Personality: Pages 17-19
How does psychology differ from false explanations of behavior?

1. Commonsense; everyday
2. false
3. Barnum

## Scientific Research—How to Think Like a Psychologist: Pages 19-20

How is the scientific method applied in psychological research?

1. measurement
2. problem; results
3. valid (or useful)
4. definitions
5. theory
6. abstract; results

## A Brief History of Psychology—Psychology's Family Album: 23-26

How did the field of psychology emerge?

1. knowledge
2. laboratory; Wundt
3. experience
4. adapt
5. Watson
6. stimuli; response
7. positive
8. thinking
9. whole
10. greater
11. unconscious
12. Freud; psychodynamic
13. free will; growth
14. image
15. potentials

## Psychology Today—Three Complementary Perspectives on Behavior: Pages 26-28

What are the contemporary perspectives in psychology?

1. blend
2. humanism; cognitive
3. neuroscience
4. optimal
5. diversity (or differences)

## Psychologists—Guaranteed Not to Shrink: Pages 29-31

What are the major specialties in psychology?

1. clinical
2. drugs
3. psychotherapy
4. Master's
5. specialties
6. basic

## The Psychology Experiment—Where Cause Meets Effect: Pages 32-35

How is an experiment performed?

1. Cause; experiment
2. varied
3. change
4. independent
5. Dependent
6. prevent
7. subjects
8. experimental; control
9. characteristics
10. identical; independent
11. significant; chance
12. combine

## Double Blind—On Placebos and Self-Fulfilling Prophecies: Pages 35-36

What is a double-blind experiment?

1. placebo
2. single; double
3. expected
4. prophecies

## Nonexperimental Research Methods—Different Strokes: Pages 37-42

What nonexperimental research methods do psychologists use?

1. natural
2. effect; observer
3. records
4. correlation (or relationship)
5. zero
6. perfect
7. minus
8. increases

30

9. decreases
10. predictions
11. curved
12. case

13. heredity
14. natural
15. sample
16. biases

17. gender
18. untruthful (or inaccurate); courtesy bias

## Psychology in the Media—Separating Fact from Fiction: Pages 43-44
How good is psychological information found in the popular media?

1. Skepticism
2. unreliable (or inaccurate)

3. control
4. causation

5. valid (or scientific)

# CONNECTIONS

## Psychology—The ABCs of Behavior Pages 12-17
What is psychology and what are its goals?

1. h
2. f
3. j
4. a

5. l
6. c
7. g
8. b

9. i
10. d
11. e
12. k

## Critical Thinking—Take It with a Grain of Salt: Pages 16-17
What is critical thinking?

1. e
2. d

3. c
4. a

## Pseudopsychologies—Palms, Planets and Personality: Pages 17-19
How does psychology differ from false explanations of behavior?

1. g
2. f
3. e

4. c
5. b

6. a
7. d

## Scientific Research—How to Think Like a Psychologist: Pages 19-20
How is the scientific method applied in psychological research?

1. b
2. c

3. e
4. d

5. f
6. a

## A Brief History of Psychology—Psychology's Family Album: Pages 23-26
How did the field of psychology emerge?

1. a
2. h
3. d

4. b
5. j
6. e

7. c
8. f

31

## Psychology Today—Three Complementary Perspectives on Behavior: Pages 26-28

What are the contemporary perspectives in psychology?

1. e
2. c
3. a
4. b
5. d
6. f

## The Psychology Experiment—Where Cause Meets Effect: Pages 32-36

How is an experiment performed?

1. h
2. b
3. c
4. a
5. d
6. e
7. f
8. g
9. i

## Nonexperimental Research Methods—Different Strokes: Pages 37-42

What nonexperimental research methods do psychologists use?

1. h
2. b
3. c
4. a
5. d
6. e
7. f
8. g
9. i
10. h

## Psychology in the Media—Separating Fact from Fiction: Pages 43-44

How good is psychological information found in the popular media?

1. c
2. b
3. a
4. f
5. e
6. d

# CHECK YOUR MEMORY

## Psychology—The ABCs of Behavior Pages 12-17

What is psychology and what are its goals?

1. F
2. F
3. T
4. F
5. F
6. T
7. F
8. F
9. T

## Critical Thinking—Take It with a Grain of Salt: Pages 16-17

What is critical thinking?

1. F
2. F
3. T
4. T
5. F

## Pseudopsychologies—Palms, Planets and Personality: Pages 17-19

How does psychology differ from false explanations of behavior?

1. F
2. F
3. F
4. T
5. F

32

## Scientific Research—How to Think Like a Psychologist: Pages 19-20
How is the scientific method applied in psychological research?

1. T
2. F
3. T
4. F
5. T
6. F

## A Brief History of Psychology—Psychology's Family Album: Pages 23-26
How did the field of psychology emerge?

1. F
2. T
3. F
4. T
5. F
6. T
7. T
8. F
9. T
10. T
11. T
12. F
13. F
14. T
15. F
16. T

## Psychology Today—Three Complementary Perspectives on Behavior: Pages 26-28
What are the contemporary perspectives in psychology?

1. F
2. F
3. T
4. F
5. T
6. F

## Psychologists—Guaranteed Not to Shrink: Pages 29-31
What are the major specialties in psychology?

1. F
2. T
3. F
4. F
5. T
6. T
7. T

## The Psychology Experiment—Where Cause Meets Effect: Pages 32-35
How is an experiment performed?

1. F
2. T
3. F
4. T

## Double Blind—On Placebos and Self-Fulfilling Prophecies: Pages 35-36
What is a double-blind experiment?

1. T
2. F
3. F
4. T

## Nonexperimental Research Methods—Different Strokes: Pages 37-42

What nonexperimental research methods do psychologists use?: Pages 37-42

| | | | | | |
|---|---|---|---|---|---|
| 1. F | | 6. F | | 11. F | |
| 2. T | | 7. F | | 12. T | |
| 3. F | | 8. F | | 13. T | |
| 4. F | | 9. F | | 14. F | |
| 5. F | | 10. T | | 15. T | |

## Psychology in the Media—Separating Fact from Fiction: Pages 43-44

How good is psychological information found in the popular media?

| | | | | | |
|---|---|---|---|---|---|
| 1. F | | 4. F | | 7. T | |
| 2. T | | 5. F | | 8. F | |
| 3. F | | 6. F | | | |

# FINAL SURVEY AND REVIEW

## Psychology—The ABCs of Behavior

What is psychology and what are its goals?

1. science; profession
2. behavior; mental
3. overt; behavior
4. observation
5. planned or structured
6. method
7. Developmental
8. Learning
9. theorists; traits
10. perception; sense (or sensory)
11. Comparative
12. Biopsychologists; behavior
13. Cognitive
14. Gender
15. social
16. Cultural; behavior
17. evolution; behavior
18. human; animal
19. describe; predict

## Critical Thinking—Take It with a Grain of Salt

What is critical thinking?

1. compare; critique
2. evaluate; evidence
3. scientific; evidence

## Pseudopsychologies—Palms, Planets and Personality

How does psychology differ from false explanations of behavior?

1. Commonsense; everyday
2. pseudo-psychologies
3. positive; Barnum

34

## Scientific Research—How to Think Like a Psychologist
How is the scientific method applied in psychological research?

1. measurement; repeatable
2. problem; hypothesis
3. valid (or useful)
4. operational
5. theory
6. introduction; methods

## A Brief History of Psychology—Psychology's Family Album
How did the field of psychology emerge?

1. philosophy
2. laboratory; Wundt
3. experience; introspection
4. adapt
5. Watson
6. stimuli; response
7. reinforcement
8. thinking; conditioning
9. whole
10. whole
11. unconscious
12. Freud; psychodynamic
13. free will; potential
14. self-image
15. self-actualization

## Psychology Today—Three Contemporary Perspectives on Behavior
What are the contemporary perspectives in psychology?

1. eclectic
2. behaviorism; biopsychology
3. neuroscience; neural
4. Positive
5. diversity (or differences)
6. values; norms

## Psychologists—Guaranteed Not to Shrink
What are the major specialties in psychology?

1. emotional; clinical
2. drugs
3. psychoanalysis
4. Master's
5. specialties
6. basic; applied

## The Psychology Experiment—Where Cause Meets Effect
How is an experiment performed?

1. Cause; experiment
2. experiment; varied
3. variable
4. independent
5. Dependent
6. Extraneous
7. subjects
8. independent; control
9. characteristics; randomly
10. identical; independent
11. statistically; chance
12. meta-analysis

## Double Blind—On Placebos and Self-Fulfilling Prophecies
What is a double-blind experiment?

1. placebo
2. single-blind; double-blind
3. experimenter
4. prophecies

## Nonexperimental Research Methods—Different Strokes
What nonexperimental research methods do psychologists use?

1. Naturalistic
2. observer; observer
3. records
4. correlation (or relationship
5. -1.00; zero
6. +1.00; perfect
7. plus
8. positive
9. decreases
10. predictions; causation
11. line; curved
12. case

13. heredity
14. natural
15. survey; sample

16. biases
17. gender

18. untruthful (or inaccurate); courtesy bias

## Psychology in the Media—Separating Fact from Fiction
How good is psychological information found in the popular media?

1. Skepticism; critical
2. biased

3. control
4. correlation; causation

5. valid (or scientific)
6. examples; generalization

# MASTERY TEST

1. d, p. 12
2. b, p. 14
3. b, p. 15
4. d, p. 22
5. b, pp. 22-23
6. a, p. 12
7. c, p. 26
8. b, p. 31
9. d, p. 27
10. a, p. 29
11. d, p. 31
12. d, p. 30
13. c, p. 16
14. a, p. 17
15. b, p. 17

16. d, p. 18
17. a, p. 18
18. c, p. 43
19. d, p. 33
20. c, p. 37
21. a, p. 38
22. b, p. 21
23. c, p. 35
24. a, p. 35
25. c, p. 33
26. d, p. 44
27. c, p. 33
28. d, p. 38
29. d, p. 37
30. b, p. 33

31. c, p. 37
32. d, p. 33
33. c, p. 21
34. d, p. 39
35. a, p. 39
36. d, p. 35
37. a, p. 24
38. c, p. 40
39. a, p. 40
40. b, p. 12
41. b, p. 31
42. c, p. 40
43. c, p. 42

# Brain and Behavior

## Chapter Overview

Communication between neurons begins when the dendrite and soma of a neuron combine neural input and send it down the axon to the axon terminals for output across the synapse to other neurons. The firing of an action potential is basically an electrical event. Communication between neurons is chemical: Neurotransmitters cross the synapse, attach to receptor sites, and excite or inhibit the receiving cell.

Chemicals called neuropeptides regulate activity in the brain. All behavior can be traced to networks of neurons. The brain can "rewire " itself and even grow new nerve cells in response to changing environmental conditions.

The nervous system can be divided into the central nervous system and the peripheral nervous system, which includes the somatic (bodily) and autonomic (involuntary) nervous systems. The brain carries out most of the "computing" in the nervous system

The spinal cord connects the brain to the peripheral nervous system and can process simple reflex arcs. The peripheral nervous system carries sensory information to the brain and motor commands to the body. "Vegetative" and automatic bodily processes are controlled by the autonomic nervous system, which has a sympathetic branch and a parasympathetic branch.

A major brain research strategy involves the localization of function to link specific structures in the brain with specific psychological or behavioral functions. Brain structure is investigated though dissection, CT scans and MRI scans, clinical case studies, electrical stimulation, ablation, deep lesioning, electrical recording, microelectrode recording, EEG recording, PET scans, and fMRI scans.

The human cerebral cortex is largely responsible for our ability to use language, make tools, acquire complex skills, and live in complex social groups. The cerebral cortex is divided into left and right hemispheres connected by the corpus callosum. Each hemisphere is divided into four lobes, the frontal lobes, the parietal lobes, the temporal lobes, and the occipital lobes. The human brain is marked by advanced corticalization, or enlargement of the cerebral cortex.

The most basic functions of the lobes of the cerebral cortex are as follows: frontal lobes—motor control, speech, abstract thought, and sense of self; parietal lobes—bodily sensation; temporal lobes—hearing and language; occipital lobes—vision. Damage to any of these areas will impair the named functions. Primary sensory and motor areas are found on the lobes of the cerebral cortex. Association areas on the cortex are neither sensory nor motor in function. They are related to more complex skills such as language, memory, recognition, and problem solving. Damage to either Broca's area or Wernicke's area causes speech and language problems known as aphasias.

The major parts of the brain can be subdivided into the forebrain, midbrain, and hindbrain. The subcortex includes hindbrain and midbrain brain structures as well as the lower parts of the forebrain, below the cortex. The medulla contains centers essential for reflex control of heart rate, breathing, and other "vegetative" functions. The cerebellum maintains coordination, posture, and muscle tone. The reticular formation directs sensory and motor messages, and part of it, known as the RAS, acts as an activating system for the cerebral cortex. The thalamus carries sensory information to the cortex. The hypothalamus exerts powerful control over eating, drinking, sleep cycles, body temperature, and other basic motives and behaviors. The limbic system is strongly related to emotion. It also contains distinct reward and punishment areas and an area known as the hippocampus that is important for forming memories.

Endocrine glands serve as a chemical communication system within the body. The ebb and flow of hormones from the endocrine glands entering the bloodstream affect behavior, moods, and personality. Many of the endocrine glands are influenced by the pituitary (the "master gland"), which is in turn influenced by the hypothalamus. Thus, the brain controls the body through both the fast nervous system and the slower endocrine system.

Brain dominance and brain activity determine if you are right-handed, left-handed, or ambidextrous. Most people are strongly right-handed. A minority are strongly left-handed. A few have moderate or mixed hand preferences or they are ambidextrous. Thus, handedness is not a simple either/or trait. Left-handed people tend to be less strongly lateralized than right-handed people.

# Learning Objectives

### Theme: Brain activity is the source of human consciousness, intelligence, and behavior.

| GQ: How do nerve cells operate and communicate? |
|---|
| LO 2.1  Name the basic unit that makes up the nervous system, state what it is specifically designed to do, and list and describe its four parts. |
| LO 2.2  Explain how a nerve impulse (*action potential*) occurs and how it is an all-or-nothing event. Include the terms *resting potential, threshold, ion channels,* and *negative after-potential*. |
| LO 2.3  Describe the difference between the nature of a nerve impulse and the nature of the communication between neurons. Explain how nerve impulses are carried from one neuron to another. Include an explanation of *receptor sites*; the types of *neurotransmitters*; and the functions of *neuropeptides, enkephalins,* and *endorphins*. |
| LO 2.4  Differentiate a *nerve* from a *neuron*. Describe the effect of *myelin* on the speed of the nerve impulse. Describe how *neurilemma* repairs neurons and explain what determines whether or not a neuron or nerve will regenerate. Include the current research techniques for alleviating brain damage. |
| GQ: What are the major parts of the nervous system? |
| LO 2.5  Chart the various subparts of the human nervous system and explain their functions. |
| LO 2.6  Describe the *spinal cord* and explain the mechanism of the *reflex arc*, including the types of neurons involved. |
| GQ: How is the brain studied? |
| LO 2.7  Describe the *localization of function* strategy. Differentiate between structural and functional imaging methods. |
| LO 2.8  Describe the following techniques for studying the brain: *CT scan, MRI, clinical study, electrical brain stimulation, ablation, deep lesioning, microelectrode recording, EEG, PET scan* and *functional MRI*. Explain why *CT scans* and *MRIs* are different from the other techniques. |

| |
|---|
| **GQ: Why is the human cerebral cortex so important and what are its parts?** |
| LO 2.9  Describe the main difference between the brains of lower and higher animals and differences between the brains of people who score high on mental tests and those who score low. Include a description of the *cerebrum* and *cerebral cortex* and an explanation of *corticalization*. |
| LO 2.10  Describe the two *hemispheres* of the brain, the *corpus callosum*, and the problem of *spatial neglect*; explain how and why the brain is "split" and the resulting effects; and differentiate the functions of right and left hemispheres. |
| LO 2.11  Describe the functions of each of the following parts of the brain as well as the resulting effects of damage to these areas: a. *occipital lobes*; b. *parietal lobes* (include the *somatosensory area*); c. *temporal lobes*; d. *frontal lobes* (include the motor cortex); e. *association areas* (include *Broca's* and *Wernicke's areas*). Describe the causes and effects of *aphasia*, *agnosia* and *facial agnosia* and compare the sex differences in the hemispheric responsibility for language. |
| **GQ: What are the major parts of the subcortex?** |
| LO 2.12  List the three areas of the *subcortex* and explain the function of each of the following parts of the subcortex: a. *hindbrain* (*brainstem*) including: 1. the *medulla*; 2. the *pons*; 3. the *cerebellum*, and 4. the *reticular formation*; and b. *forebrain* including: 1. the *thalamus* and 2. the *hypothalamus*. |
| LO 2.13  Name the structures that comprise the *limbic system*; explain its overall function, the specific functions of the *amygdala* and the *hippocampus,* and the significance of "pleasure" and "aversive" areas in the limbic system; and list the six basic functions of the brain. |
| **GQ: Does the glandular system affect behavior?** |
| LO 2.14  Explain the purpose of the *endocrine system*; describe the action of *hormones* in the body; and describe the effects that the following glands have on the body and behavior: a. *pituitary* (include a description of *dwarfism*, *giantism*, and *acromegaly*); b. *pineal*; c. *thyroid* (include a description of *hyperthyroidism* and *hypothyroidism*); d. *adrenal medulla*; and e. *adrenal cortex* (include a description of *virilism*, *premature puberty*, and the problem of *anabolic steroids*). |
| **GQ: In what ways do right- and left-handed individuals differ?** |
| LO 2.15  Describe *brain dominance* and *handness*, including their relationship to speech; whether handedness is inherited; how the dominant hemisphere is determined; and the incidence, advantages, and disadvantages of being right-or left-handed. |

# RECITE AND REVIEW

## Neurons-Building a "Biocomputer": Pages 48-52

How do nerve cells operate and communicate?

1.  The _____ and nervous system are made up of linked nerve cells called _____ , which pass information from one to another through synapses.

2.  The brain consists of approximately _____ neurons, which carry information.

3.  The basic conducting fibers of neurons are _____ , but dendrites (a receiving area), the soma (the cell body and also a receiving area), and _____ terminals (the branching ends of a neuron) are also involved in communication.

4.  A _____ refers to an inactive neuron's electrical charge (-60 to -70 millivolts).

5. The firing of an action potential (_____ _____ ) is basically electrical, whereas communication between neurons is chemical.

6. An action potential occurs when the _____ potential is altered enough to reach the threshold for firing. At that point, sodium _____flow into the axon, through _____channels.

7. The negative action potential occurs because potassium ions flow out of the _____ , restoring the resting potential.

8. The _____ potential is an all-or-nothing event.

9. The action potential leaps from gap to gap of the _____ in a process called salutatory conduction.

10. Neurons release neurotransmitters at the synapse. These cross to _____ sites on the receiving cell, causing it to be excited or inhibited. For example, the transmitter chemical acetylcholine activates _____ .

11. Some neurotransmitters act to _____ (move it closer to firing) the next neuron, and some neurotransmitters act to inhibit (make firing less likely) the next neuron.

12. Disturbances of any neurotransmitters found in the brain can have serious consequences, such as too _____ dopamine can cause muscle tremors of Parkinson's disease or too _____ dopamine can cause schizophrenic symptoms.

13. Chemicals called neuropeptides do not carry messages directly. Instead, they _____ the activity of other neurons.

14. Opiate-like neural regulators called enkephalins and endorphins are released in the brain to relieve _____ and stress.

15. _____ may help explain how some women who suffer from severe premenstrual pain and distress have unusually low endorphin levels.

16. A neuron may receive both excitatory and _____ messages.

17. _____ refers to the brain's capacity to change in response to experience

18. PET and fMRI scans show that brains of individuals with spider phobias and aphasias have developed _____changes as a result of learned experiences.

40

# The Nervous System—Wired for Action: Pages 53-56

What are the major parts of the nervous system?

1. _____ are made of large bundles of axons.

2. The axons of most neurons in the peripheral nervous systm are covered by the _____ which aids in repair to damaged nerve fibers.

3. The nervous system can be divided into the _____ nervous system (the brain and spinal cord) and the _____ nervous system.

4. The CNS includes the _____ (bodily) and _____ (involuntary) nervous systems.

5. The autonomic system has two divisions: the _____ (emergency, activating) branch and the _____ (sustaining, conserving) branch.

6. Thirty-one pairs of spinal _____ leave the spinal cord. Twelve pairs of cranial _____ leave the brain directly. Together, they carry sensory and motor messages between the brain and the body.

7. The simplest _____ is a reflex arc, which involves a sensory neuron, a connector neuron, and a _____ neuron.

8. The production of new _____ cells is called neurogenesis.

# Research Methods—Charting the Brain's Inner Realms: Pages 56-59

How is the brain studied?

1. Brain research methods have included dissection, ablation, deep lesioning, electrical recording, stimulation, micro-electrode recording, EEG recording, and _____ studies.

2. Computer-enhanced techniques are providing three-dimensional _____ of the living human brain and its _____. Examples of such techniques are CT scans, MRI scans, and PET scans.

3. The _____ scan produces images of the brain by using X-rays, the _____ scan produces images of the brain by using a magnetic field, and the _____ scan produces images of the brain as well as the activities of the brain by detecting positrons emitted by a weak radioactive glucose in the brain.

4. Using a PET scan, Haier and colleagues found that intelligence is related to _____ : A less

    efficient brain works much harder than a more efficient brain.

5. The functional MRI uses MRI technology to make brain activity _____ .

# The Cerebral Cortex—My, What a Big Brain You Have!: Pages 59-67
Why is the human cerebral cortex so important, and what are its parts?

1. The human _____ is marked by advanced corticalization, or enlargement of the cerebral

    _____ , which covers the outside surface of the cerebrum.

2. Neurological _____ signs result from brain abnormalities or injuries and do not include

    obvious behavioral symptoms but rather they include such behavioral signs as clumsiness,

    gait, and poor hand-eye coordination.

3. "Split brains" have been created by _____ the corpus callosum. The split-brain individual

    shows a remarkable degree of independence between the right and left _____ .

4. The_____cerebral hemisphere contains speech or language "centers" in most people.

    It also specializes in calculating, judging time and rhythm, and ordering complex movements.

5. The_____ hemisphere is largely nonverbal. It excels at spatial and perceptual skills,

    visualization, and recognition of _____, faces, and melodies.

6. Another way to summarize specialization in the brain is to say that the _____ hemisphere

    is good at analysis and processing information sequentially; the_____ hemisphere

    processes information simultaneously and holistically.

7. The most basic functions of the lobes of the cerebral cortex are as follows: occipital lobes—

    _____; parietal lobes—bodily sensation; temporal lobes— _____and language;

    frontal lobes—motor control, speech, and abstract thought.

8. Mirror neurons may be a cause of _____ _____ _____ .

9. Association areas _____ and process information.

10. Damage to either Broca's area or Wernicke's area causes _____ and language problems known as aphasias.

11. Damage to Broca's area causes problems with _____ and pronunciation. Damage to Wernicke's area causes problems with the _____ of words.

12. Damage in other association areas may cause agnosia, the inability to _____ objects by sight. This disability can sometimes impair the ability to recognize _____, a condition called facial agnosia.

13. Research conducted by Haier and his colleague has shown brain_____ in males and females particularly involving the concentration of gray and white _____ of the brain.

## The Subcortex—At the Core of the (Brain) Matter: Pages 67-70
What are the major parts of the subcortex?

1. All of the brain areas below the _____ are called the subcortex.

2. The medulla contains centers essential for reflex control of _____, breathing, and other "vegetative" functions.

3. The pons connects the medulla with_____ brain areas and it influences _____ and arousal.

4. The cerebellum maintains _____, posture, and muscle tone.

5. The _____ lies inside the medulla and the brainstem, influences_____, and does not mature until_____. It also directs sensory and motor messages, and part of it, known as the RAS, acts as a(n) ____ system for the cerebral cortex.

6. The thalamus carries _____information to the cortex. The hypothalamus exerts powerful control over eating, drinking, sleep cycles, body temperature, and other basic_____and behaviors.

7. The limbic system is strongly related to_____and motivated behavior. It also contains distinct reward and punishment areas.

8. A part of the limbic system called the amygdala is related to _____. An area known as the hippocampus is important for forming _____.

## The Endocrine System—My Hormones Made Me Do It: Pages 70-72

Does the glandular system affect behavior?

1. The endocrine system provides _____ communication in the body through the release of _____ into the bloodstream. Endocrine glands influence moods, behavior, and even personality.

2. Many of the endocrine glands are influenced by the pituitary (the "_____ gland"), which is in turn influenced by the hypothalamus.

3. The pituitary supplies _____ hormone. Too little GH causes _____ ; too much causes giantism or acromegaly.

4. Body rhythms and _____ cycles are influenced by melatonin, secreted by the pineal gland.

5. The thyroid gland regulates _____ . Hyperthyroidism refers to an overactive thyroid gland; hypothyroidism to an underactive thyroid.

6. The adrenal glands supply _____ and norepinephrine to activate the body. They also regulate salt balance, responses to stress, and they are a secondary source of _____ hormones.

7. Most drugs like anabolic steroids are synthetic versions of _____ .

## Psychology in Action: Handedness—Are you Dexterous or Sinister?: Pages 73-75

In what ways to right- and left-handed individuals differ?

1. Hand dominance ranges from strongly left- to strongly right-handed, with _____ handedness in between.

2. Ninety percent of the population is basically _____ ,10 percent _____

3. The vast majority of people are right-handed and therefore _____ brain dominant for motor skills. Ninety-seven percent of right-handed persons and 68 percent of the left-handed also produce _____ from the left hemisphere.

4. _____ people in the past were forced to _____ as right-handed people; therefore, there are fewer left-handed older people living than right-handed older people.

5. In general, the _____ are less strongly lateralized in brain function than are _____ persons.

# CONNECTIONS

## Neurons-Building a "Biocomputer": Pages 48-52
How do nerve cells operate and communicate?

1. _____ soma
2. _____ neurilemma
3. _____ axon collateral
4. _____ myelin
5. _____ dendrites
6. _____ axon terminals
7. _____ axon

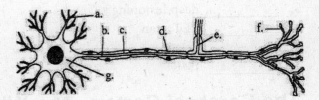

## The Nervous System—Wired for Action: Pages 53-56
What are the major parts of the nervous system?

1. _____ spinal cord
2. _____ autonomic system
3. _____ parasympathetic branch
4. _____ peripheral nervous system
5. _____ sympathetic branch
6. _____ brain
7. _____ somatic system

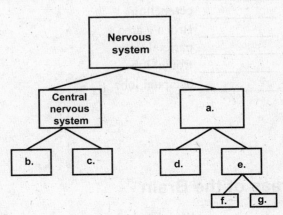

# Research Methods—Charting the Brain's Inner Realms: Pages 56-59

How is the brain studied?

1. _____ CT scan
2. _____ EEG
3. _____ deep lesioning
4. _____ PET scan
5. _____ ablation
6. _____ fMRI

a. brain waves
b. radioactive glucose
c. surgery
d. electrode
e. computerized X-rays
f. brain activity

# The Cerebral Cortex—My, What a Big Brain You Have! Pages 59-67

Why is the human cerebral cortex so important, and what are its parts?

1. _____ Wernicke's area
2. _____ temporal lobe
3. _____ cerebellum
4. _____ Broca's area
5. _____ parietal lobe
6. _____ frontal lobe
7. _____ occipital lobe

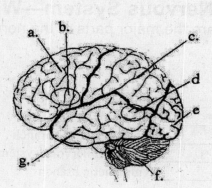

## Areas of the Brain

1. _____ Wernicke's Area
2. _____ Broca's area
3. _____ facial agnosia
4. _____ aphasia
5. _____ motor cortex
6. _____ somatosensory area

a. language impairment
b. language production
c. language comprehension
d. receives bodily sensations
e. controls voluntary movements
f. impaired facial recognition

## The Subcortex—At the Core of the (Brain) Matter: Pages 67-70

What are the major parts of the subcortex?

1. _____ midbrain
2. _____ reticular formation
3. _____ cerebrum
4. _____ medulla
5. _____ hypothalamus
6. _____ corpus callosum
7. _____ pituitary
8. _____ spinal cord
9. _____ thalamus

## The Endocrine System—My Hormones Made Me Do It: Pages 70-72

Does the glandular system affect behavior?

1. _____ hypopituitary dwarfism
2. _____ pituitary
3. _____ anabolic steroids
4. _____ testes
5. _____ pineal gland
6. _____ thyroid gland
7. _____ acromegaly
8. _____ adrenal glands

a. testosterone
b. metabolism
c. growth hormone
d. epinephrine
e. melatonin
f. synthetic of testosterone
g. too much growth hormone
h. too little growth hormone

# CHECK YOUR MEMORY

## Neurons-Building a "Biocomputer": Pages 48-52
How do nerve cells operate and communicate?

1. The dendrites receive incoming information from the neurilemma.    TRUE or FALSE

2. Human axons may be up to a meter long.    TRUE or FALSE

3. The resting potential is about plus 70 millivolts.    TRUE or FALSE

4. The interior of the axon becomes positive during an action potential.    TRUE or FALSE

5. The action potential is an all-or-nothing event.    TRUE or FALSE

6. The negative after-potential is due to an inward flow of potassium ions.    TRUE or FALSE

7. Nerve impulses travel faster in axons surrounded by myelin.    TRUE or FALSE

8. In nonmyelinated axons, salutatory conduction occurs.    TRUE or FALSE

9. Neurotransmitters activate other neurons; neuropeptides activate muscles and glands.
   TRUE or FALSE

10. Enkephalins are neuropeptides.    TRUE or FALSE

11. Our brains do not change in response to experience.    TRUE or FALSE

12. Many drugs imitate, duplicate, or block neurotransmitters to excite or inhibit an action potential.
   TRUE or FALSE

## The Nervous System—Wired for Action: Pages 53-56
What are the major parts of the nervous system?

1. The peripheral nervous system consists of the brain and spinal cord.    TRUE or FALSE

2. The neurilemma helps damaged nerve cell fibers regenerate after an injury.    TRUE or FALSE

3. Neurons in the brain and spinal cord must last a lifetime; damage to them is usually permanent.
   TRUE or FALSE

4. The word *autonomic* means "self-limiting."    TRUE or FALSE

5. The parasympathetic branch quiets the body and returns it to a lower level of arousal.
   TRUE or FALSE

6. Researchers have had some success in stimulating regrowth of cut nerve fibers in the spinal cord.
   TRUE or FALSE

7. The sympathetic system generally controls voluntary behavior.    TRUE or FALSE

8. Thirty-one cranial nerves leave the brain directly.   TRUE or FALSE

9. "Fight-or-flight" emergency reactions are produced by the autonomic nervous system.
   TRUE or FALSE

10. Activity in the parasympathetic system increases heart rate and respiration.   TRUE or FALSE

11. In a reflex arc, motor neurons carry messages to effector cells.   TRUE or FALSE

12. A person is born with all of the brain cells that she will ever have.

## Research Methods—Charting the Brain's Inner Realms: Pages 56-59
How is the brain studied?

1. Deep lesioning in the brain is usually done surgically.   TRUE or FALSE

2. Micro-electrodes are needed in order to record from single neurons.   TRUE or FALSE

3. CT scans form "maps" of brain activity.   TRUE or FALSE

4. Electroencephalography records waves of electrical activity produced by the brain.
   TRUE or FALSE

5. Radioactive glucose is used to make PET scans.   TRUE or FALSE

6. The fMRI uses X-ray technology to provide images of brain action.   TRUE or FALSE

7. According to Richard Haier, a less efficient brain works harder and still accomplishes less than a more efficient brain because a less efficient brain uses less glucose to process information. TRUE or FALSE

## The Cerebral Cortex—My, What a Big Brain You Have! Pages 59-67
Why is the human cerebral cortex so important, and what are its parts?

1. Elephants have brain-body ratios similar to those of humans.   TRUE or FALSE

2. The corpus callosum connects the right and left brain hemispheres.   TRUE or FALSE

3. The cerebellum makes up a large part of the cerebral cortex.   TRUE or FALSE

4. Much of the cerebral cortex is made up of gray matter.   TRUE or FALSE

5. Damage to the left cerebral hemisphere usually causes spatial neglect.   TRUE or FALSE

6. The right half of the brain mainly controls left body areas.   TRUE or FALSE

7. Roger Sperry won a Nobel prize for his work on corticalization.   TRUE or FALSE

8. Neurological soft signs include clumsiness, awkward gait, and poor hand-eye coordination.
   TRUE or FALSE

49

9. Cutting the reticular formation produces a "split brain."   TRUE or FALSE

10. Information from the right side of vision is sent directly to the right cerebral hemisphere.
    TRUE or FALSE

11. The right hemisphere tends to be good at speaking, writing, and math.   TRUE or FALSE

12. The left hemisphere is mainly involved with analysis.   TRUE or FALSE

13. The right hemisphere sees overall patterns and general connections. The left brain focuses on small details.   TRUE or FALSE

14. Both brain hemispheres are normally active at all times.   TRUE or FALSE

15. The motor cortex is found on the occipital lobes.   TRUE or FALSE

16. The somatosensory area is located on the parietal lobes.   TRUE or FALSE

17. Electrically stimulating the motor cortex causes movement in various parts of the body.
    TRUE or FALSE

18. Large parts of the lobes of the brain are made up of association cortex.   TRUE or FALSE

19. Damage to either brain hemisphere usually causes an aphasia.   TRUE or FALSE

20. A person with Broca's aphasia might say "pear" when shown an apple.   TRUE or FALSE

21. Damage to Wernicke's area causes the condition known as mindblindness.   TRUE or FALSE

22. Women are much more likely than men to use both cerebral hemispheres for language processing.
    TRUE or FALSE

23. Research has shown women have more white matter and men have more grey matter in their brains.
    TRUE or FALSE

# The Subcortex—At the Core of the (Brain) Matter: Pages 67-70
What are the major parts of the subcortex?

1. The cerebrum makes up much of the medulla.   TRUE or FALSE

2. Injury to the medulla may affect breathing.   TRUE or FALSE

3. Injury to the cerebellum affects attention and wakefulness.   TRUE or FALSE

4. The reticular formation is the switching station for sensory messages and is fully developed at birth.
   TRUE or FALSE

5. Smell is the only major sense that does not pass through the thalamus.   TRUE or FALSE

6. Stimulating various parts of the limbic system can produce rage, fear, pleasure, or arousal.
   TRUE or FALSE

7. The hippocampus is associated with hunger and eating.   TRUE or FALSE

8. The amydala appears to play a role in phobias and anxiety.   TRUE or FALSE

## The Endocrine System—My Hormones Made Me Do It: Pages 70-72
Does the glandular system affect behavior?

1. Androgens ("male" hormones) are related to the sex drive in both men and women.
   TRUE or FALSE

2. Hormones secreted during times of high emotion tend to increase memory loss.
   TRUE or FALSE

3. After watching violent scenes, men had high levels of testosterone in their bloodstream.
   TRUE or FALSE

4. If too little growth hormone is released, a person may experience hypopituitary drawfism.
   TRUE or FALSE

5. Activity of the pituitary is influenced by the hypothalamus.    TRUE or FALSE

6. A person who is slow, sleepy, and overweight could be suffering from hypothyroidism.
   TRUE or FALSE

7. Virilism and premature puberty may be caused by problems with the adrenal glands.
   TRUE or FALSE

8. Steroid drugs may cause sexual impotence and breast enlargement in males.    TRUE or FALSE

9. There is much evidence to support that steroids do improve performance, which is why all major sports organizations ban the use of steroids.    TRUE or FALSE

## Psychology in Action: Handedness: Pages 73-75
In what ways to right- and left-handed individuals differ?

1. Left-handers have an advantage in fencing, boxing, and baseball.    TRUE or FALSE

2. Most left-handed persons produce speech from their right hemispheres.    TRUE or FALSE

3. To a degree left or right handedness is influenced by heredity, especially by a gene on the X chromosome.    TRUE or FALSE

4. On average, left-handed persons die at younger ages than right-handed persons do.
   TRUE or FALSE

# FINAL SURVEY AND REVIEW

## Neurons-Building a "Biocomputer"
How do nerve cells operate and communicate?

1.  The brain and nervous system are made up of linked nerve cells called _____, which pass information from one to another through synapses.

2.  The brain consists of approximately 100 billion neurons, which carry _____ .

3.  The basic conducting fibers of neurons are axons, but _____ (a receiving area), the _____ (the cell body and also a receiving area), and axon terminals (the branching ends of a neuron) are also involved in communication.

4.  A resting potential refers to an electrical charge (-60 to -70 millivolts) of an _____ .

5.  The firing of an _____ _____ (nerve impulse) is basically electrical, whereas communication between neurons is chemical.

6.  An action potential occurs when the resting potential is altered enough to reach the _____ for firing. At that point, _____ ions flow into the axon, through ion channels.

7.  The negative action potential occurs because _____ ions flow out of the axon, restoring the resting potential.

8.  The action potential is an _____ event.

9.  The action potential leaps from gap to gap of the myelin in a process called _____ _____ .

10. Neurons release _____ at the synapse. These cross to receptor sites on the receiving cell, causing it to be excited or inhibited. For example, the transmitter chemical _____ activates muscles.

11. Some neurotransmitters act to excite the receiving neuron by increasing its ability to _____ an action potential, and some neurotransmitters act to inhibit the receiving neuron by _____ its ability to fire.

52

12. Disturbances of any neurotransmitters found in the brain can have serious consequences, such as too little dopamine can cause muscle tremors of _____ or too much dopamine can cause _____.

13. Chemicals called _____ do not carry messages directly. Instead, they regulate the activity of other neurons.

14. Opiate-like neural regulators called enkephalins and _____ are released in the brain to relieve pain and stress.

15. Neural regulators may help explain how some women who suffer from severe premenstrual pain and distress have unusually _____ levels.

19. A neuron may receive both _____ and inhibitory messages.

20. Neuoroplasticity refers to the brain's capacity to change in response to _____ .

21. PET and fMRI scans show that brains of individuals with spider phobias and aphasias have developed _____ changes as a result of learned experiences.

# The Nervous System—Wired for Action
## What are the major parts of the nervous system?

1. Nerves are made of large bundles of _____ .

2. The axons of most neurons in the _____ nervous systm are covered by the neurilemma which aids in repair to damaged nerve fibers.

3. The nervous system can be divided into the _____ nervous system (the_____ and spinal cord) and the peripheral nervous system.

4. The CNS includes the _____ (bodily) and _____ (involuntary) nervous systems.

5. The autonomic system has two divisions: the _____ (emergency, activating) branch and the _____ (sustaining, conserving) branch.

7. Thirty-one pairs of _____ nerves leave the spinal cord. Twelve pairs of nerves leave the brain directly. Together, these nerves carry sensory and _____ messages between the brain and the body.

8. The simplest behavior is a _____ _____, which involves a sensory neuron, an neuron, and a _____ neuron.

9. The production of new brain cells is called _____.

# Research Methods—Charting the Brain's Inner Realms
How is the brain studied?

1. Conventional brain research relies on _____ (separation into parts), staining, ablation, deep lesioning, electrical recording, electrical _____ , micro-electrode recording, EEG recording, and clinical studies.

2. Computer-enhanced techniques are providing three-dimensional images of the living human brain and its activities. Examples of such techniques are CT scans, _____ scans, and _____ scans, which record brain activity.

3. The CT scan produces images of the brain by using _____, the MRI scan produces images of the brain by using a_____, and the PET scan produces images of the brain as well as the activities of the brain by detecting positrons emitted by a weak _____in the brain.

4. Using a PET scan, Haier and colleagues found that intelligence is related to brain efficiency: A _____ efficient brain works much harder than a _____ efficient brain.

5. The _____ uses MRI technology to make brain activity visible.


# The Cerebral Cortex—My, What a Big Brain You Have!
# Pages
Why is the human cerebral cortex so important, and what are its parts?

1. The human brain is marked by advanced _____, or enlargement of the cerebral cortex, which covers the outside surface of the _____.

2. Neurological _____ _____ result from brain abnormalities or injuries and do not include obvious behavioral symptoms but rather they include such behavioral signs as clumsiness, gait, and poor hand-eye coordination.

3. "Split brains" have been created by cutting the _____ _____. The split-brain individual shows a remarkable degree of independence between the right and left _____ .

4. The left cerebral _____ contains speech or language "centers" in most people. It also specializes in calculating, judging time and rhythm, and ordering complex _____.

5. The right hemisphere is largely nonverbal. It excels at _____ and perceptual skills, visualization, and recognition of patterns, _____, and melodies.

6. Another way to summarize specialization in the brain is to say that the left hemisphere is good at _____ and processing information sequentially; the right hemisphere processes information _____ and holistically.

7. The most basic functions of the lobes of the cerebral _____ are as follows: occipital lobes - vision; parietal lobes—bodily _____; temporal lobes—hearing and language; frontal lobes—motor control, _____, and abstract thought.

8. _____ _____ may be a cause of autism spectrum disorders .

9. Association areas combine and _____ information.

10. Damage to either Broca's area or Wernicke's area causes speech and language problems known as _____ .

11. Damage to _____ area causes problems with speech and pronunciation. Damage to _____ area causes problems with the meaning of words.

12. Damage in other association areas may cause _____ , the inability to identify objects by sight. This disability can sometimes impair the ability to recognize faces, a condition called _____ _____ .

13. Research conducted by Haier and his colleague has shown brain specialization in males and females particularly involving the concentration of _____ and _____ matter of the brain.

# The Subcortex—At the Core of the (Brain) Matter
What are the major parts of the subcortex?

1. All of the brain areas below the cortex are called the _____ .

2. The _____ contains centers essential for reflex control of heart rate, breathing, and other "vegetative" functions.

3. The _____ connects the medulla with higher brain areas and it influences sleep and arousal.

4. The _____ maintains coordination, posture, and muscle tone.

5. The _____ lies inside the medulla and the brainstem, influences attention, and does not mature until adolescence. It also directs sensory and motor messages, and part of it, known as the RAS, acts as an activating system for the _____ _____.

6. The _____ carries sensory information to the cortex. The _____ exerts powerful control over eating, drinking, sleep cycles, body temperature, and other basic motives and behaviors.

7. The _____ system is strongly related to emotion and motivation. It also contains distinct _____ and punishment areas.

8. The part of the limbic system called the _____ is related to fear. An area known as the _____ is important for forming lasting memories.

## The Endocrine System—My Hormones Made Me Do It
Does the glandular system affect behavior?

1. The _____ system provides chemical communication in the body through the release of hormones into the _____ .

2. Many of the endocrine glands are influenced by the _____ (the "master gland"), which is in turn influenced by the _____ .

3. The _____ supplies growth hormone. Too little GH causes dwarfism; too much causes giantism or _____ .

4. Body rhythms and sleep cycles are influenced by _____, secreted by the _____ gland.

5. The thyroid gland regulates metabolism. Hyperthyroidism refers to an _____ thyroid gland; hypothyroidism refers to an _____ thyroid.

6. The _____ glands supply epinephrine and norepinephrine to activate the body. They also regulate salt balance, responses to _____ , and they are a secondary source of sex hormones.

7. Most drugs like anabolic steroids are _____ versions of testosterone.

# Psychology in Action: Handedness

In what ways to right- and left-handed individuals differ?

1. _____ _____ ranges from strongly left- to strongly right-handed, with

   _____ handedness in between.

2. _____ percent of the population is basically right-handed, _____ percent left-

   handed.

3. The vast majority of people are _____ and therefore _____ brain dominant for

   motor skills. Ninety-seven percent of right-handed persons and 68 percent of the left-handed

   produce speech from the _____ hemisphere.

4. Left-handed people in the past were forced to _____ as _____ people; therefore,

   there are fewer left-handed older people living than right-handed older people.

5. In general, the left-handed are less strongly _____ in brain function than are right-handed

   persons.

# MASTERY TEST

1. At times of emergency, anger, or fear, what part of the nervous system becomes more active?
   a. corpus callosum of the forebrain
   b. sympathetic branch of the ANS
   c. parasympathetic branch of the PNS
   d. Broca's area

2. The highest and largest brain area in humans is the
   a. cerebrum.
   b. cerebellum.
   c. frontal lobes.
   d. gray matter of the callosum.

3. A tumor in which brain area would most likely cause blind spots in vision?
   a. occipital lobe
   b. temporal lobe
   c. somatosensory area
   d. association cortex

4. Neurotransmitters are found primarily in
   a. the spinal cord.
   b. neurilemmas.
   c. synapses.
   d. motor neurons.

5. Enkephalins are an example of
   a. acetylcholine blockers.
   b. neuropeptides.
   c. receptor sites.
   d. adrenal hormones.

6. Electrically stimulating a portion of which brain area would produce movements in the body?
   a. occipital lobe
   b. frontal lobe
   c. parietal lobe
   d. temporal lobe

7. When a neuron reaches its threshold, a(n) _____ occurs.
   a. volume potential
   b. ion potential
   c. action potential
   d. dendrite potential

8. A person's ability to work as a commercial artist would be most impaired by damage to the
   a. left temporal lobe.
   b. right cerebral hemisphere.
   c. left cerebral hemisphere.
   d. frontal association cortex.

9. Electrically stimulating the brain would most likely produce anger if it activated the
   a. association cortex.
   b. limbic system.
   c. parasympathetic branch.
   d. reticular activating system.

10. Information in neurons usually flows in what order?
   a. soma, dendrites, axon
   b. dendrites, soma, axon
   c. dendrites, myelin, axon terminals
   d. axon, soma, axon terminals

11. Regulating the activity of other neurons is most characteristic of
   a. neuropeptides
   b. acetylcholine
   c. reflex arcs
   d. resting potentials

12. Nerve impulses occur when _____ rush into the axon.
    a. sodium ions
    b. potassium ions
    c. negative charges
    d. neurotransmitters

13. Experiments involving the grafting of nerve cells have been
    a. unsuccessful at present.
    b. successful in animals.
    c. successful only in the peripheral nervous system.
    d. successful only in the CNS.

14. A person who says "bife" for bike and "seep" for sleep probably suffers from
    a. Broca's aphasia.
    b. Wernicke's aphasia.
    c. functional agnosia.
    d. the condition known as "mindblindness."

15. Damage to which part of the limbic system would most likely impair memory?
    a. thalamus
    b. hypothalamus
    c. amygdala
    d. hippocampus

16. Involuntary changes in heart rate, blood pressure, digestion, and sweating are controlled by the
    a. thoracic nerves.
    b. parietal lobes.
    c. somatic system.
    d. autonomic system.

17. In which of the following pairs are both structures part of the forebrain?
    a. medulla, hypothalamus
    b. cerebrum, cerebellum
    c. medulla, thalamus
    d. cerebrum, thalamus

18. Which of the following is a specialized type of X-ray?
    a. PET scan
    b. CT scan
    c. MRI scan
    d. EEG scan

19. Which two problems are associated with the pituitary gland?
    a. dwarfism, acromegaly
    b. virilism, acromegaly
    c. mental retardation, dwarfism
    d. giantism, premature puberty

59

20. The cerebral hemispheres are interconnected by the
    a. reticular system.
    b. cerebellum.
    c. cerebrum.
    d. corpus callosum.

21. Damage to which of the following would most likely make it difficult for a person to play catch with a ball?
    a. reticular formation
    b. limbic system
    c. cerebellum
    d. association cortex

22. Speech, language, calculation, and analysis are special skills of the
    a. right cerebral hemisphere.
    b. limbic system.
    c. left cerebral hemisphere.
    d. right somatosensory area.

23. The usual flow of information in a reflex arc is
    a. cranial nerve, connector neuron, spinal nerve.
    b. sensory neuron, connector neuron, motor neuron.
    c. effector cell, interneuron, connector neuron.
    d. sensory neuron, connector neuron, reflex neuron.

24. A person will "hear" a series of sounds when which area of the cortex is electrically stimulated?
    a. frontal lobe
    b. parietal lobe
    c. occipital lobe
    d. temporal lobe

25. Which of the following pairs contains the "master gland" and its master?
    a. pineal—thalamus
    b. thyroid—RAS
    c. pituitary—hypothalamus
    d. adrenal—cortex

26. Many basic motives and emotions are influenced by the
    a. thalamus.
    b. hypothalamus.
    c. corpus callosum.
    d. cerebellum.

27. Both surgical ablation and _____ remove brain tissue.
    a. the MEG technique
    b. tomography
    c. micro-electrode sampling
    d. deep lesioning

28. Which of the following techniques requires access to the interior of the brain?
    a. micro-electrode recording
    b. EEG recordings
    c. PET scanning
    d. functional MRI

29. Which of the following statements about handedness is false?
    a. Like eye color, handedness is inherited from one's parents.
    b. A majority of left-handers produce speech from the left hemisphere.
    c. The left-handed are less lateralized than the right-handed.
    d. Left-handedness is an advantage in boxing and fencing.

30. Negative after-potentials are caused by the outward flow of _____ from the axon.
    a. negative charges
    b. potassium ions
    c. neurotransmitters
    d. sodium ions

31. Scott was challenged to catch a dollar bill as fast as he could with his thumb and index finger as it fell between them. Scott was successful one time out of five trials. Which statement best explains why Scott failed to catch the dollar bill?
    a. Scott's injury to the temporal lobe has caused him to not see when the dollar bill falls.
    b. This simple yet common test signifies that Scott has serious cognitive deficits and must seek a specialist immediately.
    c. From the time Scott processes the information to when his brain tells the muscles to grab the dollar bill, the dollar bill has already slipped by.
    d. none of the above

32. People with Parkinson's disease lack or have very little of the neurotransmitter_____.
    a. endorphins
    b. epinephrine
    c. serotonin
    d. dopamine

33. Which statement correctly reflects the findings of Haier and his colleagues on the relationship between intelligence and brain efficiency?
    a. A less efficient brain works much harder than a more efficient brain.
    b. A more efficient brain works much harder than a less efficient brain.
    c. A less efficient brain uses less glucose when processing information.
    d. A more efficient brain uses more glucose when processing information.

34. A healthy 75-year-old brain has _____ neurons than it did at age 25.
    a. far few
    b. a few less
    c. as many
    d. more

35. Upon waking up, Natasha experienced such behavioral symptoms as clumsiness and an awkward gait. Natasha is displaying neurological _____ .
    a. hard signs
    b. soft signs
    c. external signs
    d. mental signs

36. In regards to brain concentration and specialization, men have been shown to have more _____ matter than women and women have been shown to have more _____ matter than men.
    a. hard; soft
    b. soft; hard
    c. white; grey
    d. grey; white

37. Mirror neurons may play a role in which of the following disorders?
    a. autism spectrum
    b. schizophrenia
    c. depression
    d. stroke

# SOLUTIONS

## RECITE AND REVIEW

### Neurons-Building a "Biocomputer": Pages 48-52
How do nerve cells operate and communicate?

1. brain; neurons
2. 100 billion;
3. axons; axon
4. resting potential
5. nerve; impulse
6. resting; ions; ion
7. axon
8. action
9. myelin
10. receptor; muscles
11. excite
12. little; much
13. regulate
14. pain
15. excitatory
16. experience
17. neurological

### The Nervous System—Wired for Action: Pages 53-56
What are the major parts of the nervous system?

1. axons
2. peripheral
3. myelin; Neurilemma
4. central; brain
5. bodily; involuntary
6. emergency; activiating
7. nerves; nerves
8. behavior, motor
9. brain

## Research Methods—Charting the Brain's Inner Realms: Pages 56-59
How is the brain studied?

1. electrical; clinical
2. images; activity
3. CT; MRI; PET
4. brain efficiency
5. visible

## The Cerebral Cortex—My, What a Big Brain You Have!: Pages 59-67
Why is the human cerebral cortex so important, and what are its parts?

1. brain; cortex
2. soft; awkward
3. cutting; hemisphers
4. left; writing
5. right; patterns
6. left; right
7. vision; hearing
8. autism spectrum disorders
9. combine
10. speech
11. grammar; meaning
12. identify; faces
13. specialization; matter

## The Subcortex—At the Core of the (Brain) Matter: Pages 67-70
What are the major parts of the subcortex?

1. cortex
2. heart; rate
3. higher; sleep
4. coordination
5. reticular formation; attention; adolescence; activating
6. sensory; motives
7. emotion
8. fear; phobias
9. memories

## The Endocrine System—My Hormones Made Me Do It: Pages 70-72
Does the glandular system affect behavior?

1. chemical; hormones
2. master
3. growth; dwarfism
4. sleep
5. metabolism
6. epinephrine; sex
7. testosterone

## Psychology in Action: Handedness: Pages 73-75
In what ways to right- and left-handed individuals differ?

1. inconsistent
2. right-handed; left-handed
3. left; speech
4. Left-handed; masquerade
5. left-handed; right-handed

# CONNECTIONS
## Neurons-Building a "Biocomputer": Pages 48-52
How do nerve cells operate and communicate?

1. g.
2. d.
3. e.
4. c.
5. a.
6. f.
7. b.

63

## The Nervous System—Wired for Action: Pages 53-56

What are the major parts of the nervous system?

1. c. or b.
2. e.
3. f. or g.
4. a.
5. f. or g.
6. c. or b.
7. d.

## Research Methods—Charting the Brain's Inner Realms: Pages 56-59

How is the brain studied?

1. e.
2. a.
3. d.
4. b.
5. c.

## The Cerebral Cortex—My, What a Big Brain You Have!: Pages 59-67

Why is the human cerebral cortex so important, and what are its parts?

1. d.
2. g.
3. f.
4. b.
5. c.
6. a.
7. e.

### Areas of the Brain

1. c.
2. b.
3. f.
4. a.
5. e.
6. d.

## The Subcortex—At the Core of the (Brain) Matter: Pages 67-70

What are the major parts of the subcortex?

1. d.
2. e.
3. a.
4. g.
5. i.
6. b.
7. h.
8. f.
9. c.

## The Endocrine System-My Hormones Made Me Do I: Pages 70-72

Does the glandular system affect behavior?

1. h.
2. c.
3. f.
4. a.
5. e.
6. b.
7. g.
8. d.

# CHECK YOUR MEMORY

### Neurons-Building a "Biocomputer": Pages 48-52
How do nerve cells operate and communicate?

| | | | |
|---|---|---|---|
| 1. F | 5. T | 9. F |
| 2. T | 6. F | 10. T |
| 3. F | 7. T | 11. F |
| 4. T | 8. F | 12. T |

### The Nervous System—Wired for Action: Pages 53-56
What are the major parts of the nervous system?

| | | | |
|---|---|---|---|
| 1. F | 5. T | 9. T |
| 2. T | 6. T | 10. F |
| 3. T | 7. F | 11. T |
| 4. F | 8. F | 12. F |

### Research Methods—Charting the Brain's Inner Realms: Pages 56-59
How is the brain studied?

| | | |
|---|---|---|
| 1. F | 3. F | 5. T |
| 2. T | 4. T | |

### The Cerebral Cortex—My, What a Big Brain You Have! Pages 59-67
Why is the human cerebral cortex so important, and what are its parts?

| | | | |
|---|---|---|---|
| 1. F | 9. F | 17. T |
| 2. T | 10. F | 18. T |
| 3. F | 11. F | 19. T |
| 4. T | 12. T | 20. F |
| 5. T | 13. T | 21. F |
| 6. T | 14. T | 22. F |
| 7. F | 15. T | 23. T |
| 8. T | 16. F | 24. T |

## The Subcortex—At the Core of the (Brain) Matter: Pages 67-70
What are the major parts of the subcortex?

| | | |
|---|---|---|
| 1. F | 3. F | 5. T |
| 2. T | 4. F | 6. T |
| 7. F | 8. T | |

## The Endocrine System—My Hormones Made Me Do It: Pages 70-72
Does the glandular system affect behavior?

| | | |
|---|---|---|
| 1. T | 4. T | 7. T |
| 2. F | 5. T | 8. T |
| 3. T | 6. T | 9. F |

## Psychology in Action: Handedness: Pages 73-75
In what ways to right- and left-handed individuals differ?

| | |
|---|---|
| 1. F | 3. T |
| 2. F | 4. F |

# FINAL SURVEY AND REVIEW

## Neurons-Building a "Biocomputer"
How do nerve cells operate and communicate?

| | | |
|---|---|---|
| 1. neurons; synapses | 7. potassium | 13. neuropeptides |
| 2. information | 8. all-or-nothing | 14. endorphins |
| 3. dendrites; soma | 9. salutatory conduction | 15. low endorphin |
| 4. inactive neuron | 10. neurotransmitters; acetylcholine | 16. inhibitory |
| 5. action; potential | 11. fire; reducing | 17. Neuroplasticity |
| 6. threshold; sodium | 12, Parkinson's disease; schizophrenia | 18. Neurological |

## The Nervous System—Wired for Action
What are the major parts of the nervous system?

| | | |
|---|---|---|
| 1. Nerves | 4. somatic; autonomic | 7. reflex; arc; connector; motor |
| 2. neurillemal | 5. sympathetic; parasympathetic | 8. neurogenesis |
| 3. central; spinal cord | 6. spinal; cranial; motor | |

## Research Methods—Charting the Brain's Inner Realms
How is the brain studied?

| | | |
|---|---|---|
| 1. dissection; stimulation | 3. X-rays; magnetic field; radioactive glucose | 4. less; more |
| 2. MRI; PET | | 5. fMRI |

## The Cerebral Cortex—My, What a Big Brain You Have!
Why is the human cerebral cortex so important, and what are its parts?

1. corticalization; cerebrum
2. soft signs
3. corpus callosum; hemispheres
4. hemisphere; movements
5. spatial; faces
6. analysis; simultaneously
7. cortex; sensation; speech
8. mirror neurons
9. process
10. aphasias
11. Broca's; Wernicke's
12. agnosia; facial; agnosia
13. gray; white

## The Subcortex—At the Core of the (Brain) Matter
What are the major parts of the subcortex?

1. subcortex
2. medulla
3. pons
4. cerebellum
5. reticular formation; cerebral; cortex
6. thalamus; hypothalamus
7. limbic; reward
8. amygdala; hippocampus

## The Endocrine System—My Hormones Made Me Do It
Does the glandular system affect behavior?

1. endocrine; bloodstream
2. pituitary; hypothalamus
3. pituitary; acromegaly
4. melatonin; pineal
5. overactive; underactive
6. adrenal; stress
7. synthetic

## Psychology in Action: Handedness
In what ways to right- and left-handed individuals differ?

1. Hand dominance; inconsistent
2. Ninety; 10
3. right-handed; left; left
4. masquerade; right-handed
5. lateralized

# MASTERY TEST

1. b, p. 59
2. a, p. 63
3. a, p. 67
4. c, p. 55
5. b, p. 55
6. b, p. 68
7. c, p. 53
8. b, p. 67
9. b, p. 72
10. b, p. 52
11. a, p. 55
12. a, p. 53
13. b, p. 58

14. a, p. 68
15. d, p. 73
16. d, p. 59
17. d, p. 72
18. b, p. 62
19. a, p. 75
20. d, p. 64
21. c, p. 71
22. c, p. 67
23. b, p. 60
24. d, p. 68
25. c, p. 75
26. b, p. 72

27. d, p. 60
28. a, p. 61
29. a, p. 79
30. b, p. 54
31. c, p. 56
32. d, p. 55
33. a, p. 64
34. c, p. 57
35. b, p. 66
36. d, p. 70
37. a, p. 74

# Human Development

## Chapter Overview

Heredity (nature) and environment (nurture) are interacting forces that are both necessary for human development. The chromosomes and genes in each cell of the body carry hereditary instructions. Most characteristics are polygenic. Maturation of the body and nervous system underlies the orderly development of motor skills, cognitive abilities, emotions, and language. Many early skills are subject to the principle of readiness. Prenatal development is influenced by environmental factors, such as various teratogens, as well as the mother's diet, health, and emotions. During sensitive periods, infants are more sensitive to specific environmental influences. Early deprivation seriously retards development, whereas deliberate enrichment of the environment has a beneficial effect on infants. In general, environment sets a reaction range within which maturation unfolds. Temperament is hereditary. Most infants fall into one of three temperament categories: easy, difficult, and slow-to-warm-up. A child's developmental level reflects heredity, environment, and the effects of the child's own behavior.

Although neonates will die if not cared for at birth, they are far from helpless. They possess adaptive reflexes, are responsive to their senses, begin to learn immediately, and are aware of their actions. Infant development is strongly influenced by heredity. However, environmental factors such as nutrition, parenting, and learning are also important. The human neonate has a number of adaptive reflexes, including the grasping, rooting, sucking, and Moro reflexes. Tests in a looking chamber reveal a number of visual preferences in the newborn. The rate of maturation varies from person to person. Also, learning contributes greatly to the development of basic motor skills. Emotions develop in a consistent order, starting with generalized excitement in newborn babies. Three of the basic emotions—fear, anger, and joy—may be unlearned.

Early social development lays a foundation for relationships with parents, siblings, friends, and relatives. Emotional attachment is a critical early event. Opportunities for social interaction increase as infants develop self-awareness and begin to actively seek guidance from adults Infant attachment is reflected by separation anxiety. The quality of attachment can be classified as secure, insecure-avoidant, or insecure-ambivalent. Secure attachment is fostered by consistent care from parents who are sensitive to a baby's signals and rhythms. High-quality day care is not harmful and can even be helpful to preschool children. Low-quality care can be risky. Meeting a baby's affectional needs is as important as meeting needs for physical care.

Studies suggest that parental styles have a substantial impact on emotional and intellectual development. Three major parental styles are authoritarian, permissive, and authoritative (effective). Authoritative parenting appears to benefit children the most. Whereas mothers typically emphasize caregiving, fathers tend to function as playmates for infants. Both caregiving styles contribute to the competence of young children. Parenting styles vary across cultures.

Language development proceeds from crying to cooing, then babbling, the use of single words, and then to telegraphic speech. Learning to use language is a cornerstone of early intellectual development. A biological predisposition to acquire language is augmented by learning. Prelanguage communication between parent and child involves shared rhythms, nonverbal signals, and turn-taking. Motherese or parentese is a simplified ransitioning from childhood to adulthood requires the formation of a personal identity, the major life task of adolescence. Identity formation is even more challenging for adolescents of ethnic descent. In western industrialized societies the transition into adulthood is further complicated as it is increasingly delayed well into the 20s.

Children develop morals and values as they grow through several levels. Lawrence Kohlberg identified preconventional, conventional, and postconventional levels of moral reasoning. Developing mature moral standards is an important task of adolescence. Most adults function at the conventional level of morality, but some never get beyond the selfish, preconventional level. Only a minority of people attain the highest, or postconventional level, of moral reasoning. Carol Gilligan distinguished between Kohlberg's justice perspective and a caring perspective. Mature adult morality likely involves both.

Erik Erikson identified a series of challenges that occur across the lifespan, ranging from a need to gain trust in infancy to the need to live with integrity in old age. Personal development does not end after adolescence. Periods of stability and transition occur throughout adulthood. We face a specific "crisis," or psychosocial dilemma at each life stage. Successful resolution of the dilemmas produces healthy development while unsuccessful outcomes make it harder to deal with later crises.

Well-being during adulthood consists of six elements: self-acceptance, positive relations with others, autonomy, environmental mastery, having a purpose in life, and continued personal growth. Every adult must find ways to successfully cope with aging. Only a minority of people experience a midlife crisis, but midlife course corrections are more common. People tend to move through repeated cycles of stability and transition throughout adulthood. Intellectual declines associated with aging are limited, especially for those who remain mentally active. Successful lives are based on happiness, purpose, meaning, and integrity. Ageism refers to prejudice, discrimination, and stereotyping on the basis of age and is especially damaging to older people. Most ageism is based on stereotypes, myths, and misinformation.

Typical emotional reactions to impending death include denial, anger, bargaining, depression, and acceptance, but not necessarily in that order or in every case. Death is a natural part of life. There is value in understanding it and accepting it.

Positive parent-child interactions occur when parents spend enjoyable time encouraging their children in a loving and mutually respectful fashion. Effective parental discipline tends to emphasize child management techniques (especially communication), rather than power assertion or withdrawal of love. Consistency is also an important aspect of effective parenting. Effective parents allow their children to express their feeling but place limits on their behavior. Much misbehavior can be managed by use of I-messages and the application of natural and logical consequences., musical style of speaking that parents use to help their children learn language.

Jean Piaget theorized that children mature through a fixed series of cognitive stages by applying a combination of assimilation and accommodation. Piaget held that children mature through a fixed series of cognitive stages. The stages and their approximate age ranges are sensorimotor (0–2), preoperational (2–7), concrete operational (7–11), and formal operations (11–adult). Caregivers should offer learning opportunities that are appropriate for a child's level of cognitive development. Learning principles provide an alternate explanation that assumes cognitive development is continuous. Recent studies of infants suggest that they are capable of thought well beyond that observed by Piaget. Lev Vygotsky's sociocultural theory emphasizes that a child's mental growth takes place in a child's zone of proximal development, where a more skillful person may scaffold the child's progress. This process helps children discover new skills and principles, and learn cultural beliefs and values.

Adolescents must form their identity and values at a time when they are also dealing with puberty. The timing of puberty can complicate the task of identity formation, a major task of adolescence.

# Learning Objectives

## *Theme: The principles of development help us better understand not only children, but our own behavior as well.*

| |
|---|
| **GQ: How do heredity and environment affect development?** |
| LO 3.1 Define *developmental psychology*. Discuss *readiness* (include how readiness is related to toilet training). Define the term *developmental level* and list the three factors that combine to determine it. |
| LO 3.2 Explain the basic mechanisms of heredity, include a description of the following terms: a. *chromosome*; b. *DNA*; c. *gene*; d. *polygenic*; e. *dominant* trait (gene); f. *recessive* trait (gene). |
| LO 3.3 Compare, contrast, and give examples of the effects of *enrichment* and *deprivation* on development. |
| **GQ: What can newborn babies do?** |
| LO 3.4 Name and describe four *adaptive reflexes* displayed by neonates. |
| LO 3.5 Describe the intellectual capabilities and the sensory preferences of a neonate. |
| LO 3.6 Discuss motor development and the concepts of *maturation*, *cephalocaudal pattern*, and *proximodistal pattern*. |
| **GQ: Of what significance is a child's emotional bond with adults?** |
| LO 3.7 Describe (in general) the course of emotional development, according to Bridges and Izard. |
| LO 3.8 Discuss *emotional attachment* (including the concept of separation anxiety). Differentiate between the three types of attachment identified by Mary Ainsworth. |
| LO 3.9 Describe Harlow's experiment dealing with *contact comfort*, and state the results of the experiment. |
| **GQ: How important are parenting styles?** |
| LO 3.10 Describe Baumrind's three major styles of parenting, including characteristics of both parents and children in each style. |
| LO 3.11 Discuss the meaning and importance of infant *affectional needs*, the range of effects of maternal *caregiving styles*, and the importance of *paternal influences* on the child. |
| **GQ: How do children acquire language?** |
| LO 3.12 List and briefly describe the sequence of language acquisition. Include the term *psycholinguist* as well as briefly discuss the role of innate factors and learning in acquiring language. Explain how parents communicate with infants before the infants can talk, including the terms *signals*, *turn-taking*, and *parentese*. |
| **GQ: How do children learn to think?** |
| LO 3.13 With regard to Piaget's theory of cognitive development: a. explain how a child's intelligence and thinking differ from an adult's (include the concept of *transformation*). b. explain the concepts of *assimilation* and *accommodation*. c. list (in order) and briefly describe each stage, listing the specific characteristics of each stage. d. explain how parents can best guide their child's intellectual development. e. evaluate the usefulness of Piaget's theory, including a review of current research on infant cognition. |
| LO 3.14 Briefly discuss Vygotsky's sociocultural theory, including how his theory differs from Piaget's theory. Define the terms *zone of proximal development* and *scaffolding*. |
| **GQ: Why is the transition from adolescence to adulthood especially challenging?** |
| LO 3.15 Define and differentiate between *adolescence* and *puberty* and describe the advantages and disadvantages of early and late maturation for males vs. females. |
| LO 3.16 With regard to the adolescent search for identity: a. explain what that means; b. explain how being a member of a minority ethnic group influences the identity search; c. discuss the concept of *emerging adulthood*. |

| |
|---|
| **GQ: How do we develop morals and values?** |
| LO 3.17 Regarding *moral development*: a. list (in order) and briefly describe each of Kohlberg's three levels of moral development; b. describe what proportions of the population appear to function at each of Kohlberg's moral development levels; and c. explain Gilligan's argument against Kohlberg's system, and describe the current status of the argument. |
| **GQ: What are the typical tasks and dilemmas through the life span?** |
| LO 3.18 List the life stages experienced by all people; define the terms *developmental milestones, developmental task*, and *psychosocial dilemma*; and explain, according to Erikson, how the resolution of the psychosocial dilemmas affects a person's adjustment to life. |
| LO 3.19 Describe the *psychosocial crisis* and the possible outcome for each of Erikson's eight life stages. Give approximate age ranges for each stage. |
| **GQ: What is involved in well-being during later adulthood?** |
| LO 3.20 Describe what a *midlife crisis* is; explain how the *midlife transition* is different for women than for men; and list Ryff's six elements of well-being in adulthood. |
| LO 3.21 Discuss the findings of gerontologists regarding the mental capabilities of older adults, including *fluid* and *crystallized* abilities and ways to stay mentally sharp and the keys to successful aging. Define *ageism* and describe some of the stereotypes that exist regarding older adults. |
| **GQ: How do people typically react to death?** |
| LO 3.22 Regarding our emotional reactions toward death: a. explain what people fear about death; b. define *thanatologist*; c. list and briefly characterize the five emotional reactions typically experienced by people facing death, according to Kubler-Ross; d. explain how to make use of this knowledge. |
| **GQ: How do effective parents discipline and communicate with their children?** |
| LO 3.23 Regarding parenting techniques, briefly discuss a. the ingredients of effective parenting. b. the effects of *physical punishment* and *withdrawal of love* and guidelines for their use. c. the elements of effective communication, according to Haim Ginott. d. Thomas Gordon's concepts of *I-messages* and *you-messages*. e. the use of *natural* and *logical consequences*. |

# RECITE AND REVIEW

## Nature and Nurture—It Takes Two to Tango: Pages 79-84
How do heredity and environment affect development?

1. Developmental psychology is the study of progressive changes in _____ and abilities, from _____ to _____ .

2. The nature-nurture debate concerns the relative contributions to development of heredity (_____ ) and environment ( _____).

3. Hereditary instructions are carried by_____(deoxyribonucleic acid) in the form of chromosomes and _____ in each cell of the body.

4. Most characteristics are polygenic (influenced by a combination of _____ ) and reflect the combined effects of dominant and recessive_____ .

5. Environment refers to all _____ conditions that affect development.

6. Prenatal development is subject to _____influences in the form of diseases, drugs, radiation, or the mother's diet and health.

7. Prenatal damage to the fetus may cause congenital problems, or_____. In contrast, genetic problems are inherited from one's parents.

8. Fetal alcohol syndrome ( _____ ) is the result of heavy _____ during pregnancy, which causes the infant to have _____ birth weight, a small head, and _____ malformations.

9. Early perceptual, intellectual, and emotional deprivation seriously retards _____.

10. Poverty increases the likelihood that children will experience various forms of_____ which may impede cognitive development and _____ achievement and increase the risk for mental illness and _____ behavior.

11. Deliberate enrichment of the _____ in infancy and early childhood has a beneficial effect on development.

12. Heredity also influences differences in temperament (the physical core of _____. Most infants fall into one of three temperament categories: easy children, _____ children, and slow-to-warm-up children.

73

13. A child's developmental level (current state of development) reflects heredity, environment, and the

    effects of the child's _____ .

# The Newborn Baby—More than Meets the Eye: Pages 85-88
What can newborn babies do?

1. The human (newborn) has a number of _____ reflexes, including the grasping, rooting, sucking, and
   Moro reflexes.

2. Newborns begin to _____ immediately and they imitate adults.

3. Tests in a looking chamber reveal a number of _____ preferences in the newborn. The

   neonate is drawn to complex, _____ , curved, and brightly-lighted designs.

4. Infants prefer human face patterns, especially _____ . In later infancy,

   interest in the unfamiliar emerges.

5. While the rate of maturation varies from child to child, the _____ is nearly universal.

6. The development of _____ control (motor development) is cephalocaudal (from

   head to toe) and proximodistal (from the _____ of the body to the extremities).

7. Emotional development begins with a capacity for _____ excitement. After that,

   the first pleasant and unpleasant emotions develop.

8. By eight to twelve months, babies display a social smile when other _____ are nearby.

# Social Development—Baby, I'm Stuck on You: Pages 89-91
Of what significance is a child's emotional bond with adults?

1. _____ development refers to the emergence of self-awareness and forming relationships

   with parents and others.

2. For optimal development in human infants, the development of an emotional attachment to their

   primary _____ is a critical early event that must occur during the _____ (within the

   first year) of infancy.

3. Infant attachment is reflected by _____ anxiety (distress when infants are away from parents).

4. The quality of attachment can be classified as _____, insecure-avoidant, or insecure-ambivalent.

5. Having a secure attachment style tends to promote caring, _____, and understanding in adulthood while having an avoidant attachment style tends to promote _____ toward intimacy and commitment to others. An ambivalent attachment style tends to promote _____ feelings about love and friendship in adulthood.

6. The relationship between quality of attachment and the type of caregiving that is provided appears to be _____ in all cultures.

7. High-quality day care does not _____ children; high-quality care can, in fact, accelerate some areas of development.

8. Some characteristics of high-quality day care include having a _____ number of children per caregiver, trained caregivers, an overall group size of _____ children, and minimal staff turnover.

9. An infant's affectional_____ are every bit as important as more obvious needs for physical care.

# Parental Influences—Life with Mom and Dad: Pages 91-94
How important are parenting styles?

1. Parental styles (patterns of parental care) have a substantial impact on emotional and intellectual _____.

2. Maternal influences (the effects _____ have on their children) tend to center on caregiving.

3. Paternal influences differ in their impact because_____ tend to function as a playmate for the infant.

4. Authoritarian parents enforce rigid _____ and demand strict obedience to _____.

5. Overly permissive parents give little _____ and don't hold children accountable for their actions.

6. Authoritative (_____) parents supply firm and consistent guidance, combined with love and affection.

75

7.  Caregiving styles among various ethnic groups tend to reflect each culture's _____and

    _____ . For example, fathers in Arab-American families tend to be strong authority figures,

    demanding absolute obedience.

## Language Development—Fast-Talking Babies: Pages 94-96
How do children acquire language?

1.  Language development proceeds from control of_____, to cooing, then babbling, the use

    of single words, and then to telegraphic _____.

2.  The patterns of early speech suggest a _____ predisposition to acquire language.

3.  Psycholinguists (psychologists who study _____ ) believe that innate language

    predispositions are augmented by _____ .

4.  Prelanguage communication between parent and child involves shared rhythms, nonverbal

    _____ , and turn-taking.

5.  Parents help children learn language by using distinctive caretaker _____ or parentese.

## Cognitive Development—Think Like a Child: Pages 97-102
How do children learn to think?

1.  The intellects of children are _____ abstract than those of adults. Jean Piaget theorized that

    _____ growth occurs through a combination of assimilation and accommodation.

2.  Piaget also held that children go through a fixed series of cognitive_____ . These are:

    sensorimotor (0-2), preoperational (2-7), _____ operational (7-11), and formal _____

    (11-adult).

3.  Object permanence (the ability to understand that _____ continue to _____when

    they are out of sight) emerges during the _____ stage while conservation (the ability to

    understand that mass, weight, and volume remain_____ when the shape of objects

    changes) emerges during the _____ stage.

4. Unlike the preoperational stage of development, when children exhibit _____, children in the formal operational stage of development are less egocentric and can think _____, hypothetically, and theoretically.

5. Learning theorists dispute the idea that cognitive development occurs in _____. Recent studies suggest infants are capable of levels of thinking beyond that observed by _____.

6. A one-step-ahead strategy that takes into account the child's level of _____ development helps adapt instruction to a child's needs.

7. According to the sociocultural theory of Russian scholar Lev Vygotsky, a child's interactions with others are most likely to aid _____ development if they take place within the child's _____ of proximal _____.

8. Adults help children learn how to think by scaffolding, or_____ , their attempts to solve problems or discover principles.

9. During their collaborations with adults, children learn important cultural_____and values.

## Psychology in Action: Effective Parenting—Raising Healthy Children: Pages 112-114

How do effective parents discipline and communicate with their children?

1. Parental _____ involves setting guidelines for acceptable behavior.

2. Methods of controlling a child's behavior may include _____ _____ , withdrawal of love, or management techniques.

3. Children who experience frequent _____ punishment may demonstrate increased _____ and behavior problems.

4. The discipline methods of _____ _____ and withholding of love are related to low self-esteem.

5. Consistent discipline involves maintaining _____ rules of conduct.

6. It is often more effective to _____ good behavior rather than punish misbehavior.

7. Making a distinction between feelings and _____ is the key to clear communication.

77

8. Effective parental _____ focuses on I-messages instead of you-messages.

9. Parents can make effective use of natural consequences (intrinsic effects) and _____

   _____ (rational and reasonable effects).

## Adolescence and Young Adulthood—The Best of Times, the Worst of Times: Pages 102-104

Why is the transition from adolescence to adulthood especially challenging?

1. Adolescence is a culturally defined _____ status. Puberty is a _____ event.

2. Early maturation is beneficial mostly for _____; its effects are mixed for

3. Establishing a clear sense of personal identity is a major task of _____ . One danger of

   _____ maturation is premature identity formation.

4. For many young people in North America a period of emerging adulthood stretches from the late

   to the_____ .

5. By taking pride in their ethnic heritage, teenagers from different ethnic groups have_____

   self-esteem, a better self-image, and a stronger ethnic _____ when compared to teens who do

   not take pride in their ethnic identity.

6. As more people enroll in colleges and delay starting a family, the period of _____

   adulthood for adolescents has been pushed back from the late teens to the _____ .

7. Remaining dependent on their parents for economic support, the_____are individuals

   who are trapped between adolescence and _____ . They are recognized in England as

   "Kippers," and in Germany as "Nesthocker."

## Moral Development—Growing a Conscience: Pages 104-106

How do we develop morals and values?

1. Lawrence Kohlberg theorized that _____ development passes through a series of stages

   revealed by _____ reasoning about _____ dilemmas.

2. Kohlberg identified preconventional, conventional, and postconventional levels of moral

   _____ .

3. Some psychologists have questioned whether measures of moral development should be based only on a morality of _____ . Adults appear to base moral choices on either _____ or caring, depending on the situation.

4. _____ can be described as combining justice and caring (reason and emotion) when making the best moral judgment.

## The Story of a Lifetime—Rocky Road or Garden Path?: Pages 106-108

What are the typical tasks and dilemmas through the life span?

1. _____ milestones are or prominent landmarks in personal development.

2. According to Erik Erikson, each life stage involves a specific psychosocial _____ .

3. During childhood these are: trust versus mistrust, autonomy versus_____ and doubt, initiative versus_____ , and industry versus _____ .

4. In _____ , identity versus role confusion is the principal dilemma.

5. In young adulthood we face the dilemma of intimacy versus_____ . Later, generativity versus _____ becomes prominent.

6. Old age is a time when the dilemma of integrity versus _____ must be faced.

## Later Adulthood: Will You Still Need Me When I'm 64?: Pages 108-110

What is involved in well-being during later adulthood?

1. Well-being at midlife is related to self-acceptance, positive relationships, autonomy, mastery, a _____ in life, and continued personal _____ .

2. A midlife crisis affects many people during middle adulthood, but this is by no means _____ .

3. A transition period during midlife can provide individuals with opportunities for personal growth or make "_____ corrections" as it allows individuals to _____ their identities, their goals, and prepare for old age.

5. The greatest losses occur for fluid abilities (which require _____ or rapid learning); crystallized abilities (stored up _____ and skills) show much less decline and may actually improve.

6. Ageism refers to prejudice, discrimination, and stereotyping on the basis of _____ . It affects people of all ages, but is especially damaging to _____ people.

7. People who work in fields that require speed and skill often reach their _____ performance between the ages of 30 and 50. To maintain _____ levels of _____ as they age, individuals should practice their skills on a regular basis.

# Death and Dying—The Final Challenge: Pages 110-111
How do people typically react to death?

1. Older people fear the circumstances of _____ more than the fact that it will occur.

2. Typical emotional reactions to impending death are denial, _____ , bargaining, _____ , and acceptance.

3. One approach to death is the hospice movement, which is devoted to providing humane care to persons who are _____ .

4. Initial shock is followed by pangs of _____ . Later, apathy, dejection, and depression may occur. Eventually, grief moves toward _____ , an acceptance of the loss.

# CONNECTIONS

## Nature and Nurture—It Takes Two to Tango: Pages 84-90

How do heredity and environment affect development?

1. _____ gene
2. _____ readiness
3. _____ congenital problems
4. _____ heredity
5. _____ sensitive period
6. _____ environment
7. _____ enrichment
8. _____ prenatal period
9. _____ FAS
10. _____ temperament

a. DNA area
b. ability for rapid learning
c. nature
d. nurture
e. conception to birth
f. prenatal alcohol exposure
g. magnified environmental impact
h. personality characteristics
i. "birth defects"
j. stimulating environment

## The Newborn—More Than Meets the Eye: Pages 90-95

What can newborn babies do?

1. _____ grasping reflex
2. _____ rooting reflex
3. _____ Moro reflex
4. _____ neonate
5. _____ motor development
6. _____ familiar faces
7. _____ maturation

a. palm grip
b. startled embrace
c. food search
d. control of muscles and movement
e. newborn infant
f. physical growth
g. preferred pattern

## Social Development—Baby, I'm Stuck on You: Pages 95-101

Of what significance is a child's emotional bond with adults?

1. _____ secure attachment
2. _____ insecure-avoidant
3. _____ affectional needs
4. _____ separation anxiety
5. _____ social referencing
6. _____ cooperative play
7. _____ high-quality day care

a. love and attention
b. social development
c. anxious emotional bond
d. positive emotional bond
e. emotional distress
f. observing reactions of others
g. trained caregivers

## Parental Influences—Life with Mom and Dad: Pages 101-106

How important are parenting styles?

1. _____ resilient
2. _____ Asian-American families
3. _____ optimal caregiving
4. _____ paternal influence
5. _____ authoritative style
6. _____ authoritarian style
7. _____ permissive style

a. proactive educational interactions
b. strict obedience
c. bounce back after hardship
d. firm and consistent guidance
e. little guidance
f. playmates
g. interdependence

## Language Development—Fast-Talking Babies: Pages 106-109

How do children acquire language?

1. _____ biological predisposition
2. _____ cooing
3. _____ Vygotsky
4. _____ babbling
5. _____ telegraphic speech
6. _____ turn-taking
7. _____ Noam Chomsky
8. _____ parentese

a. vowel sounds
b. vowels and consonants
c. caretaker speech
d. "Mama gone."
e. hereditary readiness for language
f. psycholinguists
g. conversational style of communication
h. sociocultural theory

## Cognitive Development—Think Like a Child: Pages 109-118

How do children learn to think?

1. _____ assimilation
2. _____ accommodation
3. _____ sensorimotor stage
4. _____ preoperational stage
5. _____ concrete operations
6. _____ formal operations
7. _____ hothousing
8. _____ scaffolding
9. _____ Piaget

a. changing existing mental patterns
b. geocentricism
c. applying mental patterns
d. abstract principles
e. conservation
f. object permanence
g. skilled support for learning
h. forced teaching
i. stage theory of cognitive development

## Adolescence and Young Adulthood—The Best of Times, The Worst of Times: Pages 132-135

Why is the transition from adolescence to adulthood especially challenging?

1. _____ adolescence
2. _____ puberty
3. _____ twixters
4. _____ early-maturing boys
5. _____ emerging adulthood
6. _____ identity

a. sexual maturation
b. extended into the mid 20s
c. cultural status
d. teen's task
e. dominant, self-assured, and popular
f. trapped in the "maturity gap"

## Moral Development—Growing a Conscience: Pages 135-137

How do we develop morals and values?

1. _____ Carol Gilhgan
2. _____ Lawrence Kohlberg
3. _____ preconventional
4. _____ conventional
5. _____ postconventional

a. moral dilemma of justice
b. social contract/individual principles
c. good boy or girl/respect for authority
d. avoiding punishment or seeking pleasure
e. focused on the ethics of caring

## The Story of a Lifetime—Rocky Road or Garden Path?: Pages 122-125

What are the typical tasks and dilemmas through the life span?

1. _____ Erik Enkson
2. _____ optimal development
3. _____ developmental milestones
4. _____ trust versus mistrust
5. _____ developmental task
6. _____ autonomy versus shame and doubt
7. _____ initiative versus guilt
8. _____ industry versus inferiority

a. received praise versus lacking support
b. self-control versus inadequacy
c. love versus insecurity
d. freedom to choose versus criticism
e. psychosocial dilemmas
f. mastered developmental tasks
g. notable events or marker
h. skills to be attained

## Later Adulthood: Will you Still Need Me When I'm 64?: Pages 138-141

What is involved in well-being during later adulthood?

| | | | |
|---|---|---|---|
| 1. | _____ fluid abilities | a. | life change |
| 2. | _____ transition period | b. | accumulated knowledge |
| 3. | _____ crystallized ablities | c. | adult development |
| 4. | _____ ageism | d. | common prejudice |
| 5. | _____ midlife crisis | e. | requires speed or rapid learning |
| 6. | _____ Roger Gould | f. | last chance for achievement |

## Death and Dying—The Final Challenge: Pages 146-152

How do people typically react to death?

| | | | |
|---|---|---|---|
| 1. | _____ hospice | a. | expert on death |
| 2. | _____ thanatologist | b. | care for the dying |
| 3. | _____ Elizabeth Kubler-Ross | c. | acceptance of loss |
| 4. | _____ bargaining | d. | five stages of impending death |
| 5. | _____ resolution | e. | reaction to impending death |

# CHECK YOUR MEMORY

## Nature and Nurture—It Takes Two to Tango: Pages 84-90

How do heredity and environment affect development?

1. Developmental psychology is the study of progressive changes in behavior and abilities during childhood.   TRUE or FALSE

2. Each cell in the human body (except sperm cells and ova) contains 23 chromosomes.
   TRUE or FALSE

3. The order of organic bases in DNA acts as a genetic code.   TRUE or FALSE

4. Two brown-eyed parents cannot have a blue-eyed child.   TRUE or FALSE

5. Identical twins have identical genes.   TRUE or FALSE

6. More children have a slow-to-warm up temperament than a difficult temperament.   TRUE or FALSE

7. Teratogens are substances capable of causing birth defects.   TRUE or FALSE

8. Many drugs can reach the fetus within the intrauterine environment.   TRUE or FALSE

9. To prevent FAS, the best advice to pregnant women is to get plenty of rest, vitamins, and good nutrition.   TRUE or FALSE

10. Poverty is associated with retarded emotional and intellectual development.   TRUE or FALSE

11. In animals, enriched environments can actually increase brain size and weight.   TRUE or FALSE

12. Factors that influence developmental levels are heredity, environment, and one's own behavior.

    TRUE or FALSE

## The Newborn—More Than Meets the Eye: Pages 90-95
What can newborn babies do?

1.   The Moro reflex helps infants hold onto objects placed in their hands.   TRUE or FALSE

2.   As early as 9 weeks of age, infants can imitate actions a full day after seeing them.

    TRUE or FALSE

3.   Babies begin to show a preference for looking at their mother's face over a stranger's face just a

    few hours after they are born.   TRUE or FALSE

4.   Three-day-old infants prefer to look at simple colored backgrounds, rather than more complex patterns.

    TRUE or FALSE

5.   After age 2, familiar faces begin to hold great interest for infants.   TRUE or FALSE

6.   Most infants learn to stand alone before they begin crawling.   TRUE or FALSE

7.   Motor development follows a top-down, center-outward pattern.   TRUE or FALSE

8.   Anger and fear are the first two emotions to emerge in infancy.   TRUE or FALSE

9.   An infant's social smile appears within one month after birth.   TRUE or FALSE

## Social Development—Baby, I'm Stuck on You: Pages 95-101
Of what significance is a child's emotional bond with adults?

1.   Most infants have to be 15 weeks old before they can recognize themselves on television.

    TRUE or FALSE

2.   Securely attached infants turn away from mother when she returns after a period of separation.

    TRUE or FALSE

3.   *Separation anxiety disorder* is the medical term for homesickness.   TRUE or FALSE

4.   A small number of children per caregiver is desirable in day care settings.   TRUE or FALSE

## Parental Influences—Life with Mom and Dad: Pages 101-106
How important are parenting styles?

1.   Fathers typically spend about half their time in caregiving and half playing with the baby.

    TRUE or FALSE

2. Paternal play tends to be more physically arousing for infants than maternal play is.
   TRUE or FALSE

3. Since mothers spend more time caring for infants, mothers are more important than fathers.
   TRUE or FALSE

4. Authoritarian parents view children as having adult-like responsibilities.   TRUE or FALSE

5. Permissive parents basically give their children the message "Do it because I say so."
   TRUE or FALSE

6. The children of authoritarian parents tend to be independent, assertive, and inquiring.
   TRUE or FALSE

7. Asian cultures tend to be group-oriented and they emphasize interdependence among individuals.
   TRUE or FALSE

8. Severely punished children tend to be defiant and aggressive.   TRUE or FALSE

9. An authoritarian style of parenting is most effective since it focuses on pampering the child's every need.   TRUE or FALSE

## Language Development—Fast-Talking Babies: Pages 106-109
How do children acquire language?

1. The single-word stage begins at about 6 months of age.   TRUE or FALSE

2. "That red ball mine." is an example of telegraphic speech.   TRUE or FALSE

3. Noam Chomsky believes that basic language patterns are innate.   TRUE or FALSE

4. The "terrible twos" refers to the two-word stage of language development.   TRUE or FALSE

5. The "I'm going to get you" game is an example of prelanguage communication.
   TRUE or FALSE

6. Parentese is spoken in higher pitched tones with a musical inflection.   TRUE or FALSE

7. Parentese language used by mothers and fathers to talk to their infants does more harm than good to their infants' language development.   TRUE or FALSE

## Cognitive Development—Think Like a Child: Pages 109-118
How do children learn to think?

1. According to Piaget, children first learn to make transformations at about age 3.   TRUE or FALSE

2. Assimilation refers to modifying existing ideas to fit new situations or demands.   TRUE or FALSE

3. Cognitive development during the sensorimotor stage is mostly nonverbal.   TRUE or FALSE

4. Reversibility of thoughts and the concept of conservation both appear during the concrete operational stage.   TRUE or FALSE

5. Three-year-old children are surprisingly good at understanding what other people are thinking.
TRUE or FALSE

6. An understanding of hypothetical possibilities develops during the preoperational stage.
TRUE or FALSE

7. Playing peekaboo is a good way to establish the permanence of objects for children in the sensorimotor stage.   TRUE or FALSE

8. Contrary to what Piaget observed, infants as young as 3 months of age show signs of object permanence.
TRUE or FALSE

9. Hothousing or the forced teaching of children to learn reading or math is encouraged to accelerate their intellectual development and to prevent apathy.   TRUE or FALSE

10. A criticism of Piaget's theory of cognitive development is that he underestimated the impact of cultural influence on children's mental development.   TRUE or FALSE

11. Vygotsky's key insight was that children's thinking develops through dialogues with more capable persons.   TRUE or FALSE

12. Learning experiences are most helpful when they take place outside of a child's zone of proximal development.   TRUE or FALSE

13. Scaffolding is like setting up temporary bridges to help children move into new mental territory.
TRUE or FALSE

14. Vygotsky empasized that children use adults to learn about their culture and society.
TRUE or FALSE

## Adolescence and Young Adulthood—The Best of Times, The Worst of Times: Pages 132-135
Why is the transition from adolescence to adulthood especially challenging?

1. The length of adolescence varies in different cultures.   TRUE or FALSE

2. Early maturation tends to enhance self-image for boys.   TRUE or FALSE

3. Early-maturing girls tend to date sooner and are more likely to get into trouble.
TRUE or FALSE

4. By taking pride in their ethnic heritage, teenagers from different ethnic groups have reduced self-esteem, a negative self-image, and a weakened ethnic identity.   TRUE or FALSE

5. Being able to think about hypothetical possibilities helps adolescents in their search for identity.
TRUE or FALSE

6. Early maturation can contribute to adopting a foreclosed identity.   TRUE or FALSE

7. Twixters are not able to make important decisions in their life, such as a career choice, simply because they are stuck in between childhood and adolescence.   TRUE or FALSE

## Moral Development—Growing a Conscience: Pages 135-137

How do we develop morals and values?

1. Lawrence Kohlberg used moral dilemmas to assess children's levels of moral development.
   TRUE or FALSE

2. At the preconventional level, moral decisions are guided by the consequences of actions, such as punishment or pleasure.   TRUE or FALSE

3. The traditional morality of authority defines moral behavior in the preconventional stage.
   TRUE or FALSE

4. Most adults function at the conventional level of moral reasoning.   TRUE or FALSE

5. All children will achieve Kohlberg's conventional level of moral development, and approximately 80 percent of all adults will achieve the postconventional level of morality.   TRUE or FALSE

6. Both men and women may use justice or caring as a basis for making moral judgments.
   TRUE or FALSE

## The Story of a Lifetime—Rocky Road or Garden Path?: Pages 122-125

What are the typical tasks and dilemmas through the life span?

1. Learning to read in childhood and establishing a vocation as an adult are typical life stages.
   TRUE or FALSE

2. Psychosocial dilemmas occur when a person is in conflict with his or her social world.
   TRUE or FALSE

3. Initiative versus guilt is the first psychosocial dilemma a child faces.   TRUE or FALSE

4. Answering the question "Who am I?" is a primary task during adolescence.   TRUE or FALSE

5. Generativity is expressed through taking an interest in the next generation.   TRUE or FALSE

## Later Adulthood: Will you Still Need Me When I'm 64?: Pages 138-141

What is involved in well-being during later adulthood?

1.  According to Gould, building a workable life is the predominant activity between ages 16 to 18.
    TRUE or FALSE

2.  A crisis of urgency tends to hit people around the age of 30.    TRUE or FALSE

3.  Levinson places the midlife transition in the 40-55 age range.    TRUE or FALSE

4.  Only a small minority of the men studied by Levinson experienced any instability or urgency at midlife.
    TRUE or FALSE

5.  During the mid-life transition, women are less likely than men to define success in terms of a key event.
    TRUE or FALSE

6.  Wealth is one of the primary sources of happiness in adulthood.    TRUE or FALSE

7.  Having a sense of purpose in life is one element of well-being during adulthood.    TRUE or FALSE

8.  Crystallized abilities are the first to decline as a person ages.    TRUE or FALSE

9.  Ageism refers to prejudice and discrimination toward the elderly.    TRUE or FALSE

10. Few elderly persons become senile or suffer from mental decay.    TRUE or FALSE


## Death and Dying—The Final Challenge: Pages 146-152

How do people typically react to death?

1.  Most of the deaths portrayed on television are homicides.    TRUE or FALSE

2.  The "Why me" reaction to impending death is an expression of anger.    TRUE or FALSE

3.  Trying to be "good" in order to live longer is characteristic of the denial reaction to impending death.
    TRUE or FALSE

4.  It is best to go through all the stages of dying described by Kübler-Ross in the correct order.
    TRUE or FALSE

5.  To help reduce the feeling of isolation, Kirsti Dyer suggests that family members or friends should try
    to be respectful, genuine, aware of nonverbal cues, or just be there for the dying person.
    TRUE or FALSE

## Effective Parenting—Raising Healthy Children
## Pages 115-118

How do effective parents discipline and communicate with their children?

1.  Consistency of child discipline is more important than whether limits on children's behavior are strict or lenient.

    TRUE or FALSE

2.  Encouragement means giving recognition for effort and improvement.

    TRUE or FALSE

3.  Logical consequences should be stated as you-messages.

    TRUE or FALSE

# FINAL SURVEY AND REVIEW

## Nature and Nurture—It Takes Two to Tango

How do heredity and environment affect development?

1.  _____ psychology is the study of _____ changes in behavior and abilities, from birth to death.

2.  The nature-nurture debate concerns the relative contributions to development of_____ (nature) and _____ (nurture).

3.  Hereditary instructions are carried by DNA ( _____ acid) in the form of_____ ("colored bodies") and genes in every cell.

4.  Most characteristics are _____ (influenced by a combination of genes) and reflect the combined effects of dominant and _____ genes.

5.  _____ refers to all external conditions that affect development.

6.  During pregnancy, _____ development is subject to environmental influences in the form of diseases,_____, _____, or the mother's diet and health.

7.  Prenatal damage to the fetus may cause_____ problems, or birth defects. In contrast, _____ problems are inherited from one's parents.

90

8. _____ _____ _____ (FAS) is the result of heavy drinking

   during _____, which causes the infant to have _____ birth weight, a small head, and

   _____ malformations.

9. Early perceptual and intellectual _____ seriously retards development.

10. _____ increases the likelihood that children will experience various forms of

    deprivation which may impede _____ development and educational achievement and increase a

    risk for _____ illness and _____ behavior.

11. Deliberate _____ of the environment in infancy and early childhood has a beneficial

    effect on development.

12. Heredity also influences differences in _____ (the physical foundations of personality).

    Most infants fall into one of three categories: _____ children, difficult children, and

    _____ children.

13. A child's _____ (current state of development) reflects heredity,

    environment, and the effects of the child's own behavior.

# The Newborn Baby—More than Meets the Eye
What can newborn babies do?

1. The human neonate (newborn) has a number of adaptive reflexes, including the _____ ,

   rooting, _____ , and _____ reflexes.

2. Newborns begin to learn immediately and they _____ (mimic) adults.

3. Tests in a _____ reveal a number of visual preferences in the newborn. The

   neonate is drawn to _____ , circular, curved, and brightly-lighted designs.

4. Infants prefer _____ patterns, especially familiar faces. In later infancy,

   interest in the _____ emerges.

5. While the _____ of maturation varies from child to child, the order is nearly _____ .

6. The development of muscular control ( _____ development) is _____ (from head

   to toe) and _____ (from the center of the body to the extremities.)

91

7. Emotional development begins with a capacity for general _____ . After that the first

   _____ and _____ emotions develop.

8. By eight to twelve months, babies display a _____ smile when other people are nearby.

# Social Development—Baby, I'm Stuck on You
## Of what significance is a child's emotional bond with adults?

1. Social development refers to the emergence of self- _____ and forming _____

   with parents and others.

2. For optimal development in human infants, the development of an emotional attachment to their

   primary _____ is a critical early event that must occur during the _____ (within the first

   year) of infancy.

3. Infant attachment is reflected by separation _____ (distress when infants are away from

   parents).

4. The quality of attachment can be classified as secure, insecure- _____ , or

   insecure- _____ .

5. Having a _____ attachment style tends to promote caring, supportiveness, and

   understanding while having an _____ attachment style tends to promote resistance toward

   intimacy and commitment to others. An _____ attachment style tends to promote mixed

   feelings about love and friendship.

6. The relationship between quality of attachment and the type of _____ that is provided

   appears to be _____ in all cultures.

7. _____ day care does not harm children; excellent care can, in fact, _____ some

   areas of development.

8. Some characteristics of high-quality day care include having a _____ number of children

   per caregiver, trained caregivers, an overall group size of _____ children, and

   minimal _____ turnover.

9. An infant's _____ needs are every bit as important as more obvious needs for physical care.

# Parental Influences—Life with Mom and Dad
How important are parenting styles?

1. _____ (patterns of parental care) have a substantial impact on emotional and intellectual development.

2. _____ influences (the effects mothers have on their children) tend to center on _____ .

3. _____ influences differ in their impact because fathers tend to function as a _____ for the infant.

4. _____ parents enforce rigid rules and demand strict obedience to authority.

5. Overly _____ parents give little guidance and don't hold children accountable for their actions.

6. _____ (effective) parents supply firm and consistent guidance, combined with love and affection.

7. Caregiving styles among various ethnic groups tend to reflect each culture's _____ . For example, fathers in Arab-American families tend to be strong _____ figures, demanding absolute obedience.

# Language Development—Fast-Talking Babies
How do children acquire language?

1. Language development proceeds from control of crying, to _____ , then _____ , the use of single words, and then to _____ speech (two-word sentences).

2. The patterns of early speech suggest a biological _____ to acquire language.

3. _____ (psychologists who study language) believe that innate language predispositions are augmented by learning.

4. _____ communication between parent and child involves shared rhythms, nonverbal signals, and _____-taking.

5. Parents help children learn language by using distinctive caretaker speech or_____ .

# Cognitive Development—Think Like a Child
How do children learn to think?

1. The intellects of children are less _____ than those of adults. Jean Piaget theorized that cognitive growth occurs through a combination of _____ and accommodation.

2. Piaget also held that children go through a fixed series of _____ stages. The stages are: _____ (0-2), _____ (2-7), concrete operational (7-11), and formal operations (11-adult).

3. _____ (the ability to understand that objects continue to exist when they are out of sight) emerges during the _____ stage while _____ (the ability to understand that mass, weight, and volume remain unchanged when the shape of objects changes) emerges during the _____ stage.

4. Unlike the preoperational stage of development, when children exhibit egocentrism, children in the _____ stage of development are less egocentric and can think abstractly, hypothetically, and theoretically.

5. _____ theorists dispute the idea that cognitive development occurs in stages. Recent studies suggest infants are capable of levels of _____ beyond that observed by Piaget.

6. A _____ strategy that takes into account the child's level of cognitive development helps adapt instruction to a child's needs.

7. According to the_____ theory of Russian scholar Lev _____, a child's interactions with others are most likely to aid cognitive development if they take place within the child's zone of _____ development.

8. Adults help children learn how to think by _____ , or supporting, their attempts to solve problems or discover principles.

9. During their collaborations with others, children learn important_____ beliefs and values.

# Adolescence and Young Adulthood—The Best of Times, the Worst of Times
Why is the transition from adolescence to adulthood especially challenging?

1. _____ is a culturally defined social status. _____ is a biological event.

2. Early _____ is beneficial mostly for boys; its effects are mixed for girls.

3. Establishing a clear sense of personal _____ is a major task of adolescence. One danger of early maturation is premature _____ formation.

4. For many young people in North America a period of _____ stretches from the late teens to the mid-twenties.

5. By taking pride in their ethnic heritage, teenagers from different ethnic groups have _____ self-esteem, a better self-image, and a stronger ethnic _____ when compared to teens who do not take pride in their ethnic identity

6. As more people enroll in colleges and delay starting a family, the period of _____ for adolescence has been pushed back from the late teens to the mid 20s.

7. Remaining dependent on their parents for _____ support, the twixters are individuals who are trapped between _____ and _____ . They are recognized in England as "Kippers," and in Germany as "Nesthocker."

# Moral Development—Growing a Conscience
How do we develop morals and values?

1. Lawrence Kohlberg theorized that moral development passes through a series of stages revealed by moral _____ about moral _____ .

2. Kohlberg identified _____ , conventional, and postconventional levels of moral reasoning.

3. Some psychologists have questioned whether measures of moral development should be based only on a morality of justice. Adults appear to base moral choices on either justice or _____ , depending on the _____ .

4. Wisdom can be described as combining _____ and _____ (reason and emotion) when making the best moral judgment.

# The Story of a Lifetime—Rocky Road or Garden Path?
What are the typical tasks and dilemmas through the life span?

1. Developmental _____ are prominent landmarks in personal development.

2. According to Erik _____ , each life stage involves a specific _____ dilemma.

95

3. During childhood these are: _____ versus mistrust, _____versus shame and doubt, initiative versus guilt, and _____ versus inferiority.

4. In adolescence, _____ versus_____ confusion is the principal dilemma.

5. In young adulthood we face the dilemma of _____ versus isolation. Later, _____ versus stagnation becomes prominent.

6. Old age is a time when the dilemma of _____ versus despair must be faced.

# Later Adulthood: Will You Still Need Me When I'm 64?
What is involved in well-being during later adulthood?

1. Well-being at midlife is related to self-_____ , positive relationships, _____, mastery, a purpose in life, and continued personal growth.

2. A _____ affects many people during middle-adulthood, but this is by no means universal.

3. A _____ during midlife can provide individuals with opportunities for personal growth or make "midcourse corrections" as it allows individuals to _____ their identities, their goals, and prepare for old age.

4. The greatest losses occur for_____ abilities (which require speed or rapid learning); _____ abilities (stored up knowledge and skills) show much less decline and may actually improve.

5. _____ refers to prejudice, discrimination, and stereotyping on the basis of age. It affects people of all ages, but is especially damaging to older people.

# Death and Dying—The Final Challenge
How do people typically react to death?

1. Older people fear the _____ of death more than the fact that it will occur.

2. Typical emotional reactions to impending death are _____, anger,_____ , depression, and acceptance.

3. One approach to death is the _____ movement, which is devoted to providing humane care to persons who are dying.

4. Initial _____is followed by _____ of grief. Later, apathy, dejection, and _____ may occur. Eventually, grief moves toward resolution, an acceptance of the loss.

# Psychology in Action: Effective Parenting—Raising Healthy Children

How do effective parents discipline and communicate with their children?

1. Parental discipline involves setting guidelines for _____ behavior.

2. Methods of controlling a child's behavior may include power assertion, withdrawal of love, or _____ _____ .

3. Children who experience frequent physical punishment may demonstrate increased aggression and behavior problems.

4. The _____ methods of physical punishment and _____ of love are related to low self-esteem.

5. _____ discipline involves maintaining stable rules of conduct.

6. It is often more effective to reward good behavior rather than _____ misbehavior.

7. Making a distinction between _____ and behavior is the key to clear _____ .

8. Effective parental communication focuses on _____ instead of you-messages.

9. Parents can make effective use of _____ _____ (intrinsic effects) and logical consequences (rational and reasonable effects).

# MASTERY TEST

1. According to Erikson, a conflict between trust and mistrust is characteristic of
   a. infancy.
   b. adolescence.
   c. marriage.
   d. old age.

2. Identity formation during adolescence is aided by
   a. cognitive development.
   b. attaining the preoperational stage.
   c. emotional bargaining.
   d. you-messages from parents.

3. Premature identity formation is one of the risks of early
   a. generativity.
   b. preoccupation with imaginary audiences.
   c. trust-mistrust resolution.
   d. puberty.

4.  The thought "It's all a mistake" would most likely occur as part of which reaction to impending death?
    a.  anger
    b.  freezing up
    c.  denial
    d.  bargaining

5.  The choice of whether to use justice or caring to make moral decisions depends on the _____ a person faces.
    a.  situation
    b.  punishment
    c.  level of authority
    d.  exchange

6.  Seeking approval and upholding law, order, and authority are characteristics of what stage of moral development?
    a.  preconventional
    b.  conventional
    c.  postconventional
    d.  postformal

7.  The universal patterns of the human growth sequence can be attributed to
    a.  recessive genes.
    b.  environment.
    c.  polygenic imprinting.
    d.  heredity.

8.  Exaggerated or musical voice inflections are characteristic of
    a.  prelanguage turn-taking.
    b.  parentese.
    c.  telegraphic speech.
    d.  prompting and expansion.

9.  The emotion most clearly expressed by newborn infants is
    a.  joy.
    b.  fear.
    c.  anger.
    d.  excitement.

10. An infant startled by a loud noise will typically display
    a.  a Moro reflex.
    b.  a rooting reflex.
    c.  a Meltzoff reflex.
    d.  an imprinting reflex.

11. Ideas about Piaget's stages and the cognitive abilities of infants are challenged by infants' reactions to
    a. hypothetical possibilities.
    b. impossible events.
    c. turn-taking.
    d. separation anxiety.

12. The largest percentage of children display what type of temperament?
    a. easy
    b. difficult
    c. slow-to-warm-up
    d. generic

13. A child might begin to question the idea that Santa Claus's sack could carry millions of toys when the child has grasped the concept of
    a. assimilation.
    b. egocentricism.
    c. conservation.
    d. reversibility of permanence.

14. In most areas of development, heredity and environment are
    a. independent.
    b. interacting.
    c. conflicting.
    d. responsible for temperament.

15. By definition, a trait that is controlled by a dominant gene cannot be
    a. eugenic.
    b. hereditary.
    c. carried by DNA.
    d. polygenic.

16. _____ development proceeds head-down and center-outward.
    a. Cognitive
    b. Motor
    c. Prelanguage
    d. Preoperational

17. After age 2, infants become much more interested in
    a. bonding.
    b. nonverbal communication.
    c. familiar voices.
    d. unfamiliar faces.

18. According to Piaget, one of the major developments during the sensorimotor stage is emergence of the concept of
    a. assimilation.
    b. accommodation.
    c. object permanence.
    d. transformation.

19. Poverty is to deprivation as early childhood stimulation is to
    a. imprinting.
    b. enrichment.
    c. responsiveness.
    d. assimilation.

20. According to Erikson, developing a sense of integrity is a special challenge in
    a. adolescence.
    b. young adulthood.
    c. middle adulthood.
    d. late adulthood.

21. The smallest number of Levinson's subjects experienced midlife as a(n)
    a. last chance.
    b. period of serious decline.
    c. time to start over.
    d. escape from dominance.

22. According to Erikson, a dilemma concerning _____usually follows one that focuses on identity.
    a. trust
    b. industry
    c. initiative
    d. intimacy

23. Skills that rely on fluid abilities could be expected to show declines beginning in
    a. adolescence.
    b. young adulthood.
    c. middle adulthood.
    d. late adulthood

24. Which of the following is a common myth about old age?
    a. Most elderly persons are isolated and neglected.
    b. A large percentage of the elderly suffer from senility.
    c. A majority of the elderly are dissatisfied with their lives.
    d. All of the preceding are myths.

25. Gould's study of adult development found that a crisis of _____ is common between the ages of 35 and 43.
    a. urgency
    b. questions
    c. dominance
    d. stability

26. A period of _____ has been extended from the late teens to the mid 20s because young people are _____ .
    a. emerging adulthood; prolonging their identity exploration
    b. emerging adolescence; actively exploring their love and worldviews
    c. puberty; immature and irresponsible
    d. none of the above

27. Kohlberg believed that moral development typically begins _____ and continues into adulthood with _____ percent of adults achieving postconventional morality.
    a. at the onset of puberty; 50
    b. in childhood; 20
    c. in early adolescence; 40
    d. in late adolescence; 80

28. Consonants first enter a child's language when the child begins
    a. babbling.
    b. cooing.
    c. the single word stage.
    d. turn-taking.

29. Insecure attachment is revealed by
    a. separation anxiety.
    b. seeking to be near the mother after separation.
    c. turning away from the mother after separation.
    d. social referencing.

30. A healthy balance between the rights of parents and their children is characteristic of
    a. authoritarian parenting.
    b. permissive parenting.
    c. authoritative parenting.
    d. consistent parenting.

31. Studies of infant imitation
    a. are conducted in a looking chamber.
    b. confirm that infants mimic adult facial gestures.
    c. show that self-awareness precedes imitation.
    d. are used to assess the quality of infant attachment.

32. According to Vygotsky, children learn important cultural beliefs and values when adults provide _____ to help them gain new ideas and skills.
    a. scaffolding
    b. proactive nurturance
    c. imprinting stimuli
    d. parentese

33. One thing that all forms of effective child discipline have in common is that they
    a. are consistent.
    b. make use of punishment.
    c. involve temporary withdrawal of love.
    d. emphasize you-messages.

34. Children who are securely attached to their parents tend to _____ when they interact with others.
    a. be anxious and remote
    b. be resilient and curious
    c. dislike direct physical contact
    d. lack social skills

35. Parents who use a(n) _____ form of parenting tend to teach their children to manage and control their emotions and to use positive coping skills.
    a. authoritative
    b. authoritarian
    c. overly permissive
    d. power assertion

# SOLUTIONS

## RECITE AND REVIEW

### How do heredity and environment affect development?: Pages 79-84

1. behavior; birth; death
2. nature; nurture
3. DNA; genes
4. genes; genes
5. external
6. environmental
7. birth; defects
8. FAS; drinking; low; facial
9. development
10. deprivation; educational delinquent
11. environment
12. personality; difficult
13. own; behavior

### What can newborn babies do? What influence does maturation have on early development?: Pages 85-88

1. neonate; adaptive
2. learn
3. visual; circular
4. familiar; faces
5. order
6. muscular; center
7. general
8. people

### Of what significance is a child's emotional bond with parents?: Pages 89-91

1. Social
2. caregivers; sensitive period
3. separation
4. secure
5. supportiveness; resistance; mixed
6. universal
7. harm
8. small; 12 to 15
9. needs

### How important are parenting styles?: Pages 91-94

1. development
2. mothers
3. fathers
4. rules; authority
5. guidance
6. effective
7. customs; beliefs

### How do children acquire language?: Pages 94-96

1. crying; speech
2. biological
3. language; learning
4. signals
5. speech

### How do children learn to think?: Pages 97-102

1. less; intellectual
2. stages; concrete; operations
3. objects; exist; sensorimotor;
4. egocentrism; abstractly
5. stages; Piaget
6. cognitive
7. cognitive; zone; development
8. supporting
9. beliefs unchanged; concrete operational

## How do effective parents discipline and communicate with their children?: Pages 112-114

1. discipline
2. power assertion
3. physical; aggression
4. physical punishment
5. stable
6. reward
7. behavior
8. communication
9. logical consequences

## Why is the transition from adolescence to adulthood especially challenging?: Pages 102-104

1. social; biological
2. boys; girls
3. adolescence; early
4. teens; mid-twenties
5. higher; identity
6. emerging; mid 20s
7. twixters; adulthood

## How do we develop morals and values?: Pages 104-106

1. moral; moral; moral
2. reasoning
3. justice; justice
4. Wisdom

## What are the typical tasks and dilemmas through the life span?: Pages 106-108

1. developmental
2. dilemma
3. shame; guilt; inferiority
4. adolescence
5. isolation; stagnation
6. despair

## What is involved in well-being during later adulthood?: Pages 108-110

1. purpose; growth
2. universal
3. midcourse; reevaluate
4. speed; knowledge
5. age; older

## How do people typically react to death?: Pages 110-111

1. death
2. anger; depression
3. dying
5. grief; resolution

# CONNECTIONS

## How do heredity and environment affect development? Pages 84-90

1. a.
2. b.
3. i
4. c.
5. g.
6. d.
7. j.
8. e.
9. f.
10. h.

104

## What can newborn babies do? Pages 90-95

1. b.  
2. c.  
3. b.  

4. e.  
5. d.  
6. g.  

7. f.  

## Of what significance is a child's emotional bond with parents? Pages 95-101

1. d.  
2. c.  
3. a.  

4. e.  
5. f.  
6. b.  

7. g.  

## How important are parenting styles? Pages 101-106

1. c.  
2. g.  
3. a.  

4. f  
5. d  
6. b  

7. e.  

## How do children acquire language? Pages 106-109

1. e.  
2. a.  
3. h.  

4. b.  
5. d.  
6. g.  

7. f.  
8. c.  

## How do children learn to think? Pages 109-118

1. c.  
2. a.  
3. f.  

4. b.  
5. e.  
6. d.  

7. h.  
8. g.  
9. i.  

## Why is the transition from adolescence to adulthood especially challenging? Pages 132-135

1. c.  
2. a.  

3. f.  
4. e.  

5. b.  
6. d.  

## How do we develop morals and values? Pages 135-137

1. e.  
2. a.  

3. d.  
4. c.  

5. b.  

## What are the typical tasks and dilemmas through the life span? Pages 122-125

1. e.  
2. f.  
3. g.  

4. c.  
5. h.  
6. b.  

7. d.  
8. a.

## What is involved in well-being during later adulthood? Pages 138-141

3.  b.
4.  d.
5.  f.
6.  c.

## How do people typically react to death? Pages 146-152

1.  b.
2.  a.
3.  d.
4.  e.
5.  c.

# CHECK YOUR MEMORY

## How do heredity and environment affect development? Pages 84-90

1.  F
2.  F
3.  T
4.  F
5.  T
6.  T
7.  T
8.  T
9.  F
10. T
11. T
12. T

## What can newborn babies do? Pages 90-95

1.  F
2.  F
3.  T
4.  F
5.  F
6.  F
7.  F
8.  F
9.  F

## Of what significance is a child's emotional bond with parents? Pages 95-101

1.  F
2.  F
3.  F
4.  T

## How important are parenting styles? Pages 101-106

1.  F
2.  T
3.  F
4.  T
5.  F
6.  F
7.  T
8.  T
9.  F

## How do children acquire language? Pages 106-109

1.  F
2.  F
3.  T
4.  F
5.  T
6.  T
7.  F

## How do children learn to think? Pages 109-115

| | | |
|---|---|---|
| 1. F | 6. F | 11. T |
| 2. F | 7. T | 12. F |
| 3. T | 8. T | 13. T |
| 4. T | 9. F | 14. T |
| 5. F | 10. T | |

## Why is the transition from adolescence to adulthood especially challenging? Pages 132-135

| | | |
|---|---|---|
| 1. T | 4. F | 7. F |
| 2. T | 5. T | |
| 3. T | 6. T | |

## How do we develop morals and values? Pages 135-137

| | | |
|---|---|---|
| 1. T | 3. F | 5. F |
| 2. T | 4. T | 6. T |

## What are the typical tasks and dilemmas through the life span? Pages 122-125

| | | |
|---|---|---|
| 1. F | 3. F | 5. T |
| 2. T | 4. T | |

## What is involved in well-being during later adulthood? Pages 138-141

| | | |
|---|---|---|
| 1. F | 5. T | 9. F |
| 2. F | 6. F | 10. T |
| 3. F | 7. T | |
| 4. F | 8. F | |

## How do people typically react to death? Pages 146-149

| | | |
|---|---|---|
| 1. T | 3. F | 5. T |
| 2. T | 4. F | |

## How do effective parents discipline their children? Pages 115-118

| | | |
|---|---|---|
| 1. T | 2. T | 3. F |

# FINAL SURVEY AND REVIEW

## How do heredity and environment affect development?

1. Developmental; progressive
2. heredity; environment
3. deoxyribonucleic; chromosomes
4. polygenic; recessive
5. Environment
6. prenatal; drugs; radiation
7. congenital; genetic
8. Fetal alcohol syndrome; pregnancy; low; facial
9. deprivation
10. Poverty; cognitive; mental; delinquent
11. enrichment
12. temperament; easy; slow-to-warm-up
13. development; level

## What can newborn babies do?

1. grasping; sucking; Moro
2. imitate
3. looking; chamber; complex
4. human; face; unfamiliar
5. rate; universal
6. motor; cephalocaudal; proximodistal
7. excitement; pleasant; unpleasant
8. social

## Of what significance is a child's emotional bond with parents?

1. awareness; relationships
2. caregivers; sensitive period
3. anxiety
4. avoidant; ambivalent
5. secure; avoidant; abivalent;
6. caregiving; universal
7. High-quality; accelerate
8. small; 12 to 15; staff
9. affectional

## How important are parenting styles?

1. Parental styles
2. maternal; caregiving
3. Paternal; playmate
4. Authoritarian
5. permissive
6. Authoritative
7. beliefs; authority

## How do children acquire language?

1. cooing; babbling; telegraphic
2. predisposition
3. Psycholinguists
4. Prelanguage; turn
5. parentese

## How do children learn to think?

1. abstract; assimilation
2. cognitive; sensorimotor; preoperational
3. Object permanence; sensorimotor; conservation; concrete operational
4. formal operational
5. Learning; thinking
6. one-step-ahead
7. sociocultural; Vygotsky; proximal
8. scaffolding
9. cultural

## How do effective parents discipline and communicate with their children?

1. acceptable
2. management
3. punishment; behavior

4. discipline; withholding
5. Consistent
6. punish

7. feelings; communication
8. I-messages
9. natural consequences

## Why is the transition from adolescence to adulthood especially challenging?

1. Adolescence; Puberty
2. maturation
3. identity; identity

4. emerging adulthood
5. higher; identity
6. emerging adulthood

7. economic; adolescence; adulthood

## How do we develop morals and values?

1. reasoning; dilemmas
2. preconventional

3. caring; situation
4. justice; caring

## What are the typical tasks and dilemmas through the life span?

1. milestones
2. Erikson; psychosocial

3. trust; autonomy; industry
4. identity; role

5. Intimacy; generativity
6. integrity

## What is involved in well-being during later adulthood?

1. acceptance; autonomy
2. midlife crisis

3. transition period; reevaluate

4. fluid; crystallized
5. Ageism

## How do people typically react to death?

1. circumstances
2. denial; bargaining

3. hospice
4. shock; pangs; depression

# MASTERY TEST

1. a, p. 106
2. a, p. 85
3. d, p. 102
4. c, p. 111
5. a, p. 105
6. b, p. 105
7. d, p. 79
8. b, p. 96
9. d, p. 88
10. a, p. 85
11. b, p. 100
12. a, p. 84

13. c, p. 99
14. b, p. 79
15. d, p. 80
16. b, p. 87
17. d, p. 86
18. c, p. 97
19. b, p. 83
20. d, p. 108
21. c, p. 109
22. d, p. 107
23. b, p. 110
24. d, p. 110

25. a, p. 109
26. a, p. 104
27. b, p. 105
28. a, p. 94
29. c, p. 90
30. c, p. 92
31. b, p. 85
32. a, p. 101
33. a, p. 112
34. b, p. 92
35. a, p. 92

# Sensation and Reality

## Chapter Overview

The senses act as data reduction systems. Studies in psychophysics relate physical energies to the sensations we experience. Both absolute and difference thresholds have been identified for various senses. There is evidence that subliminal perception occurs, but the effect is weak. Sensory analysis and coding influence what we experience. Sensory processing is localized in specific parts of the brain.

The visible spectrum is transduced by rods and cones (photoreceptors) in the retina leading to the construction of visual experience by the brain. The visible spectrum consists of a narrow range of radiation. Four common visual defects are myopia hyperopia, presbyopia, and astigmatism. Rods specialize in peripheral vision, night vision, seeing black and white, and detecting movement. Cones specialize in color vision, acuity, and daylight vision.

Our ability to see colors is explained by the trichromatic theory (in the retina) and by the opponent-process theory (in the visual system beyond the eyes). The rods and cones differ in color sensitivity. Total color blindness is rare, but 8 percent of males and 1 percent of females are red-green color-weak. Color weakness is a sex-linked trait carried on the X chromosome

Dark adaptation, an increase in sensitivity to light, is caused mainly by increased concentration of visual pigments in both the rods and the cones but mainly by rhodopsin recombining in the rods. Vitamin A deficiencies may cause night blindness.

Sound waves are transduced by the eardrum, auditory ossicles, oval window, cochlea, and ultimately, hair cells. Frequency theory explains how we hear tones up to 4,000 hertz; place theory explains tones above 4,000 hertz. Two basic types of hearing loss are conductive hearing loss and sensorineural hearing loss. Noise-induced hearing loss is a common form of sensorineural hearing loss.

Olfaction and gustation are chemical senses responsive to airborne or liquefied molecules. It is suspected that humans are sensitive to pheromones. The lock and key theory of olfaction partially explains smell. In addition, the location of the olfactory receptors in the nose helps identify various scents. Sweet and bitter tastes are based on a lock-and-key coding of molecule shapes. Salty and sour tastes are triggered by a direct flow of ions into taste receptors.

The somesthetic senses include the skin senses, kinesthesis, and the vestibular senses. The skin senses are touch, pressure, pain, cold, and warmth. Sensitivity to each is related to the number of receptors found in an area of skin. Distinctions can be made among various types of pain. According to sensory conflict theory, motion sickness is caused by a mismatch of visual, kinesthetic, and vestibular sensations.

Incoming sensations are affected by sensory adaptation, by selective attention, and by sensory gating. Selective gating of pain messages apparently takes place in the spinal cord. Gate control theory proposes an explanation for many pain phenomena, except phantom limb pain.

Pain can be reduced or controlled by altering factors that affect pain intensity. Pain is greatly affected by anxiety, control over the stimulus, attention, and the interpretation placed on an experience. Pain can be reduced by controlling these factors through distraction, reinterpretation, and counterirritation.

# Learning Objectives

### Theme: The principles of development help us better understand not only children, but our own behavior as well.

| |
|---|
| **GQ: How do heredity and environment affect development?** |
| LO 3.1 Define *developmental psychology*. Discuss *readiness* (include how readiness is related to toilet training). Define the term *developmental level* and list the three factors that combine to determine it. |
| LO 3.2 Explain the basic mechanisms of heredity, include a description of the following terms: a. *chromosome*; b. *DNA*; c. *gene*; d. *polygenic*; e. *dominant* trait (gene); f. *recessive* trait (gene). |
| LO 3.3 Compare, contrast, and give examples of the effects of *enrichment* and *deprivation* on development. |
| **GQ: What can newborn babies do?** |
| LO 3.4 Name and describe four *adaptive reflexes* displayed by neonates. |
| LO 3.5 Describe the intellectual capabilities and the sensory preferences of a neonate. |
| LO 3.6 Discuss motor development and the concepts of *maturation*, *cephalocaudal pattern*, and *proximodistal pattern*. |
| **GQ: Of what significance is a child's emotional bond with adults?** |
| LO 3.7 Describe (in general) the course of emotional development, according to Bridges and Izard. |
| LO 3.8 Discuss *emotional attachment* (including the concept of separation anxiety). Differentiate between the three types of attachment identified by Mary Ainsworth. |
| LO 3.9 Describe Harlow's experiment dealing with *contact comfort*, and state the results of the experiment. |
| **GQ: How important are parenting styles?** |
| LO 3.10 Describe Baumrind's three major styles of parenting, including characteristics of both parents and children in each style. |
| LO 3.11 Discuss the meaning and importance of infant *affectional needs*, the range of effects of maternal *caregiving styles*, and the importance of *paternal influences* on the child. |
| **GQ: How do children acquire language?** |
| LO 3.12 List and briefly describe the sequence of language acquisition. Include the term *psycholinguist* as well as briefly discuss the role of innate factors and learning in acquiring language. Explain how parents communicate with infants before the infants can talk, including the terms *signals*, *turn-taking*, and *parentese*. |
| **GQ: How do children learn to think?** |
| LO 3.13 With regard to Piaget's theory of cognitive development: a. explain how a child's intelligence and thinking differ from an adult's (include the concept of *transformation*). b. explain the concepts of *assimilation* and *accommodation*. c. list (in order) and briefly describe each stage, listing the specific characteristics of each stage. d. explain how parents can best guide their child's intellectual development. e. evaluate the usefulness of Piaget's theory, including a review of current research on infant cognition. |
| LO 3.14 Briefly discuss Vygotsky's sociocultural theory, including how his theory differs from Piaget's theory. Define the terms *zone of proximal development* and *scaffolding*. |
| **GQ: Why is the transition from adolescence to adulthood especially challenging?** |
| LO 3.15 Define and differentiate between *adolescence* and *puberty* and describe the advantages and disadvantages of early and late maturation for males vs. females. |
| LO 3.16 With regard to the adolescent search for identity: a. explain what that means; b. explain how being a member of a minority ethnic group influences the identity search; c. discuss the concept of *emerging adulthood*. |

| |
|---|
| **GQ: How do we develop morals and values?** |
| LO 3.17  Regarding *moral development*: a. list (in order) and briefly describe each of Kohlberg's three levels of moral development; b. describe what proportions of the population appear to function at each of Kohlberg's moral development levels; and c. explain Gilligan's argument against Kohlberg's system, and describe the current status of the argument. |
| **GQ: What are the typical tasks and dilemmas through the life span?** |
| LO 3.18  List the life stages experienced by all people; define the terms *developmental milestones, developmental task*, and *psychosocial dilemma*; and explain, according to Erikson, how the resolution of the psychosocial dilemmas affects a person's adjustment to life. |
| LO 3.19  Describe the *psychosocial crisis* and the possible outcome for each of Erikson's eight life stages. Give approximate age ranges for each stage. |
| **GQ: What is involved in well-being during later adulthood?** |
| LO 3.20  Describe what a *midlife crisis* is; explain how the *midlife transition* is different for women than for men; and list Ryff's six elements of well-being in adulthood. |
| LO 3.21  Discuss the findings of gerontologists regarding the mental capabilities of older adults, including *fluid* and *crystallized* abilities and ways to stay mentally sharp and the keys to successful aging. Define *ageism* and describe some of the stereotypes that exist regarding older adults. |
| **GQ: How do people typically react to death?** |
| LO 3.22  Regarding our emotional reactions toward death: a. explain what people fear about death; b. define *thanatologist*; c. list and briefly characterize the five emotional reactions typically experienced by people facing death, according to Kubler-Ross; d. explain how to make use of this knowledge. |
| **GQ: How do effective parents discipline and communicate with their children?** |
| LO 3.23  Regarding parenting techniques, briefly discuss a. the ingredients of effective parenting. b. the effects of *physical punishment* and *withdrawal of love* and guidelines for their use. c. the elements of effective communication, according to Haim Ginott. d. Thomas Gordon's concepts of *I-messages* and *you-messages*. e. the use of *natural* and *logical consequences*. |

# RECITE AND REVIEW

## Psychophysics—The Limits of Sensibility: Pages 119-123

In what ways are our senses limited?

1. Psychophysics is the study of _____ stimuli and the _____ they evoke.

2. The senses act as _____ reduction systems that select, _____ , and code sensory information.

3. Sensory organs transduce physical energies into _____ impulses.

4. The _____ amount of physical energy necessary to produce a _____ defines the absolute threshold.

5. For the sense of vision, a person can detect a candle flame from approximately _____ miles away on a clear dark night and for the sense of hearing, a person can detect the ticking of a watch from _____ feet away under quiet conditions.

6. A person's sensitivity to pitch ranges from _____ hertz to 20,000 hertz.

7. Threatening or anxiety-provoking stimuli may _____ the threshold for recognition, an effect called perceptual _____.

8. Any stimulus _____ the level of conscious awareness is said to be subliminal.

9. There is evidence that subliminal perception occurs, but subliminal advertising is largely _____.

10. The amount of _____ necessary to produce a just noticeable difference (or JND) in a stimulus defines a _____ threshold.

11. In general, the amount of change needed to produce a JND is a constant proportion of the original stimulus_____ . This relationship is known as Weber's _____.

12. In fact, many sensory systems act as feature _____ .

13. Phosphenes and visual pop-out are examples of feature detection and _____ coding in action.

14. A good example of sensory analysis is the identification of basic _____ features in a stimulus pattern.

15. Sensory response can be partially understood in terms of _____ localization in the brain. That is, the area of the brain _____ ultimately determines which type of sensory experience we have.

## Vision—Catching Some Rays: Pages 123-127
How does the visual system function?

1. The _____ spectrum consists of electromagnetic radiation in a narrow range.

114

2. The electromagnetic spectrum ranges from violet, with a _____ of 400 nanometers, to red, with a _____ of 700 nanometers.

3. Hue refers to a color's name, which corresponds to its_____ . Saturated or "pure" colors come from a _____ band of wavelengths. Brightness corresponds to the amplitude of light waves.

4. The eye is in some ways like a digital camera. At its back lies an array of photoreceptors, called _____ and _____ , that make up a light-sensitive layer called the retina.

5. Vision is focused by the _____ of the cornea and lens and by changes in the _____ of the lens, called accommodation.

6. Four common visual defects, correctable with glasses, are myopia ( _____ ), hyperopia (farsightedness), presbyopia (loss of _____ ), and astigmatism (in which portions of vision are out of focus).

7. The amount of light entering the eye is controlled by movements of the iris, which dilates ( _____ ) and constricts ( _____ ) the pupil.

8. In the retina, the _____ specialize in night vision, black and white reception, and motion detection.

9. The _____ , found exclusively in the fovea and otherwise toward the middle of the eye, specialize in _____ vision, acuity (perception of fine detail), and daylight vision.

10. Individual cells in the visual cortex of the brain act as feature _____ to analyze visual information.

11. After the visual stimulus is processed in the primary visual cortex, further processing of the stimulus occurs via the _____ pathway which determines "what" type of object it is and the _____ pathway which determines "where" the object is in the visual field.

12. The _____ supply much of our peripheral vision. Loss of peripheral vision is called tunnel vision.

## Color Vision—There's More To It Than Meets the Eye: Pages 127-131
How do we perceive colors?

1.  The rods and cones differ in color _____ . Yellow-green is brightest for cones; blue-green for the rods (although they will see it as colorless).

2.  In the _____ , color vision is explained by the trichromatic theory. The theory says that three types of_____ exist, each most sensitive to red, green, or blue.

3.  Three types of light-sensitive visual pigments are found in the _____ , each pigment is most sensitive to either red, green, or blue light.

4.  Trichromatic theory was unable to explain why people experience _____ or visual sensations that persist after a color stimulus is removed.

5.  Beyond the retina, the visual system analyzes colors into _____ messages. According to the opponent-process theory, color information can be coded as either red or green, yellow or blue, and _____ messages.

6.  Ultimately, color experiences are constructed in the _____ . This is apparent when you look at a stimulus that produces simultaneous contrast.

7.  _____ color blindness is rare, but 8 percent of males and 1 percent of females are red-green color blind or color weak.

8.  Color blindness is a sex-linked trait carried on the X ( _____ ) chromosome and passed from mother to son.

9.  The Ishihara test is used to detect

## Dark Adaptation—Let There Be Light!: Pages 131-132
How do we adjust to the dark?

1.  Dark adaptation, an _____ in sensitivity to light, is caused by increased concentrations of visual pigments in the _____ and the _____ .

2. In order for individuals to move from a bright room into a dark room without undergoing dark adaptation, which acquires approximately _____ minutes to see clearly, _____ lights must be on since rods are insensitive to them.

3. Most dark adaptation is the result of increased rhodopsin concentrations in the _____ . Vitamin A deficiencies may cause _____ blindness by impairing the production of rhodopsin.

# Hearing—Good Vibrations: Pages 132-135
## What are the mechanisms of hearing?

1. Sound waves are the stimulus for hearing. Sound travels as waves of compression (_____) and rarefaction (_____) in the air.

2. The _____ of a sound corresponds to the frequency of sound waves. Loudness corresponds to the amplitude (_____) of sound waves.

3. Sound waves are transduced by the _____, auditory ossicles, oval window, cochlea, and ultimately, the _____ cells in the organ of Corti.

4. The frequency theory says that the _____ of nerve impulses in the auditory nerves matches the _____ of incoming sounds (up to 4000 hertz).

5. Place theory says that _____ tones register near the base of the cochlea and _____ tones near its tip.

6. Three basic types of hearing loss are _____ hearing loss, conduction hearing loss, and noise-induced hearing loss.

7. Conduction hearing loss can often be overcome with a hearing aid. _____ hearing loss can sometimes be alleviated by cochlear implants.

8. Noise-induced hearing loss can be prevented by avoiding excessive exposure to _____ sounds. Sounds above 120 decibels pose an immediate danger to hearing. Two warning signs of noise-induced hearing loss are temporary threshold _____ and tinnitus.

9. _____ is also known as biosonar.

## Smell and Taste—The Nose Knows When the Tongue Can't Tell: Pages 135-138

How do the chemical senses operate?

1. Olfaction (_____) and gustation (_____) are chemical senses responsive to airborne or liquefied molecules.

2. Research on dysomnia (_____ to detect a single odor) suggests there are receptors for specific odors; approximately _____ different types of receptors are available to produce _____ different combinations of odors that an individual can detect.

3. The lock and key theory partially explains smell. In addition, the_____ of the olfactory receptors in the nose helps identify various scents.

4. It is suspected that humans are also sensitive to _____ signals called pheromones, although the evidence remains preliminary. Pheromones may be sensed by the vomeronasal _____.

5. There are about _____ types of smell receptors.

6. The top outside edges of the tongue are responsive to sweet, salty, sour, and _____ tastes. It is suspected that a fifth taste quality called umami also exists.

7. Taste also appears to be based in part on lock-and-key _____ of molecule shapes.

8. Chemical senses of _____ and _____ operate together to allow us to experience the flavor of food.

## The Somesthetic Senses—Flying by the Seat of Your Pants: Pages 138-142

What are the somesthetic senses?

1. The somesthetic senses include the _____ senses, vestibular senses, and kinesthetic senses (receptors that detect muscle and joint positioning).

2. The skin senses include touch, _____ , pain, cold, and warmth. Sensitivity to each is related to the _____ of receptors found in an area of skin.

3. Distinctions can be made among various types of pain, including visceral pain, somatic pain, referred pain, warning system pain, and_____ system pain.

4.  Various forms of motion sickness are related to messages received from the vestibular system, which senses gravity and _____ movement.

5.  The otolith organs detect the pull of _____ and rapid head movements.

6.  The movement of _____ within the semicircular canals, and the movement of the _____ within each ampulla, detects head movement and positioning.

7.  According to sensory conflict theory, motion sickness is caused by a _____ of visual, kinesthetic, and vestibular sensations. Motion sickness can be avoided by minimizing sensory conflict.

# Adaptation, Attention, and Gating—Tuning In and Tuning Out: Pages 142-144
## Why are we more aware of some sensations than others?

1.  Incoming sensations are affected by sensory adaptation (a _____ in the number of nerve impulses sent).

2.  Because of physiological nystagmus (involuntary tremors of the eye muscles), vision does not undergo sensory _____ . Physiological nystagmus causes thousands of tiny movements of the _____ muscles to ensure detection of images falling on unfatigued rods and cones.

3.  Selective attention (selection and diversion of messages in the brain) and sensory_____ (blocking or alteration of messages flowing toward the brain) also alter sensations.

4.  Selective gating of pain messages apparently takes place in the _____. Gate control theory proposes an explanation for many pain phenomena.

5.  "Runner's high," the painkilling effects of the Chinese medical art of acupuncture, and other pain phenomena appear to be explained by the release of a _____ -like chemical in the brain, called beta-endorphin.

6.  The brain creates a neuromatrix of one's body to process one's sense of _____ self. This neuromatrix does not recognize that an actual part of the body no longer exists and continues to process nearby sensory stimulations as pain coming from the missing limb.

7.  Most amputees have phantom _____ sensations long after losing a limb.

## Psychology in Action: Controlling Pain—This Won't Hurt a Bit: Pages 145-147

How can pain be reduced in everyday situations?

1. Pain can be reduced by _____ anxiety and redirecting attention to stimuli other than the pain stimulus.

2. Feeling that you have control over a stimulus tends to _____ the amount of pain you experience.

3. The interpretation placed on a _____ affects how painful it is perceived to be.

4. Sending _____ pain messages to the spinal cord can close the gates to more severe pain. This effect is called counterirritation.

5. _____ is used by pain clinics to reduce people's experiences of _____ by introducing an additional, less intense pain signal such as a mild electrical current to the brain through the fast nerve fiber.

# CONNECTIONS

## Psychophysics—The Limits of Sensibility: Pages 119-123

In what ways are our senses limited?

1. _____ feature detectors     a. selects, analyzes, and filters information
2. _____ transducer     b. a system converting a source into another
3. _____ sensory coding     c. "seeing" stars produced by the retina
4. _____ data transduction system     d. picking up a stimulus pattern
5. _____ pop-out     e. converts features into neural messages
6. _____ phosphenes     f. detecting a slant among vertical lines

## Sensory Limitations (continued)

1. _____ Weber's Law     a. physical stimulus and sensation experienced
2. _____ psychophysics     b. smallest amount detected
3. _____ subliminal perception     c. detectable change between 2 stimuli
4. _____ absolute threshold     d. increased in constant proportion
5. _____ perceptual defense     e. blocking disturbing stimulus
6. _____ difference threshold     f. perceived below threshold of consciousness

## Vision—Catching Some Rays: Pages 123-127

How does the visual system function?

1. _____ ciliary muscle
2. _____ iris
3. _____ cornea
4. _____ blind spot
5. _____ lens
6. _____ fovea
7. _____ retinal veins
8. _____ optic nerve
9. _____ aqueous humor
10. _____ pupil
11. _____ retina

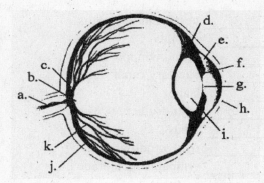

## Vision (continued)

1. _____ presbyopia
2. _____ cones
3. _____ tunnel vision
4. _____ myopia
5. _____ rods
6. _____ hyperopia
7. _____ visual acuity
8. _____ blind spot

a. sensitive to light
b. sensitive to colors
c. effect of optic nerve
d. nearsightedness
e. farsighted due to aging
f. Farsightedness
g. sharpness of images on retina
h. loss of peripheral vision

## Color Vision—There's More to It Than Meets the Eye: Pages 127-131

How do we perceive colors?

1. _____ afterimages
2. _____ opponent-process theory
3. _____ cause of color-blind
4. _____ visual pigments
5. _____ trichromatic theory
6. _____ ishihara test

a. 3 cones sensitive to red, green, and blue
b. process colors in "either-or" messages
c. image remained after stimulus is gone
d. light-sensitive chemicals in photoreceptors
e. determining color-blindness
f. sex-linked trait on the X chromosome

## Hearing—Good Vibrations: Pages 132-135
What are the mechanisms of hearing?

1. _____ vestibular apparatus
2. _____ cochlea
3. _____ round window
4. _____ auditory canal
5. _____ stapes
6. _____ auditory nerve
7. _____ incus
8. _____ oval window
9. _____ tympanic membrane
10. _____ malleus

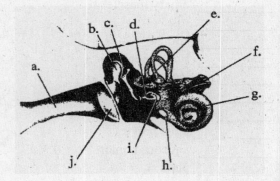

## Hearing (continued)

1. _____ loudness
2. _____ stereocilia
3. _____ conduction hearing loss
4. _____ auditory ossicles
5. _____ sensorineural hearing loss
6. _____ tympanic membrane
7. _____ place theory
8. _____ pitch
9. _____ frequency theory

a. frequency of wave
b. amplitude of wave
c. eardrum
d. hammer, anvil, stirrup
e. "bristles"
f. process impulse up to 4,000 hertz
g. impulse processed in different places
h. damaged hair cells
i. sound blockage in external and middle ear

## Smell and Taste—The Nose Knows When the Tongue Can't Tell: Pages 135-138
How do the chemical senses operate?

1. _____ lock and key theory
2. _____ taste buds
3. _____ olfaction
4. _____ umami
5. _____ dysomnia
6. _____ pheromones
7. _____ gustation

a. sense of smell
b. sense of taste
c. loss of smell
d. similar to chemical molecules' shapes
e. airborne chemical signals
f. receptor for taste
g. "brothy"

## The Somesthetic Senses—Flying by the Seat of Your Pants: Pages 138-142

What are the somesthetic senses?

1. _____ warning system
2. _____ sensory conflict theory
3. _____ vestibular senses
4. _____ reduced motion sickness
5. _____ kinesthetic senses
6. _____ reminding system

a. sense body damage may be occurring
b. senses body movement
c. semicircular canals and otolith organs
d. sense body damage has occurred
e. reduce sensory conflicts by not moving head
f. sensory mismatch

## Adaptation, Attention, and Gating—Tuning In and Tuning Out: Pages 142-147

Why are we more aware of some sensations than others? How can pain be reduced in everyday situations?

1. _____ selective attention
2. _____ neuromatrix
3. _____ beta-endorphin
4. _____ sensory gating
5. _____ counterirritation
6. _____ acupuncture
7. _____ sensory adaptation

a. habituating to a stimulus
b. focus on a sensory input
c. facilitate or block sensory input
d. insert needles to relieve pain
e. painkilling chemicals
f. ice packs and hot-water bottles
g. produces phantom pain

# CHECK YOUR MEMORY

## Psychophysics—The Limits of Sensibility: Pages 119-123

In what ways are our senses limited?

1. The electromagnetic spectrum includes ultraviolet light and radio waves.   TRUE or FALSE

2. Each sensory organ is sensitive to a select range of physical energies.   TRUE or FALSE

3. The artificial vision system described in the text is based on electrodes implanted in the retina.   TRUE or FALSE

4. The retina responds to pressure as well as light.   TRUE or FALSE

5. It takes only one photon striking the retina to produce a sensation of light.   TRUE or FALSE

6. Humans can hear sounds from 2 to 2,000 hertz.   TRUE or FALSE

7. It is possible to taste 1 teaspoon of sugar dissolved in 2 gallons of water.   TRUE or FALSE

8. Some music fans have been harmed by subliminal backmasking.   TRUE or FALSE

9. The JND for loudness is 1/10.   TRUE or FALSE

10. Weber's law applies mainly to stimuli in the mid-range.   TRUE or FALSE

11. Subliminal self-help tapes and messages flashed on TV for 1/30 of a second have shown to directly influence individuals' behavior.   TRUE or FALSE

## Vision—Catching Some Rays: Pages 123-127
How does the visual system function?

1. A nanometer is one-millionth of a meter.   TRUE or FALSE

2. The functions of a human eye have often been compared to a digital camera.   TRUE or FALSE

3. The lens of the eye is about the size and thickness of a postage stamp.   TRUE or FALSE

4. Farsightedness is corrected with a convex lens.   TRUE or FALSE

5. The myopic eye is longer than normal.   TRUE or FALSE

6. There are more rods than cones in the eyes.   TRUE or FALSE

7. Hubel and Wiesel directly recorded activity in single cells in the visual cortex.   TRUE or FALSE

8. The blind spot is the point where the optic nerve leaves the eye.   TRUE or FALSE

9. The fovea contains only retinal arteries and veins.   TRUE or FALSE

10. If your vision is 20/12 like Gordon Cooper, an American astronaut, you would be able to see 8 feet farther than someone who has 20/20 vision.   TRUE or FALSE

11. Vision rated at 20/200 is better than average.   TRUE or FALSE

12. Visual acuity decreases near the edges of the retina.   TRUE or FALSE

13. If the ventral pathway is damaged, one will not be able to process what the object is in his/her visual field. TRUE or FALSE

## Color Vision—There's More to It Than Meets the Eye: Pages 127-131
How do we perceive colors?

1. Blue emergency lights and taxiway lights are used because at night they are more visible to the cones.

   TRUE or FALSE

2. The trichromatic theory of color vision assumes that black and white sensations are produced by the rods.

   TRUE or FALSE

3.  According to the opponent-process theory it is impossible to have a reddish green or yellowish blue.

    TRUE or FALSE

4.  The afterimage produced by staring at a red object is green.   TRUE or FALSE

5.  Visual pigments bleach, or breakdown chemically, when struck by light.   TRUE or FALSE

6.  Yellow-blue color weakness is very rare.   TRUE or FALSE

7.  In the U.S. and Canada, stoplights are always on the bottom of traffic signals.   TRUE or FALSE

## Dark Adaptation—Let There Be Light!: Pages 131-132
How do we adjust to the dark?

1.  Complete dark adaptation takes about 12 minutes.   TRUE or FALSE

2.  Dark adaptation can be preserved by working in an area lit with red light.   TRUE or FALSE

## Hearing—Good Vibrations: Pages 132-135
What are the mechanisms of hearing?

1.  Sound cannot travel in a vacuum.   TRUE or FALSE

2.  The visible, external portion of the ear is the malleus.   TRUE or FALSE

3.  The hair cells are part of the organ of Corti.   TRUE or FALSE

4.  Hunter's notch occurs when the auditory ossicles are damaged by the sound of gunfire.

    TRUE or FALSE

5.  Cochlear implants stimulate the auditory nerve directly.   TRUE or FALSE

6.  Deaf children can learn spoken language close to a normal rate if they have cochlear implants

    before the age of 2.   TRUE or FALSE

7.  A 40 decibel sound could be described as quiet.   TRUE or FALSE

8.  A 100 decibel sound can damage hearing in less than 8 hours.   TRUE or FALSE

9.  Every 20 decibels increases sound energy by a factor of 10.   TRUE or FALSE

10. Only blind people are able to learn how to echolocate.   TRUE or FALSE

## Smell and Taste—The Nose Knows When the Tongue Can't Tell: Pages 135-138
How do the chemical senses operate?

1.  At least 1000 different types of olfactory receptors exist.   TRUE or FALSE

2.  Etherish odors smell like garlic.   TRUE or FALSE

125

3. Dysomnia can be caused by exposure to chemical odors.    TRUE or FALSE

4. Human pheromones (if they exist) are sensed as a subtle, perfume-like odor.    TRUE or FALSE

5. Flavors are greatly influenced by odor, as well as taste.    TRUE or FALSE

6. Taste buds are found throughout the mouth, not just on the tongue.    TRUE or FALSE

7. Umami is a pleasant "brothy" taste.    TRUE or FALSE

8. Women are more likely to be supertasters.    TRUE or FALSE

9. PTC tastes bitter to about 70 percent of those tested.    TRUE or FALSE

10. The sense of taste tends to be weaker in early childhood than it is later as the body matures.
    TRUE or FALSE

## The Somesthetic Senses—Flying by the Seat of Your Pants: Pages 138-142
What are the somesthetic senses?

1. Free nerve endings can produce any of the basic skin sensations.    TRUE or FALSE

2. Vibration is one of the five basic skin sensations.    TRUE or FALSE

3. Areas of the skin that have high concentrations of pain receptors are no more sensitive to pain than other areas of the body.    TRUE or FALSE

4. Visceral pain is often felt at a location on the surface of the body.    TRUE or FALSE

5. Small nerve fibers generally carry warning-system pain messages.    TRUE or FALSE

6. Pain originating in the heart may be felt all the way down the left arm.    TRUE or FALSE

7. Most physical skills rely on dynamic touch, which combines touch sensations with kinesthetic information.    TRUE or FALSE

8. The semicircular canals are especially sensitive to the pull of gravity.    TRUE or FALSE

9. Motion sickness is believed to be related to the body's reactions to being poisoned.
    TRUE or FALSE

10. A horizontal body position tends to intensify motion sickness.    TRUE or FALSE

## Adaptation, Attention, and Gating—Tuning In and Tuning Out: Pages 142-144
Why are we more aware of some sensations than others?

1. Unlike other receptor cells, the rods and cones do not undergo sensory adaptation.
   TRUE or FALSE

2. If you wear a ring, you are rarely aware of it because of sensory gating.    TRUE or FALSE

3. The "seat-of-your-pants" phenomenon is related to selective attention.    TRUE or FALSE

4. Stabilized visual images appear brighter and more intense than normal.   TRUE or FALSE

5. Mild electrical stimulation of the skin can block reminding system pain.   TRUE or FALSE

6. Mild electrical stimulation of the skin causes a release of endorphins in free nerve endings.
   TRUE or FALSE

7. The neuromatrix best explains phantom limb pain experienced by many amputees.
   TRUE or FALSE

## How can pain be reduced in everyday situations?: Pages 145-147

1. High levels of anxiety tend to amplify the amount of pain a person experiences.
   TRUE or FALSE

2. Prepared childbirth training helps women feel in control of the birth process.
   TRUE or FALSE

3. Physical relaxation exercises can be used to lower anxiety in situations involving pain.
   TRUE or FALSE

4. As a means of reducing pain, hot-water bottles are an example of counterirritation.
   TRUE or FALSE

# FINAL SURVEY AND REVIEW

## Psychophysics—The Limits of Sensibility
In what ways are our senses limited?

1. Psychophysics is the study of physical stimuli stimuli and the sensations they evoke.

2. The senses act as data _____ reduction systems that select, analyze , and _____
   sensory information.

3. Sensory organs _____ physical energies into nerve impulses.

4. The minimum amount of physical energy necessary to produce a sensation defines the
   _____ threshold.

5. For the sense of vision, a person can detect a candle flame from approximately _____ miles
   away on a clear dark night and for the sense of hearing, a person can detect the ticking of a watch
   from _____ feet away under quiet conditions.

6. A person's sensitivity to pitch ranges from _____ hertz to 20,000 hertz.

7. Threatening or anxiety-provoking stimuli may raise the _____ for recognition, an effect called _____ defense..

8. Any stimulus below the level of conscious awareness is said to be _____.

9. There is evidence that subliminal perception occurs, but subliminal _____ is largely ineffective.

10. The amount of change necessary to produce a _____ _____ difference (or JND) in a stimulus defines a _____ threshold.

11. In general, the amount of _____ needed to produce a JND is a constant proportion of the original stimulus intensity. This relationship is known as _____ law.

12. In fact, many sensory systems act as _____ detectors.

13. _____ and visual pop-out are examples of feature detection and sensory _____ coding in action.

14. A good example of _____ _____ is the identification of basic perceptual features in a stimulus pattern.

15. Sensory response can be partially understood in terms of sensory _____ in the brain. That is, the _____ of the brain activated ultimately determines which type of sensory experience we have.

# Vision—Catching Some Rays
How does the visual system function?

1. The visible spectrum consists of _____ radiation in a narrow range.

2. The visible spectrum ranges from violet, with a wavelength of _____, to red with a wavelength of _____ .

3. _____ refers to a color's name, which corresponds to its wavelength. Saturated or "pure" colors come from a narrow band of wavelengths. Brightness corresponds to the _____ of light waves.

4.  The eye is in some ways like a digital camera. At its back lies an array of _____ , called rods and cones, that make up a light-sensitive layer called the_____ .

5.  Vision is focused by the shape of the _____ and lens and by changes in the shape of the lens, called _____ .

6.  Four common visual defects, correctable with glasses, are_____ (nearsightedness), hyperopia (farsightedness), presbyopia (loss of accommodation), and _____ (in which portions of vision are out of focus).

7.  The amount of light entering the eye is controlled by movements of the _____ , which _____ (enlarges) and _____ (narrows) the pupil.

8.  In the retina, the rods specialize in night vision, black and white reception, and _____ detection.

9.  The cones, found exclusively in the _____ and otherwise toward the middle of the eye, specialize in color vision, _____ (perception of fine detail), and daylight vision.

10. Individual cells in the visual _____ of the brain act as feature detectors to analyze visual information.

11. After the visual stimulus is processed in the primary visual cortex, further processing of the stimulus occurs via the ventral pathway which determines "_____" type of object it is and the dorsal pathway which determines "_____" the object is in the visual field.

12. The rods supply much of our _____ vision. Loss of _____ vision is called tunnel vision.

# Color Vision—There's More To It Than Meets the Eye
## How do we perceive colors?

1.  The rods and cones differ in color sensitivity. _____ -green is brightest for cones; _____ -green for the rods (although they will see it as colorless).

2.  In the retina, color vision is explained by the _____ theory. The theory says that three types of cones exist, each most sensitive to red, green, or blue.

3.  Three types of light-sensitive visual_____ are found in the cones, each is most sensitive to either red, green, or blue light.

129

4.    _____ theory was unable to explain why people experience _____ or visual sensations that persist after a color stimulus has been removed.

5.    Beyond the retina, the visual system analyzes colors into either-or messages. According to the _____ theory, color information can be coded as either _____ , yellow or blue, and black or white messages.

6.    Ultimately, _____ experiences are constructed in the brain. This is apparent when you look at a stimulus that produces simultaneous _____ .

7.    Total color blindness is rare, but 8 percent of males and 1 percent of females are _____ color-blind or color weak.

8.    Color blindness is a _____ trait carried on the X (female) chromosome and passed from _____ to son.

9.    The _____ test is used to detect color blindness.

# Dark Adaptation—Let There Be Light!
## How do we adjust to the dark?

1.    Dark adaptation, an increase in sensitivity to light, is caused by increased concentrations of _____ in the rods and the cones.

2.    In order for individuals to move from a bright room into a dark room without undergoing dark adaptation, which acquires approximately _____ minutes to see clearly, _____ lights must be on since _____ are insensitive to them.

3.    Most dark adaptation is the result of increased _____ concentrations in the rods. Vitamin _____ deficiencies may cause night blindness.

# Hearing—Good Vibrations
## What are the mechanisms of hearing?

1.    Sound waves are the stimulus for hearing. Sound travels as waves of _____ (peaks) and _____ (valleys) in the air.

2.    The pitch of a sound corresponds to the _____ of sound waves. Loudness corresponds to the _____ (height) of sound waves.

130

3. Sound waves are transduced by the eardrum, auditory _____, oval window, cochlea, and ultimately, the hair cells in the organ of _____.

4. The frequency theory says that the frequency of nerve impulses in the _____ matches the frequency of incoming sounds (up to 4000 hertz).

5. Place theory says that high tones register near the _____ of the cochlea and low tones near its _____ .

6. Three basic types of hearing loss are sensorineural hearing loss, conduction hearing loss, and _____ hearing loss.

7. Conduction hearing loss can often be overcome with a hearing aid. Sensorineural hearing loss can sometimes be alleviated by   implants.

8. Noise-induced hearing loss can be prevented by avoiding excessive exposure to loud sounds. Sounds above _____ pose an immediate danger to hearing. Two warning signs of noise-induced hearing loss are temporary threshold shift and a ringing in the ears, called _____ .

9. Echolocation is also known as _____ .

## Smell and Taste—The Nose Knows When the Tongue Can't Tell
How do the chemical senses operate?

1. _____ (smell) and _____ (taste) are chemical senses responsive to airborne or liquefied molecules.

2. Research on _____ (inability to detect a single odor) suggests there are receptors for specific odors; approximately _____ different types of receptors are available to produce _____ different combination of odors that an individual can detect.

3. There are about 1000 types of _____ receptors.

4. It is suspected that humans are also sensitive to chemical signals called _____ , which may be sensed by the _____ organ.

5. The _____ theory partially explains smell. In addition, thelocation of the olfactory receptors in the nose helps identify various scents.

6.  The top outside edges of the tongue are responsive to _____ , _____ ,_____ , and bitter tastes. It is suspected that a fifth taste quality called _____ also exists.

7.  Taste also appears to be based in part on lock-and-key coding of _____ shapes.

8.  Chemical senses of_____and _____ operate together to allow us to experience the flavor of food.

# The Somesthetic Senses—Flying by the Seat of Your Pants
## What are the somesthetic senses?

1.  The somesthetic senses include the skin senses, vestibular senses, and _____ senses (receptors that detect muscle and joint positioning).

2.  The skin senses include touch, pressure,_____ , cold, and warmth. Sensitivity to each is related to the number of _____ found in an area of skin.

3.  Distinctions can be made among various types of pain, including visceral pain, somatic pain, _____ pain, _____ system pain, and reminding system pain.

4.  Various forms of motion sickness are related to messages received from the _____ system, which senses gravity and head movement.

5.  The _____ organs detect the pull of gravity and rapid head movements.

6.  The movement of fluid within the _____canals, and the movement of the crista within each _____ , detects head movement and positioning.

7.  According to _____ theory, motion sickness is caused by a mismatch of visual, kinesthetic, and vestibular sensations. Motion sickness can be avoided by minimizing sensory conflict.

# Adaptation, Attention, and Gating—Tuning In and Tuning Out
## Why are we more aware of some sensations than others?

1.  Incoming sensations are affected by sensory _____ (a decrease in the number of nerve impulses sent).

2.  Vision does not undergo sensory adaptation due to physiological _____ (involuntary tremors of the eye muscles) which causes thousands of tiny movements of the _____ muscles to ensure detection of images falling on _____ rods and cones.

3. Selective _____ (selection and diversion of messages in the brain) and sensory gating (blocking or alteration of messages flowing toward the brain) also alter sensations.

4. Selective gating of pain messages apparently takes place in the spinal cord. _____ Theory proposes an explanation for many pain phenomena.

5. "Runner's high," the painkilling effects of the Chinese medical art of_____ , and other pain phenomena appear to be explained by the release of a morphine-like chemical in the brain, called beta-_____ .

6. The brain creates a _____of one's body to process one's sense of bodily self. This neuromatrix does not recognize that an actual part of the body no longer exists and continues to process nearby sensory stimulations as _____ coming from the missing limb.

7. Most amputees have_____ limb sensations long after losing a limb.

# Psychology in Action: Controlling Pain—This Won't Hurt a Bit

How can pain be reduced in everyday situations?

1. Pain can be reduced by lowering anxiety and redirecting _____ to stimuli other than the pain stimulus.

2. Feeling that you have _____over a stimulus tends to reduce the amount of pain you experience.

3. The _____ or meaning placed on a stimulus affects how painful it is perceived to be.

4. Sending mild pain messages to the spinal cord can close the gates to more severe pain. This effect is called _____.

5. _____ is used by pain clinics to reduce people's experiences of pain by introducing an additional, _____ intense pain signal such as a mild electrical current to the brain through the fast nerve fiber.

# MASTERY TEST

1. A person with tunnel vision has mainly lost the ability to use the _____ for _____ vision.
   a. cones; foveal
   b. photoreceptors; color
   c. iris; retinal
   d. rods; peripheral

2. Sensory conflict theory attributes motion sickness to mismatches between what three systems?
   a. olfaction, kinesthesis, and audition
   b. vision, kinesthesis, and the vestibular system
   c. kinesthesis, audition, and the somesthetic system
   d. vision, gustation, and the skin senses

3. Which of the following types of color blindness is most common?
   a. yellow-blue, male
   b. yellow-blue, female
   c. red-green, female
   d. red-green, male

4. A reasonable conclusion about subliminal perception is that
   a. subliminal stimuli have weak effects.
   b. backmasking poses a serious threat to listeners.
   c. subliminal tapes are more effective than subliminal advertising.
   d. subliminal perception applies to hearing, but not to vision.

5. Which of the following does not belong with the others?
   a. Pacinian corpuscle
   b. Merkle's disk
   c. vomeronasal organ
   d. free nerve endings

6. The fact that the eyes are only sensitive to a narrow band of electromagnetic energies shows that vision acts as a(n)_____ system.
   a. opponent-process
   b. gate-control
   c. central biasing
   d. data reduction

7. Which theory of color vision best explains the fact that we do not see yellowish blue?
   a. trichromatic
   b. chromatic gating
   c. Ishihara hypothesis
   d. opponent-process

8. A person with inflamed kidneys feels pain in her hips. This is an example of
   a. warning system pain.
   b. referred pain.
   c. somatic pain.
   d. vestibular pain.

9. Hubel and Wiesel found that nerve cells in the visual cortex of the brain respond most to specific
   a. phosphenes.
   b. perceptual features.
   c. areas of the visible spectrum.
   d. numbers of photons.

10. Which of the following pain control strategies makes use of gate control theory?
    a. counterirritation
    b. distraction and reinterpretation
    c. anxiety reduction
    d. gaining control over pain stimuli

11. Because it is a sex-linked trait, color blindness occurs _____ in men than women.
    a. as often.
    b. less often
    c. more often
    d. sometimes more often, sometimes less often

12. According to Weber's law, the _____ is a constant proportion of the original intensity of a stimulus.
    a. absolute threshold
    b. JND
    c. phosphene
    d. sensory limen

13. Dark adaptation is closely related to concentrations of _____ in the _____ .
    a. retinal; aqueous humor
    b. photopsin; cones
    c. rhodopsin; rods
    d. photons; optic nerve

14. Sensory analysis tends to extract perceptual _____ from stimulus patterns.
    a. thresholds
    b. features
    c. transducers
    d. amplitudes

15. Which pair of terms is most closely related?
    a. hyperopia—color blindness
    b. astigmatism—presbyopia
    c. myopia—astigmatism
    d. hyperopia—presbyopia

16. The painkilling effects of acupuncture are partly explained by _____ theory and the release of _____ .
    a. lock-and-key; pheromones
    b. gate control; pheromones
    c. gate control; endorphins
    d. lock-and-key; endorphins

17. Three photons of light striking the _____ defines the _____ for vision.
    a. retina; absolute threshold
    b. cornea; difference threshold
    c. iris; upper limen
    d. cornea; JND

18. According to the _____ theory of hearing, low tones cause the greatest movement near the _____ of the cochlea.
    a. place; outer tip
    b. frequency; outer tip
    c. place; base
    d. frequency; base

19. Where vision is concerned, physiological nystagmus helps prevent
    a. sensory gating.
    b. tunnel vision.
    c. sensory adaptation.
    d. night blindness.

20. Which of the following best represents the concept of a transducer?
    a. Translating English into Spanish.
    b. Copying a computer file from one floppy disk to another.
    c. Speaking into a telephone receiver.
    d. Turning water into ice.

21. Visual pop-out is closely related to which sensory process?
    a. transduction
    b. feature detection
    c. difference thresholds
    d. perception below the limen

22. Rods and cones are to vision as _____ are to hearing.
    a. auditory ossicles
    b. vibrations
    c. pinnas
    d. hair cells

23. You lose the ability to smell floral odors. This is called _____ and it is compatible with the _____ theory of olfaction.
    a. dysomnia; lock and key
    b. anhedonia; place
    c. tinnitus; gate-control
    d. sensory adaptation; molecular

24. Which two dimensions of color are related to the wavelength of electromagnetic energy?
    a. hue and saturation
    b. saturation and brightness
    c. brightness and hue
    d. brightness and amplitude

25. Temporary threshold shifts are related to
    a. conduction hearing loss.
    b. sensorineural hearing loss.
    c. noise-induced hearing loss.
    d. damage to the ossicles.

26. The existence of the blind spot is explained by a lack of
    a. rhodopsin.
    b. peripheral vision.
    c. photoreceptors.
    d. activity in the fovea.

27. Which of the following normally has the most effect on the amount of light entering the eye?
    a. fovea
    b. iris
    c. aqueous humor
    d. cornea

28. In vision, a loss of accommodation is most associated with aging of the
    a. iris.
    b. fovea.
    c. lens.
    d. cornea.

29. Visual acuity and color vision are provided by the _____ found in large numbers in the _____ of the eye.
    a. cones; fovea
    b. cones; periphery
    c. rods; fovea
    d. rods; periphery

30. Children who are born deaf have a good chance at learning spoken language at an almost normal rate if they receive cochlear implants before they reach the age of:
    a. 2
    b. 9
    c. 12
    d. 16

31. Standing 8 feet farther away than Jacob who has 20/20 vision, Paul is able to identify the furry animal as a mouse. An optometrist might conclude that Paul has a better than average acuity and he has _____ vision.
    a. 20/8
    b. 20/18
    c. 20/12
    d. 20/80

32. S. K. suffered damage to her _____ pathway since she could not identify "what" types of objects were in her visual field, and she did not suffer damage to her _____ pathway since she could still identify "where" the objects were in her visual field.
    a. lateral; ventral
    b. ventral; dorsal
    c. dorsal; lateral
    d. dorsal; ventral

33. Submarine and airplane crewmen are able to move from a well-lit room to a dark room without having to undergo dark adaptation; this is due to the _____ lights in the room.
    a. yellow
    b. green
    c. blue
    d. red

34. Sensory adaptation does not occur with vision because of _____ , which produces the involuntary tremors of eye muscles.
    a. dysomnia
    b. perceptual defense
    c. physiological nystagmus
    d. feature detectors

# Solutions

# RECITE AND REVIEW

## Psychophysics—The Limits of Sensibility: Pages 119-123
In what ways are our senses limited?

1. physical; sensations
2. nerve
3. data; analyze
4. minimum; sensation
5. 30; 20
6. 20
7. raise; defense
8. below
9. ineffective
10. change; difference
11. intensity; law
12. detectors
13. sensory
14. perceptual
15. sensory; activated

## Vision—Catching Some Rays: Pages 123-127
How does the visual system function?

1. visible
2. wavelength; wavelength
3. wavelength; narrow
4. rods; cones
5. shape; shape
6. nearsightedness; accommodation
7. enlarges; narrows
8. rods
9. cones; color
10. detectors
11. ventral; dorsal
12. rods

## Color Vision—There's More to It Than Meets the Eye: Pages 127-131
How do we perceive colors?

1. sensitivity
2. retina; cones
3. cones
4. afterimages
5. either-or; black or white
6. brain
7. Total
8. female
9. color blindness

## Dark Adaptation—Let There Be Light!: Pages 131-132
How do we adjust to the dark?

1. increase; rods; cones
2. 30; red
3. rods; night

## Hearing—Good Vibrations: Pages 132-135
What are the mechanisms of hearing?

1. peaks; valleys
2. pitch; height
3. eardrum; hair
4. frequency; frequency
5. high; low
6. nerve
7. Nerve
8. loud; shifts
9. Echolocation

## Smell and Taste—The Nose Knows When the Tongue Can't Tell: Pages 135-138

How do the chemical senses operate?

1. smell; taste
2. inability; 400; 10,000
3. location
4. chemical; organ
5. 1000
6. bitter
7. coding
8. smell; taste

## The Somesthetic Senses—Flying by the Seat of Your Pants: Pages 138-142

What are the somesthetic senses?

1. skin
2. pressure; number
3. reminding
4. head
5. gravity
6. fluid; crista
7. mismatch

## Adaptation, Attention, and Gating—Tuning In and Tuning Out: Pages 142-144

Why are we more aware of some sensations than others?

1. reduction (or decrease)
2. adaptation; eye
3. gating
4. spinal; cord
5. morphine(or opiate)
6. bodily
7. limb

## Psychology in Action: Controlling Pain—This Won't Hurt a Bit: Pages 145-147

How can pain be reduced in everyday situations?

1. lowering
2. reduce
3. stimulus
4. mild
5. Counterirritation; pain

# CONNECTIONS

## Psychophysics—The Limits of Sensibility: Pages 119-123

In what ways are our senses limited?

1. d
2. b
3. e
4. a
5. f
6. c

## Sensory Limitations (continued)

1. d
2. a
3. f
4. b
5. e
6. c

140

## Vision—Catching Some Rays: Pages 123-127

How does the visual system function?

| | | | | | |
|---|---|---|---|---|---|
| 1. | d | 5. | i | 9. | e |
| 2. | f | 6. | c | 10. | g |
| 3. | h | 7. | k | 11. | j |
| 4. | b | 8. | a | | |

## Vision (continued)

| | | | | | |
|---|---|---|---|---|---|
| 1. | e | 4. | d | 7. | g |
| 2. | b | 5. | a | 8. | c |
| 3. | h | 6. | f | | |

## Color Vision—There's More to It Than Meets the Eye: Pages 127-131

How do we perceive colors?

| | | | | | |
|---|---|---|---|---|---|
| 1. | c | 3. | f | 5. | a |
| 2. | b | 4. | d | 6. | e |

## Hearing—Good Vibrations: Pages 132-135

What are the mechanisms of hearing?

| | | | | | |
|---|---|---|---|---|---|
| 1. | e | 5. | d | 9. | j |
| 2. | g | 6. | f | 10. | b |
| 3. | h | 7. | c | | |
| 4. | a | 8. | i | | |

## Hearing (continued)

| | | | | | |
|---|---|---|---|---|---|
| 1. | b | 4. | d | 7. | g |
| 2. | e | 5. | h | 8. | a |
| 3. | i | 6. | c | 9. | f |

## Smell and Taste—The Nose Knows When the Tongue Can't Tell: Pages 135-138

How do the chemical senses operate?

| | | | | | |
|---|---|---|---|---|---|
| 1. | d | 4. | g | 7. | b |
| 2. | f | 5. | c | | |
| 3. | a | 6. | e | | |

## The Somesthetic Senses—Flying by the Seat of Your Pants: Pages 138-142

What are the somesthetic senses?

1. a
2. f
3. c
4. e
5. b
6. d

## Adaptation, Attention, and Gating—Tuning In and Tuning Out and Psychology in Action: Controlling Pain—This Won't Hurt a Bit: Pages 142-147

Why are we more aware of some sensations than others? How can pain be reduced in everyday situations?

1. b
2. g
3. e
4. c
5. f
6. d
7. a

# CHECK YOUR MEMORY

## Psychophysics—The Limits of Sensibility: Pages 119-123

In what ways are our senses limited?

1. T
2. T
3. F
4. T

## Vision—Catching Some Rays: Pages 123-127

How does the visual system function?

1. F
2. T
3. F
4. T
5. T
6. T
7. T
8. T
9. F
10. T
11. F
12. T
13. T

## Color Vision—There's More to It Than Meets the Eye: Pages 127-131

How do we perceive colors?

1. F
2. T
3. T
4. T
5. T
6. T
7. F
8. F
9. T

## Color Vision—There's More to It Than Meets the Eye: Pages 127-131

How do we perceive colors?

1. F
2. T

## Hearing—Good Vibrations: Pages 132-135
What are the mechanisms of hearing?

| | | | | | |
|---|---|---|---|---|---|
| 1. | T | 5. | T | 9. | T |
| 2. | F | 6. | T | 10. | F |
| 3. | T | 7. | T | | |
| 4. | F | 8. | T | | |

## Smell and Taste—The Nose Knows When the Tongue Can't Tell: Pages 135-138
How do the chemical senses operate?

| | | | | | |
|---|---|---|---|---|---|
| 1. | T | 5. | T | 9. | T |
| 2. | F | 6. | T | 10. | F |
| 3. | T | 7. | T | | |
| 4. | F | 8. | T | | |

## The Somesthetic Senses—Flying by the Seat of Your Pants: Pages 138-142
What are the somesthetic senses?

| | | | | | |
|---|---|---|---|---|---|
| 1. | T | 5. | F | 9. | T |
| 2. | F | 6. | T | 10. | F |
| 3. | F | 7. | T | | |
| 4. | T | 8. | F | | |

## Adaptation, Attention, and Gating—Tuning In and Tuning Out: Pages 142-144
Why are we more aware of some sensations than others?

| | | | | | |
|---|---|---|---|---|---|
| 1. | F | 4. | F | 7. | T |
| 2. | F | 5. | T | | |
| 3. | T | 6. | F | | |

## Psychology in Action: Controlling Pain—This Won't Hurt a Bit: Pages 145-147
How can pain be reduced in everyday situations?

| | | | |
|---|---|---|---|
| 1. | T | 3. | T |
| 2. | T | 4. | T |

# FINAL SURVEY AND REVIEW

## Psychophysics—The Limits of Sensibility
In what ways are our senses limited?

1. Psychophysics
2. reduction; code
3. transducer;
4. absolute
5. 30; 20
6. 20

7. threshold; perceptual
8. subliminal
9. advertising
10. just noticeable; difference
11. change; Weber's

12. feature
13. Phosphenes; coding
14. sensory analysis
15. localization; area

## Vision—Catching Some Rays
How does the visual system function?

1. electromagnetic
2. 400 nanometers; 700 nanometers
3. Hue; amplitude
4. photoreceptors; retina

5. cornea; accommodation
6. myopia; astigmatism
7. iris; dilates; constricts
8. motion

9. fovea; acuity
10. cortex
11. what; where
12. peripheral; peripheral

## Color Vision—There's More to It Than Meets the Eye
How do we perceive colors?

1. Yellow; blue
2. trichromatic
3. pigments

4. Trichromatic; afterimages
5. opponent-process; red or green
6. color; contrast

7. red-green
8. sex-linked; mother
9. Ishihara

## Dark Adaptation—Let There Be Light!
How do we adjust to the dark?

1. visual pigments
2. 30; red; rods
3. rhodopsin; A

## Hearing—Good Vibrations
What are the mechanisms of hearing?

1. compression; rarefaction
2. frequency; amplitude
3. ossicles; Corti

4. auditory nerves
5. base; tip
6. stimulation

7. cochlear
8. 120 decibels; tinnitus
9. Biosonar

## Smell and Taste—The Nose Knows When the Tongue Can't Tell

How do the chemical senses operate?

1. Olfaction; gustation
2. dysomnia; 400; 10,000
3. receptors
4. pheromones; vomeronasal
5. lock; and; key
6. sweet; salty; sour; umami
7. molecule
8. smell; taste

## The Somesthetic Senses—Flying by the Seat of Your Pants

What are the somesthetic senses?

1. kinesthetic
4. vestibular
5. otolith
2. pain; receptors
6. semicircular; ampulla
7. sensory conflict
3. referred; warning

## Adaptation, Attention, and Gating—Tuning In and Tuning Out

Why are we more aware of some sensations than others?

1. adaptation
2. nystagmus; eye; unfatigued
3. attention
4. Gate control
5. acupuncture; endorphin
6. neuromatrix; pain
7. phantom

## Psychology in Action: Controlling Pain—This Won't Hurt a Bit

How can pain be reduced in everyday situations?

1. attention
2. control
3. interpretation
4. counterirritation
5. Counterirritation; less

# MASTERY TEST

1. d, p. 127
2. b, p. 140
3. d, p. 129
4. a, p. 120
5. c, p. 137
6. d, p. 119
7. d, p. 128
8. b, p. 139
9. b, p. 121
10. a, p. 146
11. c, p. 131
12. b, p. 120
13. c, p. 128
14. b, p. 121
15. d, p. 124
16. c, p. 143
17. a, p. 120
18. a, p. 134
19. c, p. 142
20. c, p. 142
21. b, p. 121
22. d, p. 133
23. a, p. 136
24. a, p. 123
25. c, p. 135
26. c, p. 124
27. b, p. 124
28. c, p. 124
29. a, p. 126
30. a, p. 135
31. c, p. 126
32. b, p. 127
33. d, p. 131
34. c, p. 142

# Perceiving the World

## Chapter Overview

Perception is an active process of constructing sensations into a meaningful mental representation of the world. Perceptions are based on simultaneous bottom-up and top-down processing.

Attention, motivation, values, and emotions influence perception. Attention is selective, and may be divided. Attention is closely related to stimulus intensity, repetition, contrast, change, and incongruity. The phenomenon called inattentional blindness suggests that there can be no perception without attention. When a stimulus is repeated without change, the orientation response undergoes habituation.

The Gestalt principles of organization bring order to our perceptions. The following Gestalt principles help organize sensations: figure and ground; nearness, similarity, continuity, closure, contiguity, common region, and combinations of the preceding. Perceptual organization shifts for ambiguous stimuli. Perceptual organization may be thought of as a hypothesis held until evidence contradicts it.

Perceptual constancies allow us to find regularity in the constantly changing energy patterns reaching our senses. In vision, the image projected on the retina is constantly changing, but the external world appears stable and undistorted because of size, shape, and brightness constancy.

Various visual cues are used to construct the experience of depth. A basic, innate capacity for depth perception is present soon after birth. Depth perception depends on binocular depth cues of retinal disparity and convergence and the monocular depth cue of accommodation. Monocular "pictorial" depth cues also underlie depth perception, including linear perspective, relative size, height in the picture plane, light and shadow, overlap, texture gradients, aerial haze, and motion parallax. The moon illusion can be explained by the apparent-distance hypothesis.

Perceptual learning influences the top-down organization and interpretation of sensations. Studies of inverted vision show that even the most basic organization is subject to a degree of change. Active movement speeds adaptation to a new perceptual environment. Perceptual judgments are almost always related to context.

Perceptual sets often lead us to perceive or misperceive what we expect to see. Suggestion, motives, emotions, attention, and prior experience combine in various ways to create perceptual sets, or expectancies.

The bulk of the evidence to date is against the existence of ESP. Parapsychology is the study of purported psi phenomena, including telepathy, clairvoyance, precognition, and psychokinesis. Research in parapsychology remains controversial. Stage ESP is based on deception and tricks.

Awareness of the factors which can distort perception is the key to improving perceptual accuracy. Perception is an active construction of events, which contributes to the surprising unreliability of eyewitness testimony. Eyewitness accuracy is further damaged by weapon focus and a number of similar factors. Perceptual accuracy is enhanced by reality testing, dishabituation, and conscious efforts to pay attention. It is also valuable to break perceptual habits, to beware of perceptual sets, and to be aware of the influence of motives and emotions on perceptions.

# Learning Objectives

*Theme: We actively construct our perceptions out of the information provided by our senses and our past experience; the resulting perceptions are not always accurate representations of events.*

| |
|---|
| **GQ: In general, how do we construct our perceptions?** |
| LO 5.1  Define *perception* and explain how *bottom-up processing* and *top-down processing* together result in *perceptual constructions*. |
| **GQ: Is perception altered by attention, motives, and emotions?** |
| LO 5.2  Distinguish between *selective attention* and *divided attention*; list the factors that affect attention; and explain how *inattentional blindness* can affect what one perceives. |
| LO 5.3  Differentiate *habituation* from sensory adaptation; describe the *orientation response*; and explain the boiled frog syndrome and how it may affect the ultimate survival of humans. |
| **GQ: What basic principles do we use to group sensations into meaningful patterns?** |
| LO 5.4  Give examples of the following as they relate to the organization of perception: a. *figure-ground* (include the concept of reversible figures); b. nearness; c. similarity; d. continuity; e. closure (include the concept of illusory figures); f. contiguity; g. common region. |
| LO 5.5  Explain what a *perceptual hypothesis* is and define and give an example of an ambiguous stimulus and an impossible figure. |
| **GQ: What are perceptual constancies and what is their role in perception?** |
| LO 5.6  Describe the following *constancies*: a. *size*; b. *shape*; c. *brightness*. |
| **GQ: How is it possible to see depth and judge distance?** |
| LO 5.7  Discuss *depth perception* and describe the research regarding this perceptual ability; describe the special visual adaptations found among birds. |
| LO 5.8  Describe the following cues for depth perception and indicate in each case whether the cue is *monocular* or *binocular*: a. accommodation; b. convergence; c. retinal disparity (include the term *stereoscopic vision*). |
| LO 5.9  Describe the following two-dimensional, monocular, *pictorial depth cues* and give examples of how artists use them to give the appearance of three-dimensional space: a. linear perspective; b. relative size; c. height in the picture plane; d. light and shadow; e. overlap; f. texture gradients; g. aerial perspective; h. relative motion (motion parallax). |
| LO 5.10  Describe the phenomenon of the *moon illusion*. Include in your explanation the *apparent distance hypothesis* and a description of the work of the Kaufmans. |
| **GQ: What effect does learning have on perception?** |
| LO 5.11  Define the terms *perceptual learning* and *perceptual habit* and explain how perceptual habits allow learning to affect perception and how the Ames room poses problems for organization and for a person's perceptual habits. |
| LO 5.12  Describe the research which demonstrates the brain's sensitivity to perceptual features of the environment; discuss the effects of culture on this sensitivity; and explain how the results of the inverted vision experiments support the concept of perceptual habits and why active movement is so important to adapting to inverted vision. |
| LO 5.13  Explain the concept of *context*; differentiate between *illusions* and *hallucinations*; and describe the *Charles Bonnet syndrome*, the *stroboscopic movement* illusion, the *Müller-Lyer* illusion, and the *size-distance invariance*. |

| |
|---|
| **GQ: To what extent do we see what we expect to see?** |
| LO 5.14  Explain how motives and perceptual expectancies may influence perception and describe perceptual sets. |
| **GQ: Is extrasensory perception possible?** |
| LO 5.15  Define *extrasensory perception, parapsychology, and psi phenomenon* and describe the following purported psychic abilities: a. *clairvoyance*; b. *telepathy*; c. *precognition*; d. *psychokinesis*. |
| LO 5.16  Describe the research with *Zener cards*; explain why most psychologists remain skeptical about psi abilities and *stage ESP*; and state the best conclusion to make about *psi* events. |
| **GQ: How can I learn to perceive events more accurately?** |
| LO 5.17  Explain the phrase "We see what we believe" and why most eyewitness testimony is inaccurate, (regardless of one's confidence). Include the concept of weapon focus. |
| LO 5.18  Explain how a person can more accurately perceive the world. Include the terms *reality testing* and *dishabituation*; Maslow's theory of perceptual awareness; and the seven ways to become a better eyewitness to life. |

# RECITE AND REVIEW

## Perception: That Extra Step: Pages 150-151
In general, how do we construct our perceptions?

1. _____ experience is created when a person _____ and understands patterns.

2. Perceptions may be based on_____ or bottom-up processing of information.

3. Bottom-up processing, perceptions begin with the organization of low-level _____. In top-down processing, previous knowledge is used to rapidly _____ sensory information.

## Perception and Attention—May I Have Your ... Attention!: Pages 151-154
Is perception altered by attention, motives, and emotions?

1. _____attention refers to giving priority to some sensory messages while excluding others.

2. Attention acts like a _____ or narrowing of the information channel linking the senses to perception.

3. Attention may also be divided among various activities. Divided attention suggests that our _____ for storing and thinking about information is limited.

4. Attention is aroused by _____ stimuli, by repetition (with variation), by stimulus contrast, _____ , or incongruity.

5. _____blindness refers to people's inability to _____ a stimulus that is right in front of their eyes because they were too busy focusing on another stimulus.

6. Attention is accompanied by an orientation response (OR). When a stimulus is repeated without _____ , the orientation response _____ , an effect known as habituation.

7. Personal motives and _____ often alter perceptions by changing the evaluation of what is seen or by altering attention to specific details.

## Perceptual Organization—Getting It All Together: Pages 154-156

What basic principles do we use to group sensations into meaningful patterns?

1. The most basic organization of sensations is a division into figure and ground ( _____ and _____ ). Reversible figures, however, allow figure-ground organization to be reversed.

2. A number of factors, identified by the Gestalt psychologists, contribute to the _____ of sensations. These are nearness, _____ , continuity, closure, contiguity, ____ region, and combinations of the preceding.

3. Stimuli near one another tend to be perceptually _____ together. So, too, do stimuli that are similar in _____ . Continuity refers to the fact that perceptions tend to be organized as simple, uninterrupted patterns.

4. Closure is the tendency to _____ a broken or incomplete pattern. Contiguity refers to nearness in ____ and space. Stimuli that fall in a defined area, or common region, also tend to be grouped together.

5. _____ psychologists are also known as human factors _____ . These specialists make Machine _____ and controls compatible with human _____ and motor capacities.

6. The most effective _____ _____ engineering follows the principles of natural design.

7. Basic elements of line drawings, especially the edges of _____ and parallel edges, appear to be universally recognized.

8. A perceptual organization may be thought of as an _____ held until evidence contradicts it. Camouflage patterns disrupt perceptual _____ , especially figure-ground perceptions.

9. Perceptual organization shifts for ambiguous _____ , which may have more than one interpretation. An example is Necker's _____ . Impossible figures resist stable organization altogether.

# Perceptual Constancies—Taming an Unruly World: Pages 157-159

What are perceptual constancies, and what is their role in perception?

1. Perception is the process of assembling sensations into _____ that provide a usable mental of the world.

2. In vision, the retinal _____ changes from moment to moment, but the external world appears stable and undistorted because of _____ constancies.

3. In size and shape _____ , the perceived sizes and shapes of objects remain the same even though their retinal images change size and shape. The apparent brightness of objects remains stable (a property called brightness constancy) because each reflects a _____ proportion of light.

4. Perceptual constancies are partly native (_____ ) and partly empirical ( _____ ).

# Depth Perception—What If the World Were Flat?: Pages 159-165

How is it possible to see depth and judge distance?

1. _____ perception is the ability to perceive three-dimensional space and judge distances.

2. Depth perception is present in basic form soon after _____ , as shown by testing with the visual cliff and other methods. As soon as infants become active _____ , they refuse to cross the visual cliff.

3. Depth perception depends on the muscular cues of accommodation (bending of the _____ ) and convergence (inward movement of the _____ ).

4. The area of binocular vision is _____ in some birds than in humans. However, birds and other animals may have extremely _____ fields of view.

5. A number of pictorial _____ , which will work in _____ paintings, drawings, and photographs, also underlie normal depth perception.

6. Some pictorial cues are: linear perspective (the apparent convergence of _____ _____), relative size (more distant objects appear _____ ), height in the _____ plane, light and shadow (shadings of light), and overlap or interposition (one object overlaps another).

151

7. Additional pictorial cues include: texture gradients (textures become _____ in the distance), aerial haze (loss of color and detail at large distances), and relative _____ or _____ parallax (differences in the apparent movement of objects when a viewer is moving).

8. All the pictorial cues are monocular depth cues (only _____ _____ is needed to make use of them).

9. The moon illusion refers to the fact that the moon appears _____ near the horizon than it does when overhead.

10. The moon illusion appears to be explained by the apparent _____ hypothesis, which emphasizes the greater number of depth cues present when the moon is on the _____.

# Perceptual Learning—What If the World Were Upside Down?: Pages 165-171
What effect does learning have on perception?

1. Perceptual _____ refers to the changes in the brain due to _____ that alters how we process sensory information.

2. Organizing and interpreting sensations is greatly influenced by learned perceptual _____. An example is the Ames room, which looks rectangular but is actually distorted so that objects in the room appear to change _____.

3. Sensitivity to perceptual _____ is also partly learned. Studies of inverted vision show that even the most basic organization is subject to a degree of change. Active _____ speeds adaptation to new perceptual environments.

4. European Americans can be described as individualistic as they tend to focus on the _____ and personal control. This focus influences their perceptual habits to pay attention to _____ in the environment rather than the surrounding ground.

5. East Asians can be described as collective as they tend to focus on _____ relationships and social responsibilities. This focus also influences East Asians' perceptual habits to pay _____ attention to the surrounding ground.

6. Perceptual _____ (misleading perceptions) differ from hallucinations (perceptions of nonexistent stimuli).

7. Illusions are often related to perceptual _____ . One of the most familiar of all illusions, the Müller-Lyer illusion, seems to be related to perceptual learning based on experience with box-shaped _____ and rooms.

8. Linear perspective, _____invariance relationships, and mislocating the end-points of the _____ also contribute to the Müller-Lyer illusion.

9. Stereoscopic vision ( _____ sight) relies on retinal disparity to determine the depth of objects that are within 50 feet of us.

10. People who have lost touch with reality may experience _____ that involve auditory, visual, touch, smell, or taste sensations created by the brain without proper environmental input.

11. " _____ hallucinations" are created by the brain to interpret sensory input received by partially _____ individuals who "see" objects appearing and disappearing in front of their eyes.

## Perceptual Expectancies—On Your Mark, Get Set: Pages 171-172
To what extent do we see what we want to see?

1. Attention, prior experience, suggestion, and motives combine in various ways to create perceptual sets, or _____ . A perceptual set is a readiness to perceive in a particular way, induced by strong expectations.

2. Perceptual _____ are often created by suggestion.

## Extrasensory Perception—Do You Believe in Magic?: Pages 172-175
Is extrasensory perception possible?

1. Parapsychology is the study of purported _____ phenomena, including clairvoyance (perceiving events at a distance),_____ ("mind reading"), precognition (perceiving future events), and psychokinesis (mentally influencing inanimate objects).

2. Clairvoyance, telepathy, and precognition are purported types of extrasensory _____.

3. Research in parapsychology remains controversial owing to a variety of problems. _____ and after-the-fact reinterpretation are problems with "natural" ESP episodes.

4. With no evidence supporting the existence of ESP, psychologists strongly suggest that people be _____ of those who claim to have _____ abilities. For example, the owner of the "Miss Cleo" TV-psychic operation made $1 billion from people who believed "Miss Cleo" was a psychic.

5. Many studies of ESP overlook the impact of statistically unusual outcomes that are no more than runs of _____ .

6. The bulk of the evidence to date is _____ the existence of ESP. Very few positive results in ESP research have been replicated (_____ ) by independent scientists.

7. Stage ESP is based on _____ and tricks.

# Psychology in Action: Perception and Objectivity— Believing Is Seeing: Pages 176-178
How can I learn to perceive events more accurately?

1. Perception is an _____ reconstruction of events. This is one reason why eyewitness testimony is surprisingly _____ .

2. In many crimes, eyewitness accuracy is further damaged by weapon _____. Similar factors, such as observer stress, brief exposure times, cross-racial inaccuracies, and the wording of questions can _____ eyewitness accuracy.

3. Perceptual accuracy is enhanced by reality _____ , dishabituation, and conscious efforts to pay _____ .

4. It is also valuable to break perceptual habits, to _____ frames of reference, to beware of perceptual sets, and to be aware of the ways in which motives and emotions influence perceptions.

# CONNECTIONS

## Perception: That Extra Step and Perception and Attention—May I Have Your ... Attention!: Pages 150-154

In general, how do we construct our perceptions? Is perception altered by attention, motives, and expectations?

1. _____ top-down
2. _____ bottom-up
3. _____ selective attention
4. _____ inattention blindness
5. _____ orientation response
6. _____ advertising

a. bottle neck
b. perceptual expectancy
c. undetected stimulus
d. low-level features
e. double take
f. sex and anxiety

## Perceptual Organization—Getting It All Together: Pages 154-156

What basic principles do we use to group sensations into meaningful patterns?

1. _____ continuity
2. _____ common region
3. _____ closure
4. _____ nearness
5. _____ reversible figure
6. _____ similarity

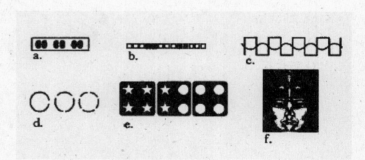

## Perceptual Constancies—Taming an Unruly World: Pages 157-159

What are perceptual constancies, and what is their role in perception?

1. _____ native perception
2. _____ empirical
3. _____ perception
4. _____ shape constancy
5. _____ brightness constancy

a. interpreting sensory input
b. interpretation based on prior knowledge
c. produced same brightness when light changes
d. same shape when viewed at various angles
e. natural and inborn perceptions

# Depth Perception—What if the World Were Flat?: Pages 159-165

How is it possible to see depth and judge distance?

1. _____ texture gradients
2. _____ stereoscopic vision
3. _____ convergence
4. _____ an impossible figure
5. _____ light and shadow
6. _____ relative size
7. _____ Necker's cube
8. _____ overlap
9. _____ retinal disparity
10. _____ linear perspective

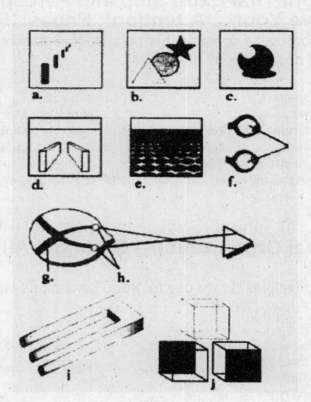

# Depth Perception (continued)

1. _____ binocular depth cue
2. _____ woodcock
3. _____ monocular depth cue
4. _____ mismatch
5. _____ visual cliff
6. _____ ponzo illusion

a. infant depth perception
b. convergence
c. stereoscopic vision
d. moon illusion
e. accommodation
f. 360 degree view

## Perceptual Learning—What if the World Were Upside Down?: Pages 165-171

What effect does learning have on perception?

| | | | |
|---|---|---|---|
| 1. | _____ Zulu | a. | stroboscopic movement |
| 2. | _____ motion picture | b. | diminished Müller-Lyer illusion |
| 3. | _____ illusions | c. | imaginary sensation |
| 4. | _____ perceptual habits | d. | result from perceptual learning |
| 5. | _____ hallucination | e. | partially blinded perception of images |
| 6. | _____ sane hallucination | f. | misleading perception of real sensations |

## Perceptual Expectancies—On Your Mark, Get Set: Pages 172-178

Is extrasensory perception possible? Can I learn to perceive events more accurately?

| | | | |
|---|---|---|---|
| 1. | _____ dishabituation | a. | run of luck |
| 2. | _____ decline effect | b. | study of ESP |
| 3. | _____ perceptual awareness | c. | mind reader |
| 4. | _____ Zener cards | d. | clairvoyance test |
| 5. | _____ Uri Geller | e. | "Miss Cleo" |
| 6. | _____ telepathy | f. | ability to move objects |
| 7. | _____ parapsychology | g. | associated with surrender to experience |
| 8. | _____ psychokinesis | h. | Zen and attention |
| 9. | _____ Psi events | i. | stage ESP |
| 10. | _____ psychic fraud | j. | J. B. Rhine |

# CHECK YOUR MEMORY

## Perception: That Extra Step: Pages 150-151

In general, how do we construct our perceptions?

1. Sensations automatically lead to a person's experience.   TRUE or FALSE

2. The way that a person assembles sensation into meaningful patterns is called perception.   TRUE or FALSE

3. Putting a jigsaw puzzle together relies primarily on top-down processing.   TRUE or FALSE

## Perception and Attention—May I Have Your ... Attention!: Pages 151-154

Is perception altered by attention, motives, and expectations?

1. Messages passing through the "bottleneck" of selective attention appear to prevent other messages from passing through.   TRUE or FALSE

2. As skills become automated, they free mental capacity for other activities.   TRUE or FALSE

3. Repetitious stimuli must vary a little to gain attention, otherwise repetition leads to habituation.
   TRUE or FALSE

4. Failing to see a pedestrian crossing a street because one is busy using a cell phone while driving is referred to as attentional blindness.   TRUE or FALSE

5. Enlarged pupils and brain-wave changes typically accompany the OR.   TRUE or FALSE

6. Humans are especially sensitive to slow, gradual changes that occur over very long time periods.
   TRUE or FALSE

7. Inattenional blindness refers to the fact that paying close attention to one stimulus can prevent a person from seeing other stimuli that are nearby.   TRUE or FALSE

8. Emotional stimuli can shift attention away from other information.   TRUE or FALSE

9. Analyzing information into small features and then building a recognizable pattern is called top-up processing.   TRUE or FALSE

10. Perceptual sets are frequently created by suggestion.   TRUE or FALSE

## Perceptual Organization—Getting It All Together: Pages 154-156

What basic principles do we use to group sensations into meaningful patterns?

1. Basic figure-ground organization is learned at about age 2.   TRUE or FALSE

2. Illusory figures are related to the principle of closure.   TRUE or FALSE

3. Contiguity refers to our tendency to see lines as continuous.   TRUE or FALSE

4. Common region refers to the tendency to see stimuli that are close together as one unit.      TRUE or FALSE

5. Pre-existing ideas actively guide our interpretation of sensations in many cases.
   TRUE or FALSE

6. Necker's cube and the "three-pronged widget" are impossible figures.
   TRUE or FALSE

## Perceptual Constancies—Taming an Unruly World: Pages 157-159

What are perceptual constancies, and what is their role in perception?

1. Perception involves selecting, organizing, and integrating sensory information.
   TRUE or FALSE

2. Some perceptual abilities must be learned after sight is restored to the previously blind.
   TRUE or FALSE

3. Newborn babies show some evidence of size constancy.    TRUE or FALSE

4. Houses and cars look like toys from a low-flying airplane because of shape constancy.
   TRUE or FALSE

5. Drunkenness impairs brightness constancy, but size and shape constancy are not usually affected.
   TRUE or FALSE

6. Brightness constancy does not apply to objects illuminated by different amounts of light.
   TRUE or FALSE

## Depth Perception—What If the World Were Flat?: Pages 159-165

How is it possible to see depth and judge distance?

1. Depth perception is partly learned and partly innate.    TRUE or FALSE

2. Human depth perception typically begins to develop at about 2 weeks of age.    TRUE or FALSE

3. Most infants, when coaxed by their mothers, will crawl cross the visual cliff.    TRUE or FALSE

4. All depth cues are basically binocular.    TRUE or FALSE

5. Accommodation and convergence are muscular depth cues.    TRUE or FALSE

6. Accommodation acts as a depth cue primarily for distances greater than 4 feet from the eyes.    TRUE or FALSE

7. Convergence acts as a depth cue primarily for distances less than 4 feet from the eyes.
   TRUE or FALSE

8. The brain is sensitive to mismatches in information received from the right and left eyes.
   TRUE or FALSE

9. Depth perception is actually as good when using just one eye as it is when both eyes are open.
   TRUE or FALSE

10. With one eye closed, the pictorial depth cues no longer provide information about depth and
    distance.    TRUE or FALSE

11. Changing the image size of an object implies that its distance from the viewer has changed, too.
    TRUE or FALSE

12. In a drawing, the closer an object is to the horizon line, the nearer it appears to be to the viewer.
    TRUE or FALSE

13. Aerial perspective is most powerful when the air is exceptionally clear.   TRUE or FALSE

14. When an observer is moving forward, objects beyond the observer's point of fixation appear to move forward too.   TRUE or FALSE

15. Accommodation is a binocular depth cue.   TRUE or FALSE

16. Some familiarity with drawings is required to use overlap as a depth cue.   TRUE or FALSE

17. The moon's image is magnified by the dense atmosphere near the horizon.   TRUE or FALSE

18. More depth cues are present when the moon is viewed near the horizon.   TRUE or FALSE

## Perceptual Learning—What If the World Were Upside Down?: Pages 165-171

What effect does learning have on perception?

1. A lack of relevant perceptual experience makes it difficult to judge upside-down faces.
   TRUE or FALSE

2. Stimuli that lie above the horizon line in a scene are more likely to be perceived as "figure" than as "ground."   TRUE or FALSE

3. The Ames room is primarily used to test the effects of inverted vision.   TRUE or FALSE

4. Cats who grow up surrounded by horizontal stripes are unusually sensitive to vertical stripes when they reach maturity.   TRUE or FALSE

5. People who wear inverting goggles say that eventually the visual world turns right side up again.
   TRUE or FALSE

6. Perception is most accurate during active interactions with one's surroundings.   TRUE or FALSE

7. If your adaptation level for judging weight is 30 pounds, you would judge a 30-pound object as "heavy."   TRUE or FALSE

8. Hearing voices when no one is speaking is an example of a perceptual illusion.   TRUE or FALSE

9. Seeing images appearing and disappearing because one is partially blind can be described as "sane hallucination."   TRUE or FALSE

10. Perceptual illusions are usually not noticeable until measurements reveal that our perceptions are inaccurate or distorted.   TRUE or FALSE

11. According to Richard Gregory, the arrowhead-tipped line in the Müiller-Lyer illusion looks like the outside corner of a building.    TRUE or FALSE

12. Zulus rarely see round shapes and therefore fail to experience the Müller-Lyer illusion.

    TRUE or FALSE

# Perceptual Expectancies—On Your Mark, Get Set: Pages 172-175

Is extrasensory perception possible?

1. Uri Geller was one of the first researchers in parapsychology to use the Zener cards.
   TRUE or FALSE

2. Psychokinesis is classified as a psi event, but not a form of ESP.    TRUE or FALSE

3. Prophetic dreams are regarded as a form of precognition.    TRUE or FALSE

4. Strange coincidences are strong evidence for the existence of ESP.    TRUE or FALSE

5. The Zener cards eliminated the possibility of fraud and "leakage" of information in ESP experiments.
   TRUE or FALSE

6. "Miss Cleo" is one of the few people who truly have psychic abilities.    TRUE or FALSE

7. Stage ESP relies on deception, sleight of hand, and patented gadgets to entertain the audience.
   TRUE or FALSE

8. Belief in psi events has declined among parapsychologists in recent years.    TRUE or FALSE

9. A skeptic of psi means that a person is unconvinced and is against the idea that psi exists.
   TRUE or FALSE

# Psychology in Action: Perception and Objectivity— Believing Is Seeing: Pages 176-178

Can I learn to perceive events more accurately?

1. In many ways we see what we believe, as well as believe what we see.    TRUE or FALSE

2. The more confident an eyewitness is about the accuracy of his or her testimony, the more likely it is to be accurate.    TRUE or FALSE

3. The testimony of crime victims is generally more accurate than the testimony of bystanders.
   TRUE or FALSE

4. Victims tend to not notice detail information such as the appearance of their attacker because they fall prey to weapon focus.    TRUE or FALSE

5. Reality testing is the process Abraham Maslow described as a "surrender" to experience.
   TRUE or FALSE

# FINAL SURVEY AND REVIEW

## Perception: That Extra Step
In general, how do we construct our perceptions?

1. Perceptual _____ is created when a person recognizes and _____ patterns.

2. Perceptions may be based on top-down or bottom-up _____ of information.

3. _____ perceptions begin with the organization of low-level features. In _____ processing, previous knowledge is used to rapidly organize sensory information.

## Perception and Attention—May I Have Your … Attention!
Is perception altered by attention, motives, and expectations?

1. _____ _____ refers to giving priority to some sensory messages while excluding others.

2. Attention acts like a bottleneck or narrowing of the information _____ linking the senses to perception.

3. Attention may also be split among various activities. _____ attention suggests that our capacity for storing and thinking about information is limited.

4. Attention is aroused by intense stimuli, by repetition (with variation), by stimulus_____, change, or _____.

5. _____ blindness refers to people's inability to detect a stimulus that is right in front of their eyes because they were too busy focusing on another stimulus or activity.

6. Attention is accompanied by an _____ _____ (OR). When a stimulus is repeated without change, the OR decreases, an effect known as _____ .

7. Personal _____ and values often alter perceptions by changing the evaluation of what is seen or by altering attention to specific details.

# Perceptual Organization—Getting It All Together
What basic principles do we use to group sensations into meaningful patterns?

1.  The most basic organization of sensations is a division into _____ and _____ (object and background).

2.  A number of factors, identified by the _____ psychologists, contribute to the organization of sensations. These are _____, similarity, continuity, _____, contiguity, common region, and combinations of the preceding.

3.  Stimuli near one another tend to be perceptually grouped together. So, too, do stimuli that are similar in appearance. _____ refers to the fact that perceptions tend to be organized as simple, uninterrupted patterns.

4.  _____ refers to nearness in time and space. Stimuli that fall in a defined area, or common region, also tend to be grouped together.

5.  Basic elements of line drawings, especially the edges of surfaces and_____ _____, appear to be universally recognized.

6.  A perceptual organization may be thought of as an hypothesis held until evidence contradicts it. _____ patterns disrupt perceptual organization, especially figure-ground perceptions.

7.  Perceptual organization shifts for _____ stimuli, which may have more than one interpretation. An example is _____ cube. Impossible _____ resist stable organization altogether.

# Perceptual Constancies—Taming an Unruly World
What are perceptual constancies, and what is their role in perception?

1.  Perception is the process of assembling _____ into patterns that provide a usable _____ _____of the world.

2.  In vision, the _____image changes from moment to moment, but the external world appears stable and undistorted because of perceptual _____.

3.  In size and shape constancy, the perceived sizes and shapes of objects remain the same even though their retinal images change size and shape. The apparent _____ of objects remains stable (a property called brightness constancy) because each reflects a constant _____ of_____.

4. Perceptual constancies are partly _____ (inborn) and partly _____ (learned).

# Depth Perception—What If the World Were Flat?
How is it possible to see depth and judge distance?

1. Depth perception is the ability to perceive _____ space and judge distances.

2. Depth perception is present in basic form soon after birth, as shown by testing with the _____ and other methods. As soon as infants become active crawlers they refuse to cross the deep side of the _____ _____.

3. Depth perception depends on the muscular cues of_____(bending of the lens) and _____ (inward movement of the eyes).

4. The area of _____ vision is smaller in some birds than in humans. However, birds and other animals may have extremely wide_____ _____ _____.

5. A number of _____ cues, which will work in flat paintings, drawings, and photographs, also underlie normal depth perception.

6. Some of these cues are: _____ _____ (the apparent convergence of parallel lines), relative size (more distant objects appear smaller), height in the picture plane, light and shadow (shadings of light), and overlap or _____ (one object overlaps another).

7. Additional pictorial cues include: texture _____ (textures become finer in the distance), aerial haze (loss of color and detail at large distances), and relative motion or motion (differences in the apparent movement of objects when a viewer is moving).

8. All the pictorial cues are _____ depth cues (only one eye is needed to make use of them).

9. The moon illusion refers to the fact that the moon appears larger near the _____ .

10. The moon illusion appears to be explained by the _____ _____ hypothesis, which emphasizes the greater number of _____ _____ present when the moon is on the horizon.

# Perceptual Learning—What If the World Were Upside Down?
What effect does learning have on perception?

1. _____ _____refers to the changes in the brain due to learning that alters how we process sensory information.

2. Organizing and interpreting sensations is greatly influenced by learned _____ _____. An example is the _____ room, which looks rectangular but is actually distorted so that objects in the room appear to change size.

3. European Americans can be described as _____ as they tend to focus on the _____ and personal control. This focus influences their perceptual habits to pay attention to _____ in the environment rather than the surrounding ground.

4. East Asians can be described as _____ as they tend to focus on interpersonal relationships and _____ responsibilities. This focus also influences East Asians' perceptual habits to pay attention to the surrounding ground.

5. Sensitivity to perceptual features is also partly learned. Studies of _____ vision show that even the most basic organization is subject to a degree of change. Active movement speeds to new perceptual environments.

6. Perceptual _____ (misleading perceptions) differ from _____ (perceptions of nonexistent stimuli).

7. Illusions are often related to perceptual habits. One of the most familiar of all illusions, the _____ illusion, involves two equal-length lines tipped with arrowheads and V's. This illusion seems to be related to perceptual learning based on experience with box-shaped buildings and rooms.

8. Linear perspective, size-distance _____ relationships, and mislocating the _____ of the lines also contribute to the Müller-Lyer illusion.

9. _____ (three-dimensional sight) relies on retinal disparity to determine the depth of objects that are within 50 feet of us.

10. People who have lost touch with _____ may experience hallucinations that involve auditory, _____, touch, smell, or taste sensations created by the brain without proper environmental input.

11. "_____ hallucinations" are created by the brain to interpret sensory input received by partially blind individuals who "see" objects appearing and disappearing in front of their eyes.

# Perceptual Expectancies—On Your Mark, Get Set
To what extent do we see what we want to see?

1. Attention, prior experience, suggestion, and motives combine in various ways to create _____, or expectancies. A _____ _____ is a readiness to perceive in a particular way, induced by strong expectations.

2. Perceptual expectancies are often created by _____ .

# Extrasensory Perception—Do You Believe in Magic?
Is extrasensory perception possible?

1. _____ is the study of purported psi phenomena, including clairvoyance (perceiving events at a distance), telepathy ("mind reading"), _____ (perceiving future events), and psychokinesis (mentally influencing inanimate objects).

2. Clairvoyance, telepathy, and precognition are purported types of_____ perception.

3. Research in parapsychology remains controversial owing to a variety of problems. Coincidence and after-the-fact _____ are problems with "natural" ESP episodes.

4. With no evidence supporting the existence of ESP, psychologists strongly suggest that people be _____ of those who claim to have _____ abilities. For example, the owner of the "Miss Cleo" TV-psychic operation made $1 billion from people who believed "Miss Cleo" was a psychic.

5. Many studies of ESP overlook the impact of _____ unusual outcomes that are no more than runs of luck.

6. The bulk of the evidence to date is against the existence of ESP. Very few positive results in ESP research have been _____ (repeated) by independent scientists.

7. _____ ESP is based on deception and tricks.

# Psychology in Action: Perception and Objectivity—Believing Is Seeing
Can I learn to perceive events more accurately?

1. Perception is an active _____ of events. This is one reason why eyewitness testimony is surprisingly inaccurate.

2.  In many crimes, eyewitness accuracy is further damaged by _____ focus. Similar factors, such as observer _____, brief exposure times, cross-racial inaccuracies, and the wording of questions can lower eyewitness accuracy.

3.  Perceptual accuracy is enhanced by reality testing, _____ , and conscious efforts to pay attention.

4.  It is also valuable to break _____ _____, to broaden frames of reference, to beware of perceptual sets, and to be aware of the ways in which motives and emotions influence perceptions.

# MASTERY TEST

1.  The Ames room creates a conflict between
    a.  horizontal features and vertical features.
    b.  attention and habituation.
    c.  top-down and bottom-up processing.
    d.  shape constancy and size constancy.

2.  Weapon focus tends to lower eyewitness accuracy because it affects
    a.  selective attention.
    b.  the adaptation level.
    c.  perceptions of contiguity.
    d.  dishabituation.

3.  Stereograms create an illusion of depth by mimicking the effects of
    a.  accommodation.
    b.  convergence.
    c.  retinal disparity.
    d.  stroboscopic motion.

4.  Which perceptual constancy is most affected by sitting in the front row at a movie theater?
    a.  size constancy
    b.  shape constancy
    c.  brightness constancy
    d.  depth constancy

5.  The fact that American tourists in London tend to look in the wrong direction before stepping into crosswalks is based on
    a.  habituation.
    b.  perceptual habits.
    c.  adaptation levels.
    d.  unconscious transference.

6. When they look at drawings and photographs, people are more likely to notice unexpected objects. This is explained by the effects of _____ on perception.
   a. pictorial depth cues
   b. selective attention
   c. habituation
   d. figure-ground organization

7. Size constancy
   a. is strongest when objects are above the horizon line.
   b. is affected by experience with seeing objects of various sizes.
   c. requires that objects be illuminated by light of the same intensity.
   d. all of the preceding

8. Adaptation to visual distortions is most rapid if people are allowed to
   a. remain immobile.
   b. move actively.
   c. move their eye muscles.
   d. habituate their adaptation levels.

9. Perceptual categories and perceptual expectancies tend to promote
   a. top-down processing.
   b. bottom-up processing.
   c. divided attention.
   d. reality testing.

10. Both internal frames of reference and external _____ alter the interpretation given to a stimulus.
    a. reconstructions
    b. bottlenecks
    c. accommodations
    d. contexts

11. Which of the following cues would be of greatest help to a person trying to thread a needle?
    a. light and shadow
    b. texture gradients
    c. linear perspective
    d. overlap

12. The American woodcock has a narrow band of _____ but an unusually wide _____.
    a. monocular vision; spectral sensitivity
    b. accommodation; field of view
    c. binocular vision; field of view
    d. spectral sensitivity; binocular range

13. Which of the following purported paranormal phenomena is NOT a form of ESP?
    a. clairvoyance
    b. telepathy
    c. precognition
    d. psychokinesis

14. Size-distance invariances contribute to which of the following?
    a. Müller-Lyer illusion
    b. the stroboscopic illusion
    c. perceptual hallucinations
    d. changes in a person's adaptation level

15. The visual cliff is used primarily to test infant
    a. size constancy.
    b. figure-ground perception.
    c. depth perception.
    d. adaptation to spatial distortions.

16. Which of the following organizational principles is based on nearness in time and space?
    a. continuity
    b. closure
    c. contiguity
    d. size constancy

17. Which of the following is both a muscular and a monocular depth cue?
    a. convergence
    b. relative motion
    c. aerial perspective
    d. accommodation

18. The problem with "natural" ESP occurrences is that it is usually impossible to rule out
    a. the fact that they are replicated.
    b. the possibility that they are caused by habituation.
    c. the ganzfeld effect.
    d. coincidences.

19. Which of the following is not part of the explanation of the Müller-Lyer illusion?
    a. aerial perspective
    b. accommodation
    c. living in a "square" culture
    d. mislocating the ends of the lines

20. The term_____ refers to our limited capacity for storing and thinking about information.
    a. selective attention
    b. habituated attention
    c. divided attention
    d. selective expectancy

21. A previously blind person has just had her sight restored. Which of the following perceptual experiences is she most likely to have?
    a. perceptual set
    b. size constancy
    c. linear perspective
    d. figure-ground

22. An artist manages to portray a face with just a few unconnected lines. Apparently the artist has capitalized on
    a. closure.
    b. contiguity.
    c. the reversible figure effect.
    d. the principle of camouflage.

23. The "boiled frog syndrome" is related to the idea that _____ elicit attention.
    a. repetition, habituation, and categories
    b. expectancies, constancies, and ambiguities
    c. change, contrast, and incongruity
    d. continuity, camouflage, and similarity

24. The most basic source of stereoscopic vision is
    a. accommodation.
    b. retinal disparity.
    c. convergence.
    d. stroboscopic motion.

25. Necker's cube is a good example of
    a. an ambiguous stimulus.
    b. an impossible figure.
    c. camouflage.
    d. a binocular depth cue.

26. Enlarged pupils, a pause in breathing, and increased blood flow to the head are associated with
    a. brightness constancy.
    b. the onset of habituation.
    c. reality testing.
    d. an orientation response.

27. Skeptics regard the decline effect as evidence that _____ occurred in an ESP test.
    a. replication
    b. cheating
    c. a run of luck
    d. leakage

28. Which of the following is a binocular depth cue?
    a. accommodation
    b. convergence
    c. linear perspective
    d. motion parallax

29. Ambiguous stimuli allow us to hold more than one perceptual
    a. gradient.
    b. parallax.
    c. constancy.
    d. hypothesis.

30. Increased perceptual awareness is especially associated with
    a. dishabituation.
    b. unconscious transference.
    c. high levels of stress.
    d. stimulus repetition without variation.

31. Joan, failing to see a pedestrian crossing the street because she is too busy using a cell phone, is an example of
    a. attentional blindness.
    b. perceptual habits.
    c. inattentional blindness.
    d. apparent-distance hypothesis.

32. Megan screams out loud saying "Insects are crawling everywhere!" when none are present and Hilda, who is partially blind, claims that people are disappearing and appearing in front of her eyes. Megan is experiencing _____ because she is seeing objects that are not present in her environment and Hilda is experiencing _____ since her brain in trying to seek meaningful patterns from her sensory input.
    a. hallucinations; "sane hallucinations"
    b. hallucinations; inattentional blindess
    c. illusions; extrasensory perception (ESP)
    d. none of the above

# SOLUTIONS

## RECITE AND REVIEW

### Perception: That Extra Step: Pages 150-151
In general, how do we construct our perceptions?

1. Perceptual;
   recognizes
2. top-down
3. features;
   organize

### Perception and Attention—May I Have Your ... Attention!: Pages 151-154
Is perception altered by attention, motives, and expectations?

1. Selective
2. bottleneck
3. capacity
4. intense; change
5. Inattentional; detect
6. change; decreases
7. values

### Perceptual Organization—Getting It All Together: Pages 154-156
What basic principles do we use to group sensations into meaningful patterns?

1. object; background
2. organization similarity; common
3. grouped; appearance
4. complete; time
5. surfaces
6. hypothesis; organization
7. stimuli; cube

### Perceptual Constancies—Taming an Unruly World: Pages 157-159
What are perceptual constancies, and what is their role in perception?

1. patterns; model
2. image; perceptual
3. constancy; constant
4. inborn; learned

### Depth Perception—What If the World Were Flat?: Pages 159-165
How is it possible to see depth and judge distance?

1. Depth
2. birth; crawlers
3. lens; eyes
4. smaller; wide
5. cues; flat
6. parallel lines; smaller; picture
7. finer; motion; motion
8. one eye
9. larger
10. distance; horizon

## Perceptual Learning—What If the World Were Upside Down?: Pages 165-171
What effect does learning have on perception?

1. learning; learning
2. habits; size
3. features; movement
4. self; figures
5. interprersonal; more
6. context; level; medium
7. illusions
8. habits; buildings
9. size-distance; lines
10. three-dimensional
11. hallucinations
12. Sane; blind

## Perceptual Expectancies—On Your Mark, Get Set: Pages 171-172
To what extent do we see what we want to see?

1. expectancies
2. expectancies (or sets)

## Extrasensory Perception—Do You Believe in Magic?: Pages 172-175
Is extrasensory perception possible?

1. psi; telepathy
2. perception
3. Coincidence
4. skeptical; psychic
5. luck
6. against; repeated
7. deception

## Psychology in Action: Perception and Objectivity—Believing Is Seeing: Pages 176-178
Can I learn to perceive events more accurately?

1. active; inaccurate
2. focus; lower
3. testing; attention
4. broaden

# CONNECTIONS

## Perception: That Extra Step and Perception and Attention— May I Have Your ... Attention!: Pages 150-154
In general, how do we construct our perceptions?
Is perception altered by attention, motives, and expectations?

1. b
2. d
3. a
4. c
5. e
6. f

## Perceptual Organization—Getting It All Together: Pages 154-156
What basic principles do we use to group sensations into meaningful patterns?

1. c
2. e
3. d
4. a
5. f
6. b

## Perceptual Constancies—Taming an Unruly World: Pages 157-159
What are perceptual constancies, and what is their role in perception?

1. e          3. a          5. c
2. b          4. d

## Depth Perception—What If the World Were Flat?: Pages 159-165
How is it possible to see depth and judge distance?

1. e          5. c          9. h
2. g          6. a          10. d
3. f          7. j
4. i          8. b

## Depth Perception (continued)

1. b          3. e          5. a
2. f          4. c          6. d

## Perceptual Learning—What If the World Were Upside Down?: Pages 165-171
What effect does learning have on perception?

1. b          3. f          5. c
2. a          4. d          6. e

## Extrasensory Perception—Do You Believe in Magic?: Pages 172-175
Is extrasensory perception possible?

1. h          5. i          9. j
2. a          6. c          10. e
3. g          7. b
4. d          8. f

# CHECK YOUR MEMORY

## Perception: That Extra Step: Pages 150-151
In general, how do we construct our perceptions?

1. F          2. T          3. F

## Perception and Attention—May I Have Your ... Attention!: Pages 151-154

Is perception altered by attention, motives, and expectations?

| | | | | | |
|---|---|---|---|---|---|
| 1. T | | 5. T | | 9. F | |
| 2. T | | 6. F | | 10. T | |
| 3. T | | 7. T | | | |
| 4. F | | 8. T | | | |

## Perceptual Organization—Getting It All Together: Pages 154-156

What basic principles do we use to group sensations into meaningful patterns?

| | | | | | |
|---|---|---|---|---|---|
| 1. F | | 3. F | | 5. T | |
| 2. T | | 4. T | | 6. F | |

## Perceptual Constancies—Taming an Unruly World: Pages 157-159

What are perceptual constancies, and what is their role in perception?

| | | | | | |
|---|---|---|---|---|---|
| 1. T | | 3. T | | 5. F | |
| 2. T | | 4. F | | 6. T | |

## Depth Perception—What If the World Were Flat?: Pages 159-165

How is it possible to see depth and judge distance?

| | | | | | |
|---|---|---|---|---|---|
| 1. T | | 8. T | | 14. T | |
| 2. T | | 9. F | | 15. F | |
| 3. F | | 10. F | | 16. F | |
| 4. F | | 11. T | | 17. F | |
| 5. T | | 12. F | | 18. F | |
| 6. F | | 13. F | | | |
| 7. F | | | | | |

## Perceptual Learning—What If the World Were Upside Down?: Pages 165-171

What effect does learning have on perception?

| | | | | | |
|---|---|---|---|---|---|
| 1. T | | 6. T | | 11. T | |
| 2. F | | 7. T | | 12. T | |
| 3. F | | 8. F | | 13 F | |
| 4. F | | 9. F | | | |
| 5. F | | 10. T | | | |

## Extrasensory Perception—Do You Believe in Magic?: Pages 172-175
Is extrasensory perception possible?

1.  F
2.  T
3.  T

4.  F
5.  F
6.  F

7.  T
8.  T
9.  F

## Psychology in Action: Perception and Objectivity—Believing Is Seeing: Pages 176-178
Can I learn to perceive events more accurately?

1. T
2. F

3. F
4. F

5. T
6. F

# FINAL SURVEY AND REVIEW

## Perception: That Extra Step
In general, how do we construct our perceptions?

1.  experience; understands

2.  processing

3.  Bottom-up; top-down

## Perception and Attention—May I Have Your ... Attention!
Is perception altered by attention, motives, and expectations?

1.  Selective; attention
2.  channel
3.  Divided

4.  contrast; incongruity
5.  Inattentional

6.  orientation; response; habitation
7.  motives

## Perceptual Organization—Getting It All Together
What basic principles do we use to group sensations into meaningful patterns?

1.  figure; ground figures
2.  Gestalt; nearness; closure
3.  Closure

4.  Contiguity
5.  parallel; edges
6.  Camouflage

7.  ambiguous; Necker's;

## Perceptual Constancies—Taming an Unruly World
What are perceptual constancies, and what is their role in perception?

1.  sensations; mental; model
2.  retinal; constancies

3.  brightness; proportion; light
4.  native; empirical

## Depth Perception—What If the World Were Upside Down?

How is it possible to see depth and judge distance?

1. three-dimensional
2. visual; cliff; visual; cliff
3. accommodation; convergence
4. binocular; fields; of; view
5. pictorial
6. linear; perspective; interposition
7. gradients; parallax
8. monocular
9. horizon
10. apparent; distance; depth; cues

## Perceptual Learning—What If the World Were Flat?

What effect does learning have on perception?

1. Perceptual; learning
2. perceptual; habits; Ames
3. individualistic; self; figures
4. collective; social; more
5. inverted; adaptation
6. illusions; hallucinations
7. Müller-Lyer
8. invariance; end-points
9. Stereoscopic vision
10 reality; visual
11. Sane

## Perceptual Expectancies—On Your Mark, Get Set

To what extent do we see what we want to see?

1. expectancies
2. suggestion

## Extrasensory Perception—Do You Believe in Magic?

Is extrasensory perception possible?

1. Parapsychology; precognition
2. extrasensory
3. reinterpretation
4. skeptical; psychic
5. statistically
6. replicated
7. Stage

## Psychology in Action: Perception and Objectivity—Believing Is Seeing

How can I learn to perceive events more accurately?

1. reconstruction
2. weapon; stress
3. dishabituation
4. perceptual; habits

177

# MASTERY TEST

1. d, p. 166
2. a, p. 151
3. c, p. 160
4. b, p. 170
5. b, p. 166
6. b, p. 151
7. b, p. 157
8. b, p. 168
9. a, p. 151
10. d, p. 168
11. d, p. 163
12. c, p. 158
13. d, p. 172

14. a, p. 170
15. c, p. 159
16. c, p. 156
17. d, p. 162
18. d, p. 173
19. a, p. 170
20. c, p. 152
21. d, p. 154
22. a, p. 155
23. c, p. 154
24. b, p. 160
25. a, p. 156
26. d, p. 153

27. c, p. 174
28. b, p. 160
29. d, p. 156
30. a, p. 177
31. c, p. 153
32. a, p. 169

# States of Consciousness

## Chapter Overview

Altered states of consciousness are differentiated from normal waking awareness by changes in the quality and pattern of mental activity. Consciousness is a core feature of mental life. Cultural conditioning greatly affects what altered states a person recognizes, seeks, considers normal, and attains.

Sleep an innate biological rhythm necessary for survival. Moderate sleep loss mainly affects vigilance and performance on routine or boring tasks and may lead to involuntary microsleeps. Extended sleep loss may produce a temporary sleep-deprivation psychosis. Sleep patterns show some flexibility, but 7 to 8 hours remains average. The amount of daily sleep decreases steadily from birth to old age.

According to the dual process hypothesis, sleep "refreshes" the body and brain and helps form lasting memories. Sleep occurs in four stages. Stage 1 is light sleep, and stage 4 is deep sleep. The sleeper cycles through stages 1 through 4 several times each night. The two most basic sleep states are rapid eye movement (REM) sleep and non-REM (NREM) sleep. REM sleep is strongly associated with dreaming and help us store important memories. NREM sleep brings overall brain activation levels down, "calming" the brain.

Sleep disorders are serious health problems that should be corrected when they persist. Insomnia may be temporary or chronic. Behavioral approaches to managing insomnia are quite effective. Sleepwalking, sleeptalking, and sleepsex occur during NREM sleep. Nightmares occur in REM sleep, whereas night terrors occur in NREM sleep. Sleep apnea is one source of insomnia and daytime hypersomnia (sleepiness). Apnea is suspected as one cause of sudden infant death syndrome (SIDS) and most healthy infants should sleep face up or on their sides. Narcolepsy (sleep attacks) and cataplexy are caused by a sudden shift to REM patterns during normal waking hours.

Whether dreams have deeper, symbolic meaning is still debated. According to the psychodynamic view, dreams express unconscious wishes through dream symbols. The activation-synthesis model, however, portrays dreaming as a random physiological process. The neurocognitive view of dreams holds that dreams are continuous with waking thoughts and emotions. Most dream content is about familiar settings, people, and actions. Positive and negative emotions occur about equally in dreams.

Hypnosis is an altered state characterized by narrowed attention and increased suggestibility. Not all psychologists agree that hypnotic effects require an alteration of consciousness. Stage hypnotism takes advantage of typical stage behavior and uses deception to simulate hypnosis. Hypnosis appears capable of producing relaxation, controlling pain, altering perceptions, and changing subjective experience.

Both concentrative meditation and mindfulness meditation can be used to focus attention, alter consciousness, and reduce stress. Major benefits are its ability to interrupt anxious thoughts and to elicit the relaxation response. Brief exposure to sensory deprivation can also elicit the relaxation response.

Under proper conditions, sensory deprivation may help break long-standing habits.

Psychoactive drugs affect the brain in ways that alter consciousness. Most psychoactive drugs can be placed on a scale ranging from stimulation to depression. Psychoactive drugs are highly prone to abuse. Drug abuse is related to personal maladjustment, the reinforcing qualities of drugs, peer group influences, and expectations about drug effects.

Drugs may cause a physical dependence (addiction), a psychological dependence, or both. Drug use can be classified as experimental, recreational, situational, intensive, and compulsive. Drug abuse is most often associated with the last three.

Stimulant drugs are readily abused because of the period of depression that often follows stimulation. The greatest risks are associated with amphetamines (especially methamphetamine), cocaine, MDMA, and nicotine, but even caffeine can be a problem. Nicotine includes the added risk of lung cancer, heart disease, and other health problems.

Barbiturates, tranquilizers, and alcohol are depressant drugs. The overdose level for barbiturates and GHB is close to the intoxication dosage, making them dangerous drugs. Mixing barbiturates, tranquilizers, or GHB and alcohol may result in a fatal drug interaction. Alcohol is the most heavily abused drug in common use today.

Marijuana is subject to an abuse pattern similar to alcohol. Studies have linked chronic marijuana use with lung cancer, various mental impairments, and other health problems.

Collecting and interpreting your dreams can promote self-awareness. Freud held that the meaning of dreams is hidden by condensation, displacement, symbolization, and secondary elaboration. Hall emphasizes the setting, cast, plot, and emotions of a dream. Cartwright's view of dreams as feeling statements and Perls' technique of speaking for dream elements are also helpful. Dreams may be used for creative problem solving, especially when dream awareness is achieved through lucid dreaming.

# Learning Objectives

### Theme: Understanding states of consciousness can promote self-awareness and enhance personal effectiveness.

| |
|---|
| **GQ: What is an altered state of consciousness?** |
| LO 6.1  Define *consciousness, waking consciousness,* and *altered state of consciousness (ASC) and* list causes of an ASC. Distinguish first-person and third-person points of view. |
| **GQ: What are the effects of sleep loss or changes in sleep patterns?** |
| LO 6.2  Describe some of the basic characteristics of sleep. Include what skills one is able to perform when asleep, sleep as a *biological rhythm,* and the concept of *microsleep.* |
| LO 6.3  Describe the symptoms of two or three days of sleep deprivation and discuss temporary *sleep deprivation psychosis.* |
| LO 6.4  Discuss the concept of *sleep patterns.* Include the characteristics of long and short sleepers and the relationship between age and sleep needs. |
| **GQ: Why do we sleep?** |
| LO 6.5  Explain the four stages of sleep, briefly describing the events in each stage. |
| LO 6.6  Describe the dual process hypothesis of sleep. Differentiate between the two basic states of sleep, *REM* and *NREM* and describe the symptoms of REM behavior disorder and the occurrence of hypnopompic hallucinations. |

| |
|---|
| **GQ: What are some sleep disorders and unusual sleep events?** |
| LO 6.7  List factors that contribute to sleep problems in American society and describe the following sleep disturbances (Table 6.1): a. *hypersomnia*; b. periodic limb movement syndrome; c. restless legs syndrome; d. sleep drunkenness; and e. sleep-wake schedule disorder. |
| LO 6.8  List and describe the characteristics and treatments of the three types of *insomnia*. List some remedies for *insomnia*. |
| LO 6.9  Describe and differentiate between sleepwalking and sleeptalking and *nightmares vs. night terrors*. State three steps that can be used to eliminate nightmares. |
| LO 6.10  Describe the sleep disorder known as *sleep apnea* including its nature, cause, treatments, and relationship to *SIDS*. Describe some possible causes of SIDS and the sleep position which seems to minimize *SIDS* in infants. |
| LO 6.11  Describe *narcolepsy* and *cataplexy*. |
| **GQ: Do dreams have meaning?** |
| LO 6.12  Explain the relationship between REM sleep and dreaming; tell how many times per night most people dream and how long dreams usually last; and discuss the cause and symptoms of REM rebound. |
| LO 6.13  Explain how *psychodynamic theories* view dreams, discuss the *activation-synthesis hypothesis* concerning dreaming, and outline *neurocognitive dream theory*. |
| **GQ: What is hypnosis?** |
| LO 6.14  Define *hypnosis*; describe the history of hypnosis from Mesmer through its use today; distinguish between state and nonstate theories of hypnosis, including the concept of the *hidden observer*. |
| LO 6.15  List four factors common to all hypnotic techniques; define the *basic suggestion effect*; and explain how a person's *hypnotic susceptibility* can be determined. |
| LO 6.16  Explain six conclusions concerning what can and cannot be achieved with hypnosis and describe five features of the stage that are used by *stage hypnotists* to perform their acts. |
| **GQ: Do meditation and sensory deprivation have any benefits?** |
| LO 6.17  Define the *relaxation response* and describe how might it explain the benefits of both *meditation* and *sensory deprivation*. Describe the two foms of *meditation* and *REST*. |
| **GQ: What are the effects of the more commonly used psychoactive drugs?** |
| LO 6.18  Define the term *psychoactive drug*; describe how various drugs affect the nervous system; differentiate *physical dependence* from *psychological dependence*; and describe five different patterns of drug use. |
| LO 6.19  Describe the following frequently abused drugs in terms of their effects, possible medical uses, side effects or long term symptoms, organic damage potential, and potential for physical and/or psychological dependence: a. amphetamines (including amphetamine psychosis); b. cocaine (including the three signs of abuse); c. MDMA (ecstasy); d. caffeine (include the term *caffeinism*); e. nicotine; f. barbiturates; g. GHB; h. *tranquilizers* (include the concept of *drug interaction*); i. alcohol; j. *hallucinogens* (including marijuana). |
| LO 6.20  Define *alcohol myopia*, *binge drinking*, and *moderated drinking*; and discuss the various treatment methods for alcoholism. |
| **GQ: How can dreams be used to promote personal understanding?** |
| LO 6.21  Explain how Freud, Hall, Cartwright, and Perls analyzed dreams; outline procedures for using dreams to improve creativity; and describe lucid dreaming. Include an explanation of Freud's four *dream processes*. |

# RECITE AND REVIEW

## States of Consciousness—The Many Faces of Awareness: Page 182
What is an altered state of consciousness?

1. States of _____ that differ from normal, alert, _____ consciousness are called altered states of consciousness (ASCs).

2. ASCs involve distinct shifts in the quality and _____ of mental activity.

3. Altered states are especially associated with _____ and _____, hypnosis, meditation, _____ deprivation, and psychoactive drugs.

4. Cultural conditioning greatly affects what altered states a person recognizes, seeks, considers _____, and attains.

## Sleep—A Nice Place to Visit: Pages 182-185
What are the effects of sleep loss or changes in sleep patterns?

1. Sleep is an innate biological _____ essential for _____ .

2. Higher animals and people deprived of sleep experience _____ microsleeps.

3. Moderate sleep loss mainly affects alertness and self-motivated performance on _____ or boring tasks.

4. Extended sleep _____ can (somewhat rarely) produce a _____ sleep-deprivation psychosis, marked by confusion, delusions, and possibly hallucinations.

5. _____ change during puberty increases adolescents need for _____ , which many lack since they tend to stay up late and get up early for school. This pattern causes them to experience hypersomnia (excessive daytime_____ ).

6. The "storm and stress" that adolescents experience may, in part, be caused by _____ of sleep.

7. Biological _____ within the body are closely tied to sleep, activity levels, and energy cycles.

8 Sleep patterns show some flexibility, but 7 to 8 hours remains average. The unscheduled human sleep-waking cycle averages slightly more than, but cycles of _____ and _____ tailor it to 24-hour days.

9. The amount of daily sleep _____ steadily from birth to old age and switches from multiple sleep-wake cycles to once-a-day sleep periods.

10. Adapting to_____ or _____ sleep cycles is difficult and inefficient for most people.

# Stages of Sleep—The Nightly Roller-Coaster: Pages 185-188
## Why Do We Sleep?

1. Sleepiness is associated with the accumulation of a sleep hormone in the _____ and spinal cord.

2. Sleep depends on which of _____ opposed sleep and waking systems in the _____ is dominant at any given moment.

3. Sleep occurs in _____ stages defined by changes in behavior and brain _____ recorded with an electroencephalograph (EEG).

4. Stage 1, _____ sleep, has small irregular brain waves. In stage 2, _____ spindles appear. _____ waves appear in stage 3. Stage 4, or deep sleep, is marked by almost pure delta waves.

5. Sleepers_____ between stages 1 and 4 (passing through stages 2 and 3) several times each night.

6. There are two basic sleep states, rapid eye _____ (REM) sleep and non-REM (NREM) sleep.

7. REM sleep is much more strongly associated with _____ than non-REM sleep is.

8. _____ and REMs occur mainly during stage 1 sleep, but usually not during the first stage 1 period.

9. Hypnopompic hallucinations occur when individuals experience sleep _____ upon awakening from sleep.

10. A day of_____ exertion generally leads to an increase in NREM sleep, which allows our body to recover from bodily fatigue. A day of    would lead to an increase in REM sleep.

11. Dreaming is accompanied by sexual and _____ arousal but relaxation of the skeletal _____ People who move about violently while asleep may suffer from _____ behavior disorder.

183

# Sleep Disturbances—Showing Nightly: Sleep Wars!: Pages 189-192

What are some sleep disorders and unusual sleep events?

1. Insomnia, which is difficulty in getting to sleep or staying asleep, may be _____ or chronic.

2. When insomnia is treated with drugs, sleep quality is often _____ and drug-dependency insomnia may develop. _____ insomnia is also a risk.

3. The amino acid tryptophan, found in bread, pasta, and other foods, helps promote_____ .

4. Behavioral approaches to managing insomnia, such as relaxation, sleep restriction,_____ control, and paradoxical _____ are quite effective.

5. _____ (somnambulism) and sleeptalking occur during NREM sleep in stages 3 and 4.

6. Night terrors occur in_____ sleep, whereas nightmares occur in _____ sleep.

7. Nightmares can be eliminated by the method called imagery _____ .

8. During sleep apnea, people repeatedly stop_____. Apnea is suspected as one cause of _____ infant death syndrome (SIDS).

9. The first _____ months are critical for babies who are at risk for SIDS. Other factors include the baby being _____ , and breathing through an open _____ .

10. The phrase " _____ to sleep" refers to the safest position for most babies: their _____ .

# Dreams—A Separate Reality?: Pages 192-194

Do dreams have meaning?

1. People will experience REM _____ if they are deprived of REM sleep the night before.

2. People deprived of REM sleep showed an urgent need to _____ and mental disturbances the next day. However, total sleep loss seems to be more important than loss of a single sleep _____ .

3. The Freudian, or psychodynamic, view is that dreams express unconscious_____ , frequently hidden by dream symbols.

4. Allan Hobson and Robert McCarley's _____-synthesis model portrays dreaming as a physiological process. The brain, they say, creates dreams to explain _____ and motor messages that occur during REM sleep.

5. According to _____ dream theory, dreams often reflect ordinary waking concerns.

6. Calvin Hall found that most dream content is about _____ settings, people, and actions. Dreams more often involve negative _____ than positive _____ .

# Hypnosis—Look into My Eyes: Pages 194-197
## What is hypnosis?

1. Hypnosis is an altered state characterized by narrowed attention and _____ suggestibility.

2. In the 1700s, Franz Mesmer (whose name is the basis for the term mesmerize) practiced " _____ magnetism," which was actually a demonstration of the power of _____ .

3. Theories regarding hypnosis can be divided into _____ and nonstate theories.

4. Mentally moving an object back and forth, such as a ring that is dangling from a string you are holding, is the result of _____ (your own suggestive power made your hand move in small increments).

5. The core of hypnosis is the _____ suggestion effect—a tendency to carry out suggested actions as if they were involuntary. However, a hypnotized person will not perform behaviors that he or she deems to be _____ or repulsive.

6. People vary in hypnotic susceptibility; _____ out of 10 can be hypnotized, as revealed by scores on the Stanford Hypnotic Susceptibility _____ .

7. Hypnosis appears capable of producing relaxation, controlling _____ , and altering perceptions.

8. Stage hypnotism takes advantage of typical stage behavior, _____ suggestibility, responsive subjects, disinhibition, and _____ to simulate hypnosis.

## Meditation and Sensory Deprivation—Chilling, the Healthy Way: Pages 197-199

Do meditation and sensory deprivation have any benefits?

1. _____ focuses attention and interrupts the typical flow of thoughts.

2. Two major forms of meditation include _____ and mindfulness meditation.

3. The core of meditation may be the _____ response

4. Sensory deprivation takes place when there is a major reduction in the amount or variety of sensory _____ available to a person.

5. Prolonged sensory deprivation is stressful and disruptive, leading to_____ distortions.

6. Brief or mild sensory deprivation can enhance sensory sensitivity and induce deep _____.

7. Sensory deprivation also appears to aid the breaking of long-standing _____ and promotes creative thinking. This effect is the basis for Restricted Environmental Stimulation Therapy (REST).

8. Mindfulness is associated with self-knowledge and _____.

## Drug-Altered Consciousness—The High and Low of It: Pages 199-201

What are the effects of the more commonly used psychoactive drugs?

1. A psychoactive drug is a substance that affects the brain in ways that _____ consciousness.

2. Drugs alter the activities in the brain by _____ and blocking neurotransmitters (_____ that carry messages between neurons) to produce feelings of pleasure.

3. Most psychoactive drugs can be placed on a scale ranging from stimulation to _____. Some, however, are best described as hallucinogens (drugs that alter _____impressions).

4. Drugs may cause a physical dependence ( _____ ) or a psychological dependence, or both.

5. Prolonged use of a drug can lead to drug tolerance (a _____ response to a drug) whereby the abuser must _____ the amount of a drug to receive the same desired effect.

6. Drug use can be classified as experimental, recreational, situational, intensive, and _____'__. Drug abuse is most often associated with the last three.

# Uppers—Amphetamines, Cocaine, MDMA, Caffeine, Nicotine: Pages 201-206

1. The physically addicting drugs are alcohol, amphetamines, barbiturates, cocaine, codeine, GHB, heroin, methadone, morphine, tobacco, and tranquilizers. All psychoactive drugs can lead to _____ dependence.

2. Amphetamines, known as "bennies," "dex," "go," and "_____," are synthetic stimulants that produce a rapid drug _____ . Abusers typically go on binges that last for several days until they "_____," suffering from _____, confusion, depression, uncontrolled irritability, and aggression.

3. Stimulant drugs are readily abused because of the period of that often follows stimulation. The greatest risks are associated with amphetamines, cocaine, MDMA, and nicotine, but even _____can be a problem.

4. Methamphetamine, known as "_____," "speed," "meth," or "crystal," is cheaply produced in labs and can be snorted,_____ , or eaten.

5. Repeated use of amphetamine can cause brain damage and amphetamine _____. Amphetamine psychosis can cause the abuser to act on their delusions and risk _____ -injury or injury to _____ .

6. Signs of cocaine abuse are: compulsive use, loss of _____, and a disregard for.

7. Users of MDMA are likely to risk an _____in body temperature, liver damage, and unsafe sex. In addition, _____brain cells may be damaged, which could increase levels of anxiety or depression.

8. MDMA or "_____," which is similar to amphetamine, has been linked with numerous deaths and with mental impairment.

9. Caffeine can be found in coffee, _____, soft drinks, and chocolate. It stimulates the brain by _____chemicals that inhibit nerve activities.

10. _____includes the added risk of lung cancer, heart disease, and other health problems.

11. The smoking of cigarettes releases carcinogens ( _____ -causing substances) in the air, which expose people to_____smoke and places them at risk for developing lung cancer.

12. Up to _____ of those who quit smoking relapse within one year.

# Downers—Sedatives, Tranquilizers, and Alcohol: Pages 206-210

1. Barbiturates are _____ drugs whose overdose level is close to the intoxication dosage, making them dangerous drugs. Common street names for barbiturates are "downers," "_____ heavens," "_____ hearts," "goofballs," " _____ ladies," and "rainbows."

2. The depressant drug _____ (gamma-hydroxybuyrate) can cause coma, breathing failure, and death in relatively low doses. GHB is commonly called "goop," "scoop," "max," or "_____ Home Boy."

3. Benzodiazepine tranquilizers, such as _____ , are used to lower anxiety. When abused, they have a strong _____ potential.

4. _____ , a tranquilizer, also known as "roofies" and the "_____ -rape drug," is odorless and tasteless and is sometimes used to spike drinks.

5. Mixing barbiturates and alcohol may result in a fatal _____ interaction (in which the joint effect of two drugs exceeds the effects of adding one drug's effects to the other's).

6. Every year in the United States, 75,000 people die of _____ -related deaths. Binge drinking (having _____ or more drinks in a short time) is responsible for 14,000 college student deaths a year.

7. People who undergo detoxification (the _____ of poison) often experience unpleasant symptoms of drug _____.

# Hallucinogens—Tripping the Light Fantastic: Pages 210-212

1. Marijuana ("pot," "herb," and "_____ ") is a hallucinogen subject to an _____ pattern similar to alcohol. Studies have linked chronic marijuana use with memory impairment, lung cancer, reproductive problems, immune system disorders, and other health problems.

2.  _____ , the main active chemical in marijuana, accumulates in the cerebral cortex and reproductive organs.

3.  Potential problems caused by frequent marijuana use are short-term _____ loss and a decline in learning, _____ , and thinking abilities. In addition, people who smoke more joints a week tend to score four points lower on IQ tests.

## Psychology in Action: Exploring and Using Dreams: Pages 212-215
How can dreams be used to promote personal understanding?

1.  Freud held that the meaning of dreams is _____ by four dream _____ he called condensation, displacement, symbolization, and secondary elaboration.

2.  Calvin Hall emphasizes the setting, cast, _____ , and emotions of a dream.

3.  Rosalind Cartwright's view of dreams as feeling statements and Fritz Perls' technique of _____ for dream elements are also helpful.

4.  Dreams may be used for _____ problem solving, especially when dream control is achieved through lucid dreaming (a dream in which the dreamer feels capable of normal thought and action).

# CONNECTIONS

## States of Consciousness—The Many Faces of Awareness: Pages 182-185
What is an altered state of consciousness? What are the effects of sleep loss or changes in sleep patterns?

| | | | |
|---|---|---|---|
| 1. _____ hypersomnia | a. | over nine hours |
| 2. _____ Randy Gardner | b. | few seconds of repeated sleep |
| 3. _____ ASC | c. | body clocks |
| 4. _____ microsleep | d. | sleep deprivation |
| 5. _____ short sleep cycles | e. | 2 to 1 ratio of awake versus sleep |
| 6. _____ long sleepers | f. | excessive sleepiness |
| 7. _____ sleep pattern | g. | mental awareness |
| 8. _____ biological rhythm | h. | daydreaming |
| 9. _____ consciousness | i. | infancy |

# Sleep—A Nice Place to Visit: Pages 185-188
Why Do We Sleep?

| | | | |
|---|---|---|---|
| 1. _____ alpha waves | a. reflex muscle contraction |
| 2. _____ beta waves | b. images created upon awakening |
| 3. _____ delta waves | c. relaxed |
| 4. _____ hypnic jerk | d. sexual arousal |
| 5. _____ hypnopompic hallucinations | e. stage 2 of sleep |
| 6. _____ sleep spindles | f. stage 4 of sleep |
| 7. _____ NREM sleep | g. awake, alert |
| 8. _____ REM sleep | h. produces sleep stages 1-4 |

# Stages of Sleep—The Nightly Roller-Coaster: Pages 189-192
What are some sleep disorders and unusual sleep events?

| | |
|---|---|
| 1. _____ sleep drunkenness | a. violent actions |
| 2. _____ hypersomnia | b. fatal to infants |
| 3. _____ stimulus control | c. remedy for insomnia |
| 4. _____ nightmares | d. slow awakening |
| 5. _____ narcolepsy | e. stages 3 and 4 of NREM |
| 6. _____ SIDS | f. sudden daytime REM sleep |
| 7. _____ tryptophan | g. during REM sleep |
| 8. _____ REM behavior disorder | h. sleep inducing foods |
| 9. _____ drug-dependency insomnia | i. excessive sleepiness |
| 10. _____ sleepwalking | j. sleep loss caused by *Nytol* |

# Dreams—A Separate Reality: Pages 192-194
Do dreams have meaning?

| | |
|---|---|
| 1. _____ integrate memories | a. unconscious meanings |
| 2. _____ dream symbols | b. wish fulfillment |
| 3. _____ REM rebound | c. extra dream time |
| 4. _____ activation-synthesis hypothesis | d. reflect daily events |
| 5. _____ Sigmund Freud | e. function of REM sleep |
| 6. _____ Calvin Hall | f. neural firing triggering memories |

## Hypnosis—Look Into My Eyes and Meditation and Sensory Deprivation—Chilling, the Healthy Way: Pages 194-199

What is hypnosis? Do meditation and sensory deprivation have any benefits?

| | | | |
|---|---|---|---|
| 1. _____ | mesmerize | a. | flotation tank |
| 2. _____ | use tricks | b. | hypnotize |
| 3. _____ | pain relief | c. | self-hypnosis |
| 4. _____ | REST | d. | hypnosis effect |
| 5. _____ | autosuggestion | e. | sensory deprivation visions |
| 6. _____ | hypnagogic images | f. | stage hypnosis |
| 7. _____ | relaxation response | g. | single focal point |
| 8. _____ | mindfulness meditation | h. | nonjudgemental awareness |
| 9. _____ | concentrative meditation | i. | physiological pattern |

## Drug-Altered Consciousness—the High and Low of It: Pages 199-201

What are the effects of the more commonly used psychoactive drugs?

| | | | |
|---|---|---|---|
| 1. _____ | drug tolerance | a. | cocaine rush |
| 2. _____ | amphetamine | b. | cancer agent |
| 3. _____ | dopamine | c. | addiction |
| 4. _____ | nicotine | d. | sedative |
| 5. _____ | carcinogen | e. | hallucinogen |
| 6. _____ | barbiturate | f. | detoxification |
| 7. _____ | AA | g. | loss of pleasure |
| 8. _____ | alcohol treatment | h. | stimulant |
| 9. _____ | THC | i. | self-help group |
| 10. _____ | anhedonia | j. | insecticide |

## Psychology in Action: Exploring and Using Dreams: Pages 212-215

How can dreams be used to promote personal understanding?

| | | | |
|---|---|---|---|
| 1. _____ | displacement | a. | redirect actions toward safer images |
| 2. _____ | symbolization | b. | combining events into one image |
| 3. _____ | secondary elaboration | c. | nonliteral forms of dream content |
| 4. _____ | lucid dream | d. | feels awake while dreaming |
| 5. _____ | condensation | e. | add details to make dreams logical |

# CHECK YOUR MEMORY

## States of Consciousness—The Many Faces of Awareness: Page 182
What is an altered state of consciousness?

1.  The quality and pattern of mental activity changes during an ASC.   TRUE or FALSE

2.  All people experience at least some ASCs.   TRUE or FALSE

3.  According to Thomas Nagel, through the use of objective studies of behavior and the first-person point of view, psychologists are able to understand the consciousness of animals.
    TRUE or FALSE

4.  Both sensory overload and monotonous stimulation can produce ASCs.   TRUE or FALSE

5.  Almost every known religion has accepted some ASCs as desirable.   TRUE or FALSE

## Sleep—A Nice Place to Visit: Pages 182-185
What are the effects of sleep loss or changes in sleep patterns?

1.  Through sleep learning it is possible to master a foreign language.   TRUE or FALSE

2.  A total inability to sleep results in death.   TRUE or FALSE

3.  Even after extended sleep loss, most symptoms are removed by a single night's sleep.
    TRUE or FALSE

4.  Hallucinations and delusions are the most common reaction to extended sleep deprivation.
    TRUE or FALSE

5.  Physical changes during puberty increase adolescents' need for sleep.   TRUE or FALSE

6.  Without scheduled light and dark periods, human sleep rhythms would drift into unusual patterns.
    TRUE or FALSE

7.  The average human sleep-wake cycle lasts 23 hours and 10 minutes.   TRUE or FALSE

8.  Short sleepers are defined as those who average less than 5 hours of sleep per night.
    TRUE or FALSE

9.  Shortened sleep cycles, such as 3 hours of sleep to 6 hours awake, are more efficient than sleeping once a day.   TRUE or FALSE

## Stages of Sleep—The Nightly Roller-Coaster: Pages 185-188
Why Do We Sleep?

1.  Sleep is promoted by a chemical that accumulates in the bloodstream.    TRUE or FALSE

2.  Body temperature drops as a person falls asleep.    TRUE or FALSE

3.  A hypnic jerk is a sign of serious problems.    TRUE or FALSE

4.  Delta waves typically first appear in stage 2 sleep.    TRUE or FALSE

5.  About 45 percent of awakenings during REM periods produce reports of dreams.
    TRUE or FALSE

6.  REM sleep occurs mainly in stages 3 and 4.    TRUE or FALSE

7.  REM sleep increases when a person is subjected to daytime stress.    TRUE or FALSE

8.  The average dream only lasts 3 to 4 minutes.    TRUE or FALSE

9.  Most people change positions in bed during REM sleep.    TRUE or FALSE

10. REM behavior disorder causes people to briefly fall asleep and become paralyzed during the day.
    TRUE or FALSE

11. Approximately 30 percent of individuals have experienced hypnopompic hallucinations upon

    awakening from their sleep.    TRUE or FALSE

## Sleep Disturbances—Showing Nightly: Sleep Wars!: Pages 189-192
What are some sleep disorders and unusual sleep events?

1.  Bread, pasta, pretzels, cookies, and cereals all contain melatonin.    TRUE or FALSE

2.  Caffeine, alcohol, and tobacco can all contribute to insomnia.    TRUE or FALSE

3.  The two most effective behavioral treatments for insomnia are sleep restriction and stimulus control.
    TRUE or FALSE

4.  Sleepwalking occurs during NREM periods, sleeptalking during REM periods.
    TRUE or FALSE

5.  People who have NREM night terrors usually can remember very little afterward.
    TRUE or FALSE

6.  Imagery rehearsal is an effective way to treat recurrent nightmares.    TRUE or FALSE

7.  REM sleep appears to help the brain process memories formed during the day.
    TRUE or FALSE

8. People who take barbiturate sleeping pills may develop drug-dependency insomnia.
TRUE or FALSE

9. Newborn babies spend 8 or 9 hours a day in REM sleep.    TRUE or FALSE

10. Sleep apnea does not increase the risk of having a heart attack. This is only a myth.
TRUE or FALSE

## Dreams—A Separate Reality: Pages 192-194
Do dreams have meaning?

1. REM rebound refers to people having more REM sleep when they do not get enough REM sleep the night before.    TRUE or FALSE

2. The favorite dream setting is outdoors.    TRUE or FALSE

3. People report feeling more negative emotions when they are awakened during REM sleep.
TRUE or FALSE

4. Pleasant emotions are more common in dreams than unpleasant emotions.    TRUE or FALSE

5. According to Freud, dreams represent thoughts and wishes expressed as images.
TRUE or FALSE

6. The activation-synthesis hypothesis emphasizes the unconscious meanings of dream symbols.
TRUE or FALSE

7. The activation-synthesis hypothesis does believe that dreams are created from memories or past experiences.    TRUE or FALSE

## Hypnosis—Look into My Eyes: Pages 194-197
What is hypnosis?

1. The Greek word hypnos means "magnetism."    TRUE or FALSE

2. Only about 4 people out of 10 can be hypnotized.    TRUE or FALSE

3. Hypnosis is an example of animal magnetism.    TRUE or FALSE

4. Physical strength cannot be increased with hypnosis.    TRUE or FALSE

5. Hypnosis is better at changing subjective experiences than behaviors.    TRUE or FALSE

6. Stage hypnotists look for responsive volunteers who will cooperate and not spoil the show.
TRUE or FALSE

7. Autosuggestion is used by people who believe they have psychic abilities.    TRUE or FALSE

8. Hypnosis is not a valuable tool since its main purpose is entertainment.    TRUE or FALSE

# Meditation and Sensory Deprivation—Chilling, the Healthy Way: Pages 197-199

Do meditation and sensory deprivation have any benefits?

1. Brain scans show changes in the activity of the frontal lobes during meditation.   TRUE or FALSE

2. During mindfulness meditation, one attends to a single focal point.   TRUE or FALSE

3. Sensory deprivation is almost always unpleasant, and it usually causes distorted perceptions.   TRUE or FALSE

4. Sensory sensitivity temporarily increases after a period of sensory deprivation.   TRUE or FALSE

5. Prolonged sensory deprivation produces deep relaxation.   TRUE or FALSE

6. REST is a form of brainwashing used during the Vietnam war.   TRUE or FALSE

# Drug-Altered Consciousness—the High and Low of It: Pages 199-201

What are the effects of the more commonly used psychoactive drugs?

1. Abuse of any psychoactive drug can produce physical dependence.   TRUE or FALSE

2. People who believe they have used too many drugs and feel they need to reduce their drug use are in need of professional help.   TRUE or FALSE

3. Amphetamines are used to treat narcolepsy and hyperactivity.   TRUE or FALSE

4. Amphetamine is more rapidly metabolized by the body than cocaine is.   TRUE or FALSE

5. Ecstasy and amphetamine reduce the production of neurotransmitters in the brain.   TRUE or FALSE

6. Cocaine ("coke" or "snow") produces feelings of alertness, euphoria, well-being, powerfulness, boundless energy, and pleasure.   TRUE or FALSE

7. MDMA is chemically similar to amphetamine.   TRUE or FALSE

8. MDMA is widely used by college students (1 in 20 students has tried Ecstasy).   TRUE or FALSE

9. Disregarding consequences is a sign of cocaine abuse.   TRUE or FALSE

10. Caffeine can increase the risk of miscarriage during pregnancy.   TRUE or FALSE

11. Unlike other drugs, caffeine does not cause dependency or side effects.   TRUE or FALSE

12. Twenty-five cigarettes could be fatal for a nonsmoker.   TRUE or FALSE

13. Regular use of nicotine leads to drug tolerance, and often to physical addiction.   TRUE or FALSE

14. Every cigarette reduces a smoker's life expectancy by 7 minutes.   TRUE or FALSE

15. Secondary smoke only causes harm to the person who smokes, not those around them.

    TRUE or FALSE

16. In order to stop smoking, tapering off is generally more successful than quitting abruptly.

    TRUE or FALSE

17. One of the most effective ways to stop smoking is to schedule the number of cigarettes smoked each day.

    TRUE or FALSE

18. There have been no known deaths caused by barbiturate overdoses.   TRUE or FALSE

19. GHB, a hallucinogen, can be easily purchased over the Internet.   TRUE or FALSE

20. It is legal and safe to drive as long as blood alcohol level does not exceed 0.8.   TRUE or FALSE

21. Drinking alone is a serious sign of alcohol abuse.   TRUE or FALSE

22. To pace alcohol intake, you should limit drinking primarily to the first hour of a social event or party.

    TRUE or FALSE

23. Over 80 percent of fraternity and sorority members in the U.S. have engaged in binge drinking.

    TRUE or FALSE

24. Alcoholics Anonymous (AA) and Secular Organizations for Sobriety are organizations that seek
    to make money from drug abusers.   TRUE or FALSE

25. Hallucinogens generally affect brain transmitter systems.   TRUE or FALSE

26. THC receptors are found in large numbers in the cerebellum of the brain.   TRUE or FALSE

27. People who smoke marijuana on a regular basis report that they are satisfied with their lives, earn more
    money, and are healthier than nonusers at the age of 29.   TRUE or FALSE

28. Pregnant mothers who use marijuana may increase the risk that their babies will have trouble
    succeeding in goal-oriented tasks.   TRUE or FALSE

29. Drug abuse is frequently part of general pattern of personal maladjustment.   TRUE or FALSE

30. The negative consequences of drug use typically follow long after the drug has been taken.
    TRUE or FALSE

## Psychology in Action: Exploring and Using Dreams: Pages 212-215

How can dreams be used to promote personal understanding?

1. Displacement refers to representing two or more people with a single dream image.
   TRUE or FALSE

2. Secondary elaboration is the tendency to make a dream more logical when remembering it.
   TRUE or FALSE

3. According to Calvin Hall, the overall emotional tone of a dream is the key to its meaning.
   TRUE or FALSE

4. Alcohol decreases REM sleep.    TRUE or FALSE

5. It is basically impossible to solve daytime problems in dreams.    TRUE or FALSE

6. Lucid dreams either occur or they don't; there is no way to increase their frequency.
   TRUE or FALSE

# FINAL SURVEY AND REVIEW

## States of Consciousness—The Many Faces of Awareness

What is an altered state of consciousness?

1. States of awareness that differ from normal, alert, waking_____ are called altered states
   of _____ (ASCs).

2. ASCs involve distinct shifts in the quality and pattern of _____ .

3. Altered states are especially associated with sleep and dreaming, _____ , meditation, sensory
   _____ , and psychoactive drugs.

4. _____ conditioning greatly affects what altered states a person recognizes, seeks, considers
   normal, and attains.

## Sleep—A Nice Place to Visit

What are the effects of sleep loss or changes in sleep patterns?

1. Sleep is an _____ rhythm essential for survival.

2. Higher animals and people deprived of sleep experience involuntary _____ (a brief shift to
   sleep patterns in the brain).

3. Moderate sleep loss mainly affects _____ and self-motivated performance on routine or boring tasks.

4. Extended sleep loss can (somewhat rarely) produce a temporary sleep-deprivation _____, marked by confusion, _____ , and possibly hallucinations.

5. _____change during puberty increases adolescents' need for sleep, which many lack since they tend to stay up late and get up early for school. This pattern causes them to experience _____ (excessive daytime sleepiness).

6. The "storm and stress" that adolescents experience may, in part, be caused by _____ of sleep.

7. _____rhythms within the body are closely tied to sleep, activity levels, and energy cycles.

8. Sleep patterns show some flexibility, but 7 to 8 hours remains average. The unscheduled human _____ averages slightly more than 24 hours , but cycles of light and dark tailor it to 24-hour days.

9. The amount of daily sleep decreases steadily from birth to _____and switches from _____ sleep-wake cycles to once-a-day sleep periods.

10. Adapting to shorter or longer _____is difficult and inefficient for most people.

## Stages of Sleep—The Nightly Roller-Coaster
Why Do We Sleep?

1. Sleepiness is associated with the accumulation of a sleep _____ in the brain and

   _____ .

2. Sleep depends on which of two _____ sleep and waking _____ in the brain is dominant at any given moment.

3. Sleep occurs in 4 stages defined by changes in behavior and brain waves recorded with an _____ (EEG).

4. Stage 1, light sleep, has small irregular brain waves. In stage 2, sleep _____ appear. Delta waves appear in stage 3. Stage 4, or deep sleep, is marked by almost pure _____

   _____

5. Sleepers alternate between stages _____ and _____ (passing through stages _____ and _____ ) several times each night.

6. There are two basic sleep states, _____  _____ movement (REM) sleep and non-REM (NREM) sleep.

7. _____ sleep is much more strongly associated with dreaming than _____ sleep is.

8. Dreams and REMs occur mainly during _____ sleep, but usually not during the first _____ period.

9. _____ hallucinations occur when individuals experience sleep paralysis upon _____ from sleep.

10. A day of physical exertion generally leads to an increase in _____ sleep, which allows our body to recover from bodily fatigue. A day of stress would lead to an increase in _____ sleep.

11. Dreaming is accompanied by sexual and emotional _____ but _____ of the skeletal muscles. People who move about violently while asleep may suffer from REM behavior _____ .

# Sleep Disturbances—Showing Nightly: Sleep Wars!
## What are some sleep disorders and unusual sleep events?

1. Insomnia, which is difficulty in getting to sleep or staying asleep, may be temporary or _____ .

2. When insomnia is treated with drugs, sleep quality is often lowered and drug-_____ insomnia may develop. Rebound _____ is also a risk.

3. The amino acid _____ , found in bread, pasta, and other foods, helps promote sleep.

4. Behavioral approaches to managing insomnia, such as relaxation, sleep _____ , stimulus control, and _____ intention are quite effective.

5. Sleepwalking ( _____ ) and sleeptalking occur during _____ sleep in stages 3 and 4.

6. Night terrors occur in _____ sleep, whereas nightmares occur in _____ sleep.

7. Nightmares can be eliminated by the method called _____  _____ .

8. During sleep _____ , people repeatedly stop breathing. _____ is suspected as one cause of sudden _____  _____ syndrome.

199

9. The first _____ months are critical for babies who are at risk for SIDS. Other factors include the baby being a _____ , and breathing through an open _____ .

10. The phrase "_____ to sleep" refers to the safest position for most babies: their _____ .

# Dreams—A Separate Reality?
Do dreams have meaning?

1. People will experience _____ if they are deprived of REM sleep the night before.

2. People deprived of _____ sleep showed an urgent need to dream and _____ disturbances the next day. However, _____ amount of sleep loss seems to be more important than loss of a single sleep stage.

3. The Freudian, or _____ , view is that dreams express unconscious wishes, frequently hidden by dream _____ .

4. Allan Hobson and Robert McCarley's activation- _____ model portrays dreaming as a physiological process. The brain, they say, creates dreams to explain sensory and _____ messages that occur during REM sleep.

5. According to neurocognitive dream theory, dreams often reflect _____ waking concerns.

6. Calvin _____ found that most dream content is about familiar settings, people, and actions. Dreams more often involve _____ emotions than _____ emotions.

# Hypnosis—Look into My Eyes
What is hypnosis?

1. Hypnosis is an altered state characterized by narrowed attention and increased _____ .

2. In the 1700s, Franz _____ (whose name is the basis for the term _____ ) practiced "animal magnetism," which was actually a demonstration of the power of suggestion.

3. Theories regarding hypnosis can be divided into state and _____ theories.

4. Mentally moving an object back and forth, such as a ring that is dangling from a string you are holding, is the result of _____ (your own suggestive power made your hand move in small increments).

5. The core of hypnosis is the basic _____ effect—a tendency to carry out suggested actions as if they were _____ .

200

6. People vary in hypnotic susceptibility; 8 out of 10 can be hypnotized, as revealed by scores on the _____ Hypnotic Susceptibility Scale.

7. Hypnosis appears capable of producing _____ , controlling pain, and altering perceptions.

8. _____ takes advantage of typical stage behavior, waking suggestibility, responsive subjects, disinhibition, and deception to _____ hypnosis.

## Meditation and Sensory Deprivation—Chilling, the Healthy Way

Do meditation and sensory deprivation have any benefits?

1. Meditation focuses _____ and interrupts the typical flow of thoughts.

2. Two major forms of meditation include concentrative and _____ meditation.

3. The core of _____ may be the relaxation response

4. Sensory deprivation takes place when there is a major reduction in the amount or variety of _____ _____ available to a person.

5. _____ sensory deprivation is stressful and disruptive, leading to perceptual distortions.

6. Brief or mild sensory _____ can induce deep _____ .

7. Sensory deprivation also appears to aid the breaking of long-standing habits and promotes creative thinking. This effect is the basis for _____ _____ Stimulation Therapy (REST).

8. Mindfulness is associated with _____ and well-being.

## Drug-Altered Consciousness—The High and Low of It

What are the effects of the more commonly used psychoactive drugs?

1. A psychoactive drug is a substance that affects the brain in ways that alter _____ .

2. Drugs alter the activities in the brain by mimicking and blocking _____ (chemicals that carry messages between neurons) to produce feelings of pleasure.

3. Most psychoactive drugs can be placed on a scale ranging from _____ to _____ . Some, however, are best described as _____ (drugs that alter sensory impressions).

4.  Drugs may cause a physical _____ (addiction) or a psychological _____ , or both.

5.  Prolonged use of a drug can lead to drug _____ (a reduced response to a drug) whereby the abuser must _____ the amount of a drug to receive the same desired effect.

6.  Drug use can be classified as experimental, _____ , situational, intensive, and compulsive. Drug abuse is most often associated with the last three.

# Uppers—Amphetamines, Cocaine, MDMA, Caffeine, Nicotine

1.  The _____ _____ drugs are alcohol, amphetamines, barbiturates, cocaine, codeine, GHB, heroin, methadone, morphine, tobacco, and tranquilizers. All psychoactive drugs can lead to psychological dependence.

2.  Stimulant drugs are readily abused because of the period of depression that often follows stimulation. The greatest risks are associated with amphetamines, _____ , MDMA, and nicotine, but even caffeine can be a problem.

3.  _____ , known as "bennies," "dex," "go," and "uppers," are synthetic stimulants that produce a rapid drug _____ .

4.  _____ , known as "crank," "speed," "meth," or "crystal," is cheaply produced in labs and can be snorted, injected, or eaten.

5.  Repeated use of amphetamine can cause brain damage and amphetamine _____. Amphetamine psychosis can cause the abuser to act on their delusions and risk _____ -injury or injury to others.

6.  Signs of cocaine abuse are: compulsive use, loss of _____ , and the disregard for

    _____

7.  Users of MDMA are likely to risk an _____ in body temperature, liver damage, and unsafe sex. _____ brain cells may be damaged, which could increase anxiety level or lead to depression.

8.  MDMA or "Ecstasy," which is similar to _____ , has been linked with numerous deaths and with _____ impairment.

9. _____ can be found in coffee, tea, soft drinks, and chocolate. It stimulates the brain by _____ chemicals that inhibit nerve activities.

10. Nicotine (smoking) includes the added risk of _____ _____ , heart disease, and other health problems.

11. The smoking of cigarettes releases _____ (cancer-causing substances) in the air, which expose people to secondhand smoke and places them at risk for developing lung cancer.

12. Up to ninety percent of those who quit smoking _____ within one year.

# Downers—Sedatives, Tranquilizers, and Alcohol

1. Barbiturates are depressant drugs whose overdose level is close to the intoxication dosage, making them dangerous drugs. Common street names for _____ are "downers," "blue heavens," "purple hearts," "goofballs," "pink ladies," and "rainbows."

2. The _____ drug GHB ( _____ ) can cause coma, breathing failure, and death in relatively low doses. _____ is commonly called "goop," "scoop," "max," or "Georgia Home Boy."

3. _____ tranquilizers, such as Valium, are used to lower anxiety. When abused, they have a strong addictive potential.

4. _____ , a tranquilizer, also known as "roofies" and the "date-rape drug," is odorless and tasteless and is sometimes used to spike drinks.

5. Mixing barbiturates and _____ may result in a fatal drug _____ (in which the joint effect of two drugs exceeds the effects of adding one drug's effects to the other's).

6. Every year in the United States, 75,000 people die of _____ -related deaths. _____ drinking (having five or more drinks in a short time) is responsible for 14,000 college student deaths a year.

7. People who undergo _____ (the removal of poison) often experience unpleasant symptoms of drug _____ .

# Hallucinogens—Tripping the Light Fantastic

1. Marijuana is a _____ subject to an abuse pattern similar to alcohol. Studies have linked chronic marijuana use with memory impairment, _____ cancer, reproductive problems, immune system disorders, and other health problems.

2. _____ , the main active chemical in marijuana, accumulates in the _____ cortex and reproductive organs.

3. Potential problems caused by frequent marijuana use are short-term _____ loss and decline in learning, _____ , and thinking abilities. In addition, people who smoke five or more joints a week tend to score four points _____ on IQ tests.

## Psychology in Action: Exploring and Using Dreams
How can dreams be used to promote personal understanding?

1. Freud held that the meaning of dreams is hidden by the dream processes he called _____ , displacement, symbolization, and _____ elaboration.

2. Calvin Hall emphasizes the setting, _____ , plot, and emotions of a dream.

3. Rosalind Cartwright's view of dreams as _____ statements and Fritz _____ technique of speaking for dream elements are also helpful.

4. Dreams may be used for creative problem solving, especially when dream control is achieved through _____ dreaming (a dream in which the dreamer feels capable of normal thought and action).

# MASTERY TEST

1. Delirium, ecstasy, and daydreaming all have in common the fact that they are
   a. forms of normal waking consciousness.
   b. caused by sensory deprivation.
   c. perceived as subjectively real.
   d. ASCs.

2. The street drug GHB is
   a. chemically similar to morphine.
   b. a depressant.
   c. capable of raising body temperature to dangerous levels.
   d. a common cause of sleep-deprivation psychosis.

3. Which of the following does not belong with the others?
   a. nicotine
   b. caffeine
   c. cocaine
   d. codeine

4. Sleep spindles usually first appear in stage _____ , whereas delta waves first appear in stage
   _____.
   a. 1; 2
   b. 2; 3
   c. 3; 4
   d. 1; 4

5. Which of the following is NOT one of the dream processes described by Freud?
   a. condensation
   b. illumination
   c. displacement
   d. symbolization

6. Which of the following most clearly occurs under hypnosis?
   a. unusual strength
   b. memory enhancement
   c. pain relief
   d. age regression

7. Alcohol, amphetamines, cocaine, and marijuana have in common the fact that they are all
   a. physically addicting.
   b. psychoactive.
   c. stimulants.
   d. hallucinogens.

8. Emotional arousal, blood pressure changes, and sexual arousal all primarily occur during
   a. REM sleep.
   b. NREM sleep.
   c. Delta sleep.
   d. stage 4 sleep.

9. The REST technique makes use of
   a. sensory deprivation.
   b. hypodynamic imagery.
   c. hallucinogens.
   d. a CPAP mask.

10. Mesmerism, hypnosis, hypnotic susceptibility scales, and stage hypnotism all rely in part on
    a. disinhibition.
    b. rapid eye movements.
    c. suggestibility.
    d. imagery rehearsal.

11. Shortened sleep-waking cycles overlook the fact that sleep
    a. must match a 3 to 1 ratio of time awake and time asleep.
    b. is an innate biological rhythm.
    c. is caused by a sleep-promoting substance in the blood.
    d. cycles cannot be altered by external factors.

12. A focal point is to concentrative meditation as _____ is to mindfulness meditation.
    a. openness
    b. attention
    c. mantra
    d. worry

13. Which of the following statements about sleep is true?
    a. Learning math or a foreign language can be accomplished during sleep.
    b. Some people can learn to do without sleep.
    c. Calvin Hall had hallucinations during a sleep deprivation experiment.
    d. Randy Gardner slept for 14 hours after ending his sleep deprivation.

14. Amphetamine is very similar in effects to
    a. narcotics and tranquilizers.
    b. methaqualone.
    c. codeine.
    d. cocaine.

15. Microsleeps would most likely occur
    a. in stage 4 sleep.
    b. in a 3 to 1 ratio to microawakenings.
    c. in conjunction with delusions and hallucinations.
    d. during sleep deprivation.

16. Sleepwalking, sleeptalking, and severe nightmares all have in common the fact that they
    a. are REM events.
    b. are NREM events.
    c. are sleep disorders.
    d. can be controlled with imagery rehearsal phase in the development of a drinking problem.

17. In its milder forms, sensory deprivation sometimes produces
    a. cataplectic images.
    b. deep relaxation.
    c. tryptophanic images.
    d. REM symbolizations.

18. The basic suggestion effect is closely related to
    a. hypnosis.
    b. sensory enhancement after sensory deprivation.
    c. hypersomnia.
    d. the frequency of dreaming during REM sleep.

19. A person who feels awake and capable of normal action while sleeping has experienced
    a. lucid dreaming.
    b. the basic suggestion effect.
    c. sleep drunkenness.
    d. REM rebound.

20. Which of the following is a hallucinogen?
    a. LSD
    b. THC
    c. hashish
    d. all of the preceding

21. The two most basic states of sleep are
    a. stage 1 sleep and stage 4 sleep.
    b. REM sleep and NREM sleep.
    c. Alpha sleep and Delta sleep.
    d. Alpha sleep and hypnic sleep.

22. Thinking and perception become dulled in the condition known as
    a. alcohol rebound.
    b. alcohol apnea.
    c. alcohol anhedonia.
    d. alcohol myopia.

23. Learning to use a computer would most likely be slowed if you were _____ each night.
    a. deprived of a half hour of NREM sleep
    b. allowed to engage in extra REM sleep
    c. prevented from dreaming
    d. awakened three times at random

24. By definition, compulsive drug use involves
    a. dependence.
    b. experimentation.
    c. repeated overdoses.
    d. anhedonia.

25. A particularly dangerous drug interaction occurs when _____ and _____ are combined.
    a. alcohol; amphetamine
    b. barbiturates; nicotine
    c. alcohol; barbiturates
    d. amphetamine; codeine

26. Narcolepsy is an example of
    a. a night terror.
    b. a sleep disorder.
    c. a tranquilizer.
    d. an addictive drug.

27. Sleep restriction and stimulus control techniques would most likely be used to treat
    a. insomnia.
    b. narcolepsy.
    c. sleepwalking.
    d. REM behavior disorder.

28. In addition to the nicotine they contain, cigarettes release
    a. dopamine.
    b. tryptophan.
    c. noradrenaline.
    d. carcinogens.

29. Disguised dream symbols are to psychodynamic dream theory as sensory and motor messages are to
    a. the Freudian theory of dreams.
    b. the activation-synthesis hypothesis.
    c. Fritz Perls' methods of dream interpretation.
    d. paradoxical intention.

30. Which is the most frequently used drug in North America?
    a. caffeine
    b. nicotine
    c. marijuana
    d. cocaine

31. Joan is 14 years old and is experiencing _____ throughout the day because she tends to stay up late and gets up early.
    a. insomnia
    b. narcolepsy
    c. hypersomnia
    d. hypnopompic

32. Gene was awakened throughout the night for a sleep study and did not receive enough REM sleep. The next night, he was allowed to sleep without interruption. Gene would be likely to experience
    a. insomnia.
    b. REM rebound.
    c. sleep waking disorder.
    d. REM behavior disorder.

33. To impress his friends of his ability, Eric holds a string with a ring attached and mentally made the ring swing back and forth. Eric used _____ , which means that as he thought about moving the ring, he made micromuscular movements with his fingers to move the string.
    a. autosuggestion
    b. telekinesis
    c. hypnotic susceptibility
    d. stimulus control

34. Nicotine and opiates stimulate the brain by _____ neurotransmitters.
    a. eliminating
    b. blocking
    c. suppressing
    d. mimicking

35. Upon awakening from sleep, Zack cannot move and as he struggles, he feels evil presences standing over him whispering to each other. Suddenly he hears screams coming from somewhere in his bedroom. Within moments, the evil presences disappear, Zack is able to move again, and realizes the screaming was from the radio. Zack just experienced
    a. a nightmare.
    b. paradoxical hallucinations.
    c. hypnopompic hallucinations.
    d. lucid dreaming neurotransmitters.

# Solutions

## RECITE AND REVIEW

### States of Consciousness—The Many Faces of Awareness: Page 182
What is an altered state of consciousness?

1. awareness; waking
2. pattern
3. sleep; dreaming; sensory
4. normal

### Sleep—A Nice Place to Visit: Pages 182-185
What are the effects of sleep loss or changes in sleep patterns?

1. rhythm; survival
2. involuntary
3. routine
4. loss; temporary
5. Physical; sleep; sleepiness
6. Lack
7. rhythms
8. slightly more than; light; dark
9. decreases
10. Shorter; longer

### Stages of Sleep—The Nightly Roller-Coaster: Pages 185-188
Why Do We Sleep?

1. brain
2. two; brain
3. 4; waves
4. light; sleep; Delta
5. alternate
6. movement
7. dreaming
8. Dreaming
9. paralysis
10. physical; stress
11. emotional; muscles; REM

## Sleep Disturbances—Showing Nightly: Sleep Wars!: Pages 189-192

What are some sleep disorders and unusual sleep events?

1. temporary
2. lowered; Rebound
3. sleep
4. stimulus; intention

5. Sleepwalking
6. NREM; REM
7. rehearsal
8. breathing; sudden

9. six; preemie; mouth;
10. Back; backs

## Dreams—A Separate Reality?: Pages 192-194

Do dreams have meaning?

1. rebound
2. dream; stage

3. wishes
4. activation; sensory

5. Neurocognitive familiar; emotions;
6. emotions

## Hypnosis—Look into My Eyes: Pages 194-197

What is hypnosis?

1. increased
2. animal; suggestion
3. state

4. autosuggestion
5. basic; immoral
6. 8; Scale

7. pain
8. waking; deception

## Meditation and Sensory Deprivation—Chilling, the Healthy Way: Pages 197-199

Do meditation and sensory deprivation have any benefits?

1. Meditation
2. concentrative
3. relaxation

4. stimulation
5. perceptual
6. relaxation

7. habits
8. well-being

## Drug-Altered Consciousness—the High and Low of It: Pages 199-201

What are the effects of the more commonly used psychoactive drugs?

1. alter (affect or change)
2. mimicking; chemicals

3. depression; sensory
4. addiction

5. reduced; increase
6. compulsive

## Uppers—Amphetamines, Cocaine, MDMA, Caffeine, Nicotine: Pages 201-206

1. psychological
2. uppers; tolerance; crash; fatigue
3. depression; caffeine
4. crank; injected

5. psychosis; self; others
6. control; consequences
7. increase; serotonergic
8. Ecstasy

9. tea; blocking
10. Nicotine (or Smoking)

11. cancer- second-hand
12. ninety percent

## Downers—Sedatives, Tranquilizers, and Alcohol: Pages 206-210

1. depressant; blue; purple; pink
2. GHB; Georgia
3. Valium; addictive
4. Rohypnol; date
5. Drug
6. five
7. removal; withdrawal

## Hallucinogens—Tripping the Light Fantastic: Pages 210-212

1. weed; abuse
2. THC
3. memory; attention; five

## How can dreams be used to promote personal understanding?: Pages 212-215

1. hidden; processes
2. plot
3. speaking
4. creative

# CONNECTIONS

## States of Consciousness—The Many Faces of Awareness and Sleep—A Nice Place to Visit: Pages 182-185

What is an altered state of consciousness? What are the effects of sleep loss or changes in sleep patterns?

1. f
2. d
3. h
4. b
5. i
6. a
7. e
8. c
9. g

## Stages of Sleep—The Nightly Roller-Coaster: Pages 185-188

Why Do We Sleep?

1. c
2. g
3. f
4. a
5. b
6. e
7. h
8. d

## Sleep Disturbances—Showing Nightly: Sleep Wars!: Pages 189-192

What are some sleep disorders and unusual sleep events?

1. d
2. i
3. c
4. g
5. f
6. b
7. h
8. a
9. j
10. e

## Dreams—A Separate Reality?: Pages 192-194

Do dreams have meaning?

1. e
2. a
3. c
4. f
5. b
6. d

## Hypnosis—Look into My Eyes and Meditation and Sensory Deprivation—Chilling, the Healthy Way: Pages 194-199

What is hypnosis? Do meditation and sensory deprivation have any benefits?

| | | |
|---|---|---|
| 1. b | 4. a | 7. i |
| 2. f | 5. c | 8. h |
| 3. d | 6. e | 9. g |

## Drug-Altered Consciousness—the High and Low of It: Pages 199-201

What are the effects of the more commonly used psychoactive drugs?

| | | |
|---|---|---|
| 1. c | 5. b | 9. e |
| 2. h | 6. d | 10. g |
| 3. a | 7. i | |
| 4. j | 8. f | |

## Psychology in Action: Exploring and Using Dreams: Pages 212-214

How can dreams be used to promote personal understanding?

| | | |
|---|---|---|
| 1. a | 3. e | 5. b |
| 2. c | 4. d | |

# CHECK YOUR MEMORY

## States of Consciousness—The Many Faces of Awareness: Page 182

What is an altered state of consciousness?

| | | |
|---|---|---|
| 1. T | 3. T | 5. T |
| 2. T | 4. T | |

## Sleep—A Nice Plate to Visit: Pages 182-185

What are the effects of sleep loss or changes in sleep patterns?

| | | |
|---|---|---|
| 1. F | 4 F | 7. F |
| 2. T | 5 T | 8. T |
| 3. T | 6. T | 9. F |

## Stages of Sleep—The Nightly Roller-Coaster: Pages 185-188
Why Do We Sleep?

1. F
2. T
3. F
4. F

5 F
6. F
7. T
8. F

9. F
10. F
11. T

## Sleep Disturbances—Showing Nightly: Sleep Wars!: Pages 189-192
What are some sleep disorders and unusual sleep events?

1. T
2. T
3. T
4. F

5 T
6. T
7. T
8. T

9. T
10. F

## Dreams—A Separate Reality?: Pages 192-194
Do dreams have meaning?

1. T
2. F
3. F

4. F
5. T
6. F

7. T

## Hypnosis—Look into My Eyes: Pages 194-197
What is hypnosis?

1. F
2. F
3. F

4. T
5. T
6. T

7. F
8. F

## Meditation and Sensory Deprivation—Chilling, the Healthy Way: Pages 197-199
Do meditation and sensory deprivation have any benefits?

1. T
2. F

3. F
4. T

5. F
6. F

## Drug-Altered Consciousness—the High and Low of It: Pages 199-201
What are the effects of the more commonly used psychoactive drugs?

1. F
2. T
3. T
4. F
5. F

6. T
7. T
8. T
9. T
10. T

11. F
12. T
13. T
14. T
15. F

213

| 16. T | 21. T | 26. F |
|-------|-------|-------|
| 17. T | 22. T | 27. F |
| 18. F | 23. T | 28. T |
| 19. F | 24. F | 29. T |
| 20. F | 25. T | 30. T |

## Psychology in Action: Exploring and Using Dreams: Pages 212-215

How can dreams be used to promote personal understanding?

| 1. | F | 3. | F | 5. | F |
|----|---|----|---|----|---|
| 2. | T | 4. | F | 6. | F |

# FINAL SURVEY AND REVIEW

## States of Consciousness—The Many Faces of Awareness

What is an altered state of consciousness?

1. consciousness; consciousness
2. mental; activity
3. hypnosis; deprivation
4. Cultural

## Sleep—A Nice Place to Visit

What are the effects of sleep loss or changes in sleep patterns?

| 1. innate; biological | 5. Physical; hypersomnia | 9. old; age; multiple |
|-----------------------|--------------------------|------------------------|
| 2. microsleeps | 6. lack | 10. sleep; cycles |
| 3. alertness | 7. Circadian | |
| 4. psychosis; delusions | 8. sleep-waking cycle | |

## Stages of Sleep—The Nightly Roller Coaster

Why Do We Sleep?

| 1. hormone; spinal; cord | 5. 1; 4; 2; 3 | 9. Hypnopompic; awakening |
|--------------------------|----------------|----------------------------|
| 2. opposed; systems | 6. rapid; eye | 10. NREM; REM |
| 3. electroencephalograph | 7. REM; non-REM | 11. arousal; relaxation; disorder |
| 4. spindles; delta; waves | 8. stage 1; stage 1 | |

## Sleep Disturbances—Showing Nightly: Sleep Wars!

What are some sleep disorders and unusual sleep events?

| 1. chronic | 5. somnambulism; NREM | 9. six; preemie; mouth; teenager |
|------------|------------------------|-----------------------------------|
| 2. dependency | 6. NREM; REM | 10. *Back*backs |
| 3. tryptophan | 7. imagery; rehearsal | |
| 4. restriction; paradoxical | 8. apnea; Apnea; infant; death | |

# Dreams—A Separate Reality?
Do dreams have meaning?

1. REM rebound
2. REM; mental; total
3. REM; sleep
4. Hall; negative; positive
5. psychodynamic; symbols
6. synthesis; motor

# Hypnosis—Look into My Eyes
What is hypnosis?

1. suggestibility
2. Mesmer; mesmerize
3. Braid
4. Stanford
5. suggestion; involuntary
6. autosuggestion
7. relaxation
8. Stage hypnotism; simulate

# Meditation and Sensory Deprivation—Chilling, the Healthy Way
Do meditation and sensory deprivation have any benefits?

1. attention
2. mindfulness
3. meditation
4. sensory; stimulation
5. Prolonged
6. deprivation; relaxation
7. Restricted; Environmental
8. self-knowledge

# Drug-Altered Consciousness—the High and Low of It
What are the effects of the more commonly used psychoactive drugs?

1. consciousness
2. neurotransmitters
3. stimulation; depression; hallucinogens
4. dependence; dependence
5. tolerance; increase
6. recreational

# Uppers—Amphetamines, Cocaine, MDMA, Caffeine, Nicotine

1. physically; addicting
2. cocaine
3. Amphetamines; tolerance
4. Methamphetamine
5. psychosis; self
6. control; consequences
7. increase; Serotonergic
8. amphetamine; mental
9. Caffeine; blocking
10. lung; cancer
11. carcinogens

# Downers—Sedatives, Tranquilizers, and Alcohol

1. barbiturates
2. depressant; gamma-hydroxybuyrate; GHB
3. Benzodiazepine
4. Rohypnol
5. alcohol; interaction
6. alcohol; Binge
7. Alcohol; crucial
8. detoxification; withdrawal

# Hallucinogens—Tripping the Light Fantastic

1. hallucinogen; lung
2. THC; cerebral
3. memory; attention; lower

## Psychology in Action: Exploring and Using Dreams
How can dreams be used to promote personal understanding?

1. condensation; secondary
2. cast
3. feeling; Perls'
4. lucid

# MASTERY TEST

| | | |
|---|---|---|
| 1. d, p. 182 | 13. d, p. 183 | 25. c, p. 207 |
| 2. b, p. 206 | 14. d, p. 200 | 26. b, p. 192 |
| 3. d, p. 199 | 15. d, pp. 183-184 | 27. a, p. 189 |
| 4. b, p. 186 | 16. c, p. 190 | 28. d, p. 205 |
| 5. b, p. 212 | 17. b, p. 183 | 29. b, p. 192 |
| 6. c, p. 194 | 18. a, p. 195 | 30. a, p. 204 |
| 7. b, p. 199 | 19. a, p. 214 | 31. c, p. 183 |
| 8. a, p. 186 | 20. d, p. 200 | 32. b, p. 192 |
| 9. a, p. 198 | 21. b, p. 186 | 33. a, p. 194 |
| 10. c, p. 182 | 22. d, p. 207 | 34. d, p. 201 |
| 11. b, p. 183 | 23. c, p. 187 | 35. c, p. 188 |
| 12. a, p. 197 | 24. a, p. 200 | |

# Conditioning and Learning

## Chapter Overview

Learning is a relatively permanent change in behavior due to experience. Two basic forms of learning are classical conditioning and operant conditioning.

Classical conditioning is also called respondent or Pavlovian conditioning. Classical conditioning occurs when a neutral stimulus is associated with an unconditioned stimulus (which reliably elicits an unconditioned response). After many pairings of the NS and the US, the NS becomes a conditioned stimulus that elicits a conditioned response. Learning is reinforced during acquisition of a response. Withdrawing reinforcement leads to extinction (although some spontaneous recovery of conditioning may occur). It is apparent that stimulus generalization has occurred when a stimulus similar to the CS also elicits a learned response. In stimulus discrimination, people or animals learn to respond differently to two similar stimuli. Conditioning often involves simple reflex responses, but emotional conditioning is also possible.

In operant conditioning (or instrumental learning), the consequences that follow a response alter the probability that it will be made again. Positive and negative reinforcers increase responding; punishment suppresses responding; nonreinforcement leads to extinction. Various types of reinforcers and different patterns of giving reinforcers greatly affect operant learning. Four types of schedules of partial reinforcements are fixed ratio, variable ratio, fixed interval, and variable interval. Fixed ratio produces a high response rate while variable interval produces a slow and steady response rate; variable interval produces a strong resistance to extinction. Operant conditioning procedures have been used to study animal cognition.

Informational feedback (knowledge of results) also facilitates learning and performance. Antecedent stimuli (those that precede a response) influence operant learning, through stimulus generalization, discrimination, and stimulus control. Shaping, a form of operant conditioning, uses successive approximation to train animals to perform tricks.

Learning, even simple conditioning, is based on acquiring information. Higher level cognitive learning involves memory, thinking, problem solving, and language. At a simpler level, cognitive maps, latent learning, and discovery learning show that learning is based on acquiring information. Learning also occurs through observation and imitating models. Observational learning imparts large amounts of information that would be hard to acquire in other ways.

Operant principles can be applied to manage one's own behavior and to break bad habits. A mixture of operant principles and cognitive learning underlies self-regulated learning—a collection of techniques to improve learning in school.

# Learning Objectives

## *Theme: The principles of learning can be used to understand and manage behavior.*

| |
|---|
| **GQ: What is learning?** |
| LO 7.1 Define *learning* and distinguish between *associative learning* and *cognitive learning*. Define *reinforcement;* explain the role of reinforcement in conditioning; and differentiate between *antecedents* and *consequences*, and explain how they are related to *classical* and *operant conditioning*. |
| **GQ: How does classical conditioning occur?** |
| LO 7.2 Briefly describe the history of *classical conditioning* and give examples of how classical conditioning takes place, utilizing the following terms: a. *neutral stimulus* (NS); b. *conditioned stimulus* (CS); c. *unconditioned stimulus* (UCS); d. *unconditioned response* (UCR); e. *conditioned response* (CR). |
| LO 7.3 Explain how *reinforcement* occurs during the *acquisition* of a classically conditioned response; describe *higher-order conditioning*; and discuss the *informational view* of *classical conditioning*. |
| LO 7.4 Describe and give examples of the following concepts as they relate to *classical conditioning*: a. *extinction*; b. *spontaneous recovery*; c. *stimulus generalization*; and d. *stimulus discrimination*. |
| **GQ: Does conditioning affect emotions?** |
| LO 7.5 Describe the relationship between *classical conditioning* and reflex responses and explain what a *conditioned emotional response* (CER) is and how it is acquired. Include the process of *desensitization* and the concept of *vicarious classical conditioning*. |
| **GQ: How does operant conditioning occur?** |
| LO 7.6 Define *operant conditioning*, including Thorndike's *law of effect*, and differentiate between the terms *reward* and *reinforcement*. |
| LO 7.7 Explain *operant conditioning* in terms of the informational view; define response-contingent reinforcement; and describe the deterimental effect of delaying reinforcement and how *response chaining* can counteract this effect. |
| LO 7.8 Explain why *superstitious behavior* develops and why it persists; describe the process of *shaping*; and explain how *extinction* and *spontanous recovery* occur in operant conditioning and how reinforcement and extinction are involved in negative attention-seeking behavior. |
| LO 7.9 Compare and contrast *positive reinforcement*, *negative reinforcement*, and the two types of *punishment* and give an example of each. |
| **GQ: Are there different kinds of operant reinforcement?** |
| LO 7.10 Define and give examples of *primary reinforcers*, *secondary reinforcers*, *tokens*, and *social reinforcers*. Include an explanation of how *secondary reinforcers* become reinforcing. |
| LO 7.11 Define *feedback* and *knowledge of results*. Explain how conditioning techniques can be applied to energy conservation and instructional programs. Include a description of *programmed instruction*, *computer-assisted instruction*, and *serious games*. |
| **GQ: How are we influenced by patterns of reward?** |
| LO 7.12 Compare and contrast the effects of *continuous* and *partial reinforcement* and describe, give an example of, and explain the effects of the following schedules of partial reinforcement: a. *fixed ratio* (FR); b. *variable ratio* (VR); c. *fixed interval* (FI); and d. *variable interval* (VI). |
| LO 7.13 Explain the concept of *stimulus control* and describe the processes of *generalization* and *discrimination* as they relate to operant conditioning. |

| GQ: What does punishment do to behavior? |
|---|
| LO 7.14  Explain how *punishers* can be defined by their effects on behavior; discuss the three factors that reduce the effectiveness of *punishment;* and differentiate the effects of severe punishment from mild punishment. |
| LO 7.15  List the three basic tools available to control simple learning (*reinforcement, nonreinforcement,* and *punishment)* and the seven guidelines which should be followed when using *punishment*. Discuss problems associated with an overreliance on punishment. |
| GQ: What is cognitive learning? |
| LO 7.16  Define *cognitive learning*; describe the concepts of a *cognitive map* and *latent learning*; and explain the difference between *discovery learning* and *rote learning*. |
| GQ: Does learning occur by imitation? |
| LO 7.17  Discuss the four factors that determine whether *observational learning* (*modeling*) will occur; describe Bandura's Bo-Bo doll; explain why what a parent does may be more important than what a parent says; and briefly describe the general conclusion that can be drawn from studies on the effects of TV violence on children. |
| GQ: How does conditioning apply to practical problems? |
| LO 7.18  Briefly describe the seven steps in a behavioral self-management program; explain how *self-recording* and behavioral contracts can aid a self-management program; and describe five strategies for changing bad habits. Include a explanation of the *Premack principle*. |

# RECITE AND REVIEW

## What is Learning—Does Practice Make Perfect?: Pages 219-220

What is learning?

1. Learning is a relatively permanent change in_____due to experience. To understand learning we must study antecedents (events that _____responses) and consequences (events that _____ responses).

2. Classical, or respondent _____ , and instrumental or operant _____ are two basic types of learning.

3. In classical conditioning, a previously neutral _____ is associated with a stimulus that elicits a response. In operant conditioning, the pattern of voluntary _____ is altered by consequences.

4. Both types of conditioning depend on reinforcement. In classical conditioning, learning is _____ when a US follows the NS or CS. _____ reinforcement is based on the consequences that follow a response.

## Classical Conditioning—Does the Name Pavlov Ring a Bell?: Pages 220-222

How does classical conditioning occur?

1. Classical conditioning, studied by Ivan Pavlov, occurs when a _____ stimulus (NS) is associated with an unconditioned stimulus (US). The US triggers a reflex called the unconditioned _____ (UR).

2. If the NS is consistently paired with the US, it becomes a conditioned _____ (CS) capable of producing a response by itself. This response is a conditioned ( _____ ) response (CR).

## Principles of Classical Conditioning—Here's Johnny: Pages 222-224

1. During acquisition of classical conditioning, the conditioned stimulus must be consistently followed by the unconditioned _____ .

2. Higher-order conditioning occurs when a well-learned conditioned stimulus is used as if it were an unconditioned _____, bringing about further learning.

3. When the CS is repeatedly presented alone, extinction takes place. That is, _____ is weakened or inhibited.

4. After extinction seems to be complete, a rest period may lead to the temporary reappearance of a conditioned _____. This is called spontaneous recovery.

5. Through stimulus generalization, stimuli _____ to the conditioned stimulus will also produce a response.

6. Generalization gives way to _____ discrimination when an organism learns to respond to one stimulus, but not to similar stimuli.

7. From an informational view, conditioning creates expectancies (or expectations about events), which alter _____ patterns.

8. In classical conditioning, the CS creates an expectancy that the US will _____ it.

## Classical Conditioning in Humans—An Emotional Topic: Pages 224-225
Does conditioning affect emotions?

1. A reflex is an inborn, _____ -and-response connection.

2. Conditioning applies to visceral or emotional responses as well as simple _____ . As a result, _____ emotional responses (CERs) also occur.

3. Irrational fears called phobias may be CERs that are extended to a variety of situations by _____ generalization.

4. The conditioning of emotional responses can occur vicariously ( _____ ) as well as directly. Vicarious classical conditioning occurs when we _____ another person's emotional responses to a stimulus.

## Operant Conditioning—Can Pigeons Play Ping-Pong?: Pages 226-229
How does operant conditioning occur?

1. Operant conditioning (or instrumental _____ ) occurs when a voluntary action is followed by a reinforcer.

2. Reinforcement in operant conditioning _____ the frequency or probability of a response. This result is based on what Edward L. Thorndike called the law of _____ .

3. An operant reinforcer is any event that follows a _____ and _____ its probability.

4. Learning in operant conditioning is based on the expectation that a response will have a specific _____ .

5. To be effective, operant _____ must be _____ contingent.

6. Delay of reinforcement reduces its effectiveness, but long _____ of responses may be built up so that a _____ reinforcer maintains many responses.

7. Superstitious behaviors (unnecessary responses) often become part of _____ chains because they appear to be associated with reinforcement.

8. In a process called shaping, complex _____ responses can be taught by reinforcing successive approximations (ever closer matches) to a final desired response.

221

9. If an operant response is not reinforced, it may extinguish (disappear). But after extinction seems complete, it may temporarily reappear (spontaneous _____ ).

10. In positive reinforcement, _____ or a pleasant event follows a response. In negative reinforcement, a response that _____ discomfort becomes more likely to occur again.

11. Punishment _____ responding. Punishment occurs when a response is followed by the onset of an aversive event or by the removal of a positive event (response _____ ).

## Operant Reinforcers—What's Your Pleasure?: Pages 230-234
Are there different kinds of operant reinforcement?

1. Primary reinforcers are "natural," physiologically-based rewards. Intra-cranial stimulation of " _____ centers" in the _____ can also serve as a primary reinforcer.

2. Secondary reinforcers are _____ . They typically gain their reinforcing value by association with primary reinforcers or because they can be _____ for primary reinforcers. Tokens and money gain their reinforcing value in this way.

3. Human behavior is often influenced by social reinforcers, which are based on learned desires for attention and _____ from others.

4. Feedback, or knowledge of _____ , aids learning and improves performance.

5. Programmed instruction breaks learning into a series of small steps and provides immediate _____ .

6. Computer-assisted _____ (CAI) does the same, but has the added advantage of providing alternate exercises and information when needed.

7. Variations of _____ are instructional games and educational simulations.

## Partial Reinforcement—Las Vegas, a Human Skinner Box?: Pages 234-236
How are we influenced by patterns of reward?

1. Reward or reinforcement may be given continuously (after every _____ ), or on a schedule of _____ reinforcement. The study of schedules of reinforcement was begun by B. F. Skinner.

2. Partial reinforcement produces greater resistance to extinction. This is the partial reinforcement

   _____ .

3. The four most basic schedules of reinforcement are _____ ratio (FR), variable ratio (VR),

   _____ interval (FI), and variable interval (VI).

4. FR and VR schedules produce _____ rates of responding. An FI schedule produces

   moderate rates of responding with alternating periods of activity and inactivity. VI schedules

   produce _____ , steady rates of responding and strong resistance to extinction.

# Stimulus Control—Red Light, Green Light: Pages 236-238

1. Stimuli that _____ a reinforced response tend to control the response on future occasions

   (stimulus control). The effect of stimulus control can be described as _____ a stimulus,

   performing a behavior, and getting a reward.

2. Two aspects of stimulus control are generalization and _____ .

3. In generalization, an operant response tends to occur when stimuli _____ to those preceding

   reinforcement are present.

4. In discrimination, responses are given in the presence of discriminative stimuli associated with

   reinforcement ( _____ ) and withheld in the presence of stimuli associated with

   nonreinforcement ( _____ ).

# Punishment—Putting the Brakes on Behavior: Pages 238-241
What does punishment do to behavior?

1. A punisher is any consequence that _____ the frequency of a target behavior.

2. Punishment is most effective when it is _____ , consistent, and intense.

3. Mild punishment tends only to temporarily _____ responses that are also reinforced or were

   acquired by reinforcement.

4. Three basic tools used by teachers and parents to control behaviors are reinforcement, _____, and punishment, which _____ responses, causes responses to be extinguished, and _____ responses, respectively.

5. Spanking a child _____ seem to show signs of long-term effects if it is backed up with supportive parenting techniques. However, if the spanking is severe, frequent, or paired with a harsh parenting technique, spanking may _____ damage a child.

6. The undesirable side effects of punishment include the conditioning of fear; the learning of _____ and avoidance responses; and the encouragement of aggression.

7. Reinforcement and nonreinforcement are better ways to change behavior than punishment. When punishment is used, it should be _____ and combined with reinforcement of alternate _____ .

# Cognitive Learning—Beyond Conditioning: Pages 241-243
## What is cognitive learning?

1. Cognitive learning involves higher mental processes, such as understanding, knowing, or anticipating. Evidence of cognitive learning is provided by cognitive _____ (internal representations of spatial relationships) and latent (hidden) _____ .

2. Discovery learning emphasizes insight and _____ , in contrast to rote learning.

# Modeling—Do as I Do, Not as I Say: Pages 243-246
## Does learning occur by imitation?

1. Much human learning is achieved through _____ , or modeling. Observational learning is influenced by the personal characteristics of the _____ and the success or failure of the _____ behavior.

2. Observational learning involves attention, remembering, _____ , and outcome of reproduction.

3. Television characters can act as powerful _____ for observational learning. Televised violence increases the likelihood of aggression by viewers.

224

4. People who play violent video games such as Mortal Kombat are prone to act _____ toward others.

## Psychology in Action: Behavioral Self-Management—A Rewarding Project: Pages 247-248
How does conditioning apply to practical problems?

1. Operant principles can be readily applied to manage behavior in everyday settings. Self-management of behavior is based on self-reinforcement, self-recording, _____ , and behavioral contracting.

2. Prepotent, or frequent, high-probability _____ , can be used to reinforce low-frequency responses. This is known as the Premack _____ .

3. Attempts to break bad habits are aided by reinforcing alternate _____ , by extinction, breaking _____ chains, and _____ cues or antecedents.

4. In school, self-regulated_____typically involves all of the following: setting learning _____ , planning learning strategies, using self-instruction, monitoring progress, evaluating yourself, reinforcing _____ , and taking corrective action when required.

# CONNECTIONS

## What is Learning—Does Practice Make Perfect?: Pages 219-220
What is learning?

1. _____ respondent conditioning
2. _____ antecedents
3. _____ meat powder
4. _____ spontaneous recovery
5. _____ bell
6. _____ salivation
7. _____ consequences
8. _____ expectancies
9. _____ CS used as US
10. _____ desensitization
11. _____ extinction
12. _____ acquisition

a. before responses
b. Pavlov's CS
c. after responses
d. higher-order conditioning
e. Pavlovian conditioning
f. US missing
g. reinforcement period
h. UR
i. Pavlov's US
j. extinction of fear
k. informational view
l. incomplete extinction

225

## Classical Conditioning in Humans—An Emotional Topic and Operant Conditioning—Can Pigeons Play Ping-Pong?: Pages 224-229

Does conditioning affect emotions? How does operant conditioning occur?

1. _____ response cost
2. _____ shaping
3. _____ negative reinforcement
4. _____ law of effect
5. _____ Skinner
6. _____ instrumental learning
7. _____ punishment
8. _____ amygdala

a. operant conditioning
b. CER
c. time out
d. learned reinforcer
e. increased responding
f. approximations
g. decreased responding
h. Edward Thorndike

## Operant Reinforcers—What's Your Pleasure?: Pages 230-234

Are there different kinds of operant reinforcement?

1. _____ primary reinforcer
2. _____ secondary reinforcer
3. _____ token economy
4. _____ approval
5. _____ carbon footprint calculator
6. _____ CAI

a. nonlearned reinforcer
b. social reinforcer
c. Chimp-O-Mat
d. educational simulations
e. feedback on resource consumption
f. conditioning chamber

## Partial Reinforcement—Las Vegas, a Human Skinner Box?: Pages 234-236

How are we influenced by patterns of reward?

1. _____ stimulus control
2. _____ continuous reinforcement
3. _____ partial reinforcement
4. _____ fixed ratio
5. _____ variable ratio
6. _____ variable interval
7. _____ fixed interval
8. _____ study animal cognition

a. resistance to extinction
b. reinforcement schedule
c. paper due every two weeks
d. operant conditioning research
e. high response rate
f. antecedent stimuli
g. steady response rate
h. reinforce all correct responses

# Punishment—Putting the Brakes on Behavior: Pages 238-241

What does punishment do to behavior?

1. _____ punishment
2. _____ avoidance learning
3. _____ severe punishment
4. _____ escape learning
5. _____ counter conditioning
6. _____ fear and aggression

a. lying to prevent discomfort
b. side effects of punishment
c. suppresses a response
d. running away
e. reward alternate behavior
f. can stop a behavior permanently

# Cognitive Learning—Beyond Conditioning, Modeling—Do as I Do, Not as I Say, and Psychology in Action: Behavioral Self-Management—A Rewarding Project: Pages 241-248

What is cognitive learning? Does learning occur by imitation? How does conditioning apply to practical problems?

1. _____ cognitive map
2. _____ Premack principle
3. _____ observational learning
4. _____ modeling
5. _____ self-recording
6. _____ rote learning
7. _____ televised violence
8. _____ discovery learning
9. _____ latent learning

a. insight
b. imitation
c. mental image of campus
d. learning through repetition
e. Albert Bandura
f. hidden learning
g- can produce aggression
h. self-management program
i. use repeated behavior as reinforcer

# CHECK YOUR MEMORY

## What is Learning—Does Practice Make Perfect?: Pages 219-220

What is learning?

1. Learning to press the buttons on a vending machine is based on operant conditioning.

   TRUE or FALSE

2. In classical conditioning, the consequences that follow responses become associated with one another.   TRUE or FALSE

3. Getting compliments from friends could serve as reinforcement for operant learning.

   TRUE or FALSE

## Classical Conditioning—Does the Name Pavlov Ring a Bell?: Pages 220-222

How does classical conditioning occur?

1.  Ivan Pavlov studied digestion and operant conditioning in dogs.   TRUE or FALSE

2.  Pavlov used meat powder to reinforce conditioned salivation to the sound of a bell.
    TRUE or FALSE

3.  Many cancer patients unknowingly have undergone classical conditioning as they associate food
    eaten before receiving chemo treatments with the sickness generated by the treatments.
    TRUE or FALSE

4.  To reduce the chances of developing an aversion to food before undergoing chemotherapy, cancer
    patients can flavor their food with hot pepper sauce.   TRUE or FALSE

5.  During successful conditioning, the NS becomes a CS.   TRUE or FALSE

6.  During acquisition, the CS is presented repeatedly without the US.   TRUE or FALSE

7.  The optimal delay between the CS and the US is 5 to 15 seconds.   TRUE or FALSE

8.  Spontaneous recovery occurs when a CS becomes strong enough to be used like a US.
    TRUE or FALSE

9.  Discriminations are learned when generalized responses to stimuli similar to the CS are extinguished.
    TRUE or FALSE

## Principles of Classical Conditioning—Here's Johnny: Pages 224-225

Does conditioning affect emotions?

1.  Narrowing of the pupils in response to bright lights is learned in early infancy.
    TRUE or FALSE

2.  Emotional conditioning involves autonomic nervous system responses.   TRUE or FALSE

3.  Stimulus generalization helps convert some CERs into phobias.   TRUE or FALSE

4.  Pleasant music can be used as a UR to create a CER.   TRUE or FALSE

5.  To learn a CER vicariously, you would observe the actions of another person and try to imitate them.
    TRUE or FALSE

6.  Many phobias, fears that persist even when no real danger exists, may begin as unconditioned
    emotional responses.   TRUE or FALSE

## Operant Conditioning—Can Pigeons Play Ping-Pong?: Pages 226-229

How does operant conditioning occur?

1. In operant conditioning, learners actively emit responses.   TRUE or FALSE

2. Rewards are the same as reinforcers.   TRUE or FALSE

3. The Skinner box is primarily used to study classical conditioning.   TRUE or FALSE

4. Reinforcement in operant conditioning alters how frequently involuntary responses are elicited.
   TRUE or FALSE

5. Operant reinforcers are most effective when they are response-contingent.   TRUE or FALSE

6. Operant learning is most effective if you wait a minute or two after the response is over before
   reinforcing it.   TRUE or FALSE

7. Response chains allow delayed reinforcers to support learning.   TRUE or FALSE

8. Superstitious responses appear to be associated with reinforcement, but they are not.
   TRUE or FALSE

9. Teaching a pigeon to play Ping-Pong would most likely make use of the principle of response cost.
   TRUE or FALSE

10. Children who misbehave may be reinforced by attention from parents.   TRUE or FALSE

11. Negative reinforcement is a type of punishment that is used to strengthen learning.
    TRUE or FALSE

12. Putting a pair of gloves on to stop the pain caused by the cold outside air is an example of negative
    reinforcement.   TRUE or FALSE

13. You have stopped offering advice to a friend because she turned distant every time you gave her
    advice is an example of punishment.   TRUE or FALSE

14. Both response cost and negative reinforcement decrease responding.   TRUE or FALSE

## Operant Reinforcers—What's Your Pleasure?: Pages 230-234

Are there different kinds of operant reinforcement?

1. Food, water, grades, and sex are primary reinforcers.   TRUE or FALSE

2. ICS is a good example of a secondary reinforcer.   TRUE or FALSE

3. Social reinforcers are secondary reinforcers.   TRUE or FALSE

4. Attention and approval can be used to shape another person's behavior.   TRUE or FALSE

5.  The effects of primary reinforcers may quickly decline as the person becomes satiated.
    TRUE or FALSE

6.  The Chimp-O-Mat accepted primary reinforcers and dispensed secondary reinforcers.
    TRUE or FALSE

7.  7.  People are more likely to recycle used materials if they receive weekly feedback about how much they have recycled.   TRUE or FALSE

8.  CAI is another term for informational feedback.   TRUE or FALSE

9.  In sports, feedback is most effective when a skilled coach directs attention to important details.
    TRUE or FALSE

10. The final level of skill and knowledge is almost always higher following CAI than it is with conventional methods.   TRUE or FALSE

## Partial Reinforcement—Las Vegas, a Human Skinner Box?: Pages 234-236
How are we influenced by patterns of reward?

1.  Continuous reinforcement means that reinforcers are given continuously, regardless of whether or not responses are made.   TRUE or FALSE

2.  An FR-3 schedule means that each correct response produces 3 reinforcers.   TRUE or FALSE

3.  The time interval in FI schedules is measured from the last reinforced response.  TRUE or FALSE

4.  In business, commissions and profit sharing are examples of FI reinforcement.   TRUE or FALSE

5.  Antecedent stimuli tend to control when and where previously rewarded responses will occur.
    TRUE or FALSE

6.  Stimulus control refers to noticing an event occurring, performing a behavior, then getting a reward for the behavior.   TRUE or FALSE

7.  Stimulus generalization is the primary method used to train dogs to detect contraband.
    TRUE or FALSE

8.  S+ represents a discriminative stimulus that precedes a nonreinforced response.   TRUE or FALSE

## Punishment—Putting the Brakes on Behavior: Pages 238-241
What does punishment do to behavior?

1.  Like reinforcement, punishment should be response-contingent.   TRUE or FALSE

2.  Punishment is most effective if it is unpredictable.   TRUE or FALSE

3. Speeding tickets are an example of response cost.   TRUE or FALSE

4. Mild punishment causes reinforced responses to extinguish more rapidly.   TRUE or FALSE

5. Generally, punishment should be the last resort for altering behavior.   TRUE or FALSE

6. An apparatus known as a shuttle box is used to study escape and avoidance learning.
   TRUE or FALSE

7. Punishment does not have to be consistent to extinguish a behavior quickly as long as positive behaviors are reinforced.   TRUE or FALSE

8. It is usually best to provide discipline making liberal use of punishment.   TRUE or FALSE

9. For humans, avoidance learning is reinforced by a sense of relief.   TRUE or FALSE

10. Punishment frequently leads to increases in aggression by the person who is punished.
    TRUE or FALSE

# Cognitive Learning—Beyond Conditioning: Pages 241-243
## What is cognitive learning?

1. Cognitive learning involves thinking, memory, and problem solving.   TRUE or FALSE

2. Animals learning their way through a maze memorize the correct order of right and left turns to make.   TRUE or FALSE

3. Typically, reinforcement must be provided in order to make latent learning visible.
   TRUE or FALSE

4. In many situations, discovery learning produces better understanding of problems.
   TRUE or FALSE

5. Rote learning produces skills through insight and understanding.
   TRUE or FALSE

# Modeling—Do as I Do, Not as I Say: Pages 243-246
## Does learning occur by imitation?

1. Modeling is another term for discovery learning.   TRUE or FALSE

2. After a new response is acquired through modeling, normal reinforcement determines if it will be repeated.   TRUE or FALSE

3. Successful observational learning requires two steps: observing and reproducing the behavior.
   TRUE or FALSE

4. Children imitate aggressive acts performed by other people, but they are not likely to imitate cartoon characters.   TRUE or FALSE

5. Violence on television causes children to be more violent.   TRUE or FALSE

6. Playing violent video games tends to increase aggressive behavior in children and young adults.
TRUE or FALSE

## Psychology in Action: Behavioral Self-Management—A Rewarding Project: Pages 247-248
How does conditioning apply to practical problems?

1. Choosing reinforcers is the first step in behavioral self-management.
TRUE or FALSE

2. 2.   Self-recording can be an effective way to change behavior, even without using specific reinforcers.   TRUE or FALSE

3. A prepotent response is one that occurs frequently.   TRUE or FALSE

4. To use extinction to break a bad habit, you should remove, avoid, or delay the reinforcement that is supporting the habit.   TRUE or FALSE

5. It is necessary to use cues or antecedents when breaking a bad habit.   TRUE or FALSE

6. In a behavioral contract, you spell out what response chains you are going to extinguish.
TRUE or FALSE

7. Self-regulated learners actively seek feedback in both formal and informal ways.
TRUE or FALSE

# FINAL SURVEY AND REVIEW

## What is Learning—Does Practice Make Perfect?
What is learning?

1. Learning is a relatively permanent change in behavior due to experience. To understand learning we must study _____ (events that precede responses) and _____ (events that follow responses).

2. Classical, or _____ conditioning, and instrumental or _____ conditioning are two basic types of learning.

3. In classical conditioning, a previously _____ stimulus is associated with a stimulus that elicits a response. In operant conditioning, the pattern of voluntary responses is altered by _____ .

4. Both types of conditioning depend on _____ . In classical conditioning, learning is reinforced when a _____ follows the NS or CS. Operant reinforcement is based on the consequences that follow a response.

## Classical Conditioning—Does the Name Pavlov Ring a Bell?

How does classical conditioning occur?

1. Classical conditioning, studied by _____ _____ , occurs when a neutral stimulus (NS) is associated with an _____ stimulus (US). The US triggers a _____ called the unconditioned response (UR).

2. If the NS is consistently paired with the US, it becomes a _____ stimulus (CS) capable of producing a response by itself. This response is a _____ (learned) response (CR).

## Principles of Classical Conditioning—Here's Johnny

1. During acquisition of classical conditioning, the conditioned stimulus must be consistently followed by the _____ _____ .

2. _____ conditioning occurs when a well-learned conditioned stimulus is used as if it were an unconditioned stimulus, bringing about further learning.

3. When the CS is repeatedly presented alone, _____ takes place. That is, conditioning is weakened or inhibited.

4. After extinction seems to be complete, a rest period may lead to the temporary reappearance of a conditioned response. This is called _____ .

5. Through stimulus _____ , stimuli similar to the conditioned stimulus will also produce a response.

6. Generalization gives way to stimulus _____ when an organism learns to respond to one stimulus, but not to similar stimuli.

7. From an _____ view, conditioning creates expectancies (or expectations about events), which alter response patterns.

8. In classical conditioning, the _____ creates an expectancy that the _____ will follow it.

233

# Classical Conditioning in Humans—An Emotional Topic
## Does conditioning affect emotions?

1. A _____ is an inborn, stimulus-and-_____ connection.

2. Conditioning applies to visceral or emotional responses as well as simple reflexes. As a result, conditioned_____ responses (CERs) also occur.

3. Irrational fears called_____ may be CERs that are extended to a variety of situations by stimulus _____ .

4. The conditioning of emotional responses can occur secondhand as well as directly. _____ classical conditioning occurs when we observe another person's emotional responses to a stimulus.

# Operant Conditioning—Can Pigeons Play Ping-Pong?
## How does operant conditioning occur?

1. Operant conditioning (or _____ learning) occurs when a voluntary action is followed by a reinforcer.

2. Reinforcement in operant conditioning increases the frequency or _____ of a response. This result is based on what Edward L. _____ called the law of effect.

3. An operant reinforcer is any event that follows a _____ and _____ its probability.

4. Learning in operant conditioning is based on the _____ that a response will have a specific effect.

5. To be effective, operant reinforcement must be response_____ .

6. Delay of reinforcement_____ its effectiveness, but long chains of responses may be built up so that a single _____ maintains many responses.

7. _____ behaviors (unnecessary responses) often become part of response chains because they appear to be associated with reinforcement.

8. In a process called_____, complex operant responses can be taught by reinforcing successive _____ (ever closer matches) to a final desired response.

9. If an operant response is not reinforced, it may _____ (disappear). But after extinction seems complete, it may temporarily reappear ( _____ recovery).

10. In _____ reinforcement, reward or a pleasant event follows a response. In _____ reinforcement, a response that ends discomfort becomes more likely to occur again.

11. Punishment decreases responding. Punishment occurs when a response is followed by the onset of an _____ event or by the removal of a_____ event (response cost).

## Operant Reinforcers—What's Your Pleasure
### Are there different kinds of operant reinforcement?

1. _____ reinforcers are "natural," physiologically-based rewards. Intra-cranial _____ of "pleasure centers" in the brain can also serve as a primary reinforcer.

2. _____ reinforcers are learned. They typically gain their reinforcing value by association with _____ reinforcers or because they can be exchanged for _____ reinforcers. Tokens and money gain their reinforcing value in this way.

3. Human behavior is often influenced by _____ reinforcers, which are based on learned desires for attention and approval from others.

4. Feedback, or_____ of results, aids learning and improves performance.

5. Programmed _____ breaks learning into a series of small steps and provides immediate feedback.

6. _____ (CAI) does the same, but has the added advantage of providing alternate exercises and information when needed.

7. Variations of CAI are_____ games and _____ simulations.

## Partial Reinforcement—Las Vegas, A Human Skinner Box?
### How are we influenced by patterns of reward?

1. Reward or reinforcement may be given continuously (after every response), or on a _____ of partial reinforcement. The study of schedules of reinforcement was begun by B. F. _____ .

2. Partial reinforcement produces greater resistance to_____. This is the _____ reinforcement effect.

3. The four most basic schedules of reinforcement are fixed and variable _____ (FR and VR), and fixed and variable _____ (FI and VI).

235

4. _____ and _____ schedules produce high rates of responding. An _____ schedule produces moderate rates of responding with alternating periods of activity and inactivity. VI schedules produce slow, steady rates of responding and strong resistance to_____ .

# Stimulus Control—Red Light, Green Light

1. Stimuli that precede a reinforced response tend to control the response on future occasions. This is called _____ _____ .

2. The effect of stimulus control can be described as _____ a stimulus, _____ a behavior, and getting a reward.

3. Two aspects of stimulus control are_____ and _____ .

4. In_____ , an operant response tends to occur when stimuli similar to those preceding reinforcement are present.

5. In_____ , responses are given in the presence of discriminative stimuli associated with reinforcement (S+) and withheld in the presence of stimuli associated with nonreinforcement (S-).

# Punishment—Putting the Brakes on Behavior
What does punishment do to behavior?

1. A_____ is any consequence that decreases the frequency of a target behavior.

2. Punishment is most effective when it is immediate, _____, and intense.

3. Mild punishment tends only to temporarily suppress responses that are also _____ in some way.

4. Three basic tools used by teachers and parents to control behaviors are _____ , nonreinforcement, and punishment, which _____ responses, causes responses to be _____ , and suppresses responses, respectively.

5. Spanking a child does not seem to show signs of long-term effects if it is backed up with_____ parenting techniques. However, if the spanking is severe, frequent, or paired with a harsh parenting technique, spanking may _____ damage a child.

6. The undesirable side effects of punishment include the conditioning of fear; the learning of escape and _____ responses; and the encouragement of _____ against others

7. _____ and _____ are better ways to change behavior than punishment.

# Cognitive Learning—Beyond Conditioning
## What is cognitive learning?

1. Cognitive learning involves higher mental processes, such as understanding, knowing, or anticipating. Evidence of cognitive learning is provided by _____ (internal representations of spatial relationships) and _____ (hidden) learning.

2. Discovery learning emphasizes insight and understanding, in contrast to _____ learning.

# Modeling—Do as I Do, Not as I Say
## Does learning occur by imitation?

1. Much human learning is achieved through imitation, or _____ . _____ is influenced by the personal characteristics of the model and the success or failure of the model's behavior.

2. _____ learning involves attention, remembering, reproduction, and outcome of reproduction.

3. Television characters can act as powerful models for _____ learning. Televised violence increases the likelihood of aggression by viewers.

4. People who play violent video games such as Mortal Kombat are prone to act _____ toward others.

# Psychology in Action: A Rewarding Project
## How does conditioning apply to practical problems?

1. Operant principles can be readily applied to manage behavior in everyday settings. Self-management of behavior is based on self-reinforcement, self-recording, feedback, and behavioral _____ .

2. Prepotent, or frequent, high-probability responses, can be used to _____ low-frequency responses. This is known as the _____ principle.

3. Attempts to break bad habits are aided by reinforcing _____ responses, by extinction, breaking response _____ , and removing cues or _____ .

237

4. In school, self-regulated learning typically involves all of the following: setting learning goals, planning learning _____ , using self-instruction, monitoring progress, evaluating yourself, _____ successes, and taking corrective action when required.

# MASTERY TEST

1. Tokens are a good example of
   a. secondary reinforcers.
   b. the effects of ICS on behavior.
   c. noncontingent reinforcers.
   d. generalized reinforcers.

2. The principle of feedback is of particular importance to
   a. CERs.
   b. ICS.
   c. CAI.
   d. higher-order conditioning.

3. As a coffee lover, you have become very efficient at carrying out the steps necessary to make a cup of espresso. Your learning is an example of
   a. response chaining.
   b. spontaneous recovery.
   c. vicarious reinforcement.
   d. secondary reinforcement.

4. To teach a pet dog to use a new dog door, it would be helpful to use
   a. the Premack principle.
   b. shaping.
   c. respondent conditioning.
   d. delayed reinforcement.

5. To test for the presence of classical conditioning, you would omit the
   a. CS.
   b. US.
   c. CR.
   d. S+.

6. Which of the following does not belong with the others?
   a. Thorndike
   b. Skinner
   c. Pavlov
   d. instrumental learning

7. To teach a child to say "Please" when she asks for things, you should make getting the requested item
    a. the CS.
    b. a token.
    c. a negative reinforcer.
    d. response contingent.

8. Money is to secondary reinforcer as food is to
    a. ICS.
    b. prepotent responses.
    c. primary reinforcer.
    d. negative reinforcer.

9. Whether a model is reinforced has a great impact on
    a. discovery learning.
    b. latent learning.
    c. observational learning.
    d. self-regulated learning.

10. One thing that classical and operant conditioning have in common is that both
    a. were discovered by Pavlov.
    b. depend on reinforcement.
    c. are affected by the consequences of making a response.
    d. permanently change behavior.

11. To shape the behavior of a teacher in one of your classes, you would probably have to rely on
    a. tokens.
    b. primary reinforcers.
    c. negative attention seeking.
    d. social reinforcers.

12. The concept that best explains persistence at gambling is
    a. partial reinforcement.
    b. continuous reinforcement.
    c. fixed interval reinforcement.
    d. fixed ratio reinforcement.

13. Which of the following is NOT a common side effect of mild punishment?
    a. escape learning
    b. avoidance learning
    c. aggression
    d. accelerated extinction

14. With respect to televised violence, it can be said that TV violence
    a. causes viewers to be more aggressive.
    b. makes aggression more likely.
    c. has no effect on the majority of viewers.
    d. vicariously lowers aggressive urges.

15. Which of the following types of learning is most related to the consequences of making a response?
    a. Pavlovian conditioning
    b. classical conditioning
    c. operant conditioning
    d. respondent conditioning

16. Which combination would most likely make a CER into a phobia?
    a. CER-discrimination
    b. CER-desensitization
    c. CER-response cost
    d. CER-generalization

17. Many people were traumatized by watching media coverage of the September 11th terrorist attacks. This is an example of
    a. avoidance learning.
    b. escape learning.
    c. vicarious extinction.
    d. vicarious conditioning.

18. A loud, unexpected sound causes a startle reflex; thus, a loud sound could be used as an _____ in conditioning.
    a. NS
    b. CR
    c. UR
    d. US

19. Antecedents are to _____ as consequences are to _____.
    a. discriminative stimuli; reinforcers
    b. shaping; response chaining
    c. conditioned stimuli; cognitive maps
    d. punishment; negative reinforcement

20. The use of self-recording to change personal behavior is closely related to the principle of
    a. response chaining.
    b. feedback.
    c. two-factor reinforcement.
    d. stimulus control.

21. _____ typically only temporarily suppresses reinforced responses.
    a. Negative reinforcement
    b. Extinction
    c. Mild punishment
    d. Stimulus generalization

240

22. In general, the highest rates of responding are associated with
    a. delayed reinforcement.
    b. variable reinforcement.
    c. interval reinforcement.
    d. fixed ratio reinforcement.

23. A child who has learned, through classical conditioning, to fear sitting in a dentist's chair becomes frightened when he is placed in a barber's chair. This illustrates the concept of
    a. stimulus generalization.
    b. spontaneous recovery.
    c. higher-order discrimination.
    d. vicarious conditioning.

24. The informational view of learning places emphasis on the creation of mental
    a. expectancies.
    b. reinforcement schedules.
    c. contracts.
    d. antecedents.

25. For some adults, blushing when embarrassed or ashamed is probably a _____ first formed in childhood.
    a. conditioned stimulus
    b. CAI
    c. discriminative stimulus
    d. CER

26. Learning to obey traffic signals is related to the phenomenon called
    a. stimulus control.
    b. spontaneous recovery.
    c. avoidance learning.
    d. modeling.

27. To be most effective, punishment should be combined with
    a. response costs.
    b. aversive stimuli.
    c. delayed feedback.
    d. reinforcement.

28. Involuntary responses are to _____ conditioning as voluntary responses are to _____ conditioning.
    a. classical; respondent
    b. classical; operant
    c. operant; classical
    d. operant; instrumental

29. Negative attention seeking by children demonstrates the impact of _____ on behavior.
    a.  operant extinction
    b.  social reinforcers
    c.  response costs
    d.  prepotent responses

30. Which consequence increases the probability that a response will be repeated?
    a.  punishment
    b.  response cost
    c.  nonreinforcement
    d.  negative reinforcement

31. Successive approximations are used in _____ to train animals to perform tricks.
    a.  observational conditioning
    b.  classical conditioning
    c.  shaping
    d.  latent learning

32. Putting on a pair of gloves to stop your hands from hurting while working in the cold weather demonstrates
    a.  positive reinforcement.
    b.  negative reinforcement.
    c.  punishment.
    d.  response cost.

33. Wanting to do some light reading while his roommate drove, Cody picked up a magazine. After a few minutes, Cody felt nauseated and had to stop reading. To avoid getting sick in the future, Cody no longer reads while riding in a car. This illustrates
    a.  positive reinforcement.
    b.  negative reinforcement.
    c.  punishment.
    d.  response cost.

34. Introducing an energy tax to reduce people's tendency to waste energy or polluting the environment utilizes _____ , a form of operant conditioning.
    a.  positive reinforcement
    b.  negative reinforcement
    c.  punishment
    d.  response cost

35. _____ gives students enough freedom and guidance to actively think and gain knowledge.
    a.  Guided discovery
    b.  Latent discovery
    c.  Observational learning
    d.  Classical learning

36. Which of the following is the correct sequence when using observational learning?
    a. attention, rewards, reproduction, and remembering
    b. attention, remembering, reproduction, and rewards
    c. rewards, remembering, attention, and reproduction
    d. remembering, rewards, attention, and reproduction

37. Increased aggression and violence among children and adolescents has been attributed to
    a. watching violent TV programs.
    b. playing violent video games.
    c. imitating others' aggressive behaviors.
    d. all the preceding.

38. Before going in for his first chemotherapy, Blake had a bread bowl crab soup from his favorite soup and sandwich shop. After his session, he gets nauseous and vomits as a result of the chemotherapy. Since then, Blake cannot eat crab soup as it makes him nauseous. In this example, the unconditioned stimulus is _____ and the conditioned stimulus is _____ .
    a. crab soup; nausea
    b. soup and sandwich shop; crab soup
    c. chemotherapy; crab soup
    d. chemotherapy; nausea

# SOLUTIONS

## RECITE AND REVIEW

### What Is Learning—Does Practice Make Perfect?: Pages 219-220
What is learning?

1. behavior; precede; follow
2. conditioning; conditioning
3. stimulus; responses
4. reinforced; Operant

### Classical Conditioning—Does the Name Pavlov Ring a Bell?: Pages 220-222
How does classical conditioning occur?

1. neutral; response
2. stimulus; learned

### Principles of Classical Conditioning—Here's Johnny: Pages 222-224

1. stimulus
2. stimulus
3. conditioning
4. response
5. similar
6. stimulus
7. response
8. follow

## Classical Conditioning in Humans—An Emotional Topic: Pages 224-225

Does conditioning affect emotions?

1. stimulus
2. reflexes; conditioned
3. stimulus
4. secondhand; observe

## Operant Conditioning—Can Pigeons Play Ping-Pong?: Pages 226-229

How does operant conditioning occur?

1. learning
2. increases; effect
3. response; increases
4. effect
5. reinforcement; response
6. chains; single
7. response
8. operant
9. recovery
10. reward; ends
11. decreases; cost

## Operant Reinforcers—What's Your Pleasure?: Pages 230-234

Are there different kinds of operant reinforcement?

1. pleasure; brain
2. learned; exchanged
3. approval
4. results
5. feedback
6. instruction
7. CAI

## Partial Reinforcement—Las Vegas, a Human Skinner Box?: Pages 234-236

How are we influenced by patterns of reward?

1. response; partial
2. effect
3. fixed; fixed
4. high; slow

## Stimulus Control—Red Light, Green Light: Pages 236-238

1. precede; noticing
2. discrimination
3. similar
4. S+; S-

## Punishment—Putting the Brakes on Behavior: Pages 238-241

What does punishment do to behavior?

1. decreases
2. immediate
3. suppress
4. nonreinforcement; strengthens; suppresses
5. does not; emotionally
6. escape
7. mild; responses

## Cognitive Learning—Beyond Conditioning: Pages 241-243

What is cognitive learning?

1. maps; learning
2. understanding

## Modeling—Do as I Do, Not as I Say: Pages 243-246
Does learning occur by imitation?

1. imitation; model; model's
2. reproduction
3. models
4. aggressively

## Psychology in Action: Behavioral Self-Management—A Rewarding Project: Pages 247-248
How does conditioning apply to practical problems?

1. feedback
2. responses; principle
3. responses; response; removing
4. learning; goals; successes

# CONNECTIONS

## What is Learning—Does Practice Make Perfect and Classical Conditioning—Does the Name Pavlov Ring a Bell?: Pages 219-222
What is learning? How does classical conditioning occur?

1. e
2. a
3. i
4. l
5. b
6. h
7. c
8. k
9. d
10. j
11. g
12. g

## Principles of Classical Conditioning—Here's Johnny and Classical Conditioning in Humans—An Emotional Topic: Pages 224-229
Does conditioning affect emotions? How does operant conditioning occur?

1. c
2. f
3. e
4. h
5. d
6. a
7. g
8. b

## Operant Reinforcers—What's Your Pleasure?: Pages 230-234
Are there different kinds of operant reinforcement?

1. a
4. b
2. f
5. e
3. c
6. d

## Partial Reinforcement—Las Vegas, a Human Skinner Box?: Pages 234-236
How are we influenced by patterns of reward?

1. f
2. h
3. a
4. e
5. c
6. g
7. b
8. d

## Punishment—Putting the Brakes on Behavior: Pages 238-241
What does punishment do to behavior?

| | | |
|---|---|---|
| 1. c | 3. f | 5. e |
| 2. a | 4. d | 6. b |

## Cognitive Learning—Beyond Conditioning, Modeling—Do as I Do, Not as I Say, and Psychology in Action: Behavioral Self-Management—A Rewarding Project: Pages 241-248
What is cognitive learning? Does learning occur by imitation? How does conditioning apply to practical problems?

| | | |
|---|---|---|
| 1. c | 4. b | 7. g |
| 2. i | 5. h | 8. a |
| 3. e | 6. d | 9. f |

# CHECK YOUR MEMORY

## What Is Learning—Does Practice Make Perfect?: Pages 219-220
What is learning?

| | | |
|---|---|---|
| 1. T | 2. F | 3. T |

## Classical Conditioning—Does the Name Pavlov Ring a Bell?: Pages 220-222
How does classical conditioning occur?

| | | |
|---|---|---|
| 1. F | 4. F | 7. F |
| 2. T | 5. T | 8. F |
| 3. T | 6. F | 9. T |

## Classical Conditioning in Humans—An Emotional Topic: Pages 224-225
Does conditioning affect emotions?

| | | |
|---|---|---|
| 1. F | 3. T | 5. F |
| 2. T | 4. F | 6. T |

## Operant Conditioning—Can Pigeons Play Ping-Pong?: Pages 226-229
How does operant conditioning occur?

| | | |
|---|---|---|
| 1. T | 7. T | 13. T |
| 2. F | 8. T | 14. F |
| 3. F | 9. F | |
| 4. F | 10. T | |
| 5. T | 11. F | |
| 6. F | 12. T | |

## Operant Reinforcers—What's Your Pleasure?: Pages 230-234
Are there different kinds of operant reinforcement?

| | | | | | |
|---|---|---|---|---|---|
| 1. | F | 5. | T | 9. | T |
| 2. | F | 6. | F | 10. | F |
| 3. | T | 7. | T | | |
| 4. | T | 8. | F | | |

## Partial Reinforcement—Las Vegas, a Human Skinner Box?: Pages 234-236
How are we influenced by patterns of reward?

| | | | | | |
|---|---|---|---|---|---|
| 1. | F | 4. | F | 7. | F |
| 2. | F | 5. | T | 8. | F |
| 3. | T | 6. | T | | |

## Punishment—Putting the Brakes on Behavior: Pages 238-241
What does punishment do to behavior?

| | | | | | |
|---|---|---|---|---|---|
| 1. | T | 5. | T | 9. | T |
| 2. | F | 6. | T | 10. | T |
| 3. | T | 7. | F | | |
| 4. | F | 8. | F | | |

## Cognitive Learning—Beyond Conditioning: Pages 241-243
What is cognitive learning?

| | | | | | |
|---|---|---|---|---|---|
| 1. | T | 3. | T | 5. | F |
| 2. | F | 4. | T | | |

## Modeling—Do as I Do, Not as I Say: Pages 243-246
Does learning occur by imitation?

| | | | | | |
|---|---|---|---|---|---|
| 1. | F | 3. | F | 5. | F |
| 2. | T | 4. | F | 6. | T |

## Psychology in Action: Behavioral Self-Management—A Rewarding Project: Pages 247-248
How does conditioning apply to practical problems?

| | | | | | |
|---|---|---|---|---|---|
| 1. | F | 4. | T | 7. | T |
| 2. | T | 5. | F | | |
| 3. | T | 6. | F | | |

# FINAL SURVEY AND REVIEW

## What Is Learning—Does Practice Make Perfect?
What is learning?

1. antecedents; consequences
2. respondent; operant
3. neutral; consequences
4. reinforcement; US

## Classical Conditioning—Does the Name Pavlov Ring a Bell?
How does classical conditioning occur?

1. Ivan; Pavlov; unconditioned; reflex
2. conditioned; conditioned

## Principles of Classical Conditioning—Here's Johnny

1. unconditioned; stimulus
2. Higher-order
3. extinction
4. spontaneous recovery
5. generalization
6. discrimination
7. informational
8. CS; US

## Classical Conditioning in Humans—An Emotional Topic
Does conditioning affect emotions?

1. reflex; response
2. emotional
3. phobia; generalization
4. Vicarious

## Operant Conditioning—Can Pigeons Play Ping-Pong?
How does operant conditioning occur?

1. instrumental
2. probability; Thorndike
3. response; increases
4. expectation
5. contingent
6. reduces; reinforcer
7. Superstitious
8. shaping; approximations
9. extinguish; spontaneous
10. positive; negative
11. aversive; positive

## Operant Reinforcers—What's Your Pleasure?
Are there different kinds of operant reinforcement?

1. Primary; stimulation
2. Secondary; primary; primary
3. social
4. knowledge
5. instruction
6. Computer-assisted instruction
7. instructional; educational

## Partial Reinforcement—Las Vegas, a Human Skinner Box?
How are we influenced by patterns of reward?

1. schedule; Skinner
2. extinction; partial
3. ratio; interval
4. FR; VR; FI; extinction

248

## Stimulus Control—Red Light, Green Light

1. stimulus; control
2. noticing; performing
3. generalization; discrimination
4. generalization
5. discrimination

## Punishment—Putting the Brakes on Behavior
What does punishment do to behavior?

1. punisher
2. consistent
3. reinforced
4. reinforcement; strengthens; extinguished
5. supportive; emotionally
6. avoidance; aggression
7. Reinforcement; nonreinforcement

## Cognitive Learning—Beyond Conditioning
What is cognitive learning?

1. cognitive; maps; latent
2. rote

## Modeling—Do as I Do, Not as I Say
Does learning occur by imitation?

1. modeling; Observational; teaming
2. Observational
3. observational
4. aggressively

## Psychology in Action: Behavioral Self-Management—A Rewarding Project
How does conditioning apply to practical problems?

1. contracting
2. reinforce; Premack
3. alternate; chains; antecedents
4. strategies; reinforcing

# MASTERY TEST

1. a, p. 230
2. c, p. 232
3. a, p. 227
4. b, p. 228
5. b, p. 220
6. c, p. 226
7. d, p. 227
8. c, p. 230
9. c, p. 243
10. b, p. 219
11. d, p. 231
12. a, p. 234
13. d, p. 239
14. b, p. 245

15. c, p. 220
16. d, p. 224
17. d, p. 225
18. d, p. 221
19. a, p. 237
20. b, p. 230
21. c, p. 238
22. d, p. 236
23. a, p. 223
24. a, p. 222
25. d, p. 224
26. a, p. 236
27. d, p. 229
28. b, p. 224

29. b, p. 229
30. d, p. 229
31. c, p. 228
32. b, p. 229
33. c, p. 229
34. d, p. 229
35. a, p. 243
36. b, p. 243
37. d, p. 245
38. c, p. 221

# Memory

## Chapter Overview

Remembering is an active process. Memories are frequently lost, altered, revised, or distorted. Memory systems allow us to encode, store, and retrieve information. The three stages of memory hold information for increasingly longer periods. The best way to remember depends partly on which memory system you are using. Sensory memories are encoded as iconic memories or echoic memories. Short-term memories tend to be encoded by sound, and long-term memories by meaning.

Short-term memory briefly holds small amounts of information in conscious awareness. Selective attention determines what information moves from sensory memory on to STM. STM has a capacity of about 5 to 7 bits of information, but this limit can be extended by chunking. Short-term memories are brief and very sensitive to interruption or interference but can be kept alive by maintenance rehearsal.

Long-term memory stores large amounts of meaningful information for long periods of time. LTM serves as a general storehouse for meaningful information. Elaborative encoding helps us form long-term, relatively permanent memories. LTM seems to have an almost unlimited storage capacity. Constructive processing tends to alter memories. LTM is highly organized. Current research explores the structure of memory networks. In redintegration, memories are reconstructed, as one bit of information leads to others, which then serve as cues for further recall. LTM contains procedural and declarative memories. Declarative memories can be semantic or episodic.

Memories may be revealed by recall, recognition, relearning, or priming. The tip-of-the-tongue state shows that memory is not an all-or-nothing event. Recall, recognition, and relearning mainly measure explicit memories. Other techniques, such as priming, are necessary to reveal implicit memories.

Forgetting can occur because of failures of encoding, of storage, or of retrieval. Forgetting occurs most rapidly immediately after learning. Failure to encode information is a common cause of "forgetting." Forgetting in sensory memory and STM is due to a failure of storage through a decay of memory traces. Decay of memory traces may also explain some LTM losses. Failures of retrieval occur when information that resides in memory is not retrieved. A lack of memory cues can produce retrieval failure. State-dependent learning is related to the effects of memory cues. Much forgetting in STM and LTM is caused by retroactive and proactive interference. Memories can be consciously suppressed or may be unconsciously repressed. Extreme caution is warranted when evaluating "recovered" memories.

Lasting memories are recorded by changes in the activity, structure, and chemistry of brain cells. It takes time to consolidate memories. In the brain, memory consolidation takes place in the hippocampus. Intensely emotional experiences can result in flashbulb memories. After memories have been consolidated, they appear to be stored in the cortex of the brain.

"Photographic" memory (eidetic imagery) occurs when a person is able to project an image onto a blank surface. Some people have naturally superior memories, but everyone can learn to improve his or her memory. Eidetic imagery is rarely found in adults. However, many adults have internal memory images, which can be very vivid. Exceptional memory may be based on natural ability or learned strategies. Usually it involves both.

Excellent memory abilities are based on using strategies and techniques that make learning efficient and that compensate for natural weaknesses in human memory. Memory can be improved by using feedback, recitation, and rehearsal, by selecting and organizing information, and by using the progressive part method, spaced practice, overlearning, and active search strategies. When you are learning, you should also keep in mind the effects of serial position, sleep, review, cues, and elaboration.

Memory systems (mnemonics) greatly improve immediate memory. However, conventional learning tends to create the most lasting memories. Mnemonic systems use mental images and unusual associations to link new information with familiar memories already stored in LTM. Effective mnemonics tend to rely on mental images and bizarre or exaggerated mental associations.

# Learning Objectives

### Theme: Memory is not like a tape recorder or a video camera: Memories change as they are stored and retrieved.

| |
|---|
| **GQ: How does memory work?** |
| LO 8.1  Define *memory* and explain the three stages of memory. Describe the three memory stores as specified in the Atkinson-Schiffrin model. |
| LO 8.2  Describe *sensory memory*, including how *iconic memories* and *echoic memories* function in this memory system, and explain how information is transferred from *sensory memory* to *short-term memory*. |
| LO 8.3  Describe *short-term memory* in terms of capacity, how information is encoded, permanence, and susceptibility to interference. Include the concept of *working memory*. |
| LO 8.4  Describe *long-term memory* in terms of permanence, capacity and the basis on which information is stored; explain how one's culture affects memory and the relationship between *short-term* and *long-term memory*. |
| **GQ: What are the features of short-term memory?** |
| LO 8.5  Explain the "magic number" seven; describe *chunking*; and explain how the two types of *rehearsal* affect memory. |
| **GQ: What are the features of long-term memory?** |
| LO 8.6  Discuss the permanence of memory including the work of Penfield and the Loftuses. |
| LO 8.7  Explain how memories are constructed. Include the concepts of *constructive processing* and pseudo-memories. Apply thse ideas to the memory jamming theory of advertising. |
| LO 8.8  Discuss the effects of hypnosis on memory and how a *cognitive interview* can improve eyewitness memories. |
| LO 8.9  Briefly describe how long-term memories are organized, including the *network model* and *redintegrative memories*. |
| LO 8.10  Differentiate *procedural* (skill) *memory* from *declarative* (fact) *memory* and define and give examples of the two kinds of *declarative memory* (*semantic* and *episodic*). |
| **GQ: How is memory measured?** |
| LO 8.11  Explain the *tip-of-the tongue phenomenon* (including the *feeling of knowing* and déjà vu). |
| LO 8.12  Describe and give an example of each of the following ways of measuring memory: a. *recall* (include the *serial position effect*); b. *recognition* (compare to *recall* and include the concept of distractors); c. *relearning* (include the concept of savings). |
| LO 8.13  Distinguish between *explicit* and *implicit* memories. Include a discussion of *priming*. |

| |
|---|
| **GQ: Why do we forget?** |
| LO 8.14 Explain Ebbinghaus' *curve of forgetting*. |
| LO 8.15 Discuss the following explanations of forgetting: a. *encoding failure*; b. storage failure, including *decay* and *disuse*; and c. retrieval failure, including *cue-dependent forgetting*; *state-dependent learning*; *interference* (list and explain the two types of interference and how they are investigated in the laboratory); *positive* and *negative transfer:* and *repression* (differentiate it from *suppression*). |
| LO 8.16 Describe the false memory syndrome. |
| **GQ: How does the brain form and store memories?** |
| LO 8.17 Describe *retrograde* and *anterograde amnesia,* and the role of *consolidation* in memory, including the effects of ECS. Describe how *flashbulb memories* are formed. |
| LO 8.18 Name the structure in the brain that is responsible for switching information from STM to LTM. Include a discussion of the engram and the relationship between learning and neurotransmitters. |
| **GQ: What are "photographic" memories?** |
| LO 8.19 Describe the concepts of *internal imagery* and *eidetic imagery* and their effects on long-term memory and explain how these abilities are different from having an exceptional memory. |
| **GQ: How can I improve my memory?** |
| LO 8.20 Describe how each of the following encoding strategies can improve memory: a. *rehearsal*; b. selection; c. organization; d. whole versus part learning; e. *serial position effect;* f. cues; g. *overlearning*; and h. *spaced practice*. |
| LO 8.21 Describe how each of the following encoding strategies can improve memory: a. recitation (including knowledge of results); b. review; c. strategies to aid recall (including the *cognitive interview*); d. extension of memory intervals; e. sleep; and f. hunger. |
| **GQ: Are there any tricks to help me with my memory?** |
| LO 8.22 Define *mnemonic;* explain four basic principles of using mnemonics; and three techniques for using mnemonics to remember things in order. |

# RECITE AND REVIEW

## Stages of Memory—Do You Have a Mind Like a Steel Trap? Or a Sieve?: Pages 252-255

How does memory work?

1. Memory is an active _____ . _____ is first encoded (changed into the form in which it will be retained).

2. Next it is _____ in memory. Later it must be retrieved to be put to use.

3. Humans appear to have _____ interrelated memory systems. These are sensory memory, _____ memory (STM), and _____ memory (LTM).

4. Sensory memory holds an _____ copy of what is seen or heard, in the form of an icon ( _____ ) or echo (sound sensation).

5. Short-term memories tend to be stored as _____ . Long-term memories are stored on the basis of _____ , or importance.

6. STM acts as a _____ storehouse for small amounts of information. It provides a working memory where thinking, mental arithmetic, and the like take place. LTM acts as a_____ storehouse for meaningful information.

7. Cultural values impact the types of_____we tend to store. American culture emphasizes the individual; therefore, American memories are _____-focused. The Chinese culture emphasizes group membership; therefore, Chinese memories are of social events, which include _____ members, friends, and others.

## Short-Term Memory—Do You Know the Magic Number?: Pages 255-256
What are the features of short-term memory?

1. Sensory memory is exact, but very brief, lasting only a few _____ or less. Through selective attention, some information is transferred to _____ .

2. The digit-span test reveals that STM has an average upper limit of about 7 _____of information. However, this can be extended by chunking, or recoding information into _____ units or groups.

3. The "_____ number" 7 (plus or minus 2) refers to the limitation of _____ memory discovered by George Miller. Nelson Cowan believes that the limitation of short-term memory is_____ than the "magic number" 7.

4. Short-term memories are brief and very sensitive to _____ , or interference; however, they can be prolonged by maintenance rehearsal (silent_____ ).

5. Elaborative rehearsal, which emphasizes meaning, helps transfer information from _____ to LTM. Elaborative rehearsal links new information with existing _____ and is superior to _____ learning.

## Long-Term Memory—Where the Past Lives: Pages 256-261
What are the features of long-term memory?

1. LTM seems to have an almost unlimited storage capacity. However, LTM is subject to constructive processing, or ongoing revision and _____ . As a result, people often have pseudo-memories ( _____ memories) that they believe are true.

2. LTM is highly_____ to allow retrieval of needed information. The pattern, or structure, of memory networks is the subject of current memory research. Network_____ portray LTM as a system of linked ideas.

3. Redintegrative memories unfold as each added memory provides a cue for retrieving the next _____ . Seemingly forgotten memories may be reconstructed in this way.

4. Within long-term memory, declarative memories for _____ seem to differ from procedural memories for _____ .

5. _____ memories may be further categorized as semantic memories or episodic memories.

6. Semantic memories consist of basic factual knowledge that is almost immune to _____ .

7. Episodic memories record _____ experiences that are associated with specific times and places.

8. _____ may lead to memory jamming, which can lead people to remember enjoying a product more than they actually did.

# Measuring Memory—The Answer Is on the Tip of My Tongue: Pages 261-264

How is memory measured?

1. The tip-of-the-tongue _____ shows that memory is not an all-or-nothing event. Memories may be revealed by _____ , recognition, or relearning.

2. In recall, memory proceeds without specific cues, as in an _____ exam. Recall of listed information often reveals a serial position effect ( _____ items on the list are most subject to errors).

3. A common test of _____ is the multiple-choice question. _____ is very sensitive to the kinds of distractors (wrong choices) used.

4. In relearning, "forgotten" material is learned again, and memory is indicated by a _____ score.

5. Recall, recognition, and relearning mainly measure explicit _____ that we are aware of having. Other techniques, such as priming, are necessary to reveal implicit_____ , which are unconscious.

# Forgetting in LTM—Why We, uh, Let's See; Why We, uh…Forget!: Pages 264-270

Why do we forget?

1. Forgetting and memory were extensively studied by Herman Ebbinghaus, whose _____ of forgetting shows that forgetting is typically most rapid immediately _____ learning.

2. Ebbinghaus used nonsense syllables to study memory. The forgetting of _____ material is much _____ than shown by his curve of forgetting.

3. Failure to encode _____ is a common cause of "forgetting."

4. Forgetting in sensory memory and STM probably reflects decay of memory _____ in the nervous system. Decay or _____ of memories may also account for some LTM loss, but most forgetting cannot be explained this way.

5. Often, forgetting is cue dependent. The power of cues to trigger memories is revealed by state-dependent _____, in which bodily _____ at the time of learning and of retrieval affect memory.

6. Much _____ in both STM and LTM can be attributed to interference of memories with one another.

7. When recent learning _____ with retrieval of prior learning, retroactive interference has occurred. If old memories _____ with new memories, proactive interference has occurred.

8. Repression is the _____ of painful, embarrassing, or traumatic memories.

9. Repression is thought to be unconscious, in contrast to suppression, which is a attempt to avoid thinking about something.

10. Experts are currently debating the validity of childhood memories of _____ that reappear after apparently being repressed for decades.

11. Independent evidence has verified that some recovered memories are _____ . However, others have been shown to be _____ .

12. In the absence of confirming or disconfirming _____ , there is currently no way to separate true memories from fantasies. Caution is advised for all concerned with attempts to retrieve supposedly hidden memories.

# Memory and the Brain—Some "Shocking" Findings: Pages 270-273

How does the brain form and store memories?

1. Retrograde_____ and the effects of electroconvulsive_____ (ECS) may be explained by the concept of consolidation.

2. Consolidation theory holds that engrams (permanent _____ ) are formed during a critical period after learning. Until they are consolidated, long-term memories are easily destroyed.

3. The hippocampus is a_____structure associated with the consolidation of memories.

4. Flashbulb memories, which seem especially vivid, are created at emotionally significant times. While such memories may not be accurate, we tend to place great _____ in them.

5. The search within the brain for engrams has now settled on changes in individual _____ cells.

6. The best-documented changes are alterations in the amounts of transmitter _____released by nerve cells.

7. Forming lasting memories depend on _____ potentiation which occurs when a connection between two brain cells grows stronger as they become more _____ at the same time. These cells will then respond more strongly to incoming messages from other cells.

# Exceptional Memory—Wizards of Recall: Pages 273-275

What are "photographic" memories?

1. Eidetic imagery (photographic memory) occurs when a person is able to project an _____onto an external surface. Such images allow brief, nearly complete recall by some children.

2. Eidetic imagery is rarely found in _____ . However, many adults have internal images, which can be very vivid and a basis for remembering.

3. Exceptional memory can be learned by finding ways to directly store information in_____ . Learning has no effect on the limits of _____ . Some people may have naturally superior memory abilities that exceed what can be achieved through learning.

## Improving Memory—Keys to the Memory Bank: Pages 275-278

How can I improve my memory?

1. Memory can be improved by using feedback, recitation, and rehearsal, by selecting

   and _____ information, and by using the progressive _____ method, spaced practice,

   overlearning, and active search strategies.

2. The effects of serial _____ , sleep, review, cues, and elaboration should also be kept in
   mind when studying or memorizing.

## Psychology in Action: Mnemonics—Memory Magic: Pages 279-280

Are there any tricks to help me with my memory?

1. Mnemonic techniques avoid rote learning and work best during the_____ stages of
   learning.

2. Mnemonic systems, such as the_____ method, use mental images and unusual associations
   to link new information with familiar memories already stored in_____ . Such strategies
   give information personal meaning and make it easier to recall.

# CONNECTIONS

## Stages of Memory—Do You Have a Mind Like a Steel Trap? Or a Sieve?: Pages 252-255

How does memory work?

1. _____ storage
2. _____ encoding
3. _____ sensory memory
4. _____ echos and icons
5. _____ working memory

a. hard drive
b. STM
c. lasts for two to three seconds
d. keyboard
e. sensory memory

## Memory: Pages 252-255 (continued)

1. _____ selective attention
2. _____ long-term memory
3. _____ incoming information
4. _____ encoding for LTM
5. _____ sensory memory
6. _____ short-term memory
7. _____ rehearsal buffer

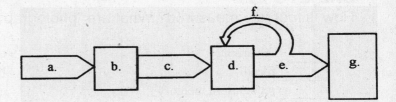

## Short-Term Memory—Do You Know the Magic Number?: Pages 255-256

What are the features of short-term memory?

1. _____ semantic memory
2. _____ long-term memory
3. _____ procedural memory
4. _____ sensory memory
5. _____ episodic memory
6. _____ short-term memory
7. _____ declarative memory

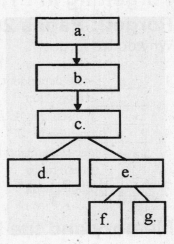

## Short-Term Memory: Pages 255-256 (continued)

1. _____ chunking
2. _____ skill memory
3. _____ revised memories
4. _____ seven information bits
5. _____ false memory
6 _____ memory structure

a. magic number
b. recoding
c. constructive processing
d. network model
e. procedures
f. pseudo-memory

## Measuring Memory—The Answer Is on the Tip of My Tongue and Exceptional Memory—Wizards of Recall: Pages 261-264 and 273-275

How is memory measured? What are "photographic" memories?

1. _____ relearning
2. _____ recall
3. _____ recognition memory
4. _____ false positive
5. _____ implicit memory
6 _____ memory prediction
7. _____ eidetic imagery
8. _____ serial position effect
9. _____ explicit memory

a. retrieval of facts
b. middle items are least recalled
c. multiple-choice questions
d. photographic memory
e. conscious memories
f. memories that are outside of awareness
g. memory test
h. feeling of knowing
i. mistaken recognition

## Forgetting in LTM—Why We, uh, Let's See; Why We, uh ... Forget!: Pages 264-270

Why do we forget?

1. _____ state dependent
2. _____ suppression
3. _____ nonsense syllable
4. _____ repression
5. _____ cue-dependent memory
6 _____ interference
7. _____ Ebbinghaus

a. WOL
b. forgetting curve
c. in same frame of mind
d. a stimulus linked to a memory
e. motivated forgetting
f. conscious forgetting
g. prevent retrieval of information

## Memory and the Brain—Some "Shocking" Findings and Improving Memory—Keys to the Memory Bank: Pages 270-273 and 275-278

How does the brain form and store memories? How can I improve my memory?

1. _____ memory trace
2. _____ recitation
3. _____ amnesia
4. _____ memory expert
5. _____ hippocampus
6 _____ order of events
7. _____ decay
8. _____ spaced practice
9. _____ erases memory
10. _____ rehearsal

a. disuse of memory
b. mnemonist
c. ECS
d. engram
e. memory loss
f. form a story
g. mental review
h. summarize out loud
i. consolidation of memories
j. study in short periods

# CHECK YOUR MEMORY

## Stages of Memory—Do You Have a Mind Like a Steel Trap? Or a Sieve?: Pages 252-255

How does memory work?

1. Incoming information must be encoded before it is stored in memory.  TRUE or FALSE

2. Sensory memories last for a few minutes or less.   TRUE or FALSE

3. A memory that cannot be retrieved has little value.   TRUE or FALSE

4. Selective attention influences what information enters STM.   TRUE or FALSE

5. Working memory is another name for sensory memory.   TRUE or FALSE

6. Errors in long-term memory tend to focus on the sounds of words.   TRUE or FALSE

7. Generally, the more you know, the more new information you can store in long-term memory.
   TRUE or FALSE

8. The type of memory people store is not affected by their cultural values.   TRUE or FALSE

## Short-Term Memory—Do You Know the Magic Number?: Pages 255-256

What are the features of short-term memory?

1. For many kinds of information, STM can store an average of 5 bits of information.
   TRUE or FALSE

2. Nelson Cowan coined the term "magic number."   TRUE or FALSE

3. Chunking recodes information into smaller units that are easier to fit into STM.
   TRUE or FALSE

4. The more times a short-term memory is rehearsed, the better its chance of being stored in LTM.
   TRUE or FALSE

5. On average, short-term memories last only about 18 minutes, unless they are rehearsed.
   TRUE or FALSE

6. Maintenance rehearsal keeps memories active in sensory memory.   TRUE or FALSE

261

# Long-Term Memory—Where the Past Lives: Pages 256-261

What are the features of long-term memory?

1. The surface of the brain records the past like a movie, complete with soundtrack.
   TRUE or FALSE

2. Long-term memory is *relatively* permanent as we tend to update, change, lose, or revise our old memories.   TRUE or FALSE

3. Being confident about a memory tells little about the true accuracy of the memory.
   TRUE or FALSE

4. Long-term memories appear to be organized alphabetically for speedy access.   TRUE or FALSE

5. False memory refers to having memories that never happened.   TRUE or FALSE

6. Hypnosis increases false memories more than it does true ones.   TRUE or FALSE

7. Recalling events from different viewpoints is part of doing a cognitive interview.
   TRUE or FALSE

8. Cognitive interview and standard questioning produce the same percentage of correct recall given by eyewitnesses.   TRUE or FALSE

9. Knowing how to swing a golf club is a type of declarative memory.   TRUE or FALSE

10. A person lacking declarative memory might still remember how to solve a mechanical puzzle.
    TRUE or FALSE

11. Semantic memories are almost immune to forgetting.   TRUE or FALSE

12. Semantic memories are a type of declarative memory.   TRUE or FALSE

13. Episodic memories have no connection to particular times and places.   TRUE or FALSE

# Measuring Memory—The Answer Is on the Tip of My Tongue: Pages 261-264

How is memory measured?

1. Remembering the first sound of a name you are trying to recall is an example of the tip-of-the-tongue state.   TRUE or FALSE

2. Tests of recognition require verbatim memory.   TRUE or FALSE

3. The serial position effect measures the strength of the feeling of knowing.   TRUE or FALSE

4. Recognition tends to be a more sensitive test of memory than recall.   TRUE or FALSE

5. False positives and distractors greatly affect the accuracy of relearning tests.
   TRUE or FALSE

6. Recall, recognition, and relearning are used to measure explicit memories.   TRUE or FALSE

7. Priming is used to activate explicit (hidden) memories.   TRUE or FALSE

# Forgetting in LTM—Why We, uh, Let's See; Why We, uh ... Forget!: Pages 264-270

## Why do we forget?

1. Ebbinghaus chose to learn nonsense syllables so that they would all be the same length.
   TRUE or FALSE

2. Ebbinghaus's curve of forgetting levels off after 2 days, showing little further memory loss after that.
   TRUE or FALSE

3. Ebbinghaus's curve of forgetting only applies to memories of nonsense syllables.
   TRUE or FALSE

4. The magic card trick demonstrates our ability to focus and pay attention.   TRUE or FALSE

5. Dividing attention between studying and other activities such as watching television can improve
   encoding.   TRUE or FALSE

6. Decay of memory traces clearly applies to information in STM.   TRUE or FALSE

7. Disuse theories of forgetting answer the question: Have I been storing the information in the first place?
   TRUE or FALSE

8. In order to remember something, the memory must be available and accessible.   TRUE or FALSE

9. Information learned under the influence of a drug may be best remembered when the drugged state
   occurs again.   TRUE or FALSE

10. If you are in a bad mood, you are more likely to remember unpleasant events.   TRUE or FALSE

11. Categorizing a person as a member of a group tends to limit the accuracy of memories about the
    person's appearance.   TRUE or FALSE

12. Sleeping tends to interfere with retaining new memories.   TRUE or FALSE

13. You learn information A and then information B. If your memory of B is lowered by having first
    learned A, you have experienced retroactive interference.   TRUE or FALSE

14. Interference only applies to the initial stage of learning. Learned information is permanent and
    can be easily retrieved.   TRUE or FALSE

15. Unconsciously forgetting painful memories is called negative transfer.   TRUE or FALSE

16. A conscious attempt to put a memory out of mind is called repression.   TRUE or FALSE

17. Elizabeth Loftus demonstrated the ease of implanting false memories by simply suggesting to Alan Alda that he does not like hard-boiled eggs, which he later avoided eating at a picnic.
    TRUE or FALSE

18. Suggestion and fantasy are elements of many techniques used in attempts to recover repressed memories.   TRUE or FALSE

19. Unless a memory can be independently confirmed, there is no way to tell if it is real or not.
    TRUE or FALSE

# Memory and the Brain—Some "Shocking" Findings: Pages 270-273
How does the brain form and store memories?

1. Retrograde amnesia is a gap in memories of events preceding a head injury.   TRUE or FALSE

2. People with damage to the hippocampus typically cannot remember events that occurred before the damage.   TRUE or FALSE

3. In the early 1920s, Karl Lashley found the location of engrams in the brain.   TRUE or FALSE

4. Storing memories alters the activity, structure, and chemistry of the brain.   TRUE or FALSE

5. Enhancing memory is now possible by taking a memory pill.   TRUE or FALSE

6. Electrically stimulating the hippocampus can decrease long-term potentiation.   TRUE or FALSE

7. Flashbulb memories tend to be formed when an event is surprising or emotional.
   TRUE or FALSE

8. The confidence we have in flashbulb memories is well placed—they are much more accurate than most other memories.   TRUE or FALSE

# Exceptional Memory—Wizards of Recall: Pages 273-275
What are "photographic" memories?

1. Eidetic images last for 30 seconds or more.   TRUE or FALSE

2. About 8 percent of all children have eidetic images.   TRUE or FALSE

3. Eidetic imagery becomes rare by adulthood.   TRUE or FALSE

4. Mr. S. (the mnemonist) had virtually unlimited eidetic imagery.   TRUE or FALSE

5. Practice in remembering one type of information increases the capacity of STM to store other types of information, too.   TRUE or FALSE

6. All contestants in the World Memory Championship performed poorly on tasks that prevented the use of learned strategies.   TRUE or FALSE

## Improving Memory—Keys to the Memory Bank and Psychology in Action: Mnemonics—Memory Magic: Pages 275-280

How can I improve my memory? Are there any tricks to help me with my memory?

1. Recitation is a good way to generate feedback while studying.    TRUE or FALSE

2. Elaborative rehearsal involving "why" questions improve memory.    TRUE or FALSE

3. Overlearning is inefficient; you should stop studying at the point of initial mastery of new information.    TRUE or FALSE

4. Massed practice is almost always superior to spaced practice.    TRUE or FALSE

5. When learning, it helps to gradually extend how long you remember new information before reviewing it again.    TRUE or FALSE

6. Roy G. Biv is a mnemonic for the notes on a musical staff.    TRUE or FALSE

7. Many mnemonics make use of mental images or pictures.    TRUE or FALSE

8. Mnemonics often link new information to familiar memories.    TRUE or FALSE

9. The keyword method is superior to rote learning for memorizing vocabulary words in another language.    TRUE or FALSE

# FINAL SURVEY AND REVIEW

## Stages of Memory—Do You Have a Mind Like a Steel Trap? Or a Sieve?

How does memory work?

1. Memory is an active system. Information is first _____ (changed into the form in which it will be retained).

2. Next it is stored in memory. Later it must be _____ to be put to use.

3. Humans appear to have 3 interrelated memory systems. These are _____ memory, _____ memory (STM), and long-term memory (LTM).

4. Sensory memory holds an exact copy of what is seen or heard, in the form of an _____ (image) or _____ (sound sensation).

5. _____ memories tend to be stored as sounds. _____ memories are stored on the basis of meaning, or importance.

265

6. _____ acts as a temporary storehouse for small amounts of information. It provides a _____ memory where thinking, mental arithmetic, and the like take place. LTM acts as a permanent storehouse for _____ information.

7. _____ values impact the types of memories we tend to store. American culture emphasizes the individual; therefore, American memories are_____-focused. The Chinese culture emphasizes _____ membership; therefore, Chinese memories are of social events, which include family members, friends, and others.

# Short-Term Memory—Do You Know the Magic Number?
## What are the features of short-term memory?

1. _____ memory is exact, but very brief, lasting only a few seconds or less. Through _____ _____ , some information is transferred to STM.

2. The _____test reveals that STM has an average upper limit of about 7 bits of information. However, this can be extended by chunking, or_____information into larger units or groups.

3. The " _____ ☐ 7 (plus or minus 2) refers to the limitation of short-term memory discovered by George_____. Nelson Cowan believes that the limitation of short-term memory is _____ than the "magic number" 7.

4. Short-term memories are brief and very sensitive to interruption or_____; however, they can be prolonged by _____ rehearsal (silent repetition).

5. _____ rehearsal, which emphasizes meaning, helps transfer information from STM to LTM and is superior to _____ _____ .

# Long-Term Memory—Where the Past Lives
## What are the features of long-term memory?

1. LTM seems to have an almost unlimited storage capacity. However, LTM is subject to _____ processing, or ongoing revision and updating. As a result, people often have _____ (false memories) that they believe are true.

2. LTM is highly organized to allow retrieval of needed information. The pattern, or structure, of memory _____ is the subject of current memory research. _____ models portray LTM as a system of linked ideas.

3. _____ memories unfold as each added memory provides a cue for retrieving the next memory. Seemingly forgotten memories may be reconstructed in this way.

4. Within long-term memory, _____ memories for facts seem to differ from _____ memories for skills.

5. Declarative memories may be further categorized as _____ memories or _____ memories.

6. _____ memories consist of basic factual knowledge that is almost immune to forgetting.

7. _____ memories record personal experiences that are associated with specific times and places.

8. Advertising may lead to _____ _____, which can lead people to remember enjoying a product more than they actually did.

# Measuring Memory—The Answer Is on the Tip of My Tongue
## How is memory measured?

1. The _____-of-the-_____ state shows that memory is not an all-or-nothing event. Memories may be revealed by recall, _____, or relearning.

2. In _____, memory proceeds without specific cues, as in an essay exam. Remembering a list of information often reveals a _____ _____ effect (middle items on the list are most subject to errors).

3. A common test of recognition is the _____-choice question. Recognition is very sensitive to the kinds of _____ (wrong choices) used.

4. In _____, "forgotten" material is learned again, and memory is indicated by a savings score.

5. Recall, recognition, and relearning mainly measure _____ memories that we are aware of having. Other techniques, such as priming, are necessary to reveal _____ memories, which are unconscious.

267

# Forgetting in LTM—Why We, uh, Let's See; Why We, uh...Forget!

Why do we forget?

1. Forgetting and memory were extensively studied by Herman _____ , whose curve of forgetting shows that forgetting is typically most rapid immediately after learning.

2. Ebbinghaus used _____ syllables to study memory. The forgetting of meaningful material is much slower than shown by his curve of forgetting.

3. Failure to _____ information is a common cause of "forgetting."

4. Forgetting in _____ memory and _____ probably reflects decay of memory traces in the nervous system. Decay or disuse of memories may also account for some_____ loss, but most forgetting cannot be explained this way.

5. Often, forgetting is_____ dependent. The power of_____ to trigger memories is revealed by_____ learning, in which bodily states at the time of learning and of retrieval affect memory.

6. Much forgetting in both STM and LTM can be attributed to _____of memories with one another.

7. When recent learning interferes with retrieval of prior learning, _____ interference has occurred. If old memories interfere with new memories, _____ interference has occurred.

8. _____ is the forgetting of painful, embarrassing, or traumatic memories.

9. _____ is thought to be unconscious, in contrast to _____, which is a conscious attempt to avoid thinking about something.

10. Experts are currently debating the validity of childhood memories of abuse that reappear after apparently being _____for decades.

11. Independent evidence has verified that some _____ memories are true. However, others have been shown to be false.

12. In the absence of confirming or disconfirming evidence, there is currently no way to separate true memories from_____ . Caution is advised for all concerned with attempts to retrieve supposedly hidden memories.

# Memory and the Brain—Some "Shocking" Findings

How does the brain form and store memories?

1. _____ amnesia and the effects of _____ shock (ECS) may be explained by the concept of consolidation.

2. Consolidation theory holds that _____ (permanent memory traces) are formed during a critical period after learning. Until they are_____, long-term memories are easily destroyed.

3. The _____is a brain structure associated with the consolidation of memories.

4. _____ memories, which seem especially vivid, are created at emotionally significant times. While such memories may not be _____, we tend to place great confidence in them.

5. The search within the brain for engrams has now settled on changes in individual_____ _____.

6. The best-documented changes are alterations in the amounts of _____ chemicals released by nerve cells.

7._____ occurs when a connection between two brain cells grow stronger as they become more active at the same time. These cells then respond more strongly to incoming messages from other cells. This process appears to affect the_____ of lasting memories.

# Exceptional Memory—Wizards of Recall

What are "photographic" memories?

1. _____ (photographic memory) occurs when a person is able to project an image onto an external surface. Such images allow brief, nearly complete recall by some children.

2. _____is rarely found in adults. However, many adults have internal images, which can be very vivid and a basis for remembering.

3. _____ memory can be learned by finding ways to directly store information in LTM. Learning has no effect on the _____ of STM. Some people may have naturally superior memory abilities that exceed what can be achieved through learning.

## Improving Memory—Keys to the Memory Bank
How can I improve my memory?

1. Memory can be improved by using_____ (knowledge of results), recitation, and rehearsal, by _____and organizing information, and by using the progressive part method, spaced practice, overlearning, and active_____strategies.

2. The effects of _____ position, sleep, review, cues, and_____ (connecting new information to existing knowledge) should also be kept in mind when studying or memorizing.

## Psychology in Action: Mnemonics—Memory Magic
Are there any tricks to help me with my memory?

1. Mnemonic techniques avoid _____ learning and work best during the _____ stages of learning.

2. _____systems, such as the keyword method, use mental images and unusual associations to link new information with familiar memories already stored in LTM. Such strategies give information personal meaning and make it easier to recall.

# MASTERY TEST

1. The meaning and importance of information has a strong impact on
   a. sensory memory.
   b. eidetic memory.
   c. long-term memory.
   d. procedural memory.

2. Pseudo-memories are closely related to the effects of
   a. repression.
   b. suppression.
   c. semantic forgetting.
   d. constructive processing.

3. The occurrence of _____ implies that consolidation has been prevented.
   a. retrograde amnesia
   b. hippocampal transfer
   c. suppression
   d. changes in the activities of individual nerve cells

4. Most of the techniques used to recover supposedly repressed memories involve
   a. redintegration and hypnosis.
   b. suggestion and fantasy.
   c. reconstruction and priming.
   d. coercion and fabrication.

5. Most daily memory chores are handled by
   a. sensory memory and LTM.
   b. STM and working memory.
   c. STM and LTM.
   d. STM and declarative memory.

6. Three key processes in memory systems are
   a. storage, organization, recovery.
   b. encoding, attention, reprocessing.
   c. storage, retrieval, encoding.
   d. retrieval, reprocessing, reorganization.

7. Procedural memories are to skills as _____ memories are to facts.
   a. declarative
   b. short-term
   c. redintegrative
   d. eidetic

8. An ability to answer questions about distances on a map you have seen only once implies that some memories are based on
   a. constructive processing.
   b. redintegration.
   c. internal images.
   d. episodic processing.

9. The first potential cause of forgetting that may occur is
   a. engram decay.
   b. disuse.
   c. cue-dependent forgetting.
   d. encoding failure.

10. The persistence of icons and echoes is the basis for
    a. sensory memory.
    b. short-term memory.
    c. long-term memory.
    d. working memory.

11. Priming is most often used to reveal
    a. semantic memories.
    b. episodic memories.
    c. implicit memories.
    d. eidetic memories.

12. "Projection" onto an external surface is most characteristic of
    a.   sensory memories.
    b.   eidetic images.
    c.   memory jamming.
    d.   mnemonic images.

13. Chunking helps especially to extend the capacity of
    a.   sensory memory.
    b.   STM.
    c.   LTM.
    d.   declarative memory.

14. There is presently no way to tell if a "recovered" memory is true or false unless independent
    _____ exists.
    a.   evidence
    b.   amnesia
    c.   elaboration
    d.   consolidation

15. Taking an essay test inevitably requires a person to use
    a.   recall.
    b.   recognition.
    c.   relearning.
    d.   priming.

16. A savings score is used in what memory task?
    a.   recall
    b.   recognition
    c.   relearning
    d.   priming

17. _____ rehearsal helps link new information to existing memories by concentrating
    on meaning.
    a.   Redintegrative
    b.   Rote
    c.   Maintenance
    d.   Elaborative

18. Middle items are neither held in STM nor moved to LTM. This statement explains the
    a.   feeling of knowing.
    b.   serial position effect.
    c.   déjà vu.
    d.   semantic forgetting curve.

19. According to the curve of forgetting, the greatest decline in the amount recalled occurs during the _____ after learning.
    a.  first hour
    b.  second day
    c.  third to sixth days
    d.  retroactive period

20. Work with brain stimulation, truth serums, and hypnosis suggests that long-term memories are
    a.  stored in the hippocampus.
    b.  relatively permanent.
    c.  unaffected by later input.
    d.  always redintegrative.

21. Which of the following is most likely to improve the accuracy of memory?
    a.  hypnosis
    b.  constructive processing
    c.  the serial position effect
    d.  memory cues

22. To qualify as repression, forgetting must be
    a.  retroactive.
    b.  proactive.
    c.  unconscious.
    d.  explicit.

23. Which of the following typically is NOT a good way to improve memory?
    a.  massed practice
    b.  overlearning
    c.  rehearsal
    d.  recall strategies

24. A witness to a crime is questioned in ways that re-create the context of the crime and that provide many memory cues. It appears that she is undergoing
    a.  retroactive priming.
    b.  the progressive part method.
    c.  retroactive consolidation.
    d.  a cognitive interview.

25. One thing that is clearly true about flashbulb memories is that
    a.  they are unusually accurate.
    b.  we place great confidence in them.
    c.  they apply primarily to public tragedies.
    d.  they are recovered by using visualization and hypnosis.

26. One common mnemonic strategy is the
    a. serial position technique.
    b. feeling of knowing tactic.
    c. network procedure.
    d. keyword method.

27. A perspective that helps explain redintegrative memories is
    a. the feeling of knowing model.
    b. recoding and chunking.
    c. the network model.
    d. mnemonic models.

28. Which of the following is NOT considered a part of long-term memory?
    a. echoic memory
    b. semantic memory
    c. episodic memory
    d. declarative memory

29. You are very thirsty. Suddenly you remember a time years ago when you became very thirsty while hiking. This suggests that your memory is
    a. proactive.
    b. state dependent.
    c. still not consolidated.
    d. eidetic.

30. After memorizing 5 lists of words you recall less of the last list than a person who only memorized list number five. This observation is explained by
    a. reactive processing.
    b. reconstructive processing.
    c. proactive interference.
    d. retroactive interference.

31. On a TV game show, you are asked which way Lincoln's head faces on a penny. You are unable to answer correctly and you lose a large prize. Your memory failure is most likely a result of
    a. the serial position effect.
    b. repression.
    c. encoding failure.
    d. priming.

32. Who coined the term "magic number" 7 (plus or minus 2)?
    a. George Miller
    b. Nelson Cowan
    c. Herman Ebbinghaus
    d. Karl Lashley

33. People from the United States tend to recall memories that focus on what they did in a particular event while people from China tend to recall memories that focus on their interactions with family members and friends. Recalling different memories of similar events is the result of
    a. cultural influence.
    b. mnemonic strategy.
    c. eidetic imagery.
    d. pseudo-memory.

34. False memory is likely to occur if hypnosis is used in conjunction with
    a. a medical doctor conducting the procedure.
    b. the presence of a loved one.
    c. misleading questions.
    d. both A and B.

35. To reduce false identification from eyewitnesses, police should
    a. have witnesses view all the pictures of people at one time.
    b. have witnesses view pictures of people one at a time.
    c. use hypnosis since it has proven to be a reliable source data gathering.
    d. not use eyewitness testimonies since they are not reliable.

36. The tendency for eyewitnesses to better identity members of their own ethnic group than other groups is best explained by
    a. eidetic memory.
    b. serial position effect.
    c. sensory memory.
    d. categorization effect.

37. A card dealer asks you to silently pick out a card from the six cards laid out in front of you and to memorize it. Without knowing the card you picked, he takes your card away and presents to you the other five cards. To perform this trick properly, the dealer hopes that
    a. you failed to encode the other five cards as you memorize the card you picked.
    b. you do have eidetic memory.
    c. you believe that he can read your mind.
    d. the serial position effect does influence your memory.

38. To form lasting memories, the brain appears to use the mechanism of _____; a process that occurs when a connection between brain cells grow stronger as they become more active at the same time.
    a. encoding
    b. transience
    c. long-term potentiation
    d. elaboration

# SOLUTIONS

## RECITE AND REVIEW

### Stages of Memory—Do You Have a Mind Like a Steel Trap? Or a Sieve?: Pages 252-255
How does memory work?

1. system; Information
2. stored
3. 3; short-term; long-term
4. exact; image
5. sounds; meaning
6. temporary; permanent
7. memories; self; family

### Short-Term Memory—Do You Know the Magic Number?: Pages 255-256
What are the features of short-term memory?

1. seconds; STM
2. bits; larger
3. magic; short-term; lower
4. interruption; repetition
5. STM; memories; rote

### Long-Term Memory—Where the Past Lives: Pages 256-261
What are the features of long-term memory?

1. updating; false
2. organized; models
3. memory
4. facts; skills
5. Declarative
6. forgetting
7. personal
8. Advertising

### Measuring Memory—The Answer Is on the Tip of My Tongue: Pages 261-264
How is memory measured?

1. state; recall
2. essay; middle
3. recognition; Recognition
4. savings
5. memories; memories

### Forgetting in LTM—Why We, uh, Let's See; Why We, uh ... Forget!: Pages 264-270
Why do we forget?

1. curve; after
2. meaningful; slower
3. information
4. traces; disuse
5. learning; states
6. forgetting
7. interferes; interfere
8. forgetting
9. conscious
10. abuse
11. true; false
12. evidence

## Memory and the Brain—Some "Shocking" Findings: Pages 270-273

How does the brain form and store memories?

1. amnesia; shock
2. memory traces
3. brain
4. nerve
5. Confidence
6. long-term; active
7. long-term; active

## Exceptional Memory—Wizards of Recall: Pages 273-275

What are "photographic" memories?

1. image
2. adults
3. LTM; STM

## Improving Memory—Keys to the Memory Bank: Pages 275-278

How can I improve my memory?

1. organizing; part
2. position

## Psychology in Action: Mnemonics—Memory Magic: Pages 279-280

Are there any tricks to help me with my memory?

1. initial
2. keyword; LTM

# CONNECTIONS

## Stages of Memory—Do You Have a Mind Like a Steel Trap? Or a Sieve?: Pages 252-255

How does memory work?

1. a
2. d
3. c
4. e
5. b

## Stages of Memory (continued)

1. c
2. g
3. a
4. e
5. b
6. d
7. f

## Short-Term Memory—Do You Know the Magic Number?: Pages 255-256

What are the features of short-term memory?

1. f or g
2. c
3. d
4. a
5. f or g
6. b
7. e

## Short-Term Memory (continued)

| | | | | | |
|---|---|---|---|---|---|
| 1. | b | 3. | c | 5. | f |
| 2. | e | 4. | a | 6. | d |

## Measuring Memory—The Answer Is on the Tip of My Tongue and Exceptional Memory—Wizards of Recall: Pages 261-264 and 273-275

How is memory measured? What are "photographic" memories?

| | | | | | |
|---|---|---|---|---|---|
| 1. | g | 4. | i | 7. | d |
| 2. | a | 5. | f | 8. | b |
| 3. | c | 6. | h | 9. | e |

## Forgetting in LTM—Why We, uh, Let's See; Why We, uh ... Forget!: Pages 264-270

Why do we forget?

| | | | | | |
|---|---|---|---|---|---|
| 1. | c | 4. | e | 7. | b |
| 2. | f | 5. | d | | |
| 3. | a | 6. | g | | |

## Memory and the Brain—Some "Shocking" Findings and Improving Memory—Keys to the Memory Bank: Pages 270-273 and 275-278

How does the brain form and store memories? How can I improve my memory?

| | | | | | |
|---|---|---|---|---|---|
| 1. | d | 5. | i | 9. | c |
| 2. | h | 6. | f | 10. | g |
| 3. | e | 7. | a | | |
| 4. | b | 8. | j | | |

# CHECK YOUR MEMORY

## Stages of Memory—Do You Have a Mind Like a Steel Trap? Or a Sieve?: Pages 252-255

How does memory work?

| | | | | | |
|---|---|---|---|---|---|
| 1. | T | 4. | T | 7. | T |
| 2. | F | 5. | F | 8. | F |
| 3. | T | 6. | F | | |

## Short-Term Memory—Do You Know the Magic Number?: Pages 255-256

What are the features of short-term memory?

| | | | | | |
|---|---|---|---|---|---|
| 1. | T | 3. | F | 5. | F |
| 2. | F | 4. | T | 6. | F |

## Long-Term Memory—Where the Past Lives: Pages 256-261
What are the features of long-term memory?

| | | |
|---|---|---|
| 1. F | 6. T | 11. T |
| 2. T | 7. T | 12. T |
| 3. T | 8. F | 13. F |
| 4. F | 9. F | |
| 5. T | 10. T | |

## Measuring Memory—The Answer Is on the Tip of My Tongue: Pages 261-264
How is memory measured?

| | | |
|---|---|---|
| 1. T | 4. T | 7. F |
| 2. F | 5. F | |
| 3. F | 6. T | |

## Forgetting in LTM—Why We, uh, Let's See; Why We, uh ... Forget!: Pages 264-270
Why do we forget?

| | | |
|---|---|---|
| 1. F | 8. T | 15. F |
| 2. T | 9. T | 16. F |
| 3. F | 10. T | 17. T |
| 4. F | 11. T | 18. T |
| 5. F | 12. F | 19. T |
| 6. T | 13. F | |
| 7. F | 14. F | |

## Memory and the Brain—Some "Shocking" Findings: Pages 270-273
How does the brain form and store memories?

| | | |
|---|---|---|
| 1. T | 4. T | 7. T |
| 2. F | 5. F | 8. F |
| 3. F | 6. T | |

## Exceptional Memory—Wizards of Recall: Pages 273-275
What are "photographic" memories?

| | | |
|---|---|---|
| 1. T | 3. T | 5. F |
| 2. T | 4. F | 6. F |

## Improving Memory—Keys to the Memory Bank and Psychology in Action: Mnemonics—Memory Magic: Pages 275-280

How can I improve my memory? Are there any tricks to help me with my memory?

| | | | | | |
|---|---|---|---|---|---|
| 1. | T | 4. | F | 7. | T |
| 2. | T | 5. | T | 8. | T |
| 3. | F | 6. | F | 9. | T |

# FINAL SURVEY AND REVIEW

## Stages of Memory—Do You Have a Mind Like a Steel Trap? Or a Sieve?:

How does memory work?

1. encoded
2. retrieved
3. sensory; short-term

4. icon; echo
5. Short-term; Long-term
6. STM; working; meaningful

7. Cultural; self; group

## Short-Term Memory—Do You Know the Magic Number?

What are the features of short-term memory?

1. Sensory; selective; attention
2. digit-span; recoding

3. magic number; Miller; lower
4. interference; maintenance

5. Elaborative; rote learning

## Long-Term Memory—Where the Past Lives

What are the features of long-term memory?

1. constructive; pseudo-memories
2. networks; Network
3. Redintegrative

4. declarative; procedural
5. semantic; episodic
6. Semantic

7. Episodic
8. memory jamming

## Measuring Memory—The Answer Is on the Tip of My Tongue

How is memory measured?

1. tip; tongue; recognition
2. recall; serial; position

3. multiple; distractors
4. relearning

5. explicit; implicit

## Forgetting in LTM—Why We, uh, Let's See; Why We, uh ... Forget!: Pages 264-270

Why do we forget?

1. Ebbinghaus
4. sensory; STM; LTM
5. cue; cues; state-dependent
6. interference
7. retroactive; proactive

2. nonsense
8. Repression
9. Repression; suppression
10. repressed
11. recovered

3. encode
12. fantasies

## Memory and the Brain—Some "Shocking" Findings
How does the brain form and store memories?

1. Retrograde; electroconvulsive
2. engrams; consolidated
3. hippocampus
4. Flashbulb; accurate
5. nerve; cells
6. transmitter
7. Long term; potentiation; formation

## Exceptional Memory—Wizards of Recall
What are "photographic" memories?

1. Eidetic imagery
2. Eidetic imagery
3. Exceptional; limits

## Improving Memory—Keys to the Memory Bank
How can I improve my memory?

1. feedback; selecting; search
2. serial; elaboration

## Psychology in Action: Mnemonics—Memory Magic
Are there any tricks to help me with my memory?

1. rote; initial;
2. Mnemonic

# MASTERY TEST

1. c, p. 254
2. d, p. 257
3. a, p. 270
4. b, p. 269
5. c, p. 253
6. c, p. 252
7. a, p. 260
8. c, p. 273
9. d, p. 265
10. a, p. 252
11. c, p. 263
12. b, p. 273
13. b, p. 255
14. a, p. 269
15. a, p. 262
16. c, p. 263
17. d, p. 256
18. b, p. 262
19. a, p. 264
20. b, p. 253
21. d, p. 266
22. c, p. 270
23. a, p. 277
24. d, p. 258
25. b, p. 271
26. d, p. 280
27. c, p. 259
28. a, p. 260
29. b, p. 267
30. c, p. 268
31. c, p. 265
32. a, p. 255
33. a, p. 254
34. c, p. 258
35. b, p. 258
36. d, p. 266
37. a, p. 265
38. c, p. 273

# Cognition, Language, Creativity and Intelligence

## Chapter Overview

Thinking is an internal representation of external stimuli or situations. Three basic units of thought are images, concepts, and language (or symbols). Mental images may be retrieved from memory or created to solve problems. Images can be three-dimensional, they can be rotated in space, and their size may change. Kinesthetic images are used to represent movements and actions.

A concept is a generalized idea of a class of objects or events. Concept formation may be based on positive and negative instances or rule learning. Concept identification frequently makes use of prototypes. Concepts may be conjunctive, disjunctive, or relational. Word meaning can be both denotative and connotative.

Language encodes events as symbols for easy mental manipulation. The study of meaning in language is called *semantics*. Bilingualism is a valuable ability. Language carries meaning by combining a set of symbols according grammar, which includes syntax. True languages are productive and can be used to generate new ideas. Complex gestural systems, such as American Sign Language, are true languages. Primates have been taught American Sign Language and similar systems. It remains controversial whether or not primates are capable of very basic language use.

Expert problem solving is based on learned mental heuristics and highly organized knowledge. The solution to a problem may be arrived at mechanically, but mechanical solutions are often inefficient. Solutions by understanding usually begin with discovery of the general properties of an answer, followed by a functional solution. Problem solving is aided by heuristics. Experts are not naturally smarter than novices. When understanding leads to a rapid solution, insight has occurred. Insight can be blocked by fixations.

To be creative, a solution must be practical and sensible as well as original. Creative thinking requires divergent thought. Tests of creativity measure these qualities. Creativity can be enhanced by strategies that promote divergent thinking. Five stages often seen in creative problem solving are orientation, preparation, incubation, illumination, and verification. Not all creative thinking fits this pattern. Studies suggest that the creative personality has a number of characteristics, most of which contradict popular stereotypes. There is only a very small correlation between IQ and creativity. Some creative thinking skills can be learned.

Intuitive thinking often leads to errors. Wrong conclusions may be drawn when an answer seems highly representative of what we already believe is true. Emotions also lead to intuitive thinking and poor choices. Another problem is ignoring the base rate of an event. Clear thinking is usually aided by framing a problem in broad terms.

Intelligence refers to the general capacity (or g-factor) to act purposefully, think rationally, and deal effectively with the environment. In practice, intelligence is operationally defined by intelligence tests, which provide a useful but narrow estimate of real-world intelligence. The first intelligence test was assembled by Alfred Binet. A modern version of Binet's test is the *Stanford-Binet Intelligence Scale*. Another major intelligence test is the *Wechsler Adult Intelligence Scale* (WAIS). Group intelligence tests are also available.

There is a wide range of mental abilities. Everyone has special aptitudes. Most people score in the mid-range on intelligence tests. Only a small percentage of people have exceptionally high or low IQ scores. People with IQs in the gifted or "genius" range of above 140 tend to be superior in many respects. A high IQ reveals potential, but it does not guarantee success. The term *intellectually disabled* is applied to those whose IQ falls below 70 or who lack various adaptive behaviors. About 50 percent of the cases of intellectual disability are organic. The remaining cases are of undetermined cause. The majority of people who are intellectually disabled can master basic adaptive behaviors and with support they can find a place in the community.

The definition of intelligence and the assumption that intelligence is mainly inherited have been called into question. Traditional IQ tests measure linguistic, logical- mathematical, and spatial abilities. It is likely that we all use other types of intelligence in daily life. Many psychologists have begun to forge broader definitions of intelligence, such as Howard Gardner's theory of multiple intelligences. Real-world intelligence combines a fast nervous system, learned knowledge and skills, an acquired ability to manage one's own thinking, and problem solving. *Artificial intelligence* refers to any artificial system that can perform tasks that require intelligence when done by people. Intelligence is determined by both heredity and environment.

Traditional IQ tests are not universally valid for all cultural groups and often suffer from a degree of cultural bias. IQ is merely an index of intelligence. Intelligence is narrowly defined by most tests. IQ is related to achievement in school, but many other factors are also important. Outside school, the connection between IQ and achievement is weaker. The use of standard IQ tests for educational placement of students has been prohibited by law in some states.

## Learning Objectives

*Theme: Thinking, language, problem solving, and creativity underlie intelligent behavior. Measuring intelligence is worthwhile, but tests provide limited definitions of intelligent behavior.*

| |
|---|
| **GQ: What is the nature of thought?** |
| LO 9.1  Define *cognition* and list the three basic units of thought. |
| **GQ: In what ways are images related to thinking?** |
| LO 9.2  Describe mental imagery, synesthesia, and the properties of mental images; explain how both stored and created images may be used to solve problems (including how the size of a mental image may be important); and describe how kinesthetic imagery aids thinking. |
| **GQ: What are concepts?** |
| LO 9.3  Define the terms *concept* and *concept formation;* explain how they aid thought processes; and describe how they are learned. |
| LO 9.4  Define the terms *conjunctive concept*, *relational concept*, *disjunctive concept*, and *prototype*; explain the difference between the *denotative* and the *connotative meaning* of a concept or word; describe how the *connotative meaning* of a concept or word is measured; and discuss problems associated with social stereotypes and all-or-nothing thinking. |

| |
|---|
| **GQ: What is the role of language in thinking?** |
| LO 9.5  Explain how language aids thought, and define semantics |
| LO 9.6  Discuss bilingual education, including the concepts of additive and subtractive *bilingualism* and *two-way bilingual education*. |
| LO 9.7  Briefly describe the following components of a language and their related concepts: a. symbols; b. *phonemes*; c. *morphemes*; and d. *grammar* or *syntax* (including *transformation rules* and productivity). Include a discussion of gestural languages. |
| LO 9.8  Explain the extent to which primates have been taught to use language and describe both the criticisms and practical value of attempts to teach language to primates. |
| **GQ: What do we know about problem solving?** |
| LO 9.9  Differentiate between *mechanical problem-solving* and *problem-solving through understanding*. Discuss *heuristics* and how they aid problem-solving and explain how novices differ from experts. |
| LO 9.10  Tell how each of the following contribute to *insight*: a. selective encoding; b. selective combination; c. selective comparison. |
| LO 9.11  Explain and give examples of how *fixation* and *functional fixedness* block problem-solving and describe the four common barriers to problem solving. |
| **GQ: What is creative thinking?** |
| LO 9.12  Describe the following four kinds of thought: a. *inductive*; b. *deductive*; c. *logical*; d. *illogical*. |
| LO 9.13  Describe the following characteristics of creative thinking: a. fluency; b. flexibility; c. originality. Describe how the ability to think divergently can be measured; explain the relationship of creativity to divergent and convergent thinking; describe the five stages of creative thinking and discuss the five qualities which characterize creative persons. |
| **GQ: How accurate is intuition?** |
| LO 9.14  Define *intuition* and explain the following three common intuitive thinking errors: a. representativeness (include *representativeness heuristic*); b. underlying odds (*base rate*); c. *framing*. Include a brief description of what it means to have *wisdom*. |
| **GQ: How is human intelligence defined and measured?** |
| LO 9.15  Describe Binet's role in intelligence testing; give a general definition of *intelligence*; and explain what an operational definition of intelligence is. |
| LO 9.16  Describe the five cognitive factors measured by the *Stanford-Binet Intelligence Scales, Fifth Edition* (SB5) and explain how these cognitive factors may be viewed differently in other cultures. |
| LO 9.17  Define *mental age* and *chronological age*; use examples to show how they are used to compute an *intelligence quotient* (IQ); and differentiate between this IQ (MA/CA x 100) and *deviation* IQs; regarding the types of intelligence tests: a. distinguish the Wechsler tests from the Stanford-Binet tests; and b. distinguish between *group* and *individual intelligence tests*. |
| **GQ: How much does intelligence vary from person to person?** |
| LO 9.18  Describe Terman's study of gifted children; list five popular misconceptions concerning genius and their corrections; explain how Terman's successful subjects differed from the less successful ones; and describe how gifted children are identified. |
| LO 9.19  List two possible explanations for the exceptional abilities of autistic savants; state the dividing line between normal intelligence and intellectually disabled; and describe the degrees of *intellectual disability*; differentiate between familial and organic intellectual disability and describe each of the following organic conditions: a. fetal damage; b. birth injuries; c. metabolic disorders; and d. genetic abnormalities. |
| **GQ: What are some controversies in the study of intelligence?** |
| LO 9.20  Contrast the definition of intelligence as a *"g" factor* with the theory of *multiple intelligences*. |
| LO 9.21  Define the term *artificial intelligence*; describe what it is based on and its potential uses and limitations. |
| LO 9.22  Describe the studies that provide evidence for the hereditary view of intelligence and for the environmental view of intelligence. Include a discussion of the *twin studies*, the adoption studies, and the finding that Western IQ scores are rising rapidly. |
| **GQ: Are IQ tests fair to all cultural and racial groups?** |
| LO 9.23  Explain how IQ tests may be unfair to certain groups, and describe the term *culture-fair test*; state the arguments against the claim that IQ differences among races being due to genetic inheritance; discuss the general validity of IQ testing and the advantages and disadvantages of standardized testing in public schools. |

# RECITE AND REVIEW

## What is Thinking?—Brains Over Brawn: Page 284
What is the nature of thought?

1. Cognition is the _____ processing of information involving daydreaming, _____ solving, and reasoning.

2. Thinking is the manipulation of_____ representations of external problems or situations.

3. Three basic units of thought are images, concepts, and _____ or symbols.

## Mental Imagery—Does a Frog Have Lips?: Pages 284-286
In what ways are images related to thinking?

1. Most people have internal images of one kind or another. Images may be based on information stored in memory or they may be _____ .

2. Sometimes images cross normal_____ boundaries in a type of imagery called synesthesia.

3. The size of images used in problem solving may _____ . Images may be three-dimensional and they may be rotated in _____ to answer questions.

4. Many of the systems in the brain that are involved in processing _____ images work in reverse to create mental images.

5. Kinesthetic images are created by memories of_____ or by implicit (unexpressed) _____ . Kinesthetic sensations seem to help structure thinking for many people.

## Concepts—I'm Positive, It's a Whatchamacallit: Pages 286-288
What are concepts?

1. A concept is a generalized idea of a of objects or events.

2. Forming concepts may be based on experiences with _____and negative instances.

3. Concepts may also be acquired by learning rules that define the _____.

4. Concepts may be classified as conjunctive (" _____ " concepts), disjunctive (" _____ " concepts), or relational concepts.

5.  In practice, we frequently use prototypes (general _____ of the concept class) to identify concepts.

6.  The denotative meaning of a word or concept is its dictionary _____ . Connotative meaning is _____ or emotional.

7.  Two common thinking errors are _____ thinking (thinking in black and white terms) and use of social stereotypes (inaccurate and oversimplified images of _____ _____).

8.  Connotative meaning can be measured with the semantic differential. Most connotative meaning involves the dimensions _____, strong-weak, and active-passive.

# Language—Don't Leave Home Without It: Pages 288-292
## What is the role of language in thinking?

1.  Language allows events to be encoded into _____ for easy mental manipulation.

2.  Thinking in language is influenced by meaning. The study of _____ is called semantics.

3.  Language is built out of phonemes (basic speech _____) and morphemes (speech sounds collected into _____ units).

4.  Learning a second _____ (bilingualism) during the elementary school years is most likely to benefit students who participate in _____ bilingual education.

5.  Language carries meaning by combining a set of symbols or signs according to a set of _____ (grammar), which includes rules about word _____ (syntax).

6.  Various sentences are created by applying transformation _____ to simple statements.

7.  A true language is productive, and can be used to generate new ideas or possibilities. American Sign Language (ASL) and other _____ languages used by the deaf are true languages.

8.  Animal communication is relatively limited because it lacks symbols that can be _____ easily.

9.  Attempts to teach chimpanzees ASL and other nonverbal systems suggest to some that primates are capable of language use. However, others believe that the chimps are merely using _____ _____ .

10. Studies that make use of lexigrams ( _____ word-symbols) provide the best evidence yet of animal language use.

# Problem Solving—Getting an Answer in Sight: Pages 293-297
## What do we know about problem solving?

1. The solution to a problem may be found mechanically (by trial and error or by _____ application of rules). However, mechanical solutions are frequently inefficient or ineffective, except where aided by_____.

2. Often a _____ solution is achieved through an algorithm, a _____set of rules that always leads to a correct solution.

3. Solutions by understanding usually begin with discovery of the _____ properties of an answer. Next comes proposal of a number of functional_____.

4. Problem solving is frequently aided by heuristics. These are strategies that typically_____ the search for solutions.

5. Expert human problem solving is based on organized _____ and acquired strategies, rather than some general improvement in thinking ability. Expertise also allows more automatic _____ of problems.

6. When understanding leads to a rapid _____ , insight has occurred. Three elements of insight are _____ encoding, selective combination, and selective comparison.

7. The ability to apply _____ comparison (comparing old solutions to new problems) effectively can be influenced by our culture.

8. Insights and other problem solving attempts can be blocked by fixation (a tendency to repeat solutions).

9. Functional fixedness is a common _____ , but emotional blocks, cultural values, learned conventions, and perceptual _____ are also problems.

# Creative Thinking—Down Roads Less Traveled: Pages 297-301
## What is creative thinking?

1. _____ may be deductive or inductive, logical or illogical.

2. Creative thinking requires divergent thought, characterized by fluency, flexibility, and _____ . Creativity is also marked by problem_____ , the active discovery of problems to be solved.

3. To be creative, a solution must be _____ and sensible as well as original.

4. Divergent thinking involves generating many _____ from one starting point.

5. Tests of _____, such as the Unusual Uses Test, the Consequences Test, and the Anagrams Test, measure the capacity for divergent thinking.

6. Five stages often seen in creative problem solving are orientation, _____ , incubation, illumination, and verification.

7. Not all creative thinking fits this pattern. Much creative activity is based on incremental problem solving (many small _____).

8. Studies suggest that creative persons share a number of identifiable general traits, _____ abilities, thinking _____, and personality characteristics. There is a small correlation between IQ and creativity.

## Intuitive Thought—Mental Shortcut? Or Dangerous Detour?: Pages 301-303
How accurate is intuition?

1. People often make decisions _____, rather than logically.

2. Intuitive thinking often leads to _____ . Wrong conclusions may be drawn when an answer seems highly representative of what we already believe is _____. (That is, when people apply the representativeness heuristic.)

3. Another problem is allowing emotions such as _____ , hope, _____ , or disgust to guide _____ in decision making.

4. An additional problem is ignoring the base rate (or underlying _____ ) of an event.

5. Clear thinking is usually aided by stating or framing a problem in _____ terms.

## Human Intelligence—The IQ and You: Pages 304-307
How is human intelligence defined and measured?

1. The first practical _____ _____ was assembled in 1904, in Paris, by Alfred Binet.

2. Intelligence refers to one's general capacity to act purposefully, think _____, and deal effectively with the _____ .

3. In practice, writing an intelligence test provides an operational _____ of intelligence.

4. One limitation of traditional intelligence testing is its _____ to other cultural groups. Because children from various cultures are taught different skills, _____ intelligence tests have been implemented to accurately assess individuals' intellectual abilities and to reduce biases.

5. A modern version of Binet's test is the *Stanford-Binet* _____ , *Fifth Edition.*

6. The Stanford-Binet measures _____ reasoning, general knowledge, quantitative reasoning, visual-spatial processing, and working _____ .

7. Intelligence is expressed in terms of an intelligence _____ (IQ). IQ is defined as mental age (MA) divided by chronological age (CA) and then multiplied by _____ . Mental age is the intellectual capacity of a group of people at a certain age and chronological age is a person's actual age.

8. An "average" IQ of _____ occurs when mental age _____ chronological age.

9. Modern IQ tests no longer calculate _____ directly. Instead, the final score reported by the test is a deviation IQ, which gives a person's _____ intellectual standing in his or her age group.

10. A second major intelligence test is the *Wechsler* _____ *Intelligence Scale, Third Edition* (WAIS-III). The WAIS-III measures both verbal and performance ( _____ ) intelligence.

11. Intelligence tests have also been produced for use with _____ of people.

12. The *Scholastic Assessment Test* (SAT) is a _____ scholastic aptitude test. Although narrower in scope than IQ tests, it bears some similarities to them.

# Variations in Intelligence—Curved Like a Bell: Pages 308-310

How much does intelligence vary from person to person?

1. People with IQs above 140 are considered to be in the _____ or "genius" range.

2. By criteria other than _____ , a large proportion of children might be considered gifted or talented in one way or another.

3. Autistic savants have exceptional abilities in music, mechanics, _____ , and remembering names or _____ .

4. The term _____ disabled is applied to those whose IQ falls below _____ or who lack various adaptive behaviors.

290

5. About _____ percent of the cases of intellectual disability are organic, being caused by _____ injuries, fetal damage, metabolic disorders, or genetic abnormalities. The remaining cases are of undetermined cause.

6. Many cases of subnormal intelligence are thought to be the result of familial intellectual disability (a low level of _____ stimulation in the home, poverty, and poor nutrition).

## Questioning Intelligence—How Intelligent Are Intelligence Tests?: Pages 310-314

What are some controversies in the study of intelligence?

1. Howard Gardner believes that _____ IQ tests define intelligence too narrowly. According to Gardner, intelligence consists of abilities in language, logic and _____, _____ and spatial thinking, music, kinesthetic skills, intrapersonal skills, interpersonal skills, and naturalist skills.

2. Artificial intelligence refers to any artificial _____ that can perform tasks that require _____ when done by people.

3. Two principal areas of artificial intelligence research are _____ simulations and expert systems.

4. Studies of eugenics (selective _____ for desirable characteristics) in animals suggest that intelligence is influenced by heredity.

5. Studies of family relationships in humans, especially comparisons between fraternal twins and identical twins (who have identical _____ ), also suggest that intelligence is partly_____ .

6. However, environment is also important, as revealed by changes in tested intelligence induced by _____ environments and improved education.

7. Early childhood education programs such as Head Start provide longer-term stimulating intellectual experiences for _____ children.

8. An overall average increase of 15 IQ points during the last 30 years has been attributed to _____ factors such as improved education, nutrition, and technology (e.g., complexity of the Internet and computer software)

9. _____ therefore reflects the combined effects of heredity and environment.

## Psychology in Action: Culture, Race, IQ, and You: Pages 314-316
Are IQ tests fair to all cultural and racial groups?

1. Traditional IQ tests often suffer from a degree of cultural _____ that makes them easier for some groups and harder for others.

2. To reduce the influence of verbal skills, cultural background, and _____ level when measuring the IQ of people from another culture (e.g., China) or from a different background (e.g., poor community), culture- _____ tests have been implemented.

3. Culture-fair tests try to measure intelligence in ways that are not strongly affected by _____ background, but no test is entirely _____ -free.

4. Differences in the average IQ scores for various racial groups are based on environmental differences, not _____ .

5. _____ is merely an index of intelligence based tests that offer a narrow definition of intelligence.

# CONNECTIONS

## What is Thinking?—Brains Over Brawn and Mental Imagery—Does a Frog Have Lips?: Pages 284-286
What is the nature of thought? In what ways are images related to thinking?

1. _____ cognition
2. _____ internal representation
3. _____ language
4. _____ mental rotation
5. _____ reverse vision
6. _____ synesthesia
7. _____ stored images
8. _____ kinesthetic imagery

a. imagined movements
b. remembered perceptions
c. brain imaging
d. mental expression
e. implicit actions
f. thinking
g. crossed senses
h. symbols and rules

## Concepts—I'm Positive, It's a Whatchamacallit: Pages 286-288

What are concepts?

| | |
|---|---|
| 1. _____ concept | a. objective meaning |
| 2. _____ connotative meaning | b. mental class |
| 3. _____ social stereotypes | c. ideal or model |
| 4. _____ prototype | d. semantic differential |
| 5. _____ denotative concept | e. two or more features |
| 6 _____ disjunctive concept | f. details of features and nearby area |
| 7. _____ relational concept | g. at least one existing feature |
| 8. _____ conjunctive concept | h. faulty, oversimplified concepts |

## Language—Don't Leave Home Without It: Pages 288-292

What is the role of language in thinking?

| | |
|---|---|
| 1. _____ word meanings | a. meaningful unit |
| 2. _____ additive bilingualism | b. ASL |
| 3. _____ morpheme | c. semantics |
| 4. _____ phoneme | d. lexigrams |
| 5. _____ "hidden" grammar | e. language sound |
| 6 _____ Washoe | f. fluent in two languages |
| 7. _____ bilingual | g. reduced competency in both languages |
| 8. _____ subtractive bilingualism | h. increased overall competency |
| 9. _____ Kanzi | i. transformation rules |

## Problem Solving—Getting an Answer in Sight: Pages 293-297

What do we know about problem solving?

| | |
|---|---|
| 1. _____ algorithm | a. mechanical solution |
| 2. _____ insight | b. thinking strategy |
| 3. _____ trial-and-error | c. element of insight |
| 4. _____ random search strategy | d. knowledge plus rules |
| 5. _____ expert versus novice | e. a clear, sudden solution |
| 6 _____ heuristic | f. trial-and-error |
| 7. _____ understanding | g. learned set of rules |
| 8. _____ selective comparison | h. acquired strategies |
| 9. _____ fixation | i. blind to alternatives |
| 10. _____ expert system | j. deep comprehension |

# Creative Thinking—Down Roads Less Traveled: Pages 297-301

What is creative thinking?

| | | | |
|---|---|---|---|
| 1. | _____ fluency | a. | way a problem is stated |
| 2. | _____ flexibility | b. | many types of solutions |
| 3. | _____ originality | c. | one correct answer |
| 4. | _____ logical | d. | follow explicit rule |
| 5. | _____ convergent thinking | e. | moment of insight |
| 6 | _____ Anagrams Test | f. | underlying odds |
| 7. | _____ representativeness heuristic | g. | quick and impulsive thought |
| 8. | _____ framing | h. | many solutions |
| 9. | _____ illumination | i. | measures divergent thinking |
| 10. | _____ thin-slicing | j. | novelty of solutions |
| 11. | _____ base rate | k. | leads to giving choice greater weight |
| 12. | _____ intuition | l. | uses the cognitive unconscious |

# Human Intelligence—The IQ and You and Variations in Intelligence—Curved Like a Bell: Pages 304-310

How is human intelligence defined and measured? How much does intelligence vary from person to person?

| | | | |
|---|---|---|---|
| 1. | _____ IQ | a. | relative standing |
| 2. | _____ normal curve | b. | absurdities |
| 3. | _____ deviation IQ | c. | Wechsler test |
| 4. | _____ average IQ | d. | block design |
| 5. | _____ Binet | e. | first intelligence test |
| 6. | _____ WAIS | f. | bell shape |
| 7. | _____ verbal reasoning | g. | digit span |
| 8. | _____ memory test | h. | MA/CA * 100 |
| 9. | _____ performance test | i. | IQ of 70 |
| 10. | _____ mentally retarded | j. | IQ of 100 |

# Questioning Intelligence—How Intelligent Are Intelligence Tests?: Pages 310-314

What are some controversies in the study of intelligence?

| | | | |
|---|---|---|---|
| 1. | _____ general ability | a. | duplicate specific human behavior |
| 2. | _____ AI | b. | "people smart" and "nature smart" |
| 3. | _____ multiple intelligence | c. | computer chess player |
| 4. | _____ fraternal twins | d. | artificial intelligence |
| 5. | _____ identical twins | e. | one egg |
| 6. | _____ computer simulation | f. | two eggs |
| 7. | _____ Deep Blue | g. | g-factor |

# CHECK YOUR MEMORY

## What is Thinking?—Brains Over Brawn: Page 284
What is the nature of thought?

1. Cognitive psychology is the study of sensation, memory, and learning.   TRUE or FALSE

2. Images, concepts, and language may be used to mentally represent problems.   TRUE or FALSE

3. Images are generalized ideas of a class of related objects or events.   TRUE or FALSE

4. Blindfolded chess players mainly use concepts to represent chess problems and solutions.
   TRUE or FALSE

## Mental Imagery—Does a Frog Have Lips?: Pages 284-286
In what ways are images related to thinking?

1. Mental images are used to make decisions, change feelings, and to improve memory.
   TRUE or FALSE

2. Experiencing color sensations while listening to music is an example of mental rotation.
   TRUE or FALSE

3. Mental images may be used to improve memory and skilled actions.   TRUE or FALSE

4. In an imagined space, it is easiest to locate objects placed above and below yourself.
   TRUE or FALSE

5. The visual cortex is activated when a person has a mental image.   TRUE or FALSE

6. The more the image of a shape has to be rotated in space, the longer it takes to tell if it matches another view of the same shape.   TRUE or FALSE

7. People who have good imaging abilities tend to score high on tests of creativity.   TRUE or FALSE

8. The smaller a mental image is, the harder it is to identify its details.   TRUE or FALSE

9. People with good synesthetic imagery tend to learn sports skills faster than average.
   TRUE or FALSE

## Concepts—I'm Positive, It's a Whatchamacallit: Pages 286-288
What are concepts?

1. Concept formation is typically based on examples and rules.   TRUE or FALSE

295

2. Prototypes are very strong negative instances of a concept.    TRUE or FALSE

3. "Greater than" and "lopsided" are relational concepts.    TRUE or FALSE

4. Classifying things as absolutely right or wrong may lead to all-or-nothing thinking.
   TRUE or FALSE

5. The semantic differential is used to rate the objective meanings of words and concepts.
   TRUE or FALSE

6. Social stereotypes are accurate, oversimplified concepts people use to form mental images of groups
   of people.    TRUE or FALSE

# Language—Don't Leave Home Without It: Pages 288-292
What is the role of language in thinking?

1. Encoding is the study of the meanings of language.    TRUE or FALSE

2. The Stroop interference test shows that thought is greatly influenced by language.
   TRUE or FALSE

3. People can easily name the color of the word without the meaning of the word interfering with
   their thought processing.    TRUE or FALSE

4. Morphemes are the basic speech sounds of a language.    TRUE or FALSE

5. Syntax is a part of grammar.    TRUE or FALSE

6. Noam Chomsky believes that a child who says, "I drinked my juice," has applied the semantic
   differential to a simple, core sentence.    TRUE or FALSE

7. Similar universal language patterns are found in both speech and gestural languages, such as ASL.
   TRUE or FALSE

8. ASL has 600,000 root signs.    TRUE or FALSE

9. True languages are productive, thus ASL is not a true language.    TRUE or FALSE

10. If one is fluent in ASL, one can sign and understand other gestural languages such as Yiddish Sign.
    TRUE or FALSE

11. Animal communication can be described as productive.    TRUE or FALSE

12. Chimpanzees have never learned to speak even a single word.    TRUE or FALSE

13. One of Sarah chimpanzee's outstanding achievements was mastery of sentences involving
    transformational rules.    TRUE or FALSE

14. Some "language" use by chimpanzees appears to be no more than simple gestures.
    TRUE or FALSE

15. Only a minority of the things that language-trained chimps "say" have anything to do with food.
TRUE or FALSE

16. Language-trained chimps have been known to hold conversations when no humans were present.
TRUE or FALSE

17. Kanzi's use of grammar is on a par with that of a 2-year-old child.    TRUE or FALSE

## Problem Solving—Getting an Answer in Sight: Pages 293-297
What do we know about problem solving?

1. Except for the simplest problems, mechanical solutions are typically best left to computers.
TRUE or FALSE

2. An algorithm is a learned set of rules (grammar) for language.    TRUE or FALSE

3. Karl Dunker's famous tumor problem could only be solved by trial-and-error.    TRUE or FALSE

4. In solutions by understanding, functional solutions are usually discovered by use of a random search strategy.    TRUE or FALSE

5. Working backward from the desired goal to the starting point can be a useful heuristic.
TRUE or FALSE

6. In problem solving, rapid insights are more likely to be correct than those that develop slowly.
TRUE or FALSE

7. Selective encoding refers to bringing together seemingly unrelated bits of useful information.
TRUE or FALSE

8. An advantage of selective comparison is our ability to solve problems in all cultures.
TRUE or FALSE

9. Functional fixedness is an inability to see new uses for familiar objects.    TRUE or FALSE

10. Learned barriers in functional fixedness refer to our habits causing us to not identify other important elements of a problem.    TRUE or FALSE

11. Much human expertise is based on acquired strategies for solving problems.    TRUE or FALSE

12. Chess experts have an exceptional ability to remember the positions of chess pieces placed at random on a chessboard.    TRUE or FALSE

## Creative Thinking—Down Roads Less Traveled:
## Pages 297-301
What is creative thinking?

1. In inductive thinking, a general rule is inferred from specific examples.    TRUE or FALSE

2. Fluency and flexibility are measures of convergent thinking.    TRUE or FALSE

3. In convergent thinking, there is one correct answer.    TRUE or FALSE

4. Creative thinking often involves divergent problem solving.    TRUE or FALSE

5. Creative thinkers typically apply reasoning and critical thinking to novel ideas after they produce them.    TRUE or FALSE

6. Creative ideas combine originality with feasibility.    TRUE or FALSE

7. Creative problem solving temporarily stops during the incubation period.    TRUE or FALSE

8. Much creative problem solving is incremental, rather than being based on sudden insights or breakthroughs.    TRUE or FALSE

9. Creative people have an openness to experience and they have a wide range of knowledge and interests.    TRUE or FALSE

10. An IQ score of 120 or above means that a person is creative.    TRUE or FALSE

11. Most creative people like Vincent Van Gogh and Edgar Allan Poe tend to become insane later in life.    TRUE or FALSE

12. Most people who are mentally ill are not especially creative. In fact, the more severely disturbed a person is, the less creative she or he is likely to be.    TRUE or FALSE

13. Maslow believed that living creatively is part of reaching our full potential.    TRUE or FALSE

## Intuitive Thought—Mental Shortcut? Or Dangerous Detour?:
## Pages 301-303
How accurate is intuition?

1. It is possible to draw true conclusions using faulty logic.    TRUE or FALSE

2. It is possible to draw false conclusions using valid logic.    TRUE or FALSE

3. Intuition is a quick, impulsive insight into the true nature of a problem and its solution.    TRUE or FALSE

4. To form accurate intuitive judgment of teachers, students must observe at least 20 minutes of the teacher's teaching ability.    TRUE or FALSE

5. The probability of two events occurring together is lower than the probability of either one occurring alone.   TRUE or FALSE

6. The representativeness heuristic is the strategy of stating problems in broad terms.
TRUE or FALSE

7. Being logical, most people do not let their emotions interfere when making important decisions.
TRUE or FALSE

8. Framing refers to the way in which a problem is stated or structured.   TRUE or FALSE

9. People who are intelligent are also wise because they live their lives with openness and tolerance.
TRUE or FALSE

# Human Intelligence—The IQ and You: Pages 304-307
## How is human intelligence defined and measured?

1. Alfred Binet's first test was designed to measure mechanical aptitude.   TRUE or FALSE

2. Lewis Terman helped write the original Stanford-Binet intelligence test.   TRUE or FALSE

3. The Stanford-Binet intelligence test measures three intelligence factors: knowledge, quantitative reasoning, and visual-spatial processing.   TRUE or FALSE

4. The Stanford-Binet intelligence test does include a memory task (repeating a series of digits) to determine a person's ability to use his/her short-term memory.   TRUE or FALSE

5. Mental age refers to average mental ability for a person of a given age.   TRUE or FALSE

6. Mental age can't be higher than chronological age.   TRUE or FALSE

7. IQ is equal to MA times CA divided by 100.   TRUE or FALSE

8. An IQ will be greater than 100 when CA is larger than MA.   TRUE or FALSE

9. Average intelligence is defined as an IQ from 90 to 109.   TRUE or FALSE

10. Modern IQ tests give scores as deviation IQs.   TRUE or FALSE

11. Being placed in the 84th percentile means that 16 percent of your peers received IQ scores higher than you and 84 percent have IQ scores lower than you.   TRUE or FALSE

12. An advantage of the Stanford-Binet intelligence test is that it can be applied cross-culturally.
TRUE or FALSE

13. The WISC is designed to test adult performance intelligence.   TRUE or FALSE

14. The digit symbol task is considered a performance subtest of the WAIS.   TRUE or FALSE

## Variations in Intelligence—Curved Like a Bell: Pages 308-310

How much does intelligence vary from person to person?

1. Only 12 people out of 100 score above 130 on IQ tests.   TRUE or FALSE

2. Gifted persons are more likely to succeed in adulthood if they have a high degree of intellectual determination.   TRUE or FALSE

3. Talking in complete sentences at age 2 is regarded as a sign of giftedness.   TRUE or FALSE

4. The performances of many autistic savants appear to result from intense practice.   TRUE or FALSE

5. A person must have an IQ of 80 or below to be classified as mentally retarded.   TRUE or FALSE

6. Familial retardation is a genetic condition that runs in families.   TRUE or FALSE

7. Intellectual disability caused by birth injuries is categorized as an organic problem.
   TRUE or FALSE

## Questioning Intelligence—How Intelligent Are Intelligence Tests?: Pages 310-314

What are some controversies in the study of intelligence?

1. Howard Gardner's theory of multiple intelligences states that traditional measures of language, logic, and math skills have little to do with intelligence.   TRUE or FALSE

2. Gardner suggests that each of us has eight different types of intelligence such as being "people smart," "word smart," etc.   TRUE or FALSE .

3. In general, artificial intelligence lacks the creativity and common sense of human intelligence.
   TRUE or FALSE

4. AI is frequently based on a set of rules applied to a body of information.   TRUE or FALSE

5. Computer simulations are used to test models of human cognition.   TRUE or FALSE

6. The IQs of fraternal twins reared together are more similar than those of other siblings.
   TRUE or FALSE

7. The IQs of identical twins are more alike than those of fraternal twins.   TRUE or FALSE

8. Intelligence is approximately 50 percent hereditary.   TRUE or FALSE

9. Children adopted into higher status homes tend, on average, to have higher adult IQs.
   TRUE or FALSE

10. The increased complexity and use of video games, the Internet, and television programs have lowered the IQ score by 15 points over the last 30 years.   TRUE or FALSE

## Psychology in Action: Culture, Race, IQ, and You: Pages 314-316
Are IQ tests fair to all cultural and racial groups?

1. The Dove Test was designed to be culturally biased.   TRUE or FALSE

2. The Stanford-Binet, Wechsler's, and the SAT are all culture-fair tests.   TRUE or FALSE

3. The small difference in average IQ scores for African Americans and Anglo Americans is explained by cultural and environmental differences.   TRUE or FALSE

4. IQ scores predict later career success.   TRUE or FALSE

5. Changing intelligence tests would result in a change in the IQ scores of people taking the tests. TRUE or FALSE

# FINAL SURVEY AND REVIEW

## What is Thinking?—Brains Over Brawn
What is the nature of thought?

1. _____ is the mental processing of information involving daydreaming, problem solving, and reasoning.

2. Thinking is the manipulation of internal _____ of external problems or situations.

3. Three basic units of thought are _____ , _____ , and language or _____ .

## Mental Imagery—Does a Frog Have Lips?
In what ways are images related to thinking?

1. Most people have internal images of one kind or another. Images may be based on _____ in memory or they may be created.

2. Sometimes images cross normal sense boundaries in a type of imagery called _____ .

3. The _____ of images used in problem solving may change. Images may be three-dimensional and they may be _____ in space to answer questions.

4. Many of the systems in the _____ that are involved in processing_____ images work in reverse to create _____ images.

301

5.  Kinesthetic images are created by memories of actions or by _____ (unexpressed) actions.

    Kinesthetic sensations seem to help structure thinking for many people.

## Concepts—I'm Positive, It's a Whatchamacallit
What are concepts?

1.  A concept is a_____ idea of a class of objects or events.

2.  Forming concepts may be based on experiences with positive and_____ _____.

3.  Concepts may also be acquired by learning _____ that define the concept.

4.  Concepts may be classified as _____ ("and" concepts), _____ ("_____

    or" concepts), or relational concepts.

5.  In practice, we frequently use _____ (general models of the concept class) to identify concepts.

6.  The _____ meaning of a word or concept is its dictionary definition. _____

    meaning is personal or emotional.

7.  Two common thinking errors are _____ thinking (thinking in black and white terms) and

    use of _____ (inaccurate and oversimplified images of social groups).

8.  Connotative meaning can be measured with the _____ differential. Most connotative

    meaning involves the dimensions good-bad, _____, and _____.

## Language—Don't Leave Home Without It
What is the role of language in thinking?

1.  Language allows events to be _____ into symbols for easy mental manipulation.

2.  Thinking in language is influenced by meaning. The study of meaning is called _____.

3.  Language is built out of_____ (basic speech sounds) and _____ (speech sounds

    collected into meaningful units).

4.  Learning a second language ( _____ ) during the elementary school years is most likely

    to benefit students who participate in _____ education.

5.  Language carries meaning by combining a set of symbols or signs according to a set of rules

    ( _____ ), which includes rules about word order ( _____ ).

302

6. Various sentences are created by applying _____ rules to simple statements.

7. A true language is _____ , and can be used to generate new ideas or possibilities.

   _____ Language (ASL) and other gestural languages used by the deaf are true languages.

8. Animal communication is relatively limited because it lacks _____ that can be rearranged easily.

9. Attempts to teach chimpanzees ASL and other nonverbal systems suggest to some that _____ are capable of language use. However, others believe that the chimps are merely using simple gestures to get food and other_____.

10. Studies that make use of_____(geometric word-symbols) provide the best evidence yet of animal language use.

# Problem Solving—Getting an Answer in Sight
## What do we know about problem solving?

1. The solution to a problem may be found _____ (by trial and error or by rote application of rules). However, _____ solutions are frequently inefficient or ineffective, except where aided by computer.

2. Often a rote solution is achieved through an _____ , a learned set of rules that always leads to a correct solution.

3. Solutions by _____ usually begin with discovery of the general properties of an answer. Next comes proposal of a number of _____ (workable) solutions.

4. Problem solving is frequently aided by _____. These are strategies that typically narrow the search for solutions.

5. Expert human problem solving is based on _____ knowledge and acquired _____ rather than some general improvement in thinking ability. Expertise also allows more processing _____ of problems.

6. When understanding leads to a rapid solution, _____has occurred. Three elements of _____ are _____ , selective combination, and selective comparison.

7. The ability to apply selective comparison (comparing _____ solutions to new problems) effectively can be influenced by our_____ .

8.  Insights and other problem solving attempts can be blocked by _____ (a tendency to repeat wrong solutions).

9.  _____ fixedness is a common fixation, but emotional _____, cultural _____, learned conventions, and perceptual habits are also problems.

# Creative Thinking—Down Roads Less Traveled
## What is creative thinking?

1.  Thinking may be deductive or_____, _____or illogical.

2.  Creative thinking requires _____ thought, characterized by _____ , flexibility, and originality. Creativity is also marked by_____, the active discovery of problems to be solved.

3.  To be creative, a solution must be practical and sensible as well as _____.

4.  _____ thinking involves generating many possibilities from one starting point.

5.  Tests of creativity, such as the Unusual _____ Test, the Consequences Test, and the Anagrams Test, measure the capacity for _____ thinking.

6.  Five stages often seen in creative problem solving are orientation, preparation,_____, _____ , and verification.

7.  Not all creative thinking fits this pattern. Much creative activity is based on _____ problem solving (many small steps).

8.  Studies suggest that creative persons share a number of identifiable general traits, thinking abilities, thinking styles, and _____ characteristics. There is a small _____ between IQ and creativity.

# Intuitive Thought—Mental Shortcut? Or Dangerous Detour?
## How accurate is intuition?

1.  People often make decisions intuitively, rather than _____.

2.  Intuitive thinking often leads to errors. Wrong conclusions may be drawn when an answer seems highly _____ of what we already believe is true. (That is, when people apply the representativeness _____ .

3. Another problem is allowing _____ such as fear, hope, anxiety, or disgust to guide thinking in _____ making.

4. An additional problem is ignoring the _____ _____ (or underlying probability) of an event.

5. Clear thinking is usually aided by stating or _____ a problem in broad _____ terms.

# Human Intelligence—The IQ and You
## How is human intelligence defined and measured?

1. Intelligence refers to one's general capacity to act _____ , _____ rationally, and deal effectively with the environment.

2. In practice, writing an intelligence test provides an _____ definition of intelligence.

3. One limitation of traditional intelligence testing is its applicability to various _____ groups. Because children from various cultures are taught different skills, _____ intelligence tests have been implemented to accurately assess individuals' intellectual abilities and to reduce biases.

4. The first practical intelligence test was assembled in 1904, in Paris, by _____ _____.

5. A modern version of Binet's test is the _____ *Intelligence* _____ *Scales, Fifth Edition.*

6. The Stanford-Binet measures fluid reasoning, general knowledge, _____ reasoning, _____ - spatial processing, and working memory.

7. Intelligence is expressed in terms of an intelligence quotient (IQ). IQ is defined as _____ _____ (MA) divided by _____ _____ (CA) and then multiplied by 100. Mental age is the _____ capacity of a group of people at a certain age and chronological age is a person's actual age in years.

8. An "average" IQ of 100 occurs when _____ age equals _____ age.

9. Modern IQ tests no longer calculate IQs directly. Instead, the final score reported by the test is a _____ _____ , which gives a person's relative intellectual standing in his or her age group.

10. A second major intelligence test is the _____ *Adult Intelligence Scale, Third Edition* (WAIS-III). The WAIS-III measures both _____ and performance (nonverbal) intelligence.

11. Intelligence tests have also been produced for use with _____ of people.

305

12. The *Scholastic Assessment Test* (SAT) is a _____ _____ test. Although narrower in scope than IQ tests, it bears some similarities to them.

# Variations in Intelligence—Curved Like a Bell
How much does intelligence vary from person to person?

1. People with IQs above _____ are considered to be in the gifted or "genius" range.

2. By criteria other than IQ, a large proportion of children might be considered _____ or _____ in one way or another.

3. Autistic _____ have exceptional abilities in music, mechanics, math, and remembering names or numbers.

4. The term _____ disabled is applied to those whose IQ falls below 70 or who lack various adaptive behaviors.

5. About 50 percent of the cases of intellectual disability are _____ , being caused by birth injuries, fetal damage, metabolic disorders, or _____ abnormalities. The remaining cases are of undetermined cause.

6. Many cases of subnormal intelligence are thought to be the result of _____ intellectual disability (a low level of intellectual stimulation in the home, poverty, and poor nutrition).

# Questioning Intelligence—How Intelligent Are Intelligence Tests?
What are some controversies in the study of intelligence?

1. Howard _____ believes that traditional IQ tests define intelligence too narrowly. According to Gardner, intelligence consists of abilities in _____ , logic and math, visual and spatial thinking, _____ , kinesthetic skills, intrapersonal skills, interpersonal skills, and naturalist skills.

2. Artificial intelligence refers to any _____ that can perform tasks that require intelligence when done by _____ .

3. Two principal areas of artificial intelligence research are computer simulations and _____ .

4. Studies of _____ (selective breeding for desirable characteristics) in animals suggest that intelligence is influenced by heredity.

5. Studies of family relationships in humans, especially comparisons between _____ twins and _____ twins, also suggest that intelligence is partly hereditary.

306

6. However, _____ is also important, as revealed by changes in tested intelligence induced by stimulating _____ and improved education.

7. Early childhood _____ programs such as Head Start provide longer-term stimulating intellectual experiences for disadvantaged children.

8. An overall average increase of 15 IQ points during the last 30 years has been attributed to _____ factors such as improved education, nutrition, and _____ (e.g., the complexity of the Internet and computer software).

9. Intelligence therefore reflects the combined effects of _____ and _____ .

## Psychology in Action: Culture, Race, IQ, and You
Are IQ tests fair to all cultural and racial groups?

1. Traditional IQ tests often suffer from a degree of _____ bias that makes them easier for some groups and harder for others.

2. _____ tests try to measure intelligence in ways that are not strongly affected by cultural background, but no test is entirely culture-free.

3. Differences in the average IQ scores for various racial groups are based on _____ differences, not heredity.

4. IQ is merely an _____ of intelligence based tests that offer a narrow definition of intelligence.

# MASTERY TEST

1. The mark of a true language is that it must be
   a. spoken.
   b. productive.
   c. based on spatial grammar and syntax.
   d. capable of encoding conditional relationships.

2. Computer simulations and expert systems are two major applications of
   a. AI.
   b. ASL.
   c. brainstorming.
   d. problem framing.

3. Failure to wear automobile seat belts is an example of which intuitive thinking error?
   a. allowing too much time for incubation
   b. framing a problem broadly
   c. ignoring base rates
   d. recognition that two events occurring together are more likely than either one alone

4. One thing that images, concepts, and symbols all have in common is that they are
   a. morphemes.
   b. internal representations.
   c. based on reverse vision.
   d. translated into micro movements.

5. To decide if a container is a cup, bowl, or vase, most people compare it to
   a. a prototype.
   b. its connotative meaning.
   c. a series of negative instances.
   d. a series of relevant phonemes.

6. During problem solving, being "cold," "warm," or "very warm" is closely associated with
   a. insight.
   b. fixation.
   c. automatic processing.
   d. rote problem solving.

7. The Anagrams Test measures
   a. mental sets.
   b. inductive thinking.
   c. logical reasoning.
   d. divergent thinking.

8. "Either-or" concepts are
   a. conjunctive.
   b. disjunctive.
   c. relational.
   d. prototypical.

9. Which term does not belong with the others?
   a. selective comparison
   b. functional fixedness
   c. learned conventions
   d. emotional blocks

10. The random search strategy is a type of
    a. prototype.
    b. heuristic.
    c. functional solution.
    d. form of intuitive thought.

11. An incremental view of creative problem solving CONTRASTS most directly with which stage of creative thought?
    a. orientation
    b. preparation
    c. illumination
    d. verification

12. While trying to solve a problem, Ed has generated as many solutions as he can think of, an example of
    a. intuition.
    b. divergent thinking.
    c. feasible solutions.
    d. selective comparison.

13. The difference between prime beef and dead cow is primarily a matter of
    a. syntax.
    b. conjunctive meaning.
    c. semantics.
    d. the productive nature of language.

14. Synaesthesia is an unusual form of
    a. imagery.
    b. heuristic.
    c. insight.
    d. daydreaming.

15. Which of the listed terms does NOT correctly complete this sentence: Insight involves selective
    a. encoding.
    b. combination.
    c. comparison.
    d. fixation.

16. Which of the following is LEAST likely to predict that a person is creative?
    a. high IQ
    b. a preference for complexity
    c. fluency in combining ideas
    d. use of mental images

17. The underlying probability of an event is its
    a. frame.
    b. base rate.
    c. selective comparison.
    d. thin-slice.

18. Language allows events to be _____ into _____ .
    a. translated; concepts
    b. fixated; codes
    c. rearranged; lexigrams
    d. encoded; symbols

19. "A triangle must be a closed shape with three sides made of straight lines." This statement is an example of a
    a. prototype.
    b. positive instance.
    c. conceptual rule.
    d. disjunctive concept.

20. Fluency, flexibility, and originality are all measures of
    a. inductive thinking.
    b. selective comparison.
    c. intuitive framing.
    d. divergent thinking.

21. The form of imagery that is especially important in music, sports, dance, and martial arts is
    a. kinesthetic imagery.
    b. synesthetic imagery.
    c. prototypical imagery.
    d. conjunctive imagery.

22. Among animals trained to use language, Kanzi has been unusually accurate at
    a. using proper syntax.
    b. substituting gestures for lexigrams.
    c. expressing conditional relationships.
    d. forming spoken words.

23. Random search strategies are most similar to
    a. selective encoding.
    b. automatic processing.
    c. trial-and-error problem solving.
    d. the orientation phase of problem solving.

24. Looking for analogies and delaying evaluation are helpful strategies for increasing
    a. divergent thinking.
    b. convergent thinking.
    c. functional fixedness.
    d. concept formation.

25. Comparing two three-dimensional shapes to see if they match is easiest if only a small amount of _____ is required.
    a. conceptual recoding
    b. mental rotation
    c. concept formation
    d. kinesthetic transformation

26. The good-bad dimension on the semantic differential is closely related to a concept's
    a. disjunctive meaning.
    b. conjunctive meaning.
    c. connotative meaning.
    d. denotative meaning.

27. Most computer models of human problem solving are based on some form of
    a. base rate framing.
    b. means-ends analysis.
    c. divergent search strategy.
    d. representativeness heuristic.

28. The largest number of people are found in which IQ range?
    a. 80-89
    b. 90-109
    c. 110-119
    d. below 70

29. Questions that involve copying geometric shapes would be found in which ability area of the SB5?
    a. fluid reasoning
    b. quantitative reasoning
    c. visual-spatial processing
    d. working memory

30. The *Scholastic Assessment Test* is really a
    a. special aptitude test.
    b. multiple aptitude test.
    c. general intelligence test.
    d. test of performance intelligence.

31. On the average, the smallest changes in IQ would be expected between the ages of
    a. 2 and 10.
    b. 10 and 15.
    c. 2 and 18.
    d. 30 and 40.

32. A combination of high ability and general retardation is found in
    a. autistism.
    b. Down syndrome.
    c. the adapted developmentally disabled.
    d. savants.

33. The distribution of IQ scores closely matches
    a. an inverted U curve.
    b. a normal curve.
    c. a g-factor curve.
    d. Bell's percentiles.

34. Which of the following is fixed at birth?
    a. IQ
    b. genes
    c. giftedness
    d. MA

35. Separate collections of verbal and performance subtests are a feature of the
    a. WAIS.
    b. *Dove Test*.
    c. CQT.
    d. SAT.

36. Westernized nations have shown large average IQ gains in a single generation. These findings support the idea that intelligence is influenced by
    a. nature.
    b. environment.
    c. genetics.
    d. the hereditary g-factor.

37. Intellectual disability is formally defined by deficiencies in
    a. aptitudes and self-help skills.
    b. intelligence and scholastic aptitudes.
    c. language and spatial thinking.
    d. IQ and adaptive behaviors.

38. A 12-year-old child, with an IQ of 100, must have an MA of
    a. 100.
    b. 12.
    c. 10.
    d. 15.

39. The *Stanford-Binet Intelligence Scale* was based on the work of Binet and
    a.  Terman.
    b.  Wechsler.
    c.  Gardner.
    d.  Feuerstein.

40. A test deliberately written to be culturally biased is the
    a.  WAIS.
    b.  SB5.
    c.  Dove Test.
    d.  SOMPA test battery.

41. A person's relative intellectual standing in his or her age group is revealed by
    a.  the age quotient.
    b.  the digit symbol index.
    c.  chronological age.
    d.  deviation IQ.

42. Creating an intelligence test provides a(n) _____ definition of intelligence.
    a.  valid
    b.  reliable
    c.  operational
    d.  chronological

43. For large groups, the greatest similarity in IQs would be expected between
    a.  identical twins.
    b.  fraternal twins.
    c.  siblings reared together.
    d.  parents and their children.

44. An intelligence test specifically designed for use with children is the
    a.  WAIS-III.
    b.  Dove Test.
    c.  WISC-IV.
    d.  *Savant Developmental Scale.*

45. A type of intellectual disability that appears to be based largely on the effects of poor environment is
    a.  fetal damage.
    b.  metabolic disorder.
    c.  genetic abnormality.
    d.  familial retardation.

46. Culture-fair tests attempt to measure intelligence without being affected by a person's
    a.  verbal skills.
    b.  cultural background.
    c.  educational level.
    d.  all of the preceding.

313

47. Which of the five Stanford-Binet Intelligence Scales measures how well people can imagine and correctly determine their location by following written instructions?
    a. fluid reasoning
    b. visual-spatial processing
    c. knowledge
    d. working memory

48. The argument that people from different regions and cultures are taught to understand the world differently by using different kinds of knowledge and mental abilities suggests that a(n) _____ is necessary to measure intelligence accurately.
    a. Stanford-Binet Intelligence Scale
    b. culture-fair test
    c. SAT
    d. WAIS

49. An average increase of 15 IQ points during the last 30 years has been attributed to
    a. an increase in the complexity of the Internet and computer software.
    b. people working harder and playing less.
    c. an increase in intelligent people having more children.
    d. none of the above.

# SOLUTIONS

## RECITE AND REVIEW

### What is Thinking?—Brains Over Brawn: Page 284
What is the nature of thought?

1. mental; problem
2. internal
3. language

### Mental Imagery—Does a Frog Have Lips?: Pages 284-286
In what ways are images related to thinking?

1. created
2. sense
3. change; space
4. visual
5. actions; actions

### Concepts—I'm Positive, It's a Whatchamacallit: Pages 286-288
What are concepts?

1. class groups
2. positive
3. concept
4. and; either-or
5. models
6. definition; personal
7. all-or-nothing; social;
8. good-bad

# Language—Don't Leave Home without It: Pages 288-292

What is the role of language in thinking?

1. symbols
2. meaning
3. sounds; meaningful
4. language; two-way

5. rules; order
6. rules
7. gestural
8. rearranged

9. simple gestures
10. geometric

# Problem Solving—Getting an Answer in Sight: Pages 293-297

What do we know about problem solving?

1. rote; computer
2. rote; learned
3. general; solutions

4. narrow
5. knowledge; processing
6. solution; selective

7. selective
8. wrong
9. fixation; habits

# Creative Thinking—Down Roads Less Traveled: Pages 297-301

What is creative thinking?

1. Thinking
2. originality; finding
3. practical
4. possibilities

5. Creativity
6. preparation
7. steps
8. thinking; styles

# Intuitive Thought—Mental Shortcut? Or Dangerous Detour: Pages 301-303

How accurate is intuition?

1. intuitively
2. errors; true

3. fear; anxiety; thinking
4. probability

5. broad

# Human Intelligence—The IQ and You: Pages 304-307

How is human intelligence defined and measured?

1. intelligence; test
2. rationally; environment
3. definition
4. applicability; culture-fair

5. *Intelligence Scales*
6. fluid; memory
7. quotient; 100
8. 100; equals
9. IQ's; relative

10. *Adult*; nonverbal
11. groups
12. group

# Variations in Intelligence—Curved Like a Bell: Pages 308-310

How much does intelligence vary from person to person?

1. gifted
4. developmentally; 70

2. motivated
5. 50; birth

3. math; numbers
6. intellectual

## Questioning Intelligence—How Intelligent Are Intelligence Tests?: Pages 310-314

What are some controversies in the study of intelligence?

1. traditional; math; visual
2. system; intelligence
3. computer

4. breeding
5. genes; hereditary
6. stimulating

7. disadvantaged
8. environmental
9. Intelligence

## Psychology in Action: How Intelligent Are Intelligent Tests?: Pages 314-316

Are IQ tests fair to all cultural and racial groups?

1. bias
2. educational; fair

3. cultural; culture
4. genetics (or heredity)

5. IQ

# CONNECTIONS

## What is Thinking?—Brains over Brawn and Mental Imagery—Does a Frog Have Lips?: Pages 284-286

What is the nature of thought? In what ways are images related to thinking?

1. f
2. d
3. h

4. a
5. c
6. g

7. b
8. e

## Concepts—I'm Positive, It's a Whatchamacallit: Pages 286-288

What are concepts?

1. b
2. d
3. h

4. c
5. a
6. g

7. f
8. e

## Language—Don't Leave Home without It: Pages 288-292

What is the role of language in thinking?

1. c
2. h
3. a

4. e
5. j
6. b

7. f
8. g
9. d

## Problem Solving—Getting an Answer in Sight: Pages 293-297

What do we know about problem solving?

1. g
2. e
3. a
4. f

5. h
6. b
7. j
8. c

9. i
10. d

## Creative Thinking—Down Roads Less Traveled: Pages 297-303

What is creative thinking? How accurate is intuition?

| | | | | | |
|---|---|---|---|---|---|
| 1. | h | 5. | c | 9. | e |
| 2. | b | 6. | i | 10. | l |
| 3. | j | 7. | k | 11. | f |
| 4. | d | 8. | a | 12. | g |

## Human Intelligence—The IQ and You and Variations in Intelligence—Curved Like a Bell: Pages 304-310

How is human intelligence defined and measured? How much does intelligence vary from person to person?

| | | | | | |
|---|---|---|---|---|---|
| 1. | h | 5. | e | 9. | d |
| 2. | f | 6. | c | 10. | i |
| 3. | a | 7. | b | | |
| 4. | j | 8. | g | | |

## Questioning Intelligence—How Intelligent Are Intelligence Tests?: Pages 310-314

What are some controversies in the study of intelligence?

| | | | | | |
|---|---|---|---|---|---|
| 1. | g | 4. | f | 7. | c |
| 2. | d | 5. | e | | |
| 3. | b | 6. | a | | |

# CHECK YOUR MEMORY

## What is Thinking?—Brains Over Brawn: Page 284

What is the nature of thought?

| | | | |
|---|---|---|---|
| 1. | F | 3. | F |
| 2. | T | 4. | F |

## Mental Imagery—Does a Frog Have Lips?: Pages 284-286

In what ways are images related to thinking?

| | | | | | |
|---|---|---|---|---|---|
| 1. | T | 4. | T | 7. | T |
| 2. | F | 5. | T | 8. | T |
| 3. | T | 6. | T | 9. | F |

## Concepts—I'm Positive, It's a Whatchamacallit: Pages 286-288

What are concepts?

| | | |
|---|---|---|
| 1. T | 3. T | 5. F |
| 2. F | 4. T | 6. F |

## Language—Don't Leave Home Without It: Pages 288-292

What is the role of language in thinking?

| | | |
|---|---|---|
| 1. F | 8. F | 15. T |
| 2. T | 9. F | 16. T |
| 3. F | 10. F | 17. T |
| 4. F | 11. F | |
| 5. T | 12. F | |
| 6. F | 13. F | |
| 7. T | 14. T | |

## Problem Solving—Getting an Answer in Sight: Pages 293-297

What do we know about problem solving?

| | | |
|---|---|---|
| 1. T | 5. T | 9. T |
| 2. F | 6. T | 10. F |
| 3. F | 7. F | 11. T |
| 4. F | 8. F | 12. F |

## Creative Thinking—Down Roads Less Traveled: Pages 297-301

What is creative thinking?

| | | |
|---|---|---|
| 1. T | | |
| 2. F | 6 T | 10. F |
| 3. T | 7. F | 11. F |
| 4. T | 8. T | 12. T |
| 5. T | 9. T | 13. T |

## Intuitive Thought—Mental Shortcut? Or Dangerous Detour?: Pages 301-303

How accurate is intuition?

| | | |
|---|---|---|
| 1. T | 4  F | 7. F |
| 2. T | 5. T | 8. T |
| 3. F | 6. F | 9 F |

## Human Intelligence—The IQ and You: Pages 304-307

How is human intelligence defined and measured?

| | | |
|---|---|---|
| 1. F | 6. F | 11.F |
| 2. F | 7. F | 12.F |
| 3. T | 8. T | 13.T |
| 4. T | 9. T | |
| 5. F | 10.T | |

## Variations in Intelligence—Curved Like a Bell: Pages 308-310

How much does intelligence vary from person to person?

| | | |
|---|---|---|
| 1. F | 4. T | 7. T |
| 2. T | 5. F | |
| 3. T | 6. F | |

## Questioning Intelligence—How Intelligent Are Intelligence Tests?: Pages 310-314

What are some controversies in the study of intelligence?

| | | |
|---|---|---|
| 1. F | 5. T | 9. F |
| 2. T | 6. T | 10.T |
| 3. T | 7. T | |
| 4. T | 8. T | |

## Psychology in Action: Culture, Race, IQ, and You: Pages 314-316

Are IQ tests fair to all cultural and racial groups?

| | |
|---|---|
| 1. T | 3. T |
| 2. F | 4. F |

# FINAL SURVEY AND REVIEW

## What is Thinking?—Brains Over Brawn
What is the nature of thought?

1. Cognition
2. representations
3. images; concepts; symbols

## Mental Imagery—Does a Frog Have Lips?
In what ways are images related to thinking?

1. information; stored
2. synesthesia
3. size; rotated
4. brain; visual; mental
5. implicit

## Concepts—I'm Positive, It's a Whatchamacallit
What are concepts?

1. generalized
2. negative; instances
3. rules
4. conjunctive; disjunctive; either-
5. prototypes
6. denotative; Connotative
7. all-or-nothing; social stereotypes
8. semantic; strong-weak; active-passive

## Language—Don't Leave Home without It
What is the role of language in thinking?

1. encoded
2. semantics
3. phonemes; morphemes
4. bilingualism; two-way bilingual
5. grammar; syntax
6. transformation
7. productive; American Sign
8. symbols
9. primates; reinforcers
10. lexigrams

## Problem Solving—Getting an Answer in Sight
What do we know about problem solving?

1. mechanically; mechanical
2. algorithm
3. understanding; functional
4. heuristics
5. organized; strategies; automatic
6. insight; insight; selective encoding
7. old; culture
8. fixation
9. Functional; blocks; values

## Creative Thinking—Down Roads Less Traveled
What is creative thinking?

1. inductive; logical
2. divergent; fluency; problem finding
3. original
4. possibilities
5. Uses; divergent
6. incubation; illumination
7. incremental
8. personality; correlation

320

# Intuitive Thought—Mental Shortcut? Or Dangerous Detour?
How accurate is intuition?

1. logically
2. representative; heuristic
3. emotions; decision
4. base; rate
5. framing;

# Human Intelligence—The IQ and You
How is human intelligence defined and measured?

1. purposefully; think
2. operational
3. cultural; culture-fair
4. Alfred; Binet
5. *Stanford-Binet*
6. quantitative; visual
7. mental; age; chronological; age; intellectual
8. mental; chronological
9. deviation; IQ
10. *Wechsler* IQ
11. groups
12. scholastic; aptitude

# Variations in Intelligence—Curved Like a Bell
How much does intelligence vary from person to person?

1. 140
2. gifted; talented
6. familial
3. savants
4. developmentally
5. organic; genetic

# Questioning Intelligence—How Intelligent Are Intelligence Tests?
What are some controversies in the study of intelligence?

1. Gardner; language; music
2. artificial system; people
3. expert systems
4. eugenics
5. fraternal; identical
6. environment; environments
7. education
8. environmental; technology
9. heredity; environment

# Culture, Race, IQ, and You
Are IQ tests fair to all cultural and racial groups?

1. cultural
2. Culture-fair
3. environmental
4. index

# MASTERY TEST

| | | | |
|---|---|---|---|
| 1. b, p. 290 | 14. a, p. 284 | 27. c, p. 312 | 40. a, p. 307 |
| 2. a, p. 312 | 15. d, p. 295 | 28. b, p. 306 | 41. c, p. 306 |
| 3. c, p. 302 | 16. a, pp. 297-298 | 29. b, p. 305 | 42. d, p. 307 |
| 4. b, p. 284 | 17. b, p. 302 | 30. c, p. 307 | 43. c, p. 312 |
| 5. a, p. 287 | 18. d, p. 284 | 31. b, p. 305 | 44. c, p. 307 |
| 6. a, p. 294 | 19. c, p. 287 | 32. d, p. 309 | 45. c, p. 310 |
| 7. d, p. 298 | 20. d, p. 298 | 33. a, p. 308 | 46. d, p. 314 |
| 8. b, p. 287 | 21. a, p. 286 | 34. b, p. 313 | 47. d, p. 305 |
| 9. a, p. 295 | 22. a, p. 292 | 35. b, p. 314 | 48. b, p. 314 |
| 10. b, p. 293 | 23. a, p. 293 | 36. b, p. 313 | 49. b, p. 313 |
| 11. c, p. 300 | 24. c, p. 295 | 37. b, p. 309 | |
| 12. b, p. 298 | 25. a, p. 287 | 38. d, p. 306 | |
| 13. c, p. 289 | 26. b, p. 287 | 39. b, p. 307 | |

# Motivation and Emotion

## Chapter Overview

Motivation refers to the dynamics of behavior. Three principal types of motives are biological, stimulus, and learned. Motives initiate, sustain, and direct activities. Motivation typically involves this sequence: need, drive, goal, and goal attainment. Behavior can be activated either by needs or by goals. The attractiveness of a goal and its ability to initiate action are related to its incentive value. Most biological motives operate to maintain homeostasis. Circadian rhythms of bodily activity are closely tied to sleep, activity, and energy cycles, which can be seriously disrupted by time zone travel and shift work.

Hunger, overeating and eating disorders are complexly determined. Hunger is influenced by a complex interplay between fullness of the stomach, blood sugar levels, metabolism in the liver, and fat stores in the body. The most direct control of eating is affected by the hypothalamus. Other factors influencing hunger are the body's set point, external eating cues, the attractiveness and variety of diet, emotions, learned taste preferences and taste aversions, and cultural values. Obesity is the result of a complex interplay of internal and external influences, diet, emotions, genetics, and exercise. The most effective way to lose weight is behavioral dieting. Anorexia nervosa and bulimia nervosa are two prominent eating disorders. Both tend to involve conflicts about self-image, self-control, and anxiety.

Both intracellular and extracellular thirst are homeostatic. Pain avoidance is episodic. The sex drive is nonhomeostatic. Thirst and other basic motives are affected by a number of bodily factors, but are primarily under the central control of the hypothalamus. Pain avoidance is unusual because it is episodic. Pain avoidance and pain tolerance are partially learned. The sex drive is also unusual in that it is non-homeostatic.

Many activities are related to needs for stimulation and our efforts to maintain desired levels of arousal. Drives for stimulation are partially explained by arousal theory. The desired level of arousal or stimulation varies from person to person. Optimal performance on a task usually occurs at moderate levels of arousal and is described by an inverted function. The Yerkes-Dodson law further states that for simple tasks the ideal arousal level is higher, and for complex tasks is lower.

Learned motives, including social motives, account for much of the diversity of human motivation. Opponent-process theory explains the operation of some acquired motives. Social motives are acquired in complex ways, through socialization and cultural conditioning. Self-confidence greatly affects motivation in everyday life.

Maslow's hierarchy of motives categorizes needs as basic and growth oriented. Lower needs in the hierarchy are assumed to be dominant over higher needs. Self-actualization, the highest and most fragile need, is reflected in meta-needs and closely related to intrinsic motivation. In some situations, external rewards can undermine intrinsic motivation, enjoyment, and creativity.

An emotion consists of physiological changes, adaptive behavior, emotional expressions, and emotional feelings. Emotions can be disruptive, but overall they help us to adapt and survive. The primary emotions can be mixed to produce more complex emotional experiences. The left hemisphere of the brain primarily processes positive emotions, while the right processes negative emotions. The amygdala provides a "quick and dirty" pathway for the arousal of fear that bypasses the cerebral cortex. Body changes that occur during emotion are caused by the hormone adrenaline and activity in the autonomic nervous system (ANS). The sympathetic branch of the ANS is primarily responsible for arousing the body, the parasympathetic branch for quieting it.

Autonomic nervous system arousal underlies emotion and is all that "lie detectors" can detect. Emotional arousal involves changes in heart rate, blood pressure, breathing rate, and the galvanic skin response (GSR). The polygraph, or "lie detector," measures emotional arousal (rather than lying). Under some circumstances, the accuracy of the lie detector can be quite low.

Basic facial expressions of fear, anger, disgust, sadness, and happiness are universally recognized. Contempt, surprise, and interest may be universal as well. Body language expresses general emotional tone rather than specific universal messages. Facial expressions reveal pleasantness versus unpleasantness, attention versus rejection, and a person's degree of emotional activation. Body positioning expresses relaxation or tension and liking or disliking. Lying can sometimes be detected from changes in illustrators or emblems and from signs of general arousal.

A variety of theories have been proposed to explain emotions. The James-Lange theory says that emotional experience follows bodily reactions. In contrast, the Cannon-Bard theory says that bodily reactions and emotional experiences occur at the same time. Schachter's cognitive theory emphasizes that labeling bodily arousal can determine what emotion you feel. Appropriate labels are chosen by attribution. The facial feedback hypothesis holds that facial expressions help define the emotions we feel. Contemporary views of emotion place greater emphasis on the effects of cognitive appraisals. Also, our feelings and actions change as elements of emotion interact. One of the best ways to manage emotion is to change your emotional appraisal of a situation.

Emotional intelligence is the ability to consciously make your emotions work for you in a wide variety of life circumstances. People who are "smart" emotionally are self-aware, empathetic, know how to use emotions to enhance thinking, decision making, and relationships, and have an ability to understand and manage emotions. Positive emotions are valuable because they tend to broaden our focus and they encourage personal growth and social connection.

# Learning Objectives

## Theme: Our behavior is energized and directed by motives and emotions.

| |
|---|
| **GQ: What is motivation? Are there different types of motives?** |
| LO 10.1  Define *motivation*. |
| LO 10.2  Describe a motivational sequence using the need reduction model; explain how the *incentive value* of a *goal* can affect motivation; and describe how *incentive value* is related to internal *need*. |
| LO 10.3  List and describe the three types of *motives* and give an example of each. |
| LO 10.4  Define *homeostasis*. |
| LO 10.5  Explain how *circadian rhythms* affect energy levels, motivation, and performance. Include an explanation of how and why shift work and jet lag may adversely affect a person and how to minimize the effects of shifting one's rhythms, including the use of melatonin. |
| **GQ: What causes hunger? Overeating? Eating disorders?** |
| LO 10.6  Discuss why hunger cannot be fully explained by the contractions of an empty stomach and describe the relationship of each of the following to hunger: a. blood sugar; b. liver; c. *hypothalamus*: 1) feeding system (lateral hypothalamus, ghrelin), 2) satiety system (ventromedial hypothalamus), 3) blood sugar regulator (paraventricular nucleus); d. GLP-1; e. a person's *set point*; and f. the release of leptin. |
| LO 10.7  Explain how each of the following is related to overeating and obesity: a. external eating cues; b. dietary content; and c. emotionality. Include a brief discussion of body mass index and explain how it is calculated. |
| LO 10.8  Describe the impact of cultural factors and taste on hunger and explain how *taste aversions* are acquired. |
| LO 10.9  Explain the paradox of "yo-yo" dieting and describe what is meant by *behavioral dieting* and how these techniques can enable you to control your weight. |
| LO 10.10  Describe the essential features of the eating disorders of *anorexia nervosa* and *bulimia nervosa*; explain what causes them; and what treatment is available for them. Include a brief discussion of the relationship of culture and ethnicity to dieting and preferred body size. |
| **GQ: Is there more than one type of thirst? In what ways are pain avoidance and the sex drive unusual?** |
| LO 10.11  Name the brain structure that appears to control thirst (as well as hunger) and differentiate *extracellular* and *intracellular thirst*. |
| LO 10.12  Explain how the drive to avoid pain and the *sex drive* differ from other biological drives and include a brief explanation of the *non-homeostatic* nature of the sex drive. |
| **GQ: How does arousal relate to motivation? Pages 333-336** |
| LO 10.13  Describe the evidence for the existence of stimulus drives for exploration, manipulation, curiosity, and stimulation; explain the *arousal theory* of motivation and the characteristics of high and low sensation-seekers; describe the inverted U function; and relate arousal to the *Yerkes-Dodson law*. |
| LO 10.14  Describe the two major components of *test anxiety* and describe four ways to reduce it. |
| **GQ: What are learned motives? Social motives? Why are they important? Why are they important?** |
| LO 10.15  Use the ideas of Solomon's *opponent-process theory* to explain how a person might learn to like hazardous, painful, or frightening pursuits. |
| LO 10.16  Define the *need for achievement* (nAch) and differentiate it from the *need for power*; relate this need for achievement to risk taking; explain the influences of drive and determination in the success of high achievers; and list eight steps to enhance self-confidence. |
| **GQ: Are some motives more basic than others?** |
| LO 10.17  List (in order) the needs found in Maslow's *hierarchy of needs*; distinguish between *basic needs* and *growth needs*; explain why Maslow's lower (physiological) needs are considered prepotent; and define and give examples of *meta-needs*. |
| LO 10.18  Distinguish between *intrinsic* and *extrinsic motivation*, and explain how each type of motivation may affect a person's interest in work, leisure activities, and creativity. |
| **GQ: What happens during emotion? Pages 341-343** |
| LO 10.19  Explain how *emotions* aid survival; describe the three major elements of emotions; list the eight *primary emotions* proposed by Plutchik; explain how a person may experience two opposite emotions simultaneously; and state which side of the brain processes positive versus negative emotions and what effect the *amygdala* has on emotion. |

| |
|---|
| **GQ: What physiological changes underlie emotion? What physiological changes underlie emotion? Can "Lie Detectors" really detect lies?** |
| LO 10.20 Describe, in general, the effects of the *sympathetic* and *parasympathetic branches* of the ANS during and after emotion; explain how the *parasympathetic rebound* may be involved in cases of sudden death; and discuss the limitations of lie detector (*polygraph*) in detecting "lies" and what it actually measures. |
| **GQ: How accurately are emotions expressed by the face and "body language"? Pages 346-348** |
| LO 10.21 Discuss Darwin's view of human emotion; differentiate between Duchenne smiles and forced smiles; describe cultural and gender differences in emotions and emotional expressions; and d. discuss *kinesics*, including the emotional messages conveyed by facial expressions and body language and the behavioral clues to lying, such as *illustrators* versus *emblems*. |
| **GQ: How do psychologists explain emotions?** |
| LO 10.22 Describe and give examples of the following theories of emotion: a. *James-Lange theory*; b. *Cannon-Bard theory*; c. *Schachter's cognitive theory*; d. the effects of *attribution* on emotion; e. the role of *appraisal;* and f. the *facial feedback hypothesis* in the contemporary model of emotion. |
| **GQ: What does it mean to have "emotional intelligence"?** |
| LO 10.23 Describe the concept of *emotional intelligence* and its five skills and briefly discuss the benefits of positive emotions. |

# RECITE AND REVIEW

## Motivation—Forces that Push and Pull: Pages 320-323
What is motivation? Are there different types of motives?

1. Motives _____ (begin), sustain (perpetuate), and direct_____.

2. Motivation typically involves the sequence _____, drive, _____, and goal

    attainment (need reduction).

3. _____ Behavior can be activated either by needs ( _____ ) or by goals ( _____ ).

4. The attractiveness of a _____ and its ability to initiate action are related to its incentive

    value (its value above and beyond its capacity to fill a _____).

5. Three principal types of motives are biological motives, stimulus motives, and _____ motives.

6. Most _____ motives operate to maintain a _____ state of bodily equilibrium called

    homeostasis.

7. Circadian _____ within the body are closely tied to sleep, activity levels, and energy

    cycles. Time zone travel and shift work can seriously disrupt _____ and bodily rhythms.

8. If you anticipate a _____ in body rhythms, you can gradually preadapt to your new

    _____ over a period of days.

9.  Body rhythms and _____ cycles are strongly influenced by the release of melatonin, a

    _____ produced at night by the pineal gland.

# Hunger—Pardon Me, My Hypothalamus Is Growling: Pages 324-331

What causes hunger? Overeating? Eating disorders?

1.  Hunger is influenced by a complex interplay between distention (fullness) of the _____ lowered

    levels of glucose ( _____ ), metabolism in the _____ , and fat stores in the body.

2.  The most direct control of eating is exerted by the hypothalamus, which has areas that act like feeding

    ( _____ ) and satiety ( _____ ) systems for hunger and eating.

3.  The lateral hypothalamus acts as a _____ system and is activated by the hormone

    _____; the ventromedial hypothalamus is part of a _____ system; the

    paraventricular nucleus influences both hunger and satiety.

4.  Other factors influencing hunger are the set point for the proportion of _____ in the body,

    external eating cues, the attractiveness and variety of _____ .

5.  A body mass index is a measure of body fat that is calculated by dividing body _____

    squared over body _____ multiplied by 703.

6.  A BMI of _____ or higher should be a cause for concern since obesity is linked to heart

    disease, high blood pressure, stroke, diabetes, and premature death.

7.  Because of the limitations of traditional dieting, changing basic eating patterns and _____ is

    usually more effective.

8.  Behavioral _____ brings about such changes by use of self-control techniques.

9.  A successful behavioral dieting approach begins with committing oneself to weight loss, _____ ,

    counting _____ , developing techniques to control overeating, and charting one's progress.

10. Hunger is also influenced by emotions, learned _____ preferences and _____

    aversions (such as bait shyness in animals), and cultural values.

11. Anorexia nervosa (self-inflicted _____ ) and bulimia nervosa ( _____ and purging) are two prominent eating disorders. About _____ of people with anorexia are male.

12. Treatments for anorexia begin with medical diet to restore weight and health then advance to _____ .

13. Both eating disorders tend to involve conflicts about self-image, self-control, and _____ . The popularity of _____ , exercise, and sports also contributes to eating disorders.

## Biological Motives Revisited—Thirst, Sex, and Pain: Pages 331-333
Is there more than one type of thirst? In what ways are pain avoidance and the sex drive unusual?

1. Like hunger, thirst and other basic motives are affected by a number of _____ factors, but are primarily under the central control of the hypothalamus in the _____ .

2. Thirst may be either intracellular (when _____ is lost from inside _____ ) or extracellular (when _____ is lost from the spaces between _____ ).

3. Pain avoidance is unusual because it is episodic (associated with particular conditions) as opposed to cyclic (occurring in regular _____ ).

4. Pain avoidance and pain tolerance are partially _____ (influenced by training).

5. The sex drive in many lower animals is related to estrus (or "heat") in _____ . The sex drive is unusual in that it is non-homeostatic (both its _____ and its reduction are sought).

6. Sex _____ in both males and females may be related to bodily levels of androgens. Levels of _____ decline with age and taking supplements may restore the sex drive.

## Stimulus Drives—Skydiving, Horror Movies, and the Fun Zone: Pages 333-336
How does arousal relate to motivation?

1. The stimulus drives reflect needs for information, exploration, manipulation, and _____ input.

2. Drives for stimulation are partially explained by arousal theory, which states that an ideal level of _____ will be maintained if possible.

3. The desired level of _____ or stimulation varies from person to person, as measured by the *Sensation-Seeking Scale* (SSS).

4. Individuals from America, Israel, and Ireland tend to score _____ on the Sensation-Seeking Scale and they are likely to engage in high-risk behaviors.

5. Optimal performance on a task usually occurs at _____ levels of arousal. This relationship is described by an inverted U function.

6. The Yerkes-Dodson law further states that for _____ tasks the ideal arousal level is higher, and for _____ tasks it is lower.

7. Test anxiety is caused by a combination of _____ worrying and heightened physiological arousal, which can be reduced with better _____ , relaxation, _____ , and restructuring thoughts.

## Learned Motives—The Pursuit of Excellence: Pages 336-338
What are learned motives? Social motives? Why are they important?

1. _____ motives are learned through socialization and cultural conditioning.

2. Opponent-process theory, which states that strong _____ tend to be followed by an opposite _____ , explains some acquired motives.

3. One of the most prominent social motives is the _____ for achievement (nAch).

4. High nAch is correlated with _____ in many situations, with occupational choice, and with moderate _____ taking.

5. Self-confidence affects _____ because it influences the challenges you will undertake, the _____ you will make, and how long you will _____ when things don't go well.

6. To enhance self-confidence, one should do the following: Set goals that are specific, _____ , and attainable, advance in _____ steps, find a role model, get expert instructions, and get _____ support.

## Motives in Perspective—A View from the Pyramid: Pages 338-341
Are some motives more basic than others?

1. Maslow's hierarchy (rank ordering) of motives categorizes needs as _____ and growth oriented.

2. _____ needs in the hierarchy are assumed to be prepotent (dominant) over _____ needs.

3. _____ -actualization, the highest and most fragile need, is reflected in meta-_____ .

4. In many situations, extrinsic motivation (that which is induced by obvious _____ rewards) can reduce intrinsic motivation, enjoyment, and creativity.

## Inside an Emotion—How Do You Feel?: Pages 341-343
What happens during emotion? Pages 341-343

1. Emotions are linked to many basic adaptive _____ , such as attacking, retreating, feeding, and reproducing.

2. Other major elements of emotion are physiological changes in the body, emotional expressions, and emotional _____ .

3. The following are considered to be primary emotions: fear, surprise, _____ , disgust, _____ , anticipation, joy, and trust (acceptance). Other emotions seem to represent mixtures of the primaries.

## Physiology and Emotion—Arousal, Sudden Death, and Lying: Pages 343-345
What physiological changes underlie emotion? Can "lie detectors" really detect lies?

1. Physical changes associated with emotion are caused by the action of adrenaline, a _____ released into the bloodstream, and by activity in the autonomic _____ (ANS).

2. The sympathetic _____ of the ANS is primarily responsible for arousing the body, the parasympathetic _____ for quieting it.

3. Sudden death due to prolonged and intense emotion is probably related to parasympathetic _____ (excess activity). Heart attacks caused by sudden intense emotion are more likely due to sympathetic _____.

4. The polygraph, or "lie detector," measures _____ by monitoring heart rate, blood pressure, breathing rate, and the galvanic skin response (GSR).

5. Asking a series of _____ and irrelevant questions may allow the detection of _____, but overall, the accuracy of the lie detector has been challenged by many researchers.

6. A polygraph makes use of such _____ questions as "Have you ever stolen anything from your place of work?" to increase the person's anxiety level. Their answers will be compared to other _____ questions for which the police are seeking answers.

7. Infrared face scans and the use of _____ in analyzing brain activity are possible alternative techniques to polygraph testing.

## Expressing Emotions—Making Faces and Talking Bodies: Pages 346-348

How accurately are emotions expressed by the face and "body language"?

1. Basic emotional expressions, such as smiling or baring one's teeth when angry, appear to be _____.

2. Facial expressions of _____, anger, disgust, _____, and happiness are recognized by people of all cultures.

3. In Western culture, women are encouraged to express such emotions as _____, fear, _____, and guilt, and men are expected to express _____ and hostility.

4. Body gestures and movements (body language) also express _____, mainly by communicating emotional _____.

5. Three dimensions of _____ expressions are pleasantness-unpleasantness, attention-rejection, and activation.

6. The study of _____ is known as kinesics.

331

## Theories of Emotion—Several Ways To Fear a Bear: Pages 348-353

How do psychologists explain emotions?

1. The James-Lange theory of emotion says that emotional experience _____ an awareness of the bodily reactions of emotion.

2. In contrast, the Cannon-Bard theory says that bodily reactions and emotional experience occur _____ _____ _____ _____ and that emotions are organized in the brain.

3. Schachter's cognitive theory of emotion emphasizes the importance of _____, or interpretations, applied to feelings of bodily arousal.

4. Also important is the process of attribution, in which bodily _____ is attributed to a particular person, object, or situation.

5. Research on attribution theory has shown that physical arousal (e.g., an _____ heart rate from exercise or fear) can be _____ to different sources such as attraction or love for someone.

6. The facial feedback hypothesis holds that sensations and information from emotional _____ help define what emotion a person is feeling.

7. Making faces does influence _____ and bodily activities through the _____ nervous system.

8. Contemporary views of emotion place greater emphasis on how _____ are appraised. Also, all of the elements of emotion are seen as interrelated and interacting.

## Psychology in Action: Emotional Intelligence—The Fine Art of Self-Control: Pages 353-354

What does it mean to have "emotional intelligence"?

1. Emotional intelligence involves the following skills: _____ -awareness, empathy, _____ -control, and an understanding of how to use _____.

2. Emotionally intelligent people are good at reading facial expressions, tone of voice, and other signs of _____

3. They also use their _____ to enhance thinking and decision making.

4. _____ emotions are not just a luxury. They tend to encourage personal growth and social connection.

5. Martin Seligman believes people can achieve genuine happiness by optimizing their natural _____, such as _____, originality, humor, _____, and generosity, to buffer them against misfortunes.

# CONNECTIONS

## Motivation—Forces That Push and Pull: Pages 320-323
What is motivation? Are there different types of motives?

1. _____ incentive value
2. _____ alexithymia
3. _____ need
4. _____ homeostasis
5. _____ learned motives
6. _____ melatonin
7. _____ circadian rhythm

a. internal deficiency
b. goal desirability
c. learned goals
d. cannot name emotions
e. steady state
f. 24-hour day cycle
g. sleep inducing hormone

## Hunger—Pardon Me, My Hypothalamus Is Growling: Pages 324-331
What causes hunger? Overeating? Eating disorders?:

1. _____ ventromedial hypothalamus
2. _____ lateral hypothalamus
3. _____ paraventricular nucleus

## Hunger—Pardon Me, My Hypothalamus Is Growling (Cont.)

1. _____ satiety system
2. _____ taste aversion
3. _____ set point
4. _____ hunger and satiety
5. _____ body mass index
6. _____ weight cycling
7. _____ changes eating habits
8. _____ feeding system

a. weight/height$^2$ x 703
b. classical conditioning
c. thermostat for fat level
d. lateral hypothalamus
e. yo-yo dieting
f. paraventricular nucleus
g. ventrornedial hypothalamus
h. behavioral dieting

## Biological Motives Revisited—Thirst, Sex, and Pain: Pages 331-333

Is there more than one type of thirst? In what ways are pain avoidance and the sex drive unusual?

1. _____ episodic drive
2. _____ non-homeostatic
3. _____ intracellular thirst
4. _____ extracellular thirst
5. _____ estrus

a. weight/height$^2$ x 703
b. result from diarrhea
c. drive to avoid incidences of pain
d. human sex drive
e. result from too much salt intake

## Stimulus Drives—Skydiving, Horror Movies, and the Fun Zone and Learned Motives—The Pursuit of Excellence: Pages 333-338

How does arousal relate to motivation? What are learned motives? Social motives? Why are they important?

1. _____ androgen
2. _____ heightened physiological arousal
3. _____ nAch
4. _____ self-confidence
5. _____ SSS
6. _____ moderate risk takers
7. _____ estrus
8. _____ inverted U function

a. standards of excellence
b. sensation seekers
c. impaired test performance
d. high in nAch
e. mixture of arousal and performance
f. change in an animal's sexual drive
g male sex hormone
h. believing that one can succeed

## Motives in Perspective—A View from the Pyramid: Pages 338-341

Are some motives more basic than others?

1. _____ safety and security
2. _____ basic needs
3. _____ love and belonging
4. _____ self-actualization
5. _____ physiological needs
6. _____ esteem and self-esteem
7. _____ growth needs

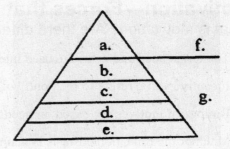

## Inside an Emotion—How Do You Feel? And Physiology and Emotion—Arousal, Sudden Death, and Lying: Pages 341-346

What happens during emotion? What physiological changes underlie emotion? Can "Lie Detectors" really detect lies?

1. _____ adrenaline
2. _____ parasympathetic rebound
3. _____ Robert Plutchik
4. _____ irrelevant questions
5. _____ polygraph
6. _____ sympathetic branch
7. _____ relevant questions
8. _____ mood

a. eight primary emotions
b. arousal-producing hormone
c. "Did you murder Hensley?"
d. nonemotional questions
e. prolonged mild emotion
f. fight or flight
g. intense emotional overreaction
h. lie detection

## Expressing Emotions—Making Faces and Talking Bodies and Psychology in Action: Emotional Intelligence—The Fine Art of Self-Control: Pages 346-348, 353-354

How accurately are emotions expressed by the face and "body language"?: How do psychologists explain emotions? What does it mean to have "emotional intelligence"?

1. _____ anxiety
2. _____ sadness
3. _____ authentic happiness
4. _____ James-Lange theory
5. _____ body language
6. _____ facial blend
7. _____ self-awareness
8. _____ Schachter's cognitive theory
9. _____ emotional intelligence

a. arousal + label then emotions
b. bodily arousal then emotions
c. mixing 2+ facial emotions
d. appraisal of loss
e. appraisal of threat
f. kinesics
g. emotional skills
h. in tune with own feelings
i. emphasize natural strengths

# CHECK YOUR MEMORY

## Motivation—Forces that Push and Pull: Pages 320-323
What is motivation? Are there different types of motives?

1. The terms need and drive are used interchangeably to describe motivation.   TRUE or FALSE

2. Incentive value refers to the "pull" of valued goals.    TRUE or FALSE

3. Biological motives are based on needs that must be met for survival.   TRUE or FALSE

4. Much of the time, homeostasis is maintained by automatic reactions within the body.

    TRUE or FALSE

5. Changes in body temperature are closely related to circadian rhythms.   TRUE or FALSE

6. Adapting to rapid time zone changes is easiest when a person travels east, rather than west.
    TRUE or FALSE

## Hunger—Pardon Me, My Hypothalamus Is Growling: Pages 324-331
What causes hunger? Overeating? Eating disorders?

1. Cutting the sensory nerves from the stomach abolishes hunger.    TRUE or FALSE

2. Lowered levels of glucose in the blood can cause hunger.   TRUE or FALSE

3. The body's hunger center is found in the thalamus.   TRUE or FALSE

4. The paraventricular nucleus is sensitive to neuropeptide Y.    TRUE or FALSE

5. Both glucagon-like peptide 1 (GLP-1) and leptin act as stop signals that inhibit eating.

    TRUE or FALSE

6. BMI is an estimation of body fat.    TRUE or FALSE

7. Dieting speeds up the body's metabolic rate.    TRUE or FALSE

8. People who diet intensely every other day lose as much weight as those who diet moderately every
    day.   TRUE or FALSE

9. Exercise makes people hungry and tends to disrupt dieting and weight loss.   TRUE or FALSE

10. Becoming emotionally upset has little impact on one's tendency to overeat. TRUE or FALSE

11. The fast-food industry promotes healthy and tasty products that have contributed to the problem
    of obesity.   TRUE or FALSE

12. "Yo-yo dieting" refers to repeatedly losing and gaining weight through the process of bingeing and purging.   TRUE or FALSE

13. Behavioral dieting changes habits without reducing the number of calories consumed.
TRUE or FALSE

14. Charting daily progress is a basic behavioral dieting technique.   TRUE or FALSE

15. The incentive value of foods is largely determined by cultural values.   TRUE or FALSE

16. Taste aversions may be learned after longer time delays than in other forms of classical conditioning.
TRUE or FALSE

17. Taste aversions tend to promote nutritional imbalance.   TRUE or FALSE

18. Many victims of anorexia nervosa overestimate their body size.   TRUE or FALSE

19. Over time, anorexics lose their appetite and do not feel hungry.   TRUE or FALSE

20. Eating disorders only occur in women.   TRUE or FALSE

## Biological Motives Revisited—Thirst, Sex, and Pain: Pages 331-333

Is there more than one type of thirst? In what ways are pain avoidance and the sex drive unusual?

1. Bleeding, vomiting, or sweating can cause extracellular thirst.   TRUE or FALSE

2. Intracellular thirst is best satisfied by a slightly salty liquid.   TRUE or FALSE

3. Tolerance for pain is largely unaffected by learning.   TRUE or FALSE

4. Castration of a male animal typically abolishes the sex drive.   TRUE or FALSE

5. Getting drunk *decreases* sexual desire, arousal, pleasure, and performance.   TRUE or FALSE

## Stimulus Drives—Skydiving, Horror Movies, and the Fun Zone: Pages 333-336

How does arousal relate to motivation?

1. It is uncomfortable to experience both very high and very low levels of arousal.
TRUE or FALSE

2. Disinhibition and boredom susceptibility are characteristics of sensation-seeking persons.
TRUE or FALSE

3. Individuals who score high on the Sensation-Seeking Scales do not engage in high-risk behaviors such as substance abuse.   TRUE or FALSE

4. For nearly all activities, the best performance occurs at high levels of arousal.   TRUE or FALSE

5. Test anxiety is a combination of arousal and excessive worry.   TRUE or FALSE

6. Being overprepared is a common cause of test anxiety.   TRUE or FALSE

## Learned Motives—The Pursuit of Excellence: Pages 336-338

What are learned motives? Social motives? Why are they important?

1. Opponent-process theory assumes that emotional responses habituate when activities are repeated. TRUE or FALSE

2. The need for achievement refers to a desire to have impact on other people.   TRUE or FALSE

3. People high in nAch generally prefer "long shots" or "sure things."   TRUE or FALSE

4. Benjamin Bloom found that high achievement is based as much on hard work as it is on talent. TRUE or FALSE

5. For many activities, self-confidence is one of the most important sources of motivation. TRUE or FALSE

## Motives in Perspective—A View from the Pyramid: Pages 338-341

Are some motives more basic than others?

1. Maslow's hierarchy of needs places self-esteem at the top of the pyramid.   TRUE or FALSE

2. Maslow believed that needs for safety and security are more potent than needs for love and belonging.   TRUE or FALSE

3. Meta-needs are the most basic needs in Maslow's hierarchy.   TRUE or FALSE

4. Maslow believed that most people are motivated to seek esteem, love and security rather than self-actualization.   TRUE or FALSE

5. Intrinsic motivation occurs when obvious external rewards are provided for engaging in an activity. TRUE or FALSE

6. People are more likely to be creative when they are intrinsically motivated.   TRUE or FALSE

7. Emotions help people survive by bonding with each other as they socialize and work together. TRUE or FALSE

8. Happy, positive moods are as equally adaptive as negative moods in influencing creativity, efficiency, and helpfulness to others.   TRUE or FALSE

## Inside an Emotion—How Do You Feel?: Pages 341-343
What happens during emotion?

1. Most physiological changes during emotion are related to the release of adrenaline into the brain.
   TRUE or FALSE

2. Robert Plutchik's theory lists contempt as a primary emotion.   TRUE or FALSE

3. For most students, elevated moods tend to occur on Saturdays and Tuesdays.   TRUE or FALSE

4. Positive emotions are processed mainly in the left hemisphere of the brain.   TRUE or FALSE

5. The brain area called the amygdala specializes in producing fear.   TRUE or FALSE

6. Our moods and motives are closely tied to circadian rhythms.   TRUE or FALSE

## Physiology and Emotion—Arousal, Sudden Death, and Lying: Pages 343-345
What physiological changes underlie emotion? Can "Lie Detectors" really detect lies?

1. The sympathetic branch of the ANS is under voluntary control and the parasympathetic branch is involuntary.   TRUE or FALSE

2. The parasympathetic branch of the ANS slows the heart and lowers blood pressure.
   TRUE or FALSE

3. Most sudden deaths due to strong emotion are associated with the traumatic disruption of a close relationship.   TRUE or FALSE

4. Although not 100% accurate, infrared face scans are 50% better at detecting lies than polygraph tests.
   TRUE or FALSE

## Expressing Emotions—Making Faces and Talking Bodies: Pages 346-348
How accurately are emotions expressed by the face and "body language"?

1. The polygraph measures the body's unique physical responses to lying.   TRUE or FALSE

2. Only a guilty person should react emotionally to irrelevant questions.   TRUE or FALSE

3. Control questions used in polygraph exams are designed to make almost everyone anxious.
   TRUE or FALSE

4. The lie detector's most common error is to label innocent persons guilty.   TRUE or FALSE

5. Children born deaf and blind express emotions with their faces in about the same way as other people do.
   TRUE or FALSE

6. An authentic, or Duchenne, smile involves the muscles near the corners of a person's eyes, not just the mouth.    TRUE or FALSE

7. The "A-okay" hand gesture means "everything is fine" around the world.    TRUE or FALSE

8. Facial blends mix two or more basic expressions.    TRUE or FALSE

9. Liking is expressed in body language by leaning back and relaxing the extremities.
TRUE or FALSE

10. Gestures such as rubbing hands, twisting hair, and biting lips are consistently related to lying.
TRUE or FALSE

11. People from Asian cultures are more likely to express anger in public than people from Western cultures.
TRUE or FALSE

12. In Western cultures, men tend to be more emotionally expressive than women.    TRUE or FALSE

## Theories of Emotion—Several Ways to Fear a Bear: Pages 348-353
How do psychologists explain emotions?

1. The James-Lange theory of emotion says that we see a bear, feel fear, are aroused, and then run.
TRUE or FALSE

2. The Cannon-Bard theory states that emotion and bodily arousal occur at the same time.
TRUE or FALSE

3. According to Schachter's cognitive theory, arousal must be labeled in order to become an emotion.
TRUE or FALSE

4. Attribution theory predicts that people are most likely to "love" someone who does not agitate, anger, and frustrate them.    TRUE or FALSE

5. Making facial expressions can actually cause emotions to occur and alter physiological activities in the body.    TRUE or FALSE

6. Emotional appraisal refers to deciding if your own facial expressions are appropriate for the situation you are in.    TRUE or FALSE

7. Suppressing emotions can impair thinking and memory because a lot of energy must be devoted to self-control.    TRUE or FALSE

8. Moving toward a desired goal is associated with the emotion of happiness.
TRUE or FALSE

9. Emotional intelligence refers to the ability to use primarily the right cerebral hemisphere to process emotional events.    TRUE or FALSE

340

## Psychology in Action: Emotional Intelligence—The Fine Art of Self-Control: Pages 353-354

What does it mean to have "emotional intelligence"?

1. People who excel in life tend to be emotionally intelligent.   TRUE or FALSE

2. People who are empathetic are keenly tuned in to their own feelings.   TRUE or FALSE

3. People who are emotionally intelligent know what causes them to feel various emotions.
   TRUE or FALSE

4. Negative emotions can be valuable because they impart useful information to us.   TRUE or FALSE

5. Positive emotions produce urges to be creative, to explore, and to seek new experiences.
   TRUE or FALSE

6. Martin Seligman believes that to be genuinely happy, people must cultivate their own natural strengths.
   TRUE or FALSE

7. A first step toward becoming emotionally intelligent is to pay attention to and value your feelings and
   emotional reactions.   TRUE or FALSE

# FINAL SURVEY AND REVIEW

## Motivation—Forces that Push and Pull

What is motivation? Are there different types of motives?

1. Motives initiate (begin), _____ (perpetuate), and _____ activities.

2. Motivation typically involves the sequence need, _____, goal, and goal _____
   (need reduction).

3. Behavior can be activated either by _____ (push) or by _____ (pull).

4. The attractiveness of a goal and its ability to initiate action are related to its _____

   _____ .

5. Three principal types of motives are _____ motives, _____ motives, and
   _____ motives.

6. Most biological motives operate to maintain a steady state of bodily equilibrium called _____ .

7. _____ rhythms within the body are closely tied to sleep, activity levels, and energy cycles.
   Travel across _____ and shift work can seriously disrupt sleep and bodily rhythms.

8. If you anticipate a change in body rhythms, you can gradually _____ to your new schedule over a period of days.

9. Body rhythms and sleep cycles are strongly influenced by the release of _____ , a hormone produced at night by the _____ gland.

# Hunger—Pardon Me, My Hypothalamus Is Growling
## What causes hunger? Overeating? Eating disorders?

1. Hunger is influenced by a complex interplay between _____ (fullness) of the stomach, lowered levels of _____ , metabolism in the liver, and fat stores in the body.

2. The most direct control of eating is exerted by the _____ , which has areas that act like feeding (start) and _____ (stop) systems for hunger and eating.

3. The _____ hypothalamus acts as a feeding system and is activated by the hormone ghrelin; the _____ hypothalamus is part of a satiety system; the paraventricular _____ influences both hunger and satiety.

4. Other factors influencing hunger are the _____ _____ for the proportion of fat in the body, external eating _____ , the attractiveness and variety of diet.

5. A _____ (BMI) is a measure of body _____ which is calculated by dividing body height squared over body weight multiplied by 703.

6. A BMI of _____ or higher should be a cause for concern since obesity is linked to _____ disease, high blood pressure, _____ , diabetes, and premature death.

7. Because of the limitations of traditional dieting, changing basic _____ patterns and habits is usually more effective.

8. _____ dieting brings about such changes by use of _____ -control techniques.

9. A successful behavioral dieting approach begins with committing oneself to weight loss, _____ , counting _____ , developing techniques to control overeating, and charting one's progress.

10. Hunger is also influenced by emotions, learned taste preferences and taste _____ (such as _____ _____ in animals), and cultural values.

11. _____ nervosa (self-inflicted starvation) and _____ nervosa (gorging and purging) are two prominent eating disorders. About _____ of people with bulimia are male.

12. Treatments for anorexia begin with _____ diet then advance to counseling.

13. Both eating disorders tend to involve conflicts about _____, self-control, and anxiety. The popularity of fitness, _____ , and sports also contributes to eating disorders.

# Biological Motives Revisited—Thirst, Sex, and Pain
Is there more than one type of thirst? In what ways are pain avoidance and the sex drive unusual?

1. Like hunger, thirst and other basic motives are affected by a number of bodily factors, but are primarily under the central control of the _____ in the brain.

2. Thirst may be either _____ (when fluid is lost from inside cells) or _____ (when fluid is lost from the spaces between cells).

3. Pain avoidance is unusual because it is _____ (associated with particular conditions) as opposed to _____ (occurring in regular cycles).

4. Pain _____ and pain _____ are partially learned.

5. The sex drive in many lower animals is related to _____ (or "heat") in females. The sex drive is unusual in that it is non- _____ (both its arousal and its reduction are sought).

6. Sex drive in both males and females may be related to bodily levels of _____. Levels of _____ decline with age and taking supplements may restore the sex drive.

# Stimulus Drives—Skydiving, Horror Movies, and the Fun Zone
How does arousal relate to motivation?

1. The _____ drives reflect needs for information, _____, manipulation, and sensory input.

2. Drives for stimulation are partially explained by _____, which states that an ideal level of physical arousal will be maintained if possible.

3. The desired level of arousal or stimulation varies from person to person, as measured by the _____ *Scale.*

4. Individuals from America, Israel, and Ireland tend to score high on the Sensation-Seeking Scale and they are likely to engage in _____ behaviors.

5. Optimal performance on a task usually occurs at moderate levels of arousal. This relationship is described by an _____ function.

6. The _____ law further states that for simple tasks the ideal arousal level is higher, and for complex tasks it is lower.

7. Test anxiety is caused by a combination of excessive _____ and heightened physiological _____ , which can be reduced with better preparation, relaxation, rehearsal, and restructuring thoughts.

# Learned Motives—The Pursuit of Excellence
What are learned motives? Social motives? Why are they important?

1. Social motives are learned through _____ and cultural conditioning.

2. _____ theory, which states that strong emotions tend to be followed by an opposite emotion, explains some acquired motives.

3. One of the most prominent social motives is the need for _____ (nAch).

4. _____ nAch is correlated with success in many situations, with occupational choice, and with moderate risk taking.

5. _____ affects motivation because it influences the challenges you will undertake, the effort you will make, and how long you will persist when things don't go well.

6. To enhance self- _____ , one should do the following: Set goals that are specific, _____ , and attainable, advance in small steps, find a role model, get expert instructions, and get _____ support.

# Motives in Perspective—A View from the Pyramid
Are some motives more basic than others?

1. Maslow's _____ (rank ordering) of motives categorizes needs as basic and oriented.

2. Lower needs in the hierarchy are assumed to be _____ (dominant) over higher needs.

3. Self-_____, the highest and most fragile need, is reflected in _____ -needs.

4. In many situations, _____ motivation (that which is induced by obvious external rewards)

   can reduce _____ motivation, enjoyment, and creativity.

# Inside an Emotion—How Do You Feel?
What happens during emotion?

1. Emotions are linked to many basic _____ behaviors, such as attacking, retreating, feeding, and reproducing.

2. Other major elements of emotion are physiological changes in the body, emotional _____, and emotional feelings.

3.

4. The following are considered to be _____ emotions: fear, surprise, sadness, disgust, anger,

   anticipation, joy, and trust (acceptance).

# Physiology and Emotion—Arousal, Sudden Death, and Lying
What physiological changes underlie emotion? Can "Lie Detectors" really detect lies?

1. Physical changes associated with emotion are caused by the action of _____ , a hormone

   released into the bloodstream, and by activity in the _____ nervous system (ANS).

2. The _____ branch of the ANS is primarily responsible for arousing the body, the branch

   for quieting it.

3. Sudden death due to prolonged and intense emotion is probably related to _____ rebound (excess

   activity). Heart attacks caused by sudden intense emotion are more likely due to _____ arousal.

4.  The _____ , or "lie detector," measures _____ by monitoring heart rate, blood pressure, breathing rate, and the galvanic skin response (GSR).

5.  Asking a series of _____ and _____ questions may allow the detection of laying, but overall, the accuracy of the lie detector has been challenged by many researchers.

6.  A _____ makes use of such control questions as "Have you ever stolen anything from your place of work?" to increase the person's anxiety level. Their answers will be compared to other _____ questions.

7.  _____ _____ scans and the use of fMRI in analyzing brain activity are possible alternative techniques to polygraph testing.

# Expressing Emotions—Making Faces and Talking Bodies
How accurately are emotions expressed by the face and "body language"?

1.  Basic emotional _____ , such as smiling or baring one's teeth when angry, appear to be unlearned.

2.  _____ expressions of fear, anger, disgust, sadness, and happiness are recognized by people of all cultures.

3.  In Western culture, _____ are encouraged to express such emotions as sadness, fear, shame, and guilt, and _____ are expected to express anger and hostility.

4.  Body gestures and movements (body language) also express _____, mainly by communicating emotional tone.

5.  Three dimensions of facial expressions are pleasantness-unpleasantness, attention-rejection, and _____ .

6.  The study of body language of is known as _____ .

# Theories of Emotion—Several Ways to Fear a Bear
How do psychologists explain emotions?

1.  The _____ -Lange theory of emotion says that emotional experience an awareness of the bodily reactions of emotion.

2. In contrast, the _____ -Bard theory says that bodily reactions and emotional experience occur at the same time and that emotions are organized in the brain.

3. Schachter's _____ theory of emotion emphasizes the importance of labels, or interpretations, applied to feelings of bodily.

4. Also important is the process of _____ , in which bodily arousal is attributed to a particular person, object, or situation.

5. Research on attribution theory has shown that _____ _____ (e.g., heart rate from exercise or fear) can be attributed to different sources such as attraction or love for someone.

6. The _____ _____ hypothesis holds that sensations and information from emotional expressions help define what emotion a person is feeling.

7. Making faces does influence _____ and bodily activities through the _____ nervous system.

8. Contemporary views of emotion place greater emphasis on how situations are _____ (evaluated). Also, all of the elements of emotion are seen as interrelated and interacting.

# Psychology in Action: Emotional Intelligence—The Fine Art of Self-control

What does it mean to have "emotional intelligence"?

1. Emotional _____ involves the following skills: self-awareness, _____ , self-control, and an understanding of how to use emotions.

2. Emotionally intelligent people are good at reading _____ expressions, tone of _____ , and other signs of emotions.

3. They also use their feelings to enhance _____ and _____ making.

4. Positive emotions are not just a luxury. They tend to encourage personal _____ and _____ connection.

5. Martin Seligman believes people can achieve genuine _____ by optimizing their natural _____ , such as kindness, originality, humor, optimism, and generosity, to buffer them against misfortunes.

# MASTERY TEST

1. Which of the following is NOT one of the signs of emotional arousal recorded by a polygraph?
   a. heart rate
   b. blood pressure
   c. pupil dilation
   d. breathing rate

2. Plain water is most satisfying when a person has _____ thirst.
   a. intracellular
   b. hypothalamic
   c. extracellular
   d. homeostatic

3. We have a biological tendency to associate an upset stomach with foods eaten earlier. This is the basis for the development of
   a. taste aversions.
   b. yo-yo dieting.
   c. bulimia.
   d. alexithymia.

4. Strong external rewards tend to undermine
   a. extrinsic motivation.
   b. intrinsic motivation.
   c. prepotent motivation.
   d. stimulus motivation.

5. Activity in the ANS is directly responsible for which element of emotion?
   a. emotional feelings
   b. emotional expressions
   c. physiological changes
   d. misattributions

6. Empathy is a major element of
   a. nAch.
   b. intrinsic motivation.
   c. emotional intelligence.
   d. the sensation-seeking personality.

7. Motivation refers to the ways in which activities are initiated, sustained, and
   a. acquired.
   b. valued.
   c. directed.
   d. aroused.

8. The psychological state or feeling we call thirst corresponds to which element of motivation?
   a. need
   b. drive
   c. deprivation
   d. incentive value

9. People who score high on the SSS generally prefer
   a. low levels of arousal.
   b. moderate levels of arousal.
   c. high levels of arousal.
   d. the middle of the V function.

10. Which facial expression is NOT recognized by people of all cultures?
   a. anger
   b. interest
   c. happiness
   d. fear

11. Learning to weaken eating cues is a useful technique in
   a. self-selection feeding.
   b. yo-yo dieting.
   c. rapid weight cycling.
   d. behavioral dieting.

12. People who score high on tests of the need for achievement tend to be
   a. motivated by power and prestige.
   b. moderate risk takers.
   c. sensation seekers.
   d. attracted to longshots.

13. Which theory holds that emotional feelings, arousal, and behavior are generated simultaneously in the brain?
   a. James-Lange
   b. Cannon-Bard
   c. contemporary
   d. attribution

14. Compared with people in North America, people in Asian cultures are less likely to express which emotion?
   a. anger
   b. jealousy
   c. curiosity
   d. fear

15. Binge eating is most associated with
    a. bulimia nervosa.
    b. alexithymia.
    c. low levels of NPY.
    d. anorexia nervosa.

16. Goals that are desirable are high in
    a. need reduction.
    b. incentive value.
    c. homeostatic valence.
    d. motivational "push."

17. _____ is to pain avoidance as _____ is to the sex drive.
    a. Non-homeostatic; episodic
    b. Episodic; non-homeostatic
    c. Non-homeostatic; cyclic
    d. Cyclic; non-homeostatic

18. A specialist in kinesics could be expected to be most interested in
    a. facial blends.
    b. circadian rhythms.
    c. sensation seeking.
    d. biological motives.

19. Coping statements are a way to directly correct which part of test anxiety?
    a. overpreparation
    b. under-arousal
    c. excessive worry
    d. compulsive rehearsal

20. Drives for exploration and activity are categorized as
    a. biological motives.
    b. learned motives.
    c. stimulus motives.
    d. extrinsic motives.

21. Sudden death following a period of intense fear may occur when _____ slows the heart to a stop.
    a. a sympathetic overload
    b. adrenaline poisoning
    c. opponent-process feedback
    d. a parasympathetic rebound

22. People who enjoy skydiving and ski jumping are very likely high in
    a. parasympathetic arousal.
    b. extrinsic motivation.
    c. their desires to meet meta-needs.
    d. the trait of sensation seeking.

23. You could induce eating in a laboratory rat by activating the
    a. lateral hypothalamus.
    b. corpus callosum.
    c. rat's set point.
    d. ventromedial hypothalamus.

24. People think cartoons are funnier if they see them while holding a pen crosswise in their teeth. This observation supports
    a. the James-Lange theory.
    b. the Cannon-Bard theory.
    c. Schachter's cognitive theory.
    d. the facial feedback hypothesis.

25. Basic biological motives are closely related to
    a. nAch.
    b. homeostasis.
    c. activity in the thalamus.
    d. levels of melatonin in the body.

26. Self-actualization is to _____ needs as safety and security are to _____ needs.
    a. growth; basic
    b. basic; meta-
    c. prepotent; basic
    d. meta-; extrinsic

27. Which of the following is NOT a core element of emotion?
    a. physiological changes
    b. emotional expressions
    c. emotional feelings
    d. misattributions

28. The effects of a "supermarket diet" on eating are related to the effects of _____ on eating.
    a. anxiety
    b. incentive value
    c. metabolic rates
    d. stomach distention

29. According to the Yerkes-Dodson law, optimum performance occurs at _____ levels of arousal for simple tasks and _____ levels of arousal for complex tasks.
    a. higher; lower
    b. lower; higher
    c. minimum; high
    d. average; high

30. Contemporary models of emotion place greater emphasis on _____, or the way situations are evaluated.
    a. appraisal
    b. attribution
    c. feedback
    d. emotional tone

31. A _____ (BMI) measures one's body fat by applying the formula: weight/height$^2$ x 703.
    a. Body Magnitude Indicator
    b. Basic Magnitude Indicator
    c. Body Mass Index
    d. Basic Mass Index

32. Which statement correctly explains why there is an obesity problem in the United States?
    a. The all-you-can-eat dining halls and restaurants tempt people to overeat.
    b. Although the food industry has made dinner easier to cook and buy, the food is high in fat and sugar.
    c. Overeating during large meals increases one's body set point.
    d. all the preceding

33. Although in some parts of the world eating monkey eyes is considered a delicacy, to Americans it is not. This difference in preference is largely influenced by
    a. cultural values.
    b. biological motives.
    c. the availability of taste buds.
    d. overdeveloped hypothalamus.

34. Bev placed herself on a strict diet of eating no other fruits except for grapefruit. Eventually, she began to crave other fruits and could not stand seeing, smelling, or tasting another grapefruit. One explanation for Bev's strong dislike of grapefruit is her body was trying to avoid nutritional imbalance by producing
    a. positive reinforcement.
    b. a taste aversion.
    c. shaping.
    d. purging.

35. The causes of anorexia have been attributed to
    a. unrealistic comparison of body image to others.
    b. seeking control.
    c. distorted body image.
    d. all the preceding.

36. Variables that aid our survival include _____ moods, which help us make better decisions and be more helpful, efficient, and creative. The ability to understand and display _____ expressions such as anger helps us communicate with others.
    a.   primary; universal
    b.   negative; natural
    c.   positive; facial
    d.   natural; primary

37. The National Academy of Sciences has concluded that polygraph tests should not be used to screen _____ since the test tends to label honest people dishonest.
    a.   immigrants
    b.   employees
    c.   government officials
    d.   mentally disturbed people

38. According to Martin Seligman, to be genuinely happy, one must
    a.   optimize one's natural strengths.
    b.   focus on fixing one's weaknesses.
    c.   strengthen negative emotions to better understand positive emotions.
    d.   balance both negative and positive emotions.

39. Two possible alternative techniques for detecting lies over polygraph testing are infrared face scans and _____.
    a.   X-Ray
    b.   fMRI
    c.   high score on the SSS
    d.   low score on the nAch

# SOLUTIONS

## RECITE AND REVIEW
### Motivation—Forces That Push and Pull: Pages 320-323

What is motivation? Are there different types of motives?

1.  initiate; activities
2.  need; goal
3.  push; pull

4.  goal; need
5.  learned
6.  biological; steady

6.  rhythms; sleep
7.  change; schedule
9.  sleep; hormone

## Hunger—Pardon Me, My Hypothalamus Is Growling: Pages 324-331

What causes hunger? Overeating? Eating disorders?

1. stomach; sugar; liver
2. start; stop
3. feeding; ghrelin; satiety
4. fat; diet
5. height; weight
6. 25
7. .habits
8. dieting
9. exercise ; calories
10. taste; taste
11. .starvation; gorging; 10%
12. counseling
13. anxiety; fitness

## Biological Motives Revisited—Thirst, Sex, and Pain: Pages 331-333

Is there more than one type of thirst? In what ways are pain avoidance and the sex drive unusual?

1. bodily; brain
2. fluid; cells; fluid; cells
3. cycles
4. learned
5. females; arousal
6. drive; testosterone

## Stimulus Drives—Skydiving, Horror Movies, and the Fun Zone: Pages 333-336

How does arousal relate to motivation?

1. sensory
2. physical arousal
3. arousal
4. high
5. moderate
6. success; risk
7. excessive; preparation; rehearsal

## Learned Motives—The Pursuit of Excellence: Pages 336-338

What are learned motives? Social motives? Why are they important?

1. Social
2. emotions; emotion
3. need
4. success; risk
5. motivation; effort; persist
6. challenging; small; social

## Motives in Perspective—A View from the Pyramid: Pages 338-341

Are some motives more basic than others?

1. basic
2. Lower; higher
3. Self; needs
4. external

## Inside an Emotion—How Do You Feel?: Pages 341-343

What happens during emotion?

1. behaviors
2. feelings
3. sadness; anger

354

## Physiology and Emotion—Arousal, Sudden Death, and Lying: Pages 343-345

What physiological changes underlie emotion? Can "Lie Detectors" really detect lies?

1. hormone; nervous system
2. branch; branch
3. rebound; arousal
4. emotional arousal
5. relevant; lying
6. control; critical
7. fMRI

## Expressing Emotions—Making Faces and Talking Bodies: Pages 346-348

How accurately are emotions expressed by the face and "body language"?

1. unlearned
2. fear; sadness
3. sadness; shame; anger
4. feelings; tone
5. facial
6. body language

## Theories of Emotion—Several Ways to Fear a Bear: Pages 348-353

How do psychologists explain emotions?

1. follows
2. at; the; same; time
3. labels
4. arousal
5. increased; attributed
6. expressions
7. emotions; autonomic
8. situations

## Psychology in Action: Emotional Intelligence—The Fine Art of Self-Control: Pages 353-354

What does it mean to have "emotional intelligence"?

1. self; self; emotions optimism
2. emotion
3. feelings (or emotions)
4. Positive
5. strengths; kindness;

# CONNECTIONS

## Motivation—Forces That Push and Pull: Pages 320-323

What is motivation? Are there different types of motives?

1. b
2. d
3. a
4. e
5. c
6. g
7. f

## Hunger—Pardon Me, My Hypothalamus Is Growling: Pages 324-331

What causes hunger? Overeating? Eating disorders?

1. b
2. a
3. c

## Hunger—Pardon Me, My Hypothalamus Is Growing (Cont.)

1. g
2. b
3. c

4. f
5. a
6. e

7. h
8. d

## Biological Motives Revisited—Thirst, Sex, and Pain: Pages 331-333
Is there more than one type of thirst? In what ways are pain avoidance and the sex drive unusual?

1. c
2. d

3. e
4. a

5. b

## Stimulus Drives—Skydiving, Horror Movies, and the Fun Zone and Learned Motives—The Pursuit of Excellence: Pages 333-338
How does arousal relate to motivation? What are learned motives? Social motives? Why are they important?

1. g
2. c
3. a

4. h
5. b
6. d

7. f
8. e

## Motives in Perspective—A View from the Pyramid: Pages 338-341
Are some motives more basic than others?

1. d
2. g
3. c

4. a
5. e
6. b

7. f

## Inside an Emotion—How Do You Feel? Physiology and Emotion— Arousal, Sudden Death, and Lying: Pages 341-346
What happens during emotion? What physiological changes underlie emotion? Can "Lie Detectors" really detect lies?

1. b
2. g
3. a

4. d
5. h
6. f

7. c
8. e

## Expressing Emotions—Making Faces and Talking Bodies and Psychology in Action: Emotional Intelligence—The Fine Art of Self-Control: Pages 346-348 and 353-354

How accurately are emotions expressed by the face and "body language"? How do psychologists explain emotions? What does it mean to have "emotional intelligence"?

1. e
2. d
3. i

4. b
5. f
6. c

7. h
8. a
9. g

# CHECK YOUR MEMORY

## Motivation—Forces That Push and Pull: Pages 320-323

What is motivation? Are there different types of motives?

1. F
2. T
3. T

4. T

5. T

6. F

## Hunger—Pardon Me, My Hypothalamus Is Growling: Pages 324-331

What causes hunger? Overeating? Eating disorders?

1. F
2. T
3. F
4. T
5. T
6. T
7. F
8. T

9. F
10. F
11. F
12. F
13. F
14. T
15. T
16. T

17. F
18. T
19. F
20. F

## Biological Motives Revisited—Thirst, Sex, and Pain: Pages 331-333

Is there more than one type of thirst? In what ways are pain avoidance and the sex drive unusual?

1. T
2. F

3. F
4. T

5. T

## Stimulus Drives—Skydiving, Horror Movies, and the Fun Zone: Pages 333-336

How does arousal relate to motivation?

1. T
2. T

3. F
4. F

5. T
6. F

357

## Learned Motives—The Pursuit of Excellence: Pages 336-338
What are learned motives? Social motives? Why are they important?

| | | |
|---|---|---|
| 1. T | 3. F | 5. T |
| 2. F | 4. T | |

## Motives in Perspective—A View from the Pyramid: Pages 338-341
Are some motives more basic than others?

| | | |
|---|---|---|
| 1. F | 4. T | 7. T |
| 2. T | 5. F | 8. F |
| 3. F | 6. T | |

## Inside an Emotion—How Do You Feel?: Pages 341-343
What happens during emotion?

| | | |
|---|---|---|
| 1. F | 3. F | 5. T |
| 2. F | 4. T | 6. T |

## Physiology and Emotion—Arousal, Sudden Death, and Lying: Pages 343-345
What physiological changes underlie emotion? Can "Lie Detectors" really detect lies?

| | |
|---|---|
| 1. F | 3. T |
| 2. T | 4. F |

## Expressing Emotions—Making Faces and Talking Bodies: Pages 346-348
How accurately are emotions expressed by the face and "body language"?

| | | |
|---|---|---|
| 1. F | 5. T | 9. F |
| 2. F | 6. T | 10. F |
| 3. T | 7. F | 11. F |
| 4. T | 8. T | 12. F |

## Theories of Emotion—Several Ways to Fear a Bear: Pages 348-353
How do psychologists explain emotions?

| | | |
|---|---|---|
| 1. F | 4. F | 7. T |
| 2. T | 5. T | 8. T |
| 3. T | 6. F | 9. F |

## Psychology in Action: Emotional Intelligence—The Fine Art of Self-Control: Pages 353-354
What does it mean to have "emotional intelligence"?

| | | |
|---|---|---|
| 1. T | 4. T | 7. T |
| 2. F | 5. T | |
| 3. T | 6. T | |

# FINAL SURVEY AND REVIEW

## Motivation—Forces that Push and Pull

What is motivation? Are there different types of motives?

1. sustain; direct
2. drive; attainment
3. needs; goals
4. incentive; value
5. biological; stimulus; learned
6. homeostasis
7. Circadian; time zones
8. preadapt
9. melatonin; pineal

## Hunger—Pardon Me, My Hypothalamus Is Growling

What causes hunger? Overeating? Eating disorders?

1. distention; glucose
2. hypothalamus; satiety
3. lateral; ventromedial; nucleus
4. set; point; cues
5. body mass index; fat
6. 25; heart; stroke
7. eating
8. Behavioral; self
9. exercise; calories
10. aversions; bait; shyness
11. Anorexia; bulimia; 25%
12. medical
13. self-image; exercise

## Biological Motives Revisited—Thirst, Sex, and Pain

Is there more than one type of thirst? In what ways are pain avoidance and the sex drive unusual?

1. hypothalamus
2. intracellular; extracellular
3. episodic; cyclic
4. avoidance; tolerance
5. estrus; homeostatic
6. androgens; testosterone

## Stimulus Drives—Skydiving, Horror Movies, and the Fun Zone

How does arousal relate to motivation?

1. stimulus; exploration
2. arousal theory
3. *Sensation-Seeking*
4. high-risk
5. inverted U
6. Yerkes-Dodson
7. worrying; arousal

## Learned Motives—The Pursuit of Excellence

What are learned motives? Social motives? Why are they important?

1. socialization
2. Opponent-process social
3. achievement
4. High
5. Self-confidence
6. confidence; challenging;

## Motives in Perspective—A View from the Pyramid

Are some motives more basic than others?

1. hierarchy; growth
2. prepotent
3. actualization; meta
4. extrinsic; intrinsic

## Inside an Emotion—How Do You Feel?

What happens during emotion?

1. adaptive
2. expressions
3. biological

## Physiology and Emotion—Arousal, Sudden Death, and Lying

What physiological changes underlie emotion? Can "Lie Detectors" really detect lies?

1. adrenaline; autonomic
2. sympathetic; parasympathetic
3. parasympathetic; sympathetic
4. polygraph;
5. relevant; irrelevant
6. polygraph; critical
7. Infrared; face

## Expressing Emotions—Making Faces and Talking Bodies

How accurately are emotions expressed by the face and "body language"?

1. expressions
2. Facial
3. women; men
4. feelings
5. activation
6. kinesics

## Theories of Emotion—Several Ways to Fear a Bear

How do psychologists explain emotions?

1. James
2. Cannon
3. cognitive; arousal
4. attribution
5. physical; arousal
6. facial; feedback
7. emotions; autonomic
8. appraised

## Psychology in Action: Emotional Intelligence—The Fine Art of Self-control

What does it mean to have "emotional intelligence"?

1. intelligence; empathy
2. facial; voice
3. thinking; decision
4. growth; social
5. happiness; strengths

# MASTERY TEST

1. c, p. 344
2. a, p. 331
3. a, p. 327
4. b, p. 339
5. c, p. 343
6. c, p. 353
7. c, p. 320
8. b, p. 320
9. c, p. 334
10. c, p. 346
11. d, p. 329
12. b, p. 337
13. b, p. 352

14. a, p. 334
15. a, p. 330
16. b, p. 321
17. b, pp. 331-332
18. a, p. 348
19. c, p. 335
20. c, p. 321
21. d, p. 344
22. d, p. 334
23. a, p. 325
24. d, p. 351
25. b, p. 322
26. a, p. 338

27. d, p. 352
28. b, p. 328
29. a, p. 335
30. a, p. 352
31. c, p. 337
32. d, p. 326
33. a, p. 328
34. b, p. 327
35. d, pp. 330-331
36. c, p. 346
37. b, p. 345
38. a, p. 354
39. b, p. 345

360

# Gender and Sexuality

## Chapter Overview

Male and female are not simple either/or categories. Sexual identity is complex, multifaceted, and influenced by biology, socialization, and learning. Biological sex consists of genetic, gonadal, hormonal, and genital sex. Sexual development begins with genetic sex and is then influenced by prenatal hormone levels. Androgen insensitivity, exposure to progestin, androgenital syndrome, and similar problems can cause a person to be born with an intersexual condition. Estrogen and androgen influence the development of different primary and secondary sexual characteristics in males and females.

Sexual orientation refers to one's degree of emotional and erotic attraction to members of the same sex, opposite sex, or both sexes. A person may be heterosexual, homosexual, or bisexual. Similar factors (heredity, biology, and socialization) underlie all sexual orientations. As a group, homosexual men and women do not differ psychologically from heterosexuals. All three sexual orientations are part of the normal range of sexual behavior.

Male and female behavior patterns are related to learned gender identity and gender role socialization. Many researchers believe that prenatal hormones exert a biological biasing effect that combines with social factors to influence psychosexual development. On most psychological dimensions, women and men are more alike than they are different. Gender identity usually becomes stable by age 3 or 4 years. Gender role socialization seems to account for most observed female–male gender differences. Parents tend to encourage boys in instrumental behaviors and girls in expressive behaviors. Gender role stereotypes often distort perceptions about the kinds activities for which men and women are suited.

People who possess both masculine and feminine traits are androgynous. Roughly one third of all persons are androgynous. Approximately 50 percent are traditionally feminine or masculine. Psychological androgyny is related to greater behavioral adaptability and flexibility.

While "normal" sexual behavior is defined differently by various cultures, adults typically engage in a wide variety of sexual behaviors. However, coercive and/or compulsive sexual behaviors are emotionally unhealthy. Sexual arousal is related to the body's erogenous zones, but mental and emotional reactions are the ultimate source of sexual responsiveness. Evidence indicates that the sex drive peaks at a later age for females than it does for males, although this difference is diminishing. Castration may or may not influence sex drive in humans. Sterilization does not alter the sex drive. Frequency of sexual intercourse gradually declines with increasing age. However, many elderly persons remain sexually active, and large variations exist at all ages. Masturbation is a common, normal, and completely acceptable behavior.

The similarities between female and male sexual responses far outweigh the differences. Sexual response can be divided into four phases: excitement, plateau, orgasm, and resolution. There do not appear to be any differences between "vaginal orgasms" and "clitoral orgasms." Fifteen percent of women are consistently multi-orgasmic, and at least 50 percent are capable of multiple orgasm. Males experience a refractory period after orgasm, and few men are multi-orgasmic. Mutual orgasm has been abandoned by most sex counselors as the ideal in lovemaking.

The most common sexual disorders are pedophilia and exhibitionism. Compulsive sexual behaviors (paraphilias) tend to emotionally handicap people. The paraphilias include pedophilia, exhibitionism, voyeurism, frotteurism, fetishism, sexual masochism, sexual sadism, and transvestic fetishism. The effects of child molestation vary greatly, depending on the severity of the molestation and the child's relationship to the molester. Exhibitionists are usually not dangerous but can escalate their sexual aggression. They can best be characterized as sexually inhibited and immature.

In the United States, a liberalization of attitudes toward sex has been paralleled by a gradual increase in sexual behavior over the last 40 years. Adolescents and young adults engage in more frequent sexual activity than they did 40 years ago. In recent years there has been a greater acceptance of female sexuality and a narrowing of differences in female and male patterns of sexual behavior. Forcible rape, acquaintance rape, and rape-supportive attitudes and beliefs are major problems in North America.

Each person must take responsibility for practicing safer sex and choosing when, where, and with whom to express sexuality. During the last 20 years the incidence of sexually transmitted diseases has steadily increased. STDs and the spread of HIV/AIDS have had a sizable impact on patterns of sexual behavior, including some curtailment of risk taking. Many sexually active people continue to take unnecessary risks with their health by failing to follow safer sex practices.

Although solutions exist for many sexual adjustment problems, good communication and a healthy relationship are the real keys to sexual satisfaction. Communication skills that foster and maintain intimacy are the key to successful relationships. Most sexual adjustment problems are closely linked to the general health of a couple's relationship. Problems with sexual function can involve desire, arousal, orgasm, or pain. Behavioral methods and counseling techniques have been developed to alleviate many sexual problems.

# Learning Objectives

*Theme: The sexes are more alike than different. Sexuality is a normal and healthy part of human behavior.*

| |
|---|
| **GQ: What are the basic dimensions of sex?** |
| LO 11.1  Distinguish between the terms *sex* and *gender*. |
| LO 11.2  List and describe the four dimensions of sex and explain how a person's sex develops. Include in your discussion a description of these conditions: a. androgen insensitivity; b. *intersexual person*; and c. androgenital syndrome. |
| LO 11.3  Differentiate *primary* from *secondary sex characteristics*; and define the following terms: a. menarche; b. ovulation; c. menopause; d. gonads; e. *estrogens*; f. *androgens*; g. *testosterone*. |
| **GQ: What is sexual orientation?** |
| LO 11.4  Define the term *sexual orientation;* discuss the various types of sexual orientation; describe the combination of influences that appears to produce *homosexuality*; and characterize the emotional adjustment of *homosexuals* versus *heterosexuals*. |
| **GQ: How does one's sense of maleness or femaleness develop?** |
| LO 11.5  Differentiate *gender identity* from *gender role*; explain the *biological biasing effect*; how gender identity is formed; and discuss the effects of socialization on gender roles, including *gender role stereotypes*, cultural variations, and *instrumental* and *expressive behaviors*. |

| |
|---|
| **GQ: What is psychological androgyny (and is it contagious)?** |
| LO 11.6 Define psychological *androgyny* and how it is measured; explain why androgyny may be adaptive. |
| **GQ: What are the most typical patterns of human sexual behavior?** |
| LO 11.7 Define *erogenous zone* and *sexual script*; discuss the differences between males and females in their degree of arousal and their *sex drives*; describe the effects of alcohol, *castration*, and aging on the sex drive; and discuss the normality and acceptability of *masturbation*. |
| **GQ: To what extent do females and males differ in sexual response?** |
| LO 11.8 List in order and briefly describe the four phases of sexual response in men and women and state the basic differences in sexual response styles of men and women. |
| **GQ: What are the most common sexual disorders?** |
| LO 11.9 Explain the difference between public and private standards of sexual behavior and what sets true sexual deviations apart from other sexual activity and list and define eight behavior patterns (*paraphilias*) that fit the definition of sexual deviation. |
| LO 11.10 Describe pedophilia (child molestation) including who does it, what the offenders are like, and the factors that affect the seriousness of the molestation. Include seven ways to recognize molestation from a child's behavior; six tactics of molesters; and ways to prevent children from being molested. |
| LO 11.11 Discuss exhibitionism, including who the offenders are, why they do it, and how one's reactions may encourage them. |
| **GQ: Have recent changes in attitudes affected sexual behavior?** |
| LO 11.12 Describe the changes that have taken place in sexual attitudes and behavior in the last 50 years; discuss how the pace of the "revolution" seems to have slowed recently; and explain what is meant by the phrase slow death of the *double standard*. |
| LO 11.13 Define *acquaintance or " date" rape* and discuss its effects; explain how gender role stereotyping may encourage the act of rape; differentiate *forcible rape* from *date rape*; and explain why rape is not viewed by experts as primarily a sexual act. |
| **GQ: What impacts have sexually transmitted diseases had on sexual behavior?** |
| LO 11.14 Explain the cause of, methods of transmission, and ways of preventing AIDS and other STDs. |
| **GQ: How can couples keep their relationship exciting? What are the most common sexual adjustment problems?** |
| LO 11.15 List four elements of a healthy sexual relationship and seven guidelines for effective communication between husbands and wives. |
| LO 11.16 Describe the following sexual problems including the nature, cause, and treatment of each: a. Desire Disorders (*hypoactive sexual desire, sexual aversion*); b. Arousal Disorders (male erectile disorder, female sexual arousal disorder); c. Orgasm Disorders (female orgasmic disorder, male orgasmic disorder, premature ejaculation); and d. Sexual Pain Disorders (dyspareunia, vaginismus). |

# RECITE AND REVIEW

## Sexual Development—Circle One: XX or XY: Pages 358-361

What are the basic dimensions of sex?

1. Physical differences between males and females can be divided into _____ and _____ sexual characteristics.

2. Primary sexual characteristics are the _____ and internal reproductive organs.

3.  Secondary sexual characteristics are bodily features such as breast development, body _____, and facial hair.

4.  Reproductive maturity in females is signaled by menarche (the onset of _____ ). Soon after, ovulation (the release of _____ , or eggs) begins.

5.  The development of sexual characteristics is influenced by androgens ( _____ sex hormones) and estrogens ( _____ sex hormones) secreted by the gonads (sex _____ ).

6.  A person's sex can be broken down into genetic sex, gonadal sex, _____ sex, genital sex, and _____ identity.

7.  Sexual development begins with _____ sex (*XX* or *XY* chromosomes). Two *X* chromosomes normally produce a _____ ; an *X* plus a *Y* produces a _____ .

8.  During prenatal sexual development, the presence of testosterone produces _____ genitals; an absence of testosterone produces _____ genitals.

9.  Androgen insensitivity, exposure to progestin, and the androgenital _____ result in _____ ambiguities called intersexualism.

10. Many researchers believe that prenatal _____ can exert a biological biasing _____ that combines with social factors present after birth to influence psychosexual development.

11. On most psychological dimensions, men and women are more _____ than they are _____ .

12. Surgical _____ with hormone therapy can alter the genital _____ and secondary sex characteristics for intersexuals (children with _____ sexual anatomy) to either male or female. However, these factors alone do not determine gender identity; socialization is also important.

## Sexual Orientation—Who Do You Love?: Pages 361-363
What is sexual orientation?

1.  Sexual orientation refers to one's degree of emotional and erotic attraction to members of the same _____ , opposite _____ , or both _____ .

2.  A person may be heterosexual, _____ , or bisexual.

364

3. A combination of hereditary, biological, social, and psychological influences combines to produce one's _____ _____. The prenatal _____ theory of homosexuality theory states that genes affect hormone levels in the developing fetus, which can affect sexual orientation.

4. Research conducted on _____ orientation or behavior by neurobiologists suggests a _____ link between mothers and children. Other theorists believe that homosexuality may have developed to _____ the male and female competition for sexual partners.

5. A national survey suggests that of every 100 people, _____ identify themselves as homosexual or _____

6. However, gay men and lesbians are frequently affected by homophobia (fear of _____ ) and heterosexism (the belief that heterosexuality is more natural than homosexuality).

7. As a group, homosexual men and women do not differ psychologically from _____ .

# Gender Development—Circle One: Masculine or Feminine: Pages 363-367
How does one's sense of maleness or femaleness develop?

1. Social factors are especially apparent in learned gender identity (a private sense of _____ or _____ ) and the effect of gender roles (patterns of behavior defined as male or female within a particular culture).

2. Gender identity, which is based to a large extent on labeling, usually becomes stable by age _____ or _____ years.

3. Gender roles contribute to the development of _____ stereotypes (oversimplified beliefs about the nature of men and women) that often distort perceptions about the kinds of occupations for which men and women are suited.

4. As a result of gender role _____ , for every $1.00 men earn in business, academia, medicine, law, sports, and politics, white _____ earn $.76, black _____ earn $.65, and Latino women earn $.55.

5. Another effect of gender role _____ is that women are _____ liked by their peers for violating _____ norms, such as holding a job that as been defined as traditionally "male."

6. Culture determines the gender _____ of males and females in each society.

7. _____ socialization (learning gender roles) seems to account for most observed male/female differences.

8. Parents tend to encourage _____ in instrumental behaviors and _____ in expressive behaviors.

9. By age _____ , _____ -segregated playing can be seen in boys and girls: Boys play _____ games that focus on superheroes, and girls play _____ games that focus on house-related activities.

## Androgyny—Are You Masculine, Feminine, or Androgynous?: Pages 367-368
What is psychological androgyny (and is it contagious)?

1. Androgyny is measured with the *Bern _____ Inventory (BSRI)*.

2. Research conducted by Sandra Bem indicates that roughly one third of all persons are androgynous (they possess both _____ and _____ traits).

3. Being _____ means that a person is independent and assertive.

4. Being _____ means that a person is nurturant and interpersonally oriented.

5. Psychological _____ appears related to greater adaptability or flexibility in behavior.

## Sexual Behavior—Mapping the Erogenous Zone: Pages 369-371
What are the most typical patterns of human sexual behavior?

1. Sexual behavior, including orgasm (sexual _____ ) is apparent soon after birth and expressed in various ways throughout life.

2. Sexual arousal is related to stimulation of the body's erogenous zones (areas that produce erotic _____ ), but cognitive elements such as _____ and images are equally important.

3. "Normal" sexual behavior is defined differently by various _____ . Also, each person uses learned sexual scripts (plots or mental plans) to guide sexual behavior.

4. There is little difference in sexual _____ between males and females.

5. Research suggests that both women and men are equal in physiological sexual _____ but differ in the _____ feelings of arousal. Women's sexual arousal is linked to their _____ responses to cues and acknowledgment from their partners of their needs and preferences.

6. Evidence suggests that the sex drive peaks at a _____ age for females than it does for males, although this difference is diminishing.

7. Sex _____ in both males and females may be related to bodily levels of androgens. As testosterone levels decline with _____ , so does _____ drive; both males and females can take testosterone supplements to restore it.

8. The belief that alcohol and other drugs enhance sex drive is a _____ . Alcohol is a depressant, which in large doses tends to _____ sexual desire, arousal, pleasure, and performance. Other drugs like _____ , amyl nitrite, barbiturates, cocaine, Ecstasy, LSD, and marijuana tend to _____ sexual responses.

9. Nocturnal _____ are a normal, but relatively minor, form of sexual release.

10. _____ (removal of the gonads) may or may not influence sex drive in humans, depending on how sexually experienced a person is. Sterilization (a vasectomy or tubal ligation) does not alter sex drive.

11. There is a gradual _____ in the frequency of sexual intercourse with increasing age.

12. Masturbation is a normal, harmless behavior practiced by a large percentage of the population. For many, masturbation is an important part of sexual self- _____ .

## Human Sexual Response—Sexual Interactions: Pages 371-373

To what extent do males and females differ in sexual response?

1. In a series of landmark studies, William _____ and Virginia Johnson directly observed sexual response in a large number of adults.

2. Human sexual response can be divided into four phases: (1) _____ ; (2) plateau; (3) _____ ; and (4) resolution.

3. There do not appear to be any differences between "vaginal _____ " and "clitoral _____ " in the female.

4. Males experience a refractory period after _____ and ejaculation.

5. Both males and females may go through all four stages in _____ or five minutes. But during lovemaking, most females typically take longer than this, averaging from 10 to 20 minutes.

6.  Mutual _____ has been abandoned by most sex counselors as the ideal in lovemaking.

7.  Fifteen percent of women are consistently _____ -orgasmic, and at least 48 percent are capable of _____ orgasm.

## Atypical Sexual Behavior—Trench Coats, Whips, Leathers, and Lace: Pages 373-374
What are the most common sexual disorders?

1.  Definitions of sexual deviance are highly _____ . Many "sexually deviant" behaviors are acceptable in private or in some _____ .

2.  Sexual _____ that often cause difficulty are called paraphilias.

3.  Some paraphilias include: pedophilia (sex with children), _____ (sexual arousal associated with inanimate objects), voyeurism (viewing the genitals of others without their permission), and _____ (displaying the genitals to unwilling viewers).

4.  Other paraphilias are: transvestic fetishism (achieving sexual arousal by wearing clothing of the opposite sex), sexual _____ (deriving sexual pleasure from inflicting pain), sexual _____ (desiring pain as part of the sex act), and frotteurism (sexually touching or rubbing against a nonconsenting person).

5.  Exhibitionists are rarely dangerous and can best be characterized as sexually _____ and immature.

6.  The effects of child molestation vary greatly, depending on the _____ of the molestation and the child's relationship to the molester.

7.  Children who have been _____ may display such signs as fear of being seen _____ , anxiety, _____ , or discomfort to references of _____ behaviors and express low self-esteem or self-worth.

8.  Child molesters tend to gain access to children through caretaking _____ and bring them to their homes. Some tactics molesters use to lull children are bribing them with _____ , encouraging them to talk about sex, and using threats to gain _____ .

## Attitudes and Sexual Behavior—The Changing Sexual Landscape: Pages 374-378
Have recent changes in attitudes affected sexual behavior?

1. Attitudes toward sexual behavior, especially the behavior of others, have become more liberal, but actual changes in sexual _____ have been more gradual.

2. Another change has been _____ and more frequent sexual activity among adolescents and young adults, including larger percentages of people who have premarital _____ .

3. Also evident are a greater acceptance of _____ sexuality and a narrowing of differences in male and female patterns of sexual _____ . In other words, the double standard is fading.

4. Acquaintance ( _____ ) rape and _____ -supportive myths and attitudes remain major problems.

5. _____ is primarily a violent crime of aggression rather than a sex crime.

6. Men now report having an average of _____ sexual partners in their lifetime, while women report an average of four.

## STDs and Safer Sex—Choice, Risk, and Responsibility: Pages 378-380
What impacts have sexually transmitted diseases had on sexual behavior?

1. Based on a recent study, approximately _____ percent of sexually active teenage _____ reported that they do not believe they will get _____ transmitted diseases (STDs) because their partners _____ show symptoms of STDs.

2. People who are sexually _____ , even with only one person, may still be engaging in risky sex from _____ contact with others through their partner's indiscretion.

3. During the last 20 years there has been a steady increase in the incidence of sexually transmitted _____ (STDs).

4. Part of this increase is due to the emergence of _____ deficiency syndrome (AIDS) caused by the human immunodeficiency _____ (HIV).

5. STDs have had a sizable impact on patterns of sexual behavior, including increased awareness of high- _____ behaviors and some curtailment of _____ taking.

6. It is predicted that over the next 20 to 30 years, the dominant group of individuals that will spread the _____ virus are heterosexuals, and unless preventions are taken, _____ million people will die of AIDS.

# Psychology in Action: Sexual Problems—When Pleasure Fades: Pages 380-385

How can couples keep their relationship exciting? What are the most common sexual adjustment problems?

1. The principal problems in sexual adjustment are _____ disorders, arousal disorders, orgasm disorders, and sexual _____ disorders.

2. Desire disorders include hypoactive _____ _____ (a loss of sexual desire) and _____ aversion (fear or disgust about engaging in sex).

3. Arousal disorders include _____ erectile disorder and _____ sexual arousal disorder.

4. Approximately 40 percent of _____ disorders result from psychogenic causes (having _____ or emotional origin) rather than physical illnesses, diseases, or _____ to the penis.

5. Both males and females have similar causes for sexual _____ disorder, which include anxiety, _____ toward their partner, depression, stress, _____ experiences, having a strict religious background, and distrust of men or women.

6. To _____ a healthy relationship through communication, people should _____ gunnysacking each other, be open about their feelings, not _____ each other's characteristics, not be mind readers, and try to understand the other's perspectives.

7. Orgasm disorders are male orgasmic disorder (retarded _____ ), premature _____ , and female orgasm disorder (an inability to reach orgasm during lovemaking).

8. Sexual pain disorders are dyspareunia ( _____ intercourse) and vaginismus ( _____ of the vagina).

9. Behavioral methods such as sensate _____ and the squeeze technique have been developed to alleviate each problem. In addition, counseling can be quite helpful.

10. However, most sexual adjustment problems are closely linked to the general health of a couple's_____.

11. For this reason, communication skills that foster and maintain _____ are the key to successful

   relationships.

# CONNECTIONS

## Sexual Development—Circle One: XX or XY?: Pages 358-361
What are the basic dimensions of sex?

1. _____ pelvic bone
2. _____ urethra
3. _____ labia minora
4. _____ ovary
5. _____ vagina
6. _____ uterus
7. _____ rectum
8. _____ fallopian tube
9. _____ clitoris
10. _____ labia majora
11. _____ urinary bladder
12. _____ cervix

## Sexual Development (Cont.)

1. _____ Cowper's gland
2. _____ glans penis
3. _____ urethra
4. _____ seminal vesicle
5. _____ vas deferens
6. _____ pelvic bone
7. _____ urinary bladder
8. _____ testis
9. _____ rectum
10. _____ urethral orifice
11. _____ epididymis
12. _____ prostate

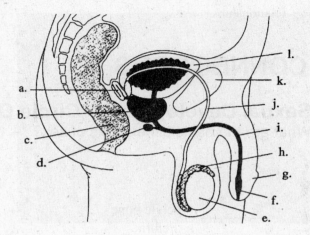

## Sexual Development (Cont.), Gender Development—Circle One: Masculine or Feminine, and Androgyny—Are You Masculine, Feminine, or Androgynous?: Pages 358-361, 363-369

What are the basic dimensions of sex? How does one's sense of maleness or femaleness develop? What is psychological androgyny (and is it contagious)?

1. _____ androgen
2. _____ estrogen
3. _____ genetic sex
4. _____ gonadal sex
5. _____ hermaphroditism
6. _____ gender identity
7. _____ gender role
8. _____ menopause
9. _____ menarche
10. _____ androgyny

a. ovaries or testes
b. cultural pattern
c. self-perception
d. female hormone
e. man-woman
f. XX or XY
g. androgenital syndrome
h. ending of menstruation
i. onset of menstruation
j. testosterone

## Sexual Orientation—Who Do You Love? And Sexual Behavior—Mapping and Erogenous Zones: Pages 361-363, 369-371

What is sexual orientation? What are the most typical patterns of human sexual behavior?

| 1. _____ masturbation | a. attracted to both sexes |
|---|---|
| 2. _____ homophobia | b. attracted to opposite sex |
| 3. _____ heterosexual | c. attracted to same sex |
| 4. _____ homosexual | d. safest sex |
| 5. _____ bisexual | e. infertility |
| 6. _____ sex drive | f. testical removal |
| 7. _____ sterilization | g. fear of homosexuality |
| 8. _____ erogenous zone | h. motivation for intercourse |
| 9. _____ castration | i. dialogue for sexual behavior |
| 10. _____ sexual script | j. productive of pleasure |

## Human Sexual Response—Sexual Interactions, Atypical Sexual Behavior—Trench Coats, Whips, Leathers, and Lace, and Attitudes and Sexual Behavior—The Changing Sexual Landscape: Pages 371-378

To what extent do males and females differ in sexual response? What are the most common sexual disorders? Have recent changes in attitudes affected sexual behavior?

| 1. _____ voyeurism | a. date rape |
|---|---|
| 2. _____ excitement phase | b. "flashing" |
| 3. _____ pedophilia | c. "peeping" |
| 4. _____ exhibitionism | d. child molesting |
| 5. _____ acquaintance rape | e. sexual climax |
| 6. _____ orgasm | f. signs of sexual arousal |

## STDS and Safer Sex—Choice, Risk, and Responsibility and Psychology in Action: When Pleasure Fades—Sexual Problems: Pages 378-385

What impacts have sexually transmitted diseases had on sexual behavior? How can couples keep their relationship exciting? What are the most common sexual adjustment problems?

1. _____ orgasmic disorder
2. _____ STD
3. _____ psychogenic
4. _____ gunnysacking
5. _____ safer sex practices
6. _____ dyspareunia
7. _____ sex

a. "dumping" saved-up complaints
b. genital pain from intercourse
c. inability to reach orgasm
d. psychological origin
e. using a condom
f. AIDS
g. a form of relational communication

# CHECK YOUR MEMORY

## Sexual Development—Circle One: XX or XY? and Gender Development—Circle One: Masculine or Feminine: Pages 358-361, 363-367

What are the basic dimensions of sex? How does one's sense of maleness or femaleness develop?

1. Primary sexual characteristics involve differences in the reproductive organs and the breasts.

   TRUE or FALSE

2. The term menarche refers to the ending of regular monthly fertility cycles in females.

   TRUE or FALSE

3. The female gonads are the ovaries.   TRUE or FALSE

4. Cowper's glands are female reproductive structures.   TRUE or FALSE

5. All individuals normally produce both androgens and testosterones.   TRUE or FALSE

6. Transsexuals are persons who have had their genetic sex altered medically.   TRUE or FALSE

7. Without testosterone, a human embryo will develop into a female.   TRUE or FALSE

8. Androgen insensitivity results in the development of female genitals.   TRUE or FALSE

9. Surgical reconstruction determines intersexuals' gender identity by altering their ambiguous genital appearance to be either male or female.   TRUE or FALSE

10. Differences in male and female scores on the SAT have declined in recent years.
TRUE or FALSE

11. Observed differences in the abilities of males and females are based on averages; they tell nothing about a particular person.    TRUE or FALSE

12. Gender identity refers to all the behaviors that are defined as male or female by one's culture.
TRUE or FALSE

13. Babies are perceived differently and treated differently when they are labeled as males than when they are labeled as females.    TRUE or FALSE

14. Women continue to receive unequal pay for work comparable to that of men.    TRUE or FALSE

15. Women of all ethnic groups receive the same unequal pay of $.76 for every $1.00 men earn.
TRUE or FALSE

16. Even though their culture is quite different, the sex roles of Tchambuli men and women are almost identical to those in North America.    TRUE or FALSE

17. Boys are allowed to roam over wider areas than girls are.    TRUE or FALSE

18. Expressive behaviors are those that directly express a person's desire to attain a goal.
TRUE or FALSE

19. Sex-segregated play means that boys and girls do not play with each other.    TRUE or FALSE

20. According to research, men who are sexually aroused are more willing to press women to have sex then men who are not sexually aroused.    TRUE or FALSE

# Androgyny—Are You Masculine, Feminine, or Androgynous?: Pages 367-368

What is psychological androgyny (and is it contagious)?

1. The BSRI consists of 20 masculine traits and 20 feminine traits.    TRUE or FALSE

2. About 50 percent of all people who take the BSRI are scored as androgynous.    TRUE or FALSE

3. Masculine men and feminine women consistently choose to engage in sex-appropriate activities.
TRUE or FALSE

4. Masculine men find it difficult to accept support from others.    TRUE or FALSE

5. Androgynous persons tend to be more satisfied with their lives than non-androgynous persons are.
TRUE or FALSE

## Sexual Orientation—Who Do You Love? and Sexual Behavior—Mapping the Erogenous Zones: Pages 361-363, 369-371

What is sexual orientation? What are the most typical patterns of human sexual behavior?

1.  Sexual scripts determine when, where, and with whom we are likely to express sexual feelings.
    TRUE or FALSE

2.  Women are less physically aroused by erotic stimuli than men are.   TRUE or FALSE

3.  Research suggests that women and men are equal in the level of physiological sexual arousal but differ in the subjective feelings of arousal.   TRUE or FALSE

4.  Differences between male and female sexuality are accurately perceived by the general public.
    TRUE or FALSE

5.  Women may engage in sexual activity at any time during their menstrual cycles.
    TRUE or FALSE

6.  More women than men have sexual dreams that result in orgasm.   TRUE or FALSE

7.  As testosterone levels decline with age, females can take testosterone supplements to restore their sex drive.   TRUE or FALSE

8.  Alcohol and other drugs enhance sexual desire, arousal, and pleasure.   TRUE or FALSE

9.  Drunkenness lowers sexual arousal and performance.   TRUE or FALSE

10. Sterilization tends to abolish the sex drive in the sexually inexperienced.   TRUE or FALSE

11. Masturbation typically ends soon after people get married.   TRUE or FALSE

12. The average frequency of sexual intercourse declines dramatically between the ages of 30 and 39.
    TRUE or FALSE

13. Your sexual orientation is revealed, in part, by who you have erotic fantasies about.
    TRUE or FALSE

14. Gay males are converted to homosexuality during adolescence by other homosexuals.
    TRUE or FALSE

15. Sexual orientation is a very stable personal characteristic.   TRUE or FALSE

16. Sexual orientation is influenced by heredity.   TRUE or FALSE

17. Hormone imbalances cause most instances of homosexuality and bisexuality.   TRUE or FALSE

18. Fifteen percent of men and 13 percent of women identify themselves as homosexual.
    TRUE or FALSE

19. A national survey suggests that of every 100 people, four identify themselves as homosexual or bisexual.   TRUE or FALSE

20. Evolutionists suggested that homosexuality may have developed to reduce male competition for female mates.   TRUE or FALSE

21. Homosexual persons tend to discover their sexual orientation at a later age than heterosexual persons do. TRUE or FALSE

# Human Sexual Response—Sexual Interactions: Pages 371-373
To what extent do males and females differ in sexual response?

1. Masters and Johnson's data on human sexuality was restricted to questionnaires and interviews. TRUE or FALSE

2. During the excitement phase of sexual response, the nipples become erect in both males and females. TRUE or FALSE

3. In males, orgasm is always accompanied by ejaculation.   TRUE or FALSE

4. Almost all women experience a short refractory period after ejaculation.   TRUE or FALSE

5. Both orgasm and resolution tend to last longer in females than they do in males.   TRUE or FALSE

6. Contemporary research has confirmed that clitoral orgasms are an inferior form of sexual response. TRUE or FALSE

7. Women tend to go through the phases of sexual response more slowly than men do. TRUE or FALSE

8. One woman in 3 does not experience orgasm during the first year of marriage.   TRUE or FALSE

# Atypical Sexual Behavior—Trench Coats, Whips, Leathers, and Lace: Pages 373-374
What are the most common sexual disorders?

1. Oral sex and masturbation are formally classified as paraphilias.   TRUE or FALSE

2. Frotteurism refers to sex with children.   TRUE or FALSE

3. Most exhibitionists are male and married.   TRUE or FALSE

4. An exhibitionist who approaches closer than arm's length may be dangerous.   TRUE or FALSE

5. In the majority of cases of child molesting, the offender is an acquaintance or relative of the child. TRUE or FALSE

6.  Child molesting is especially likely to be harmful if the molester is someone the child deeply trusts.
    TRUE or FALSE

7.  Child molesters tend to kidnap children on playgrounds in parks when caretakers are not looking.
    TRUE or FALSE

## Attitudes and Sexual Behavior—The Changing Sexual Landscape: Pages 374-378

Have recent changes in attitudes affected sexual behavior?

1.  In recent decades the gap between sexual values and actual behavior has narrowed.   TRUE or FALSE

2.  A majority of young adults continue to believe that premarital sex is unacceptable.   TRUE or FALSE

3.  The incidence of extramarital sex has not changed much in the last 40 years.   TRUE or FALSE

4.  The majority of men and women have sexual experiences before marriage.   TRUE or FALSE

5.  About 12 percent of all adult Americans are sexually abstinent.   TRUE or FALSE

6.  Women who are raped usually asked for trouble by wearing sexy clothes.   TRUE or FALSE

7.  One woman in 70 will be raped in her lifetime.   TRUE or FALSE

8.  The majority of rapists are friends or acquaintances of the victim.   TRUE or FALSE

9.  Males high in sex role stereotyping are more aroused by stories about rape than males low in sex role stereotyping.   TRUE or FALSE

## STDs and Safer Sex—Choice, Risk, and Responsibility: Pages 378-380

What impacts have sexually transmitted diseases had on sexual behavior?

1.  Many people suffering from STDs are asymptomatic.   TRUE or FALSE

2.  People who are sexually active with one partner do not have to worry about STDs or indirect sexual contact with others.   TRUE or FALSE

3.  Teenage girls today are well educated about STDs and understand that they may get STDs if they are sexually active.   TRUE or FALSE

4.  The first symptoms of AIDS may not appear for up to 7 years.   TRUE or FALSE

5.  HIV infections are spread by direct contact with body fluids.   TRUE or FALSE

6.  The AIDS epidemic has dramatically altered the sexual behavior of college students.
    TRUE or FALSE

7.  Most women who contract the HIV virus today do so through intravenous drug use.
    TRUE or FALSE

8. It is unwise to count on a partner for protection from HIV infection.   TRUE or FALSE

9. Gonorrhea can be prevented by vaccination.   TRUE or FALSE

10. Hepatitis B can be prevented by vaccination.   TRUE or FALSE

11. Chlamydia is now the most common STD among men.   TRUE or FALSE

12. Heterosexuals are predicted to be the main group of people to spread the HIV virus in the next 20 years.
   TRUE or FALSE

13. In the United States, three million people die each year from AIDS, and worldwide five million people die each year.   TRUE or FALSE

# Psychology in Action: When Pleasure Fades—Sexual Problems: Pages 381-385
How can couples keep their relationship exciting? What are the most common sexual adjustment problems?

1. In a desire disorder the person desires sex, but does not become sexually aroused.
   TRUE or FALSE

2. A person who is repelled by sex and seeks to avoid it suffers from a sexual aversion.
   TRUE or FALSE

3. Men suffering from primary erectile dysfunction have never had an erection.   TRUE or FALSE

4. The squeeze technique is the most commonly recommended treatment for erectile disorders.
   TRUE or FALSE

5. The majority of erectile dysfunctions are psychogenic.   TRUE or FALSE

6. The causes of erectile disorders include physical illnesses, diseases, and damage to the penis.
   TRUE or FALSE

7. Males' sexual arousal disorder is caused by physical illnesses, and females' sexual arousal disorder is caused by traumatic childhood experiences.   TRUE or FALSE

8. Treatment for female sexual arousal disorder usually involves sensate focus.   TRUE or FALSE

9. Female orgasmic disorder is the female equivalent of premature ejaculation in the male.
   TRUE or FALSE

10. Both males and females can experience dyspareunia.   TRUE or FALSE

11. Masters and Johnson regard all sexual problems as mutual, or shared by both parties.
   TRUE or FALSE

12. Gunnysacking is an important communication skill that all couples should master.   TRUE or FALSE

13. Rather than telling your partner what he or she thinks, you should ask her or him.   TRUE or FALSE

14. Loss of sexual interest for one's partner is inevitable in a long-term relationship.   TRUE or FALSE

# FINAL SURVEY AND REVIEW

## Sexual Development—Circle One: XX or XY
What are the basic dimensions of sex? How does one's sense of maleness or femaleness develop?

1. Physical differences between males and females can be divided into primary and secondary

   _____ _____.

2. _____ refers to the genitals _____ and reproductive organs.

3. _____ refers to bodily features such as breast development in females, body shape, and facial

   _____.

4. Reproductive maturity in females is signaled by _____ (the onset of menstruation). Soon after,

   _____ (the release of the eggs) begins.

5. The development of sexual characteristics is influenced by _____ (male sex hormones) and

   _____ (female sex hormones) secreted by the _____ (sex glands).

6. A person's sex can be broken down into _____ sex, _____ sex, hormonal sex,

   _____ sex, and gender identity.

7. Sexual development begins with genetic sex (XX or XY _____). Two X and _____

   normally produce a female; an _____ plus a _____ produces a male.

8. During prenatal sexual development, the presence of _____ produces female _____; its

   absence produces a female _____.

9. _____ insensitivity, exposure to progestin, and the androgenital syndrome result in sexual

   ambiguities called _____.

10. Many researchers believe that _____ hormones can exert a biological _____ effect

    that combines with social factors present after birth to influence psychosexual development.

11. On most _____ dimensions, men and women are more alike than they are different.

12. _____ _____ with hormone therapy can alter the genital appearance and secondary sex characteristics for _____ (children with ambiguous sexual anatomy) to either male or female. However, these factors alone do not determine gender identity; _____ is also important.

# Sexual Orientation—Who Do You Love?
## What is sexual orientation?

1. Sexual _____ refers to one's degree of emotional and erotic attraction to members of the same sex, opposite sex, or both sexes.

2. A person may be _____ , homosexual, or bisexual.

3. A combination of _____ , biological, _____ , and psychological influences combine to produce one's sexual orientation. The prenatal hormonal theory of homosexuality theory states that _____ affect hormone levels in the developing fetus, which can affect sexual orientation.

4. Research conducted on sexual _____ or behavior by neurobiologists suggests a genetic link between _____ and children. Other theorists believe that homosexuality may have developed to _____ the male and female competition for sexual partners.

5. A national survey suggests that of every 100 people, 7 identify themselves as _____ or bisexual.

6. However, gay men and lesbians are frequently affected by _____ (fear of homosexuality) and _____ (the belief that heterosexuality is more natural than homosexuality).

7. As a group, _____ men and women do not differ psychologically from _____ .

# Gender Development—Circle One: Masculine or Feminine
## How does one's sense of maleness or femaleness develop?

1. Social factors are especially apparent in learned _____ _____ (a private sense of maleness or femaleness) and the effect of _____ _____ (patterns of behavior defined as male or female within a particular culture).

2. Gender identity, which is based to a large extent on _____ , usually becomes stable by age 3 or 4 years.

3. Gender roles contribute to the development of gender role _____ (oversimplified beliefs about the nature of men and women) that often distort perceptions about the kinds of occupations for which men and women are suited.

381

4. As a result of gender role _____ , for every $1.00 men earn in business, academia, medicine, law, sports, and politics, white women earn $. _____ , black women earn $. _____ , and Latino women earn $. _____ .

4. Another effect of gender role _____ is that _____ are less liked by their peers for violating gender norms when they hold a job that as been defined as traditionally "male."

5. _____ determines gender roles of males and females in each society.

6. Gender role _____ (learning gender roles) seems to account for most observed male/female differences.

7. Parents tend to encourage boys in _____ behaviors (goal-directed actions) and girls in _____ (emotional) behaviors.

8. By age three, _____ play can be seen in boys and girls: Boys play outdoor games that focus on superheroes, and girls play indoor games that focus on house-related activities.

# Androgyny—Are You Masculine, Feminine, or Androgynous?
## What is psychological androgyny (and is it contagious)?

1. Androgyny is measured with the _____ *Sex Role Inventory (BSRI)*.

2. Research conducted by Sandra Bern indicates that roughly one _____ of all persons are androgynous (they possess both masculine and feminine traits).

3. Being masculine means that a person is _____ and assertive.

4. Being feminine means that a person is _____ (helpful and comforting) and interpersonally oriented.

5. Psychological androgyny appears related to greater _____ or flexibility in behavior.

# Sexual Behavior—Mapping the Erogenous Zone
## What are the most typical patterns of human sexual behavior?

1. Sexual behavior, including _____ (sexual climax) is apparent soon after birth and expressed in various ways throughout life.

2.   Sexual arousal is related to stimulation of the body's _____ zones (areas that produce erotic pleasure), but _____ elements such as thoughts and images are equally important.

3.   "Normal" sexual behavior is defined differently by various cultures. Also, each person uses learned sexual _____ (plots or mental _____ ) to guide sexual behavior.

4.   There is little _____ in sexual _____ between males and females.

5.   Research suggests that _____ women and men are _____ in physiological sexual arousal but _____ in the subjective feelings of arousal. Women's sexual arousal is linked to their emotional responses to cues and acknowledgment from their partners of their needs and preferences.

6.   Evidence suggests that the sex drive peaks at a later age for _____ than it does for _____ , although this difference is diminishing.

7.   Sex drive in both males and females may be related to bodily levels of _____ . As testosterone levels decline with age, so does _____ drive; both males and females can take _____ supplements to restore it.

8.   The belief that alcohol and other drugs _____ sex drive is a myth. Alcohol is a depressant, which in large doses tends to _____ sexual desire, arousal, pleasure, and performance. Other drugs like amphetamines, amyl nitrite, barbiturates, cocaine, Ecstasy, LSD, and marijuana tend to impair sexual responses.

9.   _____ orgasms, which occur during sleep, are a normal form of sexual release.

10.  Castration (removal of the gonads) may or may not influence sex drive in humans, depending on how sexually experienced a person is. _____ (a vasectomy or tubal ligation) does not alter sex drive.

11.  There is a gradual decline (or decrease) in the _____ of sexual intercourse with increasing age. However, many elderly persons remain sexually active and great variations exist at all ages.

12.  _____ is a normal, harmless behavior practiced by a large percentage of the population. For many, it is an important part of sexual self- discovery.

# Human Sexual Response—Sexual Interactions
To what extent do males and females differ in sexual response?

1.   In a series of landmark studies, William Masters and Virginia _____ directly observed sexual response in a large number of adults.

2. Human sexual response can be divided into four phases: (1) excitement; (2) _____ ; (3) orgasm; and (4) _____ .

3. There do not appear to be any differences between "_____ orgasms" and "_____ orgasms" in the female.

4. Males experience a _____ period after orgasm and ejaculation.

5. Both males and females may go through all four stages in 4 or 5 minutes. But during lovemaking, most _____ typically take longer than this, averaging from 10 to 20 minutes.

6. _____ orgasm has been abandoned by most sex counselors as the ideal in lovemaking.

7. _____ percent of women are consistently _____ , and at least 48 percent are capable of multiple orgasm.

## Atypical Sexual Behavior—Trench Coats, Whips, Leathers, and Lace
What are the most common sexual disorders?

1. Definitions of sexual deviance are highly subjective. Many "_____ _____ " behaviors are acceptable in private or in some cultures.

2. Sexual deviations that often cause difficulty are called _____ (destructive deviations in sexual preferences or behavior).

3. Some paraphilias include: _____ (sex with children), fetishism (sexual arousal associated with inanimate objects), _____ (viewing the genitals of others without their permission), and exhibitionism (displaying the genitals to unwilling viewers).

4. Other paraphilias are: _____ fetishism (achieving sexual arousal by wearing clothing of the opposite sex),
sexual sadism (deriving sexual pleasure from inflicting pain), sexual masochism (desiring pain as part of the sex act), and _____ (sexually touching or rubbing against a nonconsenting person).

5. _____ ("flashers") are rarely dangerous and can best be characterized as sexually inhibited and immature.

6. The effects of child molestation vary greatly, depending on the severity of the _____ and the child's _____ to the molester.

7. _____ who have been molested may display such signs as fear of being seen _____, anxiety, shame, or discomfort to references of _____ behaviors and express low self-esteem or self-worth.

8. Child molesters tend to gain access to children through _____ opportunities and bring them to their homes. Some tactics molesters use to lull children are _____ them with gifts, encouraging them to _____ about sex, and using threats to gain compliance.

# Attitudes and Sexual Behavior—The Changing Sexual Landscape
Have recent changes in attitudes affected sexual behavior?

1. _____ toward sexual behavior, especially the behavior of others, have become more _____, but actual changes in sexual behavior have been more gradual.

2. Another change has been earlier and more frequent sexual activity among adolescents and young adults, including larger percentages of people who have _____ intercourse.

3. Also evident are a greater acceptance of female sexuality and a narrowing of differences in male and female patterns of sexual behavior. In other words, the _____ _____ is fading.

4. _____ (date) rape and rape-supportive _____ and attitudes remain major problems.

5. Rape is primarily a violent crime of _____ rather than a sex crime.

6. Men now report having an average of seven sexual partners in their lifetime, while women report an average of _____ .

# STDs and Safer Sex—Choice, Risk, and Responsibility
What impacts have sexually transmitted diseases had on sexual behavior?

1. Based on a recent study, approximately 90 percent of _____ teenage girls reported that they do not believe they will get _____ diseases (STDs) because their partners did not show symptoms of STDs.

385

2. People who are sexually active, even with only one person, may still be engaging in _____ sex from indirect _____ with others through their partner's indiscretion.

3. During the last 20 years there has been a steady increase in the incidence of _____ _____ diseases (STDs).

4. Part of this increase is due to the emergence of acquired immune _____ syndrome (AIDS) caused by the human _____ virus (HIV).

5. _____ have had a sizable impact on patterns of sexual behavior, including increased awareness of high-risk behaviors and some curtailment of risk taking.

6. It is predicted that over the next 20 to 30 years, the dominant group of individuals that will spread the HIV virus are _____ , and unless preventions are taken, 65 million people will die of _____ .

# Psychology in Action: Sexual Problems—When Pleasure Fades

How can couples keep their relationship exciting? What are the most common sexual adjustment problems?

1. The principal problems in sexual adjustment are desire disorders, _____ disorders, _____ disorders, and sexual pain disorders.

2. Desire disorders include _____ sexual desire (a loss of sexual desire) and sexual _____ (fear or disgust about engaging in sex).

3. Arousal disorders include male _____ disorder and female sexual _____ disorder.

4. Approximately 40 percent of _____ disorders result from _____ causes (having psychological or emotional origin) rather than physical illnesses, diseases, or damage to the penis.

5. Both males and females have similar causes for sexual _____ disorder, which include _____ , hostility toward their partner, depression, stress, childhood experiences, having a _____ religious background, and distrust of men or women.

6. To maintain a _____ relationship through communication, people should _____ gunnysacking each other, be open about their _____ , not attack each other's _____ , not be mind readers, and try to understand the other's perspectives.

7. Orgasm disorders are male orgasmic disorder ( _____ ejaculation), _____ ejaculation, and female _____ disorder (an inability to reach orgasm during lovemaking).

8. Sexual pain disorders are _____ (painful intercourse) and _____ (muscle spasms of the vagina).

9. Behavioral methods such as _____ focus and the _____ technique have been developed to alleviate each problem. In addition, counseling can be quite helpful.

10. However, most sexual _____ problems are closely linked to the general health of a couple's relationship.

11. For this reason, _____ skills that foster and maintain intimacy are the key to successful relationships.

# MASTERY TEST

1. The strength of the sex drive in both men and women increases when _____ levels are higher in the body.
   a. testosterone
   b. progestin
   c. ovulin
   d. androgen

2. Worldwide, the main source of HIV infection is
   a. heterosexual sex
   b. homosexual sex
   c. intravenous drug use
   d. blood transfusions

3. Boys are encouraged to be strong, aggressive, dominant, and achieving through the process of
   a. biological biasing.
   b. sexual orienting.
   c. gender adaptation.
   d. gender role socialization.

4. Before birth, a genetic male will develop as a female if which condition exists?
   a. excessive progestin
   b. an androgen insensitivity
   c. the androgenital syndrome
   d. the testes produce testosterone

5. One of the greatest changes in attitudes toward sex is a tolerance for
   a. teenage pregnancies.
   b. the sexual behavior of others.
   c. the double standard.
   d. STDs.

6. The squeeze technique is typically used to treat
   a. dyspareunia.
   b. vaginismus.
   c. female sexual arousal disorder.
   d. premature ejaculation.

7. In a female, gonadal sex is determined by the presence of
   a. estrogens.
   b. androgens.
   c. ovaries.
   d. a vagina and uterus.

8. A policeman who accepts emotional support from others, especially from women, would most likely be scored as _____ on the BSRI.
   a. masculine
   b. feminine
   c. androgynous
   d. expressive-nurturant

9. Which of the following is POOR advice for couples who want to communicate effectively and maintain intimacy?
   a. Avoid gunnysacking.
   b. Avoid expressing anger.
   c. Don't try to win.
   d. Don't be a mind-reader.

10. The aspect of sex that is essentially formed by age 4 is
    a. gender identity.
    b. gender roles.
    c. sexual scripting.
    d. psychological androgyny.

11. In a female, broadening of the hips and breast development are
    a. primary sexual characteristics.
    b. secondary sexual characteristics.
    c. caused by the release of androgens.
    d. associated with the presence of a Y chromosome.

12. The first two phases of the sexual response cycle are
    a. excitement, arousal.
    b. arousal, orgasm.
    c. excitement, plateau.
    d. stimulation, arousal.

13. A special danger in the transmission of STDs is that many people are _____ at first.
    a. not infectious
    b. androgynous
    c. androgenital
    d. asymptomatic

14. The presence of a Y chromosome is associated with
    a. intersexualism.
    b. prenatal testosterone.
    c. menarche.
    d. the presence of progestin.

15. With respect to the behaviors parents encourage in their children, which is a correct match?
    a. controlling-female
    b. goal-oriented-female
    c. expressive-male
    d. instrumental-male

16. Which condition is LEAST likely to lower sexual performance?
    a. sterilization
    b. castration
    c. extreme alcohol intoxication
    d. sexual aversion

17. Prenatally masculinized females tend to be tomboys during childhood, an observation that supports the
    a. biological biasing effect.
    b. estrogen paradox.
    c. view that gender is genetically determined.
    d. idea that gender role socialization is dominant.

18. Which of the following increases the likelihood that a man will commit rape?
    a. drinking alcohol
    b. being high in gender role stereotyping
    c. belief in rape myths
    d. all of the preceding

19. Gender role _____ treat learned gender role differences as if they were real gender differences.
    a. labels
    b. behavior patterns
    c. stereotypes
    d. templates

20. Regarding sexual response it can be said that
    a. orgasm and resolution tend to last longer in women.
    b. a short refractory period occurs just before orgasm in males.
    c. some women skip the arousal phase of the cycle.
    d. men are incapable of having second orgasms.

21. The decline of the double standard refers to abandoning different standards for
    a. risky sex and "safe" sex.
    b. heterosexual relationships and homosexual relationships.
    c. sexuality before and after marriage.
    d. male and female sexual behavior.

22. Declines in the differences in male and female scores on the SAT call into question which concept?
    a. the androgenital syndrome
    b. the biological biasing effect
    c. gender role socialization
    d. gender identity

23. When expectations of a friendly first date clash with an attempted seduction the problem can be attributed to differences in
    a. gender roles.
    b. erogenous confrontation.
    c. gender myths.
    d. sexual scripts.

24. Which statement concerning sexual orientation is TRUE?
    a. Sexual orientation is partly hereditary.
    b. Homosexuality is caused by a hormone imbalance.
    c. Sexual orientation can be changed fairly easily.
    d. Heterosexual persons tend to discover their sexual orientation at a later date than homosexual persons do.

25. Pedophilia, fetishism, and sadism are classified as
    a. the three basic forms of child molestation.
    b. STDs.
    c. paraphilias.
    d. hormonal disorders.

26. All but one of the following is a rape myth. Which is NOT a myth?
    a.   Women who get raped ask for it in one way or another.
    b.   A majority of rapes are committed by a friend or acquaintance of the victim.
    c.   Women who are sexually active are usually lying if they say they were raped.
    d.   Many women who are raped secretly enjoy it.

27. Which of the following diseases is currently untreatable?
    a.   gonorrhea
    b.   chlamydia
    c.   syphilis
    d.   hepatitis B

28. The male sexual disorder that corresponds most closely to female sexual arousal disorder is
    a.   sexual aversion.
    b.   erectile disorder.
    c.   premature ejaculation.
    d.   dyspareunia.

29. Surgical reconstruction can alter genital appearances to either male or female for _____ or children with ambiguous sexual anatomy.
    a.   pedophilia
    b.   sexual masochism
    c.   sexual sadism
    d.   intersexuals

30. Women earn approximately $.55 to $.76 for every $1.00 men earn is the result of
    a.   gender identity.
    b.   gender role stereotyping.
    c.   sexual orientation.
    d.   androgen insensitivity.

31. To restore sex drive due to aging, both men and women can
    a.   increase their sexual activities.
    b.   take estrogen supplements.
    c.   take testosterone supplements.
    d.   eat oysters and drink wine.

32. At an early age, boys play outdoor games with other boys that focus on who's the boss, and girls play indoor games with other girls that focus on house-related activities and cooperation. This difference is the result of
    a.   gender role socialization.
    b.   sex-segregated play.
    c.   instrumental versus expressive behaviors.
    d.   all the preceding.

33. When Bem asked people to complete the BSRI, about _____ percent fell into traditional feminine or masculine categories.
    a. 15
    b. 20
    c. 35
    d. 50

34. Research suggests that physiological sexual arousal for men and women is _____ , but their subjective feelings of arousal are _____ .
    a. equal; different
    b. different; equal
    c. culturally defined; biologically defined
    d. easily measured; not measurable

35. Evolution theorists believe that homosexuality was developed
    a. to reduce male competition for female sexual partners.
    b. to explain why certain men were not physically capable of performing "manly" duties.
    c. as a result of hormonal imbalance.
    d. as a result of survival of the fittest.

36. Which of the following is NOT a tactic used by child molesters?

    a. use a chat room on the Internet to encourage children to talk about sex
    b. bribe children with gifts
    c. use threats to gain children's compliance
    d. have partners to help lure children to their homes

37. The performance gap between men and women can be traced back to
    a. heredity.
    b. women being told they cannot outperform men.
    c. availability of resources allocated to men versus women.
    d. women too busy taking care of their family to maintain their physical skills.

38. A recent study found that as high as _____ of teenage girls who are sexually active do not believe that they will get STDs because their partners did not exhibit any symptoms of STDs.
    a. 90 percent
    b. 70 percent
    c. 45 percent
    d. 35 percent

39. Cocaine and large doses of alcohol _____ sexual desire, arousal, pleasure, and performance.
    a. increase
    b. decrease
    c. do not affect
    d. enhance men's

# SOLUTIONS

## RECITE AND REVIEW

### Sexual Development—Circle One: XX or XY?: Pages 358-361
What are the basic dimensions of sex? How does one's sense of maleness or femaleness develop?

1.  primary; secondary
2.  genitals
3.  shape
4.  menstruation; ova
5.  male; female; glands
6.  hormonal; gender
7.  genetic; female; male
8.  male; female
9.  syndrome; sexual
10. hormones; effect
11. alike; different
12. reconstruction; appearance; ambiguous

### Sexual Orientation—Who Do You Love?: Pages 361-363
What is sexual orientation?

1.  sex; sex; sexes
2.  homosexual
3.  sexual; orientation; prenatal; hormonal
4.  sexual; genetic; reduce
5.  four; bisexual
6.  homosexuality
7.  heterosexuals

### Gender Development—Circle One: Masculine or Feminine: Pages 363-367
How does one's sense of maleness or femaleness develop?

1.  maleness; femaleness
2.  3; 4
3.  gender role
4.  stereotypes; women; women
5.  stereotyping; less; gender
6.  roles
7.  Gender role
8.  boys; girls
9.  three; sex; outdoor; indoor

### Androgyny—Are You Masculine, Feminine, or Androgynous? Pages 367-368
What is psychological androgyny (and is it contagious)?

1.  *Sex Role*
2.  masculine; feminine
3.  masculine
4.  feminine
5.  androgyny

## Sexual Behavior—Mapping the Erogenous Zones: Pages 369-371

What are the most typical patterns of human sexual behavior?

1. climax
2. pleasure; thoughts
3. cultures
4. responsiveness
5. arousal; subjective; emotional
6. later
7. drive; age; sex
8. myth; decrease; amphetamines; impair
9. orgasms
10. Castration
11. decline (or decrease)
12. discovery

## Human Sexual Response—Sexual Interactions: Pages 371-373

To what extent do males and females differ in sexual response?

1. Masters
2. excitement; orgasm
3. orgasms; orgasms
4. orgasm
5. 4
6. orgasm
7. multi; multiple

## Atypical Sexual Behavior—Trench Coats, Whips, Leathers, and Lace: Pages 373-374

What are the most common sexual disorders?

1. subjective; cultures
2. deviations compliance
3. fetishism; exhibitionism
4. sadism; masochism
5. inhibited
6. severity
7. molested; nude; shame; sexual
8. opportunities; gifts;

## Attitudes and Sexual Behavior—The Changing Sexual Landscape: Pages 374-378

Have recent changes in attitudes affected sexual behavior?

1. behavior
2. earlier; intercourse
3. female; behavior
4. date; rape
5. Rape
6. seven

## STDs and Safer Sex—Choice, Risk, and Responsibility: Pages 378-380

What impacts have sexually transmitted diseases had on sexual behavior?

1. 90; girls; sexually; did not
2. active; indirect
3. diseases
4. acquired immune; virus
5. risk; risk
6. HIV; 65

## Psychology in Action: When Pleasure Fades—Sexual Problems: Pages 381-385

How can couples keep their relationship exciting? What are the most common sexual adjustment problems?

1. desire; pain
2. sexual; desire; sexual
3. male; female
4. erectile; psychological; damage

5. arousal; hostility; childhood
6. maintain; avoid; attack
7. ejaculation; ejaculation
8. painful; muscle spasms

9. focus
10. relationship
11. intimacy

# CONNECTIONS

## Sexual Development—Circle One: XX or XY?: Pages 358-361

What are the basic dimensions of sex?

1. d
2. h
3. f
4. b

5. j
6. l
7. i
8. a

9. e
10. g
11. c
12. k

## Sexual Development (Cont.)

1. d
2. g
3. i
4. a

5. j
6. k
7. l
8. e

9. c
10. f
11. h
12. b

## Sexual Development (Cont.), Gender Development—Circle One: Masculine or Feminine, and Androgyny—Are you Masculine, Feminine or Androgynous?: Pages 358-361, 363-368

What are the basic dimensions of sex? How does one's sense of maleness or femaleness develop? What is psychological androgyny (and is it contagious)?

1. j
2. d
3. f
4. a

5. g
6. c
7. b
8. h

9. i
10. e

## Sexual Orientation—Who Do You Love? And Sexual Behavior—Mapping the Erogenous Zones: Pages 361-363, 369-371

What is sexual orientation? What are the most typical patterns of human sexual behavior?

| | | | | | |
|---|---|---|---|---|---|
| 1. | G. | 5. | A. | 9. | F. |
| 2. | B. | 6. | H. | 10. | I. |
| 3. | C. | 7. | E. | | |
| 4. | D. | 8. | J. | | |

## Human Sexual Response—Sexual Interactions, Atypical Sexual Behaviors—Trench Coats, Whips, Leathers, and Lace and Attitudes and Sexual Behavior—The Changing Sexual Landscape: Pages 371-378

To what extent do males and females differ in sexual response? What are the most common sexual disorders? Have recent changes in attitudes affected sexual behavior?

| | | | | | |
|---|---|---|---|---|---|
| 1. | c | 3. | d | 5. | a |
| 2. | f | 4. | b | 6. | e |

## STDs and Safer Sex—Choice, Risk, and Responsibility and Psychology in Action: When Pleasure Fades—Sexual Problems: Pages 378-385

What impacts have sexually transmitted diseases had on sexual behavior? How can couples keep their relationship exciting? What are the most common sexual adjustment problems?

| | | | | | | | |
|---|---|---|---|---|---|---|---|
| 1. | c | 3. | d | 5. | e | 7. | g |
| 2. | f | 4. | a | 6. | b | | |

# CHECK YOUR MEMORY

## Sexual Development—Circle One: XX or XY? and Gender Development—Circle One: Masculine or Feminine?: Pages 358-361, 363-367

What are the basic dimensions of sex? How does one's sense of maleness or femaleness develop?

| | | | | | |
|---|---|---|---|---|---|
| 1. | F | 9. | F | 17. | F |
| 2. | F | 10. | T | 18. | T |
| 3. | T | 11. | T | 19. | F |
| 4. | F | 12. | F | 20. | T |
| 5. | F | 13. | T | | |
| 6. | F | 14. | T | | |
| 7. | T | 15. | T | | |
| 8. | T | 16. | F | | |

## Androgyny—Are You Masculine, Feminine, or Androgynous?: Pages 367-368

What is psychological androgyny (and is it contagious)?

| | | | | | |
|---|---|---|---|---|---|
| 1. | F | 3. | 5. | 5. | T |
| 2. | F | 4. | T | | |

## Sexual Behavior—Mapping the Erogenous Zones: Pages 436-440

What are the most typical patterns of human sexual behavior?

| | | | | | |
|---|---|---|---|---|---|
| 1. | T | 8. | F | 15. | T |
| 2. | F | 9. | T | 16. | T |
| 3. | T | 10. | F | 17. | F |
| 4. | F | 11. | F | 18. | F |
| 5. | T | 12. | F | 19. | T |
| 6. | F | 13. | T | 20. | T |
| 7. | T | 14. | F | 21. | T |

## Human Sexual Response—Sexual Interactions: Pages 371-373

To what extent do males and females differ in sexual response?

| | | | | | |
|---|---|---|---|---|---|
| 1. | F | 4. | F | 7. | T |
| 2. | T | 5. | T | 8. | T |
| 3. | F | 6. | F | | |

397

## Atypical Sexual Behavior—Trench Coats, Whips, Leathers, and Lace: Pages 373-374

What are the most common sexual disorders?

| | | |
|---|---|---|
| 1. F | 4. T | 7. T |
| 2. F | 5. T | |
| 3. T | 6. T | |

## Attitudes and Sexual Behavior—The Changing Sexual Landscape: Pages 374-378

Have recent changes in attitudes affected sexual behavior?

| | | |
|---|---|---|
| 1. T | 4. T | 7. F |
| 2. F | 5. T | 8. T |
| 3. T | 6. F | 9. T |

## STDs and Safer Sex—Choice, Risk, and Responsibility: Pages 378-380

What impacts have sexually transmitted diseases had on sexual behavior?

| | | |
|---|---|---|
| 1. T | 6. F | 11. F |
| 2. F | 7. F | 12. T |
| 3. F | 8. T | 13. F |
| 4. T | 9. F | |
| 5. T | 10. T | |

## Psychology in Action: When Pleasure Fades—Sexual Problems: Pages 381-385

How can couples keep their relationship exciting? What are the most common sexual adjustment problems?

| | | |
|---|---|---|
| 1. F | 6. F | 11. T |
| 2. T | 7. F | 12. F |
| 3. T | 8. T | 13. T |
| 4. F | 9. F | 14. T |
| 5. T | 10. T | |

# FINAL SURVEY AND REVIEW

## Sexual Development—Circle One: XX or XY?
What are the basic dimensions of sex?

1. sexual; characteristics.
2. Primary sexual characteristics; interna
3. Secondary sexual characteristics; hair
4. menarche; ovulation
5. androgens; estrogens; gonads
6. genetic; gonadal; genital
7. chromosomes; X; X; Y
8. testosterone; genitals; genitals
9. Androgen; intersexualism
10. prenatal; biasing
11. psychological
12. Surgical; reconstruction; intersexuals; socialization

## Sexual Orientation—Who Do You Love?
What is sexual orientation?

1. orientation
2. heterosexual
3. hereditary; social; genes
4. orientation; mothers; reduce
5. homosexual
6. homophobia; heterosexism
7. homosexual; heterosexuals

## Gender Development—Circle One: Masculine or Feminine
How does one's sense of maleness or femaleness develop?

1. gender; identity; gender; roles
2. labeling
3. stereotypes
4. stereotypes; 76; 65; 55
5. stereotyping; women
6. Culture
7. socialization
8. instrumental; expressive
9. sex-segregated

## Androgyny—Are You Masculine, Feminine, or Androgynous?
What is psychological androgyny (and is it contagious)?

1. *Bern*
2. third
3. independent
4. nurturant
5. adaptability

## Sexual Behavior—Mapping the Erogenous Zones
What are the most typical patterns of human sexual behavior?

1. orgasm
2. erogenous; cognitive
3. scripts; plans
4. difference; behavior
5. both; equal; differ
6. females; males
7. androgens; sex; testosterone
8. enhance; decrease
9. Nocturnal
10. Sterilization
11. frequency
12. Masturbation

## Human Sexual Response—Sexual Interactions
To what extent do males and females differ in sexual response?

1. Johnson
2. plateau; resolution
3. vaginal; clitoral
4. refractory
5. females
6. Mutual
7. Fifteen; multi-orgasmic

## Atypical Sexual Behavior—Trench Coats, Whips, Leathers, and Lace

What are the most common sexual disorders?

1. sexually; deviant
2. paraphilias
3. pedophilia; voyeurism
4. transvestic; frotteurism
5. Exhibitionists
6. molestation; relationship
7. Children; nude; sexual
8. caretaking; bribing; talk

## Attitudes and Sexual Behavior—The Changing Sexual Landscape

Have recent changes in attitudes affected sexual behavior?

1. Attitudes; liberal
2. premarital
3. double; standard
4. Acquaintance; myths
5. aggression
6. four

## STDs and Safer Sex—Choice, Risk, and Responsibility

What impacts have sexually transmitted diseases had on sexual behavior?

1. sexually active; sexually transmitted
2. risky; contact
3. sexually transmitted
4. deficiency; immunodeficiency
5. STDs
6. heterosexuals; AIDS

## Psychology in Action: When Pleasure Fades—Sexual Problems

How can couples keep their relationship exciting? What are the most common sexual adjustment problems?

1. arousal; orgasm
2. hypoactive; aversion
3. erectile; arousal
4. erectile; psychogenic
5. arousal; anxiety; strict
6. healthy; avoid; feelings; characteristics
7. retarded; premature; orgasm
8. dyspareunia; vaginismus
9. sensate; squeeze
10. adjustment
11. communication

## MASTERY TEST

1. a, p. 370
2. a, p. 379
3. d, p. 364
4. b, p. 359
5. b, p. 375
6. d, p. 385
7. c, p. 358
8. c, p. 367
9. b, p. 382
10. a, p. 364
11. b, p. 360
12. c, p. 371
13. d, p. 378
14. b, p. 358
15. d, p. 366
16. a, p. 379
17. a, p. 363
18. d, p. 378
19. c, p. 364
20. a, p. 372
21. d, p. 376
22. b, p. 364
23. d, p. 369
24. a, p. 362
25. c, p. 373
26. b, p. 377
27. d, p. 378
28. b, p. 383
29. d, p. 359
30. b, p. 365
31. c, p. 370
32. d, p. 366
33. d, p. 367
34. a, p. 369
35. a, p. 362
36. d, p. 374
37. c, p. 364
38. a, p.378
39. b, p. 370

# Personality

## Chapter Overview

Personality refers to unique and enduring behavior patterns. Character is personality evaluated. Temperament refers to the hereditary and physiological aspects of one's emotional nature. Personality traits are lasting personal qualities. Personality types are categories defined by groups of shared traits. Behavior is also influenced by self-concept. Personality theories combine various ideas and principles to explain personality. Behavioral genetics suggests that heredity influences personality traits. Twin studies suggest that heredity accounts for 25 percent -50 percent of the variability in personality traits.

Allport's trait theory classifies traits as common, individual, cardinal, central, or secondary. Cattell's trait theory attributes visible surface traits to the existence of 16 underlying source traits. The five-factor model reduces traits to 5 dimensions. Traits appear to interact with situations to determine behavior.

Like other psychodynamic approaches, Sigmund Freud's psychoanalytic theory emphasizes unconscious forces and conflicts within the personality. The neo-Freudian theorists retained many of Freud's basic ideas, but modified some of them or added to them. Behavioral theories of personality emphasize learning, conditioning, and the immediate effects of the environment. Social learning theory adds cognitive elements, such as perception, thinking, expectancies, and understanding, to the behavioral view. Many differences between males and females are based on social learning. Humanistic theory emphasizes subjective experiences and needs for self-actualization. Positivistic theory focuses on characteristics that contribute to a person's well-being and life satisfaction.

Techniques typically used to assess personality are interviews, direct observation, rating scales, questionnaires, and projective tests.

Shyness is a mixture of social inhibition and social anxiety. It is marked by heightened public self-consciousness and a tendency to regard one's shyness as a lasting trait. Shyness can be lessened by changing self-defeating beliefs and by improving social skills.

# Learning Objectives

*Theme: Personality refers to the consistency we see in personal behavior patterns. Measures of personality reveal individual differences and help predict future behavior.*

| |
|---|
| **GQ: How do psychologists use the term "personality"?** |
| LO 12.1 Define the term *personality* and explain how personality differs from *character* and *temperament*. |
| LO 12.2 Describe the *trait approach* and the *type approach* to personality; discuss the stability of personality; describe the characteristics of *introverts* and *extroverts*; and explain the disadvantages of the type approach. |
| LO 12.3 Define *behavioral genetics*; explain how twin studies are used to assess the relative contribution of heredity and environment to a person's personality; and discuss how the similarities in the personalities of twins can be explained. |
| LO 12.4 Explain the terms *self-concept* and *self-esteem* and how they affect behavior and personal adjustment and explain the differences in the basis of self-esteem in Eastern and Western cultures. |
| LO 12.5 Define the term *personality theory* and describe the different psychological perspectives regarding personality theory covered in your text. |
| **GQ: Are some personality traits more basic or important than others?** |
| LO 12.6 Define *common trait, individual trait, cardinal trait, central trait, secondary trait, surface trait,* and *source trait.* |
| LO 12.7 Describe the following trait theories: a. Eysenck and the ancient Greeks; b. Rentfrow and Gosling's musical personalities; c. Gordon Allport; d. Raymond Cattell; and e. the *Five-Factor Model* of Personality. |
| LO 12.8 Explain *trait-situation interactions*. |
| **GQ: How do psychodynamic theories explain personality?** |
| LO 12.9 Discuss Freud's view of personality development, including a. the three parts of the personality; b. neurotic and moral anxiety; c. the three levels of awareness; d. the psychosexual stages and fixation; and e. the positive and negative aspects of Freud's theory. |
| LO 12.10 Define the term *neo-Freudian*; explain why many of Freud's followers eventually disagreed with him; and describe the theories of each of the following: a. Alfred Adler; b. Karen Horney; and c. Carl Jung. |
| **GQ: What do behaviorists emphasize in their approach to personality?** |
| LO 12.11 Explain how learning theorists (behaviorists) view the structure of personality. Include in your discussion the terms *situational determinants, habit, drive, cue, response,* and *reward.* |
| LO 12.12 Explain how learning theory and *social learning theory* differ and describe the role of *social reinforcement* in personality development. Include in your discussion a description of these terms: *psychological situation, expectancy, reinforcement value, self-efficacy,* and *self-reinforcement.* |
| LO 12.13 Using the behavioristic view of development, explain why feeding, toilet training, sex training, and learning to express anger or aggression may be particularly important to personality formation; and describe the role of *imitation* and *identification* in personality development. |
| **GQ: How do humanistic theories differ from other perspectives?** |
| LO 12.14 Briefly explain how the humanists set themselves apart from the Freudian and behaviorist viewpoints or personality; describe Maslow's concept of *self-actualization* and the characteristics of self-actualizers; explain what helps and hinders self-actualization; list eight steps to promote self-actualization; and describe the six human strengths that contribute to well-being and life satisfaction. |
| LO 12.15 Discuss Rogers' views of the normal or *fully functioning individual*; define his terms: *self, self-concept, incongruence, ideal self; conditions of worth, positive self-regard, organismic valuing,* and *unconditional positive regard.* |
| LO 12.16 Explain the value of *possible selves* and telling stories about ourselves. |
| LO 12.17 Compare and contrast in general terms the strengths and weaknesses of the trait, psychoanalytic, behavioristic, social learning, and humanistic theories of personality. |

| GQ: How do psychologists measure personality? |
| --- |
| LO 12.18 Discuss the following assessment techniques in terms of purpose, method, advantages, and limitations: a. structured, unstructured, and diagnostic *interviews* (include the *halo effect*); b. direct observation (combined with *rating scales*, *behavioral assessment*, and *situational testing*); c. personality *ques*tionnaires (including the MMPI-2, and validity scales); d. *projective tests* (include the Rorschach and the TAT). |
| LO 12.19 Describe the personality characteristics of sudden murderers, and explain how their characteristics are related to the nature of their homicidal actions. |
| GQ: What causes shyness? What can be done about it? |
| LO 12.20 List and describe the three elements of *shyness*; state what usually causes shyness; compare the personality of the shy and not-shy; and list and discuss the four self-defeating beliefs that can lead to shyness and possible ways to counteract these beliefs. |

# RECITE AND REVIEW

## The Psychology of Personality—Do You Have Personality?: Pages 390-394

How do psychologists use the term "personality"?

1. Personality is made up of one's unique and relatively stable _____ patterns.

2. Character is personality that has been judged or _____. That is, it is the possession of desirable qualities.

3. Temperament refers to the _____ and physiological aspects of one's emotional nature.

4. Personality traits are lasting personal qualities that are inferred from _____. Traits can even influence _____ and occupational success.

5. A personality type is a style of personality defined by having a group of related _____ or similar characteristics.

6. Two widely recognized personality _____ are an introvert (shy, self-centered person) and an extrovert (bold, outgoing person).

7. Behavior is influenced by self-concept, which is a person's perception of his or her own _____ traits.

8. Culture determines how people go about developing and maintaining _____ (self-evaluation): People with high self-esteem are confident, _____, and self-respecting, and people with low self-esteem are insecure, _____, and lack confidence.

9. _____ theories combine interrelated assumptions, ideas, and principles to explain personality.

403

10. Five major types of personality theories are: _____ , psychodynamic, behavioristic, _____ learning, and humanistic.

11. Behavioral genetics is the study of _____ behavioral traits.

12. Heredity is responsible for 25 to 50 percent of the variation in personality _____ .

13. Studies of separated _____ twins suggest that heredity contributes significantly to adult personality traits. Overall, however, personality is shaped as much, or more by differences in environment.

# The Trait Approach—Describe Yourself in 18,000 Words or Less: Pages 394-398
Are some personality traits more basic or important than others?

1. Research has found a link between personality characteristics and _____. For example, people who value aesthetic experiences, have good _____ skills, and are liberal and tolerant of others tend to prefer jazz, _____ , classical, and folk music.

2. Trait _____ attempt to specify qualities of personality that are most lasting or characteristic of a person.

3. Gordon Allport made useful distinctions between common traits (which are shared by most members of a culture) and _____ traits (characteristics of a single person).

4. Allport also identified cardinal traits (a trait that influences nearly all of a person's activities), central traits (core traits of personality), and _____ traits (superficial traits).

5. The theory of Raymond Cattell attributes visible _____ traits to the existence of 16 underlying source traits (which he identified using factor _____ ).

6. Source traits are measured by the *Sixteen _____ _____ Questionnaire (16 PF)*.

7. The outcome of the 16 PF and other personality tests may be graphically presented as a _____ profile.

8. The five-factor model of personality reduces traits to 5 _____ dimensions of personality.

9. The five factors are: extroversion, _____, conscientiousness, neuroticism, and openness to _____ . These traits have been related to differing brain chemicals and systems.

10. _____ interact with situations to determine behavior.

# Psychoanalytic Theory—Id Came to Me in a Dream: Pages 398-404

How do psychodynamic theories explain personality?

1. Psychodynamic theories focus on the inner workings of personality, especially hidden or _____ forces and internal conflicts.

2. According to Sigmund Freud's psychoanalytic theory, personality is made up of the id, _____, and superego.

3. The id operates on the pleasure _____. The ego is guided by the reality _____.

4. The _____ is made up of the conscience and the ego ideal.

5. Libido, derived from the _____ instincts, is the primary _____ running the personality.

6. Conflicts within the personality may cause neurotic _____ or moral _____ and motivate use of ego-defense mechanisms.

7. The personality operates on three levels, the _____, preconscious, and unconscious.

8. The id is completely _____ ; the ego and superego can operate at all three levels of awareness.

9. The Freudian view of personality development is based on a series of psychosexual _____ : the _____ , anal, phallic, and genital.

10. Fixations (unresolved emotional conflicts) at any stage can leave a lasting imprint on _____ .

11. Freud's theory pioneered the idea that feeding, toilet training, and early sexual experiences leave an imprint on _____ .

12. During the phallic stage of Freud's _____ stages of development, boys must confront and resolve the _____ complex and girls must confront and resolve the Electra complex.

13. Freud's theory has been influential toward the understanding of personality development for several reasons: He suggested that adult personality is formed during the _____ years of a person's life; he identified feeding, _____ training, and early sexual experiences as critical events; and he indicated that development proceeds in _____ .

14. Personality theorists who altered or revised Freud's ideas are called neo-_____ . Three prominent members of this group are Alfred Adler, Karen Horney, and Carl Jung.

# Learning Theories of Personality—Habit I Seen You Before?: Pages 404-408

What do behaviorists emphasize in their approach to personality?

1. Behavioral theories of personality emphasize _____ , conditioning, and immediate effects of the environment.

2. Learning theorists generally stress the effects of prior learning and _____ determinants of behavior.

3. Learning theorists John Dollard and Neal Miller consider _____ the basic core of personality. _____ express the combined effects of drive, cue, response, and _____ .

4. _____ learning theory adds cognitive elements, such as perception, thinking, and understanding to the behavioral view of personality.

5. Examples of social learning concepts are the _____ situation (the situation as it is perceived), expectancies (expectations about what effects a response will have), and reinforcement _____ (the subjective value of a reinforcer or activity).

6. Albert Bandura believes one's self-efficacy (belief in our _____ to produce a desired outcome) is an important aspect of expectancy. He also believes that self-efficacy beliefs influence the _____ and situations we choose to get into.

7. Some social learning theorists treat "conscience" as a case of _____ -reinforcement.

8. The behavioristic view of personality development holds that social reinforcement in four situations is critical. The critical situations are _____ , toilet or cleanliness training, sex training, and _____ or aggression training.

9. Identification (feeling emotionally connected to a person) and _____ (mimicking another person's behavior) are of particular importance in sex (or gender) training.

406

# Humanistic Theory—Peak Experiences and Personal Growth and Personality Theory—Overview and Comparison: Pages 408-414

How do humanistic theories differ from other perspectives?

1. Humanistic theory views human nature as _____ , and emphasizes subjective experience, _____ choice, and needs for self-actualization.

2. Abraham Maslow's study of self-actualizers identified characteristics they share, ranging from efficient perceptions of reality to frequent _____ (temporary moments of self-actualization).

3. The process of self-actualization involves multiple steps, some of which include being willing to change, taking _____ , examining one's motives, getting involved, and making use of _____ experiences.

4. A person's well-being and life _____ are linked to six human strengths: wisdom and knowledge, _____ , humanity, justice, _____ , and transcendence.

5. Carl Rogers' theory views the _____ as an entity that emerges when experiences that match the self-_____ are symbolized (admitted to consciousness), while those that are incongruent are excluded.

6. The incongruent person has a highly unrealistic _____ and/or a mismatch between the _____ and the ideal self.

7. The congruent or _____ functioning person is flexible and open to experiences and feelings.

8. In the development of personality, humanists are primarily interested in the emergence of a _____ and in self-evaluations.

9. As parents apply conditions of _____ (standards used to judge thoughts, feelings, and actions) to a child, the child begins to do the same.

10. Internalized conditions of worth contribute to incongruence, they damage _____ self-regard, and they disrupt the organismic _____ process.

# Personality Assessment—Psychological Yardsticks: Pages 414-420

How do psychologists measure personality?

1.  Techniques typically used for personality assessment are _____ , observation, questionnaires, and projective _____ .

2.  Structured and unstructured _____ provide much information, but they are subject to _____ bias and misperceptions. The halo effect may also _____ accuracy.

3.  Direct observation, sometimes involving situational tests, behavioral assessment, or the use of _____ scales, allows evaluation of a person's actual _____ .

4.  Personality questionnaires, such as the _____ _____ *Personality Inventory-2 (MMPI-2),* are objective and _____ , but their validity is open to question.

5.  Honesty tests, which are essentially personality _____, are widely used by businesses to make hiring decisions. Their validity is hotly debated.

## Projective Tests of Personality—Inkblots and Hidden Plots and Sudden Murderers—A Research Example: Pages 418-419

1.  Projective tests ask a subject to project thoughts or feelings onto an ambiguous _____ or unstructured situation.

2.  The *Rorschach,* or _____ test, is a well-known projective technique. A second is the _____ *Apperception Test (TAT).*

3.  The validity and objectivity of projective tests are quite _____ . Nevertheless, projective techniques are considered useful by many clinicians, particularly as part of a _____ battery.

# Psychology in Action: Barriers and Bridges—Understanding Shyness: Pages 420-422

What causes shyness? What can be done about it?

1.  Shyness is a mixture of _____ inhibition and _____ anxiety.

2.  Shy persons tend to lack social skills and they feel social anxiety (because they believe they are being _____ by others).

3.  Shy persons also have a self-defeating bias in their _____ (they tend to blame _____ for social failures).

4. Shyness is marked by heightened _____ self-consciousness (awareness of oneself as a _____ object) and a tendency to regard shyness as a lasting trait.

5. Shyness can be lessened by changing self-defeating skills _____ and by improving _____ skills.

# CONNECTIONS

## The Psychology of Personality—Do You Have Personality?: Pages 390-394

How do psychologists use the term "personality"?

1. _____ character
2. _____ trait
3. _____ Type A
4. _____ Introverts or extroverts
5. _____ melancholic
6. _____ choleric
7. _____ temperament
8. _____ phlegmatic
9. _____ sanguine

a. heart attack risk
b. hot-tempered
c. personality judged
d. cheerful
e. sluggish
f. sad, gloomy
g. lasting personal quality
h. Carl Jung
i. hereditary part of personality

## The Trait Approach—Describe Yourself in 18,000 Words or Less and Psychoanalytic Theory—Id Cam to Me in a Dream: Pages 394-404

Are some personality traits more basic or important than others? How do psychodynamic theories explain personality?

1. _____ trait situation
2. _____ behavior genetics
3. _____ 16 PF
4. _____ Big Five
5. _____ common traits
6. _____ Thanatos
7. _____ Eros
8. _____ conscience
9. _____ ego ideal
10. _____ oral stage
11. _____ anal stage
12. _____ phallic stage
13. _____ id
14. _____ Oedipus complex
15. _____ Electra complex

a. mouth
b. pride
c. genitals
d. female conflict
e. male conflict
f. death instinct
g. elimination
h. life instinct
i. guilt
j. pleasure principle
k. twin studies
l. interaction
m. source traits
n. culturally typical
o. universal dimensions

409

## Learning Theories of Personality—Habit I Seen You Before?, Humanistic Theory—Peak Experiences and Personal Growth and Personality Theories—Overview and Comparison: Pages 404-414

What do behaviorists emphasize in their approach to personality? How do humanistic theories differ from other perspectives?

1. _____ reward
2. _____ subjective experience
3. _____ expectancy
4. _____ unconditional positive regards
5. _____ situational determinants
6. _____ habits
7. _____ Karen Horney
8. _____ Carl Rogers
9. _____ Carl Jung
10. _____ Abraham Maslow
11. _____ self-efficacy
12. _____ congruence

a. anticipation
b. self-actualization
c. learned behavior pattern
d. positive reinforcer
e. external causes
f. self-image = ideal self
g. unshakable love
h. private perceptions of reality
i. fully functioning person
j. belief in one's capability
k. archetypes
l. basic anxiety

## Personality Assessment—Psychological Yardsticks and Psychology in Action: Barriers and Bridges—Understanding Shyness: Pages 414-422

How do psychologists measure personality? What causes shyness? What can be done about it?

1. _____ validity scale
2. _____ social anxiety
3. _____ MMPI
4. _____ inkblot
5. _____ private self-consciousness
6. _____ situational test
7. _____ public self-consciousness
8. _____ honesty test
9. _____ self-defeating bias
10. _____ halo effect

a. Rorschach
b. integrity at work
c. interview problem
d. personality questionnaire
e. faking good
f. Shoot Don't Shoot
g. view self as social object
h. focus on inner feelings
i. distortion in thinking
j. evaluation fears

# CHECK YOUR MEMORY

## The Psychology of Personality—Do You Have Personality?: Pages 390-394

How do psychologists use the term "personality"?

1. The term personality refers to charisma or personal style.   TRUE or FALSE

2. Personality is a person's relatively stable pattern of attitudes.   TRUE or FALSE

3. Character refers to the inherited "raw material" from which personality is formed.
   TRUE or FALSE

4. A person with genuine high self-esteem has a tendency to accurately appraise his/her own strengths and weaknesses.   TRUE or FALSE

5. In Asian cultures, self-esteem is strongly tied to personal achievement, rather than group success.
   TRUE or FALSE

6. Traits are stable or lasting qualities of personality, displayed in most situations.   TRUE or FALSE

7. Personality traits typically become quite stable by age 30 with the exception of conscientiousness and agreeability.   TRUE or FALSE

8. Paranoid, dependent, and antisocial personalities are regarded as personality types.
   TRUE or FALSE

9. Two major dimensions of Eysenck's personality theory are stable-unstable and calm-moody.
   TRUE or FALSE

10. Trait theories of personality stress subjective experience and personal growth.
    TRUE or FALSE

11. Similarities between reunited identical twins show that personality is mostly shaped by genetics.
    TRUE or FALSE

12. Intelligence, some mental disorders, temperament, and personality traits are all influenced by heredity.   TRUE or FALSE

13. Studies of identical twins show that personality traits are approximately 70 percent hereditary.
    TRUE or FALSE

14. Some of the coincidences shared by identical twins appear to be based on the fallacy of positive instances.   TRUE or FALSE

15. Unrelated people can share amazingly similar personality characteristics due to their age, gender, and living conditions.   TRUE or FALSE

# The Trait Approach—Describe Yourself in 18,000 Words or Less: Pages 394-398

Are some personality traits more basic or important than others?

1. Currently, the trait approach is the dominant method for studying personality.  TRUE or FALSE

2. Peter Rentfrow and Samuel Gosling found that one's preference to music is linked to personality characteristics.  TRUE or FALSE

3. People who are cheerful, conventional, extroverted, and reliable tend to prefer blues, jazz, and classical music.  TRUE or FALSE

4. Nearly all of a person's activities can be traced to one or two common traits.  TRUE or FALSE

5. Roughly 7 central traits are needed, on the average, to describe an individual's personality.  TRUE or FALSE

6. Allport used factor analysis to identify central traits.  TRUE or FALSE

7. The 16 PF is designed to measure surface traits.  TRUE or FALSE

8. Judging from scores on the 16 PF, airline pilots have traits that are similar to creative artists.  TRUE or FALSE

9. As one of the Big Five factors, neuroticism refers to having negative, upsetting emotions.  TRUE or FALSE

10. Extreme perfectionism typically lowers performance at school and elsewhere.  TRUE or FALSE

11. The expression of personality traits tends to be influenced by external situations.  TRUE or FALSE

12. Similarities between reunited identical twins show that personality is mostly shaped by genetics.  TRUE or FALSE

13. Intelligence, some mental disorders, temperament, and personality traits are all influenced by heredity.  TRUE or FALSE

14. Studies of identical twins show that personality traits are approximately 70 percent hereditary.  TRUE or FALSE

15. Some of the coincidences shared by identical twins appear to be based on the fallacy of positive instances.  TRUE or FALSE

16. Unrelated people can share amazingly similar personality characteristics due to their age, gender, and living conditions.  TRUE or FALSE

## Psychoanalytic Theory—Id Came to Me in a Dream: Pages 398-404

How do psychodynamic theories explain personality?

1. Freud described the id, ego, and superego as "little people" that manage the human psyche.
   TRUE or FALSE

2. The id is totally unconscious.   TRUE or FALSE

3. The ego is guided by the pleasure principle.   TRUE or FALSE

4. The superego is the source of feelings of guilt and pride.   TRUE or FALSE

5. Threats of punishment from the Thanatos cause moral anxiety.   TRUE or FALSE

6. Oral-dependent persons are gullible.   TRUE or FALSE

7. Vanity and narcissism are traits of the anal-retentive personality.   TRUE or FALSE

8. According to Freud, boys experience the Oedipus complex and girls experience the Electra complex.
   TRUE or FALSE

9. The genital stage occurs between the ages of 3 and 6, just before latency.   TRUE or FALSE

10. Boys are more likely to develop a strong conscience if their fathers are affectionate and accepting.
    TRUE or FALSE

11. Freud regarded latency as the most important stage of psychosexual development.
    TRUE or FALSE

12. Erik Erikson's psychosocial stages were derived, in part, from Freud's psychosexual stages.
    TRUE or FALSE

13. Alfred Adler believed that we are driven by basic anxiety to move toward, against, or away from others.   TRUE or FALSE

14. According to Jung, people strive for superiority by creating a unique style of life.
    TRUE or FALSE

15. Jung called the male principle the animus.   TRUE or FALSE

## Learning Theories of Personality—Habit I Seen You Before?: Pages 404-408

What do behaviorists emphasize in their approach to personality?

1. Behaviorists view personality as a collection of learned behavior patterns.   TRUE or FALSE

2. Behaviorists attribute our actions to prior learning and specific situations.   TRUE or FALSE

3. Behaviors are influenced by an interaction between the situation and previously gained knowledge.
   TRUE or FALSE

4. Knowing the consistent ways people respond to certain situations allows us to predict their personality characteristics.   TRUE or FALSE

5. According to Dollard and Miller, habits are acquired through observational learning.
   TRUE or FALSE

6. Cues are signals from the environment that guide responses.   TRUE or FALSE

7. An expectancy refers to the anticipation that making a response will lead to reinforcement.
   TRUE or FALSE

8. Self-reinforcement is highly related to one's self-esteem.   TRUE or FALSE

9. People who are depressed tend to engage in a high rate of self-reinforcement to make themselves feel better.   TRUE or FALSE

10. Social reinforcement is based on attention and approval from others.   TRUE or FALSE

11. Girls are more likely than boys to rely on indirect aggression rather than direct aggression.
    TRUE or FALSE

## Humanistic Theory—Peak Experiences and Personal Growth: Pages 408-414
How do humanistic theories differ from other perspectives?

1. Humanists believe that humans are capable of free choice.   TRUE or FALSE

2. To investigate self-actualization, Maslow studied eminent men and women exclusively.
   TRUE or FALSE

3. Self-actualizers usually try to avoid task centering.   TRUE or FALSE

4. Personal autonomy is a characteristic of the self-actualizing person.   TRUE or FALSE

5. People who live happy and meaningful lives are people who possess the traits characteristic of a self-actualizer and express such human strengths as courage, justice, and temperance.
   TRUE or FALSE

6. Information inconsistent with one's self-image is described as incongruent.   TRUE or FALSE

7. Images of our possible selves are derived from our hopes, fears, fantasies, and goals.
   TRUE or FALSE

8. Poor self-knowledge is associated with high self-esteem because people do not have to think about their own faults.   TRUE or FALSE

9. Congruence represents a close correspondence between self-image, the ideal self, and the true self.   TRUE or FALSE

10. Images of possible selves typically cause feelings of incongruence.   TRUE or FALSE

11. Rogers believed that organismic valuing is healthier than trying to meet someone else's conditions of worth.   TRUE or FALSE

12. According to the narrative approach of personality, the stories that we tell ourselves shape our personality.   TRUE or FALSE

# Personality Assessment—Psychological Yardsticks: Pages 414-420
How do psychologists measure personality?

1. Planned questions are used in a structured interview.   TRUE or FALSE

2. Computers are sometimes used to do diagnostic interviews at psychological clinics.   TRUE or FALSE

3. The halo effect may involve either a positive or a negative impression.   TRUE or FALSE

4. Personality questionnaires are used to do behavioral assessments.   TRUE or FALSE

5. Judgmental firearms training is a type of honesty test.   TRUE or FALSE

6. Items on the MMPI-2 were selected for their ability to identify persons with psychiatric problems.   TRUE or FALSE

7. The validity scale of the MMPI-2 is used to rate Type A behavior.   TRUE or FALSE

8. The psychasthenia scale of the MMPI-2 detects the presence of phobias and compulsive actions.   TRUE or FALSE

9. It is very easy to fake responses to a projective test.   TRUE or FALSE

10. The TAT is a situational test.   TRUE or FALSE

11. Habitually violent prison inmates are aggressive and over-controlled.   TRUE or FALSE

# Psychology in Action: Barriers and Bridges—Understanding Shyness: Pages 420-422
What causes shyness? What can be done about it?

1. Shyness is closely related to private self-consciousness.   TRUE or FALSE

2. Not-shy persons believe that external situations cause their occasional feelings of shyness. TRUE or FALSE

3. The odds of meeting someone interested in socializing are about the same wherever you are. TRUE or FALSE

4. Open-ended questions help keep conversations going.    TRUE or FALSE

# FINAL SURVEY AND REVIEW

## The Psychology of Personality—Do You Have Personality?
How do psychologists use the term "personality"?

1. _____ is made up of one's unique and relatively stable behavior _____ .

2. _____ is personality that has been judged or evaluated. That is, it is the possession of desirable qualities.

3. _____ refers to the hereditary and physiological aspects of one's emotional nature.

4. Personality _____ are lasting personal qualities that are inferred from behavior. Traits can even influence health and _____ success.

5. A personality _____ is a style of personality defined by having a group of related traits or similar characteristics.

6. Two widely recognized personality types are an _____ (shy, self-centered person) and an _____ (bold, outgoing person).

7. Behavior is influenced by _____ , which is a person's perception of his or her own personality traits.

8. _____ determines how people go about developing and maintaining self-esteem (self-evaluation): People with _____ self-esteem are confident, proud, and self-respecting, and people with _____ self-esteem are insecure, self-critical, and lack confidence.

9. Personality _____ combine interrelated assumptions, ideas, and principles to explain personality.

10. Five major types of personality theories are: trait, _____ , behavioristic, social learning, and _____ .

11. _____ _____ is the study of inherited behavioral traits.

12. Heredity is responsible for _____ to _____ percent of the variation in personality traits.

13. Studies of separated identical twins suggest that _____ contributes significantly to adult personality traits. Overall, however, personality is shaped as much, or more by differences in _____ .

## The Trait Approach—Describe Yourself in 18,000 Words or Less
Are some personality traits more basic or important than others?

1. Research has found a link between _____ characteristics and music. For example, people who value _____ experiences, have good _____ skills, and are liberal and tolerant of others tend to prefer jazz, blues, classical, and folk music.

2. _____ theories attempt to specify qualities of personality that are most lasting or characteristic of a person.

3. Gordon _____ made useful distinctions between _____ traits (which are shared by most members of a culture) and individual traits (characteristics of a single person).

4. He also identified _____ traits (a trait that influences nearly all of a person's activities), _____ traits (core traits of personality), and secondary traits (superficial traits).

5. The theory of Raymond _____ attributes visible surface traits to the existence of 16 underlying _____ traits (which he identified using _____ analysis).

6. _____ _____ are measured by the Sixteen Personality Factor Questionnaire (16 PF).

7. The outcome of the 16 PF and other personality tests may be graphically presented as a trait _____ .

8. The _____ model of personality reduces traits to 5 universal dimensions of personality.

9. They are: _____ , agreeableness, conscientiousness, _____ , and openness to experience. These traits have been related to differing brain chemicals and systems.

10. Traits _____ with _____ to determine behavior.

# Psychoanalytic Theory—Id Came to Me in a Dream and Psychodynamic Theories—Freud's Descendants

How do psychodynamic theories explain personality?

1.  Psychodynamic theories focus on the inner workings of _____ , especially hidden or unconscious forces and internal _____ .

2.  According to Sigmund Freud's _____ theory, personality is made up of the _____ , ego, and _____ .

3.  The id operates on the _____ principle. The ego is guided by the _____ principle.

4.  The superego is made up of the _____ and the _____ ideal.

5.  _____ , derived from the life _____ , is the primary energy running the personality.

6.  Conflicts within the personality may cause _____ anxiety or _____ anxiety and motivate use of ego-defense mechanisms.

7.  The personality operates on three levels, the conscious, _____ , and _____ .

8.  The _____ is completely unconscious; the _____ and _____ can operate at all three levels of awareness.

9.  The Freudian view of personality development is based on a series of _____ stages: the oral, anal, _____ , and genital.

10. _____ (unresolved emotional conflicts) at any stage can leave a lasting imprint on personality.

11. Freud's theory pioneered the idea that _____ , _____ training, and early sexual experiences leave an imprint on personality.

12. During the _____ stage of Freud's psychosexual stages of development, must confront and resolve the Oedipus complex and _____ must confront and resolve the Electra complex.

13. Freud's theory has been influential toward the understanding of personality development for several reasons: He suggested that _____ personality is formed during the first few years of a person's life; he identified feeding, toilet training, and early sexual experiences as _____ events; and he indicated that development proceeds in _____ .

14. Personality theorists who altered or revised Freud's ideas are called _____ -Freudians. Three prominent members of this group are Alfred _____ , Karen Horney, and Carl _____ .

# Learning Theories of Personality—Habit I Seen You Before?

What do behaviorists emphasize in their approach to personality?

1. _____ theories of personality emphasize learning, conditioning, and immediate effects of the environment.

2. Learning theorists generally stress the effects of prior learning and situational _____ of behavior.

3. Learning theorists John Dollard and Neal Miller consider habits the basic core of personality. Habits express the combined effects of _____ , _____ , response, and reward.

4. Social learning theory adds _____ elements, such as perception, thinking, and understanding to the behavioral view of personality.

5. Examples of social learning concepts are the psychological situation (the situation as it is perceived), _____ (expectations about what effects a response will have), and _____ value (the subjective value of a reinforcer or activity).

6. Albert Bandura believes one's self-_____ (belief in our ability to produce a desired outcome) is an important aspect of _____ . He also believes that _____ beliefs influence the activities and situations we choose to get into.

7. Some social learning theorists treat "conscience" as a case of self-_____ .

8. The behavioristic view of personality development holds that social reinforcement in four situations is critical. The critical situations are feeding, _____ , sex training, and anger or _____ training.

9. _____ (feeling emotionally connected to a person) and imitation (mimicking another person's behavior) are of particular importance in sex (or gender) training.

# Humanistic Theory—Peak Experiences and Personal Growth and Personality Theories—Overview and Comparison

How do humanistic theories differ from other perspectives?

1. Humanistic theory views human nature as good, and emphasizes _____ experience, free choice, and needs for self-_____ .

2. Abraham _____ , study of self- _____ identified characteristics they share, ranging from efficient perceptions of reality to frequent peak experiences.

3. The process of self- _____ involves multiple steps, some of which include being willing to change, taking responsibility, examining one's motives, getting involved, and making use of positive experiences.

4. A person's well- _____ and life satisfaction are linked to six human _____ : wisdom and knowledge, courage, humanity, justice, temperance, and transcendence.

5. Carl Rogers' theory views the self as an entity that emerges when experiences that match the self-image are _____ (admitted to consciousness), while those that are _____ are excluded.

6. The _____ person has a highly unrealistic self-image and/or a mismatch between the self-image and the _____ self.

7. The _____ or fully functioning person is flexible and open to experiences and feelings.

8. In the development of personality, humanists are primarily interested in the emergence of a self-image and in _____ .

9. As parents apply _____ of worth (standards used to judge thoughts, feelings, and actions) to a child, the child begins to do the same.

10. Internalized _____ contribute to incongruence, they damage positive self-regard, and they disrupt the _____ valuing process.

# Personality Assessment—Psychological Yardsticks
How do psychologists measure personality?

1. Techniques typically used for personality assessment are interviews, direct _____ , questionnaires, and _____ tests.

2. Structured and _____ interviews provide much information, but they are subject to interviewer _____ and misperceptions. The halo effect may also lower accuracy.

3. Direct observation, sometimes involving _____ tests, behavioral _____ , or the use of rating scales, allows evaluation of a person's actual behavior.

4. Personality questionnaires, such as the Minnesota Multiphasic _____ -2 (MMPI-2), are objective and reliable, but their _____ is open to question.

5. _____ tests, which are essentially personality questionnaires, are widely used by businesses to make hiring decisions.

## Projective Tests of Personality—Inkblots and Hidden Plots and Sudden Murderers—A Research Example
How do psychologists measure personality?

1. _____ tests ask subjects to react to an ambiguous stimulus or unstructured situation.

2. The _____ , or inkblot test, is a well-known projective technique. A second is the Thematic

3. _____ Test (TAT).

4. The _____ and objectivity of projective tests are quite low. Nevertheless, projective techniques are considered useful by many clinicians, particularly as part of a test _____ .

## Psychology in Action: Barriers and Bridges—Understanding Shyness
What causes shyness? What can be done about it?

1. Shyness is a mixture of social _____ and social anxiety.

2. Shy persons tend to lack social _____ and they feel social anxiety (because they believe they are being evaluated by others).

3. Shy persons also have a _____ bias in their thinking (they tend to blame themselves for social failures).

4. Shyness is marked by heightened public self- _____ (awareness of oneself as a _____ object) and a tendency to regard shyness as a lasting _____ .

5. Shyness can be lessened by changing _____ beliefs and by improving social _____ .

# MASTERY TEST

1. The hereditary aspects of a person's emotional nature define his or her
   a. character.
   b. personality.
   c. cardinal traits.
   d. temperament.

2. Two parts of the psyche that operate on all three levels of awareness are the
   a. id and ego.
   b. ego and superego.
   c. id and superego.
   d. id and ego ideal.

3. The four critical situations Miller and Dollard consider important in the development of personality are feeding, toilet training,
   a. sex, and aggression.
   b. cleanliness, and language.
   c. attachment, and imitation.
   d. social learning.

4. Scales that rate a person's tendencies for depression, hysteria, paranoia, and mania are found on the
   a. MMPI-2.
   b. Rorschach.
   c. TAT.
   d. 16 PF.

5. In the five-factor model, people who score high on openness to experience are
   a. intelligent.
   b. extroverted.
   c. choleric.
   d. a personality type.

6. Jung regarded mandalas as symbols of the
   a. animus.
   b. anima.
   c. self archetype.
   d. persona.

7. Maslow used the term _____ to describe the tendency to make full use of personal potentials.
   a. full functionality
   b. self-potentiation
   c. ego-idealization
   d. self-actualization

422

8.  Studies of reunited identical twins support the idea that
    a.  personality traits are 70 percent hereditary and 30 percent learned.
    b.  childhood fixations influence the expression of personality traits in adulthood.
    c.  personality traits are altered by selective mating.
    d.  personality is shaped at least as much by environment as by heredity.

9.  A person's perception of his or her own personality is the core of
    a.  temperament.
    b.  source traits.
    c.  self-concept.
    d.  trait-situation interactions.

10. Which of the following concepts is NOT part of Dollard and Miller's behavioral model of personality?
    a.  drive
    b.  expectancy
    c.  cue
    d.  reward

11. The terms structured and unstructured apply most to
    a.  the halo effect.
    b.  interviews.
    c.  questionnaires.
    d.  honesty tests.

12. Feelings of pride come from the _____ , a part of the _____ .
    a.  libido, conscience
    b.  ego ideal, superego
    c.  reality principle, superego
    d.  superego, ego

13. Four types of temperament recognized by the early Greeks are: melancholic, choleric, phlegmatic and
    a.  sanguine
    b.  sardonic
    c.  sagittarian
    d.  sagacious

14. Freud believed that boys identify with their fathers in order to resolve the _____ conflict.
    a.  Animus
    b.  Electra
    c.  Oedipus
    d.  Persona

15. Maslow regarded peak experiences as temporary moments of
    a. task-centering.
    b. congruent selfhood.
    c. self-actualization.
    d. organismic valuing.

16. Ambiguous stimuli are used primarily in the
    a. MMPI-2.
    b. Shoot-Don't-Shoot Test.
    c. Rorschach.
    d. 16 PF.

17. A person who is generally extroverted is more outgoing in some situations than in others. This observation supports the concept of
    a. trait-situation interactions.
    b. behavioral genetic determinants.
    c. situational fixations.
    d. possible selves.

18. Allport's concept of central traits is most closely related to Cattell's
    a. surface traits.
    b. source traits.
    c. secondary traits.
    d. cardinal traits.

19. According to Freud, tendencies to be orderly, obstinate, and stingy are formed during the_____ stage.
    a. genital
    b. anal
    c. oral
    d. phallic

20. Which of the following is NOT part of Carl Rogers' view of personality?
    a. possible selves
    b. organismic valuing
    c. conditions of worth
    d. congruence

21. Rating scales are primarily used in which approach to personality assessment?
    a. projective testing
    b. direct observation
    c. questionnaires
    d. the TAT technique

22. Which theory of personality places the greatest emphasis on the effects of the environment?
    a. trait
    b. psychodynamic
    c. behavioristic
    d. humanistic

23. Freudian psychosexual stages occur in the order:
    a. oral, anal, genital, phallic
    b. oral, phallic, anal, genital
    c. genital, oral, anal, phallic
    d. oral, anal, phallic, genital

24. Rogers described mismatches between one's self-image and reality as a state of
    a. moral anxiety.
    b. incongruence.
    c. basic anxiety.
    d. negative symbolization.

25. All but one of the following are major elements of shyness; which does not apply?
    a. private self-consciousness
    b. social anxiety
    c. self-defeating thoughts
    d. belief that shyness is a lasting trait

26. People who all grew up in the same culture would be most likely to have the same _____ traits.
    a. cardinal
    b. common
    c. secondary
    d. source

27. A trait profile is used to report the results of
    a. the 16 PF.
    b. situational tests.
    c. the TAT.
    d. the inkblot test.

28. An emphasis on the situational determinants of actions is a key feature of _____ theories of personality.
    a. psychodynamic
    b. projective
    c. behaviorist
    d. humanist

29. The behavioral concept most closely related to the superego is
    a. psychological situation.
    b. self-reinforcement.
    c. reinforcement value.
    d. self-concept.

30. Which two personality characteristics continue to increase as people age?
    a. creativity and organization
    b. conscientiousness and agreeability
    c. affection and trust
    d. irritability and disorganization

31. People who prefer hip-hop, soul, and electronic music tend to
    a. be talkative and forgiving.
    b. value aesthetic experiences.
    c. be conservative.
    d. enjoy taking risks.

32. Jill was invited to go snowboarding, an activity she has not done before. Jill believes she has the ability to learn snowboarding and keep up with her friends because she is a fast learner. Bandura would say that Jill is high in
    a. self-actualizing.
    b. organismic valuing.
    c. congruence.
    d. self-efficacy.

33. _____ psychologists believe that one's well-being and life satisfaction are influenced by six personality traits, including courage, temperance, and transcendence.
    a. Behavioral
    b. Positive
    c. Psychodynamic
    d. Learning

34. In Asian cultures, _____ tends to be more strongly related to group membership and the success of the group.
    a. temperament
    b. character
    c. self-esteem
    d. moral anxiety

# Solutions

## RECITE AND REVIEW

### The Psychology of Personality—Do You Have Personality?: Pages 390-394
How do psychologists use the term "personality"?

1. behavior
2. evaluated
3. hereditary
4. behavior; health

5. traits
6. types
7. personality
8. self-esteem; proud; self-critical

9. Personality
10. trait; social
11. inherited
12. traits
13. identical

### The Trait Approach—Describe Yourself in 18,000 Words or Less: Pages 394-398
Are some personality traits more basic or important than others?

1. music; verbal; blues
2. theories
3. individual
4. secondary

5. surface; analysis
6. *Personality; Factor*
7. trait
8. universal

9. agreeableness; experience
10. Traits

### Psychoanalytic Theory—Id Came to Me in a Dream: Pages 398-404
How do psychodynamic theories explain personality?

1. unconscious
2. ego
3. principle; principle
4. superego
5. life; energy
6. anxiety; anxiety

7. conscious
8. unconscious
9. stages; oral
10. personality
11. personality
12. psychosexual; Oedipus

13. first few ; toilet; stages
14. Freudians

### Learning Theories of Personality—Habit I Seen You Before?: Pages 404-408
What do behaviorists emphasize in their approach to personality?

1. learning
2. situational
3. habits; Habits; reward

4. Social
5. psychological; value
6. ability; activities

7. self
8. feeding; anger
9. imitation

## Humanistic Theory—Peak Experiences and Personal Growth: Pages 408-414

How do humanistic theories differ from other perspectives?

1. good; free
2. peak experiences
3. responsibility; positive
4. satisfaction; courage; temperance
5. self; image
6. self-image; self-image
7. fully
8. self-image
9. worth
10. positive; valuing

## Personality Assessment—Psychological Yardsticks: Pages 414-420

How do psychologists measure personality

1. interviews; tests
2. interviews; interviewer; lower
3. rating; behavior
4. *Minnesota; Multiphasic; reliable*
5. questionnaires

## How do psychologists measure personality?: Pages 414-420

1. stimulus
2. inkblot; *Thematic*
3. low; test

## Psychology in Action: Barriers and Bridges—Understanding Shyness: Pages 420-422

What causes shyness? What can be done about it?

1. social; social
2. evaluated
3. thinking; themselves
4. public; social
5. beliefs; social

# CONNECTIONS

## The Psychology of Personality—Do You Have Personality?: Pages 390-394

How do psychologists use the term "personality"?

1. c
2. g
3. a
4. h
5. f
6. b
7. i
8. e
9. d

## The Trait Approach—Describe Yourself in 18,000 Words or Less and Psychoanalytic Theory—Id Came to Me in a Dream: Pages 394-404

Are some personality traits more basic or important than others? How do psychodynamic theories explain personality?

1. l
2. k
3. m
4. o
5. n
6. f
7. h
8. i
9. b
10. a
11. g
12. c
13. j
14. e
15. d

## Learning Theories of Personality—Habit I Seen You Before?, Humanistic Theory—Peak Experiences and Personal Growth and Personality Theories—Overview and Comparison: Pages 404-414

What do behaviorists emphasize in their approach to personality? How do humanistic theories differ from other perspectives?:

| | | |
|---|---|---|
| 1. d | 5. e | 9. k |
| 2. h | 6. c | 10. b |
| 3. a | 7. l | 11. j |
| 4. g | 8. i | 12. f |

## Personality Assessment—Psychological Yardsticks and Psychology in Action: Barriers and Bridges—Understanding Shyness: Pages 414-422

How do psychologists measure personality? What causes shyness? What can be done about it?

| | | |
|---|---|---|
| 1. e | 5. h | 9. i |
| 2. j | 6. f | 10. c |
| 3. d | 7. g | |
| 4. a | 8. b | |

# CHECK YOUR MEMORY

## The Psychology of Personality—Do You Have Personality?: Pages 390-394

How do psychologists use the term "personality"?

| | | |
|---|---|---|
| 1. F | 6. T | 11. F |
| 2. F | 7. T | 12. T |
| 3. F | 8. T | 13. F |
| 4. T | 9. F | 14. T |
| 5. F | 10. F | 15. T |

## The Trait Approach—Describe Yourself in 18,000 Words or Less: Pages 394-398

Are some personality traits more basic or important than others?

| | | |
|---|---|---|
| 1. T | 5. | 10. T |
| 2. T | 6. T | 11. T |
| 3. F | 7. F | 12. T |
| 4. F | 8. F | |
| | 9. F | |

## Psychoanalytic Theory—Id Came to Me in a Dream: Pages 398-404

How do psychodynamic theories explain personality?

| | | |
|---|---|---|
| 1.  F | 6.  T | 11.  F |
| 2.  T | 7.  F | 12.  T |
| 3.  F | 8.  T | 13.  F |
| 4.  T | 9.  F | 14.  F |
| 5.  F | 10.  T | 15.  T |

## Learning Theories of Personality—Habit I Seen You Before?: Pages 404-408

What do behaviorists emphasize in their approach to personality?

| | | |
|---|---|---|
| 1.  T | 5.  T | 9.   F |
| 2.  T | 6.  T | 10.  T |
| 3.  T | 7.  T | 11.  T |
| 4.  T | 8.  T | |

## Humanistic Theory—Peak Experiences and Personal Growth, and Personality Theories—Overview and Comparison: Pages 408-414

How do humanistic theories differ from other perspectives?

| | | |
|---|---|---|
| 1.  T | 5.  T | 9.  T |
| 2.  F | 6.  T | 10. F |
| 3.  F | 7.  T | 11. T |
| 4.  T | 8.  F | 12. T |

## Personality Assessment—Psychological Yardsticks: Pages 414-420

How do psychologists measure personality?

| | | |
|---|---|---|
| 1.  T | 5.  F | 9.  F |
| 2.  T | 6.  T | 10. F |
| 3.  T | 7.  F | 11. F |
| 4.  F | 8.  T | |

## Psychology in Action: Barriers and Bridges—Understanding Shyness: Pages 420-422

What causes shyness? What can be done about it?

| | |
|---|---|
| 1.  F | 3.  F |
| 2.  T | 4.  T |

430

# FINAL SURVEY AND REVIEW

## The Psychology of Personality—Do You Have Personality?
How do psychologists use the term "personality"?

1. Personality; patterns
2. Character humanistic
3. Temperament
4. traits; occupational
5. type
6. introvert; extrovert
7. self-concept
8. Culture; high; low
9. theories
10. psychodynamic;
11. Behavioral; genetics
12. 25; 50
13. heredity; environment

## The Trait Approach—Describe Yourself in 18,000 Words or Less
Are some personality traits more basic or important than others?

1. personality; aesthetic; verbal
2. Trait
3. Allport; common
4. cardinal; central
5. Cattell; source; factor
6. Source; traits
7. profile
8. five-factor
9. extroversion; neuroticism
10. interact; situations

## Psychoanalytic Theory—Id Came to Me in a Dream
How do psychodynamic theories explain personality?

1. personality; conflicts
2. psychoanalytic; id; superego
3. pleasure; reality
4. conscience; ego
5. Libido; instincts
6. neurotic; moral
7. preconscious; unconscious
8. id; ego; superego
9. psychosexual; phallic
10. Fixations
11. feeding; toilet
12. phallic; boys; girls
13. adult; critical; stages
14. neo; Adler; Jung

## Learning Theories of Personality—Habit I Seen You Before?
What do behaviorists emphasize in their approach to personality?

1. Behavioral training;
2. determinants
3. drive; cue
4. cognitive
5. expectancies; reinforcement
6. efficacy; expectancy; self-efficacy
7. reinforcement
8. toilet or cleanliness aggression
9. Identification

## Humanistic Theory—Peak Experiences and Personal Growth
How do humanistic theories differ from other perspectives?

1. subjective; actualization
2. Maslow's; actualizers
3. Actualization
4. being; strengths

5. symbolized; incongruent
6. incongruent; ideal
7. congruent
8. self-evaluations

9. conditions
10. conditions; of; worth; organismic

## Personality Theories—Overview and Comparison
How do psychologists measure personality?

1. observation; projective
2. unstructured; bias

3. situational; assessment
4. Personality; Inventory; validity

5. Honesty

## How do psychologists measure personality?

1. Projective

2. Rorschach; Apperception

3. validity; battery

## Psychology in Action: Barriers and Bridges—Understanding Shyness
What causes shyness? What can be done about it?

1. inhibition
2. skills

3. self-defeating
4. consciousness; social; trait

5. self-defeating; skills

# MASTERY TEST

1. d, p. 389
2. b, p. 400
3. a, p. 407
4. a, p. 417
5. a, p. 423
6. c, p. 404
7. d, p. 409
8. d, p. 391
9. c, p. 392
10. b, p. 405
11. b, p. 414
12. b, p. 399
13. a, p. 393

14. c, p. 410
15. c, p. 409
16. c, p. 418
17. a, p. 398
18. b, pp. 394-395
19. b, p. 401
20. a, p. 411
21. b, p. 415
22. c, p. 394
23. d, p. 401
24. b, p. 411
25. a, p. 420
26. b, p. 394

27. a, p. 395
28. c, p. 405
29. b, p. 406
30. b, p. 390
31. a, p. 395
32. d, pp. 406-407
33. b, p. 410
34. c, p. 393

# Health, Stress, and Coping

## Chapter Overview

Health psychologists study behavioral risk factors and health-promoting behaviors. Various "lifestyle" diseases are directly related to unhealthy personal habits. To reduce lifestyle diseases, people are encouraged to adopt health-promoting behaviors, such as getting regular exercise, controlling smoking and alcohol use, maintaining a balanced diet, getting good medical care, and managing stress. In addition to health-promoting behaviors, early prevention programs and community health campaigns have been implemented.

Stress is also a major risk factor. Direct or imagined social support from family, friends, and pets can also reduce stress. The body reacts to stress in a pattern called the general adaptation syndrome (G.A.S.). In addition, stress may lower the body's immunity to disease. At work, prolonged stress can lead to burnout. Emotional appraisals greatly affect our stress reactions and coping attempts. Traumatic stressors, such as violence, torture, or natural disasters, tend to produce severe stress reactions.

Frustration and conflict are common sources of stress. Major behavioral reactions to frustration include persistence, more vigorous responding, circumvention, direct aggression, displaced aggression, and escape or withdrawal. Five major types of conflict are approach-approach, avoidance-avoidance, approach-avoidance, double approach-avoidance, and multiple approach-avoidance.

Anxiety, threat, or feelings of inadequacy frequently lead to the use of defense mechanisms. Common defense mechanisms include compensation, denial, fantasy, intellectualization, isolation, projection, rationalization, reaction formation, regression, repression, and sublimation. Learned helplessness explains some depression and some failures to cope with threat. Mastery training acts as an antidote to helplessness.

A large number of life changes can increase susceptibility to illness. However, immediate health is more closely related to the severity of daily hassles or microstressors. Intense or prolonged stress may cause psychosomatic problems. The medical model assumes that health and illness are caused by complex biological and physical sources within one's body. An alternative model, the biopsychosocial model, suggests an interplay of biological, psychological, and social factors influencing one's health and illnesses. Biofeedback may be used to combat stress and psychosomatic illnesses. People with Type A personalities run a heightened risk of suffering a heart attack. People with hardy personality traits are resistant to stress and tend to maintain positive emotions that promote creativity, seek new experiences, and appreciate life.

The *College Life Stress Inventory,* which is similar to the SRRS, can be used to rate the amount of stress an undergraduate student has experienced. A number of coping skills can be applied to manage stress. Most focus on bodily effects, ineffective behaviors, and upsetting thoughts. Meditation can also be used to reduce stress. Two benefits of meditation are its ability to interrupt anxious thoughts and its ability to elicit the relaxation response.

# Learning Objectives

## Theme: Health is affected greatly by lifestyle and behavior patterns, especially those related to stress.

| |
|---|
| **GQ: What is health psychology? How does behavior affect health?** |
| LO 13.1  Define the terms *health psychology* and *behavioral medicine.* |
| LO 13.2  List twelve *behavioral risk factors* that can adversely affect one's health; and describe the *disease-prone personality.* |
| LO 13.3  Briefly describe the relationship between health-promoting behaviors and longevity; explain how health psychologists work to lessen behavioral risks to health, including the impact of *refusal-skills training* and *community health programs*; and define *wellness.* |
| **GQ: What is stress?** |
| LO 13.4  Explain the concept of the *General Adaptation Syndrome*; list and describe its three stages; and describe how stress affects the immune system. Include the definition of *psychoneuroimmunology.* |
| LO 13.5  Explain the similarity between your body's stress reaction and emotion; and list five aspects of stress that make it more intense and damaging. Include the definitions of *stress* (contrast with *eustress*) and *pressure.* |
| LO 13.6  Define *burnout*; describe the three aspects of the problem; and explain ways that burnout can be reduced. |
| LO 13.7  Give an example of how *primary* and *secondary appraisal* are used in coping with a threatening situation; and explain how the perception of control of a stressor influences the amount of threat felt. |
| LO 13.8  Differentiate *problem-focused coping* from *emotion-focused coping*; explain how they may help or hinder each other; and describe the impact of *traumatic stress* and ways to cope with reactions to severe stress. |
| **GQ: What causes frustration and what are typical reactions to it?** |
| LO 13.9  List and describe a. the two different kinds of *frustration*; b. four factors that increase frustration; and c. five common reactions to frustration (see Fig. 13.4); explain how scapegoating is a special form of *displaced aggression*; explain how an *inflexible response* differs from persistence; and discuss three effective ways to avoid frustration. |
| **GQ: Are there different types of conflict?** |
| LO 13.10  Describe and give an example of each of the following four types of *conflict*: a. *approach-approach*; b. *avoidance-avoidance*; c. *approach-avoidance* (include the terms *ambivalence* and *partial approach*); d. *double approach-avoidance* (include the term *vacillation*); and discuss four strategies for coping with conflict. |
| **GQ: What are defense mechanisms?** |
| LO 13.11  Define the terms *anxiety* and *defense mechanism*; discuss the positive value of defense mechanisms; and describe the following defense mechanisms and give an example of each: a. *denial*; b. *repression*; c. *reaction formation*; d. *regression*; e. *projection*; f. *rationalization*; g. *compensation*; h. *sublimation.* |
| **GQ: What do we know about coping with feelings of helplessness and depression?** |
| LO 13.12  Describe the development of *learned helplessness*; relate this concept to attribution and *depression*; list problems that contribute to depression among college students and the danger signs of depression; and discuss how helplessness may be unlearned and depression can be combated. |
| **GQ: How is stress related to health and disease?** |
| LO 13.13  Discuss the relationship between life changes and long-term health; describe the SRRS; and explain how hassles are related to immediate health and how *acculturative stress* can cause problems. |

| LO 13.14 Distinguish between *psychosomatic disorders* and *hypochondria*; list some major psychosomatic disorders; compare the biopsychosocial model of health to the traditional medical model; and briefly discuss *biofeedback* in terms of the process involved and its possible applications. |
| --- |
| LO 13.15 Differentiate between *Type A* and *Type B personalities*; list strategies for reducing hostility; describe a *hardy personality* and how this personality views the world; and explain how being optimist and happy and having *social support* are related to stress reduction. |
| **GQ: What are the best strategies for managing stress?** |
| LO 13.16 Define the term *stress management;* and briefly discuss the College Life Stress Inventory. |
| LO 13.17 List the three responses that are triggered by stress; and discuss the stress management techniques that can be used to diminish or break the cycle of stress responses. |

# RECITE AND REVIEW

## Health Psychology—Here's to Your Good Health: Pages 426-430

What is health psychology? How does behavior affect health?

1. Health psychologists are interested in _____ that helps maintain and promote health. The related field of behavioral medicine applies psychology to _____ treatment and problems.

2. Most people today die from lifestyle diseases caused by unhealthy personal _____.

3. Studies have identified a number of behavioral risk factors, which increase the chances _____ of or injury.

4. A general disease-prone personality pattern also raises the risk of _____.

5. Health-promoting _____ tend to maintain good health. They include practices such as getting regular exercise, controlling _____ and alcohol use, maintaining a balanced _____ , getting good medical care, avoiding _____ deprivation, spending time with other people with healthy habits, and managing stress.

6. Health psychologists attempt to promote wellness (a positive state of _____ ) through community health _____ that educate people about risk factors and healthful behaviors.

## Stress—Thrill or Threat?: Pages 430-435

What is stress?

1. Stress occurs when we are forced to _____ or adapt to external demands.

2. Stress is more damaging in situations involving pressure (responding at full capacity for long periods), a lack of _____ , unpredictability of the stressor, and _____ or repeated emotional shocks.

435

3. In _____ settings, prolonged stress can lead to burnout, marked by emotional _____ depersonalization (detachment from others), and reduced personal accomplishment. College students can experience burnout as well.

4. The _____ (initial) appraisal of a situation greatly affects our emotional response to it. Stress reactions, in particular, are related to an appraisal of _____.

5. During a _____ appraisal some means of coping with a situation is selected. Coping may be either problem-focused (managing the situation) or emotion-focused (managing one's emotional reactions) or both.

6. _____ is intensified when a situation is perceived as a threat and when a person does not feel competent to cope with it.

7. Traumatic _____ , such as violence, torture, or natural disasters, tend to produce severe reactions.

8. Traumatic _____ leave people feeling threatened, vulnerable, and with the sense that they are losing control over their _____ .

9. Severe or _____ traumatic _____ can leave people with lasting emotional handicaps called stress disorders. For example, Americans had an elevated risk for hypertension and heart problems for three years after 9/11.

10. The body reacts to stress in a series of stages called the _____ adaptation syndrome (G.A.S.).

11. The stages of the G.A.S. are alarm, resistance, and exhaustion. Signs of impending exhaustion include _____, behavioral, and physical signs. The G.A.S. contributes to the development of _____ disorders.

12. Stress weakens the immune system and lowers the body's resistance to _____ .

# Frustration—Blind Alleys and Lead Balloons: Pages 435-437
What causes frustration and what are typical reactions to it?

1. Frustration is the negative emotional state that occurs when progress toward a _____ is _____ . Sources of frustration may be external or personal.

2. External frustrations are based on delay, failure, rejection, loss, and other direct blocking of motives. Personal frustration is related to _____ characteristics over which one has little control.

3. Frustrations of all types become more _____ as the strength, urgency, or importance of the blocked motive increases.

4. Major behavioral reactions to frustration include persistence, more _____ responding, and circumvention of barriers.

5. Other reactions to frustration are _____ aggression, displaced aggression (including scapegoating), and escape, or _____ .

6. Ways of _____ with frustration include identifying its source, determining if the source is manageable, and deciding if _____ the source is worth the effort.

## Conflict—Yes, No, Yes, No, Yes, No, Well, Maybe: Pages 438-440
Are there different types of conflict?

1. _____ occurs when we must choose between contradictory alternatives.

2. Three basic types of conflict are approach-approach (choice between two _____ alternatives), avoidance-avoidance (both alternatives are _____ ), and approach-avoidance (a goal or activity has both positive and negative aspects).

3. Approach-approach conflicts are usually the _____ to resolve.

4. Avoidance conflicts are _____ to resolve and are characterized by inaction, indecision, freezing, and a desire to escape (called _____ the field).

5. People usually remain in approach-avoidance conflicts, but fail to fully resolve them. Approach-avoidance conflicts are associated with ambivalence ( _____ feelings) and _____ approach.

6. More complex conflicts are: double approach-avoidance (both alternatives have _____ and _____ qualities) and multiple approach-avoidance (several alternatives each have good and bad qualities).

7. Vacillation (wavering between choices) is the most common reaction to double _____ conflicts.

8. Managing conflicts effectively involves not making hasty decisions, trying out a few _____ at a time, looking for _____ , and sticking with the choice.

# Psychological Defense—Mental Karate?: Pages 440-442
What are defense mechanisms?

1. Anxiety, threat, or feelings of _____ frequently lead to the use of psychological defense mechanisms. These are habitual strategies used to avoid or reduce anxiety.

2. A number of defense mechanisms have been identified, including denial, fantasy, intellectualization, isolation, projection, rationalization, _____ formation, regression, and _____ (motivated forgetting).

3. Two defense mechanisms that have some _____ qualities are compensation and sublimation.

# Learned Helplessness—Is There Hope?: Pages 442-445
What do we know about coping with feelings of helplessness and depression?

1. Learned helplessness is a learned inability to overcome obstacles or to _____ punishment.

2. Learned helplessness explains the failure to cope with some threatening situations. The symptoms of learned helplessness and depression are nearly _____.

3. Mastery _____ and hope act as antidotes to helplessness.

4. Nearly _____ percent of all college students suffer from depression due to being _____ from their families, lacking the basic skills necessary for _____ success, abusing alcohol, and feeling they are missing out on life.

5. Depression (a state of deep sadness or despondency) is a serious emotional problem. Actions and thoughts that counter feelings of helplessness tend to _____ depression.

# Stress and Health—Unmasking a Hidden Killer: Pages 445-453
How is stress related to health and disease?

1. Work with the *Social Readjustment Rating Scale (SRRS)* indicates that a large number of life _____ units (LCUs) can increase susceptibility to _____ or illness.

2. Immediate health is more closely related to the intensity and severity of daily annoyances, known as _____ or microstressors.

3. Intense or prolonged stress may damage the body in the form of psychosomatic disorders (illnesses in which _____ factors play a part).

4. Psychosomatic (mind-body) disorders have no connection to hypochondria, the tendency to imagine that one has a _____.

5. The medical model suggests one's health and illness are caused by _____ and physical sources within one's body and the _____ model suggests that three factors-biological, psychological, and social-influence one's health and illness. The term _____ _____ is being replaced with meaning response.

6. During biofeedback training, bodily processes are _____ and converted to a signal that indicates what the body is doing.

7. Biofeedback allows alteration of many bodily activities. It shows promise for promoting _____, self-regulation, and for treating some psychosomatic illnesses.

8. People with Type A ( _____ attack prone) personalities are competitive, striving, and frequently angry or hostile, and they have a chronic sense of _____ urgency.

9. _____ and hostility are especially likely to increase the chances of heart attack.

10. People who have traits of the hardy personality seem to be resistant to _____, even if they also have Type A traits.

11. People who have a hardy personality tend to be _____ and have _____ emotions such as joy, interest, and contentment. These factors reduce bodily arousal and help people find _____ solutions when they are stressed.

12. Unlike pessimists, optimists tend to deal with their problems head on, are less likely to be _____ and anxious, believe they will _____, and take better care of themselves.

13. Stress can be reduced through the mechanism of _____ support by allowing people to seek assistance and to share _____ events with friends and families.

14. Thinking about a person who provides _____ or having a _____ present can reduce one's level of stress.

439

## Psychology in Action: Stress Management: Pages 453-457
What are the best strategies for managing stress?

1. Most stress management skills focus on one of three areas: bodily effects, ineffective _____ and upsetting _____ .

2. Bodily effects can be managed with exercise, meditation, progressive_____, and guided _____ .

3. Meditation is a self-control technique that can be used to reduce _____ .

4. Benefits of_____are its ability to interrupt anxious thoughts and its ability to promote relaxation.

5. The impact of ineffective behavior can be remedied by slowing down, getting organized, striking a balance between "good stress" and _____, accepting your limits, and seeking social support.

6. A good way to control upsetting thoughts is to replace negative self-statements with _____ coping statements.

# CONNECTIONS

## Health Psychology—Here's to your Good Health and Stress—Thrill or Threat?: Pages 426-435
What is health psychology? How does behavior affect health? What is stress?

1. _____ risk factors          a. well-being
2. _____ problem-focused coping          b. people who are depressed
3. _____ wellness          c. health-promoting behavior
4. _____ burnout          d. leading cause of death
5. _____ tobacco          e. lifestyle diseases
6. _____ refusal skills          f. smoking prevention
7. _____ primary appraisal          g. ANS arousal
8. _____ managing stress          h. plans to reduce stress
9. _____ disease-prone personality          i. "Am I in trouble?"
10. _____ stress reaction          j. job stress

## Frustration—Blind Alleys and Lead Balloons and Conflict—Yes, No, Yes, No, Yes, No, Well, Maybe: Pages 435-440

What causes frustration and what are typical reactions to it? Are there different types of conflict?

| | | | |
|---|---|---|---|
| 1. | _____ frustration | a. | blocked motive |
| 2. | _____ displaced aggression | b. | psychological escape |
| 3. | _____ apathy | c. | scapegoat |
| 4. | _____ External frustration | d. | ambivalence |
| 5. | _____ avoidance-avoidance | e. | deciding on two negative alternatives |
| 6. | _____ approach-avoidance | f. | deciding on two positive alternatives |
| 7. | _____ approach-approach | g. | distress caused by outside sources |

## Psychological Defense—Mental Karate? and Learned Helplessness—Is There Hope: Pages 440-445

What are defense mechanisms? What do we know about coping with feelings of helplessness and depression?

1. _____ compensation
2. _____ denial
3. _____ fantasy
4. _____ intellectualization
5. _____ isolation
6. _____ projection
7. _____ rationalization
8. _____ reaction formation
9. _____ regression
10. _____ repression
11. _____ sublimation

a. fulfilling unmet desires in imagined activities
b. separating contradictory thoughts into "logic-tight" mental compartments
c. preventing actions by exaggerating opposite behavior
d. justifying your behavior by giving reasonable but false reasons for it
e. unconsciously preventing painful thoughts from entering awareness
f. counteracting a real or imagined weakness by seeking to excel
g. retreating to an earlier level of development
h. attributing one's own shortcomings or unacceptable impulses to others
i. protecting oneself from an unpleasant reality by refusing to perceive it
j. working off unacceptable impulses in constructive activities
k. thinking about threatening situations in impersonal terms

## What are defense mechanisms? (cont.): Pages 440-442

1. _____ defense mechanism
2. _____ feeling despondent
3. _____ learned helplessness
4. _____ mastery training

a. depression
b. Sigmund Freud
c. hope
d. shuttle box

## Stress—Thrill or Threat? and Stress and Health—Unmasking a Hidden Killer: Pages 430-435, 445-457

What is stress? How is stress related to health and disease? What are the best strategies for managing stress?

1. _____ College Life Stress Inventory
2. _____ SRRS
3. _____ hassle
4. _____ hardy personality
5. _____ psychosomatic
6. _____ modifying ineffective behavior
7. _____ Type A
8. _____ biofeedback
9. _____ coping statements
10. _____ G.A.S.

a. LCU
b. mind-body
c. self-regulation
d. cardiac personality
e. alarm reaction
f. stress resistant
g. microstressor
h. stress rating scale
i. Keep It Simple (K.I.S.)
j. stress inoculation

# CHECK YOUR MEMORY

## Health Psychology—Here's to Your Good Health: Pages 426-430

What is health psychology? How does behavior affect health?

1. Heart disease, lung cancer, and stroke are typical lifestyle diseases.   TRUE or FALSE

2. A person who is overweight doubles the chance of dying from cancer or heart disease.

   TRUE or FALSE

3. One can expect to lose up to 20 years of life expectancy if he/she is overweight by the age of 20.

   TRUE or FALSE

4. Illicit use of drugs is the second most common cause of death in the United States, after smoking.

   TRUE or FALSE

5. Behavioral risk factors such as smoking, poor diet, or alcohol abuse are linked to infectious diseases.

   TRUE or FALSE

6. People with disease-prone personalities are depressed, anxious, and hostile. TRUE or FALSE

7. Unhealthy lifestyles typically involve multiple risks. TRUE or FALSE

8. Maintaining a healthy diet means a person must live on a high-protein diet consisting of tofu and wheat grain. TRUE or FALSE

9. Moderation in drinking refers to having three to five drinks per day. TRUE or FALSE

10. School-based prevention programs have successfully increased teens' negative attitudes toward smoking. TRUE or FALSE

11. Community health campaigns provide refusal skills training to large numbers of people.

    TRUE or FALSE

12. Wellness can be described as an absence of disease. TRUE or FALSE

# Stress—Thrill or Threat?: Pages 430-435
## What is stress?

1. Unpleasant activities produce stress, whereas pleasant activities do not. TRUE or FALSE

2. Initial reactions to stressors are similar to those that occur during strong emotion.

   TRUE or FALSE

3. Short-term stresses rarely do any damage to the body. TRUE or FALSE

4. Unpredictable demands increase stress. TRUE or FALSE

5. Pressure occurs when we are faced with a stressor we can control. TRUE or FALSE

6. Burnout is especially a problem in helping professions. TRUE or FALSE

7. The opposite of burnout is positive job engagement. TRUE or FALSE

8. Stress is often related to the meaning a person places on events. TRUE or FALSE

9. The same situation can be a challenge or a threat, depending on how it is appraised.

   TRUE or FALSE

10. In a secondary appraisal, we decide if a situation is relevant or irrelevant, positive or threatening.

    TRUE or FALSE

11. When confronted by a stressor, it is best to choose one type of coping—problem focused or emotion focused. TRUE or FALSE

12. Emotion-focused coping is best suited to managing stressors you cannot control.
TRUE or FALSE

13. A distressed person may distract herself by listening to music, taking a walk to relax, or seeking emotional support from others. Such strategies illustrate problem-focused coping.
TRUE or FALSE

14. Nightmares, grief, flashbacks, nervousness, and depression are common reactions to traumatic stress.
TRUE or FALSE

15. It is possible to have stress symptoms from merely witnessing traumatically stressful events on television.   TRUE or FALSE

16. An excellent way to cope with traumatic stress is to stop all of your daily routines and isolate yourself from others.   TRUE or FALSE

17. In the stage of resistance of the G.A.S., people have symptoms of headache, fever, fatigue, upset stomach, and the like.   TRUE or FALSE

18. Serious health problems tend to occur when a person reaches the stage of exhaustion in the G.A.S.
TRUE or FALSE

19. Stress management training can actually boost immune system functioning.   TRUE or FALSE

20. Happiness and high levels of arousal due to stress have been shown to strengthen the immune system's response.   TRUE or FALSE

## Frustration—Blind Alleys and Lead Balloons: Pages 435-437
What causes frustration and what are typical reactions to it?

1. Delays, rejections, and losses are good examples of personal frustrations.   TRUE or FALSE

2. Varied responses and circumvention attempt to directly destroy or remove barriers that cause frustration.   TRUE or FALSE

3. Scapegoating is a good example of escape or withdrawal.   TRUE or FALSE

4. Abuse of drugs can be a way of psychologically escaping frustration.   TRUE or FALSE

5. Persistence must be flexible before it is likely to aid a person trying to cope with frustration.
TRUE or FALSE

## Conflict—Yes, No, Yes, No, Yes, No, Well, Maybe: Pages 438-440
Are there different types of conflict?

1. Approach-approach conflicts are fairly easy to resolve.   TRUE or FALSE

444

2. Indecision, inaction, and freezing are typical reactions to approach-approach conflicts.
   TRUE or FALSE

3. People find it difficult to escape approach-avoidance conflicts.    TRUE or FALSE

4. Wanting to eat, but not wanting to be overweight, creates an approach-approach conflict.
   TRUE or FALSE

5. People are very likely to vacillate when faced with a double approach-avoidance conflict.
   TRUE or FALSE

# Psychological Defense—Mental Karate: Pages 440-442
## What are defense mechanisms?

1. Defense mechanisms are used to avoid or distort sources of threat or anxiety.    TRUE or FALSE

2. Denial is a common reaction to bad news, such as learning that a friend has died.
   TRUE or FALSE

3. In reaction formation, a person fulfills unmet desires in imagined achievements.    TRUE or FALSE

4. A child who becomes homesick while visiting relatives may be experiencing a mild regression.
   TRUE or FALSE

5. Denial and repression are the two most positive of the defense mechanisms.    TRUE or FALSE

# Learned Helpness—Is There Hope?: Pages 442-445
## What do we know about coping with feelings of helplessness and depression?

1. The deep depression experienced by prisoners of war appears to be related to learned helplessness.
   TRUE or FALSE

2. Learned helplessness occurs when events appear to be uncontrollable.    TRUE or FALSE

3. Attributing failure to lasting, general factors, such as personal characteristics, tends to create the
   most damaging feelings of helplessness.    TRUE or FALSE

4. Mastery training restores feelings of control over the environment.    TRUE or FALSE

5. At any given time, 52 to 61 percent of all college students are experiencing the symptoms of
   depression.    TRUE or FALSE

6. Making a daily schedule will only emphasize the goals that a person cannot accomplish and will
   push him/her deeper into depression.    TRUE or FALSE

7. Depression is more likely when students find it difficult to live up to idealized images of themselves.
   TRUE or FALSE

8. Writing rational answers to self-critical thoughts can help counteract feelings of depression.
   TRUE or FALSE

## Stress and Health—Unmasking a Hidden Killer: Pages 445-453
How is stress related to health and disease?

1. Scores on the SRRS are expressed as life control units.   TRUE or FALSE

2. A score of 300 LCUs on the SRRS is categorized as a major life crisis.   TRUE or FALSE

3. According to the SRRS, being fired at work involves more LCUs than divorce does.
   TRUE or FALSE

4. Microstressors tend to predict changes in health 1 to 2 years after the stressful events took place.
   TRUE or FALSE

5. Psychosomatic disorders involve actual damage to the body or damaging changes in bodily functioning.
   TRUE or FALSE

6. A person undergoing biofeedback can sleep if he or she desires—the machine does all the work.
   TRUE or FALSE

7. Type B personalities are more than twice as likely to suffer heart attacks as Type A personalities.
   TRUE or FALSE

8. People with the hardy personality type tend to see life as a series of challenges.   TRUE or FALSE

9. People with a hardy personality have had to cope with many adversities and therefore have a negative view of life.   TRUE or FALSE

10. Both men and women will seek social support when they are stressed.   TRUE or FALSE

11. Thinking about a supportive person or having a pet present can help lower one's stress level.
    TRUE or FALSE

## Psychology in Action: Stress Management: Pages 453-457
What are the best strategies for managing stress?

1. Concern about being pregnant is the most stressful item listed on the College Life Stress Inventory.
   TRUE or FALSE

2. The harder you try to meditate the more likely you are to succeed.   TRUE or FALSE

3. Exercising for stress management is most effective when it is done daily.   TRUE or FALSE

4. Guided imagery is used to reduce anxiety and promote relaxation.   TRUE or FALSE

5. Merely writing down thoughts and feelings about daily events can provide some of the benefits of social support.   TRUE or FALSE

6. To get the maximum benefits, coping statements should be practiced in actual stressful situations.
   TRUE or FALSE

7. Persistence must be flexible before it is likely to aid a person trying to cope with frustration.

   TRUE or FALSE

8. Humor increases anxiety and emotional distress because it put problems into perspective for individuals.

   TRUE or FALSE

# FINAL SURVEY AND REVIEW

## Health Psychology—Here's to Your Good Health
What is health psychology? How does behavior affect health?

1. Health psychologists are interested in behavior that helps maintain and promote health. The related field of _____ _____ applies psychology to medical treatment and problems.

2. Most people today die from _____ diseases caused by unhealthy personal habits.

3. Studies have identified a number of behavioral _____ , which increase the chances of disease (or illness) or injury.

4. A general _____ personality pattern also raises the risk of illness (or disease).

5. Health- _____ behaviors tend to maintain good health. They include practices such as getting regular exercise, controlling smoking and alcohol use, maintaining a balanced diet, getting good medical care, avoiding sleep _____ , spending time with other people with healthy habits, and managing _____ .

6. Health psychologists attempt to promote _____ (a positive state of health) through _____ _____ campaigns that educate people about risk factors and healthful behaviors.

## Stress—Thrill or Threat?
What is stress?

1. Stress occurs when we are forced to adjust or _____ to external _____ .

2. Stress is more damaging in situations involving _____ (responding at full capacity for long periods), a lack of control, unpredictability of the _____ , and intense or repeated emotional shocks.

447

3. In work settings, prolonged stress can lead to _____ , marked by emotional exhaustion, _____ (detachment from others), and reduced personal accomplishment. College students can experience burnout as well.

4. The primary _____ of a situation greatly affects our emotional response to it. Stress reactions, in particular, are related to an _____ of threat.

5. During a secondary appraisal some means of coping with a situation is selected. Coping may be either _____ -focused (managing the situation) or _____ -focused (managing one's emotional reactions) or both.

6. Stress is intensified when a situation is perceived as a _____ and when a person does not feel _____ to cope with it.

7. _____ stressors, such as violence, torture, or natural disasters, tend to produce severe stress reactions.

8. Traumatic stresses leave people feeling threatened, vulnerable, and with the sense that they are losing _____ over their lives.

9. Severe or repeated traumatic stress can leave people with lasting emotional handicaps called _____ _____ . For example, Americans had an elevated risk for hypertension and heart problems for three years after 9/11.

10. The body reacts to stress in a series of stages called the _____ _____ _____ (G.A.S.).

11. The stages of the G.A.S. are _____ , resistance, and exhaustion. Signs of impending exhaustion include emotional, _____ , and physical signs. The G.A.S. contributes to the development of psychosomatic disorders.

12. Stress weakens the _____ system and lowers the body's resistance to disease (or illness).

# Frustration—Blind Alleys and Lead Balloons
What causes frustration and what are typical reactions to it?

1. _____ is the negative emotional state that occurs when progress toward a goal is blocked. Sources of frustration may be external or _____ .

2. _____ frustrations are based on delay, failure, rejection, loss, and other direct blocking of motives. _____ frustration is related to personal characteristics over which one has little control.

3. Frustrations of all types become more intense as the strength, urgency, or importance of the _____ _____ increases.

4. Major behavioral reactions to frustration include _____ , more vigorous responding, and _____ of barriers.

5. Other reactions to frustration are direct aggression, _____ aggression (including _____ ), and escape, or withdrawal.

6. Ways of coping with _____ include identifying its source, determining if the source is _____ , and deciding if changing the source is worth the effort.

# Conflict—Yes, No, Yes, No, Yes, No, Well, Maybe
## Are there different types of conflict?

1. Conflict occurs when we must choose between _____ alternatives.

2. Three basic types of conflict are _____ (choice between two positive alternatives), _____ (both alternatives are negative), and approach-avoidance (a goal or activity has both positive and negative aspects).

3. _____ conflicts are usually the easiest to resolve.

4. _____ conflicts are difficult to resolve and are characterized by inaction, indecision, freezing, and a desire to escape (called leaving the field).

5. People usually remain in approach-avoidance conflicts, but fail to fully resolve them. Approach-avoidance conflicts are associated with _____ (mixed feelings) and partial approach.

6. More complex conflicts are: _____ approach-avoidance (both alternatives have positive and negative qualities) and _____ approach-avoidance (several alternatives each have good and bad qualities).

7. _____ (wavering between choices) is the most common reaction to double approach-avoidance conflicts.

8. Managing _____ effectively involves not making _____ decisions, trying out a few possibilities at a time, looking for compromises, and sticking with the choice.

# Psychological Defense—Mental Karate?
## What are defense mechanisms?

1. Anxiety, threat, or feelings of inadequacy frequently lead to the use of psychological _____ _____. These are habitual strategies used to avoid or reduce _____ .

2. A number of defense mechanisms have been identified, including _____ (refusing to perceive an unpleasant reality), fantasy, intellectualization, isolation, projection, _____ (justifying one's behavior), reaction formation, regression, and repression.

3. Two defense mechanisms that have some positive qualities are _____ and _____ .

# Learned Helplessness—Is There Hope?
## What do we know about coping with feelings of helplessness and depression?

1. Learned _____ is a learned inability to overcome obstacles or to avoid _____ .

2. The symptoms of learned helplessness and _____ are nearly identical.

3. _____ training and hope act as antidotes to helplessness.

4. Nearly 80 percent of all _____ students suffer from _____ due to being isolated from their families, lacking basic skills necessary for academic success, abusing alcohol, and feeling they are missing out on life.

5. _____ (a state of deep sadness or despondency) is a serious emotional problem. Actions and thoughts that counter feelings of helplessness tend to reduce depression.

# Stress and Health—Unmasking a Hidden Killer
## How is stress related to health and disease?

1. Work with the _____ _____ _____ Scale (SRRS) indicates that a large number of life change units (LCUs) can increase susceptibility to accident or illness.

2. Immediate health is more closely related to the intensity and severity of daily annoyances, known as hassles or _____ .

3. Intense or prolonged stress may damage the body in the form of _____ disorders (illnesses in which psychological factors play a part).

4. _____ (mind-body) disorders have no connection to _____ , the tendency to imagine that one has a disease.

5. The _____ model suggests one's health and illness are caused by biological and physical sources within one's body and the biopsychosocial model suggests that three factors _____ , _____ , and _____ influences one's health and illnesses. The term placebo effect is being replaced with _____ _____ .

6. During _____ training, bodily processes are monitored and converted to a _____ that indicates what the body is doing.

7. Biofeedback allows alteration of many bodily activities. It shows promise for promoting relaxation, self- _____ , and for treating some psychosomatic illnesses.

8. People with _____ _____ (heart attack prone) personalities are competitive, striving, and frequently _____ or hostile, and they have a chronic sense of time urgency.

9. Anger and hostility are especially likely to increase the chances of _____ _____ .

10. People who have traits of the _____ personality seem to be resistant to stress, even if they also have Type A traits.

11. People who have a _____ personality tend to be optimists and have _____ emotions such as joy, interest, and contentment. These factors _____ bodily arousal and help people find creative solutions when they are stressed.

12. Unlike pessimists, _____ tend to deal with their problems head on, are _____ likely to be stressed and anxious, believe they _____ succeed, and take better care of themselves.

13. Stress can be _____ through the mechanism of social support by allowing people to seek assistance and to share positive _____ with friends and families.

14. Thinking about a _____ who provides support or having a pet present can _____ one's level of stress.

# Psychology in Action: Stress Management
What are the best strategies for managing stress?

1. Most stress management skills focus on one of three areas: bodily effects, _____ behavior, and _____ thoughts.

2. Bodily effects can be managed with exercise, meditation, _____ relaxation, and _____ imagery.

3. The impact of ineffective behavior can be remedied by slowing down, getting organized, striking a balance between "good stress" and relaxation, accepting your _____, and seeking _____ support.

4. A good way to control upsetting thoughts is to replace _____ self-statements with positive _____ statements.

5. _____ is a self-control technique that can be used to reduce stress.

6. Benefits of meditation are its ability to interrupt anxious thoughts and its ability to promote _____.

# MASTERY TEST

1. When stressful events appear to be uncontrollable, two common reactions are
   a. apathy and double-approach conflict.
   b. helplessness and depression.
   c. assimilation and marginalization.
   d. psychosomatic disorders and hypochondria.

2. The *College Life Stress Inventory* is most closely related to the
   a. SRRS.
   b. G.A.S.
   c. K.I.S.
   d. *Disease-Prone Personality Scale.*

3. We answer the question "Am I okay or in trouble?" when making
   a. negative self-statements.
   b. coping statements.
   c. a primary appraisal.
   d. a secondary appraisal.

4. Which of the following is NOT a major symptom of burnout?
   a. emotional exhaustion
   b. depersonalization
   c. reduced accomplishment
   d. dependence on co-workers

5. A child who displays childish speech and infantile play after his parents bring home a new baby shows signs of
   a. compensation.
   b. reaction formation.
   c. regression.
   d. sublimation.

6. Persistent but inflexible responses to frustration can become
   a. stereotyped behaviors.
   b. imagined barriers.
   c. negative self-statements.
   d. sublimated and depersonalized.

7. The leading cause of death in the United States is
   a. tobacco.
   b. diet/inactivity.
   c. alcohol.
   d. infection.

8. Both mountain climbing and marital strife
   a. are behavioral risk factors.
   b. are appraised as secondary threats.
   c. cause stress reactions.
   d. produce the condition known as pressure.

9. LCUs are used to assess
   a. burnout.
   b. social readjustments.
   c. microstressors.
   d. what stage of the G.A.S. a person is in.

10. Sujata is often ridiculed by her boss, who also frequently takes advantage of her. Deep inside, Sujata has come to hate her boss, yet on the surface she acts as if she likes him very much. It is likely that Sujata is using the defense mechanism called
    a. reaction formation.
    b. Type B appraisal.
    c. problem-focused coping.
    d. sublimation.

453

11. Lifestyle diseases are of special interest to _____ psychologists.
    a.   health
    b.   community
    c.   wellness
    d.   psychosomatic

12. Which of the following is NOT characteristic of the hardy personality?
    a.   commitment
    b.   a sense of control
    c.   accepting challenge
    d.   repression

13. Unhealthy lifestyles are marked by the presence of a number of
    a.   health refusal factors.
    b.   behavioral risk factors.
    c.   cultural stressors.
    d.   Type B personality traits.

14. The most effective response to a controllable stressor is
    a.   problem-focused coping.
    b.   emotion-focused coping.
    c.   leaving the field.
    d.   depersonalization.

15. Delay, rejection, failure, and loss are all major causes of
    a.   pressure.
    b.   frustration.
    c.   conflict.
    d.   helplessness.

16. There is evidence that the core lethal factor of Type A behavior is
    a.   time urgency.
    b.   anger and hostility.
    c.   competitiveness and ambition.
    d.   accepting too many responsibilities.

17. A person is caught between "the frying pan and the fire" in a(n) _____ conflict.
    a.   approach-approach
    b.   avoidance-avoidance
    c.   approach-avoidance
    d.   double appraisal

18. Which of the following is NOT one of the major health-promoting behaviors listed in the text?
    a.   do not smoke
    b.   get adequate sleep
    c.   get regular exercise
    d.   avoid eating between meals

454

19. Ambivalence and partial approach are very common reactions to what type of conflict?
    a. approach-approach
    b. avoidance-avoidance
    c. approach-avoidance
    d. multiple avoidance

20. Which of the following terms does not belong with the others?
    a. Type A personality
    b. stage of exhaustion
    c. displaced aggression
    d. psychosomatic disorder

21. Coping statements are a key element in
    a. stress inoculation.
    b. the K.I.S. technique.
    c. guided imagery.
    d. refusal skills training.

22. Which of the following factors typically minimizes the amount of stress experienced?
    a. predictable stressors
    b. repeated stressors
    c. uncontrollable stressors
    d. intense stressors

23. Scapegoating is closely related to which response to frustration?
    a. leaving the field
    b. displaced aggression
    c. circumvention
    d. reaction formation

24. The study of the ways in which stress and the immune system affect susceptibility to disease is called
    a. neuropsychosymptomology.
    b. immunohypochondrology.
    c. psychosomatoneurology.
    d. psychoneuroimmunology.

25. Refusal skills training is typically used to teach young people how to
    a. avoid drug use.
    b. cope with burnout.
    c. resist stressors at home and at school.
    d. avoid forming habits that lead to heart disease.

26. Which combination is most relevant to managing bodily reactions to stress?
    a. social support, self pacing
    b. exercise, social support
    c. exercise, negative self-statements
    d. progressive relaxation, guided imagery

27. Stress reactions are most likely to occur when a stressor is viewed as a _____ during the _____ .
    a. pressure; primary appraisal
    b. pressure; secondary appraisal
    c. threat; primary appraisal
    d. threat; secondary appraisal

28. External symptoms of the body's adjustment to stress are least visible in which stage of the G.A.S?
    a. alarm
    b. regulation
    c. resistance
    d. exhaustion

29. A perceived lack of control creates a stressful sense of threat when combined with a perceived
    a. sense of time urgency.
    b. state of sublimation.
    c. need to change secondary risk factors.
    d. lack of competence.

30. Stress, smoking, and overeating are related to each other in that they are behavioral
    a. hassles.
    b. risk factors.
    c. sources of burnout.
    d. causes of depersonalization.

31. Behavioral risk factors such as smoking cigarettes, drinking alcohol, and overeating have been linked to
    a. Type B personality.
    b. infectious diseases.
    c. high life expectancy.
    d. hardy personality.

32. Consuming no more than one to two alcoholic drinks per day, exercising three to four times a week, and eating a healthy diet are
    a. stress-induced behaviors.
    b. behavioral risk factors.
    c. health-promoting behaviors.
    d. factors that increase heart disorders.

33. Shane likes to listen to his favorite music and taking long walks in the park to relax when he is distressed or stressed. Shane's method involves
    a. defense mechanism.
    b. reaction formation.
    c. problem focused coping.
    d. emotion focused coping.

34. People with a _____ personality tend to be optimistic and have positive emotions that help them reduce and find creative solutions to stress.
    a. realistic
    b. Type A
    c. hardy
    d. high-strung

35. Real or imagined social support and encouragement from _____ can reduce one's level of stress.
    a. family members
    b. friends
    c. pets
    d. all the preceding

36. Which factor reduces one's stress or emotional distress?
    a. humor
    b. smoking
    c. high blood pressure
    d. approach-avoidance

37. Lisa's doctor suggested that her disorder has three contributing causes: biological, psychological, and social. Which model of explanation is her doctor relying on to diagnose and treat Lisa's disorder?
    a. medical
    b. biopsychosocial
    c. cognitive-behavioral
    d. cultural

# SOLUTIONS

## RECITE AND REVIEW

### Health Psychology—Here's to Your Good Health: Pages 426-430
What is health psychology? How does behavior affect health?

1. behavior; medical
2. habits
3. disease (or illness)
4. illness (or disease)
5. behaviors; smoking; diet; sleep
6. health; campaigns

### Stress—Thrill or Threat?: Pages 430-435
What is stress?

1. adjust
2. control; intense
3. work; exhaustion
4. primary; threat
5. secondary
6. Stress
7. stressors; stress
8. stresses; lives
9. repeated; stress
10. general
11. emotional; psychosomatic
12. disease (or illness)

## Frustration—Blind Alleys and Lead Balloons: Pages 435-437

What causes frustration and what are typical reactions to it?

1. goal; blocked
2. personal
3. intense
4. vigorous
5. direct; withdrawal
6. coping; changing

## Conflict—Yes, No, Yes, No, Yes, No, Well, Maybe: Pages 438-440

Are there different types of conflict?

1. Conflict
2. positive; negative
3. easiest
4. difficult; leaving
5. mixed; partial
6. positive; negative
7. approach-avoidance
8. possibilities; compromises

## Psychological Defense—Mental Karate: Pages 440-442

What are defense mechanisms?

1. inadequacy
2. reaction; repression
3. positive

## Learned Helplessness—Is There Hope?: Pages 442-445

What do we know about coping with feelings of helplessness and depression?

1. change; accident
2. hassles
3. psychological
4. disease
5. biological; placebo effect
6. monitored
7. relaxation
8. heart; time
9. Anger
   biopsychosocial;
10. stress
11. optimists; positive; creative
12. stressed; succeed
13. social; positive
14. support; pet

## Stress and Health—Unmasking a Hidden Killer: Pages 445-453

What are the best strategies for managing stress?

1. behavior; thoughts
2. relaxation; imagery
3. stress
4. meditation
5. relaxation
6. positive

# CONNECTIONS

## Health Psychology—Here's to Your Good Health and Stress—Thrill or Threat?: Pages 426-435

What is health psychology? How does behavior affect health? What is stress?

1. e
2. h
3. a
4. j
5. d
6. f
7. i
8. c
9. b
10. g

## Frustration—Blind Alleys and Lead Balloons and Conflict—Yes, No, Yes, No, Yes, No, Well, Maybe: Pages 435-440

What causes frustration and what are typical reactions to it? Are there different types of conflict?

1. a
2. c
3. b

4. g
5. e
6. d

7. f

## Psychological Defense—Mental Karate? and Learned Helplessness—Is There Hope?: Pages 440-445

What are defense mechanisms? What do we know about coping with feelings of helplessness and depression?

1. f
2. i
3. a
4. k

5. b
6. h
7. d
8. c

9. g
10. e
11. j

## What are defense mechanisms? (cont.): Pages 430-435

1. b
2. a

3. d
4. c

## Stress—Thrill or Threat? And Stress and Health—Unmasking a Hidden Killer: Pages 430-435, 442-453

What is stress? How is stress related to health and disease? What are the best strategies for managing stress?

1. h
2. a
3. g
4. f

5. b
6. i
7. d
8. c

9. j
10. e

# CHECK YOUR MEMORY

## Health Psychology—Here's to Your Good Health Pages 426-430

What is health psychology? How does behavior affect health?

1. T
2. T
3. T
4. F

5. T
6. T
7. T
8. F

9. F
10. T
11. F
12. F

## Stress—Thrill or Threat: Pages 430-435

What is stress?

| | | |
|---|---|---|
| 1. F | 8. T | 15. T |
| 2. T | 9. T | 16. F |
| 3. T | 10. F | 17. F |
| 4. T | 11. F | 18. T |
| 5. F | 12. T | 19. T |
| 6. T | 13. F | 20. F |
| 7. T | 14. T | |

## Frustration—Blind Alleys and Lead Balloons: Pages 435-437

What causes frustration and what are typical reactions to it?

| | | |
|---|---|---|
| 1. F | 3. F | 5. T |
| 2. F | 4. T | |

## Conflict—Yes, No, Yes, No, Yes, No, Well, Maybe: Pages 438-440

Are there different types of conflict?

| | | |
|---|---|---|
| 1. T | 3. T | 5. T |
| 2. F | 4. F | |

## Psychological Defense—Mental Karate: Pages 440-442

What are defense mechanisms?

| | | |
|---|---|---|
| 1. T | 3. F | 5. F |
| 2. T | 4. T | |

## Learned Helplessness—Is There Hope?: Pages 442-445

What do we know about coping with feelings of helplessness and depression?

| | | |
|---|---|---|
| 1. T | 4. T | 7. T |
| 2. T | 5. F | 8. T |
| 3. T | 6. F | |

## Stress and Health—Unmasking a Hidden Killer: Pages 445-453

How is stress related to health and disease?

| | | |
|---|---|---|
| 1. F | 5. T | 9. F |
| 2. T | 6. F | 10. F |
| 3. F | 7. F | 11. T |
| 4. F | 8. T | |

460

## Psychology in Action: Stress Management: Pages 453-457
What are the best strategies for managing stress?

| | | |
|---|---|---|
| 1. F | 4. T | 7. T |
| 2. F | 5. T | 8. F |
| 3. T | 6. T | |

# FINAL SURVEY AND REVIEW

## Health Psychology—Here's to Your Good Health
What is health psychology? How does behavior affect health?

1. behavioral; medicine stress
2. lifestyle health

3. risk factors

4. disease-prone

5. promoting; deprivation;

6. wellness; community;

## Stress—Thrill or Threat?
What is stress?

1. adapt; demands
2. pressure; stressor
3. burnout; depersonalization
4. appraisal; appraisal

5. problem; emotion
6. threat; competent
7. Traumatic
8. control
9. stress; disorders

10. general; adaptation; syndrome
11. behavioral; alarm
12. immune

## Frustration—Blind Alleys and Lead Balloons
What causes frustration and what are typical reactions to it?

1. Frustration; personal
2. External; Personal

3. blocked; motive
4. persistence; circumvention

5. displaced; scapegoating
6. frustration; manageable

## Conflict—Yes, No, Yes, No, Yes, No, Well, Maybe
Are there different types of conflict?

1. contradictory
2. approach-approach; avoidance-avoidance hasty

3. Approach-approach
4. Avoidance
5. ambivalence

6. double; multiple
7. Vacillation
8. conflicts;

## Psychological Defense—Mental Karate?
What are defense mechanisms?

1. defense; mechanisms; anxiety

2. denial; rationalization

3. compensation; sublimation

## Learned Helplessness—Is There Hope?
What do we know about coping with feelings of helplessness and depression?

1. helplessness; punishment
2. depression
3. Mastery
4. college; depression
5. Depression

## Stress and Health—Unmasking a Hidden Killer
How is stress related to health and disease?

1. Social; Readjustment; Rating
2. microstressors
3. psychosomatic
4. Psychosomatic; meaning response
   hypochondria
5. medical; biological; psychological; social
6. biofeedback; signal
7. regulation
8. Type; A; angry
9. heart attack
10. hardy
11. hardy; positive; reduce
12. optimists
13. reduced; events
14. person; reduce

## Psychology in Action: Stress Management
What are the best strategies for managing stress?

1. ineffective; upsetting
2. progressive; guided
3. limits; social
4. negative; coping
5. Meditation
6. relaxation

# MASTERY TEST

1. b, p. 443
2. a, p. 453
3. c, p. 434
4. d, p. 433
5. c, p. 441
6. a, p. 437
7. a, p. 426
8. c, p. 447
9. b, p. 446
10. a, p. 441
11. a, p. 426
12. d, p. 451
13. b, p. 427
14. a, p. 434
15. b, p. 436
16. b, p. 450
17. b, p. 438
18. d, p. 428
19. c, p. 439
20. c, p. 436
21. a, p. 456
22. a, p. 432
23. b, p. 437
24. d, p. 432
25. a, p. 429
26. d, p. 455
27. c, p. 434
28. c, p. 431
29. d, p. 434
30. b, p. 426
31. b, p. 427
32. c, p. 428
33. d, p. 434
34. c, p. 451
35. d, p. 452
36. a, p. 452
37. b, p. 449

# Psychological Disorders

## Chapter Overview

Abnormal behavior is defined by subjective discomfort, deviation from statistical norms, social nonconformity, and cultural or situational contexts. Disordered behavior is also maladaptive. Major types of psychopathology are described by DSM-IV-TR. Risk factors contributing to psychopathology include social, family, psychological, and biological factors. Psychopathology is not isolated to Western societies. Every culture recognizes the existence of psychological disorders. In the United States, insanity is a legal term, not a mental disorder.

Psychosis is a break in contact with reality. Persons suffering from delusional disorders have delusions of grandeur, persecution, infidelity, romantic attraction, or physical disease. The most common delusional disorder is paranoid psychosis. Schizophrenia is the most common psychosis. Four types of schizophrenia are: disorganized, catatonic, paranoid, and undifferentiated. Explanations of schizophrenia emphasize environmental stress, inherited susceptibility, and biochemical abnormalities.

Mood disorders involve disturbances of emotion. Two moderate mood disorders are dysthymic disorder and cyclothymic disorder. Major mood disorders include bipolar disorders and major depressive disorder. Seasonal affective disorder is another common form of depression. Biological, psychoanalytic, cognitive, and behavioral theories of depression have been proposed. Heredity is clearly a factor in susceptibility to mood disorders.

Anxiety disorders, dissociative disorders, and somatoform disorders are characterized by high levels of anxiety, rigid defense mechanisms, and self-defeating behavior patterns. Anxiety disorders include generalized anxiety disorder, panic disorder (with or without agoraphobia), agoraphobia, specific phobia, social phobia, obsessive-compulsive disorders, and posttraumatic or acute stress disorders. Dissociative disorders may take the form of amnesia, fugue, or identity disorder (multiple personality). Somatoform disorders center on physical complaints that mimic disease or disability.

Psychodynamic explanations of anxiety disorders emphasize unconscious conflicts. The humanistic approach emphasizes faulty self-images. The behavioral approach emphasizes the effects of learning, particularly avoidance learning. The cognitive approach stresses maladaptive thinking patterns.

Personality disorders are deeply ingrained maladaptive personality patterns, such as the antisocial personality. In addition to maladaptive patterns of behaviors, personality disorders are diagnosed and differentiated based on the degree of impairment. Ranging from moderate to severe impairment, some personality disorders are narcissistic, histrionic, borderline, and schizotypal.

Labeling someone with a disorder rather than the problems that people experience can dramatically influence how people with mental disorders are treated. They often are faced with prejudice and discrimination, denied jobs and housing, and accused of crimes they did not commit.

Basic approaches to treating psychological disorders are psychotherapy and medical therapies. Suicide is statistically related to such factors as age, sex, and marital status. However, in individual cases the potential for suicide is best identified by a desire to escape, unbearable psychological pain, frustrated psychological needs, and a constriction of options. Suicide can sometimes be prevented by the efforts of family, friends, and mental health professionals.

# Learning Objectives

### Theme: Judgments of abnormality are relative, but psychological disorders clearly exist and need to be classified, explained, and treated.

| |
|---|
| **GQ: How is abnormality defined?** |
| LO 14.1 Indicate the magnitude of mental health problems in this country; and define *psychopathology*. |
| LO 14.2 Describe the following ways of viewing normality, including the shortcoming(s) of each: a. subjective discomfort; b. statistical definitions; c. *social nonconformity*; d. situational context; e. cultural relativity; and indicate the two core features of abnormal behavior. |
| LO 14.3 Distinguish the term *insanity* from a *mental disorder*. |
| **GQ: What are the major psychological disorders?** |
| LO 14.4 Explain the functions of the DSM-IV-TR; and generally describe each of the following categories of mental disorders found in the DSM-IV-TR: a. *psychotic disorders;* b. *organic mental disorders*; c. *substance related disorders*; d. *mood disorders;* e. *anxiety disorders*; f. *dissociative disorders*; g. *somatoform disorders*; h. *personality disorders*; i. *sexual and gender identity disorders*; j. *substance-related disorders*. Include a description of the outdated term *neurosis* and explain why it was dropped from use. |
| LO 14.5 Define the concept of a culture-bound disorder. |
| LO 14.6 List the four general categories of risk factors for mental disorders; and explain how culture affects the labeling and incidence of mental disorders and give examples. |
| **GQ: What are the general characteristics of psychotic disorders?** |
| LO 14.7 Explain these major characteristics of psychotic disorders: a. *delusions* (including a description of the different types of delusions); b. *hallucinations*; c. emotional disturbances (including *flat affect*); d; disturbed verbal communication; and e. personality disintegration. |
| LO 14.8 Define the terms *organic psychosis* and *dementia* and give examples; and discuss *Alzheimer's disease*, including its incidence, symptoms, and types of neurological damage. |
| **GQ: What is the nature of a delusional disorder?** |
| LO 14.9 Describe the main feature of *delusional disorders;* and discuss five types of delusional disorders. |
| **GQ: What forms does schizophrenia take? What causes it?** |
| LO 14.10 Generally describe *schizophrenia,* including its frequency, typical age of onset, and symptoms; list and describe the four major types of schizophrenia; explain how *paranoid delusional disorder* and *paranoid schizophrenia* differ; and describe the general relationship between *psychosis* and violence. |
| LO 14.11 Describe the roles of the following three areas as causes of schizophrenia: a. environment (including prenatal problems, birth complications, *psychological trauma*, disturbed family environment, and deviant communication patterns; b. heredity, c. brain chemistry (including dopamine and glutamate); explain how CT, MRI, and PET scans contribute to the study of abnormal brain activity; and describe the *stress-vulnerability model*. |
| **GQ: What are mood disorders? What causes them?** |
| LO 14.12 State the incidence and characteristics of *mood disorders*, especially depression, in the general population; describe the characteristics of the moderate mood disorders: *dysthymia* and *cyclothymia*; describe the |

| characteristics of the three major mood disorders: major depression, *bipolar I* and *bipolar II;* and explain the differences between the moderate and major mood disorders. |
| --- |
| LO 14.13  Describe the possible explanations for depression; briefly discuss the symptoms of *maternity blues* and *postpartum depression*; and describe *seasonal affective disorder* (SAD), its five major symptoms, and its treatment. |
| **GQ: What problems result when a person suffers high levels of anxiety?** |
| LO 14.14  Outline the general features and characteristics of anxiety-related problems and differentiate this category from an anxiety disorder. State what is usually meant when the term *nervous breakdown* is used. |
| LO 14.15  Generally describe each of the following conditions: a. anxiety disorders (including *generalized anxiety disorder*; *panic disorder*; *agoraphobia*; *specific phobia*; and *social phobia*); b. *obsessive-compulsive disorder*; c. *stress disorders* (including *acute* stress disorder and *post-traumatic stress disorder*); d. dissociative disorders (including *dissociative amnesia*, *dissociative fugue*, and *dissociative identity disorder*); and e. somatoform disorders (including *hypochondriasis*, *somatization disorder*, *pain disorder*, and *conversion disorder*). |
| **GQ: How do psychologists explain anxiety-based disorders?** |
| LO 14.16  Discuss how each of the major perspectives in psychology view anxiety disorders: a. psychodynamic, b. humanistic (Rogers); c. humanistic-existential; d. behavioral (include the terms *self-defeating*, *avoidance learning,* and *anxiety reduction hypothesis*), e. cognitive. |
| **GQ: What is a personality disorder?** |
| LO 14.17  List and briefly describe the ten different types of personality disorders (see Table 14.7). Include an indepth discussion of the distinctive characteristics, causes, and treatment of the *antisocial personality*. |
| LO 14.18  Explain why caution is necessary when using psychiatric labels. Briefly describe Rosenhan's pseudo-patient study, and explain how his observations relate to the idea of labeling. |
| **GQ: Why do people commit suicide? Can suicide be prevented?** |
| LO 14.19  Discuss how each of the following factors affects suicide rate: a. gender, b. ethnicity; c. age, d. marital status. |
| LO 14.20  Describe the conditions which typically precede suicide and why people try to kill themselves; list the twelve warning signs of suicide and the four common characteristics of suicidal thoughts and feelings; and explain how you can help prevent suicide. |

# RECITE AND REVIEW

## Normality—What Is Normal?: Pages 460-462
How is abnormality defined?

1. *Psychopathology* refers to mental _____ themselves or to psychologically _____ behavior.

2. Formal definitions of abnormality usually take into account subjective _____ (private feelings of suffering or unhappiness).

3. Statistical definitions define abnormality as an extremely _____ or _____ score on some dimension or measure.

4. Social nonconformity is a failure to follow societal _____ for acceptable conduct.

5. Frequently, the _____ or situational context that a behavior takes place in affects judgments of normality and abnormality.

6. _____ of the preceding definitions are relative standards.

7. A key element in judgments of disorder is that a person's _____ must be maladaptive (it makes it difficult for the person to _____ to the demands of daily life.

465

8. A _____ disorder is a significant impairment in psychological functioning.

9. Insanity is a _____ term defining whether a person may be held responsible for his or her actions. Sanity is determined in _____ on the basis of testimony by expert witnesses.

# Classifying Mental Disorders—Problems by the Book: Pages 463-467
What are the major psychological disorders?

1. Major disorders and categories of psychopathology are described in the *Diagnostic and Statistical* _____ *of* _____ *Disorders* (DSM-IV-TR).

2. Psychotic disorders are characterized by a retreat from _____, by hallucinations and delusions, and by _____ withdrawal.

3. Organic mental disorders are problems caused by _____ injuries and _____.

4. Substance related disorders are defined as abuse of or dependence on _____ - or behavior-altering _____.

5. Mood disorders involve disturbances in affect, or _____.

6. Anxiety disorders involve high levels of fear or _____ and distortions in behavior that are _____ related.

7. Somatoform disorders involve physical symptoms that mimic physical _____ or injury for which there is no identifiable _____.

8. Dissociative disorders include cases of sudden amnesia, multiple _____, or episodes of depersonalization.

9. Personality disorders are deeply ingrained, unhealthy _____ patterns.

10. Sexual and gender disorders include _____ identity disorders, paraphilias, and _____ dysfunctions.

11. In the past, the term *neurosis* was used to describe milder, _____ related disorders. However, the term is fading from use.

12. Psychological disorders are recognized in every _____. For example, Native Americans who are preoccupied with death and the deceased have _____ sickness, and East Asians who experience intense anxiety that their penis, vulva, or nipples are receding into their bodies have _____ disorder.

466

# Psychotic Disorders—The Dark Side of the Moon: Pages 467-469
What are the general characteristics of psychotic disorders?

1. Psychosis is a_____ in contact with reality.

2. Some common types of delusions are depressive, _____ , grandeur, _____ , persecution, and reference.

3. Psychosis is marked by delusions, _____ (false sensations), and sensory changes.

4. Other symptoms of psychosis are disturbed emotions, disturbed communication, frozen faces, and _____ disintegration.

5. An organic psychosis is based on known injuries or _____ of the brain, such as ingestion of lead paint.

6. The most common _____ problem is dementia, a serious mental impairment in old age caused by deterioration of the_____.

7. One of the common causes of _____ is Alzheimer's disease.

# Delusional Disorders—An Enemy Behind Every Tree: Page 470
What is the nature of a delusional disorder?

1. A diagnosis of delusional disorder is based primarily on the presence of_____.

2. Delusions may concern grandeur, _____ (harassment or threat), infidelity, _____ attraction, or physical disease.

3. The most common delusional disorder is paranoid psychosis. Because they often have intense and irrational delusions of _____, paranoids may be violent if they believe they are threatened.

# Schizophrenia—Shattered Reality: Pages 470-476
What forms does schizophrenia take? What causes it?

1. Schizophrenia is distinguished by a_____ between _____ and emotion, and by delusions, hallucinations, and communication difficulties.

2.  Disorganized schizophrenia is marked by extreme _____ disintegration and silly, bizarre, or obscene behavior. _____ impairment is usually extreme.

3.  Catatonic schizophrenia is associated with stupor, _____ (inability to speak), _____ flexibility, and odd postures. Sometimes violent and agitated behavior also occurs.

4.  In paranoid schizophrenia (the most common type), outlandish delusions of grandeur and _____ are coupled with psychotic symptoms and personality breakdown.

5.  Undifferentiated schizophrenia is the term used to indicate a _____ of clear-cut patterns of disturbance.

6.  Current explanations of schizophrenia emphasize a combination of environmental _____ inherited susceptibility, and biochemical _____ in the body or brain.

7.  A number of environmental factors appear to increase the risk of developing schizophrenia. These include viral _____ during the mother's pregnancy and _____ complications.

8.  Early psychological _____ (psychological injury or shock) and a disturbed _____ environment, especially one marked by deviant communication, also increase the risk of schizophrenia.

9.  Studies of _____ and other close relatives strongly support heredity as a major factor in schizophrenia.

10. Recent biochemical studies have focused on abnormalities in brain _____ substances, especially glutamate and dopamine and their receptor sites.

11. Current explanations of schizophrenia emphasize a combination of environmental _____ , inherited susceptibility, and biochemical _____ in the body or brain.

12. Other known causes that induce schizophrenic symptoms are the hallucinogenic drug _____ and stress, which affect _____ and dopamine levels in the brain.

13. Additional abnormalities in brain structure or _____ have been detected in schizophrenic brains by the use of CT scans, MRI scans, and PET scans. _____ may be impaired in those suffering from schizophrenia.

14. The dominant explanation of schizophrenia is the _____-vulnerability model.

# Mood Disorders—Peaks and Valleys: Pages 476-480
What are mood disorders? What causes them?

1. Mood disorders primarily involve disturbances of mood or_____.

2. Long-lasting, though relatively moderate, _____ is called a dysthymic disorder.

3. Chronic, though moderate, swings in mood between _____ and _____ are called a cyclothymic disorder.

4. In a bipolar I disorder the person alternates between extreme mania and _____.

5. In a bipolar II disorder the person is mostly _____, but has had at least one episode of hypomania (mild _____ ).

6. The problem known as major depressive disorder involves extreme sadness and despondency, but no evidence of_____.

7. Major mood disorders more often appear to be endogenous (produced from_____) rather than reactions to _____ events.

8. Postpartum depression is a mild to moderate depressive disorder that affects many women after they give birth. Postpartum depression is more serious than the more common _____.

9. _____affective disorder (SAD), which occurs during the _____ months, is another common form of depression. SAD is typically treated with phototherapy.

10. Biological, psychoanalytic, cognitive, and _____ theories of depression have been proposed. Heredity is clearly a factor in susceptibility to mood disorders.

# Anxiety-Based Disorders—When Anxiety Rules: Pages 480-486
What problems result when a person suffers high levels of anxiety?

1. The term *nervous breakdown* has no formal meaning. However, "emotional breakdowns" do correspond somewhat to adjustment disorders, in which the person is overwhelmed by ongoing _____.

2. Anxiety disorders include generalized anxiety disorder (chronic_____ and worry) and panic disorder (anxiety attacks, panic, free-_____anxiety).

3. Panic disorder may occur with or without agoraphobia (fear of _____ places, unfamiliar situations, or leaving the _____ ).

4. Other anxiety disorders are agoraphobia and _____ phobia (irrational fears of specific objects or situations).

5. In the anxiety disorder called social phobia, the person fears being _____, evaluated, embarrassed, or humiliated by others in _____ situations.

6. Obsessive-compulsive disorders (obsessions and compulsions), and posttraumatic stress disorder or acute stress disorder (emotional disturbances triggered by severe_____ ) are also classified as _____ disorders.

7. Dissociative disorders may take the form of dissociative amnesia (loss of _____ and personal identity) or _____ fugue (flight from familiar surroundings).

8. A more dramatic problem is dissociative identity disorder, in which a person develops _____ personalities.

9. Somatoform disorders center on physical complaints that mimic_____ or disability.

10. In hypochondriasis, persons think that they have specific diseases, when they are, in fact _____ .

11. In a somatization disorder, the person has numerous_____ complaints. The person repeatedly seeks medical_____ for these complaints, but no organic problems can be found.

12. Somatoform pain refers to discomfort for which there is no identifiable_____ cause.

13. In conversion disorders, actual symptoms of disease or disability develop but their causes are really _____ .

14. Anxiety disorders, dissociative disorders, and somatoform disorders all involve high levels of _____, rigid_____ mechanisms, and self-defeating behavior patterns.

# Anxiety and Disorder—Four Pathways to Trouble: Pages 486-487

How do psychologists explain anxiety-based disorders?

1. The psychodynamic approach emphasizes _____ conflicts within the personality as the cause of disabling anxiety.

470

2.  The humanistic approach emphasizes the effects of a faulty_____.

3.  The behavioral approach emphasizes the effects of previous_____, particularly avoidance

4.  Some patterns in anxiety disorders can be explained by the_____ reduction hypothesis, which

    states that immediate_____ from anxiety rewards self-defeating behaviors.

5.  According to the cognitive view, distorted _____ patterns cause anxiety disorders.

# Personality Disorders—Blueprints for Maladjustment: Pages 487-489
What is a personality disorder?

1.  People with borderline_____ disorder tend to react to ordinary criticisms by feeling
    rejected and _____, which then causes them to respond with anger, self-hatred, and _____.

2.  Personality disorders are deeply ingrained _____ personality patterns.

3.  The personality disorders are: antisocial, avoidant, _____, dependent, histrionic, narcissistic,

    obsessive- _____ paranoid, schizoid, and schizotypal.

4.  Antisocial persons (sociopaths) seem to lack a _____. They are _____ shallow
    and manipulative.

5.  Possible causes attributed to people with antisocial _____ disorder include emotional

    deprivation, neglect, _____ abuse as children, and boredom due to receiving little stimulation

    from the environment.

6.  People with _____ -compulsive disorder are plagued with images or thoughts that they cannot

    force out of _____. To reduce anxiety caused by these constantly occurring images and

    thoughts, they are compelled to _____ irrational acts.

# Disorders in Perspective—Psychiatric Labeling: Pages 489-490

1.  Factors that influence the development of depression include being a woman, _____, not being

    married, having limited _____, high levels of _____, and feelings of hopelessness.

2. David Rosenhan demonstrated the damaging effects of _____ a person with a disorder in our society. They are stigmatized, _____ jobs and housing, and accused of _____ that they did not commit.

3. Treatments for psychological disorders range from hospitalization and _____ to drug therapy. Individuals diagnosed with a major disorder do respond well to drugs and psychotherapy while individuals diagnosed with _____ mental disorders can be treated successfully.

## Psychology in Action: Suicide—Lives on the Brink: Pages 490-493
Why do people commit suicide? Can suicide be prevented?

1. _____ is statistically related to such factors as age, sex, and marital status.

2. Major risk factors for suicide include _____ or _____ abuse, a prior attempt, depression, hopelessness, antisocial behavior, suicide by relatives, shame, failure, or rejection, and the availability of a _____ .

3. In individual cases the potential for suicide is best identified by a desire to _____ , unbearable psychological pain, frustrated psychological needs, and a constriction of _____ .

4. Suicidal _____ usually precede suicide threats, which progress to suicide attempts.

5. Suicide can often be prevented by the efforts of family, friends, and mental health professionals to establish _____ and rapport with the person, and by gaining day-by-day commitments from her or him.

# CONNECTIONS

## Normality—What's Normal?: Pages 460-462
How is abnormality defined? What are the major psychological disorders?

1. _____ DSM-IV-TR
2. _____ social noncomformity
3. _____ mood disorder
4. _____ somatoform disorder
5. _____ insanity
6. _____ organic disorder
7. _____ neurosis
8. _____ paraphilia
9. _____ amok

a. disobeying pubic standards
b. physical symptoms
c. legal problem
d. outdated term
e. sexual deviation
f. diagnostic manual
g. fear of germs
h. brain pathology
i. mania or depression

# Psychotic Disorders—The Dark Side of the Moon: Pages 467-470

What are the general characteristics of psychotic disorders? What is the nature of a delusional disorder?

1. _____ Psychosis
2. _____ hallucinations
3. _____ delusion
4. _____ Alzheimer's disease
5. _____ jealous type
6  _____ erotomatic type
7. _____ persecution type
8. _____ somatic type
9. _____ grandiose type

a. retreat from reality
b. false belief
c. believing a celebrity loves him/her
d. believing one has great talents
e. believing one's body is diseased
f. believing one's partner is unfaithful
g. believing one is being spied on
h. dementia
i. imaginary sensations

# Delusional Disorders—An Enemy Behind Every Tree: Pages 470-476

What forms does schizophrenia take? What causes it?

1. _____ disorganized type
2. _____ catatonic type
3. _____ undifferentiated type
4. _____ paranoid type
5. _____ psychological trauma
6  _____ twin studies
7. _____ dopamine
8. _____ stress-vulnerability

a. displaying rigidity, delusions, and disorganization
b. incoherence, bizarre thinking
c. biological and environmental influences
d. genetics of schizophrenia
e. grandeur or persecution
f. chemical messenger
g. risk factor for schizophrenia
h. stuporous or agitated

# Anxiety-Based Disorders—When Anxiety Rules: Pages 480-487

What problems result when a person suffers high levels of anxiety? How do psychologists explain anxiety-based disorders?

1. _____ cognitive explanation
2. _____ psychodynamic explanation
3. _____ behavioral explanation
4. _____ adjustment disorder
5. _____ generalized anxiety
6  _____ panic disorder
7. _____ Munchausen syndrome
8. _____ specific phobia

a. fakes own medical problems
b. fears being observed
c. conversion disorder
d. one month after extreme stress
e. caused by unconscious forces
f. within weeks after extreme stress
g. sudden attacks of fear
h. self-defeating thoughts

473

9. _____ social phobia  
10. _____ humanistic-existential  
11. _____ PTSD  
12. _____ acute stress disorder  
13. _____ glove anesthesia  
14. _____ fugue  

i. chronic worry  
j. fears objects or activities  
k. maladaptive pattern of behavior  
l. dissociation  
m. faulty self-image and no meaning in life  
n. normal life stress  

# Personality Disorders—Blueprints for Maladjustment: Pages 487-489
What is a personality disorder?

1. _____ dependent personality  
2. _____ histrionic personality  
3. _____ narcissistic personality  
4. _____ antisocial personality  
5. _____ obsessive-compulsive  
6 _____ schizoid personality  
7. _____ avoidant personality  
8. _____ borderline personality  
9. _____ paranoid personality  
10. _____ schizotypal personality  

a. self-importance  
b. rigid routines  
c. submissiveness  
d. little emotion  
e. attention seeking  
f. unstable self-image  
g. odd, disturbed thinking  
h. suspiciousness  
i. fear of social situations  
j. No conscience  

# Psychology in Action: Suicide—Lives on the Brink: Pages 490-493
What are mood disorders? What causes depression?: Pages 476-480 Why do people commit suicide? Can suicide be prevented?

1. _____ postpartum depression  
2. _____ bipolar I  
3. _____ bipolar II  
4. _____ endogenous  
5. _____ suicide  
6 _____ phototherapy  
7. _____ SAD  
8. _____ social stigma  
9. _____ acculturative stress  

a. produced from within  
b. depression and hypomania  
c. depression after childbirth  
d. light treatment  
e. leads to prejudice  
f. desire to end all pains  
g. winter depression  
h. severe mania and depression  
i. suicide risk factor for minority member

# CHECK YOUR MEMORY

## Normality—What's Normal and Classifying Mental Disorders—Problems by the Book: Pages 460-467

How is abnormality defined? What are the major psychological disorders?

1. Psychopathology refers to the study of mental disorders and to disorders themselves.
   TRUE or FALSE

2. One out of every 10 American adults will suffer from a diagnosable mental disorder in any
   given year.   TRUE or FALSE

3. Statistical definitions do not automatically tell us where to draw the line between normality
   and abnormality.   TRUE or FALSE

4. To understand how social norms define normality, a person could perform a mild abnormal behavior
   in public to observe the public's reaction.   TRUE or FALSE

5. Cultural relativity refers to making personal judgments about another culture's practices.
   TRUE or FALSE

6. All cultures classify people as abnormal if they fail to communicate with others.
   TRUE or FALSE

7. Somotoform disorders occur when a person has physical symptoms for which there is an
   identifiable physical cause.   TRUE or FALSE

8. Statistics are often used to define normality.   TRUE or FALSE

9. Being a persistent danger to oneself or others is regarded as a clear sign of disturbed psychological
   functioning.   TRUE or FALSE

10. Poverty, abusive parents, low intelligence, and head injuries are risk factors for mental disorder.
    TRUE or FALSE

11. "Organic mental disorders" is one of the major categories in DSM-IV-TR.   TRUE or FALSE

12. Keel and Klump believe that bulimia occurs primarily in Western cultures.   TRUE or FALSE

13. *Koro, locura, dhat,* and *zar* are brain diseases that cause psychosis.   TRUE or FALSE

14. Multiple personality is a dissociative disorder.   TRUE or FALSE

15. Neurosis is a legal term, not a type of mental disorder.   TRUE or FALSE

# Psychotic Disorders—The Dark Side of the Moon: Pages 467-469

What are the general characteristics of psychotic disorders?

1. The most common psychotic delusion is hearing voices.   TRUE or FALSE

2. People with depressive delusions believe that they are depressed but that they do not need therapy.
   TRUE or FALSE

3. Even a person who displays flat affect may continue to privately feel strong emotion.
   TRUE or FALSE

4. Extremely psychotic behavior tends to occur in brief episodes.   TRUE or FALSE

5. Severe brain injuries or diseases sometimes cause psychoses.   TRUE or FALSE

6. Children must eat leaded paint flakes before they are at risk for lead poisoning.   TRUE or FALSE

7. Roughly 80 percent of all cases of Alzheimer's disease are genetic.   TRUE or FALSE

# Delusional Disorders—An Enemy Behind Every Tree: Page 470

What is the nature of a delusional disorder?

1. In delusional disorders, people have auditory hallucinations of grandeur or persecution.
   TRUE or FALSE

2. Delusions of persecution are a key symptom of paranoid psychosis.   TRUE or FALSE

3. A person who believes that his body is diseased and rotting has an erotomanic type of delusional
   disorder.   TRUE or FALSE

4. Delusional disorders are common and are easily treated with drugs.   TRUE or FALSE

# Schizophrenia—Shattered Reality: Pages 470-476

What forms does schizophrenia take? What causes it?

1. One person out of 100 will become schizophrenic.   TRUE or FALSE

2. Schizophrenia is the most common dissociative psychosis.   TRUE or FALSE

3. Individuals who are mentally ill are, on average, no more violent than normal individuals.
   TRUE or FALSE

4. Silliness, laughter, and bizarre behavior are common in disorganized schizophrenia.
   TRUE or FALSE

5. Periods of immobility and odd posturing are characteristic of paranoid schizophrenia.
   TRUE or FALSE

6. At various times, patients may shift from one type of schizophrenia to another.
   TRUE or FALSE

7. Exposure to influenza during pregnancy produces children who are more likely to become schizophrenic later in life.   TRUE or FALSE

8. If one identical twin is schizophrenic, the other twin has a 46 percent chance of also becoming schizophrenic.   TRUE or FALSE

9. Excess amounts of the neurotransmitter substance PCP are suspected as a cause of schizophrenia.
   TRUE or FALSE

10. The brains of schizophrenics tend to be more responsive to dopamine than the brains of normal persons.   TRUE or FALSE

11. PET scans show that activity in the frontal lobes of schizophrenics tends to be abnormally low.
    TRUE or FALSE

12. At least three schizophrenic patients out of four are completely recovered 10 years after being diagnosed.   TRUE or FALSE

13. The stress-vulnerability model suggests that psychotic disorders are caused by a combination of environment and heredity.   TRUE or FALSE

# Mood Disorders—Peaks and Valleys: Pages 476-480
What are mood disorders? What causes depression?

1. The two most basic types of mood disorder are bipolar I and bipolar II.   TRUE or FALSE

2. In bipolar disorders, people experience both mania and depression.   TRUE or FALSE

3. If a person is moderately depressed for at least two weeks, a dysthymic disorder exists.
   TRUE or FALSE

4. A cyclothymic disorder is characterized by moderate levels of depression and manic behavior.
   TRUE or FALSE

5. Endogenous depression appears to be generated from within, with little connection to external events.
   TRUE or FALSE

6. Behavioral theories of depression emphasize the concept of learned helplessness.   TRUE or FALSE

7. Overall, women are twice as likely as men are to become depressed.   TRUE or FALSE

8. Having limited education, experiencing high levels of stress, not being married, and feeling hopeless are some characteristics that increase a woman's chance of being depressed.   TRUE or FALSE

9. Research indicates that heredity does not play a role in major mood disorder.   TRUE or FALSE

10. Postpartum depression typically lasts from about two months to a year after giving birth.
   TRUE or FALSE

11. SAD is most likely to occur during the winter, in countries lying near the equator.   TRUE or FALSE

12. Phototherapy is used to treat SAD successfully 80 percent of the time.   TRUE or FALSE

# Anxiety-Based Disorders—When Anxiety Rules: Pages 480-486
What problems result when a person suffers high levels of anxiety?

1. Anxiety is an emotional response to an ambiguous threat.   TRUE or FALSE

2. Adjustment disorders occur when severe stresses outside the normal range of human experience push people to their breaking points.   TRUE or FALSE

3. Sudden, unexpected episodes of intense panic are a key feature of generalized anxiety disorder.
   TRUE or FALSE

4. A person who fears he or she will have a panic attack in public places or unfamiliar situations suffers from acrophobia.   TRUE or FALSE

5. Arachnophobia, claustrophobia, and aviophobia are all specific phobias.   TRUE or FALSE

6. Many people who have an obsessive-compulsive disorder are checkers or cleaners.
   TRUE or FALSE

7. PTSD is a psychological disturbance lasting more than one month after exposure to severe stress.
   TRUE or FALSE

8. Multiple personality is a dissociative disorder.   TRUE or FALSE

9. Multiple personality is the most common form of schizophrenia.   TRUE or FALSE

10. Depersonalization and fusion are the goals of therapy for dissociative identity disorders.
   TRUE or FALSE

11. The word somatoform means "body form."   TRUE or FALSE

12. An unusual lack of concern about the appearance of a sudden disability is a sign of a conversion reaction.   TRUE or FALSE

# Anxiety and Disorder—Four Pathways to Trouble: Pages 486-487

How do psychologists explain anxiety-based disorders?

1. Anxiety disorders appear to be partly hereditary.   TRUE or FALSE

2. The psychodynamic approach characterizes anxiety disorders as a product of id impulses that threaten a loss of control.   TRUE or FALSE

3. Carl Rogers interpreted emotional disorders as the result of a loss of meaning in one's life.
   TRUE or FALSE

4. Disordered behavior is paradoxical, because it makes the person more anxious and unhappy in the long run.   TRUE or FALSE

5. The cognitive view attributes anxiety disorders to distorted thinking that leads to avoidance learning.
   TRUE or FALSE

# Personality Disorders—Blueprints for Maladjustment: Pages 487-489

What is a personality disorder?

1. The "emotional storms" experienced by people with borderline personality disorder is a normal process about which they and their friends have a clear understanding.   TRUE or FALSE

2. Histrionic persons are preoccupied with their own self-importance.   TRUE or FALSE

3. Personality disorders usually appear suddenly in early adulthood.   TRUE or FALSE

4. The schizoid person shows little emotion and is uninterested in relationships with others.
   TRUE or FALSE

5. "Psychopath" is another term for the borderline personality.   TRUE or FALSE

6. Sociopaths usually have a childhood history of emotional deprivation, neglect, and abuse.
   TRUE or FALSE

7. Antisocial behavior typically declines somewhat after age 20.   TRUE or FALSE

8. Antisocial personality disorders are often treated successfully with drugs.   TRUE or FALSE

## Disorders in Perspective—Psychiatric Labeling: Pages 489-490

1. Labeling a person with a disorder when they do not have it does not harm them in any way.
   TRUE or FALSE

2. People who have been successfully treated for a mental disorder are no longer a threat to society and, therefore, are not stigmatized like criminals.   TRUE or FALSE

## Psychology in Action: Suicide—Lives on the Brink: Pages 490-493
Why do people commit suicide? Can suicide be prevented?

1. The greatest number of suicides during a single day takes place at New Year's.   TRUE or FALSE

2. More men than women complete suicide.   TRUE or FALSE

3. Suicide rates steadily decline after young adulthood.   TRUE or FALSE

4. Most suicides involve despair, anger, and guilt.   TRUE or FALSE

5. People who threaten suicide rarely actually attempt it—they're just crying wolf.
   TRUE or FALSE

6. Only a minority of people who attempt suicide really want to die.   TRUE or FALSE

7. The risk of attempted suicide is high if a person has a concrete, workable plan for doing it.
   TRUE or FALSE

8. In the U.S., Caucasians have higher suicide rates than non-Caucasians.   TRUE or FALSE

# FINAL SURVEY AND REVIEW

## Normality—What Is Normal?
How is abnormality defined?

1. _____refers to mental disorders themselves or to psychologically unhealthy behavior.

2. Formal definitions of abnormality usually take into account _____ discomfort (private

   feelings of suffering or unhappiness).

3. _____definitions define abnormality as an extremely high or low score on some
   dimension or measure.

4. _____ is a failure to follow societal standards for acceptable conduct.

5. Frequently, the cultural or situational _____ that a behavior takes place in affects judgments of normality and abnormality.

6. All of the preceding definitions are _____ standards.

7. A key element in judgments of disorder is that a person's behavior must be _____ (it makes it difficult for the person to adapt to the demands of daily life).

8. A mental disorder is a significant impairment in_____ functioning.

9. _____ is a legal term defining whether a person may be held responsible for his or her actions. Sanity is determined in court on the basis of testimony by expert witnesses.

# Classifying Mental Disorders—Problems by the Book
## What are the major psychological disorders?

1. Major disorders and categories of psychopathology are described in the _____ *and* _____ *Manual of Mental Disorders* (DSM-IV-TR).

2. _____ disorders are characterized by a retreat from reality, by _____ and delusions, and by social withdrawal.

3. _____ mental disorders are problems caused by brain injuries and diseases.

4. _____ disorders are defined as abuse of or dependence on mood- or behavior-altering drugs.

5. _____ disorders involve disturbances in _____ , or emotion.

6. _____ disorders involve high levels of fear or anxiety and distortions in behavior that are anxiety related.

7. _____ disorders involve physical symptoms that mimic physical disease or injury for which there is no identifiable cause.

8. _____ disorders include cases of sudden _____, multiple personality, or episodes of depersonalization.

9. _____ disorders are deeply ingrained, unhealthy personality patterns.

10. Sexual and gender disorders include gender_____ disorders, paraphilias, and sexual

481

11. In the past, the term _____ was used to describe milder, anxiety related disorders. However, the term is fading from use.

12. Psychological disorders are recognized in every culture. For example, Native Americans who are preoccupied with death and the deceased have_____, and _____ who experience intense anxiety that their penis, vulva, or nipples are receding into their bodies have Koro disorder.

# Psychotic Disorders—The Dark Side of the Moon
What are the general characteristics of psychotic disorders?

1. _____ is a break in contact with.

2. Some common types of _____ are depressive, somatic, grandeur, influence, persecution, and _____ reference.

3. Psychosis is marked by _____ (false beliefs), hallucinations, and _____ changes.

4. Other symptoms of psychosis are disturbed emotions, disturbed_____, frozen faces, and personality _____ .

5. An _____ psychosis is based on known injuries or diseases of the brain, such as ingestion of lead paint.

6. The most common organic problem is_____ , a serious mental impairment in old age caused by deterioration of the brain.

7. One of the common causes of dementia is _____ disease.

# Delusional Disorders—An Enemy Behind Every Tree
What is the nature of a delusional disorder?

1. A _____ of _____ disorder is based primarily on the presence of delusions.

2. Delusions may concern _____ (personal importance), persecution, infidelity, romantic attraction, or physical _____ .

3. The most common delusional disorder is_____ psychosis. Because they often have intense and irrational delusions of persecution, paranoids may be_____ if they believe they are threatened.

# Schizophrenia—Shattered Reality
What forms does schizophrenia take? What causes it?

1. Schizophrenia is distinguished by a split between thought and _____, and by delusions, hallucinations, and _____ difficulties.

2. _____ schizophrenia is marked by extreme personality_____ and silly, bizarre, or obscene behavior. Social impairment is usually extreme.

3. _____ schizophrenia is associated with stupor, mutism (inability to speak), waxy _____ , and odd postures. Sometimes violent and agitated behavior also occurs.

4. In _____ schizophrenia (the most common type), outlandish delusions of _____ and persecution are coupled with psychotic symptoms and personality breakdown.

5. _____ schizophrenia is the term used to indicate a lack of clear-cut patterns of disturbance.

6. Current explanations of schizophrenia emphasize a combination of _____ stress, inherited susceptibility, and _____ abnormalities in the body or brain.

7. A number of_____ factors appear to increase the risk of developing schizophrenia. These include viral infection during the mother's pregnancy and birth complications.

8. Early _____ trauma (psychological injury or shock) and a disturbed family environment, especially one marked by    communication, also increase the risk of schizophrenia.

9. Studies of twins and other close relatives strongly support _____as a major factor in schizophrenia.

10. Recent biochemical studies have focused on abnormalities in brain transmitter substances, especially glutamate and _____ and their_____ sites.

11. Current explanations of schizophrenia emphasize a combination of_____ stress, inherited susceptibility, and _____ abnormalities in the body or brain.

12. Other known causes that induce_____symptoms are the _____ drug PCP and stress, which affect glutamate and dopamine levels in the brain.

13. Additional abnormalities in brain structure or activity have been detected in schizophrenic brains by the use of _____ scans,_____ scans, and _____ scans. Neurogenesis may be impaired in people suffering from schizophrenia.

483

14. The dominant explanation of schizophrenia is the stress- _____ model.

# Mood Disorders—Peaks and Valleys and Disorders in Perspective—Psychitatric Labeling

What are mood disorders? What causes depression?

1. Mood disorders primarily involve disturbances of_____ or emotion.

2. Long-lasting, though relatively moderate, depression is called a _____ disorder.

3. Chronic, though moderate, swings in mood between depression and elation are called a _____ disorder.

4. In a_____disorder the person alternates between extreme _____ and depression.

5. In a_____ disorder the person is mostly depressed, but has had at least one episode of _____ (mild mania).

6. The problem known as_____ disorder involves extreme sadness and despondency, but no evidence of mania.

7. _____depression is a mild to moderate depressive disorder that affects many women after they give birth. It is more serious than the more common maternity blues.

8. Major mood disorders more often appear to be _____ (produced from within) rather than reactions to external events.

9. Seasonal_____disorder (SAD), which occurs during the winter months, is another common form of depression. SAD is typically treated with (exposure to bright light).

10. _____, psychoanalytic,_____ , and behavioral theories of depression have been proposed. Heredity is clearly a factor in susceptibility to mood disorders.

# Anxiety-Based Disorders—When Anxiety Rules

What problems result when a person suffers high levels of anxiety?

1. Anxiety disorders, _____disorders, and_____disorders all involve high levels of anxiety, rigid defense mechanisms, and self-defeating behavior patterns.

2. The term nervous_____ has no formal meaning. However, people do experience _____disorders, in which the person is overwhelmed by ongoing life stresses.

484

3. Anxiety disorders include _____ anxiety disorder (chronic anxiety and worry) and _____ disorder (anxiety attacks, panic, free-floating anxiety).

4. Panic disorder may occur with or without _____ (fear of public places, unfamiliar situations, or leaving the home).

5. Other anxiety disorders are _____ (fear of public places, _____ situations, or leaving the home) and specific phobia (irrational fears of specific objects or situations).

6. In the anxiety disorder called _____, the person fears being observed, _____, embarrassed, or humiliated by others in social situations.

7. _____ -compulsive disorders and _____ stress disorder (PTSD) or _____ stress disorder (emotional disturbances triggered by severe stress) are also classified as anxiety disorders.

8. Dissociative disorders may take the form of dissociative_____ (loss of memory and personal identity) or dissociative _____ (confused identity and flight from familiar surroundings).

9. A more dramatic problem is dissociative_____, in which a person develops multiple personalities.

10. _____ disorders center on physical complaints that mimic disease or disability.

11. In _____ , persons think that they have specific diseases, when they are, in fact healthy.

12. In a _____ disorder, the person has numerous physical complaints. The person repeatedly seeks medical treatment for these complaints, but no organic problems can be found.

13. _____refers to discomfort for which there is no identifiable physical cause.

14. In _____ disorders, actual symptoms of disease or disability develop but their causes are really psychological.

# Anxiety and Disorder—Four Pathways to Trouble
How do psychologists explain anxiety-based disorders?

1. The _____ approach emphasizes unconscious conflicts within the personality as the cause of disabling anxiety.

2. The_____ approach emphasizes the effects of a faulty self-image.

3.  The _____ approach emphasizes the effects of previous learning, particularly_____ learning.

4.  Some patterns in anxiety disorders can be explained by the anxiety _____ hypothesis, which states that immediate relief from anxiety rewards _____ behaviors.

5.  According to the _____ view, distorted thinking patterns cause anxiety disorders.

# Personality Disorders—Blueprints for Maladjustment
## What is a personality disorder?

1.  People with _____ personality disorder tend to react to ordinary criticisms by feeling rejected and abandoned, which then causes them to respond with anger, self-hatred, and_____.

2.  Personality disorders are deeply _____ maladaptive personality patterns.

3.  The personality disorders are: antisocial, avoidant, borderline, _____ , histrionic, narcissistic, obsessive-compulsive, _____, schizoid, and _____ .

4.  _____ persons (sociopaths) seem to lack a conscience. They are emotionally shallow and_____ .

5.  Possible causes attributed to people with _____ personality disorder include_____ deprivation, neglect, physical abuse as_____, and boredom due to receiving little stimulation from the environment.

6.  People with _____ disorder are plagued with images or thoughts that they cannot force out of awareness. To reduce _____ caused by these constant occurring images and thoughts, they are compelled to repeat irrational acts.

# Disorders in Perspective—Psychiatric Labeling

1.  Factors that influence the development of _____ include being a woman, Latina, not being married, having limited education, high levels of stress, and feelings of_____.

2.  David Rosenhan demonstrated the damaging effects of _____ a person with a disorder in our society. They are _____, denied jobs and housing, and accused of crimes that they did not commit.

3. Treatments for psychological disorders range from hospitalization and _____ to drug therapy.

   Individuals diagnosed with a major disorder do respond well to _____ and psychotherapy while

   individuals diagnosed with _____ mental disorders can be treated successfully.

## Psychology in Action: Suicide—Lives on the Brink
Why do people commit suicide? Can suicide be prevented?

1. Suicide is _____ related to such factors as age, sex, and marital status.

2. Major _____ for suicide include alcohol or drug abuse, a prior attempt,

   depression, hopelessness, _____ behavior, suicide by relatives, shame, failure, or rejection,

   and the availability of a firearm.

3. In individual cases the potential for suicide is best identified by a desire to escape, unbearable

   psychological _____ , _____ psychological needs, and a constriction of options.

4. Suicidal thoughts usually precede suicide _____ , which progress to suicide _____.

5. Suicide can often be prevented by the efforts of family, friends, and mental health professionals

   to establish communication and _____ with the person, and by gaining day-by-day

   _____ from her or him.

# MASTERY TEST

1. The difference between an acute stress disorder and PTSD is
   a. how long the disturbance lasts.
   b. the severity of the stress.
   c. whether the anxiety is free-floating.
   d. whether dissociative behavior is observed.

2. A person is at greatest risk of becoming schizophrenic if he or she has
   a. schizophrenic parents.
   b. a schizophrenic fraternal twin.
   c. a schizophrenic mother.
   d. a schizophrenic sibling.

3. A core feature of all abnormal behavior is that it is
   a. statistically extreme.
   b. associated with subjective discomfort.
   c. ultimately maladaptive.
   d. marked by a loss of contact with reality.

4. Excess amounts of dopamine in the brain, or high sensitivity to dopamine provides one major explanation for the problem known as
   a. PTSD.
   b. schizophrenia.
   c. major depression.
   d. SAD.

5. The descriptions "aero," "claustro," and "pyro" refer to
   a. common obsessions.
   b. specific phobias.
   c. free-floating anxieties.
   d. hypochondriasis.

6. Glove anesthesia strongly implies the existence of a(n) _____ disorder.
   a. organic
   b. depersonalization
   c. somatization
   d. conversion

7. In the stress-vulnerability model of psychosis, vulnerability is primarily attributed to
   a. heredity.
   b. exposure to influenza.
   c. psychological trauma.
   d. disturbed family life.

8. A patient believes that she has a mysterious disease that is causing her body to "rot away." What type of symptom is she suffering from?
   a. bipolar
   b. delusion
   c. neurosis
   d. cyclothymic

9. Phototherapy is used primarily to treat
   a. postseasonal depression.
   b. SAD.
   c. catatonic depression.
   d. affective psychoses.

10. Psychopathology is defined as an inability to behave in ways that
    a. foster personal growth and happiness.
    b. match social norms.
    c. lead to personal achievement.
    d. do not cause anxiety.

11. Which of the following is NOT characteristic of suicidal thinking?
    a. desires to escape
    b. psychological pain
    c. frustrated needs
    d. too many options

12. Fear of using the rest room in public is
    a. a social phobia.
    b. an acute stress disorder.
    c. a panic disorder.
    d. an adjustment disorder.

13. A person who displays personality disintegration, waxy flexibility, and delusions of persecution suffers from _____ schizophrenia.
    a. disorganized
    b. catatonic
    c. paranoid
    d. undifferentiated

14. You find yourself in an unfamiliar town and you can't remember your name or address. It is likely that you are suffering from
    a. paraphilia.
    b. Alzheimer's disease.
    c. a borderline personality disorder.
    d. a dissociative disorder.

15. A major problem with statistical definitions of abnormality is
    a. calculating the normal curve.
    b. choosing dividing lines.
    c. that they do not apply to groups of people.
    d. that they do not take norms into account.

16. DSM-IV-TR primarily describes and classifies _____ disorders.
    a. mental
    b. organic
    c. psychotic
    d. cognitive

17. A person who is a frequent "checker" may have which disorder?
    a. agoraphobia
    b. somatization
    c. free-floating fugue
    d. obsessive-compulsive

18. The most direct explanation for the anxiety reducing properties of self-defeating behavior is found in
    a. an overwhelmed ego.
    b. avoidance learning.
    c. the loss of meaning in one's life.
    d. the concept of existential anxiety.

19. A person with a(n) _____ personality disorder might be described as "charming" by people who don't know the person well.
    a. avoidant
    b. schizoid
    c. antisocial
    d. dependent

20. One of the most powerful situational contexts for judging the normality of behavior is
    a. culture.
    b. gender.
    c. statistical norms.
    d. private discomfort.

21. A person who is manic most likely suffers from a(n) _____ disorder.
    a. anxiety
    b. somatoform
    c. organic
    d. mood

22. The principal problem in paranoid psychosis is
    a. delusions.
    b. hallucinations.
    c. disturbed emotions.
    d. personality disintegration.

23. A problem that may occur with or without agoraphobia is
    a. dissociative disorder.
    b. somatoform disorder.
    c. panic disorder.
    d. obsessive-compulsive disorder.

24. Hearing voices that do not exist is an almost sure sign of a _____ disorder.
    a. psychotic
    b. dissociative
    c. personality
    d. delusional

25. A conversion reaction is a type of _____ disorder.
    a. somatoform
    b. dissociative
    c. obsessive-compulsive
    d. postpartum

26. The existence, in the past, of "disorders" such as "drapetomania" and "nymphomania" suggests that judging normality is greatly affected by
    a. gender.
    b. cultural disapproval.
    c. levels of functioning.
    d. subjective discomfort.

27. Which of the following terms does NOT belong with the others?
    a. neurosis
    b. somatoform disorder
    c. personality disorder
    d. dissociative disorder

28. Threats to one's self-image are a key element in the _____ approach to understanding anxiety and disordered functioning.
    a. Freudian
    b. humanistic
    c. existential
    d. behavioral

29. Which of the following is NOT classified as an anxiety disorder?
    a. adjustment disorder
    b. panic disorder
    c. agoraphobia
    d. obsessive-compulsive disorder

30. Cyclothymic disorder is most closely related to
    a. neurotic depression.
    b. major depressive disorder.
    c. bipolar disorder.
    d. SAD.

31. Pretending to possess a delusional disorder (schizophrenia) by walking around campus on a sunny day with a raincoat on and holding an open umbrella over one's head and, when inside, continuing to hold the open umbrella over one's head is a way to
    a. understand how social norms define normality.
    b. determine how normality is defined.
    c. test cultural relativism.
    d. all the preceding

32. A person who is sometimes friendly, charming, impulsive, moody, extremely sensitive to ordinary criticisms, and suicidal has the _____ personality disorder.
    a. dependent
    b. borderline
    c. dissociative
    d. narcissistic

33. A person who is "blind" to signs that would disgust others, charming, lacks a conscience, and feels no guilt, shame, fear, loyalty, or love has the _____ personality disorder.
    a. histrionic
    b. schizoid
    c. avoidant
    d. antisocial

34. Which of the following is NOT a type of delusion?
    a. avoidant
    b. depressive
    c. reference
    d. influence

35. Which of the following statements is true of delusional disorders?
    a. The disorders are common and easily treated
    b. The main feature is a deeply held false belief
    c. Symptoms include perceiving sensations that do not exist (e.g., seeing insects crawling under their skin)
    d. The disorder is genetically linked

36. Which of the following is NOT a cause of schizophrenia?
    a. Malnutrition during pregnancy and exposure to influenza
    b. Females are more vulnerable to developing schizophrenic disorder
    c. Psychological trauma during childhood increases the risk
    d. Sensitivity to neurotransmitters dopamine and glutamate

37. Knowing that Lloyd is suffering from bipolar disorder and currently is undergoing treatment, Joan assumes that he will relapse sooner or later and, therefore, refuses to hire him as a delivery person. Joan's reaction and response to Lloyd's application reflects the impact of
    a. labeling a person with a disorder rather than the problem.
    b. prejudice and discrimination.
    c. stigmatism.
    d. all the preceding

# SOLUTIONS

## RECITE AND REVIEW

### Normality—What's Normal?: Pages 460-462
How is abnormality defined?

1. disorders; unhealthy
2. discomfort
3. high; low
4. standards
5. cultural
6. All
7. behavior; adapt
8. mental
9. legal; court

### Classifying Mental Disorders—Problems by the Book: Pages 463-467
What are the major psychological disorders?

1. *Manual; Mental*
2. reality; social
3. brain; diseases
4. mood; drugs
5. emotion
6. anxiety; anxiety
7. disease; cause
8. personality
9. personality
10. gender; sexual
11. anxiety
12. culture; Ghost; Kori

### Psychotic Disorders—The Dark Side of the Moon: Pages 467-469
What are the general characteristics of psychotic disorders?

1. break
2. somatic; influence
3. hallucinations
4. personality
5. diseases
6. organic; brain
7. dementia

### Delusional Disorders—An Enemy Behind Every Tree: Page 470
What are the general characteristics of psychotic disorder?

1. delusions
2. persecution; romantic
3. persecution

### Schizophrenia—Shattered Reality: Pages 470-476
What forms does schizophrenia take? What causes it?

1. split; thought
2. personality; Social
3. mutism; waxy
4. persecution
5. lack
6. stress; abnormalities
7. infection; birth
8. trauma; family
9. twins
10. transmitter
11. stress; abnormalities
12. PCP; glutamate
13. activity; neurogenesis
14. stress

## Mood Disorders—Peaks and Valleys: Pages 476-480

What are mood disorders? What causes depression?

1. emotion
2. depression
3. depression; elation
4. depression
5. depressed; mania
6. mania
7. within; external
8. maternity blues
9. Seasonal; winter
10. behavioral

## Anxiety-Based Disorders—When Anxiety Rules: Pages 480-486

What problems result when a person suffers high levels of anxiety?

1. life stresses
2. anxiety; floating
3. public; home
4. specific
5. observed; social
6. stress; anxiety
7. memory; dissociative
8. multiple
9. disease
10. healthy
11. physical; treatment
12. physical
13. psychological
14. anxiety; defense

## Anxiety and Disorder—Four Pathways to Trouble: Pages 486-487

How do psychologists explain anxiety-based disorders?

1. unconscious
2. self-image
3. learning; learning
4. anxiety; relief
5. thinking

## Personality Disorders—Blueprints for Maladjustment: Pages 487-489

What is a personality disorder?

1. personality; abandoned; impulsiveness
2. maladaptive
3. borderline; compulsive,
4 conscience; emotionally
5. personality; physical
6. obsessive; awareness; repeat

## Disorders in Perspective—Psychiatric Labeling: Pages 489-490

1. Latina; education; stress
2. labeling; denied; crimes
3. psychotherapy; milder

## Psychology in Action: Suicide—Lives on the Brink: Pages 490-493

Why do people commit suicide? Can suicide be prevented?

1. Suicide
2. alcohol; drug; firearm
3. escape; options
4. thoughts
5. communication

# CONNECTIONS

## Normality—What's Normal?: Pages 460-467
How is abnormality defined? What are the major psychological disorders?

1. f
2. a
3. i

4. b
5. c
6. h

7. d
8. e
9. g

## Psychotic Disorders—The Dark Side of the Moon: Pages 467-469
What are the general characteristics of psychotic disorders?

1. a
2. i
3. b

4. h
5. f
6. c

7. g
8. e
9. d

## Schizophrenia—Shattered Reality: Pages 470-476
What forms does schizophrenia take? What causes it?

1. b
2. h
3. a

4. e
5. g
6. d

7. f
8. c

## Anxiety-Based Disorders—When Anxiety Rules and Anxiety and Disorder—Four Pathways to Trouble: Pages 480-487
What problems result when a person suffers high levels of anxiety? How do psychologists explain anxiety-based disorders?

1. h
2. e
3. k
4. n
5. i

6. g
7. a
8. j
9. b
10. m

11. d
12. f
13. c
14. l

## Personality Disorders—Blueprints for Maladjustment: Pages 487-489
What is a personality disorder?

1. c
2. e
3. a
4. j

5. b
6. d
7. i
8. f

9. h
10. g

## Mood Disorders—Peaks and Valleys and Psychology in Action: Suicide—Lives on the Brink: Pages 476-480, 490-493

What are mood disorders? What causes depression? Why do people commit suicide? Can suicide be prevented?

| | | |
|---|---|---|
| 1. c | 4. a | 7. g |
| 2. h | 5. f | 8. e |
| 3. b | 6. d | 9. i |

# CHECK YOUR MEMORY

## Normality—What's Normal?: Pages 460-467

How is abnormality defined? What are the major psychological disorders?

| | | |
|---|---|---|
| 1. T | 6. T | 11. F |
| 2. F | 7. F | 12. T |
| 3. T | 8. T | 13. F |
| 4. T | 9. T | 14. T |
| 5. F | 10. T | 15. F |

## Psychotic Disorders—The Dark Side of the Moon: Pages 467-469

What are the general characteristics of psychotic disorders?

| | | |
|---|---|---|
| 1. F | 4. T | 7. F |
| 2. F | 5. T | |
| 3. T | 6. F | |

## Delusional Disorders—An Enemy Behind Every Tree: Page 470

What are the general characteristics of psychotic disorder?

| | |
|---|---|
| 1. F | 3. F |
| 2. T | 4. F |

## Schizophrenia—Shattered Reality: Pages 470-476

What forms does schizophrenia take? What causes it?

| | | |
|---|---|---|
| 1. T | 6. T | 11. T |
| 2. F | 7. T | 12. F |
| 3. T | 8. T | 13. T |
| 4. T | 9. F | |
| 5. F | 10. T | |

## Mood Disorders—Peaks and Valleys: Pages 476-480
What are mood disorders? What causes depression?

| | | | | | | |
|---|---|---|---|---|---|---|
| 1. | F | 5. | T | 9. | F | |
| 2. | T | 6. | T | 10. | T | |
| 3. | F | 7. | T | 11. | F | |
| 4. | T | 8. | T | 12. | T | |

## Anxiety-Based Disorders—When Anxiety Rules: Pages 480-486
What problems result when a person suffers high levels of anxiety?

| | | | | | | |
|---|---|---|---|---|---|---|
| 1. | T | 5. | T | 9. | F | |
| 2. | F | 6. | T | 10. | F | |
| 3. | F | 7. | T | 11. | T | |
| 4. | F | 8. | T | 12. | T | |

## Anxiety and Disorder—Four Pathways to Trouble: Pages 486-487
How do psychologists explain anxiety-based disorders?

| | | | | | | |
|---|---|---|---|---|---|---|
| 1. | T | 3. | F | 5. | F | |
| 2. | T | 4. | T | | | |

## Personality Disorders—Blueprints for Maladjustment: Pages 487-489
What is a personality disorder?

| | | | | | | |
|---|---|---|---|---|---|---|
| 1. | F | 4. | T | 7. | F | |
| 2. | F | 5. | F | 8. | F | |
| 3. | F | 6. | T | | | |

## Disorders in Perspective—Psychiatric Labeling: Pages 489-490

| | | | | |
|---|---|---|---|---|
| 1. | F | 2. | F | |

## Psychology in Action: Suicide—Lives on the Brink: Pages 490-493
Why do people commit suicide? Can suicide be prevented?

| | | | | | | |
|---|---|---|---|---|---|---|
| 1. | T | 4. | T | 7. | T | |
| 2. | T | 5. | F | 8. | T | |
| 3. | F | 6. | T | | | |

# FINAL SURVEY AND REVIEW

## Normality—What's Normal?
How is abnormality defined?

| | | | | | |
|---|---|---|---|---|---|
| 1. | Psychopathology | 4. | Social nonconformity | 7. | maladaptive |
| 2. | subjective | 5. | context | 8. | psychological |
| 3. | Statistical | 6. | relative | 9. | Insanity |

## Classifying Mental Disorders—Problems by the Book
What are the major psychological disorders?

1. *Diagnostic; Statistical*
2.
3. Psychotic; hallucinations
4. Organic
5. Substance related
6. Mood; affect

6. Anxiety
7. Somatoform
8. Dissociative; amnesia
9. Personality
10. identity; dysfunctions

11. neurosis
12. Ghost sickness; East Asians

## Psychotic Disorders—The Dark Side of the Moon
What are the general characteristics of psychotic disorders?

1. Psychosis; reality
2. delusions
3. delusions; sensory

4. communication; disintegration
5. organic
6. dementia

7. Alzheimer's

## Delusional Disorders—An Enemy Behind Every Tree
What are the general characteristics of psychotic disorder?

1. diagnosis; delusional

2. grandeur; disease

3. paranoid; violent

## Schizophrenia—Shattered Reality
What forms does schizophrenia take? What causes it?

1. emotion; communication
2. Disorganized; disintegration
3. Catatonic; flexibility
4. paranoid; grandeur
5. Undifferentiated
6. environmental; biochemical

7. environmental
8. psychological; deviant
9. heredity
10. dopamine; receptor
11. environmental; biochemical
12. schizophrenic; hallucinogenic

13. CT; MRI ; PET
14. vulnerability

## Mood Disorders—Peaks and Valleys
What are mood disorders? What causes depression?

1. mood
2. dysthymic
3. cyclothymic
4. bipolar I; mania

5. bipolar II; hypomania
6. major; depressive
7. Postpartum

8. endogenous
9. affective; phototherapy
10. Biological; cognitive

## Anxiety-Based Disorders—When Anxiety Rules
What problems result when a person suffers high levels of anxiety?

1. dissociative; somatoform
2. breakdown; adjustment
3. generalized; panic
4. agoraphobia

7. Obsessive; posttraumatic; acute
8. amnesia; fugue
9. identity; disorder
10. Somatoform

13. Somatoform; pain
14. conversion

498

5.  agoraphobia; objects or
6.  social; phobia; evaluated

11. hypochondriasis
12. somatization

## Anxiety and Disorder—Four Pathways to Trouble
How do psychologists explain anxiety-based disorders?

1.  psychodynamic
2.  humanistic

3.  behavioral; avoidance
4.  reduction; self-defeating

5.  cognitive

## Personality Disorders—Blueprints for Maladjustment
What is a personality disorder?

1.  borderline; impulsiveness children
2.  ingrained anxiety

3.  dependent; paranoid; schizotypal
4.  Antisocial; manipulative

5.  antisocial; emotional;
6.  obsessive-compulsive;

## Disorders in Perspective—Psychiatric Labeling

1.  depression; hopelessness
2.  labeling; stigmatized

3.  psychotherapy; drugs; milder

## Psychology in Action: Suicide—Lives on the Brink
Why do people commit suicide? Can suicide be prevented?

1.  statistically
2.  risk; factors; antisocial

3.  pain; frustrated
4.  threats; attempts

5.  rapport; commitments

# MASTERY TEST

1.  a, p. 481
2.  a, p. 474
3.  c, p. 462
4.  b, p. 474
5.  b, p. 482
6.  d, p. 485
7.  a, p. 476
8.  b, p. 468
9.  b, p. 479
10. a, p. 460
11. d, p. 492
12. a, p. 481
13. d, p. 471
14. d, p. 484

15. b, p. 460
16. a, p. 463
17. d, p. 482
18. b, p. 486
19. c, p. 488
20. a, p. 461
21. d, p. 477
22. a, p. 470
23. c, p. 481
24. a, p. 467
25. a, p. 484
26. b, p. 489
27. a, p. 466
28. b, p. 486

29. a, p. 481
30. c, p. 477
31. d, p. 461
32. b, p. 487
33. d, p. 487
34. a, p. 468
35. b, p. 468
36. b, p. 472
37. d. p. 489

# Therapies

## Chapter Overview

Psychotherapies may be classified as individual, group, insight, action, directive, nondirective, time-limited, positive, or supportive, and combinations of these. Primitive and superstitious approaches to mental illness have included trepanning and demonology. More humane treatment began in 1793 with the work of Philippe Pinel in Paris.

Freudian psychoanalysis seeks to release repressed thoughts and emotions from the unconscious. Brief psychodynamic therapy, such as interpersonal therapy (IPT), has largely replaced traditional psychoanalysis.

Client-centered (or person-centered) therapy is a nondirective humanistic technique dedicated to creating an atmosphere of growth. Existential therapies focus on the meaning of life choices. Gestalt therapy attempts to rebuild thinking, feeling, and acting into connected wholes.

Psychological therapies offered at a distance, including media, telephone, and internet counseling, has becomes increasingly common. Limited research is available regarding such therapy has been performed, and the value of such services remains questionable.

Behavior therapists use behavior modification techniques such as aversion therapy, systematic desensitization, operant shaping, extinction, and token economies. The tension-release method teaches people to recognize tensed muscles and learn to relax them. Of the various behavioral techniques, desensitization has been the most successful form of treatment to reduce fears, anxiety, and psychological pain.

Cognitive therapists attempt to change troublesome thought patterns. Major distortions in thinking include selective perception, overgeneralization, and all-or-nothing thinking. In rational-emotive behavior therapy, clients learn to recognize and challenge their own irrational beliefs.

Group therapies, such as psychodrama and family therapy, may be based on individual therapy methods or special group techniques. Sensitivity groups, encounter groups, and large-group awareness trainings also try to promote constructive changes.

All psychotherapies offer a caring relationship, emotional rapport, a protected setting, catharsis, explanations for one's problems, a new perspective, and a chance to practice new behaviors. Many basic counseling skills underlie the success of therapies. Successful therapists also include clients' cultural beliefs and traditions. Research has found that behavioral, cognitive-behavioral, and drug therapies are the most effective methods for treating obsessive-compulsive disorders. Because of the high cost of mental health services, future therapy may include short-term therapy; solution-focused; problem-solving approaches; master's-level practitioners; Internet services; telephone counseling; and self-help groups.

Four medical approaches to the treatment of psychological disorders are pharmacotherapy, electroconvulsive therapy, implanted electrodes, and psychosurgery. When using drugs as a form of treatment, patients must be aware of the trade-offs between the benefits and risks of drug use. Electroconvulsive Therapy (ECT) may be used with drug therapy to treat depression. When other therapeutic techniques are not effective at reducing mental illness symptoms, deep lesioning may be considered.

Mental hospitalization can serve as a treatment for psychological disorders. Prolonged hospitalization has been discouraged by deinstitutionalization and by partial-hospitalization policies. Community mental health centers attempt to prevent mental health problems before they become serious.

Cognitive and behavioral techniques such as covert sensitization, thought stopping, covert reinforcement, and desensitization can aid self-management. In most communities, competent therapists can be located through public sources or by referrals.

# Learning Objectives

**Theme: Psychotherapies are based on a common core of therapeutic principles. Medical therapies treat the physical causes of psychological disorders. In many cases, these approaches are complementary.**

| |
|---|
| **GQ: How do psychotherapies differ?** |
| LO 15.1  Define *psychotherapy*; describe each of the following aspects of therapy: a. individual therapy; b. group therapy; c. insight therapy; d. action therapy; e. directive therapy; f. non-directive therapy; g. time-limited therapy; and h. supportive therapy; and discuss what a person can expect as possible outcomes from psychotherapy. |
| **GQ: How did psychotherapy originate?** |
| LO 15.2  Briefly describe the history of the treatment of psychological problems, including trepanning, demonology, exorcism, ergotism, and the work of Pinel. |
| **GQ: Is Freudian psychoanalysis still used?** |
| LO 15.3  Discuss the development of psychoanalysis and its four basic techniques; name and describe the therapy that is frequently used today instead of psychoanalysis; and describe the criticism that helped prompt the switch, including the concept of spontaneous remission. |
| **GQ: What are the major humanistic therapies?** |
| LO 15.4  Discuss the following humanistic approaches to therapy: a. client-centered therapy; b. existential therapy; and c. Gestalt therapy. Contrast the humanistic approaches to psychoanalysis; and compare the three humanistic approaches to each other. |
| **GQ: Can therapy be conducted at a distance?** |
| LO 15.5  Discuss the advantages and disadvantages of telephone therapy, cybertherapy, and videoconferencing therapy; and describe what the APA recommends should be the extent of their activities. |
| **GQ: What is behavior therapy?** |
| LO 15.6  Contrast the goal of behavior therapy with the goal of insight therapies; define *behavior modification* and state its basic assumption. |
| LO 15.7  Explain the relationship of aversion therapy to classical conditioning; and describe how aversion therapy can be used to stop bad habits and maladaptive behaviors. |

| |
|---|
| LO 15.8  Explain how relaxation, reciprocal inhibition, and use of a hierarchy, are combined to produce systematic desensitization; and describe how desensitization therapy, vicarious desensitization therapy; virtual reality exposure; and eye movement desensitization (EMDR) are used to treat anxiety disorders, such as phobias and post-traumatic stress disorder. |
| **GQ: What role do operant principles play in behavior therapy?** |
| LO 15.9  List and briefly describe the seven operant principles most frequently used by behavior therapists; explain how nonreinforcement and time out can be used to bring about extinction of a maladaptive behavior; and describe a token economy. |
| **GQ: Can therapy change thoughts and emotions?** |
| LO 15.10  Explain what sets a cognitive therapist apart from other action therapists; describe three thinking errors which Beck said underlies depression and what can be done to correct such thinking; and discuss Ellis' rational-emotive behavior therapy and the three core ideas which serve as the basis of most irrational beliefs. |
| **GQ: Can psychotherapy be done with groups of people?** |
| LO 15.11  List the advantages of group therapy; briefly describe each of the following group therapies: a. psychodrama (include role-playing, role reversal, and mirror technique); b. family and couples therapy; and c. group awareness training (include sensitivity groups, encounter groups, and large group awareness training). Include the concept of the therapy placebo effect. |
| **GQ: What do various therapies have in common?** |
| LO 15.12  Discuss the effectiveness and strengths of each type of psychotherapy (see Table 15.2); describe the rate at which doses of therapy help people improve; and list the eight goals of psychotherapy and how they are accomplished. Include a description of a culturally-skilled therapist and the future of psychotherapy. |
| LO 15.13  List and briefly describe the nine points or tips which can help a person when counseling a friend. |
| **GQ: How do psychiatrists treat psychological disorders?** |
| LO 15.14  Describe the three types of somatic therapy, including the advantages and disadvantages of the therapy, its effects, and the types of disorders for which each is most useful: a. pharmacotherapy and the three major classes of drugs (see Table 17.4); b. electrical stimulation therapy (including ECT); and c. psychosurgery (including prefrontal lobotomy and deep lesioning techniques). |
| LO 15.15  Describe the role of hospitalization and partial hospitalization in the treatment of psychological disorders; explain what deinstitutionalization is and how halfway houses have attempted to help in the treatment of mental health; and discuss the roles of community mental health centers. |
| **GQ: How are behavioral principles applied to everyday problems? How could a person find professional help?** |
| LO 15.16  Describe how covert sensitization, thought stopping, and covert reinforcement can be used to reduce unwanted behavior. |
| LO 15.17  Give an example of how you can overcome a common fear or break a bad habit using the steps given for desensitization. |
| LO 15.18  List four indicators that may signal the need for professional psychological help and seven suggestions a person can use for finding a therapist (see Table 15.5); and describe how one can choose a psychotherapist, including the concepts of peer counselors and self-help groups. |
| LO 15.19  Summarize what is known about the importance of the personal qualities of the therapist and the client for successful therapy; and list six psychotherapy danger signals. |

# RECITE AND REVIEW

## Psychotherapy—The Talking Cure: Pages 496-497
How do psychotherapies differ?

1. Psychotherapy is any psychological technique used to facilitate _____ changes in a person's personality, _____ , or adjustment.

2. _____ therapies seek to produce personal understanding. Action therapies try to directly change troublesome thoughts, feelings, or behaviors.

3. Directive therapists provide strong_____. Nondirective therapists assist, but do not _____ their clients.

4. Supportive therapies provide on-going support, rather than actively promoting personal _____ .

5. Positive therapists seek to enhance_____ growth by nurturing _____ traits in individuals rather than trying to "fix" weakness.

6. Therapies may be conducted either individually or in groups, and they may be _____ limited (restricted to a set number of sessions).

## Origins of Therapy-Bored Out of Your Skull: Pages 497-498
How did psychotherapy originate?

1. Primitive approaches to mental illness were often based on _____ .

2. Trepanning involved boring a hole in the _____ .

3. Demonology attributed mental disturbance to supernatural forces and prescribed _____ as the cure. Many were suffering from _____, schizophrenia, dissociative disorders, or depression.

4. In some instances, the actual cause of bizarre behavior may have been ergotism or _____ fungus_____ .

5. More humane treatment began in 1793 with the work of Philippe Pinel who created the first _____ in Paris.

# Psychoanalysis—Expedition into the Unconscious: Pages 498-500

Is Freudian psychoanalysis still used?

1.  Sigmund Freud's psychoanalysis was the first formal _____ .

2.  Psychoanalysis was designed to treat cases of hysteria (physical symptoms without known _____ causes).

3.  Psychoanalysis seeks to release repressed thoughts, memories, and emotions from the _____ and resolve _____ conflicts.

4.  The psychoanalyst uses _____ association, _____ analysis, and analysis of resistance and transference to reveal health-producing insights.

5.  Freud believed that in order to uncover the individual's unconscious _____ and feelings, a psychoanalyst must conduct _____ analysis to discover the _____ content that is expressed through the manifest content of a person's dream.

6.  _____ psychodynamic therapy, such as _____ psychotherapy, (which relies on psychoanalytic theory but is brief and focused) is as effective as other major therapies.

7.  Some critics have argued that traditional psychoanalysis may frequently receive credit for _____ remissions of symptoms. However, psychoanalysis has been shown to be better than no treatment at all.

# Humanistic Therapies—Restoring Human Potential: Pages 500-502

What are the major humanistic therapies?

1.  _____ therapies try to help people live up to their potentials and to give tendencies for mental health to emerge.

2.  Carl Rogers' client-centered (or _____ -centered) therapy is nondirective and is dedicated to creating an atmosphere of _____ .

3.  In client-centered therapy, unconditional _____ regard, _____ (feeling what another is feeling), authenticity, and reflection are combined to give the client a chance to solve his or her own problems.

505

4. Existential therapies focus on the end result of the _____ one makes in life.

5. Clients in existential therapy are encouraged through confrontation and encounter to exercise free _____ , to take responsibility for their _____ , and to find _____ in their lives.

6. The goal of Gestalt therapy is to rebuild thinking, feeling, and acting into connected _____ and to help clients break through emotional blocks.

7. Frederick Perls' Gestalt therapy emphasizes immediate _____ of thoughts and feelings and discourages people from dwelling on what they ought to do.

## Therapy at a Distance—Psych Jockeys and Cybertherapy: Pages 502-503
Can therapy be conducted at a distance?

1. Media psychologists, such as those found on the radio, are supposed to restrict themselves to _____ listeners, rather than actually doing _____.

2. Telephone therapists and cybertherapists working on the _____ may or may not be competent. Even if they are, their effectiveness may be severely limited.

3. In an emerging approach called telehealth, _____ is being done at a distance, through the use of videoconferencing (two-way _____ links).

## Behavior Therapy—Healing by Learning: Pages 503-507
What is behavior therapy?

1. Behavior therapists use various behavior modification techniques that apply _____ principles to change human behavior.

2. Classical conditioning is a basic form of _____ in which existing reflex responses are _____ with new conditioned stimuli.

3. In aversion therapy, classical conditioning is used to associate maladaptive behavior with _____ or other aversive events in order to inhibit undesirable responses.

4. To be most effective, aversive _____ must be response-contingent (closely connected with responses).

5. In desensitization, gradual _____ and reciprocal inhibition break the link between fear and particular situations.

6. Classical conditioning also underlies_____ desensitization, a technique used to reduce fears, phobias, and anxieties.

7. Typical steps in desensitization are: Construct a fear hierarchy; learn to produce total _____; and perform items on the hierarchy (from least to most disturbing).

8. Desensitization may be carried out in real settings or it may be done by vividly _____ scenes from the fear hierarchy.

9. The tension-release method allows individuals, through practice, to _____ their bodies' tensed muscles and to learn to _____ them on command.

10. Desensitization is also effective when it is administered vicariously; that is, when clients watch _____ perform the feared responses.

11. In a newly developed technique, virtual _____ exposure is used to present _____ stimuli to patients undergoing desensitization.

12. Another new technique called eye-movement desensitization shows promise as a treatment for traumatic _____ and _____ disorders.

## Operant Therapies—All the World Is a Skinner Box?: Pages 508-509
What role do operant principles play in behavior therapy?

1. Behavior modification also makes use of operant principles, such as positive reinforcement, nonreinforcement, extinction, punishment, shaping, stimulus _____, and _____ out.

2. Nonreward can extinguish troublesome behaviors. Often this is done by simply identifying and eliminating _____ .

3. Time out is an extinction technique in which attention and approval are withheld following undesirable _____ .

4. Time out can also be done by _____ a person from the setting in which misbehavior occurs, so that it will not be reinforced.

507

5. Attention, approval, and concern are subtle _____ that are effective at _____ human behaviors.

6. To apply positive reinforcement and operant shaping, symbolic rewards known as tokens are often used. Tokens allow _____ reinforcement of selected target _____.

7. Full-scale use of _____ in an institutional setting produces a token economy.

8. Toward the end of a token economy program, patients are shifted to social rewards such as recognition and _____.

## Cognitive Therapy—Think Positive!: Pages 510-512
Can therapy change thoughts and emotions?

1. Cognitive therapy emphasizes changing _____ patterns that underlie emotional or behavioral problems.

2. Aaron Beck's cognitive therapy for depression corrects major distortions in thinking, including _____ perception, overgeneralization, and all-or-nothing _____.

3. The goals of cognitive therapy are to correct distorted thinking and/or teach improved coping _____.

4. In a variation of cognitive therapy called rational-emotive behavior therapy (REBT), clients learn to recognize and challenge their own irrational _____, which lead to upsetting consequences.

5. Some_____ beliefs that lead to conflicts are: I am worthless if I am not loved, I should be _____ competent, I should _____ on others who are stronger than I am, and it is easier for me to avoid difficulties than to face them.

## Group Therapy—People Who Need People: Pages 512-514
Can psychotherapy be done with groups of people?

1. Group therapy may be a simple extension of _____ methods or it may be based on techniques developed specifically for groups.

2. In psychodrama, individuals use _____ playing, _____ reversals, and the mirror technique to gain insight into incidents resembling their real-life problems.

3. In family therapy, the family group is treated as a _____ so that the entire _____ system is changed for the better.

4. Although they are not literally _____ , sensitivity groups and encounter groups attempt to encourage positive personality change.

5. In recent years, commercially offered large-group awareness _____ have become popular.

6. The therapeutic benefits of large-group techniques are questionable and may reflect nothing more than a _____ placebo effect.

# Psychotherapy—An Overview: Pages 514-517
## What do various therapies have in common?

1. After thirteen to eighteen therapy sessions, _____ percent of all patients showed an improvement, and after 6 months of therapy sessions, a majority of all patients improved.

2. To alleviate personal problems, all psychotherapies offer a caring relationship and _____ rapport in a protected _____ .

3. All therapies encourage catharsis and they provide explanations for the client's _____ .

4. In addition, psychotherapy provides a new perspective and a chance to practice new _____ .

5. Psychotherapy in the future may include short-term therapy, _____ -focused approaches, _____ -help groups, Internet services, _____ counseling, paraprofessional, and master's-level practitioners.

6. Many basic _____ skills are used in therapy. These include listening actively and helping to clarify the problem.

7. Effective therapists also focus on feelings and avoid giving unwanted _____ .

8. It helps to accept the person's perspective, to reflect thoughts and feelings, and to be patient during_____

9. In counseling it is important to use _____ questions when possible and to maintain confidentiality.

10. Therapists must establish rapport and include the patients' _____ beliefs and practices when treating them.

# Medical Therapies—Psychiatric Care: Pages 518-522

How do psychiatrists treat psychological disorders?

1. Four _____ (bodily) approaches to treatment of psychosis are pharmacotherapy (use of _____ ), electroconvulsive therapy (ECT) (brain shock for the treatment of depression), implanted electrodes, and psychosurgery (surgical alteration of the _____ ).

2. Pharmacotherapy is done with _____ tranquilizers (anti-anxiety drugs), antipsychotics (which reduce delusions and _____ ), and antidepressants ( _____ elevators).

3. All psychiatric drugs involve a trade-off between _____ and benefits.

4. ECT and _____ , especially prefrontal lobotomy, once received great acclaim for their effectiveness but recently have _____ support from professionals.

5. If psychosurgery is necessary, deep _____ , where a small targeted area in the brain is _____ , is the preferred alternative to a lobotomy.

6. _____ hospitalization is considered a form of treatment for mental disorders.

7. Prolonged hospitalization has been discouraged by deinstitutionalization (reduced use of commitment to treat mental disorders) and by _____ -hospitalization policies.

8. Half-way _____ within the community can help people make the transition from a hospital or institution to _____ living.

9. Community mental health centers were created to help avoid or minimize _____ .

10. Community mental health centers also have as their goal the prevention of mental health problems through education, consultation, and _____ intervention.

## Psychology in Action: Self-Management and Finding Professional Help: Pages 522-526

How are behavioral principles applied to everyday problems? How could a person find professional help?

1. In covert sensitization, aversive _____ are used to discourage unwanted behavior.

2. Thought stopping uses mild _____ to prevent upsetting thoughts.

3. Covert reinforcement is a way to encourage desired _____ by mental rehearsal.

4. Desensitization pairs _____ with a hierarchy of upsetting images in order to lessen fears.

5. In most communities, a competent and reputable therapist can usually be located through public sources of information or by a _____ .

6. Practical considerations such as _____ and qualifications enter into choosing a therapist. However, the therapist's personal characteristics are of equal importance.

7. Self-help _____ , made up of people who share similar problems, can sometimes add valuable support to professional treatment.

# CONNECTIONS

## Psychotherapy—The Talking Cure, Origins of Therapy—Bored Out of Your Skull, and Psychoanalysis—Expedition into the Unconscious: Pages 496-500

How do psychotherapies differ? How did psychotherapy originate? Is Freudian psychoanalysis still used?

| | | | |
|---|---|---|---|
| 1. _____ positive therapy | a. tainted rye |
| 2. _____ trepanning | b. old relationships |
| 3. _____ exorcism | c. hysteria |
| 4. _____ ergotism | d. waiting list control |
| 5. _____ Pinel | e. Bicêtre |
| 6. _____ free association | f. latent content |
| 7. _____ Freud | g. possession |
| 8. _____ dream analysis | h. enhanced personal strength |
| 9. _____ transference | i. release of evil spirits |
| 10. _____ spontaneous remission | j. saying anything on mind |

## Humanistic Therapies—Restoring Human Potential and Therapy at a Distance—Psych Jockeys and Cybertherapy: Pages 500-503

What are the major humanistic therapies? Can therapy be conducted at a distance?

| | | | |
|---|---|---|---|
| 1. _____ telephone therapy | a. reflection |
| 2. _____ authenticity | b. client centered |
| 3. _____ unconditional positive regards | c. no facades |
| 4. _____ rephrasing | d. being in the world |
| 5. _____ distance therapy | e. lack visual cues |
| 6. _____ existentialist | f. telehealth |
| 7. _____ Rogers | g. whole experiences |
| 8. _____ Gestalt therapy | h. unshakable personal acceptance |

## Behavior Therapy—Healing by Learning: Pages 503-507

What is behavior therapy?

| | | | |
|---|---|---|---|
| 1. _____ behavior modification | a. unlearned reaction |
| 2. _____ unconditional response | b. easing post-traumatic stress |
| 3. _____ virtual reality exposure | c. secondhand learning |
| 4. _____ vicarious desensitization | d. applied behavior analysis |
| 5. _____ desensitization | e. aversion therapy |
| 6. _____ EMDR | f. fear hierarchy |
| 7. _____ rapid smoking | g. computer-generated fear images |

## Operant Therapies—All the World Is a Skinner Box? And Cognitive Therapy—Think Positive!: Pages 508-512

What role do operant principles play in behavior therapy? Can therapy change thoughts and emotions?

| | | | |
|---|---|---|---|
| 1. _____ overgeneralization | a. operant extinction |
| 2. _____ cognitive therapy | b. token economy |
| 3. _____ time-out | c. Aaron Beck |
| 4. _____ REBT | d. thinking error |
| 5. _____ target behaviors | e. irrational beliefs |
| 6. _____ Gambler's fallacy | f. cognitive distortion |

## Group Therapy—People Who Need People, Psychotherapy—An Overview, and Medical Therapies—Psychiatric Care: Pages 512-522

Can psychotherapy be done with groups of people? What do various therapies have in common? How do psychiatrists treat psychological disorders?

| | | | |
|---|---|---|---|
| 1. _____ psychodrama | a. public education |
| 2. _____ family therapy | b. enhanced self-awareness |

512

| | | |
|---|---|---|
| 3. _____ | sensitivity group | c. emotional release |
| 4. _____ | encounter group | d. causes of memory loss |
| 5. _____ | media psychologist | e. prefrontal lobotomy |
| 6. _____ | therapeutic alliance | f. systems approach |
| 7. _____ | catharsis | g- drug therapy |
| 8. _____ | pharmacotherapy | h. role reversals |
| 9. _____ | ECT | i. caring relationship |
| 10. _____ | psychosurgery | j. intense interactions |

## Psychology in Action: Self-Management and Finding Professional Help: Pages 522-526

How are behavioral principles applied to everyday problems? How could a person find professional help?

| | | |
|---|---|---|
| 1. _____ | covert reinforcement | a. positive imagery |
| 2. _____ | unethical practices | b. shared problems |
| 3. _____ | qualified therapist | c. aversive imagery |
| 4. _____ | covert sensitization | d. therapist encourages dependency |
| 5. _____ | self-help group | e. American Psychiatrist Association |

# CHECK YOUR MEMORY

## Psychotherapy—The Talking Cure and Origins of Therapy—Bored Out of Your Skull: Pages 496-498

How do psychotherapies differ? How did psychotherapy originate?

1. A goal of positive therapy is to "fix" a person's weaknesses to enhance their personal strength.

   TRUE or FALSE

2. A particular psychotherapy could be both insight- and action-oriented.   TRUE or FALSE

3. With the help of psychotherapy, chances of improvement are fairly good for phobias and low self-esteem.

   TRUE or FALSE

4. Psychotherapy is sometimes used to encourage personal growth for people who are already functioning well.   TRUE or FALSE

5. Personal autonomy, a sense of identity, and feelings of personal worth are elements of mental health.

   TRUE or FALSE

6. Modern analysis of demonic possessions suggests that many patients were actually possessed by demons.   TRUE or FALSE

7. Exorcism sometimes took the form of physical torture.   TRUE or FALSE

8. Trepanning was the most common treatment for ergotism.   TRUE or FALSE

513

9. Pinel was the first person to successfully treat ergotism.   TRUE or FALSE

10. The problem Freud called hysteria is now called a somatoform disorder.   TRUE or FALSE

## Psychoanalysis—Expedition into the Unconscious: Pages 498-500

Is Freudian psychoanalysis still used?

1. During free association, patients try to remember the earliest events in their lives.
   TRUE or FALSE

2. Freud called transference "the royal road to the unconscious."   TRUE or FALSE

3. Using dream analysis, a therapist seeks to uncover the latent content or symbolic meaning of a person's dreams.   TRUE or FALSE

4. The manifest content of a dream is its surface or visible meaning.   TRUE or FALSE

5. In an analysis of resistance, the psychoanalyst tries to understand a client's resistance to forming satisfying relationships.   TRUE or FALSE

6. Therapists use direct interviewing as part of brief psychodynamic therapy.   TRUE or FALSE

7. If members of a waiting list control group improve at the same rate as people in therapy, it demonstrates that the therapy is effective.   TRUE or FALSE

## Humanistic Therapies—Restoring Human Potential: Pages 500-503

What are the major humanistic therapies? Can therapy be conducted at a distance?

1. Through client-centered therapy, Carl Rogers sought to explore unconscious thoughts and feelings.
   TRUE or FALSE

2. The client-centered therapist does not hesitate to react with shock, dismay, or disapproval to a client's inappropriate thoughts or feelings.   TRUE or FALSE

3. In a sense, the person-centered therapist acts as a psychological mirror for clients.   TRUE or FALSE

4. Existential therapy emphasizes our ability to freely make choices.   TRUE or FALSE

5. According to the existentialists, our choices must be courageous.   TRUE or FALSE

6. Existential therapy emphasizes the integration of fragmented experiences into connected wholes.
   TRUE or FALSE

7. Fritz Perls was an originator of telehealth.   TRUE or FALSE

8. Gestalt therapy may be done individually or in a group.   TRUE or FALSE

9.  Gestalt therapists urge clients to intellectualize their feelings.   TRUE or FALSE

10. The APA suggests that media psychologists should discuss only problems of a general nature.
    TRUE or FALSE

11. Under certain conditions, telephone therapy can be as successful as face-to-face therapy.
    TRUE or FALSE

12. The problem with doing therapy by videoconferencing is that facial expressions are not available to
    the therapist or the client.   TRUE or FALSE

# Behavior Therapy—Healing by Learning: Pages 503-507
What is behavior therapy?

1.  Behavior modification, or applied behavior analysis, uses classical and operant conditioning to
    directly alter human behavior.   TRUE or FALSE

2.  Aversion therapy is based primarily on operant conditioning.   TRUE or FALSE

3.  For many children, the sight of a hypodermic needle becomes a conditioned stimulus for fear
    because it is often followed by pain.   TRUE or FALSE

4.  Rapid smoking creates an aversion because people must hyperventilate to smoke at the prescribed
    rate.   TRUE or FALSE

5.  About one half of all people who quit smoking begin again.   TRUE or FALSE

6.  In aversion therapy for alcohol abuse, the delivery of shock must appear to be response-contingent
    to be most effective.   TRUE or FALSE

7.  Poor generalization of conditioned aversions to situations outside of therapy can be a problem.
    TRUE or FALSE

8.  During desensitization, the steps of a hierarchy are used to produce deep relaxation.   TRUE or FALSE

9.  Relaxation is the key ingredient of reciprocal inhibition.   TRUE or FALSE

10. Clients typically begin with the most disturbing item in a desensitization hierarchy.   TRUE or FALSE

11. Desensitization is most effective when people are directly exposed to feared stimuli.   TRUE or FALSE

12. The tension-release method is used to produce deep relaxation.   TRUE or FALSE

13. Live or filmed models are used in vicarious desensitization.   TRUE or FALSE

14. During eye-movement desensitization, clients concentrate on pleasant, calming
    images. TRUE or FALSE

## Operant Therapies—All the World Is a Skinner Box?: Pages 508-509

What role do operant principles play in behavior therapy?

1. Operant punishment is basically the same thing as nonreinforcement.   TRUE or FALSE

2. Shaping involves reinforcing ever closer approximations to a desired response.   TRUE or FALSE

3. An undesirable response can be extinguished by reversing stimulus control.   TRUE or FALSE

4. Misbehavior tends to decrease when others ignore it.   TRUE or FALSE

5. To be effective, tokens must be tangible rewards, such as slips of paper or poker chips.
   TRUE or FALSE

6. The value of tokens is based on the fact that they can be exchanged for other reinforcers.
   TRUE or FALSE

7. A goal of token economies is to eventually switch patients to social reinforcers.  TRUE or FALSE

## Cognitive Therapy—Think Positive!: Pages 510-512

Can therapy change thoughts and emotions?

1. Cognitive therapy is especially successful in treating depression.   TRUE or FALSE

2. Depressed persons tend to magnify the importance of events.   TRUE or FALSE

3. Cognitive therapy is as effective as drugs for treating many cases of depression.   TRUE or FALSE

4. Stress inoculation is a form of rational-emotive behavior therapy.   TRUE or FALSE

5. The A in the ABC analysis of REBT stands for "anticipation."   TRUE or FALSE

6. The C in the ABC analysis of REBT stands for "consequence."   TRUE or FALSE

7. According to REBT, you would hold an irrational belief if you believe that you should depend
   on others who are stronger than you.   TRUE or FALSE

8. Many problem gamblers suffer from cognitive distortions such as the gambler's fallacy and
   probability biases.  TRUE or FA:LSE

## Group Therapy—People Who Need People: Pages 512-514

Can psychotherapy be done with groups of people?

1. The mirror technique is the principal method used in family therapy.   TRUE or FALSE

2. Family therapists try to meet with the entire family unit during each session of therapy.

3. TRUE or FALSE

4. A "trust walk" is a typical sensitivity group exercise.   TRUE or FALSE

5. Sensitivity groups attempt to tear down defenses and false fronts.   TRUE or FALSE

6. Large-group awareness training has been known to create emotional crises where none existed before.
TRUE or FALSE

## Psychotherapy—An Overview: Pages 514-517
### What do various therapies have in common?

1. Half of all people who begin psychotherapy feel better after 13 to 18 sessions.   TRUE or FALSE

2. Emotional rapport is a key feature of the therapeutic alliance.   TRUE or FALSE

3. Therapy gives clients a chance to practice new behaviors.   TRUE or FALSE

4. An increase in short-term therapy, telephone counseling, and self-help groups in the future is likely the result of the high cost of mental health services.   TRUE or FALSE

5. Regarding the future of psychotherapy, experts predict that the use of psychoanalysis will increase.
TRUE or FALSE

6. Regarding the future of psychotherapy, experts predict that there will be an increase in the use of short-term therapy.   TRUE or FALSE

7. Competent counselors do not hesitate to criticize clients, place blame when it is deserved, and probe painful topics.   TRUE or FALSE

8. "Why don't you . . . Yes, but. . ." is a common game used to avoid taking responsibility in therapy.
TRUE or FALSE

9. Closed questions tend to be most helpful in counseling another person.   TRUE or FALSE

10. A necessary step toward becoming a culturally skilled therapist is to adopt the culture of your clients as your own.   TRUE or FALSE

## Medical Therapies—Psychiatric Care: Pages 518-522
### How do psychiatrists treat psychological disorders?

1. Major mental disorders are primarily treated with psychotherapy.   TRUE or FALSE

2. When used for long periods of time, major tranquilizers can cause a neurological disorder.
TRUE or FALSE

3. Two percent of all patients taking clozaril suffer from a serious blood disease.   TRUE or FALSE

4. ECT treatments are usually given in a series of 20 to 30 sessions, occurring once a day.
   TRUE or FALSE

5. ECT is most effective when used to treat depression.   TRUE or FALSE

6. To reduce a relapse, antidepressant drugs are recommended for patients with depression following
   ECT treatment.   TRUE or FALSE

7. The prefrontal lobotomy is the most commonly performed type of psychosurgery today.
   TRUE or FALSE

8. Psychosurgeries performed by deep lesioning can be reversed if necessary.   TRUE or FALSE

9. In the approach known as partial hospitalization, patients live at home.   TRUE or FALSE

10. Admitting a person to a mental institution is the first step to treating the disorder.   TRUE or FALSE

11. Deinstitutionalization increased the number of homeless persons living in many communities.
    TRUE or FALSE

12. Most half-way houses are located on the grounds of mental hospitals.   TRUE or FALSE

13. Crisis intervention is typically one of the services provided by community mental health centers.
    TRUE or FALSE

14. Most people prefer to seek help from a professional doctor over a paraprofessional because of their
    approachability.   TRUE or FALSE

## Psychology in Action: Self-Management and Finding Professional Help: Pages 522-526
How are behavioral principles applied to everyday problems? How could a person find professional help?

1. To do covert sensitization, you must first learn relaxation exercises.   TRUE or FALSE

2. Disgusting images are used in thought stopping.   TRUE or FALSE

3. Covert reinforcement should be visualized before performing steps in a fear hierarchy.
   TRUE or FALSE

4. Approximately 50 percent of all American households had someone who received mental health
   treatment.   TRUE or FALSE

5. Significant changes in your work, relationships, or use of drugs or alcohol can be signs that you
   should seek professional help.   TRUE or FALSE

6. Marital problems are the most common reason for seeing a mental health professional.
   TRUE or FALSE

7. For some problems, paraprofessional counselors and self-help groups are as effective as professional psychotherapy.   TRUE or FALSE

8. All major types of psychotherapy are about equally successful.   TRUE or FALSE

9. All therapists are equally qualified and successful at treating mental disorders.   TRUE or FALSE

# FINAL SURVEY AND REVIEW

## Psychotherapy—The Talking Cure
How do psychotherapies differ?

1. _____ is any psychological technique used to facilitate positive changes in a person's _____ , behavior, or adjustment.

2. Insight therapies seek to produce personal understanding._____ therapies try to directly change troublesome thoughts, feelings, or behaviors.

3. _____ therapists provide strong guidance. _____ therapists assist, but do not guide their clients.

4. _____ therapies provide on-going support, rather than actively promoting personal change.

5. _____ therapists seek to enhance personal growth by nurturing positive traits in individuals rather than trying to _____ weakness.

6. Therapies may be conducted either _____ or in groups, _____ they may be time limited (restricted to a set number of sessions).

## Origins of Therapy—Bored Out of Your Skull
How did psychotherapy originate?

1. _____ approaches to mental illness were often based on superstition.

2. _____ involved boring a hole in the skull.

3. _____ attributed mental disturbance to supernatural forces and prescribed exorcism as the cure. Many were suffering from epilepsy, _____ , dissociative disorders, or depression.

4. In some instances, the actual cause of bizarre behavior may have been _____ , a type of _____ poisoning.

5. More humane treatment began in 1793 with the work of Philippe _____ who created the first mental hospital in Paris.

# Psychoanalysis—Expedition into the Unconscious
Is Freudian psychoanalysis still used?

1. Sigmund _____ was the first formal psychotherapy.

2. Psychoanalysis was designed to treat cases of _____ (physical symptoms without known physical causes).

3. Psychoanalysis seeks to release _____ thoughts, memories, and emotions from the unconscious and resolve unconscious conflicts.

4. Freud believed that in order to uncover the individual's _____ desires and feelings, a psychoanalyst must conduct _____ analysis to discover the latent content of a person's dream.

5. The psychoanalyst uses free_____ , dream analysis, and analysis of _____ and transference to reveal health-producing insights.

6. Brief _____ therapy, such as interpersonal therapy, (which relies on _____ theory but is brief and focused) is as effective as other major therapies.

7. Some critics have argued that traditional psychoanalysis may frequently receive credit for spontaneous _____ of symptoms. However, psychoanalysis has been shown to be better than no treatment at all.

# Humanistic Therapies—Restoring Human Potential
What are the major humanistic therapies?

1. Humanistic therapies try to help people live up to their _____ and to give tendencies for mental health to emerge.

2. Carl _____ client-centered (or person-centered) therapy is _____ and is dedicated to creating an atmosphere of growth.

3. In client-centered therapy, _____ positive regard, empathy, authenticity, and _____ (restating thoughts and feelings) are combined to give the client a chance to solve his or her own problems.

4. _____ therapies focus on the end result of the choices one makes in life.

5. Clients in existential therapy are encouraged through _____ and _____ to exercise free will, to take responsibility for their choices, and to find meaning in their lives.

520

6. The goal of Perl's approach is to rebuild thinking, feeling, and acting into connected wholes and to help clients break through _____ _____.

7. Frederick Perls' _____ therapy emphasizes immediate awareness of thoughts and feelings and discourages people from dwelling on what they ought to do.

## Therapy at a Distance—Psych Jockeys and Cybertherapy
### Can therapy be conducted at a distance?

1. _____ psychologists, such as those found on the radio, are supposed to restrict themselves to educating listeners, rather than actually doing therapy.

2. Telephone therapists and _____ working on the Internet may or may not be competent. Even if they are, their effectiveness may be severely limited.

3. In an emerging approach called _____ , therapy is being done at a distance, through the use of _____ (two-way audio-video links).

## Behavior Therapy—Healing by Learning
### What is behavior therapy?

1. _____ therapists use various behavior _____ techniques that apply learning principles to change human behavior.

2. _____ conditioning is a basic form of learning in which existing _____ responses are associated with new conditioned stimuli.

3. In _____ therapy, classical conditioning is used to associate maladaptive behavior with pain or other aversive events in order to inhibit undesirable responses.

4. To be most effective, aversive stimuli must be _____ (closely connected with responses).

5. In desensitization, gradual adaptation and reciprocal _____ break the link between fear and particular situations.

6. Classical conditioning also underlies systematic _____ , a technique used to reduce fears, phobias, and anxieties.

7. Typical steps in desensitization are: Construct a fear_____ ; learn to produce total relaxation; and perform items on the _____ (from least to most disturbing).

521

8. Desensitization may be carried out in real settings or it may be done by vividly imagining scenes from the _____ _____ .

9. The _____-release method allows individuals, through practice, to recognize their bodies' Tensed _____ and to learn to relax them on command.

10. Desensitization is also effective when it is administered _____ ; that is, when clients watch models perform the feared responses.

11. In a newly developed technique, _____ reality _____ is used to present fear stimuli to patients undergoing desensitization.

12. Another new technique called _____ desensitization shows promise as a treatment for traumatic memories and stress disorders.

## Operant Therapies—All the World is a Skinner Box?
What role do operant principles play in behavior therapy?

1. Behavior modification also makes use of _____ principles, such as positive reinforcement, nonreinforcement, _____ (eliminating responses), _____ (molding responses), shaping, stimulus control, and time out.

2. _____ can extinguish troublesome behaviors. Often this is done by simply identifying and eliminating reinforcers.

3. Time out is an _____ technique in which attention and approval are withheld following undesirable responses.

4. Time out can also be done by removing a person from the _____ in which misbehavior occurs, so that it will not be _____ .

5. Attention, approval, and concern are subtle _____ that are effective at maintaining human

6. To apply positive reinforcement and operant shaping, symbolic rewards known as _____ are often used. Tokens allow immediate reinforcement of selected _____ behaviors.

7. Full-scale use of tokens in an institutional setting produces a _____ .

8. Toward the end of a token economy program, patients are shifted to _____ rewards such as recognition and approval.

# Cognitive Therapy—Think Positive!
## Can therapy change thoughts and emotions?

1. _____ therapy emphasizes changing thinking patterns that underlie emotional or behavioral problems.

2. Aaron _____ therapy for depression corrects major distortions in thinking, including selective perception, _____ , and all-or-nothing thinking.

3. The goals of cognitive therapy are to correct distorted thinking and/or teach improved _____ skills.

4. In a variation called _____ therapy (REBT), clients learn to recognize and challenge their own irrational beliefs, which lead to upsetting consequences.

5. Some irrational _____ that lead to conflicts are: I am _____ if I am not loved, I should be completely competent, I should _____ on others who are stronger than I am, and it is easier for me to avoid difficulties than to face them.

# Group Therapy—People Who Need People
## Can psychotherapy be done with groups of people?

1. _____ therapy may be a simple extension of individual methods or it may be based on techniques developed specifically for _____.

2. In _____ , individuals use role playing, role _____ , and the mirror technique to gain insight into incidents resembling their real-life problems.

3. In _____ therapy, the _____ group is treated as a unit so that the entire family system is changed for the better.

4. Although they are not literally psychotherapies, sensitivity groups and _____ groups attempt to encourage positive personality change.

5. In recent years, commercially offered large-group _____ trainings have become popular.

6. The therapeutic benefits of large-group techniques are questionable and may reflect nothing more than a therapy _____ effect.

# Psychotherapy—An Overview
What do various therapies have in common?

1.  After _____ therapy sessions, _____ percent of all patients showed an improvement, and after 6 months of therapy sessions, a majority of all patients improved.

2.  To alleviate personal problems, all psychotherapies offer a caring relationship and emotional _____ in a _____ setting.

3.  All therapies encourage _____ (emotional release) and they provide explanations for the client's problems.

4.  In addition, psychotherapy provides a new _____ and a chance to practice new behaviors.

5.  _____ in the future may include _____-term therapy, solution-focused approaches, self-help groups, _____ services, telephone counseling, paraprofessional, and _____ -level practitioners.

6.  _____ Many basic counseling skills are used in therapy. These include listening _____ and helping to _____ the problem.

7.  Effective therapists also focus on _____ and avoid giving unwanted advice.

8.  It helps to accept the person's_____ , to _____ thoughts and feelings, and to be patient during silences.

9.  In counseling it is important to use open questions when possible and to maintain _____ .

10. Therapists must establish rapport and include their patients' _____ beliefs and traditional practices when treating them.

# Medical Therapies—Psychiatric Care
How do psychiatrists treat psychological disorders?

1.  Four somatic approaches to treatment of psychosis are _____ (use of drugs), _____ therapy (ECT), implanted electrodes, and psychosurgery.

2.  Pharmacotherapy is done with minor tranquilizers (anti-anxiety drugs), _____ (which reduce delusions and hallucinations), and _____ (mood elevators).

3. All psychiatric drugs involve a trade-off between risks and _____ .

4. _____ therapy (ECT) and psychosurgery, especially prefrontal lobotomy, once received great acclaim for their _____ but recently have lost support from professionals.

5. If psychosurgery is necessary, _____ , where a small targeted area in the brain is destroyed, is the preferred alternative to a lobotomy.

6. _____ hospitalization is considered a form of treatment for mental_____ .

7. Prolonged hospitalization has been discouraged by _____ (reduced use of commitment to treat mental disorders) and by partial-hospitalization policies.

8. _____ houses within the community can help people make the transition from a hospital or institution to independent living.

9. _____ _____ health centers were created to help avoid or minimize hospitalization.

10. These centers have as their goal the _____ of mental health problems through education, consultation, and crisis_____ .

# Psychology in Action: Self-Management and Finding Professional Help
How are behavioral principles applied to everyday problems? How could a person find professional help?

1. In _____ sensitization, aversive images are used to discourage unwanted behavior.

2. _____ uses mild punishment to prevent upsetting thoughts.

3. Covert _____ is a way to encourage desired responses by mental rehearsal.

4. _____ pairs relaxation with a hierarchy of upsetting images in order to lessen fears.

5. In most communities, a _____ and reputable therapist can usually be located through public sources of information or by a referral.

6. Practical considerations such as cost and qualifications enter into choosing a therapist. However, the therapist's _____ _____ are of equal importance.

7. _____ groups, made up of people who share similar_____ , can sometimes add valuable support to professional treatment.

525

# MASTERY TEST

1.  To demonstrate that spontaneous remissions are occurring, you could use a
    a.  patient-defined hierarchy.
    b.  waiting list control group.
    c.  target behavior group.
    d.  short-term dynamic correlation.

2.  In desensitization, relaxation is induced to block fear, a process known as
    a.  systematic adaptation.
    b.  vicarious opposition.
    c.  stimulus control.
    d.  reciprocal inhibition.

3.  Role reversals and the mirror technique are methods of
    a.  psychodrama.
    b.  person-centered therapy.
    c.  family therapy.
    d.  brief psychodynamic therapy.

4.  One thing that both trepanning and exorcism have in common is that both were used
    a.  to treat ergotism.
    b.  by Pinel in the Bicêtre Asylum.
    c.  to remove spirits.
    d.  to treat cases of hysteria.

5.  Unconditional positive regard is a concept particularly associated with
    a.  Beck.
    b.  Frankl.
    c.  Perls.
    d.  Rogers.

6.  Many of the claimed benefits of large-group awareness trainings appear to represent a therapy
    _____ effect.
    a.  remission
    b.  education
    c.  placebo
    d.  transference

7.  Personal change is LEAST likely to be the goal of
    a.  supportive therapy.
    b.  action therapy.
    c.  desensitization.
    d.  humanistic therapy.

8. Inducing seizures is a standard part of using
   a. Gestalt therapy.
   b. antidepressants.
   c. ECT.
   d. cybertherapy.

9. Which counseling behavior does not belong with the others listed here?
   a. paraphrasing
   b. judging
   c. reflecting
   d. active listening

10. In psychoanalysis, the process most directly opposite to free association is
    a. resistance.
    b. transference.
    c. symbolization.
    d. remission.

11. Identification of target behaviors is an important step in designing
    a. a desensitization hierarchy.
    b. activating stimuli.
    c. token economies.
    d. encounter groups.

12. A person who wants to lose weight looks at a dessert and visualizes maggots crawling all over it. The person is obviously using
    a. systematic adaptation.
    b. covert sensitization.
    c. stress inoculation.
    d. systematic desensitization.

13. Which of the following is NOT a humanistic therapy?
    a. client-centered
    b. Gestalt
    c. existential
    d. cognitive

14. Not many emergency room doctors drive without using their seatbelts. This observation helps explain the effectiveness of
    a.   systematic desensitization.
    b.   aversion therapy.
    c.   covert reinforcement.
    d.   the mirror technique.

15. Telephone counselors have little chance of using which element of effective psychotherapy?
    a.   empathy
    b.   nondirective reflection
    c.   the therapeutic alliance
    d.   accepting the person's frame of reference

16. Which of the following is a self-management technique?
    a.   thought stopping
    b.   vicarious reality exposure
    c.   REBT
    d.   EMDR

17. A good example of a nondirective insight therapy is _____ therapy.
    a.   client-centered
    b.   Gestalt
    c.   psychoanalytic
    d.   brief psychodynamic

18. Which statement about psychotherapy is true?
    a.   Most therapists are equally successful.
    b.   Most techniques are equally successful.
    c.   Therapists and clients need not agree about the goals of therapy.
    d.   Effective therapists instruct their clients not to discuss their therapy with anyone else.

19. Analysis of resistances and transferences is a standard feature of
    a.   client-centered therapy.
    b.   Gestalt therapy.
    c.   REBT.
    d.   psychoanalysis.

20. Both classical and operant conditioning are the basis for
    a.   desensitization.
    b.   token economies.
    c.   behavior therapy.
    d.   aversion therapy.

21. Rational-emotive behavior therapy is best described as
    a. insight, nondirective, individual.
    b. insight, supportive, individual.
    c. action, supportive, group.
    d. action, directive, individual.

22. Deep lesioning is a form of
    a. ECT.
    b. psychosurgery.
    c. pharmacotherapy.
    d. PET.

23. Identifying and removing rewards is a behavioral technique designed to bring about
    a. operant shaping.
    b. extinction.
    c. respondent aversion.
    d. token inhibition.

24. Culturally skilled therapists must be aware of their own cultural backgrounds, as well as
    a. the percentage of ethnic populations in the community.
    b. that of their clients.
    c. the importance of maintaining confidentiality.
    d. the life goals of minorities.

25. A behavioral therapist would treat acrophobia with
    a. desensitization.
    b. aversion therapy.
    c. covert sensitization.
    d. cybertherapy.

26. Which technique most closely relates to the idea of nondirective therapy?
    a. confrontation
    b. dream analysis
    c. role reversal
    d. reflection

27. The majority of psychotherapy clients improve after _____ months of therapy.
    a. 4
    b. 6
    c. 8
    d. 12

28. Overgeneralization is a thinking error that contributes to
    a. depression.
    b. somatization.
    c. phobias.
    d. emotional reprocessing.

29. Death, freedom, and meaning are special concerns of
    a. REBT.
    b. cognitive therapy.
    c. existential therapy.
    d. psychodrama.

30. An intense awareness of present experience and breaking through emotional impasses is the heart of
    a. action therapy.
    b. Gestalt therapy.
    c. time-limited therapy.
    d. REBT.

31. The ABCs of REBT stand for
    a. anticipation, behavior, conduct.
    b. action, behavior, conflict.
    c. activating experience, belief, consequence.
    d. anticipation, belief, congruent experience.

32. Which of the following in NOT a "distance therapy"?
    a. REBT
    b. telephone therapy
    c. cybertherapy
    d. telehealth

33. Virtual reality exposure is a type of
    a. psychodrama.
    b. ECT therapy.
    c. cognitive therapy.
    d. desensitization.

34. ECT is most often used to treat
    a. psychosis.
    b. anxiety.
    c. hysteria.
    d. depression.

35. Which of the following is most often associated with community mental health programs?
    a. pharmacotherapy
    b. covert reinforcement
    c. crisis intervention
    d. REBT

36. Which of the following method(s) effectively treats obsessive-compulsive disorder?
    a. behavioral
    b. cognitive-behavioral
    c. pharmacology
    d. all of the preceding

37. Which therapy's main purpose is to enhance people's personal strengths rather than try to fix their weakness?
    a. supportive
    b. positive
    c. insight
    d. directive

38. An element of positive mental health that therapists seek to promote is
    a. dependency on therapist.
    b. a sense of identity.
    c. personal autonomy and independence.
    d. both B and C

39. Which theory relies on dream analysis to uncover the unconscious roots of neurosis?
    a. existential
    b. psychoanalytic
    c. client-centered
    d. telehealth

40. _____ has been one of the most successful behavioral therapies for reducing fears, anxieties, and psychological pains.
    a. Vicarious desensitization
    b. Virtual reality exposure
    c. Eye-movement desensitization
    d. Desensitization

41. Research suggests that, as a solution to handling people with mental illness, mental hospitals in our society are being replaced by
    a. a full-time live-in nurse.
    b. placing them in jail.
    c. medicating the mentally ill until they reach 65 years old.
    d. allowing the mentally ill to take care of themselves.

42. "There is always a perfect solution to human problems and it is awful if this solution is not found" is a typical _____ statement.
    a. irrational belief
    b. self-awareness
    c. health-promoting
    d. response-contingent

43. Experts predict that, in the near future, traditional forms of psychotherapy will be replaced by short-term, solution-focused, telephone, and self-help group therapy. This is a reflection of
    a. the lack of time available in people's busy life to seek mental health services.
    b. fewer people needing mental health services.
    c. societal pressures to reduce costs in mental health services.
    d. people being afraid to reveal their mental illness.

# SOLUTIONS

## RECITE AND REVIEW

### Psychotherapy—The Talking Cure: Pages 496-497
How do psychotherapies differ?

1. positive; behavior
2. Insight
3. guidance; guide
4. change
5. personal; positive
6. time

### Origins of Therapy—Bored Out of Your Skull: Pages 497-498
How did psychotherapy originate?

1. superstition
2. skull
3. exorcism; epilepsy
4. ergot; poisoning
5. mental hospital

### Psychoanalysis—Expedition into the Unconscious: Pages 498-500
Is Freudian psychoanalysis still used?

1. psychotherapy
2. physical
3. unconscious; unconscious
4. free; dream
5. desires; dream; latent
6. Brief; interpersonal
7. spontaneous

### Humanistic Therapies—Restoring Human Potential: Pages 500-502
What are the major humanistic therapies?

1. Humanistic
2. person; growth
3. positive; empathy
4. choices
5. will; choices; meaning
6. wholes
7. awareness

### Therapy at a Distance—Psych Jockeys and Cybertherapy: Pages 502-503
Can therapy be conducted at a distance?

1. educating; therapy
2. Internet
3. therapy; audio-video

### Behavior Therapy—Healing by Learning: Pages 503-507
What is behavior therapy?

1. learning
2. learning; associated
3. pain
4. stimuli
5. adaptation
6. systematic
7. relaxation
8. imagining
9. recognize; relax
10. models
11. reality; fear
12. memories; stress

## Operant Therapies—All the World is a Skinner Box?: Pages 508-509
What role do operant principles play in behavior therapy?

1. control; time
2. reinforcers
3. responses
4. removing
5. reinforcers; maintaining
6. immediate; behaviors
7. tokens
8. approval

## Cognitive Therapy—Think Positive!: Pages 510-512
Can therapy change thoughts and emotions?

1. thinking depend
2. selective; thinking
3. skills
4. beliefs
5. irrational; completely;

## Group Therapy—People Who Need People: Pages 512-514
Can psychotherapy be done with groups of people?

1. individual
2. role; role
3. unit; family
4. psychotherapies
5. trainings
6. therapy

## Psychotherapy—An Overview: Pages 514-517
What do various therapies have in common?

1. 50
2. emotional; setting
3. problems
4. behaviors
5. solution; self; telephone
6. counseling
7. advice
8. silences
9. open
10. traditional

## Medical Therapies—Psychiatric Care: Pages 518-522
How do psychiatrists treat psychological disorders?

1. somatic; drugs; brain
2. minor; hallucinations; mood
3. risks
4. psychosurgery; lost
5. lesioning; destroyed
6. Mental or Psychiatric
7. partial
8. houses; independent
9. hospitalization
10. crisis

## Psychology in Action: Self-Management and Finding Professional Help: Pages 522-526
How are behavioral principles applied to everyday problems? How could a person find professional help?

1. images
2. punishment
3. responses
4. relaxation
5. referral
6. cost (or fees)
7. groups

# CONNECTIONS

## Psychotherapy—The Talking Cure, Origins of Therapy—Bore Out of Your Skull, and Psychoanalysis—Expedition into the Unconscious: Pages 496-500

How do psychotherapies differ? How did psychotherapy originate? Is Freudian psychoanalysis still used?

1. h
2. i
3. g
4. a

5. e
6. j
7. c
8. f

9. b
10. d

## Humanistic Therapies—Restoring Human Potential: Pages 500-502

What are the major humanistic therapies?

1. e
2. c
3. h

4. a
5. f
6. d

7. b
8. g

## Behavior Therapy—Healing by Learning: Pages 503-507

What is behavior therapy?

1. d
2. a
3. g

4. c
5. f
6. b

7. e

## Operant Therapies—All the World Is a Skinner Box? And Cognitive Therapy—Think Positive!: Pages 508-512

What role do operant principles play in behavior therapy? Can therapy change thoughts and emotions?

1. d
2. c

3. a
4. e

5. b
6. f

## Group Therapy—People Who Need People, Psychotherapy—An Overview, and Medical Therapies—Psychiatric Care: Pages 512-522

Can psychotherapy be done with groups of people? What do various therapies have in common? How do psychiatrists treat psychological disorders?

1. h
2. f
3. b
4. j

5. a
6. i
7. c
8. g

9. d
10. e

## Psychology in Action: Self-Management and Finding Professional Help: Pages 522-526

How are behavioral principles applied to everyday problems? How could a person find professional help?

1.  a
2.  d

3.  e
4.  c

5.  b

# CHECK YOUR MEMORY

## Psychotherapy—The Talking Cure and Origins of Therapy—Bored Out of Your Skull: Pages 496-498

How do psychotherapies differ? How did psychotherapy originate?

1.  F
2.  T
3.  T
4.  T

5.  T
6.  F
7.  T
8.  F

9.  F
10. T

## Psychoanalysis—Expedition into the Unconscious: Pages 498-500

Is Freudian psychoanalysis still used?

1.  F
2.  F
3.  T

4.  T
5.  F
6.  T

7.  F

## Humanistic Therapies—Restoring Human Potential: Pages 500-502

What are the major humanistic therapies

1.  F
2.  F
3.  T
4.  T

5.  T
6.  F
7.  F
8.  T

9.  F
10. T
11. T
12. F

## Behavior Therapy—Healing by Learning: Pages 503-507

What is behavior therapy?

1.  T
2.  F
3.  T
4.  F
5.  T
6.  T

7.  T
8.  F
9.  T
10. F
11. T
12. T

13. T
14. F

## Operant Therapies—All the World Is a Skinner Box?: Pages 508-509

What role do operant principles play in behavior therapy?

| | | | | | |
|---|---|---|---|---|---|
| 1. | F | 4. | T | 7. | T |
| 2. | T | 5. | F | 8. | T |
| 3. | F | 6. | T | | |

## Cognitive Therapy—Think Positive!: Pages 510-512

Can therapy change thoughts and emotions?

| | | | | | |
|---|---|---|---|---|---|
| 1. | T | 4. | F | 7. | T |
| 2. | T | 5. | F | | |
| 3. | T | 6. | T | | |

## Group Therapy—People Who Need People: Pages 512-514

Can psychotherapy be done with groups of people?

| | | | | | |
|---|---|---|---|---|---|
| 1. | F | 3. | T | 5. | T |
| 2. | F | 4. | F | | |

## Psychotherapy—An Overview: Pages 514-517

What do various therapies have in common?

| | | | | | |
|---|---|---|---|---|---|
| 1. | T | 5. | F | 9. | F |
| 2. | T | 6. | T | 10. | F |
| 3. | T | 7. | F | | |
| 4. | T | 8. | T | | |

## Medical Therapies—Psychiatric Care: Pages 518-522

How do psychiatrists treat psychological disorders?

| | | | | | |
|---|---|---|---|---|---|
| 1. | F | 6. | T | 11. | T |
| 2. | T | 7. | F | 12. | F |
| 3. | T | 8. | F | 13. | T |
| 4. | F | 9. | T | 14. | F |
| 5. | T | 10. | F | | |

## Psychology in Action: Self-Management and Finding Professional Help: Pages 522-526

How are behavioral principles applied to everyday problems? How could a person find professional help?

| | | | | | |
|---|---|---|---|---|---|
| 1. | F | 4. | T | 7. | T |
| 2. | F | 5. | T | 8. | T |
| 3. | F | 6. | F | 9. | F |

# FINAL SURVEY AND REVIEW

## Psychotherapy—The Talking Cure
How do psychotherapies differ?

1. Psychotherapy; personality
2. Action
3. Directive; Nondirective
4. Supportive
5. Positive; "fix"
6. individually; and

## Origins of Therapy—Bored Out of Your Skull
How did psychotherapy originate?

1. Primitive
2. Trepanning
3. Demonology; schizophrenia
4. ergotism; fungus
5. Pinel

## Psychoanalysis—Expedition into the Unconscious
Is Freudian psychoanalysis still used?

1. Freud's; psychoanalysis
2. hysteria
3. repressed
4. unconscious; dream
5. association; resistance
6. psychodynamic; psychoanalytic
7. remissions

## Humanistic Therapies—Restoring Human Potential
What are the major humanistic therapies?

1. potentials
2. Rogers'; nondirective
3. unconditional; reflection
4. Existential
5. confrontation; encounter
6. emotional; blocks
7. Gestalt

## Therapy at a Distance—Psych Jockeys and Cybertherapy
Can therapy be conducted at a distance?

1. Media videoconferencing
2. cybertherapists
3. telehealth;

## Behavior Therapy—Healing by Learning
What is behavior therapy?

1. Behavior; modification
2. Classical; reflex
3. aversion
4. response-contingent
5. inhibition
6. desensitization
7. hierarchy; hierarchy
8. fear; hierarchy
9. tension; muscles
10. vicariously
11. virtual; exposure
12. eye-movement

## Operant Therapies—All the World Is a Skinner Box?
What role do operant principles play in behavior therapy?

1. operant; extinction; punishment
2. Nonreward
3. extinction
4. setting; reinforced
5. reinforcers; behaviors
6. tokens; target
7. token; economy
8. social

## Cognitive Therapy—Think Positive!
Can therapy change thoughts and emotions?

1. Cognitive
2. Beck's; overgeneralization
3. coping
4. rational-emotive behavior
5. beliefs; worthless; depend

## Group Therapy—People Who Need People
Can psychotherapy be done with groups of people?

1. Group; groups
2. psychodrama; reversals
3. family; family
4. encounter
5. awareness
6. placebo

## Psychotherapy—An Overview
What do various therapies have in common?

1. 13 to 18
2. rapport; protected
3. catharsis
4. perspective
5. Psychotherapy; short; Internet; master's
6. actively; clarify
7. feelings
8. perspective; reflect
9. confidentiality
10. cultural

## Medical Therapies—Psychiatric Care
How do psychiatrists treat psychological disorders?

1. pharmacotherapy; electroconvulsive
2. antipsychotics; antidepressants
3. benefits
4. Electroconvulsive; effectiveness
5. deep lesioning
6. Psychiatric; disorders
7. deinstitutionalization
8. Half-way
9. Community; mental
10 preventlon; intervention

## Psychology in Action: Self-Management and Finding Professional Help
How are behavioral principles applied to everyday problems? How could a person find professional help?

1. covert
2. Thought stopping
3. reinforcement
4. Desensitization
5. competent
6. personal; characteristics
7. Self-help; problems

# MASTERY TEST

1. b, p. 514
2. d, p. 505
3. a, pp. 512-13
4. c, p. 497
5. d, p. 500
6. c, p. 513
7. a, p. 496
8. c, p. 519
9. b, p. 516
10. a, p. 499
11. c, p. 505
12. b, p. 523
13. d, p. 510
14. b, p. 504
15. c, p. 502

16. a, p. 523
17. a, p. 500
18. b, p. 514
19. d, p. 498
20. c, p. 504
21. d, p. 510
22. b, p. 520
23. b, p. 508
24. b, p. 517
25. a, p. 505
26. d, p. 501
27. c, p. 514
28. a, p. 510
29. c, p. 501
30. b, p. 501

31. c, p. 510
32. a, p. 510
33. d, p. 506
34. d, p. 519
35. c, p. 521
36. d, p. 514
37. b, p. 496
38. d, p. 497
39. b, p. 498
40. d, p. 505
41. b, p. 520
42. a, p. 511
43. c, p. 51

# Social Thinking and Social Influence

## Chapter Overview

Social psychology is the study of individual behavior in social situations. Social roles, status, group structure, norms, and group cohesiveness influence interpersonal behavior. Group cohesiveness is strong for in-group members who tend to attribute positive traits to members of the group. Negative qualities tend to be attributed to out-group members.

Attribution theory summarizes how we make inferences about behavior. The fundamental attributional error is to ascribe the actions of others to internal causes. Because of an actor-observer bias, we tend to attribute our own behavior to external causes.

The beliefs and emotions, called attitudes, that people have summarize their evaluation of objects and predict or direct future actions. Attitudes consist of belief, emotional, and action components, and are learned through direct contact, interaction with others, child rearing practices, and media. Whether or not a person acts according to their attitudes can be influenced by immediate consequences, the evaluation of others, habits, and the strength of one's conviction. Attitudes are measured by open-ended interviews, social distance scales, or attitudes scales.

Attitude change can be understood in terms of reference groups, and may be a result of persuasion by others. When a person experiences inconsistency between thoughts, perceptions, and self-image, cognitive dissonance may occur which may lead to behavior change.

Social influence refers to alterations in behavior brought about by the behavior of others, and ranges from milder to stronger, ranging from mere presence to coercion. Social influence is also related to five types of social power: reward power, coercive power, legitimate power, referent power, and expert power.

The presence of others may lead to social facilitation, or, conversely, to social loafing. Proximity to others is influenced by norms governing personal space, and four basic zones include intimate, personal, social, and public distance.

Compliance with direct requests is another means by which behavior is influenced. Examples of social power include conformity, groupthink, and obedience to authority. Three types of compliance techniques are foot-in-the-door, door-in-the-face, and low-ball. Milgram's research indicates that under certain situations, people may obey authority even when they believe they are hurting another person. The most extreme form of social influence, coercion, occurs in brainwashing, which may occur during prisoner-of-war and cult recruitment and conversion situations.

Self-assertion, as opposed to aggression, involves clearly stating one's wants and needs to others. It is a method to reduce the pressure to conform, obey, and comply with others' suggestions. Learning to be assertive is accomplished by role-playing, rehearsing assertive actions, overlearning, and use of specific techniques, such as the "broken record."

# Learning Objectives

*Theme: Humans are social animals. We live in a social world in which our thoughts, feelings, and behavior are profoundly influenced by the presence of others.*

| |
|---|
| **GQ: How does group membership affect individual behavior?** |
| LO 16.1 Define *social psychology*. |
| LO 16.2 Define the following terms: a. *culture*; b. *social roles*; c. ascribed role; d. achieved role; e. *role conflict*; f. *group structure*; g. *group cohesiveness*; h. *status*; and i. *norm*. Include a description of Zimbardo's prison experiment and an explanation of how norms are formed using the idea of the *autokinetic effect*. |
| **GQ: How do we perceive the motives of others, and the causes of our own behavior?** |
| LO 16.3 Define *attribution;* state the difference between *external* and *internal causes*; explain how the consistency and distinctiveness of a person's behavior affects the attributions others make about the person; and discuss six other factors affecting attribution. |
| LO 16.4 Explain how *self-handicapping* protects a person who has a fragile self-image. |
| LO 16.5 Explain what the *fundamental attribution error* is. Include the concept of the *actor-observer bias* in making attributions. |
| **GQ: What are attitudes? How are they acquired?** |
| LO 16.6 Define *attitude*; describe the *belief, emotional*, and *action components* of an attitude; and list and give examples of six ways in which attitudes are acquired. |
| LO 16.7 Explain three reasons why people may exhibit discrepancies between attitudes and behavior and how *conviction* affects attitudes; and briefly describe the following techniques for measuring attitudes: a. *open-ended interview*, b. *social distance scale*, c. *attitude scale*. |
| **GQ: Under what conditions is persuasion most effective? What is cognitive dissonance?** |
| LO 16.8 Define *persuasion;* describe the three factors in understanding the success or failure of persuasion; list nine conditions that encourage attitude change. |
| LO 16.9 Explain *cognitive dissonance* theory; list five strategies for reducing dissonance (see Table 16.1); and describe the effect of reward or justification on dissonance. |
| **GQ: What is social influence and social power?** |
| LO 16.10 State the meaning of *social influence* and give examples of it; list and describe the five sources of *social power*. |
| **GQ: How does the mere presence of others affect behavior?** |
| LO 16.11 Define *mere presence* and distinguish between *social facilitation* and *social loafing*. |
| LO 16.12 Define *personal space* and *proxemics*; and describe the four basic interpersonal zones and the nature of the interactions that occur in each. |
| **GQ: What have social psychologists learned about conformity?** |
| LO 16.13 Define *conformity*; describe Asch's experiment on conformity; explain how *groupthink* may contribute to poor decision-making and list ways to prevent it; and describe how *group sanctions* and unanimity affect conformity. |
| **GQ: What factors lead to increased compliance?** |
| LO 16.14 Explain how *compliance* differs from simple conformity; describe the following methods of gaining compliance: a. *foot-in-the-door*; b. *door-in-the-face*; |

| |
|---|
| c. *low-ball technique*; and discuss the research that deals with *passive compliance* and how it applies to everyday behavior. |
| **GQ: Can people be too obedient?** |
| LO 16.15 Describe Milgram's study of *obedience*; and identify the factors which affect the degree of obedience. |
| **GQ: Is brainwashing actually possible? How are people converted to cult membership?** |
| LO 16.16 Define *brainwashing*; describe the techniques used in brainwashing; indicate how permanent the attitude changes brought about by brainwashing are; and describe how *cults* are able to recruit, convert, and retain their members. |
| **GQ: How does self-assertion differ from aggression?** |
| LO 16.17 Describe *assertiveness training*; describe the concept of *self-assertion* and contrast it with *aggression*; and explain how a person can learn to be more assertive using rehearsal, role-playing, *overlearning*, and the *broken record* technique. |

# RECITE AND REVIEW

## Humans in a Social Context—People, People, Everywhere: Pages 530-533

How does group membership affect individual behavior?

1. Social psychology studies how individuals behave, think, and feel in _____ situations.

2. Culture provides a broad social context for our behavior. One's position in _____ defines a variety of roles to be played.

3. _____ , which may be achieved or ascribed, are particular behavior patterns associated with social positions.

4. When two or more _____ roles are held, role conflict may occur.

5. The Stanford _____ experiment showed that destructive roles may override individual motives for behavior.

6. Positions within _____ typically carry higher or lower levels of status. High status is associated with special privileges and respect.

7. Two dimensions of a group are group structure (network of _____ , communication pathways, and power) and group cohesiveness (members' desire to _____ in the group). Group cohesion is strong for _____ members.

8. Members of the _____ identify themselves based on a combination of dimensions such as nationality, _____ , age, _____ , income, etc. People tend to attribute _____ traits to members of their in-group and negative traits to members of the _____ .

543

9. Norms are _____ of conduct enforced (formally or informally) by _____ .

10. The autokinetic effect (the illusion of _____ in a stationary light in a darkened room) has been used to demonstrate that norms rapidly form even in _____ groups.

# Social Perception—Behind the Mask: Pages 533-535
How do we perceive the motives of others, and the causes of our own behavior?

1. Attribution theory is concerned with how we make inferences about the _____ of behavior.

2. Behavior can be attributed to internal _____ or external _____ .

3. To infer _____ we take into account the _____ , the object of the action, and the setting in which the action occurs.

4. The _____ of behavior on different occasions and its distinctiveness (whether it occurs only in certain circumstances) affect the attributions we make.

5. Situational demands tend to cause us to discount _____ causes as explanations of someone's behavior.

6. Consensus in behavior (in which many people act alike) implies that their behavior has an _____ cause.

7. The fundamental attributional _____ is to ascribe the actions of others to _____ causes. This is part of the actor-observer bias, in which we ascribe the behavior of others to _____ causes, and our own behavior to _____ causes.

8. Self-handicapping involves arranging excuses for poor _____ as a way to protect your self-image or self-esteem.

# Attitudes—Belief + Emotion + Action: Pages 535-537
What are attitudes? How are they acquired?

1. Attitudes affect peoples' actions, views of the world, tastes and _____ , friendships, goals, and _____ .

2. An _____ is a mixture of belief and _____ that predisposes one to respond to other people, objects, or institutions in either a positive or negative manner.

3. Attitudes have three components, the _____ component, the emotional component and the action component.

4. Attitudes may be acquired through direct _____ , interaction with others, _____ rearing practices, or the media.

5. Whether or not people act upon their attitudes may be influenced by _____ _____ , how they expect others to evaluate their actions, habit, and strength of conviction.

6. Attitudes can be measured by _____ _____ , social distance scales, and attitude scales.

## Attitudes Change—Why the Seekers Went Public: Pages 537-540

Under what conditions is persuasion most effective? What is cognitive dissonance?

1. Any _____ which a person uses as a standard for social comparison can be called a _____ group and may influence attitudes.

2. Persuasion is a purposeful attempt to change another person's _____ or beliefs. The success of persuasion can be understood in terms of the communicator, message, and _____ .

3. _____ thoughts cause discomfort according to _____ dissonance theory.

## Social Influence—Follow the Leader: Page 540

What is social influence and social power?

1. Social influence refers to alterations in _____ brought about by the behavior of _____ .

2. Social influence ranges from mild forms such as mere _____ , to stronger forms such as conformity and _____ , to the strongest form of coercion.

3. Social influence is also related to five types of _____ reward power, coercive power, legitimate power, referent power, and expert power.

## Mere Presence—Just Because You Are There: Pages 541-542

How does the mere presence of others affect behavior?

1. The study of _____ is called proxemics.

2. Four basic spatial zones around each person's body are intimate distance (0-18 inches), _____ distance (1.5-4 feet), _____ distance (4-12 feet), and public distance (12 feet or more).

3. Norms for the use of personal space vary considerably in various _____ .

4. The tendency to perform _____ when others are present is called social facilitation, while the tendency to get _____ work done when part of a group is called social loafing.

## Conformity—Don't Stand Out: Pages 542-544
What have social psychologists learned about conformity?

1. When a person brings their _____ into agreement with the actions, _____, or values of other people without direct pressure, that person conforms.

2. The famous Asch experiments demonstrated that various _____ sanctions encourage conformity.

3. Groupthink refers to compulsive conformity in group _____ _____ . Victims of groupthink seek to maintain each other's approval, even at the cost of critical thinking.

## Compliance—A Foot in the Door: Pages 544-547
What factors lead to increased compliance?

1. Compliance with direct _____ by a person who has little or no social _____ is another means by which behavior is influenced.

2. Three strategies for inducing compliance are the _____ -in-the-door technique, the door-in-the- _____ approach, and the low-ball technique.

3. To _____ the odds with salespeople, one should know a rough _____ of the product, get the negotiated price in _____ , and compare the negotiated price with other stores to get the best deal.

4. Recent research suggests that in addition to excessive obedience to _____ , many people show a surprising passive compliance to unreasonable _____ .

## Obedience—Would You Electrocute a Stranger?: Pages 547-549
Can people be too obedient?

1. Obedience to _____ has been investigated in a variety of experiments, particularly those by Stanley Milgram.

2. _____ in Milgram's studies decreased when the victim was in the same room, when the victim and subject were face to face, when the authority figure was absent, and when others refused to obey.

## Coercion—Brainwashing and Cults: Pages 549-551

Is brainwashing actually possible? How are people converted into cult membership?

1. A person has been _____ if they are forced to _____ their beliefs against their will.

2. Brainwashing involves forced _____ change and requires a _____ audience.

3. Recruitment and _____ efforts by cults also involve _____ .

## Psychology in Action: Assertiveness Training—Standing Up for Your Rights: Pages 551-553

How does self-assertion differ from aggression?

1. Self-assertion involves clearly stating one's _____ and _____ to others.

2. Aggression expresses one's feelings and desires, but it _____ others.

3. Non-assertive behavior is self- _____ and inhibited.

4. Learning to be _____ is accomplished by role-playing and rehearsing assertive actions.

5. Self-assertion is also aided by overlearning (practice that _____ after initial mastery of a skill) and use of specific techniques, such as the "broken record" ( _____ a request until it is acknowledged).

# CONNECTIONS

## Humans in a Social Context—People, People, Everywhere: Pages 530-533

How does group membership affect individual behavior?

1. _____ culture
2. _____ ascribed role
3. _____ achieved role
4. _____ status
5. _____ cohesiveness
6. _____ norm
7. _____ autokinetic

a. privilege and importance
b. rule or standard
c. way of life
d. self-moving
e. assigned role
f. degree of attraction
g. voluntary role

# Attitudes—Belief + Emotion + Action and Attitude Change—Why the Seekers Went Public: Pages 535-540

What are attitudes? How are they acquired? Under what conditions is persuasion most effective? What is cognitive dissonance?

| | | | |
|---|---|---|---|
| 1. _____ attitude | a. | feelings toward object |
| 2. _____ cognitive dissonance | b. | deliberate attempt to change attitude |
| 3. _____ conviction | c. | average television |
| 4. _____ reference group | d. | discomfort from clashing thoughts |
| 5. _____ emotional component | e. | belief plus emotion |
| 6. _____ persuasion | f. | standard for comparison |
| 7. _____ 7-plus hours per day | g. | evokes strong feelings |

# Social Cognition—Behind the Mask and Mere Presence—Just Because You Are There: Pages 533-535, 541-542

How do we perceive the motives of others, and the causes of our own behavior? How does the mere presence of others affect behavior?

| | | | |
|---|---|---|---|
| 1. _____ intimate distance | a. | impairing performance |
| 2. _____ personal distance | b. | social inference |
| 3. _____ social distance | c. | 0-18 inches |
| 4. _____ public distance | d. | 12 feet plus |
| 5. _____ attribution | e. | 1.5-4 feet |
| 6. _____ fundamental attribution error | f. | 4-12 feet |
| 7. _____ self-handicapping | g. | overestimate internal causes |

# Social Influence—Follow the Leader: Page 540

What is social influence and social power?

| | | | |
|---|---|---|---|
| 1. _____ reward power | a. | person has power |
| 2. _____ expert power | b. | change another person's behavior |
| 3. _____ coercion | c. | mildest form of social influence |
| 4. _____ social influence | d. | has knowledge needed to obtain goal |
| 5. _____ coercive power | e. | strongest form of influence |
| 6. _____ mere presence | f. | control over desired reinforcement |
| 7. _____ authority | g. | ability to punish for failure to comply |

# Compliance—A Foot in the Door and Psychology in Action: Assertiveness Training—Standing Up for Your Rights: Pages 544-547, 551-553

What factors lead to increased compliance? How does self-assertion differ from aggression?

| | | | |
|---|---|---|---|
| 1. _____ foot-in-the-door | a. | rewards and punishments |
| 2. _____ assertiveness | b. | matching behavior |
| 3. _____ conformity | c. | self-assertion technique |

4. _____ group sanctions  d. salesperson's tactic
5. _____ obedience  e. honest expression
6. _____ broken record  f. following authority
7. _____ compliance  g. yielding to requests

# CHECK YOUR MEMORY

## Humans in a Social Context—People, People, Everywhere: Pages 530-533

How does group membership affect individual behavior?

1. The average number of first-name acquaintance links needed to connect two widely separated strangers is about 70 people.   TRUE or FALSE

2. Language and marriage customs are elements of culture.   TRUE or FALSE

3. *Son, husband,* and *teacher* are achieved roles.   TRUE or FALSE

4. The Stanford prison experiment investigated the impact of the roles "prisoner" and "guard."
   TRUE or FALSE

5. Group cohesion refers to the dimensions that define a group such as ethnicity, age, or religion.
   TRUE or FALSE

6. A group could have a high degree of structure but low cohesiveness.   TRUE or FALSE

7. "Us and them" refers to members of the in-group perceiving themselves as one unit and everyone else as the out-group.   TRUE or FALSE

8. Persons of higher status are more likely to touch persons of lower status than the reverse.
   TRUE or FALSE

9. Women are more likely to touch men than men are to touch women.   TRUE or FALSE

10. The more trash that is visible in public places, the more likely people are to litter.
    TRUE or FALSE

11. An autokinetic light appears to move about the same distance for everyone who observes it.
    TRUE or FALSE

## Attitudes—Belief + Emotion + Action: Pages 535-537

What are attitudes? How are they acquired?

1. An attitude is a mixture of action and emotion.   TRUE or FALSE

2. A research technique called the misdirected letter technique has been used to show how attitudes are linked to behavior.  TRUE or FALSE

549

3. Attitudes are expressed only through action. TRUE or FALSE

4. Eighty-five percent of American households have television sets. TRUE or FALSE

5. Social distance scales usually use a 5-point scale. TRUE or FALSE

## Attitudes Change—Why the Seekers Went Public: Pages 537-540

Under what conditions is persuasion most effective? What is cognitive dissonance?

1. Reference groups always involve face-to-face contact. TRUE or FALSE

2. More than two hundred billion dollars are spent yearly on television advertising in the U.S. and Canada. TRUE or FALSE

3. Cognitive dissonance often leads to attitude change. TRUE or FALSE

## Mere Presence—Just Because You Are There: Pages 540-541

How does the mere presence of others affect behavior?

1. Most people show signs of discomfort when someone else enters their personal space without permission. TRUE or FALSE

2. The Dutch sit closer together when talking than the English do. TRUE or FALSE

3. Social distance basically keeps people within arm's reach. TRUE or FALSE

4. Formal interactions tend to take place in the 4 to 12 foot range. TRUE or FALSE

5. The tendency to get less work done when they are part of a group rather than working individually is called social facilitation. TRUE or FALSE

## Social Cognition—Behind the Mask: Pages 533-535

How do we perceive the motives of others, and the causes of our own behavior?

1. The deliberateness of another person's behavior affects the attributions we make about it. TRUE or FALSE

2. If someone always salts her food before eating, it implies that her behavior has an external cause. TRUE or FALSE

3. Situational demands lead us to discount claims that a person's behavior is externally caused. TRUE or FALSE

4. A strong consensus in the behavior of many people implies that their behavior is externally caused.
   TRUE or FALSE

5. Getting drunk is a common form of self-handicapping.    TRUE or FALSE

6. Attributing the actions of others to external causes is the most common attributional error.
   TRUE or FALSE

7. People tend to attribute the actions of actors on television to personality instead of their playing
   characters.    TRUE or FALSE

## Conformity—Don't Stand Out, Compliance—A Foot in the Door, and Obedience—Would You Electrocute a Stranger?: Pages 542-549

What have social psychologists learned about conformity? What factors lead to increased compliance? Can people be too obedient?

1. Conformity situations occur when a person becomes aware of differences between his or her own
   behavior and that of a group.    TRUE or FALSE

2. Most subjects in the Asch conformity experiments suspected that they were being deceived in some way.
   TRUE or FALSE

3. Seventy-five percent of Asch's subjects yielded to the group at least once.    TRUE or FALSE

4. People who are anxious are more likely to conform to group pressure.    TRUE or FALSE

5. Groupthink is more likely to occur when people emphasize the task at hand, rather than the bonds
   between group members.    TRUE or FALSE

6. Rejection, ridicule, and disapproval are group norms that tend to enforce conformity.
   TRUE or FALSE

7. A unanimous majority of 3 is more powerful than a majority of 8 with 1 person dissenting.
   TRUE or FALSE

8. If you identify with a particular person, that person has referent power with respect to your behavior.
   TRUE or FALSE

9. Milgram's famous shock experiment was done to study compliance and conformity.
   TRUE or FALSE

10. Over half of Milgram's "teachers" went all the way to the maximum shock level.    TRUE or FALSE

11. Being face-to-face with the "learner" had no effect on the number of subjects who obeyed in
    the Milgram experiments.    TRUE or FALSE

12. People are less likely to obey an unjust authority if they have seen others disobey.    TRUE or FALSE

13. The foot-in-the-door effect is a way to gain compliance from another person.    TRUE or FALSE

14. The low-ball technique involves changing the terms that a person has agreed to, so that they are less desirable from the person's point of view.    TRUE or FALSE

15. Using the door-in-the-face strategy is an effective way to even the odds with salespeople for using the low-ball technique.    TRUE or FALSE

# Coercion—Brainwashing and Cults: Pages 549-551
Is brainwashing actually possible? How are people converted to cult membership?

1.  You have been coerced if you voluntarily change your behavior or beliefs.
    TRUE or FALSE

2.  Brainwashing requires a captive audience and complete control over the environment.
    TRUE or FALSE

3.  Brainwashing brings about permanent changes in attitude.    TRUE or FALSE

4.  In a cult, the leader's personality is more important than the beliefs the leader preaches.
    TRUE or FALSE

# Psychology in Action: Assertiveness Training— Standing Up for Your Rights: Pages 627-628
How does self-assertion differ from aggression?

1.  Many people have difficulty asserting themselves because they have learned to be obedient and "good."    TRUE or FALSE

2.  Self-assertion involves the rights to request, reject, and retaliate.    TRUE or FALSE

3.  Aggression does not take into account the rights of others.    TRUE or FALSE

4.  Overlearning tends to lead to aggressive responses.    TRUE or FALSE

5.  In order to be assertive, you should never admit that you were wrong.    TRUE or FALSE

6.  If someone insults you, an assertive response should include getting the person to accept responsibility for his or her aggression.    TRUE or FALSE

# FINAL SURVEY AND REVIEW

## Humans in a Social Context—People, People, Everywhere
How does group membership affect individual behavior?

1. _____ _____ studies how individuals behave, think, and feel in social situations.

2. _____ provides a broad social context for our behavior. One's position in groups defines a variety of _____ to be played.

3. Social roles, which may be _____ or _____, are particular behavior patterns associated with social positions.

4. When two or more contradictory roles are held, role _____ may occur.

5. The _____ prison experiment showed that destructive _____ may override individual motives for behavior.

6. Positions within groups typically carry higher or lower levels of _____ . _____ _____ is associated with special privileges and respect.

7. Two dimensions of a group are group _____ (network of roles, communication pathways, and power) and group _____ (members' desire to remain in the group). Group cohesion is strong for _____ members.

8. Members of the _____ identify themselves based on a combination of dimensions such as nationality, ethnicity, age, religion, income, etc. People tend to attribute _____ traits to members of their in-group and _____ traits to members of the out-group.

9. _____ are standards of conduct enforced (formally or informally) by groups.

10. The _____ effect (the illusion of movement in a _____ light in a darkened room) has been used to demonstrate that _____ rapidly form even in temporary groups.

## Social Perception—Behind the Mask
How do we perceive the motives of others, and the causes of our own behavior?

1. _____ theory is concerned with how we make inferences about the causes of behavior.

2. Behavior can be attributed to _____ causes or _____ causes.

3. To infer causes we take into account the actor, the _____ of the action, and the _____ in which the action occurs.

4. The consistency of behavior on different occasions and its _____ (whether it occurs only in certain circumstances) affect the attributions we make.

5. _____ demands tend to cause us to _____ (downgrade) internal causes as explanations of someone's behavior.

6. _____ in behavior (in which many people act alike) implies that their behavior has an external cause.

7. The _____ error is to ascribe the actions of others to internal causes. This is part of the _____ bias, in which we ascribe the behavior of others to internal causes, and our own behavior to external causes.

8. _____ involves arranging excuses for poor performance as a way to protect your self-image or self-esteem.

## Attitudes—Belief + Emotion + Action
What are attitudes? How are they acquired?

1. _____ affect peoples' actions, views of the world, tastes and _____, friendships, goals, and behavior.

2. An attitude is a mixture of _____ and emotion that predisposes one to respond to other people, objects, or institutions in either a _____ or negative manner.

3. Attitudes have three components, the _____ component, the emotional component and the action component.

4. Attitudes may be acquired through direct _____, interaction with others, _____ rearing practices, or the media.

5. Whether or not people act upon their attitudes may be influenced by immediate consequences, how they expect others to _____ their actions, habit, and strength of _____.

6. Attitudes can be measured by open-ended interview, social distance scales, and _____.

# Attitude Change—Why the Seekers Went Public
Under what conditions is persuasion most effective? What is cognitive dissonance?

1. Any group which a person uses as a standard for _____ comparison can be called a reference group and may influence _____ .

2. _____ is a purposeful attempt to change another person's attitudes or beliefs. The success of persuasion can be understood in terms of the _____ , message, and audience.

3. Contradicting thoughts cause _____ according to cognitive _____ theory.

# Social Influence—Follow the Leader
What is social influence and social power?

1. Social _____ refers to alterations in behavior brought about by the _____ of others .

2. _____ influence ranges from mild forms such as mere presence, to stronger forms such as conformity and compliance, to the strongest form of _____ .

3. Social influence is also related to five types of social power - _____ power, coercive power, legitimate power, referent power, and _____ power.

# Mere Presence—Just Because You Are There
How does the mere presence of others affect behavior?

1. The study of personal space is called _____ .

2. Four basic spatial zones around each person's body are _____ distance (0-18 inches), personal distance (1.5-4 feet), social distance (4-12 feet), and _____ distance (12 feet or more).

3. _____ for the use of personal space vary considerably in various cultures.

4. The tendency to perform better when others are present is called social _____ , while the tendency to get less work done when part of a group is called social _____ .

# Conformity—Don't Stand Out
What have social psychologists learned about conformity?

1. When a person brings their behavior into _____ with the actions, norms, or values of other people without direct _____ , that person conforms.

2.  The famous _____ experiments demonstrated that various group sanctions encourage _____ .

3.  _____ refers to compulsive conformity in group decision making. Victims of groupthink seek to maintain each other's _____ , even at the cost of critical thinking.

# Compliance—A Foot in the Door
What factors lead to increased compliance?

1.  _____ with direct requests by a person who has little or no social power is another means by which behavior is influenced.

2.  Three strategies for inducing compliance are the foot-in-the- _____ technique, the _____ -in-the-face approach, and the _____ technique.

3.  To _____ the odds with salespeople, one should know a rough _____ of the product, get the negotiated price in _____ ; and compare the negotiated price with other stores to get the best deal.

4.  Recent research suggests that in addition to excessive obedience to authority, many people show a surprising _____ compliance to unreasonable requests.

# Obedience—Would You Electrocute a Stranger?
Can people be too obedient?

1.  _____ to authority has been investigated in a variety of experiments, particularly those by Stanley _____ .

2.  Obedience in his studies _____ when the victim was in the same room, when the victim and subject were face to face, when the _____ figure was absent, and when others refused to obey.

# Coercion—Brainwashing and Cults
Is brainwashing actually possible? How are people converted into cult membership?

1.  A person has been coerced if they are _____ to change their beliefs _____ their will.

2.  _____ involves forced attitude _____ and requires a captive audience.

3.  _____ and conversion efforts by _____ also involve coercion.

556

## Psychology in Action: Assertiveness Training—Standing Up for Your Rights

How does self-assertion differ from aggression?

1. _____ involves clearly stating one's wants and needs to others.

2. _____ expresses one's feelings and desires, but it hurts others.

3. _____ behavior is self-denying and inhibited.

4. Learning to be assertive is accomplished by _____ and rehearsing assertive actions.

5. Self-assertion is also aided by _____ (practice that continues after initial mastery of a skill) and use of specific techniques, such as the " _____ _____ " (repeating a request until it is acknowledged).

# MASTERY TEST

1. Frequent television viewers _____ their chance of being harmed by another person.
   a. underestimate
   b. overestimate
   c. accurately estimate
   d. deny

2. Being an agent of an accepted social order is the basis for _____ power.
   a. coercive
   b. legitimate
   c. referent
   d. compliant

3. Randy is attempting to change another person's feelings, beliefs, and actions about an issue. Randy's behavior is an example of
   a. conformity.
   b. attitude.
   c. cognitive dissonance.
   d. persuasion.

4. We expect people to be respectful and polite at funerals because of
   a. situational demands.
   b. the door-in-the-face effect.
   c. attributional discounting.
   d. self-handicapping.

5. Which of the following is the strongest form of social influence?
   a. mere presence
   b. coercion
   c. conformity
   d. obedience

6. Which of the following is an assertiveness technique?
   a. foot-in-the-door
   b. calm absorption
   c. door-in-the-face
   d. broken record

7. The people that you identify with and whose attitudes and opinions you care about is called your
   a. proxemics.
   b. attribution.
   c. reference group.
   d. social influence.

8. "President of the United States" is
   a. an ascribed role.
   b. an achieved role.
   c. a structural norm.
   d. a cohesive role.

9. Where attribution is concerned, wants, needs, motives, or personal characteristics are perceived as
   a. external causes.
   b. situational attributions.
   c. discounted causes.
   d. internal causes.

10. Asch is to _____ experiments as Milgram is to _____ experiments.
    a. compliance; assertion
    b. conformity; obedience
    c. autokinetic; social power
    d. groupthink; authority

11. Social psychology is the scientific study of how people
    a. behave in the presence of others.
    b. form into groups and organizations.
    c. form and maintain interpersonal relationships.
    d. make inferences about the behavior of others.

12. "A person who first agrees with a small request is later more likely to comply with a larger demand." This summarizes the
    a.  low-ball technique.
    b.  set-the-hook technique.
    c.  door-in-the-face effect.
    d.  foot-in-the-door effect.

13. Large desks in business offices almost ensure that interactions with others take place at
    a.  ascribed distance.
    b.  social distance.
    c.  personal distance.
    d.  public distance.

14. Annie lies about being sick to get a day off of work. She told herself "They don't pay me enough and I really deserve and extra day off." This is an example of
    a.  conformity.
    b.  justification.
    c.  persuasion.
    d.  influence.

15. Group structure involves all but one of the following elements. Which does NOT belong?
    a.  roles
    b.  communication pathways
    c.  allocation of power
    d.  social comparisons

16. A "guard" in the Stanford prison experiment who discovers that one of the "prisoners" is a friend would very likely experience
    a.  role conflict.
    b.  a change in status.
    c.  groupthink.
    d.  a shift to coercive power.

17. Groupthink is a type of _____ that applies to decision making in groups.
    a.  conformity
    b.  social comparison
    c.  social power
    d.  obedience

18. If procrastinating on school assignments helps protect your self-image, you have used procrastination as a type of
    a.  autokinetic effect.
    b.  attributional error.
    c.  self-handicapping.
    d.  situational demand.

19. When two people view an autokinetic light at the same time, their estimates of movement
    a. polarize.
    b. normalize.
    c. cohere.
    d. converge.

20. In Milgram's studies, the smallest percentage of subjects followed orders when
    a. the teacher and learner were in the same room.
    b. the teacher received orders by phone.
    c. the teacher and learner were face to face.
    d. the experiment was conducted off campus.

21. The most basic attributional error is to attribute the behavior of others to _____ causes, even when they are caused by _____ causes.
    a. inconsistent, consistent
    b. internal, external
    c. random, distinctive
    d. situational, personal

22. Janet found that when she ran in a marathon, she performed better than when she trained alone. Her better performance when around other people is an example of
    a. social facilitation.
    b. social influence.
    c. social loafing.
    d. social power.

23. Jane has strong attitudes regarding women's rights. She recently took part in a demonstration, which is an example of the _____ of her attitudes.
    a. emotional
    b. belief
    c. conviction
    d. action

24. Which of the following methods of persuasion are used in brainwashing?
    a. mere presence
    b. compliance
    c. coercion
    d. conformity

25. Which of the following gives special privileges to a member of a group?
    a. convergent norms
    b. high cohesiveness
    c. actor-observer bias
    d. high status

26. When situational demands are strong we tend to discount _____ causes as a way of explaining another person's behavior.
    a. public
    b. internal
    c. legitimate
    d. external

27. When we are subjected to conformity pressures, the _____ of a majority is more important than the number of people in it.
    a. unanimity
    b. cohesion
    c. proximity
    d. comparison level

28. Distressed couples tend to _____ their partner's actions to negative motives.
    a. discount
    b. compare
    c. coerce
    d. attribute

29. Which of the following is NOT a component of attitudes?
    a. belief
    b. persuasion
    c. action
    d. emotional

30. _____ consists of a network of roles, communication pathways, and power in a group.
    a. Group cohesiveness
    b. Group structure
    c. Group norm
    d. Group goal

31. Members of the _____ are people who share similar values, goals, interest, and identify themselves as belonging to a same group.
    a. in-group
    b. out-group
    c. pep group
    d. essential group

32. Which tactic should one use to get someone to voluntarily comply with a request?
    a. foot-in-the-door
    b. door-in-the-face
    c. high-ball
    d. both A and B

33. Kyle has taken a psychology class and is aware of the tactics that salespeople use to hook customers into buying their products. He reviewed the cost of a car model that he is interested in from a consumer's reports guide. Having a general idea of a price, Kyle can negotiate with the salesperson, and after getting a quote from a salesperson, Kyle should
    a. buy the car immediately because the salesperson is offering him a good deal.
    b. tell the salesperson he has changed his mind and does not need a new car.
    c. tell the salesperson he cannot afford it.
    d. leave the store and compare the quoted price to other car dealers.

# SOLUTIONS

## RECITE AND REVIEW

### Humans in A Social Context—People, People, Everywhere: Pages 530-533
How does group membership affect individual behavior?

1. social
2. groups
3. Social roles
4. contradictory
5. prison
6. groups
7. roles; remain; in-group
8. in-group; ethnicity; religion; positive; out-group
9. standards; groups
10. movement; temporary

### Social Cognition—Behind the Mask: Pages 533-535
How do we perceive the motives of others, and the causes of our own behavior?

1. causes external
2. causes; causes
3. causes; actor
4. consistency
5. internal
6. external
7. error; internal; internal;
8. performance

### Attitudes—Belief + Emotion + Action: Pages 535-537
What are attitudes? How are they acquired?

1. preferences; behavior
2. attitude; emotion
3. belief
4. contact; child
5. immediate consequences
6. open-ended interview

### Attitude Change—Why the Seekers Went Public and Social Influence—Follow the Leader: Pages 537-540
Under what conditions is persuasion most effective? What is cognitive dissonance?

1. group; reference
2. attitudes; audience
3. contradicting; cognitive

## Social Influence—Follow the Leader: Page 540

What is social influence and social power?

1. behavior; others
2. presence; compliance
3. social power

## Mere Presence—Just Because You Are There: Pages 541-542

How does the mere presence of others affect behavior?

1. personal space
2. personal; social
3. cultures
4. better; less

## Conformity—Don't Stand Out: Pages 542-544

What have social psychologists learned about conformity?

1. behavior; norms
2. group
3. decision making

## Compliance—A Foot in the Door: Pages 544-547

What factors lead to increased conformity?

1. requests; power
2 .foot; face
3. even; price; writing
4. authority; requests

## Obedience—Would You Electrocute a Stranger?: Pages 547-549

Can people be too obedient?

1. authority
2. Obedience

## Coercion—Brainwashing and Cults: Pages 549-551

Is brainwashing actually possible? How are people converted into cult membership?

1. coerced; change
2. attitude; captive
3. conversion; coercion

## Psychology in Action: Assertiveness Training—Standing Up for Your Rights: Pages 551-553

How does self-assertion differ from aggression?

1. wants; needs
2. hurts
3. denying
4. assertive
5. continues; repeating

# CONNECTIONS

## Humans in a Social Context—People, People, Everywhere: Pages 530-533

How does group membership affect individual behavior?

1. c
2. e
3. g
4. a
5. f
6. b
7. d

## Social Cognition—Behind the Mask and Mere Presence—Just Because You Are There: Pages 533-535, 541-542

How do we perceive the motives of others, and the causes of our own behavior? How does the mere presence of others affect behavior?

| | | |
|---|---|---|
| 1. c | 4. d | 7. a |
| 2. e | 5. b | |
| 3. f | 6. g | |

## Attitudes—Belief + Emotion + Action and Attitude Change—Why the Seekers Went Public: Pages 535-540

What are attitudes? How are they acquired? Under what conditions is persuasion most effective? What is cognitive dissonance?

| | | |
|---|---|---|
| 1. e | 4. f | 7. c |
| 2. d | 5. a | |
| 3. g | 6. b | |

## Social Influence—Follow the Leader: Page 540

What is social influence and social power?

| | | |
|---|---|---|
| 1. f | 4. b | 7. a |
| 2. d | 5. g | |
| 3. e | 6. c | |

## Conformity—Don't Stand Out and Psychology in Action: Assertiveness Training—Standing Up for Your Rights: Pages 542-544, 551-553

What have social psychologists learned about conformity? How does self-assertion differ from aggression?

| | | |
|---|---|---|
| 1. d | 4. a | 6. c |
| 2. e | 5. f | 7. g |
| 3. b | | |

# CHECK YOUR MEMORY

## Humans in Social Context—People, People, Everywhere: Pages 530-533

How does group membership affect individual behavior?

| | | |
|---|---|---|
| 1. F | 5. F | 9. F |
| 2. T | 6. T | 10. T |
| 3. F | 7. T | 11. F |
| 4. T | 8. T | |

## Attitudes—Belief + Emotion + Action: Pages 535-537
What are attitudes? How are they acquired?

1. F

2. T

3. F

4. F

5. F

## Attitude Change—Why the Seekers Went Public: Pages 537-540
Under what conditions is persuasion most effective? What is cognitive dissonance?

1. F

2. F

3. T

## Social Cognition—Behind the Mask: Pages 533-535
How do we perceive the motives of others, and the causes of our own behavior?

1. F

2. F

3. F

4. T

5. T

6. F

7. T

## Conformity—Don't Stand Out: Pages 542-544
What have social psychologists learned about conformity?

1. T

2. F

3. T

4. T

5. F

6. F

7. T

8. T

9. F

10. T

11. F

12. T

13. T

14. T

15. F

## Coercion—Brainwashing and Cults: Pages 549-551
Is brainwashing actually possible? How are people converted into cult membership?

1. F

2. T

3. F

4. T

## Psychology in Action: Assertiveness Training—Standing Up for Your Rights: Pages 551-553
How does self-assertion differ from aggression?

1. T

2. F

3. T

4. F

5. F

6. T

# FINAL SURVEY AND REVIEW

## Humans in Social Context—People, People, Everywhere
How does group membership affect individual behavior?

1. Social; psychology
2. Culture; roles
3. achieved; ascribed
4. conflict
5. Stanford; roles
6. status; High; status
7. structure; cohesiveness; in-group
8. in-group; positive; negative
9. Norms
10. autokinetic; stationary; norms

## Social Cognition—Behind the Mask
How do we perceive the motives of others, and the causes of our own behavior?

1. Attribution
2. internal; external
3. object; setting
4. distinctiveness
5. Situational; discount
6. Consensus
7. fundamental; attributional; actor-observer
8. Self-handicapping

## Attitudes—Belief + Emotion + Action
What are attitudes? How are they acquired?

1. Attitudes; actions
2. belief; positive
3. Attitudes; action
4. interaction; media
5. evaluate; conviction
6. attitude scales

## Attitude Change—Why the Seekers Went Public
Under what conditions is persuasion most effective? What is cognitive dissonance?

1. social; attitudes
2. persuasion; communicator
3. discomfort; dissonance

## Social Influence—Follow the Leader
What is social influence and social power?

1. influence; behavior
2. social; coercion
3. reward; expert

## Mere Presence—Just Because You Are There
How does the mere presence of others affect behavior?

1. proxemics
2. intimate; public
3. Norms
4. facilitation; loafing

## Conformity—Don't Stand Out
What have social psychologists learned about conformity?

1. agreement; pressure
2. Asch; conformity
3. Groupthink; approval

## Compliance—A Foot in the Door
What factors lead to increased compliance?

1. Compliance
2. door; door; low-ball
3. even; price; writing
4. passive

## Obedience—Would You Electrocute a Stranger?
Can people be too obedient?

1. Obedience; Milgram
2. decreased; authority

## Coercion—Brainwashing and Cults
Is brainwashing actually possible? How are people converted to cult membership?

1. forced; beliefs
2. brainwashing; change
3. recruitment; cult

## Psychology in Action: Assertiveness Training—Standing Up for Your Rights
How does self-assertion differ from aggression?

1. Self-assertion
2. Aggression
3. Non-assertive
4. role-playing
5. overlearning; broken record

# MASTERY TEST

1. b, p. 526
2. b, p. 540
3. d, p. 538
4. a, p. 534
5. b, p. 540
6. d, p. 552
7. c, p. 537
8. b, p. 530
9. d, p. 533
10. b, pp. 543, 547
11. a, p. 530
12. d, p. 545
13. b, p. 542
14. b, p. 539
15. d, p. 553
16. a, p. 531
17. a, p. 543
18. c, p. 534
19. d, p. 532
20. b, p. 548
21. b, pp. 534-535
22. a, p. 541
23. d, p. 537
24. c, p. 549
25. d, p. 531
26. b, p. 534
27. a, p. 544
28. d, p. 533
29. b, pp. 535-536
30. b, p. 531
31. a, p. 531
32. d, p. 545
33. d, p. 546

# Prosocial and Antisocial Behavior

## Chapter Overview

The need to affiliate is related to needs for approval, support, friendship, information, and desires to reduce anxiety or uncertainty. Social comparison theory holds that we affiliate to evaluate our actions, feelings, and abilities. Interpersonal attraction is increased by physical proximity, frequent contact, physical attractiveness, competence, and similarity. Self-disclosure, which follows a reciprocity norm, occurs more when two people like one another. According to social exchange theory, we tend to maintain relationships that are profitable. Sternberg's triangular theory of love distinguishes between different types of love which arise from three basic components - intimacy, passion, and commitment. Adult love relationships tend to mirror patterns of emotional attachment observed in infancy and early childhood. Evolutionary psychology attributes human mating patterns to the reproductive challenges faced by men and women since the dawn of time.

Four decision points that must be passed before we give help to others are: noticing, defining an emergency, taking responsibility, and selecting a course of action. Helping is less likely at each point when other potential helpers are present. Giving help tends to encourage others to help too.

Ethologists blame aggression on instincts. Biological explanations emphasize brain mechanisms and physical factors. Aggression tends to follow frustration, especially when aggression cues are present. Social learning theory relates aggressive behavior to the influence of aggressive models. Students who plan to commit violence in school might disrupt classes, fight, join gangs, destroy property, get frustrated easily, react with extreme anger to criticism, blame others for their troubles, and use drugs.

Prejudice is a negative attitude held toward out-group members. Prejudice can be attributed to scapegoating, personal prejudice, group norms, and authoritarian personality traits. Intergroup conflict leads to hostility and stereotyping. Status inequalities tend to build prejudices. Equal-status contact and superordinate goals tend to reduce these problems.

Multiculturalism is an attempt to give equal status to different ethnic, racial, and cultural groups. To reduce conflict and misunderstanding between members of different ethnic groups, one can do the following: Be aware of stereotyping, seek individuating information, beware of just-world beliefs, understand that race is a social construction, look for commonalities, and set examples for others. Cultural awareness is a key element in promoting greater social harmony.

# Learning Objectives

*Theme: Social life is complex, but consistent patterns can be found in our positive and negative interactions with others.*

| |
|---|
| **GQ: Why do people affiliate?** |
| LO 17.1 Distinguish between *prosocial* and *antisocial behavior*. |
| LO 17.2 State the needs that appear to be satisfied by affiliation; and describe the research indicating humans have a *need to affiliate*. |
| LO 17.3 Describe *social comparison* theory; explain the diference between downward and *upward comparison*. |
| **GQ: What factors influence interpersonal attraction?** |
| LO 17.4 List and describe the factors that affect *interpersonal attraction*. Include a description of *homogamy*. |
| LO 17.5 Explain *self-disclosure*; discuss the effects of varying degrees of disclosure on interpersonal relationships; and explain the difference in gendered friendships. |
| LO 17.6 Describe the *social exchange theory* as it relates to interpersonal relationships. |
| **GQ: How do liking and loving differ?** |
| LO 17.7 Describe the three components in Sternberg's triangular theory of love. Using the theory, define *liking*, *romantic love, companionate love,* and *consummate love* (including the term *mutual absorption*). |
| LO 17.8 Define the three different love/attachment styles); define the term *evolutionary psychology;* and describe how it explains the different mating preferences of males and females. |
| **GQ: Why are bystanders so often unwilling to help in an emergency?** |
| LO 17.9 Give an example of *bystander apathy*; explain how the presence of other people can influence apathy; describe four conditions that need to exist before bystanders are likely to give help; discuss how heightened and *empathetic arousal* affect helping behavior; and state three ways in which prosocial behavior can be encouraged. |
| **GQ: How do psychologists explain human aggression?** |
| LO 17.10 Define *aggression*; and discuss the role of each of the following in aggressive behavior: a. instincts; b. biology; c. *frustration-aggression hypothesis*; d. frustration, in the form of aversive stimuli; e. *weapons effect*; and d. *social learning theory*. Include a brief description of the results of studies on the relationship between *aggressive pornography* and aggression of males toward females. |
| LO 17.11 Explain how media including television may serve as a *disinhibiting* factor with respect to aggression; present evidence to support the viewpoint that interacting with media can cause a *desensitization* to violence; list seven ways in which parents can buffer the impact of media on children's behavior; and explain how watching television can also increase prosocial behavior. |
| LO 17.12 Explain the basic principle of *anger control* and describe five strategies for controlling anger. |
| **GQ: What causes prejudice?** |
| LO 17.13 Define and differentiate *prejudice* and *discrimination*; define *implicit prejudice*; explain how *scapegoating* relates to prejudice; and distinguish between *personal* and *group prejudices*. |
| LO 17.14 Describe the characteristic beliefs (including *ethnocentrism* and *dogmatism*) and childhood experiences of the *authoritarian personality*. |
| **GQ: What can be done about prejudice and intergroup conflict?** |
| LO 17.15 Present the major characteristics of *social stereotypes* and indicate how they may lead to intergroup conflicts. Include a description of *symbolic prejudice*. |
| LO 17.16 Explain how *status inequalities* may lead to the development of stereotypes and how *equal-status contact* may reduce intergroup tension. Give an example of each situation. |
| LO 17.17 Define *superordinate goals* and include an explanation of how they can reduce conflict and hostility; and explain how a *jigsaw classroom* utilizes superordinate goals and helps reduce prejudice. |
| **GQ: How can we promote multiculturalism and social harmony?** |
| LO 17.18 Define the term *multiculturalism*; discuss eight ways in which a person can become more tolerant; and explain how a person can develop cultural awareness. |

# RECITE AND REVIEW

## The Need for Affiliation—Come Together: Pages 557-558
Why do people affiliate?

1. The need to affiliate is tied to needs for _____ , support, friendship, and _____ .

2. Additionally, research indicates that we sometimes affiliate to _____ anxiety and uncertainty.

3. Social comparison theory holds that we affiliate to _____ our actions, feelings, and abilities.

4. Social _____ are also made for purposes of self-protection and self-enhancement.

5. Downward _____ are sometimes used to make us feel better when faced with a threat. Upward

_____ may be used for self-improvement.

## Interpersonal Attraction—Social Magnetism?: Pages 558-561
What factors influence interpersonal attraction?

1. Interpersonal attraction is increased by physical proximity ( _____ ) and frequent _____ .

2. Initial acquaintance and _____ are influenced by physical attractiveness (beauty), competence (high ability), and _____ (being alike).

3. A large degree of _____ on many dimensions is characteristic of _____ selection, a pattern called homogamy.

4. Self-disclosure ( _____ oneself to others) occurs to a greater degree if two people like one another.

5. Self-disclosure follows a reciprocity _____ : Low levels of self-disclosure are met with low levels in return, whereas moderate self-disclosure elicits more personal replies.

6. Overdisclosure tends to inhibit _____ by others.

7. According to social exchange theory, we tend to maintain relationships that are profitable; that is, those for which perceived _____ exceed perceived _____ .

571

## Liking and Loving—Dating, Rating, Mating: Pages 561-563
How do liking and loving differ?

1.  Sternberg's _____ theory of love distinguishes between different types of love which arise from three basic components - _____, passion, and commitment.

2.  Romantic love is also associated with greater _____ absorption between people.

3.  Adult _____ relationships tend to mirror patterns of emotional attachment observed in infancy and early childhood.

4.  _____ , avoidant, and ambivalent patterns can be defined on the basis of how a person approaches romantic and affectionate relationships with others.

5.  Evolutionary psychology attributes human _____ patterns to the differing reproductive challenges faced by men and women since the dawn of time.

6.  David Buss's study on human mating patterns showed that men prefer _____ and physically attractive partners, and women prefer _____ partners who are industrious, high in status, and successful.

## Helping Others—The Good Samaritan: Pages 564-566
Why are bystanders so often unwilling to help in an emergency?

1.  Prosocial behavior is _____, constructive, or altruistic toward others.

2.  Bystander apathy is the unwillingness of bystanders to offer _____ to others during emergencies.

3.  Four decision points that must be passed before a person gives help are: _____ , defining an emergency, taking responsibility, and selecting a course of action.

4.  Helping is _____ likely at each point when other potential helpers are present.

5.  Helping is encouraged by general arousal, empathic _____, being in a good mood, low effort or _____ , and perceived similarity between the victim and the helper.

6.  Altruistic behaviors can be seen in people who perform acts of ___by saving people

    from various disasters, _____ their kidneys and blood, volunteering for the Peace Corps,

    and _____ children's games.

7.  A method to _____ negative stereotypes is to use individuating information, which requires

    getting to know someone on an_____ and personal level.

# Aggression—The World's Most Dangerous Animal: Pages 566-571

## How do psychologists explain human aggression?

1.  Ethologists explain aggression as a natural expression of inherited _____.

2.  Biological explanations emphasize brain mechanisms and physical factors that_____ the

    threshold (trigger point) for aggression.

3.  According to the frustration-_____ hypothesis, frustration and _____ are closely

    linked.

4.  Frustration is only one of many aversive _____that can arouse a person and make

    aggression more likely. Aggression is especially likely to occur when        cues (stimuli associated

    with aggression) are present.

5.  Social learning theory has focused attention on the role of aggressive_____ in the

    development of aggressive behavior.

6.  Aggressive _____ on television, violent video games, and violent song lyrics encourage

    aggression because they desensitize (lower the sensitivity of) _____ to violence and

    disinhibit (remove restraints against) aggressive impulses.

7.  To _____ anger, aggression, and violence, parents should_____children, avoid

    hitting children, be consistent in disciplining children, and teach children _____ ways to

    solve problems.

# Prejudice—Attitudes that Injure: Pages 571-573
What causes prejudice?

1.  Prejudice is a _____ attitude held toward members of various out-groups.

2.  Racism, ageism, and sexism are specific types of prejudice based on race, age, and _____.

3.  One theory attributes prejudice to scapegoating, which is a type of displaced _____.

4.  A second account says that prejudices may be held for personal reasons such as direct threats to a person's well being (personal prejudice) or simply through adherence to group _____ (group prejudice).

5.  Prejudiced individuals tend to have an authoritarian or dogmatic _____ , characterized by rigidity, inhibition, intolerance, and _____ -simplification.

6.  Authoritarians tend to be very ethnocentric (they use their own_____as a basis for judging all others).

# Intergroup Conflict—The Roots of Prejudice: Pages 573-579
What can be done about prejudice and intergroup conflict?

1.  Intergroup _____ gives rise to hostility and the formation of social stereotypes (over-simplified images of members of various groups).

2.  Symbolic prejudice, or prejudice expressed in _____ ways, is common today.

3.  _____ inequalities (differences in power, prestige, or privileges) tend to build prejudices.

4.  In-group beliefs of superiority, _____ , vulnerability, and distrust are common variables that promote _____ between groups.

5.  Equal-status contact (social interaction on an equal footing) tends to_____ prejudice.

6.  Superordinate _____ (those that rise above all others) usually reduce intergroup conflict.

7.  On a small scale, jigsaw _____ (which encourage cooperation through _____ interdependence) have been shown to be an effective way of combating prejudice.

## Psychology in Action: Multiculturalism—Living with Diversity: Pages 579-581

How can we promote multiculturalism and promote social harmony?

1. Multiculturalism is an attempt to give _____ status to different ethnic, racial, and cultural groups.

2. To _____ prejudice, one can do the following: Be _____ _____ of stereotyping, seek individuating information, beware of _____ -world beliefs, understand that race is a _____ construction, look for commonalities, and set examples for others.

3. Greater tolerance can be encouraged by neutralizing stereotypes with individuating information (which helps see others as _____ ).

4. Tolerance comes from looking for commonalties with others and by avoiding the effects of just-world _____ , self-fulfilling prophecies, and _____ competition.

5. _____ awareness is a key element in promoting greater social harmony. It refers to _____ one's understanding of how people from different cultures and religious backgrounds practice their _____ and traditions to _____ misunderstanding, stereotyping, and prejudice.

# CONNECTIONS

## The Need for Affiliation—Come Together and Interpersonal Attraction—Social Magnetism?: Pages 557-561

Why do people affiliate? What factors influence interpersonal attraction?

1. _____ proximity
2. _____ halo effect
3. _____ competency
4. _____ reciprocity
5. _____ need to affiliate
6. _____ social comparison
7. _____ interpersonal attraction
8. _____ social exchange

a. relating self to others
b. generalized impression
c. rewards minus costs
d. return in kind
e. a person's proficiency
f. affinity to others
g. desire to associate
h. nearness

## Helping Others—The Good Samaritan and Psychology in Action: Multiculturalism—Living with Diversity: Pages 564-566, 579-581

Why are bystanders so often unwilling to help in an emergency? What can be done to promote multiculturalism and social harmony?

| | | | |
|---|---|---|---|
| 1. | _____ social competition | a. | taking responsibility |
| 2. | _____ spreading the accountability | b. | feeling someone's anguish |
| 3. | _____ bystander apathy | c. | group rivalry |
| 4. | _____ just-world beliefs | d. | Kitty Genovese |
| 5. | _____ bystander intervention | e. | diffusion of responsibility |
| 6. | _____ empathic arousal | f. | "tossed salad" |
| 7. | _____ multiculturalism | g. | she gets what she deserves |

## Aggression—The World's Most Dangerous Animal: Pages 566-571

How do psychologists explain human aggression?

| | | | |
|---|---|---|---|
| 1. | _____ prosocial | a. | instincts |
| 2. | _____ ethology | b. | television perspective |
| 3. | _____ weapons effect | c. | reduced emotional sensitivity |
| 4. | _____ desensitization | d. | remove inhibition |
| 5. | _____ mean world | e. | aggression cue |
| 6. | _____ disinhibition | f. | altruistic |

## Prejudice—Attitudes That Injure and Intergroup Conflict—The Roots of Prejudice: Pages 571-579

What causes prejudice? What can be done about prejudice and intergroup conflict?

| | | | |
|---|---|---|---|
| 1. | _____ scapegoat | a. | unequal treatment |
| 2. | _____ authoritarianism | b. | aggression target |
| 3. | _____ implicit association test | c. | modern bias |
| 4. | _____ ethnocentric | d. | above all others |
| 5. | _____ dogmatism | e. | F scale |
| 6. | _____ discrimination | f. | group-centered |
| 7. | _____ stereotype | g. | unwarranted certainty |
| 8. | _____ symbolic prejudice | h. | simplified image |
| 9. | _____ superordinate | i. | reveals hidden prejudices |

# CHECK YOUR MEMORY

## The Need for Affiliation—Come Together: Pages 557-558
Why do people affiliate?

1. The need to affiliate is a basic human characteristic.   TRUE or FALSE

2. People who are frightened prefer to be with others who are in similar circumstances.
   TRUE or FALSE

3. Social comparisons are used to confirm objective evaluations and measurements.
   TRUE or FALSE

4. Useful social comparisons are usually made with persons similar to ourselves.   TRUE or FALSE

5. Some social comparisons are made for self-protection.   TRUE or FALSE

6. Downward social comparisons are typically made for self-improvement.   TRUE or FALSE

## Interpersonal Attraction—Social Magnetism Liking and Loving—Dating, Rating, Mating?: Pages 558-564
What factors influence interpersonal attraction? How do liking and loving differ?

1. Interpersonal attraction to someone takes weeks to develop.   TRUE or FALSE

2. Nearness has a powerful impact on forming friendships.   TRUE or FALSE

3. Physical proximity leads us to think of people as competent, and therefore worth knowing.
   TRUE or FALSE

4. The halo effect is the tendency to generalize a positive or negative first impression to other
   personal characteristics.   TRUE or FALSE

5. Physical attractiveness is closely associated with intelligence, talents, and abilities.
   TRUE or FALSE

6. Physical attractiveness has more influence on women's fates than men's.   TRUE or FALSE

7. Homogamy, marrying someone who is like oneself, does not apply to unmarried couples.
   TRUE or FALSE

8. The risk of divorce is higher than average for couples who have large differences in age and education.
   TRUE or FALSE

9. In choosing mates, women rank physical attractiveness as the most important feature.
   TRUE or FALSE

10. Self-disclosure is a major step toward friendship.   TRUE or FALSE

577

11. Overdisclosure tends to elicit maximum self-disclosure from others.   TRUE or FALSE

12. Self-disclosure through an Internet chat room can lead to genuine, face-to-face friendship.
TRUE or FALSE

13. Male friendships tend to be activity-based; women's friendships tend to be based on shared feelings and confidences.   TRUE or FALSE

14. The personal standard used to judge the acceptability of a social exchange is called the comparison level.   TRUE or FALSE

15. The statement, "I find it easy to ignore _____ 's faults" is an item on the Liking Scale.
TRUE or FALSE

16. People with an avoidant attachment style tend to form relationships that are marked by mixed emotions.
TRUE or FALSE

17. Where their mates are concerned, men tend to be more jealous over a loss of emotional commitment than they are over sexual infidelities.   TRUE or FALSE

18. Although women tend to give "polite" answers about men's infidelity, privately, they are just as angry as men are about infidelity.   TRUE or FALSE

## Helping Others—The Good Samaritan: Pages 564-566
Why are bystanders so often unwilling to help in an emergency?

1.  In the Kitty Genovese murder, no one called the police until after the attack was over.
TRUE or FALSE

2.  In an emergency, the more potential helpers present, the more likely a person is to get help.
TRUE or FALSE

3.  The first step in giving help is to define the situation as an emergency.   TRUE or FALSE

4.  Emotional arousal, especially empathic arousal, lowers the likelihood that one person will help another.   TRUE or FALSE

5.  You are more likely to help a person who seems similar to yourself.   TRUE or FALSE

6.  In many emergency situations it can be more effective to shout "Fire!" rather than "Help!"
TRUE or FALSE

## Aggression—The World's Most Dangerous Animal: Pages 566-571
How do psychologists explain human aggression?

1.  Over 75 percent of all married persons physically attack their spouses at one time or another.
TRUE or FALSE

578

2. Ethologists argue that humans learn to be aggressive by observing aggressive behavior in lower animals.    TRUE or FALSE

3. Specific areas of the brain are capable of initiating or ending aggression.    TRUE or FALSE

4. Intoxication tends to raise the threshold for aggression, making it more likely.    TRUE or FALSE

5. Higher levels of the hormone testosterone are associated with more aggressive behavior by both men and women.    TRUE or FALSE

6. The frustration-aggression hypothesis says that being aggressive is frustrating.    TRUE or FALSE

7. People exposed to aversive stimuli tend to become less sensitive to aggression cues.
   TRUE or FALSE

8. Murders are less likely to occur in homes where guns are kept.    TRUE or FALSE

9. Social learning theorists assume that instinctive patterns of human aggression are modified by learning.    TRUE or FALSE

10. American Quakers have adopted a nonviolent way of life as a way to inhibit aggression.
    TRUE or FALSE

11. According to Leonard Eron, children learn aggression from direct contact with other children and not from indirect contact of viewing TV programs that shows aggressive behaviors.    TRUE or FALSE

12. To discourage violence, parents should get themselves and their children involved in community-related activities.    TRUE or FALSE

13. The erotic content of pornography is usually more damaging than the aggressive content.
    TRUE or FALSE

14. Aggressive crimes in TV dramas occur at a much higher rate than they do in real life.
    TRUE or FALSE

15. Preferring violent TV programs at age 8 predicts higher levels of violent behavior at age 19.
    TRUE or FALSE

16. Prosocial TV programs have little effect on viewer behavior.    TRUE or FALSE

17. An important element of anger control is looking at upsetting situations as problems to be solved.
    TRUE or FALSE

18. Modeling positive ways of getting along with others can help to counteract the effects of exposure to media violence.    TRUE or FALSE

19. Children who see violence in the community tend to be less likely to engage in violence themselves.
    TRUE or FALSE

# Prejudice—Attitudes That Injure and Intergroup Conflict—The Roots of Prejudice: Pages 571-579

What causes prejudice? What can be done about prejudice and intergroup conflict?

1. Sexism is a type of prejudice.    TRUE or FALSE

2. The implicit association test reveals people's tendency to harbor hidden prejudicial views of others even when they explicitly deny it.    TRUE or FALSE

3. The term *racial profiling* refers to giving preferential treatment to some students seeking admission to college.    TRUE or FALSE

4. Scapegoating is a prime example of discrimination.    TRUE or FALSE

5. A person who views members of another group as competitors for jobs displays group prejudice.    TRUE or FALSE

6. Authoritarian persons tend to be prejudiced against all out-groups.    TRUE or FALSE

7. The F in F scale stands for fanatic.    TRUE or FALSE

8. An authoritarian would agree that people can be divided into the weak and the strong.    TRUE or FALSE

9. Dogmatic personalities are found at both ends of the political spectrum.    TRUE or FALSE

10. Social stereotypes can be positive as well as negative.    TRUE or FALSE

11. People who feel they are being evaluated in terms of a stereotype tend to become anxious, which can lower their performance and seemingly confirm the stereotype.    TRUE or FALSE

12. Children as young as age three have begun to show signs of racial bias.    TRUE or FALSE

13. Beliefs on superiority, injustice, and distrust are common variables that tend to promote conflict among members of the in-group.    TRUE or FALSE

14. Symbolic prejudice occurs when people understand the causes of prejudice and do not discriminate against minorities.    TRUE or FALSE

15. Symbolic prejudice is the most obvious and socially unacceptable form of bigotry.    TRUE or FALSE

16. Images of national enemies tend to humanize the inhabitants of other countries, making them seem less threatening.    TRUE or FALSE

17. The key to creating prejudice in Jane Elliot's experiment was her use of scapegoating to cause group conflict.    TRUE or FALSE

18. Equal-status contact tends to reduce prejudice and stereotypes.    TRUE or FALSE

19. Superordinate groups help people of opposing groups to see themselves as members of a single larger group.    TRUE or FALSE

20. Prejudice tends to be reduced when members of groups that have higher status offer to reward members of other groups for cooperating.   TRUE or FALSE

21. Presidential maps that divide states into "red" and "blue" have had the effect of decreasing between-group prejudice.   TRUE or FALSE

# Psychology in Action: Multiculturalism—Living with Diversity: Pages 579-581

How can we promote multiculturalism and promote social harmony?

1.  Multiculturalism is an attempt to blend multiple ethnic backgrounds into one universal culture.
    TRUE or FALSE

2.  A study conducted in Canada found that increasing interaction among different groups only increases negative stereotypes of both groups.   TRUE or FALSE

3.  Members of major groups in the United States rated themselves better than other groups to enhance their self-esteem.   TRUE or FALSE

4.  The emotional component of prejudicial attitudes may remain even after a person intellectually renounces prejudice.   TRUE or FALSE

5.  Both prejudiced and nonprejudiced people are equally aware of social stereotypes.
    TRUE or FALSE

6.  Individuating information forces us to focus mainly on the labels attached to a person.
    TRUE or FALSE

7.  From a scientific point of view, "race" is a matter of social labeling, not a biological reality.
    TRUE or FALSE

8.  People who hold just-world beliefs assume that people generally get what they deserve.
    TRUE or FALSE

9.  Every major ethnic group rates itself better than other groups.   TRUE or FALSE

10. The statement "Don't judge somebody until you know them. The color of their skin doesn't matter" is an example of a way to promote understanding in an ethnically diverse group of people.
    TRUE or FALSE

# FINAL SURVEY AND REVIEW

## The Need for Affiliation—Come Together
Why do people affiliate?

1. The _____ to _____ is tied to needs for approval, support, friendship, and information.

2. Additionally, research indicates that we sometimes affiliate to reduce _____ and uncertainty.

3. Social _____ theory holds that we affiliate to evaluate our actions, feelings, and abilities.

4. Social comparisons are also made for purposes of self- _____ and self-enhancement.

5. _____ comparisons are sometimes used to make us feel better when faced with a threat. _____ comparisons may be used for self-improvement.

## Interpersonal Attraction—Social Magnetism?
What factors influence interpersonal attraction?

1. Interpersonal attraction is increased by physical _____ (nearness) and frequent contact.

2. Initial acquaintance and attraction are influenced by _____ attractiveness (beauty), _____ (high ability), and similarity.

3. A large degree of similarity on many dimensions is characteristic of mate selection, a pattern called _____ .

4. _____ (revealing oneself to others) occurs to a greater degree if two people like one another.

5. Self-disclosure follows a _____ norm: Low levels of self-disclosure are met with low levels in return, whereas moderate self-disclosure elicits more personal replies.

6. _____ tends to inhibit self-disclosure by others.

7. According to social _____ theory, we tend to maintain relationships that are _____ ; that is, those for which perceived rewards exceed perceived costs.

## Loving and Liking—Dating, Rating, Mating
How do liking and loving differ?

1. _____ triangular theory of love distinguishes between different types of love which arise from three basic components - intimacy, passion, and _____ .

2. Romantic love is also associated with greater mutual _____ between people.

3. Adult love relationships tend to mirror patterns of emotional _____ observed in infancy and early childhood.

4. Secure, _____ (noncommittal), and _____ (conflicted) patterns can be defined on the basis of how a person approaches romantic and affectionate relationships with others.

5. _____ psychology attributes human mating patterns to the differing _____ challenges faced by men and women since the dawn of time.

6. David Buss's study on human mating patterns showed that _____ prefer younger and physically attractive partners, and _____ prefer older partners who are industrious, high in status, and _____ successful.

## Helping Others—The Good Samaritan
Why are bystanders so often unwilling to help in an emergency?

1. Prosocial behavior is helpful, constructive, or _____ toward others.

2. Bystander _____ is the unwillingness of bystanders to offer help to others during emergencies.

3. Four decision points that must be passed before a person gives help are: noticing, defining an _____ , taking _____ , and selecting a course of action.

4. Helping is less likely at each point when other _____ are present.

5. Helping is encouraged by general arousal, _____ arousal, being in a good mood, low effort or risk, and perceived _____ between the victim and the helper.

6. _____ behaviors can be seen in people who perform acts of heroism by _____ people from various disasters, _____ their kidneys and blood, volunteering for the Peace Corps, and coaching children's games.

7. A method to reduce negative stereotypes is to use _____ information, which requires getting to know someone on an individual and personal level.

## Aggression—The World's Most Dangerous Animal
How do psychologists explain human aggression?

1. _____ explain aggression as a natural expression of inherited instincts.

2. Biological explanations emphasize brain mechanisms and physical factors that lower the _____ (trigger point) for aggression.

583

3. According to the _____ -aggression hypothesis, _____ and aggression are closely linked.

4. Frustration is only one of many _____ stimuli that can arouse a person and make aggression more likely. Aggression is especially likely to occur when aggression_____ (stimuli associated with aggression) are present.

5. _____ _____ theory has focused attention on the role of aggressive models in the development of aggressive behavior.

6. Aggressive models on television, violent video games, and violent song lyrics encourage aggression because they _____ (lower the sensitivity of) viewers to violence and _____ (remove restraints against) aggressive impulses.

7. To _____anger, aggression, and violence, parents should supervise children, _____ hitting children, be consistent in disciplining children, and teach children _____ ways to solve problems.

# Prejudice—Attitudes that Injure
## What causes prejudice?

1. Prejudice is a negative attitude held toward members of various _____ .

2. _____ , _____ , and _____ are specific types of prejudice based on race, age, and gender.

3. One theory attributes prejudice to _____, which is a type of _____aggression.

4. A second account says that prejudices may be held for personal reasons such as direct threats to a person's well being ( _____ prejudice) or simply through adherence to group norms ( _____prejudice).

5. Prejudiced individuals tend to have an_____ or dogmatic personality, characterized by rigidity, inhibition, intolerance, and over-simplification.

6. Authoritarians tend to be very _____ (they use their own group as a basis for judging all others).

# Intergroup Conflict—The Roots of Prejudice
What can be done about prejudice and intergroup conflict?

1. Intergroup conflict gives rise to hostility and the formation of _____ _____ (over-simplified images of members of various groups).

2. _____ prejudice, or prejudice expressed in disguised ways, is common today.

3. Status _____ (differences in power, prestige, or privileges) tend to build prejudices.

4. _____ beliefs of superiority, injustice, vulnerability, and distrust are common variables that promote _____ between groups.

5. _____ contact (social interaction on an equal footing) tends to reduce prejudice.

6. _____ goals (those that rise above all others) usually reduce intergroup conflict.

7. On a small scale, _____ classrooms (which encourage cooperation through mutual _____ ) have been shown to be an effective way of combating prejudice.

# Psychology in Action: Multiculturalism—Living with Diversity
How can we promote multiculturism and promote social harmony?

1. _____ is an attempt to give equal status to different ethnic, racial, and cultural groups.

2. To reduce prejudice, one can do the following: Be _____ of stereotyping, seek individuating information, beware of _____-world beliefs, understand that race is a _____ construction, look for commonalities, and set examples for others.

3. Greater tolerance can be encouraged by neutralizing stereotypes with _____ information (which helps see others as individuals).

4. Tolerance comes from looking for commonalties with others and by avoiding the effects of _____ beliefs, _____ prophecies, and social competition.

5. Cultural _____ is a key element in promoting greater social harmony. It refers to increasing one's _____ of how people from different cultures and religious backgrounds practice their beliefs and traditions to prevent misunderstanding, _____ , and prejudice.

# MASTERY TEST

1. The weapons effect refers to the fact that weapons can serve as aggression
   a. thresholds.
   b. cues.
   c. models.
   d. inhibitors.

2. Homogamy is directly related to which element of interpersonal attraction?
   a. competence
   b. similarity
   c. beauty
   d. proximity

3. One thing that reduces the chances that a bystander will give help in an emergency is
   a. heightened arousal.
   b. empathic arousal.
   c. others who could help.
   d. similarity to the victim.

4. Suspicion and reduced attraction are associated with
   a. reciprocity.
   b. self-disclosure.
   c. competence and proximity.
   d. overdisclosure.

5. One consequence of seeing aggression portrayed on TV is a loss of emotional response, called
   a. disinhibition.
   b. disassociation.
   c. deconditioning.
   d. desensitization.

6. Conflicting feelings of anger, affection, doubt, and attraction are characteristic of what attachment style?
   a. avoidant
   b. ambivalent
   c. compliant
   d. kinetic

7.  Which view of human aggression is most directly opposed to that of the ethologists?
    a.  social learning
    b.  brain mechanisms
    c.  sociobiological
    d.  innate releaser

8.  Using social comparison for self-protection typically involves
    a.  external attributions.
    b.  comparisons with group norms.
    c.  downward comparisons.
    d.  comparison with a person of higher ability.

9.  Research suggests that the most damaging element of pornography is the
    a.  erotic content.
    b.  nudity.
    c.  aggressive content.
    d.  impersonality.

10. Creating superordinate goals is an important way to
    a.  reduce group conflict.
    b.  break the frustration-aggression link.
    c.  promote bystander intervention.
    d.  reverse self-fulfilling prophecies.

11. Children who learn good manners by watching television demonstrate that TV can promote
    a.  disinhibition.
    b.  prosocial behavior.
    c.  deconditioning.
    d.  superordinate behavior.

12. A person who is dogmatic and politically conservative would be most likely to score high on the
    a.  R Scale.
    b.  Individuation Inventory.
    c.  Social Competition Scale.
    d.  F Scale.

13. A major problem with the ethological view of human aggression is that
    a.  labeling a behavior does not explain it.
    b.  aversive stimuli alter the threshold for aggression.
    c.  it assumes that aggression begets aggression.
    d.  it assumes that aggression is related to biological processes.

14. Comparison level is an important concept in
    a.  social comparison theory.
    b.  social exchange theory.
    c.  evolutionary psychology.
    d.  social compliance theory.

15. In an experiment, most women waiting to receive a shock preferred to wait with others who
    a. were about to be shocked.
    b. did not share their fears.
    c. were trained to calm them.
    d. had been shocked the day before.

16. A key element in the effectiveness of jigsaw classrooms is
    a. deindividuation.
    b. the promotion of self-fulfilling prophecies.
    c. mutual interdependence.
    d. selecting competent student leaders.

17. A good antidote for social stereotyping is
    a. adopting just-world beliefs.
    b. creating self-fulfilling prophecies.
    c. accepting status inequalities.
    d. seeking individuating information.

18. Evolutionary theories attribute mate selection, in part, to the _____ of past generations.
    a. food-gathering habits
    b. tribal customs
    c. maternal instincts
    d. reproductive success

19. The "what is beautiful is good" stereotype typically does NOT include the assumption that physically attractive people are more
    a. likable.
    b. intelligent.
    c. honest.
    d. mentally healthy.

20. The effects of frustration on aggression are most like the effects of _____ on aggression.
    a. social learning
    b. prosocial models
    c. defining an emergency
    d. aversive stimuli

21. Which of the following factors does NOT increase interpersonal attraction?
    a. competence
    b. overdisclosure
    c. proximity
    d. similarity

22. The top three categories on which social stereotypes are based are
    a. employment, age, race.
    b. age, race, income.
    c. race, national origin, income.
    d. gender, age, race.

23. Status inequalities are to_____ as equal-status contact is to _____.
    a. dependence; independence
    b. discrimination; stereotyping
    c. prejudice; tolerance
    d. aggression; individuation

24. Young children spend about _____ hours per week in front of television or computer screens.
    a. 25
    b. 30
    c. 35
    d. 40

25. If the Earth's population were to be condensed to only 100 people, _____ of those people would be Asian.
    a. 11
    b. 14
    c. 50
    d. 61

26. If it is easier for Anglo Americans to get automobile insurance than it is for African Americans, then African Americans have experienced
    a. discrimination.
    b. scapegoating.
    c. ethnocentrism.
    d. personal prejudice.

27. The presence of other potential helpers reduces the likelihood that a bystander will offer help in an emergency during which decision point?
    a. noticing
    b. defining an emergency
    c. taking responsibility
    d. all of the decision points

28. According to Sternberg's triangular theory of love, companionate love is a combination of
    a. passion and intimacy.
    b. intimacy and commitment.
    c. decision and commitment.
    d. intimacy, passion, and commitment.

29. Racism expressed in a disguised form, so that it appears to be socially acceptable, is called _____ prejudice.
    a. secondary
    b. subjective
    c. silent
    d. symbolic

589

30. Which of the following terms refers to feelings of connectedness and affection for another person?
    a. liking
    b. intimacy
    c. passion
    d. committment

31. Beliefs concerning superiority, injustice, vulnerability, and distrust are common variables that promote
    a. cooperation from out-group members.
    b. cooperation from in-group members.
    c. hostilities between out-group members.
    d. hostilities within in-group members.

32. When a white candidate is given "the benefit of the doubt" on his/her abilities to perform a task and is hired for a position for which other black candidates are qualified, is an example of
    a. symbolic prejudice.
    b. modern racism.
    c. justice.
    d. both a and b

33. Which theory combines learning principles with cognitive processes, socialization, and modeling to explain human behavior?
    a. social learning
    b. individuating information
    c. existential
    d. multiculturalism

34. Children are exposed to about _____ acts of murder through media by the time they leave elementary school.
    a. 1000
    b. 4000
    c. 8000
    d. 10,000

35. Billy's new neighbor is from Pakistan. Because Billy wants to avoid misunderstandings and conflict when he meets and talks to his neighbor, he attends a cultural event sponsored by the Pakistani student club at his university. Billy is attempting to
    a. set an example for others in his neighborhood.
    b. increase his cultural awareness of other's culture.
    c. reduce stereotypes and prejudicial views of others.
    d. all the preceding

# SOLUTIONS

## RECITE AND REVIEW

### The Need for Affiliation—Come Together: Pages 557-558
Why do people affiliate?

1. approval; information
2. reduce
3. evaluate
4. comparisons
5. comparisons; comparisons

### Interpersonal Attraction—Social Magnetism: Pages 558-561
What factors influence interpersonal attraction?

1. nearness; contact
2. attraction; similarity
3. similarity; mate
4. revealing
5. norm
6. self-disclosure
7. rewards; costs

### Liking and Loving—Dating, Rating, Mating: Pages 561-563
How do liking and loving differ?

1. triangular; intimacy
2. mutual
3. love
4. Secure
5. mating
6. younger; older; economically

### Helping Others—The Good Samaritan: Pages 564-566
Why are bystanders so often unwilling to help in an emergency?

1. helpful
2. help
3. noticing
4. less
5. arousal; risk
6. heroism; donating; coaching
7. reduce; individual

### Aggression—The World's Most Dangerous Animal: Pages 566-571
How do psychologists explain human aggression?

1. instincts
2. lower
3. aggression; aggression
4. stimuli; aggression
5. models; nonaggressive
6. models; viewers
7. minimize; supervise;

### Prejudice—Attitudes That Injure: Pages 571-573
What causes prejudice?

1. negative
2. gender (or sex)
3. aggression
4. norms
5. personality; over
6. group

## Intergroup Conflict—The Roots of Prejudice: Pages 573-579

What can be done about prejudice and intergroup conflict?

| | | |
|---|---|---|
| 1. conflict | 4. injustice; hostilities | 7. classrooms; mutual |
| 2. disguised | 5. reduce | |
| 3. Status | 6. goals | |

## Psychology in Action: Multiculturalism—Living with Diversity: Pages 579-581

How can we promote multiculturalism and promote social harmony?

| | | |
|---|---|---|
| 1. equal beliefs; | 3. individuals | 5. Cultural; increasing; |
| 2. reduce; aware; just; social | 4. beliefs; social | prevent |

# CONNECTIONS

## The Need for Affiliation—Come Together and Interpersonal Attraction—Social Magnetism?: Pages 557-561

Why do people affiliate? What factors influence interpersonal attraction?

| | | |
|---|---|---|
| 1. h | 4. d | 7. f |
| 2. b | 5. g | 8. c |
| 3. e | 6. a | |

## Helping Others—The Good Samaritan and Psychology in Action: Multiculturalism—Living with Diversity: Pages 564-566, 579-581

Why are bystanders so often unwilling to help in an emergency? How can we promote multiculturalism and promote social harmony?

| | | |
|---|---|---|
| 1. c | 4. g | 7. f |
| 2. e | 5. a | |
| 3. d | 6. b | |

## Aggression—The World's Most Dangerous Animal: Pages 566-571

How do psychologists explain human aggression?

| | | |
|---|---|---|
| 1. f | 3. e | 5. b |
| 2. a | 4. c | 6. d |

## Prejudice—Attitudes That Injure: Pages 571-573

What causes prejudice?

| | | |
|---|---|---|
| 1. b | 4. f | 7. h |
| 2. e | 5. g | 8. c |
| 3. i | 6. a | 9. d |

# CHECK YOUR MEMORY

## The Need for Affiliation—Come Together: Pages 557-558
Why do people affiliate?

| | | |
|---|---|---|
| 1. T | 3. F | 5. T |
| 2. T | 4. T | 6. F |

## Interpersonal Attraction—Social Magnetism?: Pages 558-561
What factors influence interpersonal attraction?

| | | |
|---|---|---|
| 1. F | 7. F | 13. T |
| 2. T | 8. T | 14. T |
| 3. F | 9. F | 15. F |
| 4. T | 10. T | 16. F |
| 5. F | 11. F | 17. F |
| 6. T | 12. T | 18. T |

## Helping Others—The Good Samaritan: Pages 564-566
Why are bystanders so often unwilling to help in an emergency?

| | | |
|---|---|---|
| 1. T | 3. F | 5. T |
| 2. F | 4. F | 6. T |

## Aggression—The World's Most Dangerous Animal: Pages 566-571
How do psychologists explain human aggression?

| | | |
|---|---|---|
| 1. F | 7. F | 13. F |
| 2. F | 8. F | 14. T |
| 3. T | 9. F | 15. T |
| 4. F | 10. T | 16. F |
| 5. T | 11. F | 17. T |
| 6. F | 12. T | 18. T |
| | | 19. F |

## Intergroup Conflict—The Roots of Prejudice: Pages 573-579
What causes prejudice? What can be done about prejudice and intergroup conflict?

| | | |
|---|---|---|
| 1. T | 9. T | 17. F |
| 2. T | 10. T | 18. T |
| 3. F | 11. T | 19. T |
| 4. F | 12. T | 20. F |
| 5. F | 13. F | 21. F |
| 6. T | 14. F | |
| 7. F | 15. F | |
| 8. T | 16. F | |

## Psychology in Action: Multiculturalism—Living with Diversity: Pages 579-581

How can we promote multiculturalism and promote social harmony?

1. F
2. F
3. T
4. T
5. T
6. F
7. T
8. T
9. T
10. T

# FINAL SURVEY AND REVIEW

## The Need for Affiliation—Come Together
Why do people affiliate?

1. need; affiliate
2. anxiety
3. comparison
4. protection
5. Downward; Upward

## Interpersonal Attraction—Social Magnetism?
What factors influence interpersonal attraction?

1. proximity
2. physical; competence
3. homogamy
4. Self-disclosure
5. reciprocity
6. Overdisclosure
7. exchange; profitable

## Liking and Loving—Dating, Rating, Mating
How do liking and loving differ?

1. Sternberg's; commitment
2. absorption
3. attachment
4. avoidant; ambivalent
5. Evolutionary; reproductive
6. men; women; economically

## Helping Others—The Good Samaritan
Why are bystanders so often unwilling to help in an emergency?

1. altruistic
2. apathy
3. emergency; responsibility
4. potential; helpers
5. empathic; similarity
6. Altruistic; saving; donating
7. individuating

## Aggression—The World's Most Dangerous Animal
How do psychologists explain human aggression?

1. Ethologists
2. threshold; nonaggressive
3. frustration; frustration
4. aversive; cues
5. Social; learning
6. desensitize; disinhibit
7. minimize; avoid

## Prejudice—Attitudes That Injure
What causes prejudice?

1.    out-groups
2.    Racism; ageism; sexism
3.    scapegoating; displaced
4.    personal; group
5.    authoritarian
6.    ethnocentric

## Intergroup Conflict—The Roots of Prejudice
What can be done about prejudice and intergroup conflict?

1.  social; stereotypes
2.  Symbolic
3.  inequalities
4.  In-group; hostilities
5.  Equal-status
6.  Superordinate
7.  jigsaw; interdependence

## Psychology in Action: Multiculturalism—Living with Diversity
How can we promote multiculturalism and promote social harmony?

1.  Multiculturalism
2.  aware; just; social
3.  individuating
4.  just-world; self-fulfilling
5.  awareness; understanding; stereotyping

# MASTERY TEST

1. b, p. 568
2. b, p. 559
3. c, p. 564
4. d, p. 560
5. d, pp. 569-570
6. b, p. 562
7. a, p. 568
8. c, p. 558
9. c, p. 569
10. a, p. 577
11. b, p. 570
12. d, p. 573
13. a, p. 567
14. b, p. 560
15. a, p. 557
16. c, p. 578
17. d, p. 579
18. d, p. 562
19. c, p. 559
20. d, p. 568
21. b, p. 559
22. d, p. 574
23. c, p. 577
24. c, p. 569
25. d, p. 581
26. a, p. 572
27. d, p. 564
28. b, p. 561
29. d, p. 574
30. b, p. 561
31. c, p. 574
32. d, p. 575
33. a, p. 568
34. c, p.569
35. d, p. 581

# Applied Psychology

## Chapter Overview

Applied psychologists attempt to solve practical problems. Some major applied specialties are: clinical and counseling, industrial-organizational, environmental, educational, legal, and sports psychology.

Industrial-organizational psychologists are interested in the problems people face at work. They specialize in personnel psychology and human relations at work. Personnel psychologists try to match people with jobs by combining job analysis with various tests and selection procedures. Two basic approaches to business and industrial management are scientific management (Theory X) and human relations (Theory Y) approaches. Healthy organizations express concern for the well-being of their employees by promoting trust, promoting open confrontation to avoid "desk rage," empowering their employees, and encouraging cooperation.

Environmental psychologists study the effects of behavioral settings, physical or social environments, and human territoriality, among many other major topics. Resource consumption can be measured as an ecological footprint, while carbon footprint measures the volume of greenhouse gases consumption adds to the atmosphere. Overpopulation is a major world problem, often reflected at an individual level in crowding. Environmental psychologists are solving many practical problems—from noise pollution to architectural design.

Educational psychologists seek to understand how people learn and teachers instruct. They are particularly interested in teaching styles and teaching strategies. Two of the basic types of teaching styles are direct instruction which includes lecture, demonstration, and rote practice and discovery learning which involves active teacher-student discussion. As schools have become increasingly diverse, a third teaching style has emerged; the Universal Design for Instruction makes use of different instructional methods to accommodate the different needs of students.

The psychology of law includes courtroom behavior and other topics that pertain to the legal system. Psychologists serve various consulting and counseling roles in legal, law enforcement, and criminal justice settings.

Sports psychologists seek to enhance sports performance and the benefits of sports participation. A careful task analysis of sports skills is a major tool for improving coaching and performance. The psychological dimension contributes greatly to peak performance.

Human factors psychology considers how best to design machines and environments so they best meet human needs. Examples include designing human-computer interaction (HCI) and habitats in space.

# Learning Objectives

***Theme: Psychological principles can be used to solve practical problems in a variety of settings.***

| |
|---|
| **GQ: How is psychology applied in business and industry?** |
| LO 18.1 Define the term *applied psychology*. |
| LO 18.2 List the two main areas of interest of *industrial/organizational psychology*. |
| LO 18.3 Differentiate *Theory X* (*scientific management*) from *Theory Y* (human relations-based) *leadership styles*. Include the terms *knowledge worker*, *work efficiency* and *psychological efficiency*; and define the terms *participative management*, *management by objectives*, *self-managed teams*, and *quality circles*. |
| LO 18.4 Discuss the suitability of women for high-level leadership roles. |
| LO 18.5 List seven factors that seem to contribute the most to *job satisfaction*; and explain the concept of flexible work (including *flextime*, the *compressed workweek* and *telecommuting*) and how it is related to job satisfaction. |
| LO 18.6 Explain the purpose and results of *job enrichment*. |
| LO 18.7 Explain what is meant by *organizational culture* and *organizational citizenship*. |
| LO 18.8 Describe the activities of *personnel psychologists* by defining or describing the following areas and related concepts: a. *job analysis* (include the concept of *critical incidents*); b. *biodata* (include the concepts of *personal interviews*, the halo effect, and impression management); c. *vocational interest test*; d. *aptitude test* (include *computerized tests*); e. *assessment center* (include *situational judgement tests*, *in-basket tests*, and *leaderless group discussion*). |
| **GQ: What have psychologists learned about the effects of our physical and social environments?** |
| LO 18.9 Explain the goals of *environmental psychology*, including the three types of environments or settings of interest; and describe how people exhibit *territoriality*. |
| LO 18.10 Discuss the results of animal experiments on the effects of overcrowding and the possible implications for humans; differentiate between *crowding* and *density*; and discuss the concept of *attentional overload* and the effects of *noise pollution*. |
| LO 18.11 List eight ways people can be encouraged to reuse and recycle resources. Describe the issues involved in environmental preservation. Include references to sustainable lifestyles and *ecological footprint*. Define *social dilemma* and the *tragedy of the commons*. |
| LO 18.12 Explain how *environmental assessments* and *architectural psychology* can be used to solve environmental problems. |
| **GQ: How has psychology improved education?** |
| LO 18.13 Describe the goals of *educational psychology*; define the term *teaching strategy*; differentiate *direct instruction* from *discovery learning*; and explain the basic ideas of the Universal Design for Instruction. |
| **GQ: What does psychology reveal about juries and court verdicts?** |
| LO 18.14 Discuss the *psychology of law* and identify topics of special interest; list several problems in jury behavior; describe the process of *scientific jury selection*; and define *death-qualified jury*. |
| **GQ: Can psychology enhance athletic performance?** |
| LO 18.15 Explain the ways in which a *sports psychologist* might contribute to peak performance by an athlete; differentiate between a *motor skill* and a *motor program*; list six rules that can aid skill learning; and describe *flow* (or *peak performance*). |
| **GQ: How are tools designed to better serve human needs?** |
| LO 18.16 Define *human factors psychology*, *natural design*, and *usability testing*. Explain why understanding your task and your tools are the keys to effective tool use. |
| LO 18.17 Define *human-computer interaction* (including the *interface*, and *telepresence*). |
| LO 18.18 Discuss the following issues involved in designing space habitats like the International Space Station: privacy, sleep cycles and sensory restriction. |

# RECITE AND REVIEW

## Industrial/Organizational Psychology—Psychology at Work: Pages 584-593

How is psychology applied in business and industry?

1.  Applied psychology refers to the use of psychological principles and research methods to solve

    _____ .

2.  Major applied specialties include clinical and _____ psychology.

3.  Other applied areas are related to business, such as _____/organizational psychology.

4.  Psychology is also applied to problems that arise in the environment, in education, in law, and in

    _____ .

5.  Industrial-organizational psychologists are interested in the problems people face at _____

    and within organizations.

6.  Typically they specialize in personnel psychology and human _____ at work.

7.  Two basic approaches to business and industrial management are scientific management (Theory

    _____) and human relations approaches (Theory _____).

8.  Theory _____ is most concerned with work efficiency (productivity), whereas, Theory

    _____ emphasizes psychological efficiency (good human relations).

9.  Employees are increasingly becoming _____ workers. Two common Theory_____

    methods are _____ leadership and _____ by objectives.

10. Recently, many companies have given employees more autonomy and responsibility by creating

    self-managed _____ .

11. Below the management level, employees may be encouraged to become more involved in their

    work by participating in_____circles.

12. Job satisfaction is related to _____ , and it usually affects absenteeism, morale, employee

    turnover, and other factors that affect overall business efficiency.

599

13. Job satisfaction is usually enhanced by _____ oriented job enrichment.

14. Variations of flexible work include a _____ workweek and telecommuting.

15. Workers who fit comfortably within the _____ of a business typically show good organizational citizenship.

16. "Desk rage" (workplace _____ ) occurs from job-related _____ , work-related conflicts, people feeling that they have been treated _____ , and people perceiving that their self-esteem is threatened.

17. _____ organizations express concerns for the well-being of their employees by promoting trust, open _____ of problems, employee _____ and participation, cooperation, and full use of human potential.

18. Personnel psychologists try to match people with _____ by combining _____ analysis with a variety of selection procedures.

19. To effectively match people with jobs, it is important to identify critical incidents (situations with which _____ employees must be able to cope).

20. Personnel selection is often based on gathering biodata (detailed _____ information about an applicant).

21. The traditional _____ interview is still widely used to select people for jobs. However, interviewers must be aware of the halo effect and other sources of _____.

22. Standardized psychological _____, such as vocational interest inventories, aptitude tests, and multi-media _____ tests, are mainstays of personnel selection.

23. In the assessment center approach, in-depth _____ of job candidates are done by observing them in simulated _____ situations.

24. Two popular assessment center techniques are the in-basket test, and leaderless _____ discussions.

# Environmental Psychology—Life on Spaceship Earth: Pages 593-601

What have psychologists learned about the effects of our physical and social environments?

1. Environmental psychologists are interested in the effects of behavioral _____ , physical or _____ environments, and human territoriality, among many other major topics.

2. Territorial behavior involves defining a space as one's own, frequently by placing _____ markers (signals of ownership) in it.

3. Overpopulation is a major world problem, often reflected at an individual level in _____ .

4. Animal experiments indicate that excessive crowding can be unhealthy and lead to_____ and pathological behaviors.

5. However, human research shows that psychological feelings of _____ do not always correspond to density (the number of people in a given space).

6. One major consequence of _____ is attentional overload (stress caused when too many demands are placed on a person's attention).

7. Toxic or poisoned environments, pollution, excess consumption of natural resources, and other types of environmental_____ pose serious threats to future _____ .

8. Resource _____ can be measured in terms of an ecological footprint, while individual impact on global warming can be calculated as an individual _____ footprint.

9. A social situation that rewards actions that have undesirable long-term effects is called a _____ _____ . A situation in which people overuse scarce resources that must be shared by many people is called the tragedy of the commons.

10. Recycling can be encouraged by monetary _____ . removing barriers, persuasion, obtaining public commitment, _____ setting, and giving feedback.

11. In many cases, solutions to environmental problems are the result of doing a careful _____ assessment (an analysis of the effects environments have on behavior).

12. Architectural psychology is the study of the effects _____ have on behavior and the design

of _____ using _____ principles.

# Educational Psychology—An Instructive Topic: Pages 601-602
How has psychology improved education?

1. Educational psychologists seek to understand how people _____ and teachers

2. An effective teaching strategy involves _____ preparation, stimulus presentation, the

   learner's _____ , reinforcement, evaluation of the learner's progress, and periodic review.

3. They are particularly interested in teaching styles, such as direct instruction ( _____ and

   demonstrations) and discovery learning (active student-teacher _____ ).

4. The Universal Design for Instruction makes use of different _____ methods such as a

   lecture, a podcast of the lecture, a group activity, or an Internet discussion.

# Psychology and Law—Judging Juries: Pages 602-604
What does psychology reveal about juries and court verdicts?

1. The psychology of law includes studies of courtroom behavior and other topics that pertain to the

   _____ system.

2. Studies of mock juries ( _____ juries) show that jury decisions are often far from

   _____.

3. Psychologists are sometimes involved in jury _____. Demographic information, a

   community survey, nonverbal behavior, and looking for authoritarian _____ traits may be

   used to select jurors.

# Sports Psychology—The Athletic Mind: Pages 604-607
Can psychology enhance athletic performance?

1. Sports psychologists seek to enhance sports performance and the benefits of sports _____.

2. A careful task analysis breaks _____ _____ into their subparts.

3.  Motor skills are the core of many sports performances. Motor skills are nonverbal chains assembled into a smooth sequence.

4.  Motor skills are guided by internal _____ plans or models called motor programs.

5.  _____ performances are associated with the flow experience, an unusual mental state.

6.  Top athletes typically _____ their arousal level so that it is appropriate for the task. They also focus _____ on the task and mentally rehearse it beforehand.

7.  Most top athletes use various self-regulation strategies to _____ their performances and make necessary adjustments.

# Psychology in Action: Human Factors Psychology—Who's the Boss Here?: Pages 607-610

How are tools designed to better serve human needs?

1.  Human _____ psychology focuses on designing _____ and work environments so they are compatible with our sensory and motor capacities.

2.  In order to _____ useful tools, human factors psychologists perform usability testing, during which they directly measure how easily people learn to use a _____.

3.  Using human factors methods to design computers and _____ is referred to as human-computer _____.

4.  Human factors psychology has also been applied to space _____ , for example to reduce _____ monotony.

# CONNECTIONS

## Industrial/Organizational Psychology—Psychology at Work: Pages 584-593

How is psychology applied in business and industry?

| | | | |
|---|---|---|---|
| 1. | _____ telecommunte | a. | work at home |
| 2. | _____ I/O psychology | b. | vocational interests |
| 3. | _____ Flextime | c. | essential work problem |
| 4. | _____ Biodata | d. | variable schedule |
| 5. | _____ critical incident | e. | work efficiency |
| 6 | _____ Kuder | f. | personal history |
| 7. | _____ in-basket test | g. | work and organizations |
| 8. | _____ Theory X | h. | psychological efficiency |
| 9. | _____ quality circle | i. | discussion group |
| 10. | _____ Theory Y | j. | typical work problems |

## Environmental Psychology—Life on Spaceship Earth: Pages 593-601

What have psychologists learned about the effects of our physical and social environments?

| | | | |
|---|---|---|---|
| 1. | _____ feedback | a. | intrusive sounds |
| 2. | _____ spatial norm | b. | pollution |
| 3. | _____ territorial marker | c. | persons in area |
| 4. | _____ density | d. | volume of greenhouse gases |
| 5. | _____ social dilemma | e. | public distance |
| 6 | _____ noise pollution | f. | ownership signal |
| 7. | _____ architectural psychology | g. | tragedy of the commons |
| 8. | _____ environmental psychology | h. | solution for overcrowded buildings |
| 9. | _____ community psychology | i. | information about effects |
| 10. | _____ carbon footprint | j. | mental health |

## Educational Psychology—An Instructive Topic and Psychology and Law—Judging Juries: Pages 601-604

How has psychology improved education? What does psychology reveal about juries and court verdicts?

| | | | |
|---|---|---|---|
| 1. | _____ direct instruction | a. | favoring death penalty |
| 2. | _____ discovery learning | b. | better for facts |
| 3. | _____ jury selection | c. | simulated trial |
| 4. | _____ death-qualified jury | d. | avoid authoritarian personality |
| 5. | _____ mock jury | e. | better for thinking |

## Sports Psychology—The Athletic Mind: Pages 604-610
Can psychology enhance athletic performance? How are tools designed to better serve human needs?

1. _____ natural design
2. _____ motor program
3. _____ human factors psychology
4. _____ mental practice
5. _____ sports psychology
6 _____ satisfice
7. _____ peak performance

a. coaching styles
b. imagined performance
c. movement plan
d. flow
e. based on perceptual signals
f. achieve minimum result
g. ergonomics

# CHECK YOUR MEMORY

## Industrial/Organizational Psychology—Psychology at Work: Pages 584-593
How is psychology applied in business and industry?

1. Applied psychology can be defined as the use of learning principles to change undesirable human behavior.   TRUE or FALSE

2. Psychological research has shown that the best fire alarm is a recorded voice.   TRUE or FALSE

3. During a fire in a high-rise building, you should use the elevators, rather than the stairwell, so that you can leave as quickly as possible.   TRUE or FALSE

4. Personnel psychology is a specialty of I-O psychologists.   TRUE or FALSE

5. The basic idea of flextime is that employees can work as many or as few hours a week as they choose. TRUE or FALSE

6. One way of doing a job analysis is to interview expert workers.   TRUE or FALSE

7. To have an effective interview, one should focus on direct efforts (emphasizing positive traits and past successes) rather than indirect efforts (wearing cologne and flattering the interviewer). TRUE or FALSE

8. Impression management refers to employers seeking to certify their authority through appearances (wearing jackets and ties).   TRUE or FALSE

9. Critical incidents are serious employee mistakes identified by doing a job analysis. TRUE or FALSE

10. Use of biodata is based on the idea that past behavior predicts future behavior.   TRUE or FALSE

11. Because of their many shortcomings, personal interviews are fading from use as a way of selecting job applicants.   TRUE or FALSE

12. The halo effect is a major problem in aptitude testing.   TRUE or FALSE

13. Excessive self-promotion tends to lower the ratings candidates receive in job interviews.
TRUE or FALSE

14. "I would prefer to read a good book" is the kind of statement typically found on aptitude tests.
TRUE or FALSE

15. Multi-media computerized tests seek to present realistic work situations to job candidates.
TRUE or FALSE

16. Leaderless quality circles are a typical task applicants face in assessment centers.   TRUE or FALSE

17. Theory X assumes that workers enjoy autonomy and accept responsibility.   TRUE or FALSE

18. The main benefit of a Theory X management style is a high level of psychological efficiency among workers.   TRUE or FALSE

19. Shared leadership aims to make work a cooperative effort.   TRUE or FALSE

20. Quality circles are typically allowed to choose their own methods of achieving results as long as the group is effective.   TRUE or FALSE

21. Job satisfaction comes from a good fit between work and a person's interests, needs, and abilities.
TRUE or FALSE

22. Job enrichment involves assigning workers a large number of new tasks.   TRUE or FALSE

23. In a compressed workweek, employees work fewer hours but work on more days.
TRUE or FALSE

24. People who display organizational citizenship tend to contribute in ways that are not part of their job description.   TRUE or FALSE

25. "Desk rage" at work is associated with job stresses, threats to one's self-esteem, and conflicts with other workers.   TRUE or FALSE

26. A healthy organization encourages their employees to openly confront their problems.
TRUE or FALSE

# Environmental Psychology—Life on Spaceship Earth: Pages 593-601

What have psychologists learned about the effects of our physical and social environments?

1. Country people are less likely to help others than city people.   TRUE or FALSE

2. Environmental psychologists study physical environments rather than social environments. TRUE or FALSE

3. Assaults and burglaries are less likely near the few restaurants or bars where likely offenders hang out.   TRUE or FALSE

4. Overpopulation is one of the most serious problems facing the world today.   TRUE or FALSE

5. A dance is a behavioral setting.   TRUE or FALSE

6. Saving a place at a theater is a type of territorial behavior.   TRUE or FALSE

7. Burglars tend to choose houses to break into that have visible territorial markers.   TRUE or FALSE

8. World population doubled between 1850 and 1930. By 2050, the earth's population may exceed 10 billion.   TRUE or FALSE

9. In Calhoun's study of overcrowding in a rat colony, food and water rapidly ran out as the population increased.   TRUE or FALSE

10. High densities invariably lead to subjective feelings of crowding.   TRUE or FALSE

11. Stress is most likely to result when crowding causes a loss of control over a person's immediate social environment.   TRUE or FALSE

12. People suffering from attentional overload tend to ignore nonessential events and their social contacts are superficial.   TRUE or FALSE

13. Exposure to toxic hazards increases the risk of mental disease, as well as physical problems. TRUE or FALSE

14. Long-corridor dormitories reduce feelings of crowding and encourage friendships. TRUE or FALSE

15. Providing feedback about energy consumption tends to promote conservation of resources. TRUE or FALSE

16. Direct monetary rewards have little or no effect on whether or not people recycle. TRUE or FALSE

# Educational Psychology—An Instructive Topic: Pages 601-602

How has psychology improved education?

1. Reinforcement, evaluation, and spaced review are elements of a teaching strategy. TRUE or FALSE

2. Students of direct instruction do a little better on achievement tests than students of discovery learning do.   TRUE or FALSE

3. Students of open instruction tend to be better at thinking and problem solving than students of direct instruction.   TRUE or FALSE

4. The Universal Design for Instruction makes use of one instructional method that all students can understand.   TRUE or FALSE

## Psychology and Law—Judging Juries: Pages 602-604
What does psychology reveal about juries and court verdicts?

1. In court, attractive defendants are less likely to be found guilty than unattractive persons.
   TRUE or FALSE

2. Jurors are supposed to take into account the severity of the punishment that a defendant faces, but many don't.   TRUE or FALSE

3. Scientific jury selection is only used in laboratory studies—the practice isn't allowed in real jury trials.
   TRUE or FALSE

4. Demographic information consists of the most prominent personality traits a person displays.
   TRUE or FALSE

5. All members of a death-qualified jury must be opposed to the death penalty.   TRUE or FALSE

## Sports Psychology—The Athletic Mind: Pages 682-685
Can psychology enhance athletic performance?

1. Peak performances in sports require both mental and physical training.   TRUE or FALSE

2. Distance running tends to reduce anxiety, tension, and depression.   TRUE or FALSE

3. The most accurate marksmen are those who learn to pull the trigger just as their heart beats.
   TRUE or FALSE

4. Motor programs adapt complex movements to changing conditions.   TRUE or FALSE

5. Verbal rules add little to learning a sports skill; you should concentrate on lifelike practice.
   TRUE or FALSE

6. To enhance motor skill learning, feedback should call attention to correct responses.
   TRUE or FALSE

7. Mental practice refines motor programs.   TRUE or FALSE

8. The top athletes in most sports are the ones who have learned how to force the flow experience to occur. TRUE or FALSE

9. Better athletes often use imagery, relaxation techniques, and fixed routines to control their arousal levels. TRUE or FALSE

## Psychology in Action: Human Factors Psychology—Who's the Boss Here?: Pages 607-610
How are tools designed to better serve human needs?

1. Machines are of little use if humans can not operate them effectively.   TRUE or FALSE

2. Natural design is based on learned perceptual signals.   TRUE or FALSE

3. Including live animals and plants in space could reduce stress and boredom.  TRUE or FALSE

# FINAL SURVEY AND REVIEW

## Industrial-Organizational Psychology—Psychology at Work
How is psychology applied in business and industry?

1. Applied psychology refers to the use of psychological _____ and _____ methods to solve practical problems.

2. Major applied specialties include _____ and _____ psychology.

3. Other applied areas are related to business, such as industrial/_____ psychology.

4. Psychology is also applied to problems that arise in the natural and social _____, in _____ , in law, and in sports.

5. _____ psychologists are interested in the problems people face at work and within organizations.

6. Typically they specialize in _____ psychology (testing, selecting, and promoting employees) and human relations at work.

7. Two basic approaches to business and industrial management are_____ management (Theory X) and _____ approaches (Theory Y).

8. Theory X is most concerned with work _____ (productivity), whereas, Theory Y

609

emphasizes _____ efficiency (good human relations).

9. Employees are increasingly becoming _____ workers. Two common Theory Y methods are

    shared leadership and management by _____ .

10. Recently, many companies have given employees more autonomy and responsibility by creating

    _____ teams.

11. Below the management level, employees may be encouraged to become more involved in their work

    by participating in _____ _____ .

12. Job_____is related to productivity, and it usually affects absenteeism,_____ ,

    employee turnover, and other factors that affect overall business efficiency.

13. Job satisfaction is usually enhanced by Theory Y oriented job _____ .

14. Variations of flexible work include a compressed workweek and _____ .

15. Workers who fit comfortably within the culture of a business typically show good organizational

    _____ .

16. " _____ " (workplace anger) occurs from _____ -related stresses, work-related

    conflicts, people feeling that they have been treated unfairly, and people perceiving that their

    self-esteem is threatened.

17. _____ organizations express concerns for the well-being of their employees by promoting

    trust, _____confrontation of problems, employee empowerment and_____ ,

    cooperation, and full use of human potential.

18. _____ psychologists try to match people with jobs by combining job _____ with a

    variety of selection procedures.

19. To effectively match people with jobs, it is important to identify _____ incidents

    (situations with which competent employees must be able to cope).

20. Personnel selection is often based on gathering_____ (detailed biographical information

    about an applicant).

21. The traditional personal _____ is still widely used to select people for jobs. However,

    interviewers must be aware of the _____ effect and other sources of bias.

22. Standardized psychological tests, such as _____ interest inventories, _____ tests, and multi-media computerized tests, are mainstays of personnel selection.

23. In the _____ approach, in-depth evaluations of job candidates are done by observing them in simulated work situations.

24. Two popular assessment center techniques are the in-_____ test, and group discussions.

# Environmental Psychology—Life on Spaceship Earth

## What have psychologists learned about the effects of our physical and social environments?

1. _____ psychologists are interested in the effects of _____ settings, physical or social environments, and human territoriality, among many other major topics.

2. Territorial behavior involves defining a space as one's own, frequently by placing territorial _____ (signals of ownership) in it.

3. _____ is a major world problem, often reflected at an individual level in crowding.

4. Animal experiments indicate that excessive _____ can be unhealthy and lead to abnormal and pathological behaviors.

5. However, human research shows that psychological feelings of crowding do not always correspond to _____ (the number of people in a given space).

6. One major consequence of crowding is _____ (stress caused when too many demands are placed on a person's attention).

7. Toxic or poisoned environments, _____, excess consumption of natural _____, and other types of environmental damage pose serious threats to future generations.

8. Resource consumption can be measured in terms of an _____ footprint, while individual impact on global warming can be calculated as an individual carbon _____.

9. A social situation that rewards actions that have undesirable long-term effects is called a social dilemma. A situation in which people overuse scarce resources that must be shared by many people is called the _____ of the _____.

10. Recycling can be encouraged by _____ rewards, removing barriers, persuasion, obtaining public _____ , goal setting, and giving feedback.

11. In many cases, solutions to environmental problems are the result of doing a careful environmental _____ (an analysis of the effects environments have on behavior).

12. _____ psychology is the study of the effects buildings have on behavior and the design of buildings using psychological principles.

# Educational Psychology—An Instructive Topic
How has psychology improved education?

1. _____ psychologists seek to understand how people learn and teachers instruct.

2. An effective teaching _____ involves learner preparation, stimulus presentation, the learner's response, _____ , evaluation of the learner's progress, and periodic _____.

3. They are particularly interested in teaching styles, such as _____ (lecture and demonstrations) and _____ teaching (active student-teacher _____).

4. The _____ Design for Instruction makes use of different instructional methods such as a lecture, a podcast of the lecture, a group activity, or an Internet discussion.

# Psychology and Law—Judging Juries
What does psychology reveal about juries and court verdicts?

1. The psychology of _____ includes studies of courtroom behavior and other topics that pertain to the legal system.

2. Studies of _____ juries (simulated juries) show that jury decisions are often far from objective.

3. Psychologists are sometimes involved in jury selection. _____ information (population data), a community survey, nonverbal behavior, and looking for _____ personality traits may be used to select jurors.

# Sports Psychology—The Athletic Mind
Can psychology enhance athletic performance?

1. Sports psychologists seek to enhance sports _____ and the benefits of sports participation.

2. A careful _____ breaks sports skills into their subparts.

3. _____ skills are the core of many sports performances. Motor skills are nonverbal response _____ assembled into a smooth sequence.

4. Motor skills are guided by internal mental plans or models called _____ .

5. Peak performances are associated with the _____ experience, an unusual _____ state.

6. Top athletes typically adjust their _____ level so that it is appropriate for the task. They also focus attention on the task and mentally _____ it beforehand.

7. Most top athletes use various self-regulation _____ to evaluate their performances and make necessary adjustments.

# Human Factors Psychology—Who's the Boss Here?
How are tools designed to better serve human needs?

1. Human _____ psychology focuses on _____ machines and work environments so they are compatible with our sensory and motor capacities.

2. In order to _____ useful tools, human factors psychologists perform usability testing, during which they directly measure how easily people learn to use a _____.

3. Using human factors methods to design computers and _____ is referred to as human-computer _____.

3. Human factors psychology has also been applied to space _____, for example to reduce _____ monotony.

# MASTERY TEST

1. Praise and feedback make up what part of a teaching strategy?
   a. learner preparation
   b. stimulus presentation
   c. reinforcement
   d. review

2. Which is POOR advice for learning motor skills?
   a. Observe a skilled model.
   b. Learn only nonverbal information.
   c. Get feedback.
   d. Avoid learning artificial parts of a task.

3. Which of the following would be a question for applied psychology?
   a. How does conditioning occur?
   b. How can eyewitness memory be improved?
   c. What are the most basic personality traits?
   d. Do athletes have unusual personality profiles?

4. Signs are placed on a recycling container each week showing how many aluminum cans were deposited during the previous week. This practice dramatically increases recycling, showing the benefits of using _____ to promote recycling.
   a. feedback
   b. public commitment
   c. consumer symbolization
   d. persuasion

5. Psychological efficiency is promoted by
   a. scientific management.
   b. Theory Y.
   c. time-and-motion studies.
   d. progressive pay schedules.

6. In court, being attractive does NOT help a defendant avoid being found guilty when
   a. a majority of jurors are also attractive.
   b. the defendant is a man.
   c. the defendant is over age 30.
   d. being attractive helped the person commit a crime.

7. Which of the following is NOT a specialty of I-O psychologists?
   a. personnel psychology
   b. theories of management
   c. human relations
   d. architectural psychology

8. Dividing long-corridor dormitories into two living areas separated by a lounge
   a. makes residents feel more crowded, not less.
   b. decreases social contacts.
   c. increases energy consumption.
   d. decreases stress.

9. You leave a book on a table in the library to save your place. The book is a territorial
   a. display.
   b. marker.
   c. strategy.
   d. control.

10. When professional golfer Jack Nicklaus talks about "watching a movie" in his head before each shot, he is referring to the value of _____ for enhancing sports performance.
    a. mental practice
    b. self-regulation
    c. skilled modeling
    d. task analysis

11. What cognitive maps, behavioral settings, and crowding have in common is that all
    a. are studied by community psychologists.
    b. produce attentional overload.
    c. are studied by environmental psychologists.
    d. are characteristics of Type A cities.

12. Potentials for learning the skills used in various occupations are measured by
    a. interest tests.
    b. aptitude tests.
    c. in-basket tests.
    d. cognitive mapping.

13. To encourage creative thinking by students, a teacher would be wise to use
    a. direct instruction.
    b. demonstrations as well as lectures.
    c. discovery learning.
    d. spaced review.

14. A good job analysis should identify
    a. critical incidents.
    b. compatible controls.
    c. motor programs.
    d. essential biodata.

15. High_____ is experienced as crowding when it leads to a loss of_____one's immediate environment.
    a. overload; attention to
    b. density; control over
    c. stimulation; interest in
    d. arousal; contact with

16. Studies of flextime would most likely be done by a(n) _____ psychologist.
    a. community
    b. environmental
    c. I-O
    d. consumer

17. The halo effect is a problem in
    a. collecting biodata.
    b. scoring interest inventories.
    c. conducting interviews.
    d. aptitude testing.

18. Mental practice is one way to improve
    a. motor programs.
    b. the flow experience.
    c. the accuracy of cognitive maps.
    d. job satisfaction.

19. Joan has been given a specific sales total to meet for the month, suggesting that she works for a company that uses
    a. quality circles.
    b. job enrichment.
    c. flexi-quotas.
    d. management by objectives.

20. Which of the following computer interface provides output?
    a. keyboard
    b. display screen
    c. touch pad
    d. voice recognition

21. Planning, control, and orderliness are typical of _____ management.
    a. Theory X
    b. participative
    c. Theory Y
    d. enriched

22. A psychologist who checks demographic information, does a community survey, and looks for authoritarian traits is most likely
    a. a personnel psychologist.
    b. doing a community mental health assessment.
    c. a consumer welfare advocate.
    d. a legal consultant.

23. A very important element of job enrichment is
    a. switching to indirect feedback.
    b. increasing worker knowledge.
    c. use of bonuses and pay incentives.
    d. providing closer supervision and guidance.

24. About what percent of American business organizations have female CEOs?
    a. 5
    b. 15
    c. 25
    d. 35

25. An I/O psychologist hears someone make such claims as "He was really stressed out, and because of that he was often angry" and can predict that the individual may be experiencing
    a. "road rage."
    b. "desk rage."
    c. "private rage."
    d. "postal rage."

26. Which of the following is a method to increase employees' well-being?
    a. open confrontation of problems
    b. adhered to structured schedules
    c. employee empowerment
    d. both A and C

27. Resource consumption can be measured in terms of
    a. noise pollution.
    b. ecological footprint.
    c. conservation.
    d. carbon footprint.

28. Mrs. West uses multiple instructional approaches (lectures, group activities, and Internet discussion) in her classes to ensure each student has the opportunity to find an instructional method by which he/she can best learn the material. Mrs. West is utilizing the
    a. direct instruction.
    b. discovery learning.
    c. Universal Design for Instruction.
    d. flextime instruction.

# SOLUTIONS

## RECITE AND REVIEW

### Industrial/Organizational Psychology—Psychology at Work: Pages 584-593

How is psychology applied in business and industry?

1. practical problems
2. counseling
3. industrial
4. sports
5. work
6. relations
7. X; Y
8. X; Y
9. Y; management;

knowledge
10. teams
11. quality
12. productivity
13. Theory Y
14. compressed
15. culture
16. anger; stresses; unfairly
17. Healthy; confrontation;

empowerment
18. jobs; job
19. competent
20. biographical
21. personal; bias
22. tests; computerized
23. evaluations; work
24. group

### Environmental Psychology—Life on Spaceship Earth: Pages 593-601

What have psychologists learned about the effects of our physical and social environments?

1. settings; social
2. territorial
3. crowding behavioral
4. abnormal
5. crowding

6. crowding
7. damage; generations
8. consumption; carbon
9. social dilemma

10. rewards; goal
11. environmental
12. buildings; buildings;

### Educational Psychology—An Instructive Topic: Pages 601-602

How has psychology improved education?

1. learn; instruct
2. learner; response

3. lecture; discussion
4. instructional

### Psychology and Law—Judging Juries: Pages 602-604

What does psychology reveal about juries and court verdicts?

1. legal

2. simulated; objective

3. selection; personality

### Sports Psychology—The Athletic Mind: Pages 604-607

Can psychology enhance athletic performance?

1. participation
2. sports; skills
3. response

4. mental
5. Peak
6. adjust; attention

7. evaluate

## Psychology in Action: Human Factors Psychology—Who's the Boss Here?: Pages 607-610

How are tools designed to better serve human needs?

1. designing; sensory
2. design; machine
3. software; interaction
4. flight; sensory

# CONNECTIONS

## Industrial/Organizational Psychology—Psychology at Work: Pages 584-590

How is psychology applied in business and industry?

1. a
2. g
3. d
4. f
5. c
6. b
7. j
8. e
9. i
10. h

## Environmental Psychology—Life on Spaceship Earth: Pages 593-601

What have psychologists learned about the effects of our physical and social environments?

1. i
2. e
3. f
4. c
5. g
6. a
7. h
8. b
9. j
10. d

## Educational Psychology—An Instructive Topic and Psychology and Law—Judging Juries: Pages 601-604

How has psychology improved education? What does psychology reveal about juries and court verdicts?

1. b
2. e
3. d
4. a
5. c

## Sports Psychology—The Athletic Mind and Psychology in Action: Human Factors Psychology—Who's the Boss Here?: Pages 604-610

Can psychology enhance athletic performance? How are tools designed to better serve human needs?

1. e
2. c
3. g
4. b
5. a
6. f
7. d

# CHECK YOUR MEMORY

## Industrial/Organizational Psychology—Psychology at Work: Pages 584-590

How is psychology applied in business and industry?

| | | |
|---|---|---|
| 1. F | 10. T | 19. T |
| 2. T | 11. F | 20. F |
| 3. F | 12. F | 21. T |
| 4. T | 13. T | 22. F |
| 5. F | 14. F | 23. F |
| 6. T | 15. T | 24. T |
| 7. T | 16. F | 25. T |
| 8. F | 17. F | 26. T |
| 9. F | 18. F | |

## Environmental Psychology—Life on Spaceship Earth: Pages 593-601

What have psychologists learned about the effects of our physical and social environments?

| | | |
|---|---|---|
| 1. F | 7. F | 13. T |
| 2. F | 8. T | 14. F |
| 3. F | 9. F | 15. T |
| 4. T | 10. F | 16. F |
| 5. F | 11. T | |
| 6. T | 12. T | |

## Educational Psychology—An Instructive Topic: Pages 601-602

How has psychology improved education?

| | |
|---|---|
| 1. T | 3. T |
| 2. T | 4. F |

## Psychology and Law—Judging Juries: Pages 602-604

What does psychology reveal about juries and court verdicts?

| | | |
|---|---|---|
| 1. T | 3. F | 5. F |
| 2. F | 4. F | |

## Sports Psychology—The Athletic Mind: Pages 604-607

Can psychology enhance athletic performance?

| | | |
|---|---|---|
| 1. T | 4. T | 7. T |
| 2. T | 5. F | 8. F |
| 3. F | 6. T | 9. T |

## Psychology in Action: Human Factors Psychology—Who's the Boss Here?: Pages 607-610

How are tools designed to better serve human needs?

1.  F                    2.  F                    3.  T

# FINAL SURVEY AND REVIEW

## Industrial/Organizational Psychology—Psychology at Work

How is psychology applied in business and industry?

1.  principles; research
2.  clinical; counseling
3.  organizational
4.  environment; education
5.  Industrial-organizational
6.  personnel
7.  scientific; human; relations
8.  efficiency; psychological
9.  knowledge; shared; objectives
10. self-managed
11. quality; circles
12. satisfaction; morale
13. enrichment
14. telecommuting
15. citizenship
16. Desk rage; job
17. Healthy; open; participation
18. Personnel; analysis
19. critical
20. biodata
21. interview; halo
22. vocational; aptitude
23. assessment center
24. basket; leaderless

## Environmental Psychology—Life on Spaceship Earth

What have psychologists learned about the effects of our physical and social environments?

1.  Environmental; behavioral
2.  markers
3.  Overpopulation
4.  crowding
5.  density
6.  attentional; overload
7.  pollution; resources
8.  ecological; footpring
9.  tragedy; commons
10. monetary; commitment
11. assessment
12. Architectural

## Educational Psychology—An Instructive Topic

How has psychology improved education?

1.  Educational
2.  strategy; reinforcement; review
3.  direct instruction; open; discussion
4.  Universal

## Psychology and Law—Judging Juries

What does psychology reveal about juries and court verdicts?

1.  law authoritarian
2.  mock
3.  Demographic;

## Sports Psychology—The Athletic Mind

Can psychology enhance athletic performance?

1. performance
2. task; analysis
3. Motor; chains
4. motor; programs
5. flow; mental
6. arousal; rehearse
7. strategies

## Psychology in Action: Human Factors Psychology—Who's the Boss Here?

How are tools designed to better serve human needs?

1. factors; machines
2. tools; usability
3. computers; human
4. space; monotony

# MASTERY TEST

1. c, p. 602
2. b, p. 606
3. b, p. 585
4. a, p. 599
5. b, p. 586
6. d, p. 603
7. d, p. 594
8. d, p. 600
9. b, p. 594

10. a, p. 606
11. c, p. 594
12. b, p. 592
13. c, p. 602
14. a, p. 590
15. b, p. 596
16. c, p. 588
17. c, p. 591
18. a, p. 606

19. d, p. 587
20. b, p. 608
21. a, p. 586
22. d, p. 603
23. b, p. 589
24. c, p. 587
25. b, p. 590
26. d, p. 590
27. b, p. 597
28. c, p. 602